SUFI HERMENEUTICS

This book examines the Sufi approach to Qur'anic interpretation as exemplified in a twelfth-century Persian Qur'an commentary, Rashīd al-Dīn Maybudī's *Kashf al-asrār wa ʿuddat al-abrār* (Unveiling of Mysteries and Provision of the Righteous). Written during one of the most exciting, formative periods in Sufism's history, the commentary manifests the doctrines and the poetic language of love mysticism, which were to become essential elements of the later literature of Sufism. Dr Keeler analyses Maybudī's approach to the Qur'an, examines the mystical doctrines of the *Kashf al-asrār* and shows how Maybudī conveys these teachings through his mystical interpretations of the stories of the prophets Abraham, Moses and Joseph.

Over a decade since this book's first publication, the bibliography and notes have been updated.

Annabel Keeler is an Affiliated Researcher at the Faculty of Asian and Middle Eastern Studies and a Research Associate of Wolfson College, both at the University of Cambridge. Her research interests include Sufi exegesis, early to 'classical' Islamic mysticism, Persian literature and prophetology. As well as being the author of *Sufi Hermeneutics: The Qur'an Commentary of Rashīd al-Dīn Maybudī* (Oxford, 2006), she is co-translator of the commentary of Sahl al-Tustarī, under the title *Tafsīr al-Tustarī* (Kentucky, 2011) and co-editor of *The Spirit and the Letter: Approaches to the Esoteric Interpretation of the Qur'an* (Oxford, 2016).

The Institute of Ismaili Studies
Qur'anic Studies Series, 3
Series editor, Omar Alí-de-Unzaga

Published titles:

1. Suha Taji-Farouki, editor,
Modern Muslim Intellectuals and the Qur'an
(2004; Paperback 2006)

2. Abdullah Saeed, editor,
Approaches to the Qur'an in Contemporary Indonesia
(2005)

4. Fahmida Suleman, editor,
Word of God, Art of Man: The Qur'an and its Creative Expressions
(2007; Paperback 2010)

5. Feras Hamza and Sajjad Rizvi, editors, with Farhana Mayer,
An Anthology of Qur'anic Commentaries, Volume I: On the Nature of the Divine
(2008; Paperback 2010)

6. Toby Mayer, translator,
Keys to the Arcana: Shahrastānī's Esoteric Commentary on the Qur'an
(2009)

7. Travis Zadeh
The Vernacular Qur'an: Translation and the Rise of Persian Exegesis
(2012)

8. Martin Nguyen
Sufi Master and Qur'an Scholar: Abū'l-Qāsim al-Qushayrī and the Laṭā'if al-ishārāt
(2012)

9. Karen Bauer, editor,
Aims, Methods and Contexts of Qur'anic Exegesis (2nd/8th–9th/10th C.)
(2013)

10. Angelika Neuwirth
Scripture, Poetry and the Making of a Community: Reading the Qur'an as a Literary Text
(2014)

11. M. Brett Wilson
Translating the Qur'an in an Age of Nationalism: Print Culture and Modern Islam in Turkey
(2014)

12. Andreas Görke and Johanna Pink, editors,
Tafsīr and Islamic Intellectual History: Exploring the Boundaries of a Genre
(2014)

13. S.R. Burge, editor,
The Meaning of the Word: Lexicology and Qur'anic Exegesis
(2015)

14. Suha Taji-Farouki, editor,
The Qur'an and Its Readers Worldwide: Contemporary Commentaries and Translations (2015)

15. Annabel Keeler and Sajjad Rizvi, editors,
The Spirit and the Letter: Approaches to the Esoteric Interpretation of the Qur'an
(2016)

16. Nuha Alshaar, editor,
The Qur'an and Adab*: The Shaping of Literary Traditions in Classical Islam*
(2016)

17. Asma Hilali
The Sanaa Palimpsest: The Transmission of the Qur'an in the First Centuries AH
(2017)

Sufi Hermeneutics

The Qur'an Commentary of Rashīd al-Dīn Maybudī

Annabel Keeler

OXFORD
UNIVERSITY PRESS
in association with
THE INSTITUTE OF ISMAILI STUDIES
LONDON

OXFORD
UNIVERSITY PRESS

Great Clarendon Street, Oxford OX2 6DP

Oxford University Press is a department of the University of Oxford.
It furthers the University's objective of excellence in research, scholarship,
and education by publishing worldwide in

Oxford New York

Auckland Cape Town Dar es Salaam Hong Kong Karachi
Kuala Lumpur Madrid Melbourne Mexico City Nairobi
New Delhi Shanghai Taipei Toronto

With offices in

Argentina Austria Brazil Chile Czech Republic France Greece
Guatemala Hungary Italy Japan Poland Portugal Singapore
South Korea Switzerland Thailand Turkey Ukraine Vietnam

Oxford is a registered trade mark of Oxford University Press
in the UK and certain other countries

Published in the United States
by Oxford University Press Inc., New York

First published 2006
This paperback edition published 2017

British Library Cataloguing in Publication Data
Data available

Library of Congress Cataloging in Publication Data
Data available

Cover illustration:
Photographed by Mukhtar & Soraya Sanders of Inspiral Design
www.inspiraldesign.com
Detail of a tile section from the Great Mosque of
Yazd, Iran, fourteenth or fifteenth century.

Cover design:
Alnoor Nathani

ISBN 978-0-19-921478-5 hardback
ISBN 978-0-19-881470-2 paperback

The Institute of Ismaili Studies

THE INSTITUTE OF ISMAILI STUDIES was established in 1977 with the objectives of promoting scholarship and learning on Islam, in historical as well as contemporary contexts, and fostering a better understanding of Islam's relationship with other societies and faiths.

The Institute's programmes encourage a perspective which is not confined to the theological and religious heritage of Islam, but seeks to explore the relationship of religious ideas to broader dimensions of society and culture. The programmes thus *encourage* an interdisciplinary approach to Islamic history and thought. Particular attention is given to the issues of modernity that arise as Muslims seek to relate their heritage to the contemporary situation.

Within the Islamic tradition, the Institute promotes research on those areas which have, to date, received relatively little attention from scholars. These include the intellectual and literary expressions of Shiʿism in general and Ismailism in particular.

The Institute's objectives are realised through concrete programmes and activities organised by various departments of the Institute, at times in collaboration with other institutions of learning. These programmes and activities are informed by the full range of cultures in which Islam is practised today. From the Middle East, South and Central Asia, and Africa to the industrialised societies in the West, they consider the variety of contexts which shape the ideals, beliefs and practices of the faith.

In facilitating the *Qur'anic Studies Series* and other publications, the Institute's sole purpose is to encourage original research and analysis of relevant issues, which often leads to diverse views and interpretations. While every effort is made to ensure that the publications are of a high academic standard, the opinions expressed in these publications must be understood as belonging to their authors alone.

QUR'ANIC STUDIES SERIES

THE QUR'AN has been an inexhaustible source of intellectual and spiritual reflection in Islamic history, giving rise to ever-proliferating commentaries and interpretations. Many of these have remained a realm for specialists due to their scholarly demands. Others, more widely read, remain untranslated from the primary language of their composition. This series aims to make some of these materials from a broad chronological range —the formative centuries of Islam to the present day—available to a wider readership through translation and publication in English, accompanied where necessary by introductory or explanatory materials. The series will also include contextual-analytical and survey studies of these primary materials.

Throughout this series and others like it which may appear in the future, the aim is to allow the materials to speak for themselves. Not surprisingly, in the Muslim world where its scriptural sources continue to command passionate interest and commitment, the Qur'an has been subject to contending, often antithetical ideas and interpretations. This series takes no sides in these debates. The aim rather is to place on record the rich diversity and plurality of approaches and opinions which have appealed to the Qur'an throughout history (and even more so today). The breadth of this range, however partisan or controversial individual presentations within it may be, is instructive in itself. While there is always room in such matters for personal preferences, commitment to particular traditions of belief, and scholarly evaluations, much is to be gained by a simple appreciation, not always evident today, of the enormous wealth of intellectual effort that has been devoted to the Qur'an from the earliest times. It is hoped that through this objective, this series will prove of use to scholars and students in Qur'anic Studies as well as other allied and relevant fields.

To my parents, Denys and Angela Drower

Contents

Note on transliteration and translation xi

List of abbreviations xiii

Foreword by Gerhard Böwering xv

Preface xxi

1 Introduction 1

Part One: Hermeneutics

2 The hermeneutics of the *Kashf al-asrār* 39

3 The hermeneutics of mystical commentary in the *Kashf al-asrār* 69

Part Two: Mystical doctrine

4 The development of love mysticism in Khorasan 107

5 God and the creation 124

6 Aspects of spiritual guidance 150

7 Mystical theology and the way of love 183

Part Three: Maybudī's mystical interpretation of the stories of the prophets

Prolegomenon: Prophets in the Qur'an and in Sufi exegesis 209

8 The story of Abraham 215

9 The story of Moses 241

10 The story of Joseph 278

Conclusion 311

Bibliography 319

Index of Qur'anic citations 353

Index 359

Note on transliteration and translation

This study has followed the transliteration system used by the *International Journal of Middle East Studies* (*IJMES*), except that the Persian pronunciation of consonants in Arabic words has not been indicated (e.g. *dhikr* rather than *zikr*). The *tāʾ marbūṭa* has been rendered *-a* in passages translated from Arabic when the word is not in the construct state (e.g. *ḥaqīqa*), but *-at* in the construct form (e.g. *ḥaqīqat al-ʿishq*), or in passages translated from Persian where that form is used (e.g. *sharīʿat wa ḥaqīqat*). Only the names of less well-known places and dynasties have been transliterated. Dates are according to the *hijrī* calendar and correspond to *qamrī*, or lunar, dates. *Shamsī*, or solar, dates are indicated by 'sh'.

Translations of the Qur'an are mostly taken from Marmaduke Pickthall's *The Meaning of the Glorious Qur'an*, with some adjustment to his archaic Biblical style. Other translations have been referred to, when comparison was necessary. The Qur'anic translations cited in this study are listed below.

Abdel Haleem, Muhammad A.S. *The Qur'an: A New Translation*. Oxford, Oxford University Press, 2004.

Arberry, Arthur John. *The Koran Interpreted.* London, George Allen and Unwin, 1955.

Pickthall, Marmaduke. *The Meaning of the Glorious Koran*. First published London, Al-Furqan Publications Ltd, 1930.

Yusuf Ali, Abdullah. *The Holy Qur'an: Text, Translation and Commentary*. Cairo, al-Manār, 1938.

Abbreviations

The abbreviation of journal titles will be as in the *Index Islamicus*.

Kashf	*Kashf al-asrār wa ʿuddat al-abrār* of Rashīd al-Dīn Maybudī, Tehran, 1331-9
Ḥaqāʾiq	*Ḥaqāʾiq al-tafsīr* of Abū ʿAbd al-Raḥmān al-Sulamī, various editions listed in the bibliography
Laṭāʾif	*Laṭāʾif al-ishārāt* of Abu'l-Qāsim al-Qushayrī, Cairo, 1981
Risāla	*al-Risāla al-Qushayriyya* of Abu'l-Qāsim al-Qushayrī, Cairo, 1966
Sawāniḥ	*Sawāniḥ* of Aḥmad Ghazzālī, Tehran, 1359
Iḥyāʾ	*Iḥyāʾ ʿulūm al-dīn* of Abū Ḥāmid al-Ghazzālī, Damascus, 1417/1997
EI[1]	*Encyclopaedia of Islam*, 1st edn, Leiden, 1913-34
EI[2]	*Encyclopaedia of Islam*, 2nd edn, Leiden/London, 1960-2002
EI[r]	*Encyclopaedia Iranica*, ed. Ehsan Yarshater, London, then California, 1985-
EQ	*Encyclopaedia of The Qur'an*, ed. Jane Dammen McAuliffe. Leiden, Brill, 2001-6.
CEI	*Concise Encyclopaedia of Islam*, London, 1989
CHI	*Cambridge History of Iran*, 7 vols., Cambridge, 1968-91

List of manuscripts of *Kashf al-asrār*:

A Topkapı Sarayı (Sultan Aḥmed Library), Istanbul, MS no. 23, pre-eighth century AH, in 6 vols. (complete)

B Süleymaniye (Yeni Cami Library), Istanbul, MS no. 43, dated between AH 703 and 716, copied by Ibrāhīm b. Abī Isḥāq al-Murshidī for Faṣīḥ al-Dīn Aḥmad, 11 vols. (complete)

C Āstān-i Quds Library, Mashhad, MS no. 1232, probably sixth century AH, incomplete: from Q. 21:6 to end Q. 25

- D Istanbul University, MS no. 624, seventh or eighth century AH, incomplete: from beginning of *tafsīr* to middle of *Sūrat al-Baqara* (Q. 2)
- E Istanbul University, MS no. 625, dated AH 661, incomplete: from *Sūrat Āl ʿImrān* (Q. 3) to end of *Sūrat al-Anfāl* (Q. 8).
- F Nuru Osmaniye, Istanbul, MS no. 474, pre-700 AH, incomplete: from *Sūrat al-Anʿām* (Q. 6) to *Sūrat Yūnus* (Q. 10)

Other extant manuscripts of Maybudī's *Kashf al-asrār* can be found listed in Aḥmad Munzawī, *Fihrist-i nuskhahā-yi khaṭṭī-yi fārsī*, 6 vols. (Tehran, Regional Cultural Institute, 1969-), I, pp. 55–6, and in Ḥusayn Masarrat, *Kitābshināsī-yi Rashīd al-Dīn al-Maybudī* (Tehran, Anjuman-i āthār wa mafākhir-i farhangī, 1374sh/1995).

Foreword

Since the first half of the twentieth century, the Qur'an interpretation of the Sufi mystics has attracted the attention of scholars of Islam. Louis Massignon made the powerful argument that significant Qur'anic roots could be discovered in the mystical language that Sufism developed in the early centuries of its existence. To document his argument, he identified terms and topics of Sufi Qur'an interpretations that were included in the Arabic Sufi sources written prior to the times of Abū Ḥāmid al-Ghazzālī (d. 505/1111). In the second part of the twentieth century Henri Corbin continued this line of Sufi studies by focusing on mystical themes and symbols in the Persian sources of Islamic esoterism, especially in the period after Ghazzālī. He turned his attention not only to Sufi sources but also to Shiʿi mystical texts, of both Imami and Ismaili provenance.

One voluminous Persian Sufi commentary on the Qur'an received little attention in these studies – the massive *Kashf al-asrār*, compiled from the year 520/1126 onward by Rashīd al-Dīn Maybudī, a scholar hailing from a small town near Yazd in Iran. The Persian text was published in ten volumes about half a century ago by the persistent efforts of Ali Asghar Hekmat over eight years, from 1952 to 1960 (reprinted a number of times). In 1984, Muhammad Jawad Shariʿat added a substantial volume of indexes to this work. Since its publication, Maybudī's commentary repeatedly has been the highlight of conferences and publications in Iran but has received little attention in Western scholarship.

Annabel Keeler's hermeneutical study of this large Persian Sufi Qur'an commentary is the first major analytical study of the work in any Western language and admirably bridges this void in the field of study on Sufi hermeneutics. The reader of this monograph will value the balance between hermeneutics and doctrines that her study achieves. A special treat is the examination the monograph devotes to the sustained exposition of the stories of the prophets, Abraham, Moses and Joseph, as inspirations of mystical experience and expression. The book also includes translations of text passages that involved the author's technical labour of consulting a number of manuscripts and improving the accuracy of the actual published text of the *Kashf al-asrār* that, in its present form, is unfortunately not based on a critical edition and includes quite a number of flaws in textual clarity.

Maybudī's work is not only a *tafsīr* – the technical term for a commentary on Qur'anic verses – but also an anthology of Sufi sayings and anecdotes that are consciously combined in the work with hermeneutical insights into the inner meaning of the Qur'anic text. In the time before Maybudī, the Qur'anic commentary literature of the Sufi tradition, as compiled in Arabic, produced such standard sources as the *Ḥaqā'iq al-tafsīr* of Sulamī (d. 412/1021) and the *Laṭā'if al-ishārāt* of Qushayrī (d. 465/1072). The *Kashf al-asrār* extracts material from both sources quite freely, yet produces a different kind of Qur'anic commentary within the Sufi tradition. It funnels the Sufi Qur'an interpretation written in Arabic into a Persian framework and bases its Qur'anic hermeneutics on the concise Qur'an commentary of the famous Sufi ʿAbd Allāh Anṣārī (d. 481/1089) of Herat. In his work, Maybudī achieves a synthesis between exoteric and esoteric methods of reading the Qur'an and a fusion between strictly traditionalist doctrines and metaphorical interpretations. The characteristic mark of Maybudī's Qur'an commentary is its three-level structure (*nawbat*) that is applied equally to each of the thirty sections (*juz'*) of the Qur'an, organised as sessions (*majlis*). This tripartite structure offers Maybudī the opportunity of separating (1) literal explanations that paraphrase the Arabic text of the Qur'an in the Persian language; (2) conventional exoteric interpretations that include variant readings, accounts of the occasions of revelation, doctrinal traditions, legal implications and anecdotal illustrations; and (3) esoteric interpretations that form the substance of the genuinely mystical and esoteric Sufi commentary.

The third level, representing the mystical core of Maybudī's commentary, is identified in the introduction to the work as including 'the allegories of the mystics, the allusions of the Sufis and the subtleties of the preachers'. Maybudī clearly indicates that it is the purpose of the book to serve as a treasure trove of Qur'anic hermeneutics and edifying admonition from which the preacher can draw inspiration in his homilies before the wide public. In the last decade, M. Mahdi Rokni analysed this third level of Maybudī's Qur'anic exegesis meticulously and suggested that it revolved around three types of interpretation. One type uncovers Sufi beliefs in the quarry of the Qur'anic verses, either by discovering Sufi terms and images in the text or juxtaposing Sufi terminology with Qur'anic phrases. A second type grafts homiletic elucidations on to Qur'anic passages, thus broadening the text to offer exhortations for the reader. A third type breaks up Qur'anic verses, expanding the parts by selections from the store of tradition to enrich the inspiration of the reader.

As Annabel Keeler rightly observes, the *Kashf al-asrār* was compiled in an age when Arabic Qur'anic commentary flourished in all schools of Sunnism and Shi'ism, as highlighted by the well-known Qur'an commentaries of Zamakhsharī (d. 538/1144), Shahrastānī (d. 548/1153) and Ṭabarṣī (d. 548/1153). This medieval tradition was firmly based on the two pillars of the classical Qur'an commentary, the *Jāmiʿ al-bayān* of Ṭabarī (d. 310/923) and the *Al-Kashf wa'l-bayān* of Thaʿlabī (d. 427/1035). As well as this voluminous and highly elaborate tradition of Arabic Qur'an commentary, Maybudī could also rely on the literature of Persian Qur'an commentary that had already undergone its formative development when he began his own work. In fact, the transition in the Qur'anic commentary literature from Arabic into Persian was initiated under the Samanid ruler Manṣūr b. Nūḥ (reigned from 350/961 to 366/976), who sponsored the collaborative effort of scholars translating Qur'anic verses and stories into Persian from Ṭabarī's famous and monumental Arabic Qur'an commentary. The *Tafsīr al-Surābādī* of the Karrāmī author ʿAtīq b. Muḥammad Harawī (d. about 460/1067) and the *Tāj al-tarājim* of Ṭāhir b. Muḥammad Isfarāyinī, known as Shāhfūr (d. 471/1079), continued this Persian tradition in Saljuq times. Finally, the *Laṭā'if al-tafsār* (also known as *Tafsīr-i Zāhidī*), composed in 519/1125 by Aḥmad b. al-Ḥasan Darwajakī of Bukhara, and the massive *Rawḍ al-jinān* of Abu'l-Futūḥ Rāzī (d. 538/1144), both approximately contemporary with Maybudī, continued this tradition of Persian Qur'an commentaries into the time of the author of the *Kashf al-asrār*.

These works illustrate the extent to which Maybudī could draw on a wealth of Sufi Qur'an commentary and indicate the lead he was able to take from the Qur'an commentary tradition accessible in Persian. Furthermore, the *Kashf al-asrār* also stands in relationship to the tradition of the Persian Sufi prose treatises. Maybudī's work is by no means the first major Sufi source written in Persian. The oldest surviving substantial treatise in Persian Sufi prose, *Nūr al-murīdīn wa faẓīhat al-mudda'īn*, was composed a century before Maybudī in Transoxiana. It is a lengthy commentary by Ismāʿīl b. Muḥammad Mustamlī (d. 434/1042) of Bukhara on *Kitāb al-taʿarruf*, an early Arabic Sufi treatise by Kalābādhī (d. 380/990 or 385/995). The *Kashf al-maḥjūb*, the Persian Sufi manual written by the Ḥanafī Sufi of Ghazna, ʿAlī b. ʿUthmān Jullābī, alias Hujwīrī (d. 465/1073 or 3469/1077), is yet another major specimen of eloquent Persian Sufi prose predating Maybudī. Consideration of priority of place with regard to early Persian Sufi prose has to be given also to selections of Sufi statements, entitled *Nūr al-ʿulūm*, that, though collected later, are attributed to Abu'l-Ḥasan Kharaqānī (d. 425/1033), who was the teacher of both Abū Saʿīd b. Abi'l-Khayr Mayhanī (d. 440/1049) and Anṣārī. However the Persian hagiography of Ibn Khafīf (d. 371/982) of Shiraz, compiled by Abu'l-Ḥasan ʿAlī b. Muḥammad Daylamī, Sulamī's contemporary, is clearly a seventh/fourteenth-century Persian translation of the author's actual Arabic text. Among the Persian Sufi prose works that were authored by Maybudī's contemporaries, special attention has to be drawn to the splendid *Tamhīdāt* of ʿAyn al-Quḍāt Hamadānī (executed in 525/1131) and to the influential Persian prose works of Ghazzālī, such as the *Kīmiyā-yi saʿādat*, and the Persian poetry and prose of the *Sawāniḥ*, a work of his younger brother Aḥmad Ghazzālī (d. 520/1126).

These significant examples of early Sufi prose written in Persian demonstrate the highly developed literary environment in which Maybudī wrote his work. It was this environment that provided the basis for the magnificent flourishing of Sufi prose and poetry in Persian that marked the period from the late sixth/twelfth to the end of the seventh/thirteenth century, from Farīd al-Dīn ʿAṭṭār (d. before 617/1220) to Jalāl al-Dīn Rūmī (d. 672/1273). With regard to the seventh/fourteenth century, the influence Maybudī's Qur'an commentary had on Ḥāfiẓ (d. 792/1390), the famous Persian lyric poet of Shiraz, has been highlighted in recent years by the innovative study of Daryoush Ashouri. This study argues strongly that there exists an undeniable relationship between the terms, images and mystical attitudes found in Ḥāfiẓ's *Dīwān* and those of the *Kashf al-asrār*.

As shown by the author, the relationship of Maybudī's Qur'an commentary to that of the Ḥanbalī Sunni and Sufi master ʿAbd Allāh Anṣarī is a thorny problem which has not found a definite answer in the absence of any extant manuscript preserving Anṣārī's actual Qur'an commentary.

The internal evidence of the *Kashf al-asrār* establishes only that Maybudī frequently cites Khwāja ʿAbd Allāh Anṣārī as *Pīr-i ṭarīqat* (Master of the Path) and the *Shaykh al-Islām* with statements interpreting Qur'anic verses. It further indicates that most of these statements belong to the third level of Maybudī's commentary, indicating that Anṣārī's Qur'an interpretation was weighted toward esoteric hermeneutics. As stated in Maybudī's introduction to the work, the citations on the authority of Anṣārī were taken from a written source rather than an oral tradition. Indeed, an isolated reference in Islamic bibliography confirms Anṣārī as the author of a Qur'an commentary in the language of the Sufis. Beyond these markers, however, all other evidence about a linkage between the two scholars is circumstantial. It shows only that the Shāfiʿī Sunni Maybudī may have studied with the Ḥanbalī Sufi Anṣārī for some time, that both authors were active in Khorasan and resemble one another in combining a strict Sunni traditionalism with Sufi piety and ethics.

In her analysis of the doctrines of the *Kashf al-asrār*, Annabel Keeler reaches the apex of her study by placing the Qur'anic stories of Abraham, Moses and Joseph in the context of a 'love mysticism' that is strongly advocated by Maybudī. She finds in these prophets the basic paradigms of mystical experience and distinguishes a typology of three layers in Maybudī's vision of the prophets: (1) the historical personalities of the prophets as depicted in the literature of 'the stories of the prophets' and their underlying recitals in the Qur'an; (2) the prophets as prototypes of the spiritual wayfarer and his aspirations; and (3) the meta-historical role of the prophets in the divine plan of creation and salvation. Abraham, known as the Friend of God (*Khalīl Allāh*), presents the prototype for the mystic's friendship with God. Moses, known as the Interlocutor of God (*Kalīm Allāh*) 'brought close in communion' at the theophany of Mount Sinai, represents the mystic receiving unmediated divine inspiration and hearing God's voice without seeing the Speaker. Joseph, known as the Sincere One (*al-Ṣiddīq*) and the subject of 'the fairest story' in the Qur'an, depicts the intricate plane of love mysticism in human experience and has the invincible divine providence prevail over human design and determination. These three prophetical figures are engulfed by the light of Muhammad, known as the Beloved of God (*Ḥabīb Allāh*), who radiates as the first in creation, giving meaning to the universe, and the last of creation, the ultimate fulfillment of the divine plan of salvation.

Annabel Keeler's *Sufi Hermeneutics* is part of the new Qur'anic Studies Series published by The Institute of Ismaili Studies in London, in association with Oxford University Press. The publications in the series range from English translations and scholarly studies of classical texts to analyses of contemporary approaches to the Qur'an. Previous volumes focused on contemporary issues; Annabel Keeler's *Sufi Hermeneutics* opens a vista into the medieval world of the esoteric interpretation of the Qur'an, and illustrates the commitment of The Institute of Ismaili Studies to the study of both modern and classical Islamic texts in the field of Qur'anic Studies.

Gerhard Böwering
Yale University

Preface

Western scholarship in the field of Sufi hermeneutics has largely focused on Qur'anic commentaries written in the Arabic language. This is understandable given that Arabic, the sacred language of the Qur'an, has always been the principal language for its interpretation. Yet, from the fourth/tenth century onwards, Persian was increasingly employed for scientific and religious texts of all kinds, including Qur'anic exegesis (*tafsīr*), and in the early sixth/twelfth century the scholar and mystic Rashīd al-Dīn Maybudī demonstrated that Persian could be an effective medium for the esoteric interpretation of the Qur'an. In fact, it can be said that Maybudī's commentary, the *Kashf al-asār wa 'uddat al-abrār* (Unveiling of Mysteries and Provision of the Righteous), established the genre of Sufi *tafsīr* writing in Persian. Although it is little known outside the Persian-speaking world, Maybudī's *Kashf al-asrār* deserves far more attention than it has hitherto received, both as a source for understanding mystical hermeneutics and as a treasury of Sufi lore. In the area of Sufi interpretation, it appears to be the only extant esoteric commentary on the Qur'an dating from the first half of the sixth/twelfth century, and therefore represents a significant stage in the development of Sufi hermeneutics, between the *Laṭā'if al-ishārāt* of Abu'l-Qāsim al-Qushayrī (d. 465/1072) and the *'Arā'is al-bayān* of Rūzbihān Baqlī (d. 606/1209). At the same time, the over one thousand pages that make up Maybudī's esoteric commentary include not only detailed expositions of Sufi doctrine, but also sayings of, and anecdotes about, important figures in the history of Islamic mysticism, not to mention numerous couplets of love poetry.

Begun in the year 520/1126, the *Kashf al-asrār* is based upon and probably embodies the only surviving text of the mystical commentary on the Qur'an by the well-known Ḥanbalī Sufi, 'Abd Allāh Anṣārī of Herat (d. 481/1089). Among Anṣārī's works on Sufism, his *Manāzil al-sā'irīn*, written in Arabic, became a key work on the states and stations of the mystical path and the subject of a number of commentaries, while his *Ṭabaqāt al-ṣūfiyya*, based on the earlier work on the lives of Sufis by Abū 'Abd al-

Raḥmān al-Sulamī (d. 412/1021), was an important source for later biographies such as those of Jāmī and Farīd al-Dīn ʿAṭṭār. The eloquence of Anṣārī's Persian style, well known through his *Munājāt* (Prayers and Invocations), is much in evidence and often emulated by Maybudī in the *Kashf al-asrār*.

A unique feature of Maybudī's commentary is its arrangement in sequences of three *nawbats* (lit. turns). The Qur'an is divided into sessions of convenient length, for which Maybudī presents first a concise rendering of the meaning in Persian (*Nawbat I*), then a conventional or exoteric commentary (*Nawbat II*), and finally a mystical or esoteric commentary (*Nawbat III*). Of these three sections, it is the mystical commentary which forms by far the most interesting and original part of the work, and which is said to have influenced later Sufi commentaries on the Qur'an, such as the *Ḥadāʾiq al-ḥaqāʾiq* of Muʿīn al-Dīn Farāhī Harawī (d. 908/1502), and *Mawāhib-i ʿAliyya* of Kamāl al-Dīn Ḥusayn Wāʿiẓ Kāshifī (d. 910/1504), in Persian, and the *Rūḥ al-bayān* of Ismāʿīl Ḥaqqī Burūsawī (d. 1137/1724), in Arabic. Preserved in over fifty manuscripts, the *Kashf al-asrār* can certainly be counted as one of the most popular Persian *tafsīrs*. It appears to have enjoyed particular favour during the eighth/fourteenth and ninth/fifteenth centuries, and over thirty manuscripts date from that period. The commentary continued to be copied well into the Qājār era.

Since its publication in the 1950s, the *Kashf al-asrār* has been the subject of renewed interest in Iran. The translation of the verses (*Nawbat I*) has yielded invaluable data for linguists in their study of early New Persian in general and of the Khorasani dialect in particular. The exoteric commentary is viewed as a rich source of both Sunni and Shiʿi traditions. As a whole, the work is valued not only as one of the few extant and complete Persian commentaries on the Qur'an, but also as a work of literature in its own right, and it is regularly used as a set text for the degree in literature at various universities in Iran. Following the publication of the commentary itself, a comprehensive index, a bibliographical survey, several anthologies and the proceedings of an international conference on the *Kashf al-asrār* have been published in Iran.

However, as yet no comprehensive study has been made of the mystical hermeneutics and doctrines of the *Kashf al-asrār*. It is the purpose of this book to address these two aspects of the work, and to examine the way in which mystical doctrine and exegesis interact in the writing of a Sufi commentary on the Qur'an. Like earlier studies in the field of Sufi hermeneutics, such as those of Louis Massignon, Paul Nwyia, Gerhard Böwering and Pierre Lory, this study will therefore pay close attention to the relationship between Qur'anic word, mystical experience and the language of interpretation; but in this study, language is taken to include not only the terminology that evolved for the exposition of mystical experience, but also the newly emerging literary language that in the early sixth/twelfth century was becoming indispensable for the expression of the doctrines of mystical love. Thus, this study will consider the way in which Sufi exegesis may reflect a particular spiritual 'ethos' as well as the mystical experience of the commentator.

I have divided the study into three parts. Part one presents an analysis of the hermeneutics of the *Kashf al-asrār*; part two examines the mystical doctrines of the work; while part three illustrates the interaction of these two elements of mystical hermeneutics and doctrine by examining Maybudī's interpretation of a selection of the stories of the prophets. A brief introduction (chapter one) will serve to provide some background to the intellectual climate of the early sixth/twelfth century and to introduce the author and his work.

In the wake of developments in the field of hermeneutics by philosophers such as Schleiermacher, Heidegger, Dilthey and Gadamer, the term hermeneutics has acquired a wide application in modern scholarship which takes it far beyond the realm of scriptural interpretation. In fact, it is often used simply to mean an approach to, or way of understanding, any subject or discipline – an epistemology, even. However, the *Oxford English Dictionary* continues to define hermeneutics as 'the branch of knowledge that deals with interpretation, especially of the Bible or of literary texts'. In embarking on this study, therefore, it was necessary to locate a precise definition of the term hermeneutics that would prove suitable for the analysis of a medieval commentary on the Qur'an. This was provided by Jane Dammen McAuliffe, in her article 'Qur'ānic hermeneutics: the views of Ṭabarī and Ibn Kathīr'. In this comparative study, she presents two definitions of the term hermeneutics. She initially defines it as 'the aims and criteria of interpretation as distinct from exegesis, which denotes the practice of interpretation' and then as 'the principles and method of interpretation'. The first of these two definitions seemed to provide a promising key for understanding the hermeneutics of both exoteric and esoteric interpretation. However, as the research proceeded it became clear that this definition of hermeneutics could become more workable for the purposes of analysis if one expanded it to include 'method' (so, in a sense, this involved combining the two definitions set out by McAuliffe). Therefore apart from its general meaning of the branch of knowledge dealing with interpretation, the more specific definition of hermeneutics that is followed throughout this book is the aims, criteria and method of interpretation.

While the main focus both of this book and of Maybudī's commentary is the mystical interpretation of the Qur'an – the very title *Kashf al-asrār* (Unveiling of Mysteries) implies this – account has been taken of the fact that Maybudī chose to combine his mystical commentary with a translation and exoteric commentary. Therefore I have first examined (in chapter two) the overall hermeneutics of the *Kashf al-asrār*, on the basis both of Maybudī's own statements and of the text itself, considering in particular his reasons for combining exoteric and esoteric interpretations in one work, and for writing his commentary in Persian. I have also briefly examined the exegetical procedure of Maybudī's exoteric commentary; that is to say, I have shown how the aims and criteria of interpretation affect its practice, before passing on to the mystical hermeneutics of the work.

Maybudī does not outline any theory of mystical interpretation. However, it is possible to take advantage of his juxtaposition of exoteric and esoteric interpretations in the *Kashf al-asrār*, and, by contrasting his *Nawbat* II and *Nawbat* III commentaries on a particular passage of the Qur'an and examining the aims and criteria of each, understand more precisely the hermeneutics of mystical interpretation. Previous studies of Sufi hermeneutics, such as those of Nwyia and Böwering, have focused mainly on the doctrines and language of Sufi interpretation, and have been somewhat allusive when speaking about the *method* of interpretation. Paul Nwyia, perhaps in order to emphasize the arcane nature of Sufi interpretation, has poetically referred to it as a 'play of mirrors between the inward (*bāṭin*) of the mystic and the inward (*bāṭin*) of the scripture.' Gerhard Böwering does include a short section entitled 'Tustarī's method of Qur'anic interpretation' in his study on Sahl al-Tustarī's *tafsīr*. Here, he describes mystical exegesis as being ecstatic utterances in response to the recited Qur'an which are jotted down. He also speaks of what he calls 'key-notes, words or phrases in the verses which set off mystical thoughts or associations in the Sufi commentator'. In this book, I have attempted to examine more closely the method and procedure of mystical interpretation, drawing examples from Qushayrī's *Laṭā'if al-ishārāt* as well as from the *Kashf al-asrār*. Then, using Qushayrī's *Laṭā'if al-ishārāt* as a 'control', I have highlighted features which are peculiar to the procedure of Maybudī's mystical commentary.

My discussion of mystical doctrine in the *Kashf al-asrār* focuses on the fundamental teachings and predominant themes which Maybudī seems most concerned to communicate. In the *Kashf al-asrār*, explanations of Sufi technical terms and of the states and stations of the mystical path are not set out in any systematic order, as in a Sufi manual, but arise in different contexts whenever the author is inspired to expound them. Often they are expressed in the poetic language of allusion and metaphor, and occasionally one teaching may appear to contradict another. It has been necessary, therefore, to collate all the definitions which Maybudī gives for each technical term, before attempting to piece together a more or less coherent picture of his mystical doctrines. Whenever further clarification was needed, reference was made to Sufi manuals, or other Sufi commentaries of the fourth/tenth and fifth/eleventh centuries.

The hermeneutics of Maybudī's commentary are not examined in isolation, but within the wider context of the general development of Qur'anic hermeneutics, both in Arabic and Persian, and alongside theories of interpretation proposed by other exegetes. Likewise, the mystical teachings of the *Kashf al-asrār* are viewed against the background of doctrinal developments in Sufism up to and during the period of Maybudī, particularly in the region of Khorasan.

The two elements of hermeneutics and mystical doctrine, examined separately in the first two parts of the book, are brought together in the third, which presents a detailed account of Maybudī's mystical interpretations of the prophets Abraham, Moses and Joseph. My purpose here is to illustrate the way in which mystical doctrines are expounded *through* the exegesis of the Qur'an, and to show how the interpretations reflect the particular mystical outlook of the author (the spiritual 'ethos' referred to earlier). Of the many possible examples which could have been selected, I chose the mystical interpretations of the stories of the prophets because they constitute some of the most sustained expositions of Sufi doctrine. In each case, a brief discussion of the place which the prophets hold in the

Qur'an, in hadith literature, and in the Islamic tradition in general precedes the discussion of the esoteric interpretation of their stories. This is in keeping with Maybudī's principle of not presenting the esoteric in isolation from the exoteric. Moreover, it will be seen that often the mystical interpretations have their root in the Qur'anic or traditional identity or 'type' of the prophet.

No serious study of Maybudī's commentary can ignore the fact that it presents what at first sight appear to be two contradictory doctrinal perspectives: that of a strict and dogmatic traditionalist, who insists that knowledge can only be derived from the Qur'an and the sayings of Prophet and the pious predecessors, and who disallows all metaphorical interpretations of the Scripture; and that of an ecstatic love mystic, who sets forth allusive, poetic and often allegorical interpretations of the Qur'anic verses. One of the interesting challenges of this study has been to understand how these two apparently incongruous approaches not only co-exist, but are integrally linked in the mystical teachings of Maybudī.

A word should be said here about the use of the word 'Sufi' in this book. As a noun, I have employed this word to mean 'a proponent of Islamic mysticism' (and as an adjective, 'pertaining to Islamic mysticism'), in the form that it has been practiced, and continues to be so, among Sunni and some Shiʿi Muslims – in contradistinction to the more philosophically based form of mysticism that is commonly referred to in Iranian circles as *ʿirfān*. This is, of course, a retrospective use of the term Sufi – that is to say, during the sixth/twelfth century, the word 'Sufi', which early on was especially associated with mystics of Baghdad, had not yet gained universal currency among the mystics of Khorasan, including Maybudī, who typically used other terms, such as *ʿārif* (a mystic, or possessor of mystical knowledge or gnosis) *ʿāshiq* (mystical lover), *ahl-i ṭarīqat* (person or people of the spiritual path), or *ahl-i ḥaqīqat* (person or people of realised truth or spiritual realisation). In this book, the words Sufi and mystic/mystical will be used interchangeably. In relation to interpretation, the adjective 'mystical' will be used to refer to the nature of its content, while the term 'esoteric' will be used as an equivalent to the Arabic term *bāṭin* (inner), as distinct from *ẓāhir*, which denotes the outer meanings or exoteric interpretation of the Qur'an. Throughout the book, masculine pronouns, when not referring to a specific male-gendered personage, are intended inclusively, as are the generic terms 'man' and 'mankind'.

The research for this book has for the most part relied on the present published edition of the *Kashf al-asrār*, which, regrettably, is not a critical edition of the text. However, I have recently had access to several manuscripts of the commentary, and have consulted these manuscripts for clarification wherever I discovered in the passages that I was translating obscurities or obvious mistakes in the published text. Any amendments made on the basis of the manuscripts have been mentioned in the notes. The manuscripts consulted are listed in the editorial notes on pp. xiii and xiv.

Since the first publication of this book, a number of publications on Maybudī's *Kashf al-asrār* have appeared. A selection of those which have been brought out as monographs will be mentioned here, while some recently authored articles have been added to the bibliography. In 2007 a list of typographical errors in the published edition of the *Kashf al-asrār*, compiled by Aḥmad Mahdawī Damghānī, was published by Ayene-ye Miras under the title *Ṣawābnāma-yi aghlāṭ-i chāpī-yi mujalladāt-i dehgāna-yi tafsīr-i sharīf-i Kashf al-asrār wa ʿuddat al-abrār* (Tehran, 2007). More recently, an abridged English translation of the third *nawbat* of Maybudī's *Kashf al-asrār* (amounting to about half of the mystical commentary) by William C. Chittick has been published as *The Unveiling of Mysteries and Provision of the Righteous* by Fons Vitae in 2015. A Persian translation of the present monograph by Jawad Qasemi was published in Tehran in 2016 by Mīrās-i Maktūb. More widely in the field of Sufi Qur'an interpretation, various critical editions, several translations into English and monographs in Western languages have appeared. Among the critical editions are Ibn Barrajān's commentary, edited by Gerhard Böwering and Yousef Casewit, and the first part of Najm al-Dīn Rāzī's *Baḥr al-ḥaqāʾiq* by Mohammad Movahedi; among the translations or partial translations are the commentaries of Sahl al-Tustarī, Qushayrī, Kāshāni and Ibn ʿAjība; and monographs include one on Qushayrī's *Laṭāʾif al-ishārāt*, by Martin Nguyen, and one on Ibn Barrajān, by Yousef Casewit. In addition, a collected volume on the esoteric interpretation of the Qur'an, edited by Sajjad Rizvi and myself, has also been published. Details of all these publications and several recent articles in the field may be found in the Bibliography.

It remains for me to express my gratitude to all of those who, in numerous ways, have helped me during the course of preparing this book. Any and all mistakes, of course, are my own. I should first acknowledge the advice and encouragement given to me by the two teachers who guided me in the writing of the thesis on which this book is based, namely the late John Cooper, who was my supervisor in Cambridge until his sudden death in 1998, and Tim Winter, lecturer in Islamic Studies at the Faculty of Divinity, who oversaw the completion of the thesis. Subsequently, and despite his busy schedule, Dr Winter has always been ready to answer questions that have arisen during the preparation of the book.

In Iran, I am greatly indebted to Dr Nasrollah Pourjavady, for all the articles and books he has made available to me, for his advice on the translation of Sufi technical terms and poetical idioms, for answering countless queries, and for the many insights he has given me into the history of Sufism. I would also like to thank Dr Muhammad Husseini of the Ṭabāṭabāʾī University in Tehran. He is at present preparing a new and critical edition of the *Kashf al-asrār*, and he and his family have been more than hospitable to me, allowing me to take over their dining room table for an entire fortnight, so that I was able to spend time examining copies of different manuscripts of the *Kashf al-asrār*. I would also like to thank the translator of my book Dr Jawad Qasemi, who pointed out several errors in the referencing, and made one or two helpful suggestions on the Persian renderings of certain words.

Others to whom I would like to express my gratitude are Prof. Hermann Landolt, Prof. Wilferd Madelung, Dr Sajjad Rizvi, Dr Tobias Mayer and Farhana Mayer, all of whom made helpful comments on the book at different stages of its preparation. Among the many friends who have helped in different ways I would particularly like to mention Fatima Azzam, Aziza Spiker, Reza Pourjavady and the late Peter Avery.

I would like to acknowledge the assistance given to me by The Institute of Ismaili Studies, which in 2002 offered me a generous research fellowship, allowing me to devote one year entirely to the revision and expansion of my thesis for publication as a book. I would also like to express my appreciation to members of the team at Qur'anic Studies Unit, especially Nancy Hynes and Christina Phillips, for their painstaking efforts towards preparing the book for publication.

Last, but definitely not least, I would like to thank my family, who always help me keep my work in perspective, and especially my husband Paul, for his constant, loving support and encouragement.

1

Introduction

The intellectual climate

The twelfth century (sixth century of the *hijra*) could be described as a period of both consolidation and creativity in the history of Islamic thought. It began with the writing of Abū Ḥāmid al-Ghazzālī's great synthesis of religious knowledge, the *Iḥyā' ʿulūm al-dīn*, and ended with the development of a new school of philosophy, the *Ḥikmat al-ishrāq* or 'Philosophy of illumination' by Shihāb al-Dīn Yaḥyā al-Suhrawardī (d. 587/1191), and the regeneration of speculative theology by Fakhr al-Dīn al-Rāzī (d. 606/1209). This was also a particularly creative period for Islamic mysticism. Although in the history of Sufism, the sixth/twelfth century might appear to have been overshadowed by the many famous names of the preceding century, such as Sulamī, Qushayrī, Anṣārī and Abū Saʿīd b. Abi'l-Khayr (d. 440/1049), and dwarfed by the two mystical giants of the following century, Jalāl al-Dīn Rūmī (d. 672/1273) and Muḥyi'l-Dīn Ibn ʿArabī (d. 638/1240), it could nonetheless boast challenging and imaginative figures such as ʿAyn al-Quḍāt Hamadānī (d. 525/1131) and Rūzbihān Baqlī (d. 606/1209), as well as great mystic poets such as Sanā'ī (d. 525/1131) and Farīd al-Dīn ʿAṭṭār (d. before 617/1220). It was, moreover, an important formative period in the history of Sufism, for it saw simultaneously the evolution of the mystical doctrines of love and of a new literary language for their expression. These momentous developments were to have a profound and enduring impact on Sufism and its literature throughout the Persian-speaking world and beyond.

Such fresh departures in thought and literature were no doubt made possible by the processes of stabilisation, systematisation and synthesis that had gone before. During the course of the fifth/eleventh century, first the Ghaznavids and then the Saljuqs had gradually re-established Sunni rule over most of the Iranian plateau, capturing the lands of western Iran from the long-standing Buyid dynasty, the holy cities in the Hijaz from the Fatimids, and extending their empire as far as Syria and Anatolia. Niẓām al-Mulk (d. 485/1092), vizier first to the Saljuq sultan Alp Arslān and then to his young son Malik Shāh, took further steps to bolster the Sunni cause by setting up a chain of madrasas which specialised in the teaching of his preferred school of Shāfiʿī law. Apart from strengthening the Shāfiʿī school, the establishment of these madrasas in Baghdad, Nishapur, Herat, Merv and other important cities of the Saljuq empire helped to defuse some of the factional tension that had arisen following the systematic persecution of Shāfiʿīs and Ashʿarīs by Niẓām al-Mulk's predecessor as vizier, Abū Naṣr al-Kundurī (d. 457/1065).[1]

Though the Niẓāmiyya madrasas were by no means the first institutions of their kind, they were apparently the first to have been conceived of as a chain with a more or less standardised curriculum.[2] Each of the Niẓāmiyya madrasas also had the advantage of a generous endowment (*waqf*) which provided not only stipends for the teachers but also scholarships for the students, who resided at the academy for a number of years. Graduates of the Niẓāmiyya had enhanced status and were able to find prominent positions in society as Shāfiʿī *qāḍī*s, *faqīh*s, imams and so on.[3] Makdisi has argued that Ashʿarī theology was not, as previously supposed, a part of the *official* curriculum of the Niẓāmiyya, and this would certainly have been in keeping with the astute diplomacy of Niẓām al-Mulk.[4] Nevertheless, the vizier did to some degree attempt to promote the Ashʿarī school of theology by patronising scholars who were either proponents of, or strongly associated with, Ashʿarism, such as ʿAbd al-Malik al-Juwaynī, known as Imām al-Ḥaramayn (d. 478/1085), and Abū Ḥāmid al-Ghazzālī (d. 505/1111).[5] Moreover, it is hard to imagine that some impromptu discussion of, if not instruction in, theology did not take place in these educational establishments,[6] and since most (though not all) Shāfiʿīs followed al-Ashʿarī in theology, the promotion of Shāfiʿism already served to advance the cause of Ashʿarism.[7] In any case, Niẓām al-Mulk's intention in founding these madrasas was not to exacerbate theological tensions within the Sunni fold, but more likely to train up a body of well-grounded religious scholars who could effectively argue against the propaganda of the Ismailis[8] and of the charismatic Karrāmiyya, who were still active in Khorasan.[9]

By the end of the first quarter of the sixth/twelfth century, the religious climate might appear to have become more stable and settled. The military hold of the Ismailis had, in Iran at least, become confined to pockets in the mountain regions of the Alburz, Alamut, Quhistan and territories close to the Caspian sea, while the Karrāmiyya, having long since lost their hold on the important city of Nishapur, had moved the centre of their activities to the mountainous region of Ghur. Yet vigorous and at times violent competition between different Muslim sects and schools of thought continued throughout the century.[10] If anything, the strengthening of the Shāfiʿī/Ashʿarī position and the influential writings of Abū Ḥāmid al-Ghazzālī served to stimulate intellectual activity among ideological rivals, who sought to consolidate and promote their own beliefs, as well as making appraisals or critiques of others in works of various kinds.

The notable output of Sunni and Shiʿi heresiographical works during the sixth/twelfth century demonstrates a sharp awareness of this polemical background.[11] In the field of Qur'anic exegesis, the same century witnessed the composition of two important Shiʿi commentaries on the Qur'an, the Arabic *Majmaʿ al-bayān* of Ṭabrisī (d. 548/1153),[12] and the Persian *Rawḍ al-jinān* of Abu'l-Futūḥ Rāzī (d. mid-sixth/twelfth century);[13] an influential Muʿtazilī commentary by Abu'l-Qāsim al-Zamakhsharī (d. 538/1144);[14] and a philosophically-oriented and Ismaili-influenced commentary by the theologian Abu'l-Fatḥ al-Shahrastānī (d. 548/1153).[15] We shall see that by writing his commentary in Persian, Maybudī was trying to promote a traditionalist form of Shāfiʿī Sufism that was anti-Ashʿarī, anti-Muʿtazilī, and certainly anti-philosophy. For it is another complexity of this period that while Ghazzālī strongly criticised aspects of philosophy in a number of his works, most notably in his *Tahāfut al-falāsifa*, he was not entirely against philosophy, and his ideas and methodology reveal the influence of both philosophy and logic.[16] This may well have paved the way for later Ashʿarī theologians to adopt a more open approach not only to logic but also to philosophy, despite Ghazzālī's condemnation of the latter.[17] It is arguable that it also encouraged Sufis of the sixth/twelfth century to draw more freely on the philosophical tradition, though this may simply have been another of the possibilities that were opened up with the greater emancipation of Sufism.[18]

The patronage of Niẓām al-Mulk and the writings of Ghazzālī contributed to an enhancement of the status of Sufism during the late fifth/eleventh and early sixth/twelfth centuries. However, these two figures cannot be given the entire credit for this shift, as the process had been gradually taking place for more than a century.[19] Between the late fourth/tenth and mid-fifth/eleventh centuries, several Sufi scholars had set about documenting the teachings of Sufism and recording the lives and sayings of great mystics. These compilations, which took the form of Sufi 'manuals'[20] and biographical dictionaries or *Ṭabaqāt* works,[21] served not only to systematise and expound the doctrines of Sufism, but also to demonstrate the legitimacy of Sufism. Clearly, at this time there continued to be those among the ulema who disapproved of aspects of Sufi doctrine, but now matters were being made worse by the actions of antinomians and others, claiming to be Sufis, who were giving Sufism a bad name.[22] The works that these Sufi scholars produced were valuable in a number of ways: they preserved in writing for posterity a great deal of early Sufi lore that had hitherto mainly been transmitted through the oral tradition; they defined the parameters of Sufism, both assisting the Sufis' own self-knowledge and clarifying what Sufism was and was not for others; they stimulated the theoretical disciplines within Sufism; and (in Khorasan) they established Sufism as the mainstream over and against competing mystical and ascetic traditions.[23] For all these reasons they must certainly also have added to the credibility of Sufism, though it is doubtful that they could ever win over the most exoterically-inclined religious scholars.

By the middle of the fifth/eleventh century, it appears that the situation of Sufism within society was already changing, and Sufis were beginning to take on a more influential role both with those in power and with the populace.[24] Anecdotes in the histories of this period and in hagiographical literature indicate that celebrated mystics of the time were held in respect, and even in awe, by the Turkish sultans.[25] At the same time, charismatic Sufis like Abū Saʿīd b. Abi'l-Khayr were attracting increasingly large numbers of followers from all walks of life. On the other hand, there were the more 'conservative' Sufis, such as Qushayrī, who had standing among the ulema, and who were therefore part of that class of bureaucrats and religious scholars upon whom the Saljuq rulers depended.[26] By virtue of their religious authority, these Sufi members of the scholarly elite could also wield influence with the people, especially in the cities.[27]

Another aspect of the growing prominence of Sufism during the fifth/eleventh century was the development of the Sufi 'lodge' or *khānaqāh*. It had long been customary for Sufis to gather at a certain place to imbibe the teachings of their shaykh or *pīr*. When this was simply a case of listening to a talk or sermon, such gatherings might take place in a circle in the mosque, but when they involved Sufi ceremonies such as 'spiritual concert' (*samāʿ*), they were more likely to be held at the shaykh's home or, after his death, at a shrine close to his tomb. As places where Sufis could stay, either when in retreat or when travelling, such gathering places were known as *ribāṭ*s and *duwayra*s or, increasingly from the late fourth/tenth century on, as *khānaqāh*s. By the mid-fifth/eleventh century, it appears that in Khorasan the institution was becoming more formalised, and Abū Saʿīd is reported to have drawn up a code of rules for people in the *khānaqāh*.[28] This institutionalisation of the *khānaqāh* was no doubt associated with the growing popular appeal of Sufism and the changing role of shaykhs and *pīr*s in relation to their disciples, which appears to have been taking place in Khorasan around the same time.[29] Shaykhs such as Abū Saʿīd, and later Aḥmad Jām (d. 536/1141), were becoming more 'paternalistic', more directly involved in the day-to-day supervision of the spiritual lives of their disciples and their overall well-being.[30] Disciples, for their part, were expected to bind themselves loyally to one shaykh, rather than going from one to another in search of knowledge, as had previously been the custom.[31] The ever-growing circle of devoted followers around such figures not only attracted patronage from the wealthy and powerful, among them several of the Saljuq administrators,[32] but also accrued considerable sums from smaller donations given daily by the people of the bazaar.[33] Thus the shaykh had the additional power and responsibility of disposing wealth to the needy, not to mention offering hospitality to large numbers of followers.[34] One indication of the establishment of these institutions, and the growing respectability of Sufism during the latter part of the fifth/eleventh century, was the building and endowment of several *khānaqāh*s in different cities by Saljuq officials – Niẓām al-Mulk himself endowed at least one.[35] Toward the end of the century, *khānaqāh*s were sufficiently established and powerful as an institution for Ghazzālī to be asked to issue a fatwa concerning the administration of endowments in them.[36]

In fact, by the time Ghazzālī began to write his *Iḥyāʾ ʿulūm al-dīn*, Sufism already featured more prominently in Muslim society. *Khānaqāhs* founded by the ruling powers stood as sacred buildings alongside mosques,[37] and Sufi doctrine was being taught as part of the curriculum in several madrasas.[38] Ghazzālī's significant contribution was to provide a sound intellectual basis for the new, still fragile emancipation of Sufism, which had thus far been fostered by a favourable social and political climate. In his *Iḥyā'* and in other works, such as the *Munqidh min al-ḍalāl*, Ghazzālī argues unequivocally for the intellectual superiority of mystical knowledge. Moreover, it appears that the *Iḥyā'* and Ghazzālī's Persian work the *Kīmiyā-yi sa'ādat* were not written *exclusively* for the ulema or for a Sufi elite, but, as Hodgson has observed, 'for a private person, concerned for his own life or charged with the spiritual direction of others.'[39] In the *Iḥyā'*, Ghazzālī discusses all the Shari'a laws that are obligatory for each individual as well as almost every aspect of religious life, explaining its intellectual significance, its moral and social benefit, and how it can become a means for the purification of the soul, if not for spiritual realisation. In this work, as well as in others, Ghazzālī explicitly speaks of a threefold hierarchy of knowledge in society: the commonalty (*'āmm*), that is, those who believe in the truths of religion without questioning; the elite (*khāṣṣ*), who learn reasons for their beliefs (by whom he is implying the religious scholars and especially speculative theologians); and finally the elite of the elite (*khāṣṣ al-khawāṣṣ*), those who directly experience religious truth, namely Sufis. Hodgson has observed that for Ghazzālī, this hierarchy of knowledge also implied a moral function, such that each of the classes could teach the one below it and act as an example for it. It follows by implication that those who are lower in the hierarchy should be receptive to the knowledge of those in the class above, and that therefore 'the Shar'ī men of religion had the responsibility to receive Sufi inspiration so far as they could, and to spread the inward spirit of religion and not merely the outward doctrines, among the populace generally.' This point leads Hodgson to observe: 'Thus the high evaluation of Sufi experience as a vindication of truth had social consequences which Ghazzālī did not quite dare spell out but which he himself provided a living example of.'[40] Ghazzālī's achievement, therefore, was to have placed the spiritual and intellectual disciplines of Sufism firmly among the traditional sciences of Islam. Certainly, after him Sufism was no longer preoccupied with defending its right to existence.[41]

At the opening of the sixth/twelfth century then, the stage was set for a new and creative phase in the history of Sufism. It was during this period that the doctrines of love mysticism, which had been growing ever more prevalent during the last decades of the fifth/eleventh century, began to be fully developed and articulated. A decisive moment in this development came when Abū Ḥāmid's younger brother Aḥmad Ghazzālī (d. 520/1126) wrote his seminal treatise on love, the *Sawāniḥ*.[42] This work was important because it added an intellectual dimension to love mysticism, for it showed love to be not merely a state or a station, or an emotional yearning of the servant for his or her Lord, but a complete spiritual way, with its own metaphysic. The *Sawāniḥ* was composed in Persian, and it was Persian that became the natural and preferred language for the expression of the doctrines of love. Love mysticism, in turn, gave Persian literature a new lease of life. The love lyric (*ghazal*) gained new depths as poets ambiguously serenaded and eulogised a human/divine beloved/Beloved – this ambiguity itself being an allusion to the profound analogical, for some Sufis existential, connection between human and divine love. Even before the *ghazal*, the quatrain or *rubāʿī*, an indigenous Persian genre, had been appropriated for love mysticism. The *rubāʿī* had the added advantage of being easily incorporated into sermons and passages of prose. Persian prose itself, which had hitherto tended to be plain and functional in character, was now transformed into an artistic medium, becoming all but poetry with its use of metaphor, assonance, rhythm and rhyme. It was in the prose and poetry of this period that the metaphorical language of love mysticism became fully established, and the now familiar themes and images of the tavern and wine drinking, gambling, the ball and polo-stick, and every detail of the beloved's physiognomy became invested with symbolic meaning. These metaphors would become standard for all love-mystical literature in centuries to come.[43]

But this should be seen as a formative era in Persian Sufism not only in terms of its literary language; all of the doctrines and aspects of mystical love that were expounded in Sufi works of prose and poetry during this period can be found echoed and re-echoed in the masterpieces of later Persian poets. These include the coquetry of the Beloved; the pain of separation and the joy of union; the need to be 'cooked' by love's suffering; the moth and the candle symbolising sacrifice in the fire of love; and so on.[44]

At the same time that the doctrines of love mysticism were gaining ground in eastern Iran, Sufism was, as we have seen, increasingly reaching out to society at large; again, Persian had its role to play as a more suitable language than Arabic to address the more universal audience in Iranian lands. One aspect of this phenomenon in mystical literature is the increased use of story-telling as a popular and appealing mode of communication. Stories had always been used by preachers, of course, and were no doubt already part of the oral tradition of Sufism. Now, in addition to exemplary anecdotes about saints, parables and even animal fables were also finding their way into Sufi written works of all kinds.[45] It is probably no coincidence that during this same century, the epic *mathnawī* with its sequences of inter-related tales became established as a didactic genre of mystical poetry. The mystical *mathnawī*s of Sanāʾī, at the beginning of the sixth/twelfth century, and of ʿAṭṭār at the end, were to pave the way for Rūmī's great *mathnawī* in the century that followed.

It was in this stimulating and creative climate, then, that Rashīd al-Dīn Maybudī composed his commentary on the Qur'an. We shall find that many of these currents, the themes and doctrines of mystical love in their most artistic expression, together with the moral and theological concerns of the day, flow through the pages of the *Kashf al-asrār*.

The state of Qur'anic hermeneutics

By the time Maybudī began to compose the *Kashf al-asrār* in 520/1126, Qur'anic hermeneutics were, like most other Islamic sciences, in a state of maturity.[46] Over two centuries earlier Abū Jaʿfar al-Ṭabarī (d. 310/923), in his commentary the *Jāmiʿ al-bayān ʿan taʾwīl āy al-Qurʾān*, had not only amassed a vast number of exegetical traditions, the comments of the Prophet, the Companions and the Followers, together with their chains of transmission, he had also developed his own criteria for evaluating the different opinions on each verse, the variant readings and the arguments of the philologists and grammarians.[47]

For commentators who came after him, Ṭabarī's work was an invaluable source, although by no means the only one; there were other commentaries such as those of Muqātil b. Sulaymān (d. 150/767) and Ibn Qutayba (d. 274/887), and compilations of comments attributed to Ibn ʿAbbās (d.

68/687), Mujāhid (d. between 100/718 and 102/722) and Sufyān al-Thawrī (d. 161/778).[48] Moreover hadith collections of Bukhārī (d. 256/870), Muslim (d. 261/875) and Tirmidhī (d. 279/892) had chapters devoted to those hadiths which commented upon the Qur'an. Other sources for these commentators included the compilations of the stories of the prophets, the *Qiṣaṣ al-anbiyāʾ* of Kisāʾī (dates not known), Ibn Bishr (d. 206/821) and others; works on various aspects of lexicography and grammar, on variant readings, and on other specialized areas of exegesis, such as abrogating and abrogated verses (*al-nāsikh wa'l-mansūkh*), aspects of meaning and analogues (*wujūh wa naẓāʾir*), *majāz al-Qurʾān*, *aḥkām al-Qurʾān*, *gharīb al-Qurʾān* and so on.[49] Later exegetes would also have the benefit of further developments in the sciences of hadith in order to make their own assessments of traditions according to the content and soundness of their chains of transmission (*isnād*), and in the field of Qur'anic sciences many new works would be added on specialized topics of exegesis.

However, it was not just as a source of exegetical traditions that Ṭabarī's *Jāmiʿ al-bayān* was important; it could also be said that it laid the foundations for the development of a genre of verse-by-verse commentary on the Qur'an which treated, to a greater or lesser extent, all the conventional aspects of exegesis: the circumstances of Revelation (*asbāb al-nuzūl*), abrogating and abrogated verses (*al-nāsikh wa'l-mansūkh*), variant readings (*qirāʾāt*), stories of the prophets (*qiṣaṣ al-anbiyāʾ*), clear and ambiguous verses (*al-muḥkam wa'l-mutashābih*), questions of lexicography and grammar, and matters of law. This genre became the most widely accepted format for Qur'anic exegesis, for it could be adapted according to the sectarian or theological persuasion of the commentator.[50] It might be based entirely on received tradition, that is traditional material that has been handed down (*tafsīr bi'l-maʾthūr*), or it might involve much more of the reasoned opinion of the author (*tafsīr bi'l-raʾy*), or a combination of the two. Furthermore, greater emphasis might be placed upon one discipline; for example Zamakhsharī, whose influential commentary was mentioned earlier, greatly developed the use of grammatical and lexicographical arguments in his Muʿtazilī commentary, *al-Kashshāf ʿan ḥaqāʾiq al-tanzīl*.

Meanwhile mystical exegesis had, from about the third/ninth century onwards, separated itself from the mainstream of exoteric commentary. This may have been due to the fact that Ṭabarī had set a precedent by choosing to exclude esoteric and allegorical exegesis altogether from the

Jāmiʿ al-bayān, because, as Gilliot has suggested, his interest was essentially that of a *faqīh*.[51] On the other hand, mystical exegesis may have had a separate existence quite naturally because it demanded a different approach and was intended for a more specialised audience of people who were to some extent involved in mysticism.[52] Whilst accepting the outer meanings of the Qur'an, Sufi commentators held that the scripture also has inner meanings that pertain to, and can shed light on, spiritual states and realities. They defined this process of eliciting the inner meanings from the Qur'an as *istinbāṭ* (lit. drawing up water from a well).[53] The earliest surviving Sufi commentary on the Qur'an is the *Tafsīr al-Qurʾān al-ʿaẓīm* of Sahl b. ʿAbd Allāh al-Tustarī (d. 283/896).[54] However, the *Ḥaqāʾiq al-tafsīr* of the fifth/eleventh century Sufi Abū ʿAbd al-Raḥmān al-Sulamī (d. 412/1021) includes esoteric comments attributed to other early mystics, such as al-Ḥasan al-Baṣrī (d. 110/728), Jaʿfar al-Ṣādiq (d. 148/765), Ibn ʿAṭāʾ al-Adamī (d. 309/922)[55] and Ḥusayn b. Manṣūr al-Ḥallāj (309/922). Sulamī compiled this commentary, along with its supplement, the *Ziyādāt ḥaqāʾiq al-tafsīr*, from the oral tradition as well as from written sources.[56]

Qur'anic commentary was not only to be found in *tafsīr* works. It often appeared in religious works of a more general nature, such as Ghazzālī's *Iḥyāʾ ʿulūm al-dīn*. In Sufi works, esoteric interpretation was often implied when a Qur'anic verse was quoted to endorse some mystical teaching, while some Sufi manuals included sections on the esoteric exegesis of the Qur'an.[57]

Thus when Maybudī began to write the *Kashf al-asrār*, he had a wealth of existing exegetical material on which to draw. He also had a genre in which to work; that is, he would adhere to certain norms by including those aspects which would be expected to appear in any major commentary on the Qur'an. However, in writing the *Kashf al-asrār* he was to take an unusual step by bringing together the exoteric and esoteric exegesis of the Qur'an in one work.[58] Moreover, he chose to compose his commentary in Persian, and here he may also have been breaking new ground; at least, we so far have no extant evidence of a complete mystical commentary on the Qur'an written in Persian before the sixth/twelfth century.

The time was clearly ripe for such an enterprise, for by now Persian *tafsīr* writing had also reached a certain maturity. Whereas the earliest known Persian commentary on the Qur'an, the so-called translation of

Ṭabarī's *tafsīr* commissioned by the Samanids in the late third/ninth century, consisted of little more than a translation of the verses and storytelling, Persian *tafsīrs* written in the fourth/tenth and fifth/eleventh centuries show distinct development regarding the level of intellectual content, the extent of scholarly material and the number of Arabic quotations included.[59] Therefore, although a commentary written in Persian clearly took Qur'anic interpretation and made it accessible to a much wider public, rather than the preserve of an Arabic literary elite, it cannot be said that Persian *tafsīrs* were solely aimed at the uneducated masses. The range of 'audience' for which Persian *tafsīrs* were intended is indicated by the late fifth/eleventh century exegete Isfarāyinī, who, in the introduction to his commentary the *Tāj al-tarājim*, writes that 'the community (*ummat*) have unanimously agreed that the exegesis of the Qur'an should be read out in Persian, both at scholarly gatherings and from the *minbar*, at assemblies where everyone, the [scholarly] elite (*khāṣṣ*) and common people (*'āmm*), religious and wordly alike, is present'.[60]

Maybudī, too, appears to have intended his commentary for a wide public. In the introduction to the *Kashf al-asrār*, he states that he will write his commentary in such a way as to make it easy for those 'involved in this field'.[61] Yet the rhetorical style and scope of the content of his commentary (discussed in chapters two and three) suggest that he did not intend it exclusively for students of Qur'anic exegesis, but for a wider audience of varying intellectual ability. Moreover, the prose style of the mystical sections of the *Kashf al-asrār* is far more accessible than, for example, that of Qushayrī's *Laṭā'if al-ishārāt*, which is written in a concise elliptical style probably more suited to adepts of the Sufi path. It appears that Maybudī's mystical commentary was intended both for those who had been initiated into the practice of Sufism and for those who, though not themselves intitiated into the mystical path, were not antagonistic towards it.

This was an age when Sufism was more actively moving out into the community, particularly in Khorasan; a period when 'new-style' shaykhs (to use Jürgen Paul's expression) were playing a more prominent and influential role in the life of the community, attracting followers and patronage, often at the expense of traditional Sufis and the ulema.[62] These Sufi shaykhs were more accessible than their predecessors. No longer viewed as intellectually aloof, they were ready to go out and preach their doctrines to people in the Persian language.[63] It was also a time when preachers were known to encourage and patronise the recitation of Persian mystical and ascetic poetry, which may even have been recited alongside their sermons to enhance their popular appeal.[64]

Clearly, this was a favourable and auspicious climate for writing a mystical *tafsīr* in Persian. However, we shall see that there may also have been aesthetic reasons for Maybudī's choice of the Persian language for his commentary: it would give him more scope for the free and poetic expression of themes associated with the doctrines of love.

The author

Until the 1950s, there was some confusion as to the authorship of the *Kashf al-asrār*. Ḥājjī Khalīfa and subsequently Charles Storey attributed the commentary to Taftazānī (b. 722/1322)[65] and, because the work was based on a Qur'anic commentary by ʿAbd Allāh Anṣārī which has otherwise been lost, some manuscripts bear the title 'Anṣārī's Tafsīr'.[66] Indeed, the present printed edition is subtitled '*Maʿrūf bi-tafsīr-i Khwāja ʿAbd Allāh al-Anṣārī*'. It was Ali Asghar Hekmat who, in preparing the published edition, examined several manuscripts and finally established that the author of the work was Abu'l-Faḍl Aḥmad b. Abī Saʿd b. Aḥmad b. Mihrīzad al-Maybudī, otherwise known as Rashīd al-Dīn Maybudī.[67]

About Maybudī's life we have no information except the date of his beginning to write the *Kashf al-asrār*: 520/1126.[68] Since the commentary is likely to be the work of a man in his mature years it can be surmised that he was born some time in the second half of the fifth/eleventh century and died in the first half of the sixth/twelfth century. It has been suggested that his father was Jamāl al-Islām Abū Saʿd b. Aḥmad b. Mihrīzad, who died in 480/1087.[69] According to the histories of Yazd,[70] Jamāl al-Islām was descended from Anūshirvān the Just. One of his ancestors (perhaps a Zoroastrian) had embraced Islam after a dream in which he saw the Prophet. He later became a disciple of Ibrāhīm b. Adham (d. 166/783), leaving his position at court to take up a life of asceticism, poverty and devotion. We are told that Jamāl al-Islām was blessed with spiritual gifts from an early age. Whilst still a child he, too, had a miraculous dream of the Prophet, as a result of which[71] he became a *ḥāfiẓ* of the Qur'an and a master in all the religious sciences. Later, he outshone in scholarly debate some of the great ulema of his time, including Imām al-Ḥaramayn.[72] He is said to have 'devoted himself to guiding people on the highway of mysticism (*ʿirfān*)' and to have 'brought those straying in the sea of disobedience back to follow the Shariʿa.' Whoever followed his guidance was 'led to the shore of salvation and found prosperity in the two worlds'.[73] Jamāl al-Islām's tomb, built together with a *khānaqāh* in 748/1347, is reputed to have been the site of a number of miracles, and continued to be visited until Safavid times. His children are described as having been virtuous ascetics,[74] while his descendants are said to have been mostly virtuous and learned, and 'honoured by sultans'.[75] Among his descendants, the most celebrated seem to have been Saʿīd Ghiyāth al-Dīn ʿAlī Munshī[76] and Shihāb al-Dīn Muḥammad.[77] Of his direct descendants the only one mentioned by name is a son, Shihāb al-Dīn ʿAlī, who is described as having been 'an eminent man of religion and author of a number of works' of which one is named *Sharḥ al-ḥāwī*.[78] While no other direct descendant of Jamāl al-Dīn is named in the histories, Iraj Afshar has found the gravestone of another son, Saʿīd Muwaffaq al-Dīn Abī Jaʿfar b. Abī Saʿd b. Aḥmad b. Mihrīzad, and of a grand-daughter, the daughter of our commentator, named Fāṭima bint al-Imām Saʿīd Rashīd al-Dīn Abi'l-Faḍl b. Abī Saʿd b. Aḥmad Mihrīzad.[79]

The correspondence between the *kunya*s in these names and the name of our author seems to confirm that the latter was indeed the son of Jamāl al-Islām, and that in all likelihood he was born in the region of Yazd. The *nisba* al-Maybudī, referring to the small town of Maybud, some fifty kilometres north-west of Yazd, does not appear in the histories or on the gravestones, but since the grave of Fāṭima bint Rashīd al-Dīn is situated in the Friday mosque of Maybud, a connection with this location might be assumed.[80]

The lives of Jamāl al-Islām and his sons would have spanned the greater part of the Saljuq dynasty (429/1038-582/1186). From 433/1056 onwards, Yazd was governed by the Kākūyids, a dynasty of Daylami origin. The Kākūyids had ruled independently in parts of Western Persia during the first part of the fifth/eleventh century and then became faithful vassals to the Saljuqs, to whom they were also linked by marriage.[81] According to Bosworth, the Kākūyid governors of Yazd 'did much to beautify the town and to make it a centre of intellectual life, and under them and their epigoni, the Atabegs, Yazd enjoyed one of its most flourishing periods'.[82] After the death of Malik Shāh in 485/1092, Western Iran and Iraq underwent a period of instability as his sons Maḥmūd, Barkyārūq and Muḥammad fought out their battles for succession.[83] Yet however much the region may have been affected by this period of internecine strife, Yazd, it seems, continued to enjoy the patronage of the Kākūyids under Garshāsp b. Abī Manṣūr (d. 536/1141). During his forty-year lordship of Yazd, Manṣūr built a Friday mosque, a structure known as a Jamāʿat khāna-yi ʿAlī, a library and several qanats.[84]

In any case, Rashīd al-Dīn would have grown up before this period of upheaval. On the basis of his father's biography, we may assume that he was raised in an atmosphere of Islamic learning and mysticism. It is probable that, having completed his early education in Maybud or Yazd, he would have travelled to more established centres of learning to increase his knowledge of jurisprudence (*fiqh*) and hadith, as was the custom for young scholars. This search for knowledge might have taken him to Baghdad or Damascus in the West, or to Nishapur, Balkh, Merv or Herat in the East.[85] At some point during these scholarly travels he must have become acquainted with the teachings of ʿAbd Allāh Anṣārī of Herat.

It is not known whether or not Maybudī ever met Khwāja ʿAbd Allāh in person, but the constant reference to him as *Pīr-i Ṭarīqat* (the Master of the Way) and the prominence given to his sayings in the *Kashf al-asrār* indicate that he regarded Anṣārī as his spiritual master. In the introduction to the *Kashf al-asrār*, he states that he had 'read' or 'studied' (*ṭālaʿtu*) the *tafsīr* of ʿAbd Allāh Anṣārī; the fact that many of the sayings of Anṣārī are preceded by the words '*Pīr-i ṭarīqat guft*' (the Master of the Way said) probably signifies no more than that Anṣārī's *tafsīr* was delivered orally and written down by disciples. Although no mention of Maybudī's presence in Herat has yet been found in any of the histories or *ṭabaqāt* works, it is possible that he went there and spent some time in the circle of Anṣārī's followers at the *khānaqāh* by his tomb at Gāzurgāh, imbibing the *Anṣāriyyāt* tradition there.

This notwithstanding, there is some evidence to suggest that Maybudī may have spent a period of his life somewhere in Khorasan. First of all, some features of Khorasani dialect appear particularly in *Nawbat*s I and II of the *Kashf al-asrār*;[86] second, quotations from the works of Qushayrī and Aḥmad Ghazzālī, and the poetry of Sanāʾī, appear in the *Nawbat* III sections;[87] and third, Maybudī produced an adaptation of the *Kitāb al-fuṣūl,* a work composed by another native of Herat (discussed on p. 18). Lastly, most surviving manuscripts of the *Kashf al-asrār* were found in the region of Khorasan and present-day Afghanistan.[88] Apart from the presence of Anṣārī and his heritage in Herat, there would have been other factors to attract Maybudī to Eastern Iran. In Khorasan the late fifth/eleventh and early sixth/twelfth centuries saw both a development and crystallization of the Sufi doctrines of love, and an evolution of the Persian literary language for the expression of mystical experience. Each of these developments is much in evidence in the mystical sections of the *Kashf al-asrār*. In the absence of further biographical data, the story of Maybudī's life must, sadly, remain in the realm of conjecture. However, considerable information about his beliefs, learning and interests may be gleaned from the content of the *Kashf al-asrār*.

In jurisprudence Maybudī evidently followed the Shāfiʿī school in *fiqh*, for, when explaining a point of law, he invariably refers to al-Shāfiʿī's opinion on the matter, and, if he discusses the views of the other imams, he will usually present al-Shāfiʿī's position first. His particular reverence for ʿAlī b. Abī Ṭālib is said to be further evidence that he was a follower of al-Shāfiʿī.[89] It is probable that he, like his father, was a *ḥāfiẓ* of the Qur'an, for he shows great facility in using the Qur'an to comment upon the Qur'an.[90] We may assume that he was a traditionist (*muḥaddith*) both from his extensive use of hadith in the *Kashf al-asrār* and from the fact that he informs us of his own *Arbaʿīn,* a collection of forty hadiths with commentary.[91] The number of authorities referred to in his work, his knowledge of Arabic, his eloquent use of Persian prose and his numerous citations of Persian and Arabic poetry all attest to his erudition.

If Maybudī was a Shāfiʿī in jurisprudence (*fiqh*), it should not therefore be assumed that he was an Ashʿarī in the fundamentals of religious belief (*uṣūl al-dīn*). Although by the twelfth century Ashʿarism had been widely adopted by Shāfiʿīs, it was not universally so. Maybudī was not an Ashʿarī, a fact that is indicated by his outright rejection of speculative theology (*kalām*) and those who practise it (*mutakallimūn*),[92] and confirmed by his direct condemnation of the Ashʿarīs on two occasions in the *Kashf al-asrār*. In his commentary on those who 'wrangle concerning the Revelations of Allah' (Q. 40:56), he names Ashʿarīs along with Jahmīs, philosophers and *Ṭabāʾiʿiyān*[93] as innovators and deniers of the divine attributes (*munkirān-i ṣifāt-i Ḥaqq*).[94] Elsewhere he criticises them for their belief that the Qur'an is uncreated, but only in essence:

> The Ashʿarīs said that [all] letters, whether they be in the Qur'an or not, are created; that [what is implied by] 'the speech of God' is its meaning; and that it subsists in His essence (*qā'im ba-dhāt-i ū*), without letters or sounds. But this is not the belief of the *ahl-i sunnat wa jamāʿat* who have clear proof against this [view] in verses of the Qur'an and in the Hadith.[95]

The belief that the Qur'an was uncreated not only in meaning, but in its sounds when recited and in its letters when written, is a dogma that has been particularly associated with the Ḥanbalī school.[96] Maybudī also championed other Ḥanbalī doctrines, such as the insistence upon the *istithnā'* — that is, if the words 'I am a believer' are said they must be followed by the words 'if God wills'[97] – and above all, the doctrine that the anthropomorphic expressions in the Qur'an, such as 'He mounted (or established Himself on) the Throne' (*istawā ʿala'l-ʿarsh*),[98] and 'hand(s)' of God,[99] should be accepted literally as they are according God's intended meaning, without subjecting them to metaphorical interpretation (*ta'wīl*). This doctrine is included in the Qādirī Creed (*al-Iʿtiqād al-Qādirī*), issued by the Ḥanbalī caliph al-Qādir in 433/1041, which states: 'He is on the Throne because He so wills it and not like human beings to rest on it,' and 'only those attributes should be ascribed to Him which He himself has ascribed or those which His prophets have ascribed to Him', and 'every one of the attributes of His being which He has ascribed is an attribute of His being which man should not overlook.'[100] Maybudī is clearly following this doctrine when, concerning the 'hand' of God in Q. 5:64, he insists that it is

> a hand of attribute (*yad-i ṣifat*), a hand of essence (*yad-i dhāt*),[101] the outward meaning of which [should be] accepted, (*ẓāhir-i ān padhīrufta*), the inner meaning surrendered [to God], (*bāṭin taslīm karda*) and its reality unapprehended (*ḥaqīqat dar nayāfta*), [so that one] desists from the way of [asking] how (*rāh-i chigūnagī*), the exertion [of reason] (*taṣarruf*) and metaphorical interpretation (*ta'wīl*).[102]

Attempting to cover himself against the imputation of anthropomorphism (*tashbīh*), Maybudī goes on to explain that 'to be the same in name (*hamnām*) is not to be the same in kind (*hamsān*)'. This position, he claims, avoids the two extremes of *tashbīh* on the one hand and *taʿṭīl* (denial of the divine attributes) on the other.[103]

Given his espousal of these Ḥanbalī doctrines, we might be tempted to conclude that Maybudī had followed Anṣārī's recommendation that one should be a Shāfiʿī in law, a Ḥanbalī in theology and live the way of life of a Sufi.[104] However, Maybudī never claims any formal allegiance to the Ḥanbalī school, consistently maintaining his theological position to be that of the *ahl-i sunnat* or the *ahl-i sunnat wa jamāʿat* (people of the tradition and the community). Moreover, Maybudī quotes the words of al-Shāfiʿī as much as those of Ibn Ḥanbal in support of these doctrines.[105] Had Maybudī been a committed Ḥanbalī, one might have expected to find in the *Kashf al-asrār* a great deal more polemic against the Ashʿarīs; he must, after all, have been aware of the fierce antagonism between the two schools, which had resulted in several riots in Baghdad during the fifth/eleventh century,[106] and of Ashʿarī attempts to have Anṣārī indicted for heresy.[107] Furthermore, Maybudī makes use of precisely the kind of reasoned analogy (*qiyās*) to which Ḥanbalīs like Barbahārī (d. 329/941) and Ibn Baṭṭa (d. 387/997) objected in the writings of al-Ashʿarī. For example, in arguing the doctrine that the destiny of each person, whether he will be a believer or an unbeliever, good or bad, is pre-ordained by God, he compares God to the potter who makes some clay into bowls and some into pots.[108] As Allard explains, the Ḥanbalī objection to this kind of analogy is that to compare the qualities of God to human qualities is 'to establish an analogical rapport between the creature and God'.[109] Maybudī also argues for the doctrine of 'acquisition' (*kasb*) which became particularly associated with the Ashʿarī school.[110] All that can be said with certainty, therefore, is that our author was a Shāfiʿī who counted himself one of the *ahl-i sunnat wa jamāʿat*.[111]

Even so, if Maybudī was not, like Anṣārī, a Ḥanbalī in theology, he was very much Anṣārī's disciple in combining an uncompromising traditionalism with Sufism.[112] The following saying, quoted from Anṣārī in the *Kashf al-asrār*, summarises Maybudī's own position:

> My faith is what is heard (*samʿī*) [i.e. Revelation]; my law is what is reported (*khabarī*) [i.e. from the Prophet]; and my gnosis (*maʿrifat*) is what is found (*yāftanī*). I affirm as true what is reported; I bring to realisation what is found, and I follow what is heard; by the agent of reason (*ʿaql*), the evidence of creation, the guidance of [divine] light; by the indication of Revelation and the message of the Prophet, on condition of submission.[113]

It will be seen that traditionalist and mystical doctrines are integrally linked in Maybudī's commentary on the Qur'an.

His works

Kitāb-i arbaʿīn

In his mystical commentary of verse 41 of *Sūrat al-Raʿd* (Thunder, Q. 13), Maybudī quotes a long hadith of the Prophet, and then adds that he has explained the significance of this hadith at length in the *Kitāb-i arbaʿīn*.[114] Sarwar Mawlāʾī has suggested that the *Arbaʿīn* mentioned here may have been composed by Anṣārī rather than Maybudī, since Maybudī might in this context have been quoting Anṣārī.[115] However, this seems unlikely for two reasons. First, the passage in question is not preceded by the words '*Pīr-i ṭarīqat guft*' – Maybudī attributes this interpretation in a general manner to the 'people of allusion (*ahl-i ishārat*)' and 'masters of gnosis (*arbāb-i maʿrifat*)' – and, given the respect with which Maybudī regarded his master, he would surely have named Anṣārī had he been the author of the work. Second, neither the hadith in question, nor the mystical significance Maybudī has attached to it, appear to conform to the subject matter of Anṣārī's *Arbaʿīn*.[116] Moreover, the *arbaʿīn*, a collection of forty hadiths, often with commentary, was a popular genre for traditionists, and it is quite possible that both Maybudī and Anṣārī compiled one. In any case, no manuscript of an *arbaʿīn* by Maybudī has yet come to light.

Kitāb al-fuṣūl

Apart from the *Kashf al-asrār*, the only extant work which bears Maybudī's name is the *Kitāb al-fuṣūl*, a short treatise which has apparently survived in only one manuscript. Comprised of an introduction and six chapters, this treatise discusses the virtues of various officials of state and religion, starting with sultans and ending with scholars and *qāḍīs*.[117] According to the colophon, the work was originally composed by Abu'l-Qāsim Yūsuf b. al-Ḥusayn b. Yūsuf al-Harawī, and was 'adapted' in Persian (*istakhrajahu*) by Shaykh al-Imām al-Ḥāfiẓ Rashīd al-Dīn Abu'l-Faḍl al-Maybudī. The colophon also informs us that the manuscript was copied in the year 719/1319 by one Ḥusayn b. al-Qāḍī ʿAlī from a manuscript written in Maybudī's hand. The style of the *Fuṣūl* bears some resemblence to the third *nawbat* of the *Kashf al-asrār*, since it includes passages of rhyming prose (*sajʿ*) and poetry, both in Persian and in Arabic.

Kashf al-asrār

Qur'anic commentaries range in length from the comprehensive, such as the monumental *Jāmiʿ al-bayān* of Abū Jaʿfar al-Ṭabarī (d. 310/923), to the more condensed, such as the *Anwār al-tanzīl* of ʿAbd Allāh b. ʿUmar al-Bayḍāwī (d. 716/1316) or the *Tafsīr al-Jalālayn* of Jalāl al-Dīn al-Maḥallī (d. 864/1459) and Jalāl al-Dīn al-Suyūṭī (d. 911/1505). The *Kashf al-asrār* falls midway between these two extremes, being comparable in length to the *Tafsīr al-tibyān* of Abū Jaʿfar al-Ṭūsī (d. *c.* 460/1067), but shorter than the *Tafsīr al-kabīr* of Fakhr al-Dīn al-Rāzī (d. 606/1210). Among Persian commentaries it is one of the most extensive, being second only in length to the Shi'i commentary of Abu'l-Futūḥ Rāzī (d. mid-sixth/twelfth century).[118]

In his introduction to the *Kashf al-asrār*, Maybudī explains the unique ternary structure of his commentary. He proposes that the Qur'an should be divided into sessions (*majlis-hā*). Within each *majlis* the discourse will be further sub-divided into three 'turns' (*nawbats*). The first *nawbat* will consist of the 'literal Persian (*fārsī-yi ẓāhir*), intended to convey the meaning of the verses as succinctly as possible'. The second *nawbat*, will be the *tafsīr*, and will include: 'facets of meaning (*wujūh-i maʿānī*), the canonically accepted readings (*qirāʾāt-i mashhūr*), circumstance[s] of Revelation (*sabab-i-nuzūl*), exposition of rulings (*bayān-i aḥkām*), relevant hadiths and traditions (*akhbār wa āthār*), wonders (*nawādir*) which relate to the verses, aspects [of meaning] and analogues (*wujūh wa naẓāʾir*) and so on'. The third *nawbat* will comprise 'the allegories of mystics (*rumūz-i ʿārifān*), the allusions of Sufis (*ishārāt-i ṣūfiyān*), and the subtle "associations" of preachers (*laṭāʾif-i mudhakkirān*)'.[119]

The second and third *nawbats* of Maybudī's commentary are distinguished not only by their content but also by their literary style. *Nawbat* II presents a simple, fluent and unadorned style of prose, whereas *Nawbat* III boasts a far more artistic style, rich in metaphor and embellished with metred and rhyming prose, and numerous verses of love poetry. Another difference is that the second *nawbat* tends to have a greater Arabic content than the third; that is to say, Persian is most consistently used in the *Nawbat* III sections of the *Kashf al-asrār*. I have estimated that the proportion of Arabic in the exoteric (*Nawbat* II) sections of the *Kashf al-asrār* steadily increases during the course of the commentary, from an average of 5 per cent in the first two volumes to around 80 per cent in the last two.[120] In the *Nawbat* III sections, on the other hand, the amount of Arabic remains consistently around five per cent, but never more than 10 per cent throughout the ten volumes of the work. We might infer, therefore, that it was the *Nawbat* III sections in particular that Maybudī intended to be more universally accessible, and therefore that it was the combination of traditionalist and mystical doctrine which he presents in the third *nawbat* that he was especially concerned to disseminate. That the esoteric commentary had precedence over the exoteric commentary is, moreover, indicated by the way the verses that make up each of the sessions (*majālis*) are selected. As was stated earlier, each session usually comprises between three and fifty verses. Although Maybudī comments on all these verses in the *Nawbat* II sections, in the *Nawbat* III sections he only provides commentary for a small number of verses, sometimes as few as two or three.[121] Yet he almost always begins his mystical commentary with the first verse of each session. This suggests that it was the mystical rather than the exoteric commentary which guided the selection of verses for each session.

The sources of Maybudī's Qur'an commentary

In the introduction to the *Kashf al-asrār*, Maybudī states that he has based his commentary on the *tafsīr* of Khwāja ʿAbd Allāh Anṣārī. He explains that he had read this commentary, and finding it, despite its eloquence and depth of meaning, to be too short, decided to expand it.[122] Passages directly ascribed to Anṣārī in the *Kashf al-asrār* are preceded by the words '*Pīr-i ṭarīqat guft*', or more formally with his *laqab* (honorific title) '*Shaykh al-Islām Khwāja ʿAbd Allāh Anṣārī guft*', and are almost entirely located in the third *nawbat*, that is the mystical sections of the *Kashf al-asrār*. This would appear to endorse de Beaurecueil's view, on the basis of Ibn Rajab, that a major part of Anṣārī's now no longer extant commentary on the Qur'an was esoteric.[123]

According to Kutubī, Anṣārī began to hold sessions in which he commented on the Qur'an in the year 436/1044, when he returned to Herat after his first period of exile.[124] Then in the following year, he began for a second time to hold sessions in which he commented on the Qur'an (*aftataḥa'l-qur'ān yufassirahu thāniyan fī majālis al-tadhkīr*). At this time, it is related, Anṣārī's commentary was mainly concerned with legal matters (*al-qawl fi'l-sharʿ*), until he reached the words 'Those who believe are stauncher in their love for Allah' (Q. 2:165). Then he began to dedicate the sessions to the '[esoteric] truth' [of the Qur'an] (*aftataḥa tajrīd al-majālis fi'l-ḥaqīqa*), spending a long period of his life on this one verse.[125] Similarly, he devoted 360 sessions to Q. 21:101, 'Those for whom kindness has been decreed from Us'. We are told that he was expounding the 'hidden secrets' of each of the divine names as part of his commentary on Q. 32:17, 'No soul knows what is kept for them of joy', and had reached *al-Mumīt* (the One Who causes to die) when he was again exiled in the year 480/1088. On his return, he did not resume his commentary on the divine names, but instead changed his method of interpretation, moving more swiftly through the Qur'an so that he commented on ten verses each session. However he had only reached Q. 38:67-8 when he died in 481/1089. Thus, in this second commentary, or second series of sessions for his interpretation of the Qur'an (de Beaurecueil speaks of a second commentary, but it is not clear from Kutubī's statement whether or not in the first year of sessions he completed a commentary on the Qur'an), Anṣārī would have covered more than two-thirds of the Qur'an, of which his commentary on Q. 2:165 to 32:17 appears to have been extensive and esoteric.

To what extent did Maybudī draw upon such a work by Anṣārī? A close examination of quotations directly attributed to Anṣārī reveals that this material mostly comprises *munājāt* (intimate communings with God), aphorisms and short theological sermons, with little material that could strictly be defined as exegetical.[126] These passages aside, it is difficult to ascertain how much of the *Kashf al-asrār* has been drawn from Anṣārī's original *tafsīr*, because throughout the mystical commentary Maybudī has emulated his master's characteristic style of rhyming and metred prose.

What is certain is that Maybudī drew on a great many other works, both exegetical and otherwise, in the compilation of the *Kashf al-asrār*, although, like other writers, he often omitted to acknowledge his sources.

An exhaustive analysis of Maybudī's sources would go beyond the scope of this study; only the most important will be mentioned here. For the *Nawbat* II sections of his commentary he evidently drew on a great number of exegetical works, including the Qur'anic commentaries of Ṭabarī (d. 311/933),[127] Ibn Qutayba (d. 274/887),[128] Muqātil b. Sulaymān (d. 150/767),[129] Mujāhid (d. between 100/718 and 102/722),[130] and Sufyān al-Thawrī (d. 161/778).[131] For the *Nawbat* III sections, he again drew on numerous sources. For example, he cites esoteric comments from Sahl al-Tustarī (d. 283/896), though Böwering notes that most of these comments may be traced to the *Kitāb al-lumaʿ* of Abū Naṣr al-Sarrāj (d. 378/998), the *Qūt al-qulūb* of Abū Ṭālib al-Makkī, and the *Ḥilyat al-awliyāʾ* of Abū Nūʿaym al-Iṣfahānī (d. 430/1038).[132] He also includes numerous comments from the *Ḥaqāʾiq al-tafsīr* of ʿAbd al-Raḥmān al-Sulamī, particularly in the names of Jaʿfar al-Ṣādiq, Ibn ʿAṭāʾ al-Adamī (d. 311/923) and Abū Bakr al-Wāsiṭī (d. after 320/932). However, it is worth noting that Maybudī occasionally places the comments of these masters in a different Qur'anic context.[133] Interpretations from Sulamī's commentary are sometimes quoted in the original Arabic and sometimes rendered in Persian, and they may appear in a form which differs from existing published editions.[134] Above all, however, Maybudī drew on the *Laṭāʾif al-ishārāt* of Qushayrī, from which he derived a great number of ideas and comments.[135] In some instances, for example in his commentary on *Sūrat Yūsuf*, comments taken from the *Laṭāʾif* even outnumber quotations attributed to Anṣārī. Interpretations taken from the *Laṭāʾif* are sometimes quoted word for word in Arabic, and at other times rendered in Persian, where they often undergo some development and elaboration. Interestingly, Maybudī never once cites either the *Laṭāʾif* or its author by name. Could this be because of Qushayrī's well-known allegiance to the Ashʿarī school?

Non-exegetical Sufi works that may well have been used by Maybudī for his *Nawbat* III commentary include the *Qūt al-qulūb* of Abu Ṭālib al-Makkī (d. 382/993 or 386/996),[136] Aḥmad Ghazzālī's *Sawāniḥ*,[137] Anṣārī's *Ṣad maydān*,[138] and a work attributed to al-Ḥakīm al-Tirmidhī (d. late third/ninth century), entitled *Bayān al-farq bayn al-ṣadr wa'l-qalb wa'l-fuʾād wa'l-lubb*.[139] In addition, he would probably have drawn on other important Sufi works such as the *Kitāb al-lumaʿ* of Sarrāj and *Ḥilyat al-awliyāʾ* of Abū Nuʿaym;[140] Qushayrī's *Risāla*, Abū Ḥāmid al-Ghazzālī's *Iḥyāʾ ʿulūm al-dīn* and *Kīmiyā-yi saʿādat*,[141] and the *Rawḥ al-arwāḥ* of Aḥmad Samʿānī (d. 543/1148).[142] In addition to these written sources, Maybudī undoubtedly included in his mystical commentary an abundance of material from the oral tradition.

Apart from the writings and teachings of Anṣārī, the most perceivable influence on Maybudī's mystical commentary in terms of the interpretations of the verses was Qushayrī's *Laṭāʾif al-ishārat*, though our author evidently also drew ideas and inspiration from Samʿānī's *Rawḥ al-arwāḥ* and may well have been influenced to a degree by Aḥmad Ghazzālī's *Sawāniḥ*.[143]

NOTES

1 See Richard Bulliet, *The Patricians of Nishapur: A Study in Medieval Islamic Social History* (Cambridge, Mass., 1972), pp. 71-4; idem, 'The political-religious history of Nishapur in the eleventh century', in D. S. Richards, ed., *Islamic Civilisation: 950-1150* (Oxford and London, 1973), pp. 80-5.

2 On the development of the *madrasa* see George Makdisi, *The Rise of Colleges* (Edinburgh, 1981); idem, 'Muslim institutions of learning in eleventh-century Baghdad', *BSOAS* 24 (1961), pp. 1-56; Abdul Latif Tibawi, 'Origin and character of *al-Madrasah*', *BSOAS* 25 (1962), pp. 225-38; Johannes Pedersen [G. Makdisi] 'Madrasa', *EI²*, V, pp. 1123-34. For an account of *madrasas* in medieval Nishapur see Bulliet, *Patricians*, Appendix I, pp. 249-55.

3 Abū Isḥāq al-Shīrāzī, the first professor to the Niẓāmiyya in Baghdad, is reported to have said: 'I travelled from Baghdad to Khorasan, and I found in every town or village on my way the position of *qāḍī*, *muftī*, or *khaṭīb* held by a former pupil of mine or by one of my followers'; Tāj al-Dīn ʿAbd al-Wahhāb b. ʿAlī al-Subkī, *Ṭabaqāt al-Shāfiʿiyya al-kubrā*, ed. M.M. al-Ṭanāḥī and ʿA.M. al-Ḥulw (Cairo, 1992), III, p. 89, cited in Tibawi, 'Origin and character of *al-Madrasah*', p. 236. Marshall G.S. Hodgson (*Venture of Islam*, Chicago and London, 1974, II, p. 49) suggests that the establishment of the Niẓāmiyya *madrasas* resulted generally in an enhancement of the status of the ulema in society.

4 For Makdisi's discussion of the place of Ashʿarī theology in the Niẓāmiyya curriculum see Makdisi, *The Rise of Colleges*, Appendix A, pp. 296-304. An example of Niẓām al-Mulk's more pragmatic and diplomatic approach (as compared with his predecessor al-Kundurī) is given in de Beaurecueil's biography of Khwāja ʿAbd Allāh Anṣārī. See Serge de Laugier de Beaurecueil, *Khwādja ʿAbdullāh Anṣārī, mystique ḥanbalite* (Beirut, 1965), pp. 109-10; Bulliet, *Patricians*, p. 74, n. 39. However, it should be added that in the year 449-50/1058, when Niẓām al-Mulk founded the first Niẓāmiyya *madrasa* in Nishapur, Alp Arslān, as ruler of the Eastern Saljuq provinces, was subordinate to Tughril Beg, whose vizier, al-Kundurī, was at that time persecuting the Ashʿarīs. Under these circumstances Niẓām al-Mulk could not very well have placed Ashʿarī theology on the curriculum. See Richard Bulliet, *Islam, the View from the Edge* (New York, 1994), p. 147.

5 Both Makdisi and Frank have in different ways argued that Ghazzālī's corpus of writings is not in its entirety representative of the teachings of al-Ashʿarī in theology. See George Makdisi, 'Al-Ghazālī, disciple de Shâfiʿî en droit et théologie', in G. Makdisi, *Ghazālī, la raison et le miracle*, Islam d'hier et d'aujourd'hui 30 (Paris, 1987), pp. 45-55; Richard M. Frank, *Al-Ghazālī and the Ashʿarite School* (Durham and London, 1994). Nevertheless, Frank has observed (op. cit. ch. 3) that Ghazzālī did conform to the teachings of the Ashʿarī school when he was writing 'textbooks', or works intended for students. On Ghazzālī's principle of adapting writings to the capacity of the readers for whom they are intended see Hodgson, *Venture*, II, p. 191; Frank, *Al-Ghazālī*, pp. 96, 101.

6 Makdisi ('Muslim institutions', p. 47) admits that Niẓām al-Mulk could not afford to ignore Ashʿarism since he depended on the Ashʿarī learned men, his link with the masses in Khorasan. He also informs us (ibid.) that the vizier even

tried to bring in Ashʿarism 'through the back door' by appointing Ashʿarī preachers to the Baghdad Niẓāmiyya.

7 It may also have contributed to the promotion of Sufism in Iran, for which see Wilferd Madelung, 'Sufism and the Karrāmiyya', in W. Madelung, *Religious Trends in Early Islamic Iran* (New York, 1988), p. 47.

8 Bulliet (*Patricians*, p. 48) argues that, contrary to the prevailing view, Niẓām al-Mulk was not carrying out a campaign against the Shīʿa. There can, however, be little question about both Niẓām al-Mulk and Ghazzālī's concern to counter the propaganda of the Ismailis. See, for example, Niẓām al-Mulk's *Siyar al-mulūk* or *Siyāsat-nāma*, ed. H. Darke (repr., Tehran, 1347sh/1968), pp. 282–311; trans. by H. Darke as *The Book of Government* (London, 1960), pp. 213-25; Ghazzālī, *Al-Munqidh min al-ḍalāl*, ed. R. Ahmad (Jullandri) (Lahore, 1971), pp. 1, 33-43; trans. by R.J. McCarthy in *Freedom and Fulfillment* (Boston, 1980), pp. 61, 81-9; idem, *Faḍā'iḥ al-bāṭiniyya*, ed. ʿA. Badawī (Cairo, 1964).

9 On the Karrāmiyya see Clifford E. Bosworth, 'Karrāmiyya', *EI²*, IV, pp. 667-9; idem, 'The rise of the Karrāmiyyah in Khurasan', *MW* 50 (1960), pp. 5-14; Madelung, 'Sufism and the Karrāmiyya', pp. 39-53.

10 See Alessandro Bausani, 'Religion in the Saljuq period', *CHI*, V, pp. 284-5; Bulliet, 'Nishapur', pp. 89-90.

11 Examples of such works are a heresiography written by Sayyid Murtaḍā al-Rāzī (fl. sixth/twelfth century), the *Tabṣirat al-ʿawāmm fī maʿrifat maqālāt al-anām*, ed. A. Iqbāl (repr., Tehran, 1984), and a polemical refutation of Sunnism, the *Kitāb al-naqḍ* of ʿAbd al-Jalīl b. Abi'l-Ḥasan al-Qazwīnī (d. after 556/1161), ed. J.M. Urmawī (3 vols., Tehran, 1358sh/1980). The latter was allegedly written in response to an anonymous Sunni polemic anti-Shīʿi work entitled *Baʿḍ faḍā'iḥ al-rawāfiḍ*. Another work which is also classed as a heresiography was the survey of religious schools and sects composed by the Ashʿarī theologian Abu'l-Fatḥ Muḥammad b. ʿAbd al-Karīm al-Shahrastānī, namely, the *Kitāb al-milal wa'l-niḥal*, ed. W. Cureton (Leipzig, 1842).

12 Al-Faḍl b. al-Ḥasan al-Ṭabrisī, *Majmaʿ al-bayān fī tafsīr al-Qur'ān* (Qum, 1403/1983-4).

13 Ḥusayn b. ʿAlī Abu'l-Futūḥ Rāzī, *Rawḍ al-jinān wa rawḥ al-janān*, also known as *Tafsīr-i Shaykh Abu'l-Futūḥ Rāzī*, ed. M.J. Yāḥaqqī and M.N. Nāsiḥ (20 vols., Mashhad, 1371-5sh/1992-6).

14 Abu'l-Qāsim Maḥmūd b. ʿUmar al-Zamakhsharī, *Al-Kashshāf ʿan ḥaqā'iq al-tanzīl* (Cairo, 1972).

15 Abu'l-Fatḥ Muḥammad b. ʿAbd al-Karīm al-Shahrastānī, *Mafātīḥ al-asrār wa maṣābīḥ al-abrār*. It comprises a long introduction followed by complete commentary on the first two suras; facsimile ed. with intro. and index (2 vols., Tehran 1368sh/1989).

16 See, for example, Frank, *Al-Ghazālī*; idem, *Creation and the Cosmic System: al-Ghazālī and Avicenna* (Heidelberg, 1992); Hermann Landolt, 'Ghazālī and "*Religionswissenschaft*"', *Asiatische Studien* 45/1 (1991), pp. 19-72.

17 One notable example of the late sixth/twelfth century being Fakhr al-Dīn al-Rāzī (d. 606/1210).

18 The influence of Ibn Sīnā (d. 428/1037), for example, is evident in the writings of ʿAyn al-Quḍāt Hamadānī, such as his *Zubdat al-ḥaqā'iq* (Arabic text ed. ʿA.

ʿUsayrān with Persian trans. by M. Tadayyun [Tehran, 1379sh/2000]), and in some of the poetical works of Sanāʾī. On the latter see Kathryn V. Johnson, 'A mystical response to the claims of philosophy: Abu'l-Majd Majdūd Sanāʾī's *Sayr al-ʿibād ila'l-maʿād*', *IS* 34/3 (1995), pp. 253-95.

19 This matter has been discussed by Margaret Malamud in 'Sufi organizations and structures of authority in medieval Nishapur', *IJMES* 26 (1994), pp. 427-42.

20 For example, Abū Naṣr ʿAbd Allāh b. ʿAlī al-Sarrāj, *Kitāb al-lumaʿ fi'l-taṣawwuf*, ed. with synopsis by R.A. Nicholson, Gibb Memorial Series 22 (Leiden and London, 1914); Abū Bakr Muḥammad b. Isḥāq al-Kalābādhī (d. 390/1000), *Kitāb al-taʿarruf li-madhhab ahl al-taṣawwuf*, ed. A.J. Arberry (Cairo, 1934); trans. by A.J. Arberry as *Doctrine of the Sufis* (Cambridge, 1935; repr. 1977); Abu'l-Qāsim ʿAbd al-Karīm b. Hawāzin al-Qushayrī, *Al-Risāla al-Qushayriyya fī ʿilm al-taṣawwuf* (Cairo, 1966); trans. by B.R. von Schlegel as *The Principles of Sufism* (Berkeley 1990); ʿAlī b. ʿUthmān Jullābī Hujwīrī (d. 469/1077), *Kashf al-maḥjūb*, ed. V. Zhukovsky (Lenningrad, 1926); trans. by R.A. Nicholson as *Kashf al-maḥjūb: The Oldest Persian Treatise on Sufism* (London, 1911). During this period, Abū Ibrāhīm Ismāʿīl b. Muḥammad Mustamlī Bukhārī (d. 434/1042-3) wrote a commentary on Kalābādhī's *Kitāb al-taʿarruf*, the *Sharḥ al-taʿarruf li-madhhab ahl al-taṣawwuf*, ed. M. Rawshan (Tehran, 1363sh/1984).

21 For example, Abū Nuʿaym al-Iṣfahānī (d. 430/1038), *Ḥilyat al-awliyāʾ* (10 vols., Cairo, 1932-8); ed. M.ʿA. ʿAṭāʾ (11 vols. with index, Beirut, 1997); Abū ʿAbd al-Raḥmān al-Sulamī, *Ṭabaqāt al-ṣūfiyya*, ed. J. Pedersen (Leiden, 1960); ʿAbd Allāh Anṣārī, *Ṭabaqāt al-ṣūfiyya*, ed. S. Mawlāʾī (Tehran, 1362sh/1983-4).

22 See Kalābādhī, *Kitāb al-taʿarruf*, pp. 4-5; tr. Arberry, p. 3; Qushayrī, *Risāla*, p. 46.

23 For the latter see Jacqueline Chabbi's observations about the works of Sulamī, 'Remarques sur le développement historique des mouvements ascétiques et mystiques au Ḫurāsān', *SI* 46 (1977), pp. 20, 68-9, and part two of this study.

24 Jürgen Paul, 'Au début du genre hagiographique au Khorassan', in D. Aigle, ed., *Saints Orientaux* (Paris, 1995), pp. 15-38 and, especially, pp. 24-35. Paul's focus in this article has been on the role of Abū Saʿīd b. Abi'l-Khayr, and the later Aḥmad Jām, known as 'Zhinda Pīl' (d. 536/1141).

25 The encounter between Sultan Maḥmūd and Abu'l-Ḥasan Kharaqānī is related in *Nūr al-ʿulūm*, ed. M. Mīnuwī in *Aḥwāl wa aqwāl-i Shaykh Abu'l-Ḥasan Kharaqānī, muntakhab-i Nūr al-ʿulūm, manqūl az nuskha-yi khaṭṭī-yi Landan* (Tehran, 1980), pp. 138-40; Farīd al-Dīn ʿAṭṭār, *Tadhkirat al-awliyāʾ*, ed. M. Istiʿlāmī (6th repr.,Tehran, 1346sh/1967-8), pp. 669-70; and reported in Abū Saʿd ʿAbd al-Karīm b. Muḥammad b. Manṣūr al-Samʿānī, *Kitāb al-ansāb*, ed. M.ʿA. ʿAṭāʾ (Beirut, 1998), p. 399. The encounter is rendered in French by Christiane Tortel, *Paroles d'un soufi: Abû'l-Ḥasan Kharaqânî (960-1033)* (Paris, 1998), pp. 14-16. The encounter between Bābā Ṭāhir and Tughril Beg is related in the *Rāḥat al-ṣudūr wa āyat al-surūr* of Muḥammad b. ʿAlī b. Sulaymān al-Rāwandī, ed. M. Iqbāl (Tehran, 1364sh/1985), pp. 98-9. For numerous anecdotes about Abū Saʿīd and the Saljuqs see Muḥammad b. Munawwar b. Abī Saʿd Abī Ṭāhir b. Abī Saʿīd Mayhanī, *Asrār al-tawḥīd fī maqāmāt Shaykh Abī Saʿīd*, ed. M.R.S. Kadkanī (2 vols., Tehran, 1366sh/1987), I, pp. 58-9, 90, 115; II, pp. 115-17, 365-6; trans. with intro. and notes by J. O'Kane as *The Secrets*

of God's Mystical Oneness (California, 1992). For an encounter between Sultan Sanjar and Aḥmad Jām (Zhinda Pīl) see Khwāja Sadīd al-Dīn Muḥammad Ghaznawī, *Maqāmāt Zhinda Pīl*, ed. Ḥ.M. Sanandjī (Tehran, 1340sh/1961), pp. 30-3.

26 Malamud, 'Sufi organizations', p. 428.

27 See, for example, Bulliet, *Patricians*, pp. 69-70; Paul, 'Au début', p. 28.

28 On the history of the *khānaqāh* (var. *khānqāh* and *khāngāh*) see Muḥsin Kiyānī, *Tārīkh-i khānaqāh dar Īrān* (Tehran, 1369sh/1990). Jacqueline Chabbi, 'Khānḳāh', *EI²*, IV, pp. 1025-6; Nasrollah Pourjavady, *Du mujaddid* (Tehran, 1379sh/2002), ch. 4. On the *ribāṭ* see Jacqueline Chabbi, 'La fonction du ribat à Baghdad du Ve siècle au début du VIIe siècle', *REI* 42 (1974), pp. 101-21. Numerous *ribāṭ*s visited by Abū Saʿīd are mentioned in Ibn al-Munawwar, *Asrār al-tawḥīd*. Abū Saʿīd's rules for the *khānaqāh* are listed in Reynold A. Nicholson, *Studies in Islamic Mysticism* (1921; repr., Cambridge, 1978), p. 73. In the *Histories of Nishapur*, written in the fifth/eleventh and sixth/twelfth centuries, Abū Saʿīd is regarded as the first to have regulated the communal life in the *khānaqāh* 'according to the rules still in use today'. See Richard N. Frye, *The Histories of Nishapur*, Harvard Oriental Series 45 (The Hague, 1965), MS 2, p. 74.

29 On the change in the role of the shaykh from *shaykh al-taʿlīm* to *shaykh al-tarbiya* see Fritz Meier, 'Ḫurāsān und das Ende der klassischen Ṣūfik', in *Atti del Convegno Internazionale sul tema: La Persia nel Medioevo* (Rome, 1971), pp. 131-56; trans. by J. O'Kane in F. Meier, *Essays on Islamic Piety and Mysticism* (Leiden, 1999). But see also Laurie Silvers-Alario's reappraisal of Meier's theory, 'The teaching relationship in early Sufism: a reassessment of Fritz Meier's definition of the *shaykh al-tarbiya* and *shaykh al-taʿlīm*', *MW* 93 (2003), pp. 69-97.

30 Paul, 'Au début', pp. 32, 34.

31 Again, see Meier, 'Ḫurāsān'; Silvers-Alario 'Teaching relationship'.

32 Concerning the patronage of Niẓām al-Mulk see Ibn al-Munawwar, *Asrār al-tawḥīd*, pp. 177-80, 365-6. The poet Muʿizzī, who was unsuccessful in gaining the patronage of the vizier, accused him of 'paying no attention to anyone but religious leaders and mystics'; Niẓāmī ʿArūḍī, *Chahār Maqāla*, ed. M. Qazwīnī, Gibb Memorial Series (Leiden, 1910), p. 47; trans. by E.G. Browne as *Four Discourses*, Gibb Memorial Series (London, 1921), p. 46. Another Saljuq official who gave generous patronage to the Sufis (Abū Saʿīd as well as Qushayrī) was Abū Manṣūr Waraqānī, as related in *Asrār al-tawḥīd*, p. 115.

33 Paul, 'Au début', p. 28.

34 Ibid., p. 32; Ibn al-Munawwar, *Asrār al-tawḥīd*, pp. 223, 277.

35 This was in the city of Isfahan, and is mentioned in Ibn al-Munawwar's *Asrār al-tawḥīd*.

36 This fatwa, which was written in Persian, has recently been edited and published by Pourjavady in *Du mujaddid*, pp. 79-91.

37 Pourjavady, *Du mujaddid*, p. 81.

38 See Malamud, 'Sufi organizations', pp. 430, 431; Bulliet, *Patricians*, pp. 152, 250. Several of the *madrasa*s in Nishapur were strongly associated with Sufism; one was even called *Madrasat al-ṣūfiyya*. See Bulliet's list of *madrasa*s in *Patricians*, pp. 249-55.

39 Hodgson, *Venture*, II, p. 190.

40 Ibid. Hodgson does not mention that this threefold hierarchy had previously

been discussed by Sufis, though usually in esoteric works intended mainly for initiates, and this, one might contend, being for the reason that the earlier Sufi authors did not expect, let alone demand, the same interaction between the three classes that was being proposed by Ghazzālī.

41 That it to say, apologetics in Sufi writings would be limited to specific areas of controversy, as in for example, the *Shakwat al-gharīb* of ʿAyn al-Quḍāt, ed. ʿA. ʿUsayrān (Tehran, 1962) and the *Sharḥ-i shaṭḥiyyāt* of Rūzbihān Baqlī, ed. H. Corbin (Tehran, 1966). The ball was now in the other court, as it were, for theologians such as Ibn al-Jawzī (d. 597/1200) to attack what they found reprehensible in Sufism, as in his *Talbīs Iblīs* (Cairo, 1369/1950); trans. by D.S. Margoliouth as *The Devil's Delusion*, *IC* 9 (1935), pp. 1–21, and 12 (1938), pp. 235-40.

42 Aḥmad Ghazzālī, *Sawāniḥ*, ed. H. Ritter (Istanbul, 1942); ed. N. Pourjavady (Tehran, 1359sh/1980); trans. with intro. and glossary by N. Pourjavady as *Sawāniḥ, Inspirations from the World of Pure Spirits* (London, 1986).

43 These metaphors were later explained in detail by Maḥmūd Shabistarī in his *Gulshan-i rāz*, ed. Ṣ. Muwaḥḥid, *Majmūʿa-yi āthār-i Shaykh Maḥmūd Shabistarī* (2nd repr., Tehran, 1371sh/1992).

44 It should be added that even those poets and writers who were not counted as 'Sufis' could no longer be totally free of the influence of Sufism and its literature.

45 In Maybudī's commentary we shall see this phenomenon manifested in freer parabolic interpretations of the stories of the prophets.

46 See Hodgson, *Venture*, II, ch. 2.

47 See Claude Gilliot, *Exégèse, langue et théologie en Islam* (Paris, 1990), chs. 6 and 7.

48 On the question of whether or not these early authorities on Qur'anic exegesis can be considered as authors of complete commentaries see Claude Gilliot, 'The beginnings of Qur'ānic exegesis', in A. Rippin, ed., *The Qur'ān: Formative Interpretation* (Ashgate, 1999), pp. 1-27. The commentary ascribed to Mujāhid b. Jabr is published as *Tafsīr al-imām Mujāhid b. Jabr*, ed. ʿA.Ṭ al-Sūratī (Islamabad, 1976); ed. M.ʿA. Abu'l-Nīl (Cairo 1410/1989); and the commentary ascribed to Abū ʿAbd Allāh Sufyān b. Saʿīd b. Masrūq al-Thawrī al-Kūfī as *Tafsīr Sufyān al-Thawrī*, ed. I.ʿA. ʿArshī (Rampur, 1965; repr., Beirut, 1403/1983).

49 For the history of these various aspects of Qur'anic exegesis see Andrew Rippin, ed., *Approaches to the History of the Interpretation of the Qur'ān* (Oxford, 1988); idem, ed., *Formative Interpretation*; Jane Dammen McAuliffe *et al.*, ed., *With Reverence for the Word: Medieval Scriptural Exegesis in Judaism, Christianity, and Islam* (Oxford and New York, 2003).

50 The format also formed the basis of several Shiʿi *tafsīrs*, for example, Abū Jaʿfar Muḥammad b. al-Ḥasan al-Ṭūsī, *Al-Tibyān fī tafsīr al-Qur'ān*, ed. A.S. al-Amīn and A.Ḥ.Q. al-ʿĀmilī (10 vols., Najaf, 1959-63); al-Faḍl b. al-Ḥasan al-Ṭabrisī, *Majmaʿ al-bayān fī tafsīr al-Qur'ān*; Abu'l-Futūḥ Rāzī, *Rawḍ al-jinān wa rawḥ al-janān*. Ismaili (or Bāṭinī) exegesis, however, involved a different methodology; for references on this subject see ch. 3, n. 81. On the development of Shiʿi exegesis see Meir M. Bar-Asher, *Scripture and Exegesis in Early Imāmī Shiʿism* (Leiden, Boston and Jerusalem, 1999); Mahmoud M. Ayoub,

'The speaking Qur'ān and the silent Qur'ān: a study of the principles and development of Imāmī Shī'ī *tafsīr*', in Rippin, ed., *Approaches*, pp. 77-98.

51 Claude Gilliot, 'Parcours exégétiques: de Ṭabarī à Rāzī (Sourate 55)', *Études arabes, analyses, théorie* 1 (Paris, 1983), p. 92.

52 Qushayrī, for example, composed a separate exoteric commentary, the *Tafsīr al-kabīr*, of which apparently only a small fragment has been preserved in the MS 811, University of Leiden.

53 On the early development of Sufi exegesis see Louis Massignon, *Essai sur les origines du lexique technique de la mystique musulmane* (Paris, 1922); trans. by B. Clark as *Essay on the Origins of the Technical Language of Islamic Mysticism* (Paris, 1997); Paul Nwyia, *Exégèse coranique et langue mystique* (Beirut, 1970).

54 Sahl b. ʿAbd Allāh al-Tustarī, *Tafsīr al-Qur'ān al-ʿaẓīm* (Cairo, 1329/1911). For a detailed analysis of the hermeneutics and doctrine of Tustarī see Gerhard Böwering, *The Mystical Vision of Existence in Classical Islam: The Qur'ānic Hermeneutics of the Ṣūfī Sahl at-Tustarī (d. 283/896)* (Berlin and New York, 1980).

55 See Richard Gramlich, *Abu'l-ʿAbbās b. ʿAṭā': Sufi und Koranausleger* (Stuttgart, 1995).

56 The *Ḥaqā'iq al-tafsīr* has been edited and published by Sayyid ʿImrān (Beirut, 2001). Comments attributed to Jaʿfar al-Ṣādiq have been extracted and published by Paul Nwyia in 'Le tafsîr mystique attribué à Ǧaʿfar Ṣâdiq', Arabic text and intro. in *Mélanges de l'Université Saint-Joseph* 43 (1967), pp. 179-230; and the comments of Ibn ʿAṭā' in idem, ed., *Trois oeuvres inédites de mystiques musulmanes: Šaqīq al-Balḫī, Ibn ʿAṭā', Niffārī* (Beirut, 1973). Comments attributed to Ḥallāj in the *Ḥaqā'iq* have been assembled by Louis Massignon and are published in his *Essai sur les origines*. All these extracts have been reprinted in Nasrollah Pourjavady, ed., *Majmūʿa-yi āthār-i Abū ʿAbd al-Raḥmān al-Sulamī* (2 vols.,Tehran, 1369sh/1990). Sulamī's *Ziyādāt ḥaqā'iq al-tafsīr* has been edited by G. Böwering (Beirut, 1995).

57 For example, Sarrāj, *Lumaʿ*, and Abū Saʿd ʿAbd al-Malik b. Muḥammad al-Khargūshī, *Tahdhīb al-asrār*, ed. B.M. Bārūd (Abu Dhabi, 1999), both include sections on *mustanbaṭāt* (elicitations).

58 Maybudī's reasons for doing this will be explored in chapter two of this book.

59 See Annabel Keeler, 'Exegesis iii, in Persian', *EIr*, IX, p. 119.

60 Abu'l-Muẓaffar Shāhfūr Isfarāyinī, *Tāj al-tarājim fī tafsīr al-Qur'ān li'l-aʿājim*, ed. N.M. Harawī and ʿA.A. Ilāhī Khurāsānī (3 vols. incomplete, Tehran, 1374sh-/1995-), I, pp. 8-9.

61 *Kashf*, I, p. 1.

62 See Paul, 'Au début', pp. 15-38, especially pp. 24-35.

63 Paul ('Au début', p. 35) also speaks of a 'new style' of hagiography, of the *Maqāmāt* type, which focused on one particular Sufi shaykh, and he suggests that the anecdotes and stories compiled in these works were probably originally delivered at public gatherings of the faithful somewhere close to the tomb of the master.

64 See Johannes T.P. de Bruijn, *Of Piety and Poetry: The Interaction of Religion and Literature in the Life and Works of Ḥakīm Sanā'ī of Ghazna* (Leiden, 1983), pp. 64-8, 169-70.

65 That is to say Ḥājjī Khalīfa, in his *Kashf al-ẓunūn* (2 vols., Istanbul, 1941-7),

II, p. 1487, attributes the commentary in its full title, *Kashf al-asrārwa ʿuddat al-abrār*, to Taftāzāni. However, a little before this entry, he does list a *Kashf al-asrār* by Rashīd al-Dīn Abu'l-Faḍl Aḥmad b. Abī Saʿīd al-Maybudī, which he states is mentioned by al-Wāʿiẓ, presumably Ḥusayn al-Wāʿiẓ Kāshifī (d. 910/1504-5), the Timurid exegete who was influenced by, and drew upon, Maybudī's *Kashf al-asrār*. On the basis of Ḥājjī Khalīfa, Charles Storey initially makes the same incorrect attribution in the first edition of his *Persian Literature* (London, 1927), p. 7, but in the later edition of this work (London, 1953, I, Part 2, pp. 1190-1) amends it.

66 For an account of Anṣārī's life and list of his biographical sources see de Beaurecueil, *Khwādja ʿAbdullāh*.

67 Hekmat gives the author's name as Abu'l-Faḍl b. Abī Saʿīd in his introduction to *Kashf*, volume I (page a). However, in his introduction to volume VII (page b), having acquired two further manuscripts, he presents the name as Abu'l-Faḍl Aḥmad b. Abī Saʿd b. Aḥmad b. Mihrīzad al-Maybudī preceded by the *laqab* Rashīd al-Dīn Fakhr al-Islām. In view of the *kunya* of his father, Abū Saʿd would appear to be correct. See also Ali Asghar Hekmat, 'Une exégèse Coranique du XII siècle en Persan', *Journal Asiatique* 238 (1950), pp. 91-6; Muḥammad Muḥīṭ Ṭabāṭabāʾī, 'Dāstān-i tafsīr-i Khwāja Anṣārī', *Dānish* 1 (1328sh/1949), pp. 193-200. The *laqab* (honorific title) Rashīd al-Dīn appears on the gravestone of his daughter, for which see note 79, and in the colophon to a work attributed to Maybudī under the title *Kitāb al-fuṣūl*, for which also see p. 18.

68 This date is given in the introduction to MS 176/1376, Kitābkhāna-yi Āstān-i Quds, Mashhad. See also *Kashf*, I, p. 195, where Maybudī says: 'Look at the people of Muhammad, five hundred years and more have passed since he was taken from them and his religion and his law grow fresher every day', and other versions of the same in *Kashf*, III, p. 139; V, p. 636, and IX, p. 14.

69 Iraj Afshar, 'Iḥtīmālī dar bāb-i muʾallif-i *Kashf al-asrār*', *Yaghmā* Year 14 (1340sh/1962), p. 312; idem, 'Sang-i qabr-i barādar-i muʾallif-i *Kashf al-asrār*', *Yaghmā* Year 20 (1346sh/1968), p. 190.

70 Mustawfī, Muḥammad Mufīd (Bāfiqī), *Jāmiʿ-i Mufīdī*, ed. I. Afshar (3 vols., Tehran, 1340sh/1961), III, p. 621; Jaʿfar b. Muḥammad Jaʿfarī, *Tārīkh-i Yazd*, ed. I. Afshar, Persian Text Series 2 (Tehran, 1338sh/1960), p. 146.

71 Mustawfī, *Jāmiʿ-i Mufīdī*, III, p. 621.

72 Presumably this Imām al-Ḥaramayn was al-Juwaynī (d. 478/1085). Mustawfī names the Imām al-Ḥaramayn as Rāghib al-Iṣfahānī, or perhaps a *wa* (and) has dropped out here. Jaʿfarī merely states that Jamāl al-Islām was acquainted with Imām al-Ḥaramayn.

73 Mustawfī, *Jāmiʿ-i Mufīdī*, III, p. 622.

74 Jaʿfarī, *Tārīkh-i Yazd*, p. 121.

75 Mustawfī, *Jāmiʿ-i Mufīdī*, II, p. 624.

76 Mentioned in Jaʿfarī, *Tārīkh-i Yazd*, p. 121, as having been honoured by the Muẓaffarids (ruled in Southern Persia between 714/1314 and 795/1393).

77 Mustawfī, *Jāmiʿ-i Mufīdī*, III, p. 623.

78 Jaʿfarī, *Tārīkh-i Yazd*, p. 121.

79 Afshar, 'Sang-i qabr', p. 190; idem, 'Dukhtar-i Maybudī', *Yaghmā* Year 21 (1347sh/1969), p. 440, and (1357sh/1979); idem., 'Two twelfth-century gravestones of Yazd in Mashhad and Washington', *Studia Iranica* 2 (1973), pp. 203-4.

80 The date of Fāṭima's death is given as 562/1166, which would be consistent with the likely dates for Rashīd al-Dīn on the basis of the dating of *Kashf al-asrār*.
81 See Clifford E. Bosworth, 'Kākūyids', *EI*[2], IV, pp. 465-7; Jaʿfarī, *Tārīkh-i Yazd*, pp. 35ff.
82 Bosworth, 'Kākūyids', p. 466.
83 Clifford E. Bosworth, 'The political and dynastic history of the Iranian world (AD 1000-1217)', *CHI* V, pp. 102ff.
84 Jaʿfarī, *Tārīkh-i Yazd*, pp. 37-8.
85 All of these cities had Niẓāmiyya *madrasas*, suggesting that they were important centres of learning, though from the 1090s on, Nishapur was disturbed by factional strife. See Bulliet, *Patricians*, ch. 6; idem, 'Political-religious history'.
86 This information was given to me by Dr. ʿAlī Rawāqī in Tehran, who is making a linguistic study of Maybudī's *Kashf al-asrār* and the commentary by his contemporary Darwājakī. For information on Dr ʿAlī Rawāqī's findings on this subject, see Mihdī Dashtī, 'Taʾammul dar bara-yi tafsīr-i *Kashf al-asrār*-i Maybudi', *Majalla-yi Safīna* (Winter 1382/2003). Available at http://www.maarefquran.org/index.php/page,viewArticle/LinkID,10658.
87 Although a rigorous study of the manuscripts is required to check the authenticity of the presence of Sanāʾī's poetry in the *Kashf al-asrār*.
88 Ḥusayn Masarrat, *Kitābshināsī-yi Rashīd al-Dīn al-Maybudī* (Tehran, 1374sh/1995), p. 17.
89 Muḥammad Jawād Sharīʿat, *Fihrist-i Kashf al-asrār wa ʿuddat al-abrār* (Tehran, 1363sh/1984), p. 10. See *Kashf*, VI, p. 84, where Maybudī writes 'and he is not a believer if he does not love ʿAlī.' On the connection between al-Shāfiʿī and ʿAlī b. Abī Ṭālib see Eric Chaumont, 'al-Shāfiʿī', *EI*[2], IX, pp. 181-5, and on al-Shāfiʿī's connection with ʿAlids during his younger years see Willi Heffening, 'al-Shāfiʿī', *EI*[1], VIII, pp. 252-4.
90 The *laqab* al-Ḥāfiẓ also appears among his names in the colophon to the *Kitāb al-fuṣūl*, for which see p. 18 in the section on Maybudī's works.
91 This work is referred to in *Kashf*, V, p. 219, and is discussed on p. 18.
92 On the use of *kalām* by al-Ashʿarī and members of his school see Richard M. Frank, 'Elements in the development of the teaching of al-Ashʿarī', *Le Muséon* 104 (1991), pp. 141-90.
93 Perhaps Maybudī means here the 'Naturalists' (*Ṭabīʿiyyūn*), a category of philosophers mentioned by Ghazzālī in his *Al-Munqidh min al-ḍalāl*, ed. Ahmad, p. 18; tr. McCarthy, pp. 71-2.
94 *Kashf*, VIII, p. 486.
95 *Kashf*, VIII, p. 507.
96 And one for the defence of which its founder, Aḥmad b. Ḥanbal, was persecuted during the reign of the caliph al-Maʾmūn. On the persecution of Ibn Ḥanbal see Walter M. Patton, *Aḥmad b. Ḥanbal and the Miḥna* (Leiden, 1897).
97 *Kashf*, V, pp. 676-7. On *istithnāʾ* see W. Montgomery Watt, *The Formative Period of Islamic Thought* (Edinburgh, 1973), pp. 138-9; ʿAbd al-Qāhir b. Ṭāhir al-Baghdādī, *Uṣūl al-dīn* (Istanbul, 1928), p. 253; Henri Laoust, *La profession de foi d'Ibn Batta* (Damascus, 1958), pp. 79f.
98 For example, Q. 7:54; 10:4; 13:2; 20:5; 25:59; 32:4; 57:4.
99 For example, Q. 5:64; 36:70; 38:76; 48:10.

100 Quoted from Adam Mez, *The Renaissance of Islam*, trans. by Salahuddin Bukhsh and David S. Margoliouth (London, 1937), pp. 207-9. See George Makdisi, *Ibn ʿAqil: Religion and Culture in Classical Islam* (Edinburgh, 1997), pp. 303ff. The Muʿtazilīs (among others) believed that these anthropomorphic verses should be interpreted allegorically to preserve the transcendence of God (*tanzīh*). This will be discussed further in chapter two.

101 Compare with a statement in the anonymous *Al-Kāmil al-ikhtiṣār al-shāmil* cited by Frank ('Elements', p. 164, n. 62) according to which al-Ashʿarī's position was that God's 'hands' are 'two revealed attributes that are distinct from His essence'.

102 *Kashf*, III, p. 169. Maybudī's desisting from the 'way of [asking] how' (*rāh-i chigūnagī*) is clearly a Persian equivalent to the Arabic *bi-lā kayf*. This expression is said to go back to Mālik b. Anas (d. 179/795), though it became particularly associated with the Ashʿarī school, and was included in the creed of al-Ashʿarī (*Kitāb al-ibāna ʿan uṣūl al-diyāna*, Cairo, 1348/1929, pp. 37, 39), for which see Binyamin Abrahamov, 'The *bi-lā kayfa* doctrine and its foundation in Islamic theology', *Arabica* 42 (1995), pp. 165-79. Wesley Williams ('Aspects of the creed of Aḥmad ibn Ḥanbal: a study of anthropomorphism in early Islamic discourse', *IJMES* 34, 2002, pp. 448ff.) alleges that the expression was falsely attributed to Ibn Ḥanbal. However, a number of Ḥanbalīs, from at least al-Barbahārī (d. 329/941) onwards, adopted the doctrine. Frank ('Elements', pp. 154ff) has convincingly argued that the way that al-Ashʿarī and his school applied the term *bi-lā kayf* differed significantly from its usage by Ḥanbalīs.

103 Ibid. For a discussion of these two terms see Louis Gardet and Georges C. Anawati, *Introduction à la théologie musulmane* (Paris, 1981), pp. 56-8; Josef Van Ess, 'Tashbīh wa tanzīh', *EI²*, X, pp. 341-4.

104 This is according to a verse attributed to Anṣārī by Ibn Rajab, which reads: 'Since the person who holds the opinion of al-Ashʿarī – a devil of a human being – has veered away from the bounds of good guidance, you be a Shāfiʿī in law, adorned as a Sunni, Ḥanbalī in creed and a Sufi in your conduct.' See Ibn Rajab al-Baghdādī, *Dhayl ʿalā ṭabaqāt al-Ḥanābila*, ed. H. Laoust and S. Dahhān (2 vols., Damascus, 1370/1951), I, p. 83; de Beaurecueil, *Khwādja Abdullāh,* p. 43, n. 2. However, Muḥammad Saʿīd al-Afghānī, in his biography of Anṣārī, *ʿAbd Allāh al-Anṣārī al-Harawī, mabādiʾuhu wa ārāʾuhu'l-kalāmiyya wa'l-rūḥiyya* (Cairo, 1968), pp. 96-7, does not agree with this attribution and insists that Anṣārī was a Ḥanbalī both in *furūʿ* and *uṣūl.*

105 For example, *Kashf*, I, p. 43 and V, p. 307, where when arguing against the metaphorical interpretation of the anthropomorphic verses he cites al-Shāfiʿī's words: *al-ẓāhir amlak*. Another authority whom Maybudī cites in support of these doctrines is the Kufan traditionist Wakīʿ b. al-Jarrāḥ (d. 197/778).

106 On which see George Makdisi, 'Ashʿarī and the Ashʿarites in Islamic religious history', *SI* 17 (1962), pp. 37-80 and *SI* 18 (1963), pp. 19-39.

107 De Beaurecueil, *Khwādja Abdullāh,* pp. 103-4, 111.

108 *Kashf*, III, p. 445.

109 Michel Allard, 'En quoi consiste l'opposition faite à al-Ashʿarī par ses contemporains Ḥanbalites?' *REI* 28 (1960), p. 104; Watt, *Formative Period,* p. 295.

110 *Kashf*, II, p. 445. It should be added, however, that this doctrine was in time adopted by some Ḥanbalīs, for which see Daniel Gimaret, 'Théories de l'acte

humain dans l'école Ḥanbalite', *BEO* 29 (1977), pp. 157-78. On the doctrine of *kasb* see W. Montgomery Watt, 'The origin of the Islamic doctrine of acquisition', *JRAS* (1943), pp. 234-7; idem, *Free Will and Predestination in Early Islam* (London, 1948); Daniel Gimaret, 'Théories'; idem, *Théories de l'acte humaine en théologie musulmane* (Paris and Leuven, 1980).

111 This would to some extent endorse Makdisi's view that the Shāfiʿī school of jurisprudence was not entirely won over to Ashʿarī theology from the time of Niẓām al-Mulk onwards. See George Makdisi, *L'Islam hanbalisant* (Paris, 1983), p. 38; idem, 'Ashʿarī and the Ashʿarites'; idem, 'The Sunni revival', in Richards, ed., *Islamic Civilisation: 950-1150*, pp. 155-68, especially pp. 159-60. There is evidence, moreover, that there were in this period Shāfiʿīs with 'anthropomorphic' tendencies (see Bausani, 'Religion in the Saljuq period', p. 284), and Ḥanbalīs with Shāfiʿī tendencies. According to the *Tabṣirat al-ʿawāmm* written in the early seventh/thirteenth century by the Shiʿi author Sayyid Murtaḍā al-Rāzī, Shāfiʿīs with 'anthropomorphic' theological beliefs were to be found in the region of Hamadan, Qara, Burūjird, Isfahan, Yazd and Herat. See Henri Laoust, 'Les premières professions de foi ḥanbalites', in Louis Massignon, ed., *Mélanges Louis Massignon* (Damascus, 1956), III, pp. 31-4 on Ibn Yaʿlā's Shāfiʿī tendencies. Another 'traditionalist' Shāfiʿī almost contemporary with Maybudī was al-Taymī (d. 535/1140), for which see Binyamin Abrahamov, *Islamic Theology: Traditionalism and Rationalism* (Edinburgh, 1998), p. 1 *et passim*. For a caveat concerning Makdisi's view see Wilferd Madelung, 'The spread of Māturīdism and the Turks', repr. in W. Madelung, *Religious Schools and Sects in Medieval Islam* (London, 1970), p. 110, n. 3.

112 I am using the term 'traditionalist' as it has been used by Makdisi, and recently defined by Abrahamov (*Traditionalism*, p. ix), to mean a person who regarded 'religious knowledge as deriving from the Revelation (Qur'an), the tradition (Sunna) and the consensus (*ijmāʿ*), and preferred these sources to reason in treating religious matters'. The term 'traditionist' is here being used to mean a scholar of hadith (*muḥaddith*). See also the discussion of the designation 'traditionalist' in Christopher Melchert, 'The piety of the ḥadīth folk', *IJMES* 34 (2002), pp. 425-39.

113 *Kashf*, VI, p. 111. The inclusion of *ʿaql* in this passage shows that, as Jackson has indicated, reason does have its place with traditionalists. See Sherman Jackson, *On the Boundaries of Theological Tolerance in Islam: Abū Ḥāmid al-Ghazālī's Fayṣal al-tafriqa bayna al-Islām wa al-zandaqa* (Oxford, 2002), pp. 19ff. However, as this study will show, Maybudī's traditionalism keeps the rational faculty strictly within bounds.

114 *Kashf*, V, p. 219.

115 Anṣārī, *Ṭabaqāt al-ṣūfiyya*, ed. S. Mawlāʾī, editor's introduction, p. 18.

116 Anṣārī's *Kitāb al-arbaʿīn* consists of forty chapters, among which are: 'Exposition of the Fact that God is something (*shayʾ*)'; 'Affirmation of the Fact that God has a limit (*ḥadd*)'; 'Affirmation of the Fact that God has Sides or Directions (*jihāt*)', and so on. The work is included by Helmut Ritter in his list of manuscripts of Anṣārī's works, 'Philologica VIII', *Der Islam* 22 (1934), p. 89.

117 Ed. with intro. by M.T. Dānishpazhūh, '*Fuṣūl*-i Rashīd al-Dīn Maybudī', *Farhang-i Īrān zamīn*, Year 16 (1348sh/1969), pp. 44-89.

118 On Abu'l-Futūḥ Rāzī see Martin J. McDermott, 'Abu'l-Fotūḥ Rāzī, *EI²*, I, p. 292.

119 The word *laṭā'if* is a term that was used for subtle or interesting points, poems or anecdotes (often related to the subject of love mysticism) that came to the mind of the preacher by way of association. See Nasrollah Pourjavady, 'Laṭā'if-i Qur'ānī dar Majālis-i Sayf al-Dīn Bākharzī', *Ma'ārif* 18/1 (March 2001), pp. 3-24. However, the word *laṭā'if* was also applied without this connotation in Sufi exegesis to mean simply 'subtleties' or 'subtle insights or meanings', as in the title of Qushayrī's commentary, the *Laṭā'if al-ishārāt*, or in the saying attributed to Ja'far al-Ṣādiq designating four levels of meaning in the Qur'an, for which see p. 55.

120 By contrast, the exoteric commentaries of Isfarāyinī and Abu'l-Futūḥ Rāzī are consistently composed in Persian, with Rāzī's commentary having marginally more Arabic content than Isfarāyinī's in the form of untranslated hadiths.

121 Maybudī's reasons for limiting the number of verses he comments on in his mystical commentary will be discussed further in chapter three.

122 *Kashf*, I, p. 1. Shafī'ī Kadkanī has recently presented the theory that Khwāja 'Abd Allāh Anṣārī never wrote a *tafsīr*, and that Maybudī was probably confusing Khwāja 'Abd Allāh with another Anṣārī, one Abū Aḥmad 'Umar b. 'Abd Allāh b. Muḥammad al-Hirawī, known as 'Pīr-i Hirī', who probably died *c.* 400/1009, to whom a commentary has been attributed but not found. See Muḥammad Riḍā Shafī'ī Kadkanī, '"Pīr-i Hirī ghayr az Khwāja 'Abd Allāh Anṣārī" ast!' *Nāma-yi Bahāristān*, Year 10 (1388sh/2009), vol. 15, pp. 185-92. However, as is indicated below, there is evidence in the sources that Khwāja 'Abd Allāh did dictate a commentary on parts of the Qur'an to some of his disciples. Since no commentary attributed to either of these two masters of Herat is extant, it is not possible to verify the source on which Maybudī was drawing. Nonetheless, given Maybudī's familiarity with the doctrines, teachings and Persian style of Khwāja 'Abd Allāh, it seems unlikely that he would have confused the two authors.

123 De Beaurecueil, *Khwādja 'Abdullāh*, pp. 89-90; Ibn Rajab, *Dhayl*, I, pp. 73-4.

124 De Beaurecueil (*Khwādja 'Abdullāh*, pp. 15-16, n. 5) informs us that Abū 'Abd Allāh Ḥusayn al-Kutubī was a disciple and companion of Khwāja 'Abd Allāh's last days. His record of Anṣārī's life and teachings was used as a source by 'Abd al-Qādir Ruhāwī, whose *Kitāb al-mādiḥ wa'l-mamdūḥ* was in turn used by Ibn Rajab.

125 It is difficult to find for the word *ḥaqīqa* (Persian *ḥaqīqat*) one word in English to fit the different contexts in which it is used. In this book it will be variously translated according to the context as 'truth', 'reality', 'realised truth' or 'spiritual/inner realisation'.

126 Bo Utas in his article, 'The *Munājāt* or *Ilāhī-nāmah* of 'Abdu'llāh Anṣārī', *Manuscripts of the Middle East* 3 (1988), p. 84, has pointed out that Anṣārī's *Munājāt* are also included in his *Ṭabaqāt al-ṣūfiyya*, and that the *Ṭabaqāt* and *Kashf al-asrār* may be the oldest and most reliable sources for a part of the Anṣāriyyāt heritage that, according to de Beaurecueil (*Khwādja 'Abdullāh,* p. 287), has snowballed over the centuries. Muhammad Asif Fikrat has extracted and published *munājāt* from both these works in his *Munājāt wa guftār-i Pīr-i Harāt Khwāja 'Abdu'llāh-i Anṣārī-yi Harawī* (Kabul, 1355sh/1976). He has numbered fifteen *munājāt* from the *Ṭabaqāt* and 88 from *Kashf al-asrār*. Utas suggests that the *Kashf al-asrār*, like the *Ṭabaqāt*, probably existed as a collection of

notes taken down by Anṣārī's disciples. If, as de Beaurecueil has suggested (*Khwādja ʿAbdullāh,* p. 120, n. 2), the *Ṭabaqāt* 'reflects the teaching at intimate sessions held by Anṣārī in his own khānaqāh in Herāt', then the same might be said of material attributed to Anṣārī in the *Kashf al-asrār*. In this case it is not impossible that *munājāt* which appear in the text were spontaneous interjections by the master in the course of his teaching sessions. Other passages in the *Kashf al-asrār*, however, appear to have been taken from another work of Anṣārī, the *Ṣad maydān*, for which see p. 22 and n. 138.

127 Ṭabarī is only cited twice by name (*Kashf,* III, p. 307; V, p. 588) but Maybudī probably drew numerous hadiths from his *tafsīr.*

128 Citations too numerous to list here. Reference may be made to Sharīʿat's *Fihrist-i Kashf al-asrār wa ʿuddat al-abrār.*

129 For example in *Kashf,* III, pp. 321, 477; VI, pp. 405, 406; VII, pp. 110, 288, 440.

130 Citations both on variant readings and exegesis too numerous to be listed here.

131 Again, numerous citations. On the commentaries of Sufyān al-Thawrī and Mujāhid, see n. 48.

132 Böwering, *Mystical Vision*, p. 39. Citations of Tustarī occur in *Kashf,* I, pp. 21, 108, 161; II, p. 727; III, p. 483; VI, p. 356.

133 Such differences in context may be noted when comparing Maybudī's citations with the edition of Nwyia. For example, Jaʿfar al-Ṣādiq's comment on Q. 6:19 in Sulamī's *Ḥaqāʾiq* appears in the context of Q. 3:18 in the *Kashf al-asrār*, and his comment on Q. 9:14 appears in the context of Q. 10:57.

134 For example, *Kashf,* II, pp. 778-9 commenting on Q. 7:160, and *Kashf,* VI, p. 477, commenting on Q. 23:115. These discrepancies suggest that Maybudī may have been using a variant manuscript, or that he had derived the comments through oral transmission, and this might also account for comments with the same wording being cited in different contexts from Sulamī's original.

135 By contrast with the comments that appear to have been derived from Sulamī's *Ḥaqāʾiq*, comments taken from Qushayrī's *Laṭāʾif* almost always occur in the same Qur'anic context and usually follow the same wording as in the original, and this suggests that Maybudī had access to a written copy of the *Laṭāʾif.*

136 Both the work and the author are cited by name. See *Kashf,* III, p. 297.

137 Neither the work nor the author is cited by name, but the quatrains cited in *Kashf,* I, p. 614; V, p. 141; VII, p. 75, as well as the passage on *wilāyat-i ʿishq* (*Kashf,* I, pp. 239-40) appear to have been taken from the *Sawāniḥ*.

138 Anṣārī, *Ṣad maydān*, text and French trans. in S. de Laugier de Beaurecueil, 'Une ébauche persane des *Manāzil as-Sāʾirīn*: le *Kitāb-e Ṣad maydān* de ʿAbdullāh Anṣārī', *Mélanges Islamologiques d'Archéologie Orientale* 2 (1954), pp. 1-90; French trans. repr. in de Beaurecueil, *Chemins de Dieu* (Paris, 1985). A close correspondence, for example, can be seen between passages in *Kashf,* I, p. 128, and *Maydān*, 47; *Kashf,* I, p. 423, and *Maydān*, 57; *Kashf,* I, p. 738 and *Maydān*, 54; *Kashf,* II, pp. 94-5 and the conclusion to *Ṣad maydān*; *Kashf,* V, p. 216, and *Maydān*, 96. See Utas, 'The *Munājāt*'; Nasrollah Pourjavady, 'Iṣālat-i *Ṣad Maydān*-i Khwāja ʿAbd Allāh Anṣārī', in ʿAlī Ashraf Ṣādiqī, ed., *Yādnāma-yi Duktur Aḥmad Tafaḍḍullī* (*Tafazzoli Memorial Volume*) (Tehran, 1379sh/2001), pp. 1-15.

139 For example, *Kashf*, V, pp. 59-60. Berndt Radtke and John O'Kane (*The Concept of Sainthood in Early Islamic Mysticism*, Richmond, 1996, p. 5) list this as one of the works which may have been incorrectly attributed to Tirmidhī. In a footnote to his translation of this work, Heer suggests that it may have been composed by Abu'l-Ḥusayn al-Nūrī, author of the *Maqāmāt al-qulūb*, for which see Nicholas Heer and Kenneth L. Honerkamp, *Three Early Sufi Texts* (Louisville, 2003), p. 57. Maybudī may, therefore, equally have drawn on a work by Nūrī.

140 Regarding Maybudī's use of the works of Sarrāj and Iṣfahānī, see n. 131.

141 For example, the metaphor of the bat (*Kashf*, II, p. 397) may have been taken from the chapter on love in Ghazzālī's *Iḥyā' ʿulūm al-dīn* (6 vols., Damascus, 1417/1997), Part 4, Book 6, *Kitāb al-maḥabba wa'l-shawq wa'l-riḍā' wa'l-uns*, p. 213, or in his *Kīmiyā-yi saʿādat*, ed. Ḥ. Khadīwjam (3rd repr., Tehran, 1364sh/1985), II, p. 595.

142 Shihāb al-Dīn Aḥmad Samʿānī, *Rawḥ al-arwāḥ fī sharḥ asmā' al-Malik al-Fattāḥ*, ed. N.M. Harawī (Tehran, 1368sh/1989). A number of passages in *Kashf al-asrār* replicate almost word for word passages in *Rawḥ al-arwāḥ*. For example, *Kashf*, VII, p. 56, and *Rawḥ al-arwāḥ*, p. 2; *Kashf*, VII, p. 77, and *Rawḥ al-arwāḥ*, p. 69; *Kashf*, VI, p. 527, and *Rawḥ al-arwāḥ*, p. 130. Both ʿAli Aṣghar Ṣayfī and Akbar Naḥwī have concluded that the composition of *Rawḥ al-arwāḥ* preceded that of the *Kashf al-asrār* and thus that Maybudī drew material from Samʿānī's work. See ʿAlī Asghar Ṣayfī, 'Ta'thīr-i *Rawḥ al-arwāḥ* dar tafsīr-i *Kashf al-asrār*', in Yad Allāh Jalālī Pindarī, ed., *Yādnāma-yi Abu'l-Faḍl Rashīd al-Dīn Maybudī*, vol. I (Yazd, 1378sh/1999), pp. 356-94; and Akbar Naḥwī, 'Barkhī az manābiʿ-i fārsī-yi *Kashf al-asrār*', in Mehdī Malik Thābit, ed., *Yādnāma-yi Abu'l-Faḍl Rashīd al-Dīn Maybudī*, vol. II (Yazd, 1379sh/2000), pp. 272-84. In the introduction to his abridged translation of the *Nawbat* III sections of the *Kashf al-asrār*, Chittick notes that Maybudī appears to have obtained a copy of Samʿānī's *Rawḥ al-arwāḥ* at the time he was writing his commentary on *Sūrat al-Naḥl* (Q. 16) – at any rate, it is from this point on in the *Kashf al-asrār* that the influence of Samʿānī's work may be seen. See Chittick, tr., *The Unveiling of Mysteries and Provision of the Righteous*, Introduction, p. xiv.

143 Whilst only a small number of possible 'borrowings' from the *Sawāniḥ* may be found in the *Nawbat* III sections of *Kashf al-asrār* (see above, n. 137), and Maybudī's understanding of love differed from the metaphysical perspective of Aḥmad Ghazzālī (for which see Chapter Four, below), it is possible to trace aspects of Ghazzālī's teachings in Maybudī's discourse on love, as for example, his discussions of humanity's pre-eternal initiation into divine love (see below, p. 141 and *Kashf*, III, pp. 793-4), and his mention of *wilāyat-i ʿishq* (see below, pp. 289-92 and 300, and *Kashf*, V, 59-60). Beyond this, it is difficult to ascertain the influence of the *Sawāniḥ* on Maybudī's *Kashf al-asrār*. Even so, it is unlikely that Ghazzālī's seminal treatise on mystical love did not have some impact on wider developments in love mysticism that were taking place at the time Maybudī was writing his *tafsīr*.

PART ONE

HERMENEUTICS

2

The hermeneutics of the *Kashf al-asrār*

In this chapter I will examine the overall hermeneutics of the *Kashf al-asrār*, before passing on to the hermeneutics of his esoteric commentary in chapter three. Unlike other Sufi commentators, Maybudī did not present his esoteric commentary as a self-contained work but purposely combined it with a translation and exoteric commentary. Keeping in mind the definition of hermeneutics that was discussed in the preface, this chapter will examine the way in which Maybudī himself defines the aims, criteria and method of interpretation: for example, his attitude towards commenting according to received tradition (*tafsīr bi'l-ma'thūr*) as opposed to commenting on the basis of reasoned opinion (*tafsīr bi'l-ra'y*), and his views on the interpretation of the *mutashābihāt* and the anthropomorphic verses in the Qur'an. His principles concerning the latter will be placed in context by comparing them to those of Abū Ḥāmid al-Ghazzālī, and will be contrasted with the criteria for esoteric interpretation which Maybudī holds in common with other Sufis. Having established the overall aims and criteria of the *Kashf al-asrār*, the chapter will briefly digress to show how the content and style of Maybudī's exoteric commentary serve its hermeneutical purpose, before finally looking into the reasons behind the threefold structure of the *Kashf al-asrār*, and Maybudī's combination of exoteric and esoteric interpretations of the Qur'an.

Maybudī's hermeneutics as defined in the *Kashf al-asrār*

In his brief introduction to the *Kashf al-asrār*, Maybudī clearly indicates what he believes to be the purpose of writing a commentary on the Qur'an, stating:

> I studied the book by that unique and peerless man of his age, the Shaykh al-Islām Abū Ismāʿīl ʿAbd Allāh Muḥammad b. ʿAlī al-Anṣārī, may God sanctify his spirit, concerning the exegesis of the Qur'an and the unveiling of its meanings, and I saw that he had well-nigh attained a miracle in language and meaning, in ascertaining the truth and adorning it with jewels. Yet he had made it extremely short, taking therein the path of brevity, so that it could hardly bring the student seeking guidance (*al-mutaʿallim al-mustarshid*) to his goal or satisfy the longing of one who ponders and seeks insight (*al-mutaʾammil al-mustabṣir*). I determined, therefore, to spread the wings of discourse, loosening the reins of the tongue to expand it, combining the truths of commentary with the subtleties of admonition in a way that would be easy for those who are involved in this field.[1]

The purpose of the *Kashf al-asrār* was, therefore, not merely to supply a commentary on the Qur'an, but to provide spiritual guidance and illumination.

Maybudī does not, like other exegetes, precede his commentary with chapters setting out his hermeneutical theory.[2] In isolated places in the *Kashf al-asrār* he discusses aspects of interpretation when this is called for by the occurrence in the Qur'anic text of a word such as *taʾwīl* or *istinbāṭ*, but he reserves his more general discussion of Qur'anic exegesis for the very end, where it appears almost as an afterthought.[3] Here, in a short chapter entitled simply '*faṣl*', Maybudī begins by justifying the interpretation of the Qur'an with a hadith of the Prophet: 'Enunciate the Qur'an clearly, and inquire into what is strange in it, for God likes that it should be enunciated clearly'.[4] He then adds a citation from the Qur'an, 'and he unto whom wisdom is given, he has truly received abundant good' (Q. 2: 269) – Maybudī glosses wisdom (*ḥikma*) here as the *tafsīr* of the Qur'an – and a saying of Mujāhid, 'The people who are most beloved of God are those who are most knowledgeable concerning His revelation.' There follows a well-known tradition defining the categories of *tafsīr*, which is to be found in the introduction to Ṭabarī's *Jāmiʿ al-bayān*.[5]

> Ibn ʿAbbās has stated, 'The *tafsīr* of the Qur'an falls into four categories: that which can be understood by the learned; that of which the Arabs have knowledge; that which it is unforgivable not to know; and that the interpretation of which if anyone should claim to have knowledge, he is lying.'[6]

Maybudī proceeds to define his own criteria for interpretation and to stipulate those qualifications that he considers to be necessary for the commentator. In spite of his traditionalist outlook, he does not believe that *tafsīr bi'l-ma'thūr* (interpretation according to received tradition) can stand on its own, but advocates a combination of *tafsīr bi'l-ma'thūr* and *tafsīr bi'l-ra'y* (interpretation according to one's own reasoned opinion or judgement). Having put the case for the proponents of both *tafsīr bi'l-ma'thūr* and *tafsīr bi'l-ra'y*, he says:

> These two schools of thought tend towards opposite extremes and are inadequate. Whoever restricts himself merely to what has been handed down leaves aside much that is necessary [for exegesis]. On the other hand, anyone who deems it permissible for a person [simply to] plunge into the science of interpretation runs the risk of causing confusion and does not take note of the true import of His words 'that they may ponder its verses and that men of learning might reflect' [Q. 38:29].
> So, a person may only embark upon the exegesis of the Qur'an once [he has] mastered ten areas of knowledge: the knowledge of the [Arabic] language; of the derivation of words; of grammar; of the variant readings; of the biography of the Prophet, and of his sayings; the knowledge of the principles of jurisprudence; of the ordinances [concerning worship]; of those concerning transactions; and of those concerning gifts. When he has mastered these ten areas of knowledge and gone beyond that to comment upon the Qur'an using his reasoned opinion (*bi-ra'yihi*), then it can be said that he is [truly] practising the science of Qur'anic interpretation.[7]

The ten areas of knowledge, which Maybudī here insists must be mastered, are in fact what constitutes for him *tafsīr bi'l-ma'thūr*, and they are the *sine qua non* for any exegete who wishes to undertake *tafsīr bi'l-ra'y*.

A discussion of Qur'anic exegesis, however brief, would not be complete without some mention of the *muḥkam* ('unequivocal') and *mutashābih* ('ambiguous') verses; the understanding of these two terms, and in fact, the reading of verse Q. 3:7 in which they occur, are fundamental to any definition of the parameters and criteria of interpretation.[8] Maybudī concludes this short *faṣl* with an interesting passage on the subject.

> If someone should put the question, 'What is the wisdom in some of the Qur'an being *muḥkam* and some of it being *mutashābih*, for if it were all straightforward there would be no need for the trouble of speculation, and errors and slips of judgement would not occur?', the answer is that this is as good as asking, 'Why did the Lord of Might not give us the good things of this world without trouble and difficulties, so that His blessing would be [wholly] agreeable and His gift without hardship?' The answer would

> be that this is not without wisdom, [for] when God, exalted is He, created Adam, He distinguished him with the capacity to think and discriminate, two faculties which no other creature has. He honoured and ennobled man with these qualities saying, '[and We have] conferred upon them special favours above a great part of Our creation' [Q. 17:70], and by honouring him and ennobling him in this way He made him worthy of being His deputy, as He the Exalted said, '[and your Lord] may make you vicegerents in the earth' [Q. 7:129]. Thus He gave Adam qualities by which He Himself, exalted be His Glory, is described and named, such as knowledge (*ʿilm*), wisdom (*ḥikmat*) and clemency (*ḥilm*). Then, since He had distinguished man with thought (*fikr*) and deliberation (*rawiyyat*), whatever God gave him, He bestowed upon him just short of perfection, so that man, by means of his thought and deliberation, could make it complete, the benefit of those faculties would become manifest and he, thereby, would become worthy of his reward. This is in particular the duty of mankind, and God, exalted be His Glory, is the All-Transcending, the All-Holy [...]

Maybudī was not alone in speaking of the spiritual and intellectual benefits provided by the *mutashābih* verses,[9] but the way he has expressed this principle here is original and somewhat surprising, both in the context of the generally held concept of *iʿjāz*[10] and from one who uncompromisingly argues for the uncreatedness of the Qur'an. Moreover, Maybudī is not basing his argument on tradition but is very much employing his reasoned opinion (*ra'y*) to defend the use of *ra'y*. Such inconsistencies are not uncommon in the *Kashf al-asrār*, and do not allow the reader to be too conclusive about its author's theological views.

Maybudī has more to say about the *muḥkam* and *mutashābih* verses when he comments upon Q. 3:7. He sets out several different traditional opinions on the subject, most of which occur in Ṭabarī's *Jāmiʿ al-bayān* and need not be repeated here.[11] In this context, Maybudī (like Ṭabarī) expresses the opinion that there should be a break between the words 'and none knows its interpretation save only God' and 'those who are rooted in knowledge say'. Thus, in contrast to what was implied in the previously quoted passage, he seems here to be confirming the view (held by Ṭabarī) that the *mutashābihāt* are to be understood by God alone.[12] Yet this view is soon over-ridden when later, in the same *Nawbat* II commentary, he provides the following answer to the question of what benefit there could be in God's placing the *mutashābih* verses in the Qur'an:

> It is for the ennoblement and distinction of scholars that, with the acuity of their understanding (*minqāsh-i fahm*), they should extract the precise meaning from the [*mutashābihāt*] verses and, according to this view, be distinguished from ordinary people.[13] Furthermore, they earn God's reward in the other world, for by eliciting the meanings of the Qur'an (*istinbāṭ*) they exert their thought and reflection. If all the verses of the Qur'an were *muḥkam* there would be no need for the toil of consideration or the labour of thought and thus no attainment of this reward. Another argument is that when wise men, having pondered the *mutashābih* verses, find themselves incapable of understanding them, they realise their deficiency and weakness and walk straight in the path of servanthood, because servanthood lies in recognising one's weakness and accepting one's helplessness.[14]

Perhaps the clearest exposition of Maybudī's approach to the *mutashābihāt,* and the most significant for understanding his hermeneutics, is to be found in his *Nawbat* III commentary on Q. 3:7. He begins by stating in a somewhat allusive fashion: 'those [verses] that are manifest and clear (*ẓāhir*, *rawshan*, i.e. *muḥkam*) are for the majesty of the law (*jalāl-i sharīʿat-rā'st*); those that are difficult and obscure (*mushkil*, *ghāmiḍ*, i.e. *mutashābih*) are for the beauty of realised truth (*jamāl-i ḥaqīqat-rā'st*)'. He then explains:

> The former are manifest, so that the common people (*ʿāmma-yi khalq*) can grasp them, put into practice what they have understood, and attain favour and blessing (*nāz wa niʿmat*). The latter are difficult, so that by acquiescing in, and affirming [the apparently obscure meaning][15] the elite may attain the mystery of the Bestower of blessing (*walī-yi niʿmat*) [...] It is in order to glorify the state and honour of that work [of the spiritual elite among the believers] that God does not remove the veil of obscurity and ambiguity [from the *mutashābihāt*], and so that no uninitiated person should set foot in this alley, for not everyone is worthy of knowing the secrets of kings.'[16]

In other words, by accepting the outward ambiguity of the verses, the elite (here clearly mystics) gain access to the divine mysteries. According to Maybudī, therefore, the *mutashābihāt* verses appear to have five functions:

> To make use of those faculties by which God has distinguished man from the animals.
> To distinguish the learned (or spiritual) elite from ordinary people.
> To make wise men aware of their weakness when they are unable to understand the verses.

For the sake of spiritual realisation (*ḥaqīqat*) as opposed to the outer practice of the law (*sharīʿat*).
To preserve the divine mysteries, which can only be attained through spiritual realisation, and on the condition of a complete acquiescence in those verses which appear to be rationally obscure.

In these passages, Maybudī sometimes applies the word *khāṣṣ* (elite) to scholars of exoteric sciences and sometimes to the spiritual elite.[17] His use of the word *istinbāṭ*, a term that was commonly used among Sufis to denote the esoteric interpretation of the Qur'an,[18] is also worth noting. Maybudī himself employs the word elsewhere with the latter meaning (for which see p. 49), whereas in the statement 'by eliciting the meanings of the Qur'an (*istinbāṭ*) they exert their thought and reflection', he is clearly applying the term to the eliciting of meanings through the exertion of reason (*ta'wīl ʿaqlī*) rather than through mystical unveiling (*ta'wīl kashfī*).[19] Maybudī, it seems, was not overly concerned with precise definitions, nor was he always consistent in his use of words. This non-uniformity is also to be found in his application of the word *ta'wīl*.[20] Commenting on the latter part of Q. 3:7, he makes a clear distinction between the word *tafsīr*, 'the interpretation which treats of the circumstances of revelation, matters of law and the stories of the prophets, and which cannot be truly accomplished unless it has been taught (*ba-tawqīf*) or heard [directly from a traditionist in the customary manner] (*ba-samāʿ*)', and *ta'wīl*, 'tracing a verse back to the meaning it bears', adding the observation that 'eliciting the meaning (*istinbāṭ*) is not unlawful for the learned once they are conversant with the Book and the Sunna.'[21] What the words *tafsīr* and *ta'wīl* are representing here is *tafsīr bi'l-ma'thūr* and *tafsīr bi'l-ra'y*, respectively.

Elsewhere, Maybudī uses the words *ta'wīl* and *tafsīr* interchangeably simply to mean interpretation or explanation.[22] In Ṭabarī's time the two words were apparently synonymous, as is evidenced by the title of his commentary. Later, although it continued to be used by some commentators synonymously with *tafsīr*,[23] the word *ta'wīl* took on a more specific meaning when it was applied either to the esoteric interpretation that was practised by the Sufis and regarded with suspicion by many of the ulema or to the metaphorical interpretation practised by Muʿtazilīs, Ismailis and philosophers and generally considered to be heretical by traditionalist schools of Sunni Islam.

Maybudī could therefore use the word *ta'wīl* effectively in a pejorative sense when, on numerous occasions in the *Kashf al-asrār*, he condemns those kinds of interpretation that he considers to be heretical. His attacks are directed specifically at two kinds of *ta'wīl*: the metaphorical interpretation of the anthropomorphic verses practised by the Muʿtazilīs and others; and any interpretation which contradicts or denies the importance of the literal meanings of a verse, such as that practised by the philosophers.[24]

An interesting comparison can be made with Ghazzālī's views on metaphorical interpretation, as expressed in a number of his works.[25] In a passage from the *Kitāb qawāʿid al-ʿaqāʾid* (*The Foundations of the Articles of Faith*) in the *Iḥyāʾ*, Ghazzālī speaks sympathetically of those who disallow metaphorical interpretation:

> What is believed about Aḥmad b. Ḥanbal is that, although he knew that sitting (*al-istiwāʾ*) did not imply being established (*al-istiqrār*) [in a place] and that descending (*al-nuzūl*) did not imply movement [from place to place], he nevertheless forbade metaphorical interpretation (*al-ta'wīl*) in order to close the door and to safeguard the welfare of the people, for should the door be opened, disruption would spread, and the situation would get out of control and exceed the limits of moderation, because the limits of moderation cannot be precisely determined. Thus there is nothing wrong with this restriction, and the practice of the predecessors attests to it.

Explaining the opinion of his own school, he says:

> Another group believed in moderation (*al-iqtiṣād*) and opened the door to metaphorical interpretation of everything pertaining to God's attributes, but kept the verses pertaining to the afterlife in their apparent meanings (*ʿalā ẓawāhirihā*) and prohibited their interpretation. These were the Ashʿarīs.[26]

Ghazzālī is alluding here to the philosophers' allegorical interpretation of verses which describe the bodily resurrection and the sensible punishments in the afterlife. His (and the Ashʿarīs') objection to such interpretation was that it challenged the fundamentals of faith and was therefore heretical.[27] From the point of view of a fervent traditionalist like Maybudī, unquestioning belief in the attributes of God (which included His 'two hands',[28] His breathing,[29] His being 'in heaven'[30] and His 'ascending the Throne') should also be considered among the fundamentals of religious belief. While he condemns corporealists (*mujassima*) such as the Karrāmiyya and Hishāmiyya,[31] who describe the 'hand of God' as a limb, and he designates them as 'tending towards unbelief (*kufr*)', he equally dismisses the metaphorical interpretations of Muʿtazilīs, Qādirīs, and Twelver Shiʿa, who understand the 'hand of God' to be His power (*qudrat*) or 'His two hands' as power and blessing (*qudrat wa niʿmat*), arguing at length that their view is invalid and absurd (*bāṭil wa muḥāl*).[32]

Thus far, it might be said that the difference between Maybudī's and Ghazzālī's approach to Qur'anic interpretation was one of dogma rather than hermeneutics. Yet Maybudī goes further, insisting that verses such as: 'All that is in the heavens and earth glorifies God' (Q. 57:1) should be accepted as they are in their literal meaning. Commenting on this verse, he states:

> The Creator of the world and all its creatures [...] informs us, 'All that is in the heavens and earth: wind and fire, earth and water, mountain and sea, sun, moon and stars, trees, everything, be it animate or inanimate, praises Us in Our perfection, attests to [Our] greatness, and bears witness to Our Oneness.'
>
> [Although] that glorification and attestation of oneness perplexes the heart of man, and reason rejects it, yet the religion of Islam accepts it and creation's Creator affirms its truth.[33]

Maybudī continues his commentary on this verse by advocating that 'the fortunate ones, those who will be among the truly sincere and the friends of God in the hereafter, will accept the meaning of the verse with heart and soul, even without comprehending it', and he warns 'the noble ones' that they 'should not allow one jot of innovation to enter their hearts. When they hear something [in the Qur'an] which they cannot rationally comprehend, they should see the fault as lying entirely with their faculty of reason.'[34] In another context he lists five other verses which should be accepted in their literal meaning, even though that might go against reason: 'a wall which "would" fall into ruin' (Q. 18:77); 'garments of fire' (Q. 22:19); 'We [heaven and earth] come willingly' (Q. 41:11); 'As it [hellfire] would burst with rage' (Q. 67:8); 'The thunder hymns His praise' (Q. 13:13); 'the moon was rent in two' (Q. 54:1); and the demand of the insatiable hellfire: 'Is there more to come?' (Q. 50:30). None of these Qur'anic statements appear to involve fundamentals of religious belief; in most cases they are what might be called figurative expressions, and form part of the Qur'anic rhetoric.[35] It appears then, that Maybudī's principal objection to the metaphorical interpretation both of these 'figurative' expressions in the Qur'an and of the anthropomorphic verses, is that it allows human reason (*ʿaql*) to stray into a domain in which it does not belong.[36]

Insistence on the limits of reason, and on man's dependence upon the knowledge provided by God through His revelation and the Sunna, is a predominant theme in the *Kashf al-asrār*. Thus we find Maybudī continuing his *Nawbat* III commentary on Q. 57:1 with the following admonition:

> Do not tread the path of *taʾwīl* for that is to experiment with poison or to try to use a thorn to remove a thorn from the foot.
>
> Seek not the way of oneness with reason,
> Scratch not the eye of the spirit with thorns,
> I'll warrant, by God, there is no one
> Can have aught from God, without God.
> Deem not that there can be on the highway of religion
> Any better guide than the Qur'an and tradition,
> Only the heart of Muhammad can provide
> The key to the treasury of His secrets.[37]

However, while it is unlawful, in Maybudī's view, for philosophers, dialectical theologians and astrologers to reason about the essence and attributes of God,[38] knowledge of them may be *granted* to prophets and mystics.[39] Equally, the restrictions that Maybudī places on exoteric interpretation, which involves the exercise of reason, do not apply to esoteric interpretation. Thus, for example, while exoterically Maybudī forbids anything beyond a literal interpretation of the 'wall which "would" fall into ruin' (Q. 18:77), we find these words the subject of an interesting allegorical interpretation at the esoteric level.[40] There is, nevertheless, a caveat. In his mystical commentary on Q. 13:17, Maybudī interprets 'that which they smelt in the fire in order to make ornaments and tools' allegorically as: 'whatever they deduce and discover (*istidlāl wa kashf*) through their reflection (*tafakkur*), deliberation (*tadabbur*) and elicitation (*istinbāṭ*) concerning [the revelation]', and then interprets the word 'scum or foam' (*zabad*) in the same verse as: 'that which is in excess of [what comes through] the inspiration of God, and divinely-bestowed cognizance.' Maybudī further clarifies this principle by warning that masters of inspiration and gnosis should avoid making excessive efforts in their eliciting of meanings to the point that they go beyond the limits of what is inspired to them by God, for that excess would result in nothing better than an embellishment from Satan.[41] Thus, in the realm of mystical interpretation, Maybudī invalidates whatever issues from the exercise of human reason and effort, and allows only what is brought by divine intervention and provenance.[42]

Here again, a parallel may be drawn with the hermeneutics of Ghazzālī. Although he certainly allows more scope for the faculty of reason than Maybudī, seeing it as a tool by which one can discern those words or passages from the Qur'an that do not make sense rationally and therefore require to be interpreted metaphorically,[43] he does not allow that the rational faculty can of itself be the instrument of their interpretation.[44] The only source of such interpretation is what he calls *ʿilm al-mukāshafa*, the knowledge of mystical unveiling.[45] Explaining this term in the first book of the *Iḥyāʾ*, Ghazzālī describes it as

> tantamount to a light which appears in the heart when it is cleansed and purified of its blameworthy attributes. Through this light are disclosed many things for which names had previously been heard, and for which only general and vague meanings had been imagined, but which now become clear. Eventually one acquires true knowledge of God's essence, of His abiding and perfect attributes, of His acts, of His reasons for creating this world and the next, and of the way in which He has arranged the other world with respect to this world. One gains knowledge of the meaning of prophecy and the Prophet, and of the meaning of revelation (*waḥy*).[46]

Later, in the same book of the *Iḥyāʾ*, Ghazzālī states:

> Many are the subtle meanings of the mysteries of the Qur'an which dawn upon the hearts of those who have devoted themselves to invocation (*dhikr*) and reflection or meditation (*fikr*), but are not found in the books of commentary, and remain unknown to the best commentators.[47]

Ghazzālī's mention in this passage of the spiritual practices of invocation (*dhikr*) and reflection (*fikr*), and in the previous passage of the cleansing of the heart, is consistent with Sufi tradition as a whole, which stipulated that this knowledge – that is, the knowledge of the inner meanings of the Qur'an – would only be revealed to one the mirror of whose soul had been purified from the rust of worldliness. In the words of Ibn ʿAṭāʾ al-Adamī:

> The [esoteric] meanings alluded to in the Qur'an (*ishārāt al-qur'ān*) will only be understood by one who has purified his 'secret' (*sirr*) from all attachment to the world and everything it contains.[48]

Likewise, according to Ḥallāj:

> Only to the extent of his outward and inward piety and his mystical knowledge (*ma'rifa*) will the believer discover the inner meanings of the Qur'an.[49]

The same preconditions for esoteric interpretation are set out in Maybudī's definition of *istinbāṭ*, which occurs as part of his mystical commentary on the words 'and will they not ponder on the Qur'an' (Q. 4:82). He explains that reflecting upon the Qur'an (*andīsha dar qur'ān*) is the third of three kinds of meditation,[50] and is called 'meditation on the truth or reality' (*ḥaqīqa*) and 'unveiling' (*mukāshafa*). This is an attribute of mystics (*'ārifān*), 'who are given an illuminative vision (*dīda-yi mukāshafa'ī*) so that every veil between their hearts and the truth is lifted.' There follows a warning: this eliciting of the inner meanings of the Qur'an (*istinbāṭ*) is the preserve of those only

> who have shed all desires so that the divine grace of witnessing comes freely to them, whose hearts are full of the remembrance of God and tongues silent, whose secrets are filled with contemplation and who are oblivious of themselves; those who have seen the grandeur of the angels, found the permanency of God's Lordship and attained the profound tranquility of the ones who are wholly sincere. Anyone who is not in their state is not fit to enter the sea of the Qur'an and bring up (*istinbāṭ*) its hidden pearls. Indeed, every hour, every moment an envoy from the awe[someness] (*haybat*) and absolute perfection (*bī niyāzī*) of the Qur'an will place a hand upon his breast saying: "this knowledge is God's secret."[51]

From these varied statements, it can be concluded that Maybudī's hermeneutical theory comprised two distinct methodological approaches and sets of criteria. The first was a conventional approach to exoteric commentary, which combined *tafsir bi'l-ma'thūr* and *tafsīr bi'l-ra'y*, allowed for some interpretation of the *mutashābih* verses whilst accepting that the understanding of others must be left for God alone, and which denounced any *ta'wīl* that went against the outward meaning of the Qur'an or threatened the fundamentals of faith. The second was a mystical approach, known by the Sufis as *istinbāṭ*, for which the only criteria given are that it should not be entered into without complete purification of the soul, and that it should be received through the bestowal of divine inspiration rather than being 'produced' by the mystic's own deliberation and effort.

Before addressing Maybudī's reasons for bringing together his exoteric and esoteric interpretations of the Qur'an, the following section will briefly explore the way in which the content and rhetorical style of the *Nawbat* II sections of the *Kashf al-asrār* reflect the homiletic purpose of the commentary.

Tafsīr and homily in the *Kashf al-asrār*

A cursory look at the *Nawbat* II section of Maybudī's commentary on the first few verses of the Qur'an will suffice to show how much the *Kashf al-asrār* differs in style and content from other commentaries. The method of exegesis is, on the whole, similar to that of other exoteric commentaries, and all the conventional elements are there – matters of *asbāb al-nuzūl, qirā'a*, grammar, philology and law – but the *tafsīr* proper is constantly interwoven with edifying or devotional passages, anecdotes and personal observations. This is not to say that didactic passages are absent from other commentaries, but typically they are kept within the confines of the exegetical structure.

An example from Ṭabarī's *Jāmiʿ al-bayān* may serve to illustrate. In the commentary on the *Basmala* he says: 'Moreover, God, exalted is His praise, bestows abiding bliss and clear triumph, which He has promised in the next world in His gardens, on those who entirely believe in Him and who hold His Messenger to be truthful, who act in obedience to Him, but not on those who attribute partners to, and disbelieve in Him.'[52] This sentence, whilst bearing a salutary message, is in fact intended to explain the view held by some that the divine name *al-Raḥmān* refers to God's mercy to all creatures, while *al-Raḥīm* refers to the mercy He accords exclusively to the believers. Ṭabarī is instructing the reader, but *through* the exegesis.

Maybudī, on the other hand, often takes the commentary on a verse, phrase or word as the starting point for a homily which may be anything from a few words to several paragraphs in length. In his commentary on the *Basmala*, for example, he discusses the derivation of the divine name Allāh and explains that according to some, it comes from the verb *alihtu fi'l-shay'*, that is, 'I am bewildered or baffled by something.' He then elaborates: 'for the intellects of the wise and the understanding of the learned are dazzled [even] at the first rising [of the sun] of His Majesty, and have no hope of grasping the nature of His Attributes and Acts'. Continuing in Persian he says: 'He keeps His [true] nature behind the veil of grandeur so that no unworthy intruder should catch sight of the secrets of [His] Eternity and no troublesome impostor should attain perception of them. That hand of yours, what could it achieve by itself? What could that eye see unaided?'[53] Such passages are often personalised in this way. The suddenness of the interjection in this case may have been a matter of style, to add more urgent appeal to the words, or it may be an indication that the passage was spoken and written down by a listener.

In order to 'bring the student seeking guidance to his goal', Maybudī does not simply comment upon matters of Islamic law as they occur in the Qur'an, he expands upon them and, where a fundamental aspect of the Sharī'a is concerned, he devotes a separate section (*faṣl*) to explaining it. This in itself is not unusual for commentators on the Qur'an. But in addition to those aspects of *fiqh* which are obligatory (*farḍ* or *wājib*), and those which are legally permissible (*ḥalāl*) or forbidden (*ḥarām*), Maybudī also finds occasion to discuss activities upon which no direct guidance is given in the Qur'an, but which are considered to be praiseworthy (*mustaḥabb*) or reprehensible (*makrūh*), according to traditions either of the Prophet or the pious early Muslims (*salaf*). Thus he speaks of the virtues of archery and running races[54] and the vices of chess.[55] However directly or indirectly these comments spring from the Qur'anic text, they are there for the edification of the reader or listener. To the same end there are passages in his commentary to inspire awe at the beauty and wisdom in nature[56] and to encourage respect for the prophets,[57] and there are anecdotes to foster good *adab*, maxims and subtle observations for the understanding of human psychology.[58]

Discussions of a technical nature are never prolonged in the *Kashf al-asrār* and Maybudī appears to have been concerned to keep the text continuously varied in subject matter and style. This may be another indication of the scope of audience for which the work was intended. Where appropriate, for instance in relating the *qiṣaṣ al-anbiyā'*, he will introduce vivid and colourful details to capture the imagination and heighten dramatic moments in the story. In the commentary on *Sūrat Yūsuf* (Q. 12), when Joseph is to be sold in Egypt, we find Zulaykhā seated on a golden throne and surrounded by handmaidens, and Fāriʿa, another wealthy woman of Egypt, ready with a thousand large pearls each the weight of a gold piece and a thousand rubies; the two women are trying to outbid each other for the purchase of Joseph.[59]

Explanations about the variant readings and grammar are often left in Arabic, presumably to be passed over by readers (or listeners) not well-versed in that language, to whom they would be of little interest. On the whole, Maybudī pays rather less attention than some other commentators to variant readings, philology and grammar, which he raises only when there is some controversy over them, or when they are particularly relevant for understanding the text. He appears to be more concerned with the significance of words, and their different facets of meaning (*wujūh*) as manifested in other verses of the Qur'an. For example, when commenting on '*yawmi'l-dīn*' (Q. 1:4) he does not discuss the semantic structure of the phrase, but gives twelve different aspects of the word *dīn* as it appears in different verses of the Qur'an.[60] Similarly, he leaves aside a discussion of the derivation of the word *ism* in the *Basmala*, moving directly to the significance of mentioning God's name before performing actions, and to the idea of God's identity with His name.[61] It is noticeable that when arguing a point about the meaning or derivation of a word, Maybudī usually limits himself to citations from the Qur'an or hadith, where other exegetes additionally cite couplets of early Arabic poetry, as *shawāhid* (textual evidence), to prove a point. This is not to say that he does not at times use *shawāhid* for this purpose, but, when he quotes from Arabic poetry, it is more often to support a moral or mystical principle than a linguistic one.

Maybudī frequently uses the Qur'an to comment upon the Qur'an. There are, of course, many occasions when this method is essential for the commentator.[62] For example, Ṭabarī cites the verse Q. 40:16, '"Whose is the Kingdom (*mulk*) today?" "God's, the One, the Omnipotent"', to support his preferred reading of '*maliki yawmi'l-dīn*' (Sovereign over the Day of Reckoning) as opposed to '*māliki yawmi'l-dīn*' (Possessor of the Day of Reckoning), while he refers to Q. 5:60 in his definition of those who have incurred God's wrath (Q. 1:6). However, Maybudī's application of this method goes far beyond this conventional usage and adds great subtlety to his commentary so that a verse, or part of a verse, which may be explained in a particular way in its own context, may be seen in yet another light when it is related to another verse somewhere else in the Qur'an. It will be seen that this skill really comes into its own in his mystical commentary.

He makes liberal use of the traditions of the Prophet, His Companions and Followers, to which he seldom attaches a chain of transmission (*isnād*). Since *isnād*s had already been clearly recorded in the canonical hadith collections and in early commentaries such as that of Ṭabarī, later exegetes did not always consider it necessary to include complete chains of transmission in their works. It was common practice to refer only to the first source through whom the tradition was transmitted from the Prophet (or Companion), for example, '*ʿan Abī Hurayra anna rasūl Allāh qāla*', but Maybudī does not, as a rule, mention even this first source; he simply precedes the tradition with the words '*ʿan Muṣṭafā*' or '*ʿan al-nabī*' except when it is important to prove the authority of the tradition in the case of some dogmatic argument. He also cites a great deal of traditional material for which he does not give any source at all, preceding it with '*gufta and*', 'it is said' or 'they say.' Much of this must have been drawn from the mine of oral traditions used then, and still used by preachers and Sufis today.[63] When an important point of doctrine is involved, however, he is sure to translate the tradition and to specify the source of its transmission, sometimes supplying a full *isnād*.

In his book on Ṭabarī's *Jāmiʿ al-bayān*, Claude Gilliot writes: 'A commentary on the Qur'an is not a treatise on heresy, yet polemics against sectarian groups are not absent from it.'[64] Polemics are certainly not absent from the *Kashf al-asrār*, and Maybudī takes every opportunity in the commentary to refute doctrines which he considers to be heretical or innovative, and to argue for those doctrines which he holds to be orthodox, as the following examples will serve to illustrate. In his commentary on Q. 2:1, '*Alif lām mīm*', after citing several alternative opinions concerning the significance of the mysterious letters with which many suras begin, Maybudī says, 'The *ahl-i sunnat* say that these letters give evidence and clear [proof] of the fact that the Qur'an has letters and is eternal in its letters, and whosoever says other than this is being insolent and stubborn in the face of God and in so doing is a heretic (*mulḥid*).'[65] There follow various arguments supported by a hadith, and sayings of Ibn Ḥanbal and al-Shāfiʿī, insisting on the uncreatedness of the Qur'an. In his commentary on God's words to Moses and Aaron, 'Fear not, I am with you twain, hearing and seeing' (Q. 20:46), Maybudī says that this is proof that God has both hearing and sight:

> It is a hearing with an uncreated ear and seeing with an uncreated eye. The meaning of hearing and seeing is not knowing and comprehending as the Muʿtazilīs say, for if it were then there would be no point in saying 'hearing and seeing' for knowledge and comprehension are already present in 'I am with you'.[66]

These examples are indicative of a preoccupation with the defence of traditionalist doctrine. If Maybudī was concerned that those whom he was teaching through the *Kashf al-asrār* should know the Shariʿa, he was equally concerned that they should be firmly rooted in the theological doctrine of the *ahl al-sunna wa'l-jamāʿa*.

In concluding this discussion of Maybudī's exoteric commentary, a word should be said about *Nawbat* I. Although it was described by Storey as a literal translation into Persian,[67] it appears to have more of an interpretative function in the *Kashf al-asrār*. Maybudī sometimes renders the literal meaning of the verse in Persian, but often he presents a concise interpretation of the verse that is far from literal. Moreover, it is clear that *Nawbat* I was not intended to stand on its own, but to be an integral part of the *Kashf al-asrār*, and it sometimes appears to have a positive function in relation to *Nawbat* II. For example, when Maybudī cites a number of alternative interpretations for a Qur'anic verse, he does not always express a preference for any one of them in *Nawbat* II,[68] but his own opinion may be found in the concise interpretation of the verse in *Nawbat* I. Such is the case with the mysterious letters at the beginning of *Sūrat al-Baqara* (Q. 2.1) for which Maybudī gives several interpretations. In *Nawbat* I we find '*Alif lām mīm*' rendered: 'It is God's secret in the Qur'an.' Again, in *Nawbat* I, the last verse of *Sūrat al-Fātiḥa* (Q. 1:7) is rendered 'Unlike the Jews. And the Christians', instead of being translated 'Unlike those who have incurred God's wrath. And those who have gone astray', which would have been the literal translation. This interpretation is evidently favoured because it has the support of a Prophetic tradition.[69]

On the other hand, the rendering of a word, phrase or verse given in *Nawbat* I sometimes appears to call for some clarification. This is subsequently provided in the *Nawbat* II section. For example '*al-Raḥmān*' (I, 3) is rendered as 'Keeper of the world and Nourisher of enemies' (*jahān-dār, dushman parwar*). This is puzzling as it stands, and certainly far from a literal translation. The riddle is solved in *Nawbat* II when Maybudī (like Ṭabarī) explains the view that, in being *al-Raḥmān* God extends His mercy to all creatures, good and bad, whilst in being *al-Raḥīm* he confers mercy in particular on the believers.[70]

In this way it can be seen that *Nawbat*s I and II are subtly linked: *Nawbat* I at times anticipating what will follow in *Nawbat* II, *Nawbat* II providing clarification for *Nawbat* I. We shall now turn to the essential link which Maybudī maintains between *Nawbat*s II and III, the 'outward' and 'inward', in the *Kashf al-asrār*.

Ẓāhir and *Bāṭin*, *Sharīʿa* and *Ḥaqīqa* in the *Kashf al-asrār*

Proponents of the esoteric interpretation of the Qur'an normally took care not to belittle the importance of the literal meaning of its verses. In the *Iḥyā'* Ghazzālī writes:

> One should not neglect the learning of the outward exegesis first, for there is no hope of reaching the inward aspect [of the Qur'an] before having mastered the outward.[71]

This did not imply, however, that esoteric and exoteric exegesis should be combined in practice. Among adepts of the mystical path it was clearly understood that different levels of the meaning of the Qur'an were accorded to different levels of human understanding. The mystical commentary attributed to Jaʿfar al-Ṣādiq begins with a definition of the classes of believers for whom the different levels of meaning were intended:

> The Book of God has four aspects: the explicit (*ʿibāra*), the allusive (*ishāra*), subtleties (*laṭā'if*) and realities (*ḥaqā'iq*). The explicit is for the commonalty (*ʿawāmm*), the allusive for the elite (*khawāṣṣ*), the subtleties are for the saints (*awliyā'*) and the realities for the prophets (*anbiyā'*).[72]

Ghazzālī warns against teaching the metaphorical interpretations (*ta'wīlāt*) of the Qur'an to the common man, who would be incapable of understanding them: 'If he (the common man) were confronted with the [esoteric] interpretation of the externals, he would relinquish his study as a layman, without attaining the status of an educated man'.[73]

Against this background, what were Maybudī's reasons for bringing together the outward and inward interpretations of the Qur'an in the *Kashf al-asrār*? The suggestion that Maybudī's exoteric and esoteric commentaries might have been delivered to different audiences may be discounted because of the numerous occasions when, in the course of his mystical interpretation (*Nawbat* III), he refers back to what he has said on the matter in his exoteric commentary (*Nawbat* II).[74] Looking again at Maybudī's introduction we see that he considered Anṣārī's *tafsīr*, despite its insights and elegance of expression, to be brief and inadequate. If, as de Beaurecueil has suggested,[75] Anṣārī's original *tafsīr* was an esoteric commentary, then Maybudī did not merely expand it – he also added to it an exoteric commentary.[76] Could it thus be inferred that Maybudī did not feel that an esoteric commentary could provide sufficient guidance *without* an exoteric commentary?

Passages in the Sufi writings of the period and in the *Kashf al-asrār* itself suggest a concern to demonstrate an essential relationship between the religious law (*sharīʿa*) and the spiritual path (*ṭarīqa*), or religious law (*sharīʿa*) and spiritual realisation (*ḥaqīqa*)[77] – a concern apparently aroused by a lack of sincerity among the ulema on the one hand, and by the abandonment of religious practices by some, in the name of mysticism, on the other. In the introduction to his *Risāla,* Qushayrī decries those who

> decided to overthrow conscience and put away shame, [who] began to show indifference to religious observances and to consider fasting and prayer of no account... [moreover they] were not content with accomplishing these evils but went so far as to indicate certain higher truths and states, maintaining that they had thrown off the shackles of slavery and were assured of the truths of 'union' and now were defending God and were the channel through which His laws came but they themselves were effaced.[78]

[Later] in the *Risāla* Qushayrī says: 'No practice of the religious law (*sharīʿa*) is acceptable if not corroborated by spiritual realisation (*ḥaqīqa*) and no realisation is attained without the conditions of the religious law.'[79]

Maybudī repeatedly emphasizes the vital interdependence of the law and inward realisation in the *Kashf al-asrār*. For example in his commentary on Q. 3:85, 'Whosoever seeks as religion other than surrender to God (Islam) it will not be accepted from him, and he will be a loser in the Hereafter', he says:

> The people of gnosis (*ahl-i maʿrifat*) know another mystery about [the word] *islām: islām* (submission) is truth (*ḥaqq*) and *istislām* (self-surrender) is

> spiritual realisation (*ḥaqīqat*). *Islām* is the law (*sharīʿat*) and *istislām*, the way (*ṭarīqat*). The abode of *islām* is the breast and the abode of *istislām* is the heart. *Islām* is like the body and *istislām* is like the spirit. A body without the spirit is [no more than] a corpse; the spirit without the body cannot function (*na ba-kār ast*).[80]

Elsewhere he states: 'Inner realisation (*ḥaqīqat*) cannot be effected without the outer practice of the law (*sharīʿat*), and the outer practice of the law without inner realisation is incomplete. [Only] when these two are combined are "They the believers in truth" (Q. 8:4)'.[81] This concern, then, may well have been one reason for Maybudī's combining exoteric and esoteric exegesis in the *Kashf al-asrār*. It would also have been in line with the didactic purpose of his commentary.[82] However, another reason may have been his concern that the esoteric interpretations of the verses should never be regarded as standing in place of the exoteric interpretations, but rather as existing alongside them.

The format of the *Kashf al-asrār* not only maintains this essential link between outward and inward interpretation, and between *sharīʿa* and *ḥaqīqa*. It also allows for an important distinction to be retained – that between the ordinary believer (*ʿāmm*) and the elite (*khāṣṣ*). For as Maybudī says, 'Between the place of blessing and beneficence [of the ordinary believer, who practices the religious law] and the place of intimacy and mystery [that of the elite], there are many ups and downs.'[83] The sessions of commentary covering between three and fifty verses at a time are just short enough for the reader or listener to retain in his memory the outer meanings of the words whilst listening to the mystical commentary. At the same time they are long enough for the distinctive style of *Nawbat* III, expressing the contemplative approach of *istinbāṭ* to unfold and take its effect. Maybudī usually opens the *Nawbat* III sections with a short devotional passage in rhyming prose to place his audience in the right frame of mind to receive these mystical insights - the realm of the mystical knowledge of the Qur'an should be entered with a sense of awe.

Within the *Nawbat* III sections, we find two modes of expression: the first clear and explanatory, although usually adorned with rhyming prose and poetry; the second, the language of allusion (*ishāra*), often elliptical and abstruse. Again, this is an indication of the scope of Maybudī's audience which probably included (as previously suggested) both those initiated into the mysteries of the path, and others whom he wanted to encourage simply to attain a higher level in the outward observance of their religion.[84] An example of the more elliptical and allusive style is found in the mystical commentary on the first verse of *Sūrat al-Baqara* (Q. 2) .

(In Arabic): *Alif, lām, mīm*, intimate communication in a code of single letters is the way lovers show their partiality for each other. It is the private [message] between lover and beloved, out of sight of any rival.

Between lovers is a secret
Which no tongue may divulge
Nor pen disclose to anyone.
[...]

(In Persian): In the private chamber of love there is a secret between lovers, whose murmurings only the mystics understand. In the studio of love is a colourless colour (*rang-i bī-rang*) that only those who are blind in the distraction of their love can see.[85]

In this example the *Nawbat* III commentary presents a complete contrast to that of *Nawbat* II, in exegetical approach, style and content; at other times, it complements it. For example, in the commentary on Q. 4:103, 'When you have completed the prayer, remember God, sitting, standing and reclining', *Nawbat* II presents a full account of the movements of prayer and the merits of praying. *Nawbat* III begins with a passage in rhyming prose encouraging the performance of the prayers in view of the rewards that it will bring in the hereafter, and continues with an explanation of the significance of prayers which are made up of two, three and four *rakʿa*s:

> The servant is made up of two things, spirit and body; in the prayer of two *rakʿa*s, one *rakʿa* is in thanks for the spirit and the other in thanks for the body; and the human being contains within three precious jewels: the heart, reason and faith; the prayer of three *rakʿa*s is in thanks for these three qualities. Moreover, man embodies four humours (*ṭabʿ*). The prayer of four *rakʿa*s is in thanks for these.[86]

In this case *Nawbat* III is, like *Nawbat* II, promoting the practice of the Shariʿa, but by inspiring the believer to understand its deeper significance. At other times *Nawbat* II enters the realm of *Nawbat* III, as it were, in pointing the reader towards the way of the people of realised truth (*ahl-i ḥaqīqat*) or spiritual wayfarers (*rawandagān*). For example in his *Nawbat* II commentary on Q. 2:4, he interprets '[the people] who believe in that which is revealed to you (Muhammad) and that which was revealed before you, and are certain of the Hereafter', as '[those who] knew the path of religion and the way to travel on it and sought to approach God'. While in his commentary on the verse which follows (Q. 2:5), he interprets 'These depend on guidance from their Lord. These are the successful', as '[those who]transcended their limitations and strove to "arrive", so that they came to know and experience the realities of the revealed verses, advanced upon the path and reached their destination'. The latter interpretation is clearly a reference to practising mystics.[87] Likewise the occurrence of the word *shukr* (gratitude) in Q. 4:147 gives rise in *Nawbat* II to a discussion of gratitude, not as a moral virtue but as a station on the path of the spiritual wayfarers (*rawandagān*), a station which, Maybudī explains, is higher than other stations because it is sought purely as an end in itself, whereas patience, for example, is a means of combatting the tyranny of desire, and asceticism a way of fleeing from worldly attachments.[88]

It can be seen, then, that while *Nawbat*s II and III are mostly clearly defined in approach and content, there is nevertheless some overlap between them. Maybudī shows morality and spirituality to be as closely linked as *sharīʿa* and *ḥaqīqa*. Thus we find in *Nawbat* III the dogmatic[89] and the ethical,[90] as well as the mystical.

> My eye is ever full of the face of the Friend.
> I am happy with that eye as long as the Friend is there.
> It is wrong to distinguish between eye and Friend –
> Either it is He and not the eye, or the eye *is* He.[91]

It may be asked how mystical interpretations such as 'the eye *is* He' and 'His Throne upon earth is the heart of [His] friends'[92] can be reconciled with literalist interpretations which insist, for example, that 'God, exalted is He, is in one of the directions of the universe (*ʿālam*) and that direction is above.'[93] An answer to this can be found in a passage attributed to ʿAbd Allāh Anṣārī in Maybudī's mystical commentary on Q. 20:5:

> God's ascending the Throne is in the Qur'an. I believe in it and do not attempt to interpret it, for metaphorical interpretation (*ta'wīl*) in this case

> would be a transgression (*ṭughyān*). I accept its outer meaning and acquiesce (*taslīm*) in its inner meaning. This is the belief of the Sunnis (*sunniyān)* and their way is to accept in their hearts whatever they do not comprehend. [...] However I know that He does not occupy this exalted place out of necessity, but He indicates place by way of demonstration (*ba-ḥujjat*). The Throne does not bear God, exalted is He, for God is the Maintainer and Keeper of the Throne. The Throne of God is for those who seek God, not those who know God.[94] The one who seeks God (*Khudā-jūy*) is different from the one who knows Him (*Khudā-shinās*). For the one who seeks God He said: 'The All-merciful ascended the Throne' [Q. 20:5], and for the one who knows Him He said: 'He is with you' [Q. 57:4]. In essence (*dhāt*) He is on the Throne; in knowledge (*ʿilm*), everywhere; in communing (*ṣuḥbat*), in the spirit (*jān*); in nearness (*qurb*), in the soul (*nafs*). O noble one! When you are in the private chamber of 'He is with you' [Q. 57:4] do not let fall your gown, for [to say] 'Exalted be God, the King, the Truth,' [Q. 20:114] is fitting for Him. And do not take your ease upon the carpet of 'We are nearer to him' [Q. 56:85] for above that is 'They measure not the power of Allāh its true measure' [Q. 6:91]. Do not be presumptuous with 'and faces that day will be radiant looking towards their Lord' [Q. 75:22], for above that is 'eyes will not see Him' [Q. 6:103].
>
> Whatever bestows 'He is the First' takes away 'He is the Last'. Whatever indicates 'He is the Outward' effaces 'He is the Inward' [Q. 57:3]. Why is this? So that the believer will keep oscillating (*ṭawf*) between fear and hope, and the mystic between contraction (*qabḍ*) and expansion (*basṭ*). One cannot say that finding [Him] is impossible for that would be contradicted by the divine law; one cannot say that finding [Him] is possible for [His] Mightiness does not assent to it. [He is] the Glorious, the Mighty, Whose power and truth cannot be grasped. [He is] the Gracious, the Loving – 'He loves them and they love Him' [Q. 5:54].[95]

As the passage relates, the literal meaning of 'He ascended the throne' has its significance for ordinary believers and its significance for the mystics – 'a portion for the common people (*ʿāmm*) and a portion for the mystics and the wholly sincere (*ʿārifān wa ṣiddīqān*).'[96] In the ordinary believer it arouses a sense of awe, so that he might feel both fear and hope; for the mystic it is in order that he should not forget God's transcendence when he has come to experience His immanence. *Ṭawf* (oscillation) between one state and the other is necessary because fear and hope, *qabḍ* and *basṭ*, cannot be experienced at the same time.

In a variant of this passage, where Maybudī is commenting on Q. 6:3 ('And He is in heaven'), we are given a further insight into his understanding of the complementarity and necessary coexistence of outward received knowledge (equivalent to the literal meanings of the Qur'an) and realised truth (equivalent to the inner mystery of the verses). This time Maybudī does not attribute the passage to Anṣārī:

> In essence, [He is] in heaven; in knowledge, everywhere; in communing, in the spirit; in nearness, in the soul – the soul annihilated in Him, and He in place of the spirit that is effaced in Him. [...] Received knowledge (*khabar*) does not impair realised truth (*ḥaqīqat*), nor does realised truth invalidate received knowledge. Keep saying 'He ascended', for He is established on the Throne, but [also] keep reciting 'He is with you', because He is with you wherever you are. He does not occupy place out of necessity, He indicates place out of mercy. He made the Throne for those who seek God, not those who know Him. The one who knows Him, were he to breathe one breath without Him would tie on the *zunnār*.[97]

In the *Kashf al-asrār* every 'exoteric' doctrine is shown to have its esoteric significance. The orthodox doctrine of *qaḍā'*, which insists that everything, good or bad, is decreed by God,[98] has its mystical analogue in *tawakkul*, complete trust in God and conformity to the divine will;[99] in the acceptance of trials and afflictions as God's way of bringing His servants closer to Himself;[100] and in the realisation that ultimately seekers depend on divine intervention to bring them to the state of freedom from themselves and union with Him.[101] The traditionalist doctrine that forbids the discussion of God's essence and attributes and demands the acceptance without question of everything which God has revealed through the Book and tradition, finds its mystical counterpart in the way of love, which sees the state of union not as 'knowing' but as 'finding', and His revealing Himself as an unexpected grace which leaves the mystic dazed and confounded. In the words of Anṣārī's prayer:

> O You, Who are found, not apprehended; evident, not seen! In the unseen You are Manifest, in the manifest, Unseen. Finding You is as the sudden dawning of the day. He that finds You has no concern for sorrow or for joy. Complete for us, O Lord, that which cannot be expressed![102]

Following this examination of the overall hermeneutics of the *Kashf al-asrār*, it could be said in summary that Maybudī intended his commentary to be a homiletic work, which would provide those who studied it with everything they needed to know for the practice of their religion. Essential to that practice was unquestioning adherence to the words of the Book and the traditions of the Prophet and Predecessors. The combination of exoteric and esoteric in the *Kashf al-asrār* had distinct hermeneutical advantages, for it provided Maybudī with a 'separate space' to develop two distinct approaches to Qur'anic interpretation: one which relied on transmitted knowledge and allowed only limited use of the rational faculty, and the other which was received through divine inspiration. At the same time the juxtaposition of *Nawbat*s II and III allowed him to maintain a tangible link between these two interdependent approaches. Equally important, the bringing together of the outward and inward in the *Kashf al-asrār* was for Maybudī doctrinally sound, and essential to the didactic purpose of his commentary. On the one hand, it would remind those following the mystical path that they should not neglect the outward requirements of the Shari'a; on the other, it would encourage the believer to go beyond mere outward observance (*ri'āya*) to attain inner realisation (*ḥaqīqa*) by means of spiritual discipline (*ṭarīqa*). 'Those rooted in knowledge (*rāsikhūna fi'l-'ilm*)' says Maybudī, 'are those who learn the knowledge of the law and practice it with sincerity until eventually they find the knowledge of reality.'[103]

NOTES

1 *Kashf*, I, p. 1.
2 Ṭabarī, Ṭūsī, Zamakhsharī and Abu'l-Futūḥ Rāzī, for example, have such introductions to their commentaries.
3 *Kashf*, X, pp. 679–80.
4 Maybudī narrates this hadith on the authority of Abū Hurayra.
5 Ṭabarī, *Jāmi' al-bayān 'an ta'wīl āy al-Qur'ān*, ed. M.M. Shākir and A.M. Shākir (vols. 1–16, incomplete, Cairo, 1955–69), I, pp. 29–30; trans. by J. Cooper as *The Commentary on the Qur'ān* (Oxford, 1987), p. 34.
6 *Kashf*, X, p. 679.
7 Ibid.
8 According to Arberry's translation, Q. 3:7 reads: 'It is He who sent down unto thee the Book, wherein are verses clear (*muḥkamāt*) that are the essence of the Book (*umm al-kitāb*), and others ambiguous (*mutashābihāt*). As for those in whose hearts is swerving, they follow the ambiguous part desiring dissention, and desiring its interpretation.' The end of Q. 3:7 reads: *wa mā ya'lamu ta'wīlahu illa'llāhu wa'l-rāsikhūna fi'l-'ilmi yaqūlūna āmannā bihi kullun min 'indi rabbinā wa mā yadhdhakkaru illā ūlu'l-albāb.* There was a difference of opinion as to whether, grammatically, there should be a break between the word *Allāh* and *wa* (underlined). According to one opinion (that held by Ṭabarī and later Suyūṭī) it should

read 'and none knows its interpretation save only God. And those who are rooted in knowledge say'; according to the other (for example, that of Zamakhsharī and Ṭūsī), it should read 'and none knows its interpretation save only God and those who are rooted in knowledge, who say'. On the discussion of *muḥkamāt* and *mutashābihāt* in Qur'anic hermeneutics see Jane Dammen McAuliffe, 'Qur'ānic hermeneutics: the views of Ṭabarī and Ibn Kathīr', in A. Rippin, *Approaches to the History of the Interpretation of the Qur'ān* (Oxford and New York, 1988), pp. 46–62; Leah Kinberg, 'Muḥkamāt and Mutashābihāt (Q. verse 3/7). Implication of a Qur'ānic pair of terms in medieval exegesis', *Arabica* 35 (1988), pp. 143–72; Michel Lagarde, 'De l'ambiguité dans le Coran', *Quaderni di Studi Arabi* 3 (1985), pp. 45–62; Sahiron Syamsuddin, '*Muḥkam* and *Mutashābih*: an analytical study of al-Ṭabarī's and al-Zamakhsharī's interpretations of Q. 3:7', *Journal of Qur'anic Studies* 1/1 (1999), pp. 63–79; Stefan Wild, 'The self-referentiality of the Qur'ān: Sura 3:7 as an exegetical challenge', in McAuliffe *et al.*, eds., *With Reverence for the Word*, pp. 422–36.

9 See, for example, Ṭūsī, *Al-Tibyān fī tafsīr al-Qur'ān*, I, p. 11.

10 *I'jāz* means literally 'the rendering incapable'. From the second half of the third/ninth century on it became a technical term for the inimitability or uniqueness of the Qur'an in content and form. See Gustav E. von Grünebaum, 'Iʿdjāz', *EI²*, III, pp. 1018–20.

11 Ṭabarī, *Jāmiʿ al-bayān*, ed. Shākir and Shākir, VI, pp. 168–211. See also McAuliffe, 'Qur'ānic hermeneutics'.

12 Wild has designated the view that only God understands the meaning of the *mutashābihāt* as the 'standard reading' of Q. 3:7, and the view that those rooted in knowledge also understood it as the 'minority reading'. Although Ṭabarī clearly argued for the 'standard reading', other important early exegetes held the minority view. See Wild, 'The self-referentiality', pp. 424–5.

13 See also *Kashf*, VII, pp. 171–2, where Maybudī explains that the reason why some (not all) the verses must be *muḥkam*, and some (not all) *mutashābih*, is that it would not be in conformity with mercy and wisdom for the *'āmm* and *khāṣṣ* to be equal in knowledge.

14 *Kashf*, II, p. 19.

15 Maybudī is almost certainly understanding *mutashābihāt* to mean the anthropomorphic verses here. For further discussion see pp. 16, 46–7, 53–4.

16 *Kashf*, II, p. 24.

17 Later we shall see how Qushayrī refers to scholars of exoteric knowledge by the term *khāṣṣ* and to the elite of spiritual wayfarers by the term *khāṣṣ al-khawāṣṣ*.

18 Although the word *istinbāṭ*, meaning literally 'drawing up water from a well', was also applied to the exoteric religious sciences, it came to be used by Sufis to refer to the mystical interpretation of the Qur'an. For a discussion of the criteria for *istinbāṭ* as mystical exegesis see Sarrāj, *Lumaʿ*, pp. 105ff. For a discussion of the application of the term *istinbāṭ* in mystical exegesis see Nwyia, *Exégèse coranique*, pp. 34, 67, 163–4. Khargūshī (*Tahdhīb al-asrār*, MS Ahlwardt, fols. 2819ff; 98ff.) gives examples of mystical interpretations under the title *Fī dhikr mustanbaṭātihim*. The hermeneutics of mystical commentary will be discussed in depth in the next chapter.

19 For a discussion of these two terms in relation to Kāshānī's commentary on the Qur'an see Pierre Lory, *Les Commentaires ésotériques du Coran d'après*

'Abd al-Razzâq al-Qâshânî (Paris, 1980), p. 10.

20 *Ta'wīl* is the verbal noun from the form II of the verb *awwala*, meaning literally to bring something back to its origin or source. For a discussion of the term *ta'wīl* see Ismail Poonawala, 'Ta'wīl', *EI*[2], X, pp. 390–2; Henri Corbin, *Avicenne et le récit visionnaire: étude sur le cycle des récits avicenniens* (Paris, 1979), pp. 32ff. *et passim.*

21 *Kashf*, II, p. 20.

22 As, for example, in *Kashf*, VI, pp. 292, 534.

23 As, for example, in the titles of the commentaries of ʿAbd Allāh b. ʿUmar al-Bayḍāwī, *Anwār al-tanzīl wa asrār al-ta'wīl,* published as *Baidhawi Commentarius in Coranum*, ed. H.O. Fleischer (Leipzig, 1846–8); ʿAbd Allāh b. Aḥmad al-Nasafī (d. 701/1301–2), *Madārik al-tanzīl wa ḥaqā'iq al-ta'wīl*, ed. M.M. al-Shaʿār (Beirut, 1996). See other examples cited in Poonawala, 'Ta'wīl'.

24 For example, *Kashf*, I, p. 193; II, p. 507; V, p. 307; VI, p. 111, X, p. 486. For a philosophical approach to *ta'wīl* see Heath's discussion of the allegorical interpretation of Ibn Sīnā; Peter Heath, 'Creative hermeneutics: a comparative analysis of three Islamic approaches', *Arabica* 36 (1989), pp. 173–210; idem, *Allegory and Philosophy in Avicenna (Ibn Sīnā): With a Translation of the Book of the Prophet Muḥammad's Ascent to Heaven* (Philadelphia, 1992).

25 See, for example, Ghazzālī, *Fayṣal al-tafriqa bayn al-islām wa'l-zandaqa*, ed. S. Dunyā (Cairo, 1961); trans. in McCarthy, *Freedom and Fulfillment*, Appendix I; Ghazzālī, *Al-Iqtiṣād fi'l-iʿtiqād*, ed. I.A. Çubukçu and H. Atay (Ankara, 1962); idem, *Qānūn al-ta'wīl*, ed. M.Z. al-Kawtharī (Cairo, 1359/1940). On Ghazzālī's hermeneutics see Frank Griffel, *Apostasie und Toleranz im Islam: die Entwicklung zu al-Ġazālīs Urteil gegen die Philosophie und die Reaktionen der Philosophen* (Leiden, 2000); Jackson, *On the Boundaries*; Richard M. Frank, 'al-Ghazālī on *taqlīd*: scholars, theologians and philosophers', *Zeitschrift für Geschichte der arabisch-islamischen Wissenschaften* 7 (1991–2), pp. 207–52; Landolt, 'Ghazālī and "*Religionswissenschaft*"'; Iysa A. Bello, *The Medieval Islamic Controversy between Philosophy and Orthodoxy* (Leiden, 1989); Nicholas Heer, 'Abū Ḥāmid al-Ghazālī's esoteric interpretation of the Qur'ān', in L. Lewisohn, ed., *Classical Persian Sufism from its Origins to Rumi* (London, 1993), pp. 235–57.

26 *Iḥyā'*, Part 1, Book 2, *Kitāb qawāʿid al-ʿaqā'id*, ch. 2, pp. 135–6; trans. by N.A. Faris as *Foundations of the Articles of Faith* (Lahore, 1963), pp. 50–2; quoted in Heer, 'Abū Ḥāmid al-Ghazālī's esoteric interpretation', pp. 242–3. For a discussion of Ghazzālī's views on the metaphorical interpretation of the Qur'an see M.S. Aydin, 'Al-Ghazālī on metaphorical interpretation', in R. Bisschops and J. Francis, eds., *Metaphor, Canon and Community* (Bern, 1999), pp. 242–55; Timothy J. Gianotti, *Al-Ghazālī's Unspeakable Doctrine of the Soul* (Leiden, 2001), pp. 36, 136, 161–2.

27 See Ghazzālī's *Fayṣal*, pp. 190ff; tr. McCarthy, pp. 159ff., where he states that a person who interprets [Qur'anic verses] according to probable conjectures without apodeictic proof should not be charged with unbelief except when this interpretation concerns the fundamentals of belief (*uṣūl*). The two doctrines that he specifies here are, firstly, the resurrection of bodies and sensible rewards/punishments in the afterlife, and secondly, God's knowledge of particulars. He asserts that no one should be charged with unbelief concerning branches of faith (*furūʿ*). See ibid., pp. 191–2. See also Ghazzālī, *Tahāfut al-falāsifa*, ed. S. Dunyā (Cairo,

1947), ch. 8; trans. by S.A. Kamali as *Al-Ghazālī's Tahafut al-falasifah: Incoherence of the Philosophers* (Lahore, 1958), ch. 8; Ignaz Goldziher, *Streitschrift des Ġazālī gegen die Bāṭinijja–Sekte* (Leiden, 1916), pp. 70–1.

28 *Yadayya*, mentioned in Q. 38:75, or the 'hand of God' (*yad Allāh*), mentioned in Q. 5:63. For Maybudī's view on this see *Kashf*, III, pp. 168–71.

29 *Nafkh* mentioned in Q. 15:29. See *Kashf*, V, p. 307.

30 Mentioned in Q. 67:17.

31 Followers of Hishām b. al-Ḥakam, on whom see Wilferd Madelung, 'Hishām b. al-Ḥakam', *EI²*, III, pp. 496–8.

32 *Kashf*, III, pp. 168–71. It is interesting to note, however, that Maybudī does not follow members of the Ḥanbalī school and other traditionalists cited by Ibn al-Jawzī, who insist that the 'face (*wajh*) of God' (Q. 28:88, 30:39, 55:27), His 'soul or self' (*nafs*, Q. 5:116), leg (*sāq*, Q. 42:11), or side (*janb*, Q. 39:56) should be understood literally. See Merlin Swartz, *A Medieval Critique of Anthropomorphism: Ibn al-Jawzī's Kitāb Akhbār aṣ-ṣifāt* (Leiden, 2002), pp. 152, 185. Concerning *wajh*, Maybudī states (*Kashf*, V, p. 356) that the Arabs often make the attribute stand in place of the thing itself. The word *nafs* he interprets likewise as 'essence' explaining (*Kashf*, III, pp. 276–7) that the Arabs use this word to mean either the soul or spirit (*rūḥ*), or reality (*ḥaqīqa*), or totality (*jumla*) of a thing. Concerning the word *sāq* he quotes (*Kashf*, X, p. 196) a hadith in which the Prophet speaks of 'His leg' (cited in the *Kitāb al-tawḥīd* of Muḥammad b. Ismāʿīl al-Bukhārī's *Al-Jāmiʿ al-ṣaḥīḥ*, ed. L. Krehl and T.W. Juynboll [Leiden, 1862–1909], and in the *Kitāb al-īmān* of Muslim b. al-Ḥajjāj al-Qushayrī's *Ṣaḥīḥ bi-sharḥ al-Nawawī* [18 vols., Cairo, 1929–30]). However, this is followed by a quite different hadith narrated by Abū Mūsā al-Ashʿarī, according to which *sāq* means 'a great light', and another from Ibn ʿAbbās, which interprets the word as 'a grave matter'. For the word *janb*, Maybudī presents (*Kashf*, X, p. 433) a number of alternative interpretations cited from earlier exegetes, including that of Mujāhid, according to which *janb* means command. He then explains that in Arabic the word *janb* is often used to mean *jānib*, that is to say, beside or next to. In all of these examples, Maybudī's interpretation is based on established linguistic practice of the Arabs. Perhaps his particular concern with the God's 'hand', and His 'being seated on the Throne' was that these verses were consistently targeted for metaphorical interpretation by the Muʿtazilīs.

33 *Kashf*, IX, p. 485.

34 Ibid. See pp. 41–4 re Maybudī's mystical commentary on Q. 3:7.

35 In fact, Ghazzālī has specifically explained similar expressions in the Qur'an (for example, Q. 41:11 and Q. 17:44), as being examples of a rhetorical device known as *lisān al-ḥāl*, and argues that these expressions *should* be interpreted metaphorically. See *Iḥyā'*, Part 1, Book 2, *Kitāb qawāʿid al-ʿaqāʾid*, ch. 2, pp. 134–5. On Ghazzālī's approach to this rhetorical device in the Qur'an and *lisān al-ḥāl* or *zabān-i ḥāl* in Persian literature see Nasrollah Pourjavady, 'Zabān-i ḥāl dar adabiyyāt-i Fārsī', Part 1, *Nashr-i dānish* 2, Year 17 (Summer 1379sh/2001), pp. 25–42.

36 *Kashf*, I, pp. 334–5.

37 *Kashf*, IX, p. 486. The same advice is given in prose form in *Kashf*, III, pp. 437–8 and 457.

38 *Kashf*, I, pp. 334–5.

39 *Kashf*, V, p. 81, and I, p. 441, where Maybudī glosses a saying of Ibn ʿAṭāʾ al-Adamī with the statement: 'The generality of believers contemplate created things; the elite, God's attributes; and prophets and the elite of the elite, His essence (*dhāt*).'

40 The esoteric interpretation will be discussed in chapter nine, 'The story of Moses'.

41 *Kashf*, V, p. 192. Maybudī is here suggesting that in the practice of *istinbāṭ* there is a thin line to be drawn between 'legitimate' efforts in reflection and deliberation, and 'illegitimate' excessive effort.

42 This doctrine is likewise fundamental to the mystical doctrines of the *Kashf al-asrār*, as will be discussed in chapters four and seven.

43 See, for example, Ghazzālī, *Fayṣal*, pp. 179–83; tr. Jackson, pp. 96–100; Bello, *Controversy*, p. 53.

44 Bello, *Controversy*, p. 53; Ghazzālī, *Al-Iqtiṣād fi'l-iʿtiqād*, p. 212.

45 Heer, 'Abū Ḥāmid al-Ghazālī's esoteric interpretation', pp. 247, 248.

46 *Iḥyāʾ*, Part 1, Book 1, *Kitāb al-ʿilm*, ch. 2, p. 30; trans. by N.A. Faris as *The Book of Knowledge* (Lahore, 1962), p. 47; revised by N. Heer, 'Abū Ḥāmid al-Ghazālī's Esoteric Interpretation of the Qurʾān', p. 247. We may also note that in this passage Ghazzālī, like Maybudī, understands knowledge of the essence and attributes of God to be dependent on divine disclosure. In another context, though not using the term *ʿilm al-mukāshafa*, Ghazzālī again speaks of a God-given light, this time a light of certainty, which opens secrets in the heart, to the extent of each person's spiritual striving and purification from other than God. *Iḥyāʾ*, Part 1, Book 2, *Kitāb qawāʿid al-ʿaqāʾid*, ch. 1, pp. 123–4; tr. Faris, p. 52.

47 *Iḥyāʾ*, Part 1, Book 1, *Kitāb al-ʿilm*, ch. 6, p. 94; tr. Faris, p. 190. The same idea is implied in Ghazzālī's *Iljām al-ʿawāmm ʿan al-kalām*, when in another discussion of the allowability of *taʾwīl* for the anthropomorphic verses, Ghazzālī explains that God intended the metaphorical expressions to be understood by 'His people', that is, the saints (*awliyāʾ*) and those 'rooted in knowledge' (*al-ʿulamāʾ al-rāsikhūn*). Later in the same work he explains that those who should not be involved in *taʾwīlāt* are the *ʿawāmm*, that is to say: the man of letters, the grammarian, the traditionist, the exegete, the jurisprudent and the dialectical theologian, in fact all men of learning 'save those who have devoted themselves to learning how to swim in the seas of gnosis (*biḥār al-maʿrifa*), those who have spent their lives on it, turning their faces from this world and its passions (*shahawāt*), rejecting wealth, reputation, people and all pleasures, and purifying themselves for God'. See Ghazzālī, *Iljām al-ʿawāmm ʿan al-kalām*, ed. M.M. al-Baghdādī (Beirut, 1985), p. 67.

48 *Ḥaqāʾiq*, ed. Nwyia, 'Trois œuvres inédites', p. 155. The word *sirr*, meaning literally 'secret', is a term used by Sufis to describe a subtle centre of perception or locus of mystical experience deep within the human being. The word *sirr* suggests both the mysterious, indefinable nature of this inner 'organ', and the ineffability of the higher realities that are experienced in or through it. There is no adequate translation of this word in English, though it is sometimes rendered by such expressions such as 'innermost consciousness', 'inmost being' or 'innermost mystery'. On this subject see Shigeru Kamada, 'A study of the term *sirr* (secret) in Sufi *Laṭāʾif* theories', *Orient* 19, (1983), pp. 7–28.

49 *Ḥaqāʾiq*, ed. ʿImrān, I, p. 157; MS Or. 9433, British Library, London, fol. 45a.

50 The first is reflecting on oneself and one's state, called 'meditation upon the admonition [of religion]' (*tadabbur-i mawʿiẓa*) and is said to be an attribute of the generality of Muslims; the second, due to a lacuna in the text is not known but is said to be an attribute of ascetics. Unfortunately, all the manuscripts I have examined so far have the same lacuna.
51 *Kashf*, II, pp. 612–3. The spiritual qualification required for 'plumbing the depths of the ocean of the Qur'an' are also set out in *Kashf*, I, pp. 229–30.
52 Ṭabarī, *Jāmiʿ al-bayān*, ed. Shākir and Shākir, I, p. 149; tr. Cooper, p. 56.
53 *Kashf*, I, p. 6.
54 *Kashf*, V, pp. 23–4.
55 *Kashf*, III, pp. 14–5.
56 For example, *Kashf*, V, p. 320, on the bee.
57 *Kashf*, V, p. 9.
58 *Kashf*, V, pp. 8, 56.
59 *Kashf*, V, pp. 34–5.
60 *Kashf*, I, p. 16.
61 *Kashf*, I, pp. 4–5.
62 This was an important category in Qur'anic interpretation, supported by the well-known maxim: *wa'l-Qur'ān yufassiru baʿḍuhu baʿḍahu.* On this subject see Baha ud-Din, Khurramshahi, 'L'explication du Coran par le Coran lui-même', *Aux Sources de la Sagesse* 2/6 (1995), pp. 7–20; Muhammad A.S. Abdel Haleem, *Understanding the Qurʾān* (London, 1999), ch. 12.
63 Ignaz Goldziher, *Muhammedanische Studien* (Halle, 1888–90); trans. by C.R. Barber and S.M. Stern as *Muslim Studies* (London, 1967–71), p. 154: 'Theologians tended not to be stringent about the *isnād*s of *ḥadīth* which did not belong to the category of law, but offered pious tales, edifying maxims and ethical teachings in the name of the Prophet.'
64 Gilliot, *Exégèse*, p. 207.
65 *Kashf*, I, p. 43. We have already seen an example of his polemic against the Ashʿarīs and others concerning this same doctrine, though here it is more vehemently expressed with the accusation of heresy.
66 *Kashf*, VI, p. 128.
67 Charles A. Storey, *Persian Literature*, 2nd edn (London, 1953), I, p. 190.
68 As does Ṭabarī.
69 For these hadiths see Ṭabarī, *Jāmiʿ al-bayān*, ed. Shākir and Shākir, I, pp. 184ff; *Kashf*, I, p. 2 (*Nawbat* I); I, p. 21 (*Nawbat* II). Maybudī narrates this hadith on the authority of ʿAdī b. Ḥātim.
70 Ṭabarī, *Jāmiʿ al-bayān*, ed. Shākir and Shākir, I, p. 149; *Kashf*, I, p. 7.
71 *Iḥyāʿ*, Part 1, Book 8, *Kitāb ādāb tilāwat al-Qurʾān*, ch. 6, p. 386; trans. by Heer in 'Abū Ḥāmid al-Ghazālī's esoteric interpretation of the Qurʾān', p. 253. This view was also held by later exegetes. See, for example, the view of Ibn ʿAṭāʾ Allāh cited by Suyūṭī in *Al-Itqān fī ʿulūm al-Qurʾān,* ed. M.A. Ibrāhīm (2 vols., Cairo, 1967), II, p. 185; trans. by R. Ahmad (Jullandri) in 'Qurʾānic exegesis and classical tafsīr', *IQ* 12 (1968), p. 106. On Kāshānī's view see Lory, *Les Commentaires*, pp. 12 and 31.
72 *Ḥaqāʾiq*, ed. Nwyia, 'Le tafsîr mystique', p. 188; MS Or. 9433, fol. 2a.
73 *Iḥyāʾ*, Part 1, Book 1, *Kitāb al-ʿilm*, ch. 5, p. 77; tr. Faris, p. 152.
74 For example, *Kashf*, II, p. 495; III, p. 257; III, p. 437; V, p. 451.

75 See p. 20.
76 Further evidence for this would be that, as indicated previously, the selection of verses for the *majālis* appears to have been guided by the esoteric commentary. Again, see p. 20.
77 On the translation of the term *ḥaqīqa* see ch. 1, n. 125.
78 Qushayrī, *Risāla,* p. 46. The translation of this passage is in Valentin Zhukovsky, 'Persian Sufism', *BSOAS* 5 (1928–30), pp. 83–4.
79 *Risāla,* p. 240. See also Hujwīrī, *Kashf al-maḥjūb,* tr. R. Nicholson, pp. 383–4; Ghazzālī, *Iḥyā',* Part 1, Book 1, *Kitāb al-ʿilm,* ch. 2, p. 33; tr. Faris, p. 52; W. Montgomery Watt, *Muslim Intellectual: A Study of Al-Ghazali* (Edinburgh, 1963), p. 176.
80 *Kashf,* II, p. 197.
81 *Kashf,* IV, p. 11.
82 The fact that Qushayrī expressed the same concern but did not combine his esoteric and exoteric commentaries might be further evidence that Qushayrī's mystical commentary was addressed to a smaller circle of more experienced initiates, who were already familiar with these principles, whereas Maybudī intended his commentary for a wider audience (see p. 11).
83 *Kashf,* II, p. 24.
84 An indication of the range of his audience is given in *Kashf,* X, p. 629: 'and if you have not the strength to be among those who make the inner pilgrimage [to God], then at least perform the outer pilgrimage. If you can't be an elephant, then at least be a gnat!'
85 *Kashf,* I, p. 52.
86 *Kashf,* II, p. 677.
87 *Kashf,* I, p. 51.
88 *Kashf,* II, p. 745.
89 For example, *Kashf,* III, p. 455.
90 For example, *Kashf,* V, p. 669.
91 *Kashf,* I, p. 31. This *rubāʿī* is included in Nafīsī's collection of poetry attributed to Abū Saʿīd b. Abi'l-Khayr. See Saʿīd-i Nafīsī, *Sukhanān-i manẓūm-i Abū Saʿīd-i Abi'l-Khayr* (6th repr. Tehran, 1376sh/1997), p. 15, no. 102.
92 *Kashf,* III, p. 639.
93 *Kashf,* I, p. 123.
94 lit., 'He made the Throne for those who seek God'.
95 *Kashf,* VI, p. 111.
96 *Kashf,* III, p. 638.
97 *Kashf,* III, pp. 298–9. The *zunnār* was a girdle worn to identify Jews and Christians within Islamic society. The idea being expressed is that were the mystic to forget God for one instant, it would be as bad for him as abandoning his faith.
98 *Kashf,* X, p. 506.
99 *Kashf,* V, pp. 70–1.
100 *Kashf,* V, p. 117.
101 This doctrine will be discussed at length in part two.
102 *Kashf,* VIII, p. 205.
103 *Kashf,* II, p. 775.

3

The hermeneutics of mystical commentary in the *Kashf al-asrār*

In chapter two we saw that the *Nawbat* II and *Nawbat* III sections of the *Kashf al-asrār*, although purposely and skillfully linked, nevertheless represent two distinct approaches to the interpretation of the Qur'an: the exoteric (*ẓāhir*) and the esoteric (*bāṭin*). The present chapter will examine more closely the mystical hermeneutics of the *Kashf al-asrār*. This will involve first, looking at some theories of exegesis which may have relevance to Maybudī's mystical commentary; second, comparing Maybudī's *Nawbat* II and *Nawbat* III commentaries on a particular passage of the Qur'an in order to define more precisely the aims and criteria of his mystical commentary; and third, examining the method and practice of mystical exegesis. Here the *Kashf al-asrār* will not be studied in isolation but alongside Qushayrī's *Laṭā'if al-ishārāt*. Finally, using Qushayrī's *Laṭā'if* as a 'control', the chapter will attempt to discover to what extent the *Kashf al-asrār* represents the continuation of an existing genre, or introduces new features, and why.

Theories of levels of meaning in the scripture

At the end of the *Kashf al-asrār*, where Maybudī briefly sets out his views on the theory and criteria of exegesis, he cites a well-known tradition of Ibn 'Abbās which defines four levels of meaning in the Qur'an (or, as 'Abbās puts it, four categories of *tafsīr*): that which can be understood by the learned; that of which the Arabs have knowledge; that which it is unforgivable not to know; and that the interpretation of which if anyone should claim to know, he is lying.[1] This system does not include an esoteric level that might be accessible to those with the capacity to understand it.

Other Sufi commentators, however, have put forward fourfold theories of exegesis that include an esoteric level. Reference has already been made to the saying attributed to Jaʿfar al-Ṣādiq defining four levels of meaning in the Qur'an: the explicit, the allusive, subtleties and realities, intended for the ordinary believers, the elite, the saints and the prophets respectively.[2] Another fourfold theory of levels of meaning in the Qur'an is given by Sahl al-Tustarī in his commentary, the *Tafsīr al-Qur'ān al-ʿaẓīm*:

> Each verse of the Qur'an has four senses (*maʿānin*), a literal (*ẓāhir*), and a hidden sense (*bāṭin*), a limit (*ḥadd*) and a point of transcendency (*maṭlaʿ*). The literal sense is the recitation (*tilāwa*), the hidden sense the understanding (*fahm*) of the verse. The limit [defines what is] lawful (*ḥalāl*) and unlawful (*ḥarām*) by the verse, and the point of transcendency is the command of the heart (*ishrāf al-qalb*) over the meaning intended (*murād*), as it is understood from the vantage point of God (*fiqhan min Allāh*).[3]

An almost identical theory is to be found in the introduction to Sulamī's *Ḥaqā'iq al-tafsīr*, where it is attributed to ʿAlī b. Abī Ṭālib.[4] The theory recalls a well known hadith of the Prophet transmitted through Ibn Masʿūd, which reads:

> The Qur'an was sent down according to seven 'lectiones' (*aḥruf*). Each Qur'anic verse has an exterior (*ẓahr*) and an interior (*baṭn*). Each lectio (*ḥarf*) has a limit (*ḥadd*) and a point of transcendency (*maṭlaʿ*).[5]

As Böwering points out, this hadith is differentiating 'two levels of Qur'anic meaning, expressed by two images', or, more precisely, two levels of meaning pertaining to the verse and two pertaining to the 'lectio'.[6] More recently, Böwering has suggested that 'by blurring the distinction between *āya* and *ḥarf*, Sahl al-Tustarī transforms the hadith into a statement that collapses the two separate assertions into a composite declaration of the fourfold meaning of each Qur'anic verse.'[7] Other exegetes, certainly, interpreted the same hadith as signifying four levels of meaning. Perhaps they, like Tustarī, also had in mind the tradition narrated in several variant forms from Ibn ʿAbbās (quoted by Maybudī and referred to earlier) which defined four categories of *tafsīr*.[8] According to Ṭabarī, the *ẓahr* signifies the recitation (*tilāwa*), the *baṭn* the interpretation which is held within it (*mā baṭana min ta'wīlihi*),[9] the *ḥadd* that which is lawful and unlawful, and the *maṭla*ʿ (or *muṭṭala*ʿ),[10] reward (*thawāb*) or punishment (*ʿiqāb*) in the hereafter.[11] Al-Muḥāsibī, like Ṭabarī, interprets *ẓahr* as *tilāwa* and *baṭn* as *ta'wīl*, but he interprets *ḥadd* as 'the limit of understanding' (*muntaha'l-fahm*), and *maṭla*ʿ as 'that which one should not infringe upon by transgressing the limit through exaggeration, false interpretation or attempting to go too deep'.[12]

Böwering, along with Massignon, Van Ess, Wansbrough and Gilliot, has compared Tustarī's theory to the fourfold theory of exegesis of late patristic and early medieval Christendom.[13] The equivalent levels would be as follows:

ẓāhir (or *zahr*)	*tilāwa*	*historia*
bāṭin (or *baṭn*)	*fahm*	*allegoria*
ḥadd	*ḥalāl wa ḥarām*	*tropologia*
*maṭla*ʿ	*ishrāf al-qalb*	*anagogia*

The fourfold system of Christian exegesis was explained with a verse in circulation around the sixteenth century:

Littera gesta docet, quid credas allegoria
Moralis quid agas, quo tendas anagogia.
(The literal [sense] teaches what happened
The allegorial what you should believe
The moral what you should do
The analogical where you are going.)

The classic illustration was in the word Jerusalem, which historically was the city, allegorically the church, tropologically the soul and anagogically the Kingdom of Heaven.[14]

Gilliot observes that an equivalent fourfold system was also to be found in Jewish exegesis, with *peshat* being the literal meaning, *remez* the implied sense, *derash* the homiletic teaching, and *sod* the mystico-allegorical sense.[15] He then states: 'Nous sommes donc là sur un terrain de rencontre entre les trois traditions exégétiques, même s'il est difficile de préciser les liens de filiation qui les unissent.'[16] Böwering goes further and states: 'Both the differentiation between literal and spiritual senses widely used in Jewish biblical hermeneutics and in Christian patristic exegesis, as well as the four senses of scripture developed in the Latin tradition, may be the ultimate roots of the Islamic distinctions between *ẓāhir* and *bāṭin* and the definition of a fourfold meaning of the Qur'an'; and 'the hermeneutical similarities are striking, especially if Jaʿfar al-Ṣādiq's methodological distinction of exegetical principles is compared with the Jewish tradition and Sahl al-Tustarī's with the Christian patristic tradition'. However, he adds the caveat that 'Demonstrable historical evidence [...] remains to be proven'.[17]

An in-depth discussion about the extent to which the exegetical theories of the three traditions are comparable or may have influenced each other obviously goes beyond the scope of this study. However, in the context of a discussion of Sufi hermeneutics, three observations about this comparison need to be made. In the first place, one must not forget the criteria that the exegetes had in mind when developing these theories. This is particularly important when it comes to the allegorical level. Medieval Christian exegetes sought to interpret the New Testament as the fulfilment of the Old; for them the literal meaning in the Old Testament was the 'type' which anticipated or 'prophesied' what was to be realised in the coming of Christ.[18] In Islam, on the other hand, as Wansbrough has argued, allegory in this typological sense is more characteristic of sectarian exegesis.[19] At the same time, among Jews, Christians and Muslims there were commentators who sought an allegorical meaning for the scripture when acceptance of the literal meaning seemed contrary to reason.[20]

Second in the case of Sufi exegesis, the allegorical meaning very often *is* the tropological, mystical or anagogical meaning. This being so, it would be more appropriate to speak of allegory as one of the methods by which the moral or spiritual meaning is elicited from the literal meaning. In this case we could speak of three levels of meaning in Sufi exegesis: the literal, the moral and the mystical/anagogical. It might then be comparable to Origen's idea of the body, soul and spirit of the Scripture.[21]

Third, it has to be remembered that all these systems,whether threefold or fourfold, are *theories*. Böwering states that although both Tustarī and Jaʿfar al-Ṣādiq speak of a fourfold sense, in practice they differentiate a twofold meaning.[22] Similar observations have been made with regard to exegetical practice as opposed to exegetical theory in the works of Origen and Medieval Christian exegetes.[23]

Why then, did Tustarī and Sulamī place this tradition defining a fourfold system of Qur'anic meaning in the introductions to their commentaries? On the one hand, it may have been an attempt to justify Sufi exegesis: the mystical sense was, according to Tustarī's understanding of the word *maṭlaʿ*, one of four senses implied in a Prophetic hadith.[24] On the other hand, the theory may have been intended to convey both the idea that there can be an inner meaning (*baṭn*) beneath or beyond the literal meaning (*ẓahr*) of the Qur'anic verses, and the idea that the verses can have a multiplicity of meanings.[25] Ghazzālī gives the following explanation for this same hadith in the *Kitāb ādāb tilāwat al-Qur'ān* of the *Iḥyā'* :

> What, then, is the meaning of *ẓahr*, *baṭn*, *ḥadd* and *maṭlaʿ* ?
> ʿAlī said, 'If I wished I could load seventy camels with the exegesis of the opening sura (*al-Fātiḥa*) of the Qur'an'. What is the meaning of this, when the exoteric interpretation [of this sura] is extremely short? Abū Dardā' said, 'A man does not [truly] understand until he attributes [different] perspectives (*wujūh*) to the Qur'an.' A certain scholar said, 'For every [Qur'anic] verse there are sixty thousand understandings (*fahm*)'.

Ghazzālī proceeds to explain that the plurality of meanings is proper to the esoteric interpretation of the Qur'an.

> The Prophet's repetition of [the phrase] 'In the Name of God, the Merciful, the Compassionate' twenty times was only for the purpose of pondering (*tadabbur*) its esoteric meanings (*bāṭin maʿānīhā*). Otherwise, its explanation (*tarjuma*) and exegesis (*tafsīr*) are so obvious (*ẓāhir*) that someone like him would not need to repeat it. Ibn Masʿūd said, 'He who desires the knowledge of the ancients and the moderns should ponder the Qur'an', and that is something that cannot be attained merely by its exoteric interpretation.[26]

This is not to say that there might not be many alternative and divergent interpretations of a verse at the outer level, but, because of the various practical functions which it serves, exoteric exegesis will tend to seek one definitive reading of the text.[27] In esoteric exegesis, on the other hand, plurality of meaning has a positive function, as Sarrāj explains in his chapter on *istinbāṭ* in the *Lumaʿ*:

> The Sufis differ in their interpretations just as the formalists (*ahl al-ẓāhir*) do, but whereas differences in the latter lead to error, differences in mystical

> science do not produce this result [...] It has been said that difference of opinion amongst the authorities on exoteric science is an act of divine mercy, because he who holds the right view refutes and exposes the error of his adversary. So too, the difference of opinion amongst mystics is an act of divine mercy, because each one speaks according to his predominant state and feeling. Hence mystics of every sort – whether novices or adepts, whether engaged in works of devotion or in spiritual meditation – can derive profit from their words.[28]

Mystical commentary as *irshād*

The principle outlined by Sarrāj in the above passage could no doubt be illustrated with numerous examples from the mystical commentaries of Sulamī, Qushayrī and others. However, it can be more fully demonstrated with reference to the *Kashf al-asrār*, where the exoteric and esoteric interpretations of the Qur'an have been juxtaposed. By comparing the *Nawbat* II and *Nawbat* III commentaries on a single passage, it will be possible to highlight the fundamental difference between exoteric and esoteric exegesis, and to show how diversity of meaning has a positive function in the latter. The passage in question, sura 6 (*al-Anʿām*) vs. 75–9, tells part of the story of Abraham. The Qur'anic account reads as follows:

75. Thus did We show Abraham the kingdom of the heavens and the earth, that he might be of those possessing certainty.
76. When the night grew dark upon him he beheld a star. He said, 'This is my Lord.' But when it set he said, 'I love not things that set.'
77. And when he saw the moon uprising, he exclaimed, 'This is my Lord.' But when it set he said, 'Unless my Lord shall guide me I shall surely become of the folk who are astray.'
78. And when he saw the sun uprising, he cried, 'This is my Lord! This is greater.' And when it set he exclaimed, 'O my people I am free from all that you associate (with Him).'
79. Indeed, I have turned my face toward Him who created the heavens and earth, as one by nature upright and I am not of the idolaters.'

At an exoteric level, this passage appears to present a theological problem: how could Abraham, a prophet and therefore protected from error (*maʿṣūm*), have mistaken a star, the moon and the sun for his Lord? Like other exoteric commentaries on this passage, Maybudī's *Nawbat* II section largely comprises different attempts to solve this problem.[29] The first is to place the event in the context of Abraham's life story, for which Maybudī has recourse to traditional sources (*tafsīr bi'l-ma'thūr*). He presents a lengthy account which may be summarised thus:

> At the time of Abraham's birth, the powerful and idolatrous ruler Nimrod, for fear of an ominous dream which augured the birth of a boy who would change the religion of his people and destroy both him and his kingdom, had commanded the slaying of all baby boys. Abraham's mother, therefore, hid her new-born son in a cave, which she visited daily in order to suckle him, only to find that he was already deriving nourishment miraculously from his fingers from which flowed milk, water, honey, oil and dates.[30]

Maybudī continues his account by relating two hadiths, both of which seek to emphasize that Abraham had from earliest childhood an innate sense of the transcendent Creator. The first, for which Maybudī does not name a source, tells how one day, when Abraham's mother comes to see him in the cave, he asks her: 'Who is my Lord?' to which she replies, 'I am'. Then he asks 'Who is your lord?' to which she replies, 'Your father.' After that he asks 'Who is my father's lord?' to which she replies, 'Nimrod.' When he follows this with the inevitable question of 'Who is Nimrod's lord?' he is beaten and told to be silent. When he puts the same questions to his father, he is greeted by a similar response.

The second tradition, which Maybudī attributes to Ibn ʿAbbās, relates that when Abraham was seven years old, he tired of being confined to the cave and begged to be allowed to see what was outside. When he saw camels, horses and sheep, the earth, the sky, the mountains and the desert, he felt certain that they had a creator, and that it was this creator that was his Lord. When he saw the beauty and resplendence of a star for the first time, it was understandable that he should say, 'This is my Lord.'[31] Maybudī does not add anything here, but presumably Abraham's statement is to be attributed to his being a child who had never seen the world before but who, nevertheless, had an instinct for the truth.

If these tradition-based arguments were not acceptable,[32] other arguments could be used to clear Abraham of the imputation of error:[33] he could have been asking a rhetorical question, or using the debating device whereby the opponent's view is stated before being attacked.[34] Alternatively, Maybudī suggests, this might have been the tactful way in which Abraham taught his parents the error of their idolatry, first by appearing to follow their belief and then by demonstrating to them, stage by stage, that it was false.[35] All these exoteric interpretations seem to have been intended to assert the prophet's immunity from error (*ʿiṣma*).

When we turn to the mystical commentary, the *Nawbat* III section, we find that while the starting point is still the puzzle presented by Abraham's having called the star, moon and sun his Lord, there is nothing apologetic about the solution. Reflected upon as a *mathal*, a parable or paradigm,[36] the story no longer pertains specifically to Abraham but has a universal application.[37] Interpreted esoterically, what Abraham experienced represents a spiritual transformation, a necessary stage in the path of realisation, and is therefore relevant to all men.

Seen in the light of mystical experience, the story could be interpreted in a number of ways. Maybudī presents eight different interpretations which will be analysed in detail later, but which may be summarised here as:

1. The danger of being subject to the [divine] ruse (*makr*).[38]
2. The passage from knowledge by demonstration (*ba-istidlāl*) to knowledge by direct experience (*ba-ʿiyān*).[39]
3. The need not to be distracted from the way by the bestowal of divine graces, but to persevere towards the truth.[40]
4. Abraham's being in the state in which he sees God in everything.[41]
5. The way of the true lovers of God who remain awake at night to contemplate their Lord.[42]
6. The gradual purification of the soul from other than God.[43]
7. The way of the 'manly' man (*mard-i mardāna*)[44] who must necessarily travel upon a difficult, uncharted road before he reaches the highway of divine unity (*tawḥīd*).[45]
8. An example of being truly intoxicated with love, in which state a person no longer knows what he says, or even that he is intoxicated.[46]

Maybudī's *Nawbat* II commentary, as we saw, consisted in putting forward several alternative solutions to an apparent theological problem posed by the Qur'anic passage. Exoteric exegesis often presents several divergent opinions on a verse, with the understanding that one of these alternatives is more likely to be correct, even though a preference for any one opinion may not be expressed by the commentator himself.[47] In the case of the Abraham story, to opt for any one opinion (or solution) would be logically to preclude the others: Abraham spoke as he did *either* because he was a child seeing the heavenly bodies for the first time, *or* because he was posing a rhetorical question, *or* because he was tactfully correcting his parents. In the mystical commentary, as can be seen from the above summary, some of the interpretations appear to contradict others, for example the first and the third, as against the fifth and the eighth. However, here no one interpretation necessarily precludes the others, for diversity of meaning serves the purpose of mystical exegesis.[48] To understand this purpose more clearly, two of the interpretations listed, the fifth and sixth, will be examined in detail. The other interpretations will be examined later in this study in the chapters on Abraham and Moses.

It is characteristic of Maybudī's mystical commentary that these interpretations are not grouped together, but arise in many different contexts. The fifth mystical interpretation of the story occurs in the context of Q. 2:77, 'Are they then unaware that God knows that which they keep hidden and that which they proclaim?' There is certainly no obvious connection between this verse and the Abraham story. However, by following closely Maybudī's exegetical train of thought, it will be possible to see how he links the two. To begin with, Maybudī explains that for mystics (*'ārifān*) an allusion is sufficient:

> When they were told, '[God] knows that which they keep hidden', they shook from their secrets the dust of all otherness, and did not allow any dispersion to enter their hearts. And when they were told 'He knows what they proclaim', they acted truly and with sincerity in their dealings with other people.[49]

Maybudī continues his commentary by stressing the importance of being aware that God knows what is hidden within us: '[He says], "If you do not know that I see you, there is a fault in your faith, and if you do, then why [do you] make Me the least of those who look upon you?"'[50] The same verse (Q. 2:77) is then compared with another, 'He knows the traitor of the eyes and that which bosoms hide' (Q. 40:19), and it is in commenting upon the latter verse that Maybudī introduces the Abraham story:

> The 'traitor of the eye' is one thing for bystanders and another for wayfarers; for the devout [among the wayfarers] the treachery of the eye is that at dead of night, the time for private communing with God, they sleep, so that the opportunity for intimate seclusion and closeness with Him is lost to them. Thus it was revealed to [the prophet] David: 'O David! A person is lying in his claim to love Me if, when night comes, he sleeps away from Me. Does not every lover love to be alone with their beloved?' In this regard God praised Khalīl (Abraham). He said, 'When night grew dark upon him [...] Sleep fled from his eyes, all his gaze was upon the traces of Our creation, and in those he found solace'.[51]

By alluding to the story of Abraham, Maybudī has not only added a poetic illustration to his explanation of the verse in question (Q. 40:19), he has also provided a new insight into Abraham's having called a star, the moon and the sun his Lord: it was his taking consolation (*tasallī*) in the objects of God's creation. In this interpretation Abraham has been placed in the class of the devout (*mutaʿabbidān*). Maybudī concludes his commentary by explaining that for those at a more advanced stage of the way, the mystics (*ʿārifān*), treachery of the eye is that, at the time of separation from the Beloved, they do not weep tears of blood.

In this example it can be seen how far Maybudī has come from a literal reading or exoteric interpretation of the verse (that is, the verse he was originally commenting upon, Q. 2:77); according to his *Nawbat* II commentary, the verse was a warning to hypocrites and Jews – who were saying one thing to the believers but had another thing in their hearts – that whether they kept their thoughts secret or expressed them, God would know them all the same.[52]

A second example, and the sixth of Maybudī's mystical interpretations of the Abraham story, occurs in the context of his interpretation on Q. 9:23, 'O you who believe! Do not choose your brethren for friends if they take pleasure in disbelief rather than faith.' Maybudī begins his mystical commentary on this verse by explaining that the sign of sincerity in the affirmation of [the] Oneness [of God] (*tawḥīd*) is 'cutting oneself off from all attachments, abandoning all habits, separating oneself from acquaintances and keeping one's attention on God in every state'. Abraham is then cited as an example of one who cut himself off from all attachments:

> First of all the world in the form of a star was placed before him, then the Hereafter displayed its beauty before the eye of his friendship in the form of

> the moon. Finally his inciting soul (*nafs ammāra*) and his love for Ishmael, in as much as it was selfish and partial (*ba-ḥukm-i baʿḍiyya*)[53] showed themselves to him in the form of the sun. Khalīl looked. In none of those existent things did he find [...] a sign of permanency (*nishān-i azal*). He said 'I do not want them', 'I love not things that set.' He shunned engendered existence altogether. He gave up the world, cut off his heart from his son and submitted himself to the fire of Nimrod, saying, 'For sure, they are all an enemy to me' (Q. 26:77). Whoever, likewise, wishes to pitch his tent in the alley of conformity (*muwāfaqat*) upon the carpet of love, let him at once turn loose the mount of attachments.[54]

Two significant observations about the hermeneutics of Maybudī's mystical commentary can be made from these examples. First, it can be seen how much the interpretations differ from each other in terms of content: in the fifth interpretation Abraham is still at the stage where he finds comfort in the contemplation of God's creation, whereas in the sixth, he has reached the stage where he has cut off from everything other than God. But here the apparent contradiction is not a problem, because the concern of the commentary is not to decide what Abraham's state was when he uttered these words, but to provide different insights into the spiritual path, so that, as Sarrāj stated, 'mystics of every sort can derive profit from them.'[55] Second, the interpretations may digress some way even from what might be considered an esoteric reading of the verse it is commenting on – this is particularly the case in the fifth interpretation.

From these two points it may be concluded that the aim of Maybudī's mystical commentary, and indeed of Sufi interpretation in general, is not so much to explain the Qur'anic verses, but to explain the complexities of the mystical path in the light of or through the inspiration of the Qur'anic verses. This would confirm Nwyia's observation about early mystical exegesis as exemplified in the commentary of Jaʿfar al-Ṣādiq, that it is 'no longer a reading of the Qur'an, but a reading of [mystical] experience in [or through] the new interpretation of the Qur'an.'[56] However, it could further be stated that for mystics such as Maybudī, the contemplation of the Qur'anic verses not only opens to them spiritual insights according to their state and level of attainment, it also provides them with a powerful means of communicating this knowledge to others.[57] In this case, the hermeneutic intent of mystical commentary could be defined quite simply as *irshād* (spiritual guidance).[58]

In Maybudī's view, the presentation of a translation of the verses and an exoteric commentary was an indispensable part of this spiritual guidance. We may therefore define his overall aim in writing the commentary as *irshād*, hence the concern expressed in his introduction that the *Kashf al-asrār* should 'bring the student seeking guidance (*mustarshid*) to his goal'. The first stage of this *irshād* was to provide a basic comprehension of the Scripture through a translation of the verses (*Nawbat* I); the second was to make possible a more thorough understanding of the Qur'anic verses by means of exoteric exegesis (*Nawbat* II); and the third was to encourage advancement to greater sincerity in the practice of that which had been understood (*Nawbat* III). Thereby, the believer might advance from the level of the outward observance of the generality of believers (*ʿāmm*) to the level of the elite (*khāṣṣ*) and finally to the level of the elite of the elite (*khāṣṣ al-khawāṣṣ*).

If there were a theory of levels of meaning underlying Maybudī's commentary, the evidence suggests it would be a threefold rather than a fourfold scheme, according to the levels of attainment of the *ʿāmm*, *khāṣṣ*, and *khāṣṣ al-khawāṣṣ*.[59] Maybudī does, on one occasion, indicate a threefold system of levels of meaning when he discusses the word *fahm* (understanding):

> Knowledge by understanding (*ʿilm-i fahm*) is beyond the knowledge of *tafsīr* and *taʾwīl*. *Tafsīr* is [learned] by means of teaching and instruction (*taʿlīm wa talqīn*), and *taʾwīl* by means of guidance and God-given success (*irshād wa tawfīq*),[60] but understanding has no intermediary, for it is by divine inspiration (*ba-ilhām-i rabbānī'st*). *Tafsīr* without a teacher is worthless, and *taʾwīl* without spiritual effort (*ijtihād*) unacceptable, but the one who possesses understanding has no other teacher than God. *Tafsīr* and *taʾwīl* are [accomplished] by means of knowledge and effort (*dānish wa kūshish*), but understanding is by finding and by divine attraction (*yāft wa kashish*)[61]. Ḥasan of Baṣra said, 'I once asked Ḥudhayfa b. Yamān[62] about inner knowledge, that is knowledge by understanding. He told me that he had asked the Messenger of God about this and that he had replied, "It is knowledge (*ʿilm*) that is between God and His saints (*awliyāʾ*). No archangel, nor any created thing, can have cognisance of it."' The understanding these men have of the mysteries in the Book and the Sunna has reached a point such that the masters of outward knowledge dare not even walk around the perimeters of its sacred and revered precincts. In every letter they have found a station (*maqām*), in every word a message, and from every verse a guidance [...].[63]

Having established the aims and criteria of Maybudī's esoteric commentary, we shall now pass on to the third aspect of mystical hermeneutics, namely the 'method' of Sufi interpretation.

The method of mystical commentary

To define the hermeneutics of mystical exegesis as *irshād*, is not to suggest that it is contrived; nor is it an attempt to explain how mystical insights are inspired by the verses of the Qur'an, a process which has been aptly described by Paul Nwyia as a 'play of mirrors between the *bāṭin* of the mystic and the *bāṭin* of the scripture'.[64] Nevertheless, once the point is reached where these insights are expounded to others in a way that has come down to us in written form, it is possible to discern recurrent patterns in the way that these insights are connected to the sacred text. This we may call the 'method' of mystical exegesis.

By analysing the method of one commentator and comparing it to that of another, it will be possible not only to discover procedures that are common to both, but also to see to what extent a mystical commentary reflects the particular Sufi outlook and doctrines of its author, and, in the case of the *Kashf al-asrār*, any distinctive features that might be associated with the use of Persian as the language of commentary. For the purpose of analysis, this study has concentrated on Maybudī's mystical commentary on the first *juz'* (thirtieth part) of the Qur'an (from the beginning of the Qur'an to verse 141 of *Sūrat al-Baqara* (Q. 2)). This has ensured the inclusion of verses of different categories: legislative, eschatological, allegorical etc. For the purposes of comparison the same part of the *Laṭā'if al-ishārāt* of Qushayrī has been looked at in detail, though some reference has also been made to the *Ḥaqā'iq al-tafsīr* of Sulamī.[65]

Following the overall principle of *irshād*, the esoteric interpretations in the *Kashf al-asrār* and the *Laṭā'if al-ishārāt* seem to fall into two broad categories. The first comprises interpretations which are intended directly for spiritual guidance, either by encouraging spiritual virtue or by discouraging spiritual laxity or weakness. The second includes interpretations which are for the purpose of what shall be termed here 'edification', by increasing the knowledge of God, by encouraging love and respect for the Prophet Muhammad, by pointing to the wonder of nature and the meaning of creation, or by emphasizing the special privileges, and therefore responsibilities, given to man among created beings. These categories represent recurring patterns rather than any hard and fast rule; there may, of course, be overlapping between them.

Methodologically, interpretations for the purpose of spiritual guidance fall into several different types, according to the way in which each one is related to the verse in question. For example, they might be discussed in an analogical, allegorical, or explicative fashion, and so on. Interpretations in the second category, edification, usually take the form of explanations or comments on the verses based either on theology or on metaphysics. The following section presents some methods which are common to both Maybudī and Qushayrī, and illustrates these with examples.

Spiritual guidance

Interpretations by means of analogy

The use of analogy (*qiyās*) as a tool in exoteric exegesis has been discussed in detail by J. Wansbrough.[66] But analogy also has its place in mystical exegesis. By this method a verse which, in its outer meaning, clearly refers to a particular person, people or situation, is given wider relevance or transferred to another context.[67] Analogical interpretations usually occur in the context of verses which speak either of the state of the blessed in Paradise or of the doom of the unbelievers. A typical example is in Q. 2:7, 'God has set a seal upon their hearts and their hearing', for which both Qushayrī and Maybudī give analogical interpretations.

Qushayrī begins his commentary on this verse by explaining the Qur'anic metaphor: 'a seal upon a thing neither allows anything to enter nor to leave it'. He then explains why this metaphor is applied to the unbelievers (*al-ladhīna kafarū* mentioned in the previous verse):

> Thus God ruled that the hearts of His enemies should never be parted from ignorance and error, and that no insight (*baṣīra*) or guidance should come to them. Upon the organ of their hearing is the covering of abandonment [by God].
>
> It is blocked from perceiving His address, with respect to faith, whilst the whispering of Satan and the murmuring of their egos busies them away from giving ear to reminders of God.

Now comes the analogy, which he introduces with the phrase 'as for the elite (*khawāṣṣ*)'. By *khawāṣṣ* Qushayrī is evidently referring to the ulema, for he continues: 'concern with knowledge of the religious sciences and the agitation of [trying to] resolve questions busies their hearts away from the mysteries of God which might [otherwise] be able to enter unmediated. This latter is the situation of the *khāṣṣ al-khawāṣṣ*.'[68]

Here, Qushayrī has marked off his analogy clearly with the words 'as for (*fa-ammā*)'. Often the link is made with the word 'thus' or 'similarly' (*kadhālik*). Maybudī, however, does not usually demarcate his analogy so clearly. For example, in his commentary on the same verse he moves directly into the analogy, and using the Persian word for seal, *muhr*, explains: 'One had the seal of alienation (*bīgānagī*) placed upon his heart so that he remained in unbelief; another had the seal of confusion (*sar gardānī*), so that he remained in lassitude (*fatrat*)'. Only afterwards does Maybudī explain why the word seal, as he has understood it (that is, being 'cut off' in a certain state), may be applied to other than the unbelievers: 'Not everyone who escaped from unbelief attained to God, nor was freed from himself. He who escaped from unbelief reached acquaintance, and he who was freed from himself reached love. From acquaintance to love there are a thousand stations, and from love to the Beloved a thousand vales [to be traversed].'[69]

Sometimes an element of interpretation is required before the analogy can be made. One example is Qushayrī's commentary on Q. 2:25, which describes the state of the believers in Paradise: 'Whenever they are given sustenance from its fruit, they will say: We have been given this before'.[70] He firstly explains that, although when they are given the fruit they suppose it to be as before, when they taste it, they find it to be superior. He then makes his analogy: 'It is the same way for the possessors of realities. Their inward states are constantly being elevated, so that when one is elevated from his [previous] state, he supposes that what he will come to at that moment will be like that which preceded it, but when he experiences (lit. tastes) it, he finds it to be superior by twice as much.'[71] Another example is Maybudī's mystical commentary on the verse 'Those who believe, those who are Jews, Christians and Sabaeans – whoever believes in God and the Last Day – surely their reward is with their Lord; there shall be no fear for them, nor shall they grieve' (Q. 2:62), concerning which there is a hadith of the Prophet to the effect that only those among the people of the Book who died *before* hearing him would be saved.[72] Maybudī begins his esoteric commentary on this verse by explaining:

> However much those Jewish scribes and Christian monks strove, and whatever pains they took in keeping their religion; however far they went on the path of spiritual striving and discipline, restrained themselves from their desires and habits, cut themselves off completely from the world and worldly people and incarcerated themselves in their hermit's cell, their efforts were wasted, for the truth is that unless they believed in Muhammad and accepted his message and prophethood, you may count all their devotions as nothing and their obedience unaccepted [by God].

His analogy then follows: 'The way of the pious and the states and stations of lovers follow a similar pattern: as long as there remains with them a remnant of [worldly] attachment, their claim to having discovered the fragrant breeze of friendship is nothing but vain words.'[73]

Symbolic and allegorical interpretations

I am using the term 'symbolic interpretations' to mean those interpretations in which a noun (or pair or group of nouns) mentioned in the Qur'an is taken as a symbol or metaphor for something else. Symbolic interpretations often occur when features of nature are mentioned, such as the two seas, representing fear and hope,[74] the hills of Ṣafā and Marwa, representing purity and manliness,[75] the sun or moon representing the spiritual states of stability (*tamkīn*) and vacillation (*talwīn*).[76] They may also be given for other things such as a town (*qarya*), representing the precinct of knowledge,[77] or the rod of Moses, representing the Shari'a.[78]

Concerning the allegorical interpretation of the Qur'an, Lazarus-Yafeh correctly observed that it is rare to find in early Sufi exegesis what she called 'full-fledged allegory' – I prefer to use the term extended allegory – in which an entire sura is allegorised.[79] This extended form of allegorical interpretation appears later in Sufi exegesis, in the thirteenth and fourteenth centuries, as exemplified in the commentary of ʿAbd al-Razzāq al-Kāshānī (d. 730/1329),[80] though it is to be found much earlier in Ismaili exegesis.[81] Nevertheless, allegory in the sense of an extended metaphor[82] is quite common in earlier Sufi exegesis. Typically it occurs where a change or movement in the heavenly bodies is mentioned, for example the waxing and waning of the moon, interpreted to represent the states of 'contraction' (*qabḍ*) and 'expansion' (*basṭ*).[83] Allegorical interpretations also occur when physical or outward actions are described in the verse, such as 'entering the gate prostrate' (Q. 2:58), representing acting with rectitude and humility in religion;[84] or the ransoming of captives (Q. 2:85), representing not practising what one preaches;[85] or the command to the Children of Israel to kill themselves (Q. 2:54), representing killing the *nafs* with the sword of spiritual striving.[86] Also interpreted allegorically are stories related in the Qur'an, the so-called 'tales of the ancients' (*akhbār al-awwalīn*), such as the Companions of the Cave, and, particularly, the stories of the prophets, as has already been illustrated in Maybudī's interpretation of the story of Abraham and will be demonstrated with numerous examples in Part Three of this book. Allegorical interpretations are often introduced by the word *ishāratuhu* (Qushayrī) or *az rūy-i ishārat* (Maybudī).

Three examples may serve here to illustrate more fully the use of allegorical interpretation. The first is Qushayrī's commentary on the verse 'Any revelation that We abrogate or cause to be forgotten, We bring [in its place] one better or similar' (Q. 2:106), for which he presents an allegorical interpretation in the form of a gloss: 'that is, He moves you from one state (*ḥāl*) to one above it, or higher than it, so the branch of your union is ever verdant and blooming and the star of your favour is ever rising.' As can be seen, the allegorical interpretation has in this case been embellished with metaphors of Qushayrī's choosing. These metaphors are added to as he explains, again in the form of a gloss: '"We never take away any of the traces of worship (or service, *ʿibāda*) without exchanging them for the lights of servanthood (*ʿubūdiyya*); and We never take away any of the lights of servanthood without causing to rise in their place the moons of slavery (*ʿubūda*)."'[87]

This example illustrates an allegorical interpretation of a series of actions, in this case, two complementary acts on the part of God: the abrogating of a verse, and replacing it with one better. Two further examples, this time taken from Maybudī's commentary, will illustrate the allegorical interpretation of *akhbār al-awwalīn*. Both are taken from his interpretation of the story of the Companions of the Cave. In the first, he glosses the command 'seek refuge in the Cave; your Lord will spread for you of His mercy, and prepare for you a pillow in your plight' (Q. 18:16) thus: 'Go into the Cave of [God's] protective jealousy (*ghayrat*), in the shade of [divine] solicitude (*ʿināyat*), under the wing of His guardianship (*wilāyat*), in the world of [His] safekeeping, so that God, be He exalted, may keep you in the private enclosure of immunity from error, and clothe you with His mercy.'[88] In the second example, Maybudī interprets the words 'You would have thought that they were awake, though they were asleep' (Q. 18:18) as 'When you look at their exterior, you see them busy in the arena of work, but when you look at their secret, you will find them carefree in the orchard of the benevolence of the Majestic Lord. Outwardly they are at work; inwardly they are contemplating the pre-eternal grace.'[89]

Interpretation

An 'interpretative' method is often used when there is something unspecified or unclear in the verse. In some cases this method resembles that of certain exoteric interpretations, as in Qushayrī's mystical commentary on the words, 'Indeed I know that which you do not know' (Q. 2:30), where he has specified 'that which' to mean 'about My forgiveness of them',[90] or his interpretation of the word *kalimāt* in the verse, 'When Abraham's Lord tried him with His commands' (Q. 2:124).[91] Usually, however, the interpretation will be more esoteric, as when Qushayrī interprets the words 'Those who break the covenant of God' (Q. 2:26) to mean 'those who traverse the way of aspirancy (*irāda*),[92] but then return to the way of habit (*'āda*)'.[93]

The interpretative method also occurs in the context of the Qur'anic use of metaphors, such as the words 'Deaf, dumb, blind, they do not return' (Q. 2:18), which Qushayrī interprets as 'Deaf to hearing the calls of God with the ear of the heart, dumb, so that they do not make intimate prayer to God with the tongue of their secret (*sirr*), and blind, so that they do not see the playing out of their destinies with the eye of insight.'[94]

Another instance where interpretative commentary is called for is in the 'coining of similitudes' (*ḍarb al-amthāl*), such as the verse 'They are like one who kindles a fire. When it sheds its light around him God takes away their light and leaves them in darkness, where they cannot see' (Q. 2:17). Qushayrī interprets this as 'one who starts travelling the way of *irāda*, toils for a time, but suffers one hardship after another, and then regresses to the world, before he has attained to Reality, returning to the human darkness that he was in before'.[95] Maybudī begins his mystical commentary on this verse with a similar interpretation. However, he continues by interpreting the 'shedding of light', in the second half of the same verse, as being 'the eternal mysteries of the Qur'an', and advises those who possess hearts 'to listen to these mysteries with their heart's ear and know them, to contemplate in their secrets (*asrār*) the realities or deepest truths (*ḥaqā'iq*) [of the Qur'an], and become closely acquainted with them'.[96]

Explanation

When words such as 'guidance' (*hudā*) or 'piety' (*taqwā*) occur in the Qur'anic verses, the esoteric commentary may take the form of an explanation of the word as it should be understood by those who have undertaken to travel the spiritual path. For example, Qushayrī explains the meaning of *hudā* (Q. 2:2) as 'elucidation (*bayān*) and proof (*ḥujja*), illumination (*ḍiyā'*) and love (*maḥabba*), for one whom God protects from the darkness of ignorance, and causes to see by the lights of the intellect (*'aql*) and selects for the realities of union',[97] while the pious or God-fearing person (*muttaqī*) in the same verse is explained as being 'the one who is wary of seeing his piety and does not place any trust in it, but sees his salvation as being solely through the grace of his Lord'.[98] Maybudī explains that the command to listen (Q. 2:104) means: 'Listen, and with heart and soul accept [the Qur'an]. Look upon it with the eye of respect and a pure heart, so that the reality of listening (*ḥaqīqat-i samā'*) and the nourishment of finding (*ṭa'ām-i wujūd*) may reach your soul.'[99]

Sometimes a statement in the Qur'an is explained in terms of 'spiritual psychology' or the science of the soul. For example, Qushayrī explains the verse 'In their hearts is a disease and God increases their disease' (Q. 2:10) thus: 'In the hearts of the hypocrites is the disease of doubt, and God increases the sickness by [allowing them] to delude themselves that they have been saved by their deceiving of the Muslims'.[100] Maybudī explains Q. 2:86, 'Such are those who buy the life of this world at the price of the Hereafter. Their punishment will not be lightened, neither will they have support', in the following manner:

> Those who buy this world and sell the Hereafter, and choose the desire of their lower souls above God's good-pleasure, 'Their punishment will not be lightened', [that is] there will be no end to their punishment nor will it be alleviated, either in this world or the next. In this world their punishment is the accumulation of wealth, seeking respect and reputation and the gratification of their greed and the lust of the soul which incites [to evil]

(*nafs-i ammāra*) [...], and there is no end to that craving and greed, for it will never subside.[101]

Classification

Classification is being used here to mean taking an action, virtue or state that is mentioned in the Qur'an and showing how it may be realised by different classes of believers (for example, *ahl-i sharīʿat* and *ahl-i ḥaqīqat*, or *ʿāmm*, *khāṣṣ* and *khāṣṣ al-khawāṣṣ*), or at different levels of the human being (for example, body, heart and spirit). This kind of interpretation typically occurs either following the exhortation to accomplish a particular action or virtue, or after the description of an action or virtue being performed by the believers. For example, in his interpretation of Q. 2:3, 'and [those who] give out of what We have provided for them',[102] Qushayrī explains that 'the people of the law (*aṣḥāb al-sharīʿa*) give of their possessions (*amwāl*) but the people of spiritual realisation (*aṣḥāb al-ḥaqīqa*) give of their states (*aḥwāl*),' and then proceeds to show that which is given by the renunciants (*zāhidūn*), the worshippers (*ʿābidūn*), the aspirants (*murīdūn*) and the mystics (*ʿārifūn*). This method is frequently used by Maybudī, as when he follows the words 'And fear Me' (Q. 2:40) with a discussion of six kinds of fear: that of the repentant (*tāʾibān*), the worshippers (*ʿābidān*), the renunciants (*zāhidān*), the learned (*ʿālimān*), the mystics (*ʿārifān*) and the wholly sincere (*ṣiddīqān*).[103]

Comment

Sometimes the esoteric commentary takes the form of a personal observation, a traditional saying, or some information presented by the commentator to endorse or expand on what has been related in the verse. For example, after the words, 'And you wilt find them greediest of mankind for life – greedier than the idolaters' (Q. 2:96), Qushayrī comments: 'Love of life in this world is the result of forgetfulness of God'.[104] Maybudī finds great scope for adding his own observations, which he sometimes attributes to God or one of the prophets.[105] One example is when he comments on the verse, 'And when We made the House (at Mecca) a resort for mankind and a sanctuary' (Q. 2:125), which reads:

> He (God) said 'I have made the House for people – a house and *what* a house! I made it out of brick, but I connected it to eternity. When those who are estranged [from Me] look at it they see nothing but bricks and mortar, as a

blind man experiences only warmth from the sun. But when the lover looks, he sees beyond the bricks the mark of special designation and connection [to the divine presence]. He gives his heart and stakes his life.'[106]

Edification

Interpretations which are intended for increasing the knowledge of God, love and respect for the Prophet Muhammad, wonder at the wisdom in the created universe, or awareness of the honour and responsibility given to mankind within the creation, variously take the form of explanations of, additions to, and comments on, words, phrases or verses in the Qur'anic text.

Explanations might have a metaphysical or theological basis, as when Qushayrī comments on the verse, 'God does not shy from drawing comparisons even with something as small as a gnat or something larger' (Q. 2:26),[107] showing that, since in relation to God existence is in reality smaller than a single atom of the dust of the air, there is no difference vis-à-vis His might between the Throne and a gnat – the creation of the Throne is not harder nor the creation of the gnat easier for Him, for He is exalted beyond being affected by easiness or difficulty;[108] or when he explains the reasons for the angels protesting at God's announcement that He is about to place a vicegerent on the earth (Q. 2:30).[109] Maybudī has recourse to a (theo)logical syllogism in order to explain why God has no need to 'have a son' (Q. 2:116). He observes that God has provided everything that perishes with seed so that it will have a successor and its species will not die out. So it is with animals and plants, but for those things that will remain until the Resurrection, such as the sun, moon and stars, He has not. For the same reason, namely, that He will always remain, there is no need for God to have a son.[110]

Both Qushayrī and Maybudī interpret the verse, 'We have seen the turning of your face to heaven, [O Muhammad]' (Q. 2:144), as an indication of the Prophet's courtesy or propriety (*adab*) towards God; rather than expressing the desire that was in his heart, he waited until the words came from the divine presence: 'and We shall make you turn towards a *qibla* which will please you' (Q. 2:144). The two commentators also emphasize the special love which God has for Muhammad, 'All the servants strive to gain My good pleasure, but I seek to please you.'[111]

Qushayrī observes that the verse, 'Who has appointed the earth a resting place for you and the sky a canopy' (Q. 2:22), is an indication that God has provided for all the needs of His creation, that there is no other innovator but Him and that anyone who considers benefit or harm, good or bad as having its origin in a created thing is committing the sin of idolatry (*shirk*).[112] Maybudī, on the other hand, sees the same verse as an opportunity to wonder at the wisdom and might of the Creator Who raised the seven heavens, one above the other without anything to support or connect them, and then brought day out of night and night out of day.[113]

We might include in this category of interpretation comments which speak of the general situation of human beings, particularly their being governed by *qaḍā'* (that which has been determined by God in pre-eternity),[114] or the infinite kindness and favour which is constantly bestowed on them by God.[115] Also included are comments which elaborate upon descriptions of Paradise that are given in the verses.[116]

Diversity, digression and development in Maybudī's mystical commentary

In the examples that have been cited so far, no significant difference will have been noticed between Qushayrī's and Maybudī's mystical commentaries. However, while the two commentators certainly have themes and methods in common – not surprisingly, since Maybudī often quotes or draws upon ideas from the *Laṭā'if al-ishārāt* – there are distinct differences in the style and presentation of the two commentaries.

Overall, Maybudī's *Nawbat* III commentary appears to be substantially freer than the *Laṭā'if*. Qushayrī adheres much more closely to the Qur'anic text, and although he is presenting an esoteric interpretation, he usually acknowledges the exoteric meaning of the verse in some way, either by firstly explaining its outer meaning in the light of spiritual psychology, and then moving on to its more esoteric implication, or by showing how a particular analogy or allegory relates to the outer meaning of the verse. Maybudī, on the other hand, often interprets a word or phrase with no apparent regard to its Qur'anic context. For example, in the verse 'And (remember O Children of Israel) when We made a covenant with you and caused the Mount to tower above you' (Q. 2:63), Maybudī ignores the covenant that was made with the Children of Israel, and instead takes the word 'covenant' to mean that which was made with all men in pre-eternity, 'when the Oneness [of God] (*aḥadiyyat*) was manifested to all hearts. To one heart it was the manifestation of terror and might, to another the manifestation of gentleness and generosity.'[117]

This kind of mystical interpretation, which is not unique to Maybudī, allows Sufi exegetes considerable scope to expand the mystical content of their commentaries.[118] However, sometimes the freedom with which Maybudī draws his mystical discussion from a Qur'anic verse is surprising, as when he interprets the hardening of hearts in Q. 2:74, 'Then when your hearts were hardened', as being, in people of sincerity and strength of heart, the advanced stage of 'stability (*tamakkun*), perfection of gnosis, and the state of purity'.[119] Maybudī broadens the context of his mystical commentary in a number of other ways. Sometimes he compares one Qur'anic usage with another, as when he discusses the word *ummī* in the verse, 'And among them are illiterate people (*ummiyyūn*)' (Q. 2:78), and points out that the use of the word in this verse is a condemnation, whereas in the verse 'Those who follow the Messenger, the Prophet who can neither read nor write' (Q. 7:157) the use of the word is praise, which is an indication that 'to be the same in name is not to be equal'. This leads him on to remind those whom he is addressing that God is transcendent above all created things, and to warn them against trying to comprehend Him through groundless supposition and [mental] searching (*tawahhum wa justujū*).[120] Other methods which Maybudī uses to extend the scope of his commentary include comparing a verse with the one that precedes or follows it;[121] comparing the people mentioned in a verse with another people (for example the Children of Israel and the Muslims,[122] or disbelievers and believers);[123] and explaining why the same thing may be expressed differently in two verses.[124]

In one of the interpretations of the story of Abraham discussed previously (see pp. 77–8), we saw how, by linking the verse in question to another of similar meaning, Maybudī skillfully digressed to a subject that was neither obviously connected to the verse he was originally commenting upon nor connected to its Qur'anic context. Another form of digression simply leads out from the subject matter of the verse itself, as when, for example, he comments on the verse, 'Who has appointed the earth a resting-place for you, and the sky a canopy' (Q. 2:22). First of all he wonders at God's power and wisdom in raising the seven heavens without support. Next, he calls attention to another miracle: that of

God's bringing day out of night and night out of day. Then, turning from the macrocosm to the microcosm, he observes that even more wondrous is the fact that God has placed the light of knowledge in the 'dark blood' of the heart, and the light of vision in the dark pupil of the eye. Returning again to the theme of the alternation of darkness and light, he explains how the succession of day and night in the macrocosm is also reflected in the microcosm, for in the soul, too, there must inevitably be an alternation between the light of felicity (*dawlat*) and the darkness of affliction (*miḥnat*), and between the states of contraction (*qabḍ*) and expansion (*basṭ*).[125]

Although, as these examples show, Maybudī digresses some way from the subject of the verse in question, each step of the digression is usually endorsed or illustrated by a quote from the Qur'an, which keeps an exegetical 'thread' running through the narrative. In contrast to these rather complex interpretations, Maybudī's mystical commentary may often take the form of a simple encomium,[126] or a eulogy to God, the Prophet or the Qur'an.[127]

Two factors may account for the greater freedom and diversity of Maybudī's mystical commentary: first, his use of the Persian language, which may have been less constraining than Arabic, the traditional language of *tafsīr*; and second, the structure of the *Kashf al-asrār*. In the *Laṭā'if al-ishārāt*, Qushayrī has presented a complete mystical commentary; that is, he has in some measure commented on almost every verse of the Qur'an. His commentary, therefore, consistently follows a traditional format comprising the verse (or in some cases, two or three verses) followed by the commentary on that verse or part of it. Although Qushayrī's commentary is rich in metaphors and includes numerous couplets of poetry, his style is usually succinct, probably because he was addressing an elite audience of adepts, who were both more literate in Arabic and better versed in the Sufi path than Maybudī's wider audience. Occasionally if he wishes to say more on a subject, he will introduce a brief section (*faṣl*) on it.[128]

Maybudī, on the other hand, has already commented on all the verses of the Qur'an in the *Nawbat* II sections of the *Kashf al-asrār*. This leaves him free, in his *Nawbat* III sections, to present a mystical commentary only on those verses or part-verses which he choses or is inspired to expound upon.[129] It also gives him scope to develop the content, language and style of his commentary in a way that is fitting for the didactic purpose of his work and for the audience he is aiming to reach.

Aspects of Sufi doctrine, or words of interest which occur in the verses, are explained and discussed at length. In fact, these explanations make up the greater part of his commentary. They are often interwoven with quotations from the Qur'an and hadith, and may include poetry, usually no more than a couplet or quatrain, or one of the *munājāt* of Anṣārī, to encapsulate or give added nuance to the theme he is discussing. The topic is also frequently illustrated with an anecdote or two about well-known mystics, or, as shown in the example earlier, with stories of the prophets.

However, storytelling, poetry and poetical prose are not merely elements which are added to Maybudī's mystical commentary; they become integral to, and an essential part of, his narrative style and rhetoric.[130] Reference has already been made to the way in which Maybudī uses the storyteller's art in his *Nawbat* II commentary (see pp. 51–2), but he uses it with equal effect in his mystical commentary. The following example is taken from his commentary on the creation of Adam, where God announces to the angels 'Lo! I am about to place a viceroy in the earth' (Q. 2:30):

> The world was still and at peace. No heart yet burned with the fire of passion, nor could any breast be accused of being in love. The sea of mercy was brimming over, the treasuries of devotion fully laden. No dust of langour had yet settled on the brow of the angels' worship. The banner of their boasting 'We hymn Your praise and sanctify You' [Q. 2:30] had reached the Pleiades. In that world[131] every subtle substance fell to wishful thinking: the glorious Throne looked at its magnificence and said 'Maybe this honour [lit. saying] will be written for me'. The Footstool looked upon its power and said, 'Maybe this authority will be assigned to my name'. The seven heavens looked at their beauty and wondered, 'Will this guardianship (*wilāyat*) be given to us?' Everything had lost hope of realising its desire, and all had fallen into suspicion (*tuhmat*) and dejection (*sawdā'ī*). Suddenly from the mighty and glorious Presence the news was given to the kingdom of the angels, 'Lo! I am about to place a viceroy in the earth.' This was not a consultation with the angels; this was setting out the canons of the greatness and magnitude of Adam. Nor was it a summons for support, but a proclamation of the veneration of Adam. He said, 'The decree of Our wrath has done its work, and We have commanded the pen of beneficence (*karam*) to draw a line through the register (*dīwān*) of commandments from the world's beginning to its end, and to set down what has been decreed for all its inhabitants through the entire extent and duration of creation, so that the place of honour in every realm will be secured for the earthly Adam, his

precious breast will become luminous with the light of gnosis, and the graces of Our bounty and the wonders of Our favour towards him will be known.[132]

In this passage it can be seen how Maybudī first sets the scene, and then gradually builds the suspense leading up to the entry of Adam, in order to place the spotlight, as it were, on the uniqueness of Adam's position in the creation, and as the one solely designated for gnosis and love. Also to be noted is the personification of elements in the creation such as the Throne, Footstool and Seven Heavens, and the way Maybudī places the Qur'anic quote at the climax of the passage.

Another feature of Maybudī's narrative style in the mystical commentary is his use of poetic imagery and metaphors, particularly metaphors of wine-drinking, polo, gambling and profane love. For example, on the subject of the need for 'manliness' on the spiritual path he says:

The spirits of God's lovers are tossed about [like a ball] in [the crook of] the polo-stick of His remembrance. O brave and noble one! How long you have slept! Wake up, for it is time for morning devotions (*ṣubāḥ*), and if you are wine sick beware, for the ray of God's light (*partaw*) will be a morning draught (*ṣubūḥ*)![133]

Describing the special intimacy granted to the Prophet Muhammad, he says:

That which for hundreds of years the noble ones only tasted in sleep,[134] you taste awake, in this one instant, for the house is empty and the Beloved is yours.

Night has come, the wine is here and your lover alone,
Rise and come, my love, for the night is ours.[135]

The second of these two examples illustrates the way in which poetry is integrated with the prose. Another artistic element in the mystical commentary is Maybudī's use of *saj*ʿ. Passages of metred (*mawzūn*) and rhyming (*musajjaʿ*) prose, echoing the style of Anṣārī's *Munājāt*, occur at intervals throughout the *Nawbat* III sections of the *Kashf al-asrār*. The passages are usually quite short, often no more than a few lines. This transliterated and translated passage is an example of Maybudī's metred and rhyming prose:

> *īnt bīmārī ki ānrā kerān na, wa īnt dardī ki ānrā darmān na* [...]*bazārtar az rūz-i munāfiq rūz-i kīst? ki az azal tā abad dar bīgānagī zīst.*

> See here's a sickness that has no end! Here, a pain that has no cure! Whose fate is more wretched than that of the hypocrite, who from ever to eternity lives in alienation?[136]

The following is an example of rhyming prose:

> *āngah marā zabānī dād az luṭf-i samadānī, wa dilī dād az nūr-i rabbānī, wa chashmī az ṣunʿ-i yazdānī / tā agar gūyam ba-madad-i ū gūyam wa ba-quwwat-i ū pūyam / ba-dīdaʾ-i ū bīnam, ba-qudrat-i ū gīram.*

> Then He gave me a tongue from His eternal grace, a heart of lordly light and an eye of divine making, so that if I speak it is with His help, with His strength I discern, by His radiance I see and by His power I hold.[137]

It is not only the style of Anṣārī's *Munājāt* that is echoed in the *Nawbat* III sections of the *Kashf al-asrār,* but also the spirit. In his *Munājāt,* Anṣārī is addressing God in intimate terms; it is part of the rhetoric of Maybudī's mystical commentary that God often addresses man with a similar intimacy. In his comment on the words 'We caused the white cloud to overshadow you' (Q. 2:57), we may note again how freely he is attributing words to God:

> This is an allusion to God's grace and favour and His kindness to His servants, for the Lord of the Worlds says: 'O poor son of Adam! Why don't you make friends with Me? I desire [your] friendship. Why don't you trade with me? I am the most open-handed and generous [...] O helpless one! No one calls for you as I do. Since you are selling yourself [know that] others buy [only] what is perfect, but We buy that which is faulty. Others only invite those who are faithful, but We call for the fickle.'[138]

In these few examples it can be seen how Maybudī's commentary has found a dynamic of its own that almost takes it beyond the genre of Qur'anic exegesis, be it mystical or otherwise; the interpretation of the verses has been transformed into a narrative which seeks to communicate not simply by the ideas it contains, but by its very beauty. This development may partly be attributed to Maybudī's desire to make his commentary more appealing and to reach a wider audience.[139] In this case, these artistic features could be understood as being not simply a matter of literary style, but as intrinsic to the aim and method, and therefore to the hermeneutics, of Maybudī's mystical commentary, thus exemplifying the integration of hermeneutics with the evolution of the *language* of mystical expression. At the same time, the artistic elements that are evidenced in the *Nawbat* III sections of the *Kashf al-asrār* clearly exemplify a wider literary movement in the writing of Persian prose and poetry that was taking place in Khorasan at that time, one that was directly linked to the development of the doctrines of love in Sufism. It is this development, and the place of love within the mystical doctrines of the *Kashf al-asrār*, which will form the subject of part two of this book.

NOTES

1 Quoted p. 40.

2 See MS Or. 9433, fol. 2a. The published edition of Sulamī's *Ḥaqā'iq*, based on the Cairo MS al-Fātiḥ, includes the following anonymous statement which may be intended as a gloss: 'The expression (*'ibāra*) is to be listened to (*li'l-sam'*), the allusion (*ishāra*) is for the intellect (*li'l-'aql*), the subtleties (*laṭā'if*) are for contemplation (*li'l-mushāhada*), and the realities (*ḥaqā'iq*) are for self-surrender (*li'l-istislām*).' *Ḥaqā'iq*, ed. 'Imrān, p. 23.

3 Trans. Böwering, *Mystical Vision,* p. 139.

4 Though this attribution is incorrect according to Böwering, *Mystical Vision*, p. 140. The only difference between the two versions is the last part, which, in the theory attributed by Sulamī to 'Alī b. Abī Ṭālib, reads: 'the *maṭla'* is what God wants from, or intends for the servant by the verse' (*murīd Allāh ta'ālā min al-'abd bihā*). *Ḥaqā'iq,* ed. 'Imrān, pp. 22–3; MS Or. 9433, fol. 2a.

5 *Ḥaqā'iq*, ed. 'Imrān, p. 21; trans. Böwering, *Mystical Vision*, p. 140. This hadith is not present in the British Library manuscript. For a discussion of the different forms of the hadith see Gerhard Böwering, 'The scriptural senses in medieval Ṣūfī Qur'ān exegesis', in McAuliffe *et al.,* eds., *With Reverence for the Word*, pp. 350–1.

6 Böwering, *Mystical Vision*, p. 140. Maybudī alludes to this same hadith on two occasions. On the first (*Kashf,* III, p. 437), he also intends a twofold distinction, that of *ẓahr* and *baṭn*, but here he understands the *baṭn* to be a meaning accessible to God alone. On the second occasion (*Kashf,* VIII, p. 315), he understands the seven *aḥruf* or *dargāh*s of the Qur'an to be a reference to the seven seas (stations) which must be crossed (attained) before entering the alley (station) of *tawḥīd*.

7 Böwering, 'Scriptural senses', p. 351. Although in idem, *Mystical Vision*, p. 141, he explains Tustarī's statement of a fourfold sense as having been 'partly based on this hadith, partly on Ibn 'Abbās' four Qur'anic levels, and partly on the patristic tradition', for which see below.

8 See note 7. Some versions of this hadith go back to the Prophet, others stop

at Ibn ʿAbbās. See Gilliot, *Exégèse*, pp. 121–3.

9 Given that Ṭabarī uses the word *ta'wīl* simply to mean interpretation, and that he understands *ẓahr* to mean the recitation, he probably does not have any esoteric meaning in mind here.

10 For a discussion of whether the word should be read *maṭlaʿ* or *muṭṭalaʿ* see Josef Van Ess, *Die Gedankenwelt des Ḥāriṯ al-Muḥāsibī* (Bonn, 1961), p. 210.

11 *Jāmiʿ al-bayān*, ed. Shākir and Shākir, p. 72; tr. Cooper, p. 31. See also Gilliot, *Exégèse*, pp. 113ff.

12 Translated from Van Ess' German in *Gedankenwelt*, p. 210. Compare al-Muḥāsibī's understanding of *maṭlaʿ* with Maybudī's interpretation of the word 'scum' (*zabad*) in Q. 13:17, discussed on pp. 47–8. A saying attributed to Junayd in Sulamī's *Ziyādāt ḥaqā'iq al-tafsīr*, p. 1, reads: 'The word of God comprises four [levels or categories of] meaning: outward, inward, truth and reality' (*kalām Allāh ʿalā arbaʿa maʿānin, ẓāhir wa bāṭin wa ḥaqq wa ḥaqīqa*). Jalāl al-Dīn Rūmī too speaks of four levels of meaning in the Qur'an when he interprets another saying of the Prophet which refers to seven levels of meaning. See Jalāl al-Dīn Rūmī, *Mathnawī*, ed. R.A. Nicholson (London, 1925–40), III, lines 4242ff.; tr. Nicholson (London, 1930), IV, p. 237.

13 Massignon, *Essai sur les origines*, pp. 703ff; Van Ess, *Gedankenwelt*, p. 210; John E. Wansbrough, *Quranic Studies*, London Oriental Series 31 (Oxford, 1977), pp. 242–3; Gilliot, *Exégèse*, p. 123; Böwering, *Mystical Vision*, p. 139; idem, 'Spiritual senses', pp. 352–3.

14 Robert M. Grant (with David Tracy), *Short History of the Interpretation of the Bible*, 2nd edn (London, 1984), p. 85.

15 Gilliot, *Exégèse*, p. 121.

16 Ibid.; it translates as: 'Here, we are in an area of encounter between the three exegetical traditions, even though it is difficult to define precisely the filiation that connects them.'

17 Böwering, 'Scriptural senses', p. 353. On the previous page of the same article, the author is more cautious, stating that an analogy between the hermeneutical systems is 'tempting, though untenable, if seen as directly and historically linking Islamic hermeneutics with the principles of biblical exegesis developed in the Jewish tradition and in Christian patristic exegesis'.

18 Grant, *Short History*, ch. 4.

19 Wansbrough, *Quranic Studies*, pp. 245–6; Nwyia *Exégèse coranique*, p. 33. The use of allegory in esoteric interpretation will be discussed further below.

20 As in the case of Philo, Origen and the Muʿtazilīs. See Frances H. Colson and George H. Whitaker, *Philo* (London and Harvard, 1929), translators' introduction p. xiii; Grant, *Short History*, p. 58. This was also Ghazzālī's view, with certain caveats: See ch. 2, pp. 45 and 48, nn. 27 and 35.

21 See Karen J. Torjesen, *Hermeneutical Procedure and Theological Method in Origen's Exegesis* (Berlin and New York, 1986), p. 40; Grant, *Short History*, p. 59.

22 Böwering, *Mystical Vision*, p. 141; idem, 'Scriptural senses', p. 352.

23 Torjesen writes: 'People have understood Origen's concept of body soul and spirit in scripture to mean literal, moral and mystical senses of the Scripture. Therefore each of these meanings should be developed for each verse. However, this rarely occurs in Origen's practice of exegesis' (*Hermeneutical Procedure*, p. 40); and: 'Problems with the threefold distinction have already been noted.

Nowhere does Origen employ it with any kind of consistency. In most of his discussions he refers only to the letter and the spirit' (ibid., p. 41). See also Grant, *Short History*, p. 59: 'In actual practice, however, Origen rarely makes use of the moral sense as distinct from the other senses and he ordinarily distinguishes merely between the "letter" and the "spirit".' Again, concerning the medieval theory of four senses, Grant writes: 'In actual practice, many interpreters limited their investigations to two senses, while some of the most famous medieval exegetes interpreted the Scripture in terms of three. But four came to be regarded as an important number' (ibid.).

24 Maybudī did have access to Tustarī's commentary and could have quoted the same theory but, as we have previously noted, he made no attempt to justify mystical exegesis in the *Kashf al-asrār.*

25 Lory (*Les Commentaires,* pp. 28–9) has traced five levels of meaning in Kāshānī's commentary, while Sanā'ī also alludes to five levels of meaning in his *Ḥadīqat al-ḥaqīqa wa sharīʿat al-ṭarīqa*, ed. J. Stevenson (Calcutta 1910), p. 88 and trans. pp. 148–9; ed. M. Raḍawī (Tehran, 1950), p. 173. In his *Ziyādāt ḥaqā'iq al-tafsīr*, Sulamī cites two other sayings of Jaʿfar al-Ṣādiq (p. 2, paras. 4 and 6), which speak of nine and of seven levels of meaning (*tisʿat awjuh* and *sabʿat anwāʿ*), respectively. See Böwering, 'Scriptural senses', p. 352. On the seven levels of meaning in the *tafsīr* of Simnānī (d. 736/1336) see Henri Corbin, *En Islam Iranien* (Paris, 1971–2), III, ch. 4; idem, *L'Homme de lumière dans le soufisme iranien* (Paris, 1971); trans. by N. Pearson as *Man of Light in Iranian Sufism* (London, 1978), ch. 6.

26 Ghazzālī, *Iḥyā'*, Part 1, Book 8, *Kitāb ādāb tilāwat al-Qur'ān*, ch. 4, p. 383; trans. by M. Abul Quasem as *The Recitation and Interpretation of the Qur'ān: al-Ghazālī's Theory* (Bangi, Malaysia, 1979), pp. 87–8.

27 See Paul Nwyia, 'Un cas d'exégèse soufie: l'histoire de Joseph', in S.H. Nasr, *Mélanges Henri Corbin* (Tehran, 1977), p. 408:

> Selon la diversité des préoccupations, on vit apparaître diverses manières de lire le Coran qui étaient plus ou moins ouvertes sur un pluralisme du sens. Beaucoup de ces lectures étaient essentiellement *utilitaires* (author's emphasis): le grammairien et le philologue scrutaient le Coran au niveau de leurs préoccupations linguistiques; pour le juriste, il était un code où il puisait la solution aux problèmes qui se posait à une communauté transformée, en quelques années en un grand empire; l'historien interrogeait le Coran comme la seule source pour connaître le monde anté-islamique, tandis que, pour le dogmaticien, le Livre d'Allah devenait un arsenal où il puisait des arguments pour étayer ses thèses théologiques. Au niveau de chacune de ces lectures, il ne pouvait y avoir qu'un sense et un sense littéral, car la préoccupation utilitaire ne pouvait guère aller au-delà de ce que révélait la letter.

28 Sarrāj, *Lumaʿ*, p. 107; trans. in Nicholson's summary, ibid., p. 31. Kāshānī presents a similar idea in the introduction to his commentary. See Lory, *Les Commentaires*, p. 14.

29 For a detailed discussion of how various commentators attempted to solve this as well as other theological 'problems' raised by the story of Abraham see Norman Calder, 'Tafsīr from Ṭabarī to Ibn Kathīr: problems in the description of a genre, illustrated with reference to the story of Abraham', in G.R. Hawting

and A.K. Shareef, eds., *Approaches to the Qur'ān* (London and New York, 1993), pp. 101–40. For a discussion of how Jewish exegetes attempted to solve doctrinal problems posed in Exodus, IV, pp. 24–6, see Geza Vermes, *Scripture and Tradition in Judaism* (Leiden, 1961), pp. 178–92. On the doctrines held by different theological schools regarding immunity from error in the prophets see Émile Tyan, "Iṣma', *EI*², IV, pp. 182–4.

30 *Kashf*, III, pp. 403–4.

31 *Kashf*, III, pp. 404–5. See also Ṭabarī, *Jāmiʿ al-bayān*, ed. Shākir and Shākir, XI, pp. 478–88.

32 Ibn Kathīr would not allow any material that was solely based upon the *Isrā'īliyyāt* traditions. See Calder, 'Tafsīr', pp. 120, 121.

33 By means of reasoned opinion (*tafsīr bi'l-ra'y*).

34 Bayḍāwī, *Anwār al-tanzīl*, pp. 296–7.

35 *Kashf*, III, p. 406.

36 A reference to Q. 13:17; 24:35; 29:43.

37 Another example where a verse is given greater contextuality in *Nawbat* II, but universalised in *Nawbat* III, is to be found in *Kashf*, I, pp. 168–9 and p. 178.

38 *Kashf*, I, p. 367. The term *makr* may be defined as an illusion created by God to test the spiritual wayfarer.

39 *Kashf*, III, p. 409.

40 *Kashf*, III, p. 410.

41 *Kashf*, V, p. 474.

42 *Kashf*, I, pp. 253–4.

43 *Kashf*, IV, pp. 120–1.

44 An allusion to the tradition of 'spiritual chivalry' (*futuwwa*) in Sufism. This will be discussed in chapters four and six.

45 *Kashf*, VII, p. 309.

46 *Kashf*, I, p. 351. Maybudī cites the following couplet to illustrate this principle:

You say you are drunk? I'll wager my life you are not
For the real drunk no longer knows what drunkenness is.

Later in the *Sharḥ-i shaṭḥiyyāt*, Rūzbihān Baqlī was to explain the ecstatic utterances of some mystics as being on account of this intoxication of love. See, for example, *Sharḥ-i shaṭḥiyyāt*, pp. 86, 147, where Rūzbihān also attributes sayings of the prophets Moses and Muhammad to intoxication.

47 Maybudī seldom indicates any preference, whereas Ṭabarī frequently does, as, for example, in his commentary on Q. 1:3 and 7, and Q. 2:1, 2, 3, 5, and so on. For a discussion of the criteria which Ṭabarī used in assessing different interpretations see Gilliot, *Exégèse*, especially chs. 6 and 7.

48 As was explained in the statement of Sarrāj quoted pp. 73–4.

49 *Kashf*, I, pp. 253–4.

50 Ibid. Maybudī derives this saying from 'one of the books of God'.

51 Ibid.

52 *Kashf*, I, pp. 242ff. The exoteric commentary here is using *asbāb al-nuzūl* (circumstances of revelation) to explain the verse.

53 That is his love was an extension of his ego, and a manifestation of duality.

54 *Kashf*, IV, pp. 120–1.

55 See p. 74.

56 Nwyia, *Exégèse coranique*, p. 161.

57 Cf. Corbin's explanation of the word *hermenoia* as 'comprendre et faire comprendre' in 'Herméneutique spirituelle comparée, I. Swedenborg - II. Gnose Ismaélienne ', *Eranos-Jahrbuch* (Zurich), 33 (1965), p. 74.

58 *Irshād* appears to be equally the hermeneutic intent of Qushayrī's mystical commentary, as will be noted in the comparative analysis which follows.

59 If we were to draw any parallel with Christian exegetical theory, it might in this case be with Origen's threefold system: Origen has organised the congregation of believers into three groups which simply represent the three distinct phases through which a soul passes on its way to perfection. Origen's principle of interpretation is that there are three levels of meaning (or doctrine) in the Scripture which correspond with the differing spiritual capabilities of each of these three groups. The three different ways of reading the text can be described as three different levels of teaching. The first, the body of the Scripture, is the unexegeted text as it is read in the liturgical service of the Church. The second level, the soul of the Scripture, belongs to the general category of what is edifying. Its distinctive mark is simply that it is for those who have advanced beyond the letter but are not yet ready for the mysteries. The third level, the spirit in the Scripture, means understanding the text as a shadow of the coming blessings. Torjesen, *Hermeneutical Procedure*, p. 40.

60 Again, Maybudī seems to be understanding the word *taʾwīl* here to mean *tafsīr biʾl-raʾy* as opposed to *tafsīr biʾl-maʾthūr*. See p. 44.

61 The word *kashish* is a Sufi technical term, used in Persian as an equivalent to the Arabic word *jadhb*. Its meaning will be discussed in part two.

62 Ḥudhayfa b. al-Yamān al-ʿAbsī (d. 36/656–7), one of the earliest converts to Islam, and narrator of numerous hadiths, was particularly revered by the Sufis. See Massignon, *Essai sur les origines*, pp. 159–61.

63 *Kashf*, VI, pp. 292–3.

64 Nwyia 'Un cas d'exégèse soufie, p. 409.

65 Qushayrī's commentary was selected firstly because among Arabic mystical commentaries it was closest in date to the writing of the *Kashf al-asrār*, and secondly because, having been written some fifty to seventy years earlier than the *Kashf al-asrār*, it could be said to represent the Khorasani 'school' of Sufism at an earlier date.

66 Wansbrough, *Quranic Studies*, pp. 167–70; idem, 'Majāz al-Qurʾān: periphrastic exegesis', *BSOAS* 33 (1970), pp. 247–66.

67 Lory explains how Kāshānī uses this method, which he terms *taṭbīq*, when he interprets historical events related in the Qur'an as an allusion to spiritual states in the microcosm. See Lory, *Les Commentaires*, pp. 31–3.

68 Qushayrī, *Laṭāʾif al-ishārāt*, ed. I. Basyūnī (3 vols., Cairo, 1968–71), I, p. 60.

69 *Kashf*, I, p. 74.

70 Trans. amended on the basis of Abdel Haleem's translation.

71 *Laṭāʾif*, I, p. 70.

72 The hadith is quoted in the *Nawbat* II commentary on this verse: 'Whosoever died in the religion of Jesus, or in a state of submission (*fiʾl-islām*) before hearing me, it is well for him, and whosoever heard me today and did not believe in me will be destroyed' (*Kashf*, I, p. 214). This hadith is cited on the authority of Salmān al-Fārisī by Ṭabarī in his commentary on the same verse (Q. 2:62). See *Jāmiʿ al-bayān*, ed. Shākir and Shākir, II, p. 155.

73 *Kashf*, I, p. 218.
74 *Kashf*, IX, p. 421.
75 *Kashf*, I, p. 430.
76 *Kashf*, VIII, p. 234; or the moon, the Prophet, *Kashf*, II, p. 393; or, according to Qushayrī, the stars representing knowledge, the moon presence [with God], and the sun, gnosis. *Laṭā'if*, I, p. 116.
77 *Kashf*, I, 209.
78 *Kashf*, I, p. 211. Neither Qushayrī nor Maybudī appear to have developed any coherent system of symbols like Kāshānī, in whose commentary the sun consistently refers to the spirit, and the moon the heart. See Lory, *Les Commentaries*, pp. 39–43.
79 Hava Lazarus-Yafeh, 'Are there allegories in Sufi Qur'ān interpretation?' in McAuliffe *et al.*, eds., *With Reverence for the Word*, pp. 366–75. However, Lazarus-Yafeh's hypothesis, presented in the same article, that avoidance of 'full-fledged' allegories by the Sufis may be related to the Muslim prohibition of representational art is more difficult to accept. Moreover, her assertion that in Sufi literature in general, 'full-fledged allegories do exist but are rather rare' and that full-fledged allegories 'really only flourish in modern Arabic literature, apparently under Western influence' seems to indicate unfamiliarity with a plethora of Sufi works in Persian. The reason for this absence of 'full-fledged' or extended allegories in Sufi commentaries is, I would suggest, not a deliberate avoidance on the part of the Sufi commentators, but rather because by its very nature early Sufi exegesis proceeded from spontaneous and inspired responses to recited passages of the Qur'an, rather than the systematic application of the faculty of reason – indeed, as was discussed above, the rational faculty of itself was frowned upon as a means for eliciting the inner meanings of the Qur'an.
80 ʿAbd al-Razzāq al-Kāshānī, *Tafsīr al-Qur'ān al-karīm*, also known as *Ta'wīlāt al-Qur'ān,* and popularly and erroneously known as the *Tafsīr Ibn ʿArabī* (2 vols., Beirut, 1968); reprinted under the latter title and edited by ʿA.M. ʿAlī (Beirut, 2001). One of the best examples is Kāshānī's commentary on the twelfth sura of the Qur'an, where the entire story of Joseph has been interpreted as an allegory of the purification of the heart in its journey towards the One, with each character symbolising part of the human microcosm, for example, Joseph the Heart, Jacob the Intellect (*ʿaql*), and so on.
81 On Ismaili *ta'wīl* see Corbin, 'Herméneutique spirituelle comparée, I. Swedenborg - II. Gnose Ismaélienne'; Ismail Poonawala, 'Ismāʿīlī *ta'wīl* of the Qur'ān', in Rippin, *Approaches*, pp. 199–222; Anton M. Heinen, 'The notion of *ta'wīl* in Abū Yaʿqūb al-Sijistānī's *Book of Sources (Kitāb al-manābīʿ)*', *Hamdard Islamicus* 2/1 (1979), pp. 35–46; Hamid Haji, *A Distinguished Dāʿī under the Shade of the Fāṭimids: Ḥamīd al-Dīn al-Kirmānī (d. c. 411/1020) and His Epistles* (London, 1998).
82 See *The Shorter Oxford Dictionary*, 5th edn (Oxford, 2002), under the second definition of allegory.
83 *Kashf*, I, p. 520.
84 *Kashf*, I, p. 210.
85 *Kashf*, I, pp. 267–8.
86 *Kashf*, I, p. 197. Abdel Haleem's translation reads: 'Kill [the guilty] among you',

but Maybudī, in his *Nawbat* I, renders *fa'qtulū anfusakum* as: *khwīshtan-rā ba-kushīd* (Kill yourselves).

87 *Laṭā'if*, I, p. 111.
88 *Kashf*, V, pp. 669–70.
89 *Kashf*, V, p. 670.
90 *Laṭā'if*, I, p. 74. *Takhṣīṣ* (specifying) is one of the terms used in exoteric interpretation. See Wansbrough, *Quranic Studies*, p. 191.
91 *Laṭā'if*, I, p. 120.
92 *Irāda*. On this neologism see Timothy J. Winter, *Al-Ghazālī on Disciplining the Soul and on Breaking the Two Desires* (Cambridge, 1995), p. 84, n. A.
93 *Laṭā'if*, I, p. 65.
94 *Laṭā'if*, I, p. 66.
95 *Laṭā'if*, I, p. 65. It might be argued that this interpretation is allegorical. However the difference is that the *outward* meaning of the verse is here allegorical, whereas those interpretations which we have termed allegorical occur when the outward meaning of the verses is not (obviously) allegorical.
96 *Kashf*, I, p. 95.
97 *Laṭā'if*, I, p. 55.
98 Ibid.
99 *Kashf*, I, p. 317.
100 *Laṭā'if*, I, pp. 61–2.
101 *Kashf*, I, p. 267.
102 Trans. Abdel Haleem.
103 *Kashf*, I, p. 177. See also *Kashf*, I, p. 129, three kinds of life and three kinds of death; *Kashf*, I, p. 127, different levels of diffidence (*ḥayā'*); and *Kashf*, II, p. 238, three kinds of *taqwā*. We may detect in Maybudī's propensity for this method an echo of the structure of Anṣārī's *Manāzil al-sā'irīn* (ed. with intro. and French trans. S. de Laugier de Beaurecueil [Cairo, 1962]) in which each station is systematically broken down into three levels, each of which is then broken down into three further levels. Maybudī's application of this classification of states will be discussed further in part two of this book. On the use of this tripartite systematisation by the earlier Ḥanbalī mystic, Abū Manṣūr al-Iṣfahānī (d. 418/1027), see Abū Manṣūr Muʿammar al-Iṣfahānī, *Kitāb nahj al-khāṣṣ*, ed. with French intro. S. de Beaurecueil in ʿA. Badawī, ed., *Mélanges Taha Husain* (Cairo, 1962); ed. with Persian intro. N. Pourjavady, *Taḥqīqāt-i Islāmī* 3/1–2 (1988–9), pp. 94–149, in particular the editor's introduction, pp. 127–8.
104 *Laṭā'if*, I, p. 107.
105 The attribution of comments to God appears to be a characteristic feature of Sufi exegesis. See, for example, the comments of Abū Saʿīd Kharrāz and Abū Saʿīd al-Qurashī on Q. 12:83 and 84, Sulamī, *Ḥaqā'iq*, MS Or 9433, fols. 123a and 123b (ʿImrān's edition does not include *Sūrat Yūsuf*). Further examples from the *Kashf al-asrār* will be seen later in this book.
106 *Kashf*, I, p. 352.
107 Trans. Abdel Haleem.
108 *Laṭā'if*, I, pp. 70–1.
109 *Laṭā'if*, I, p. 75.
110 *Kashf*, I, p. 342.
111 *Laṭā'if*, I, p. 135; *Kashf*, I, pp. 404–5.

112 *Laṭā'if*, I, p. 68.
113 *Kashf*, I, p. 113.
114 *Kashf*, I, pp. 219 and 563; *Laṭā'if*, I, p. 80.
115 *Kashf*, I, pp. 208–9, 662.
116 *Laṭā'if*, I, p. 70; *Kashf*, I, p. 115.
117 *Kashf*, I, p. 219, and Maybudī's comment on the following verse.
118 Böwering has coined the term 'keynote' for a word or phrase which, irrespective of its Qur'anic context, sets off particular associations in the mind of the mystic. See *Mystical Vision*, p. 136.
119 *Kashf*, I, pp. 239–40. Those with hardened hearts are usually interpreted as those who were resistant to the words of the Qur'an, as for example in Qushayrī's *Laṭā'if*, I, p. 100, whom Maybudī in his *Nawbat* II commentary (*Kashf*, I, p. 233) specifies as being the Jews.
120 *Kashf*, I, pp. 254–5.
121 *Kashf*, I, p. 254.
122 *Kashf*, I, pp. 57, 175, 196.
123 *Kashf*, I, pp. 92–3.
124 *Kashf*, I, p. 301.
125 *Kashf*, I, p. 113. Other examples of this form of digression are: *Kashf*, I, p. 58, from *hudā*, to *firāsa*, to *mukāshafa*, to the nature of heart and soul; *Kashf*, I, p. 625, from divorce, to God's being the joiner of opposites and disliking separation, to the pain of separation; and *Kashf*, I, pp. 639–40, from the recommendation that mothers should suckle their children for two years, to God's kindness and mercy being even greater than that of mothers, to God's mercy at the Resurrection.
126 For example, *Kashf*, I, p. 352.
127 For example, *Kashf*, I, p. 278.
128 For example, *Laṭā'if*, I, p. 75.
129 Out of the verses discussed in *Nawbat* II (numbering anywhere between three and fifty), Maybudī comments on no more than ten, but often as few as two or three verses in *Nawbat* III (see also pp. 19–20).
130 Meisami has rightly pointed out that in artistic prose 'verse insertions are no mere extraneous embellishments, as is often thought, but are integral to many works'. See Julie Scott Meisami, 'Mixed prose and verse in medieval Persian literature', in J. Harris and K. Reichl, eds., *Prosimetrum: Cross-Cultural Perspectives on Narrative in Prose and Verse* (Woodbridge, 1997), p. 297.
131 That is, the world of pre-existence before the material world had come into being.
132 *Kashf*, I, pp. 139–40.
133 *Kashf*, VI, p. 492.
134 Perhaps a reference to the 'Sleepers in the Cave'? I have rendered *jawānmardān* (lit. young men, i.e. proponents of spiritual chivalry) as 'noble ones'. This term will be explained in chapter seven.
135 *Kashf*, I, p. 53.
136 *Kashf*, I, p. 75.
137 *Kashf*, 1, p. 331. This passage is followed by the well-known hadith, known as 'the hadith of supererogatory works' (*ḥadīth al-nawāfil*), for which it acts as a form of interpretation. The relevant part of the hadith reads: My servant

continues to draw near to Me with supererogatory works so that I shall I love him. When I love him I am his hearing with which he hears, his seeing with which he sees, his hand with which he strikes and his foot with which he walks. Were he to ask [something] of Me, I would surely give it to him, and were he to ask Me for refuge, I would surely grant it to him. The hadith is listed in Bukhārī, *Ṣaḥīḥ*, *Kitāb al-riqāq*, ch. 38 (al-Tawāḍuʿ), no. 2, § 6502, and is included in *An-Nawawī's Forty Ḥadīth*, Arabic text and trans. E. Ibrahim and D. Johnson-Davies (5th repr., Lebanon, 1980), no. 38. The hadith appears in a shorter version in Ibn Ḥanbal's *Al-Musnad* (Cairo, 1895), VI, p. 256, where it goes from 'so that I love him' straight to 'were he to ask something of Me'.

138 *Kashf*, I, p. 209.

139 Stories, poetry and rhyming prose were all elements in common use in the sermonising of the popular preacher. See Johannes Pedersen, 'The Islamic preacher: *wāʿiẓ*, *mudhakkir*, *qāṣṣ*', in S. Löwinger and J. Somogyi, eds., *Ignace Goldziher Memorial Volume* (2 vols., Budapest, 1948).

PART TWO

MYSTICAL DOCTRINE

4

The development of love mysticism in Khorasan

We have established that Maybudī in all likelihood travelled to Khorasan, or if not, he was certainly influenced by and drew on sources written by Khorasani mystics. We also know that his spiritual master lived and left his legacy in the Khorasani city of Herat. Thus, although the background to Sufism in the sixth/twelfth century has to some extent been discussed in chapter one, it is appropriate to discuss the spiritual background of this region, and the emergence of love mysticism there, before looking at Maybudī's place in that development.

The region of Khorasan, which until this century encompassed Eastern Iran, Transoxiana and much of present-day Afghanistan, came to be known as the land whose product is saints because of the number of mystics and sages who had been born there. These included some of the most famous and influential figures in the history of Sufism, representing many different approaches to the mystical way.[1] Among these, some of the best known are: Ibrāhīm b. Adham (d. *c.* 165/782), who was known for his poverty and asceticism;[2] al-Ḥakīm al-Tirmidhī (d. late third/ninth century), who represented a more theosophical form of mysticism;[3] Abū Yazīd Bisṭāmī (d. 261/874 or 264/877–8), commonly known in the Persian-speaking world as Bāyazīd[4] and famed for his controversial ecstatic utterances (*shaṭḥiyyāt*); Abu'l-Qāsim al-Qushayrī who was both a scholar and theologian, and known for a more more cautious approach to Sufism; the illiterate and reclusive Abu'l-Ḥasan Kharaqānī (d. 425/1033) who was one of the the most influential mystics of Khorasan;[5] the more popular and public figure of Abū Sa'īd ibn Abi'l-Khayr (d. 440/1049);[6] and Aḥmad Ghazzālī, who developed and expounded the doctrines of love mysticism.[7]

This diversity was also to be seen in a number of ascetic and mystical trends and movements which took root in Khorasan from the third/ninth century on. These included the popular and highly organised Karrāmiyya, founded by Abū ʿAbd Allāh b. Karrām (d. 260/873), and known for its ostentatious asceticism and active proselytisation;[8] the more introverted Malāmatiyya or 'way of blame', which insisted that spiritual states and stations should be concealed from others and is said to have been founded by Ḥamdūn Qaṣṣār (d. 271/884);[9] and the *futuwwa* (literally young manliness – in Persian *jawānmardī*), the pursuit of a code of chivalry for spiritual ends, one of the earliest proponents of which is said to have been Fuḍayl b. ʿIyāḍ (d. 187/803), known as the 'Shaykh of the *fityān*'.[10]

During the second/eighth and third/ninth centuries, the term *ṣūfī* was usually applied to mystics of Iraq, particularly of the Baghdad school, or to those who had trained there and then migrated elsewhere such as Abū Bakr al-Wāsiṭī (d. after 320/932).[11] In Khorasan, however, the term *ṣūfī* did not gain currency until the fourth/tenth and fifth/eleventh centuries.[12] The gradual eclipse of other mystical and ascetic movements in Eastern Iran by Sufism has been linked to the spread of the Shāfiʿī school of law, the decline of the Karrāmiyya, and the move towards a greater organisation and structure within Sufism.[13] A part of the latter process was the writing of Sufi manuals and biographies, such as the *Kitāb al-lumaʿ* of Sarrāj, the *Kitāb al-taʿarruf* of Abū Bakr al-Kalābādhī (d. 390/1000), the *Ṭabaqāt al-ṣūfiyya* of Sulamī, the *Risāla* of Qushayrī, and the *Kashf al-maḥjūb* of ʿAlī b. ʿUthmān Jullābī Hujwīrī (d. 469/1097). As noted earlier, all of these works sought to defend the religious legitimacy of Sufism and to establish it as the mainstream over and against other mystical movements, or any antinomian tendencies that were in circulation. They also served to promote the teachings of the school of Baghdad.[14] Sulamī, who was spiritually linked both to Iraq and, through his maternal uncle, to the Malāmatiyya, sought to bring together the teachings of the schools of Baghdad and Khorasan.[15] He wrote treatises on *malāmatiyya* and *futuwwa*, while his disciple, Qushayrī, included a section on *futuwwa* in his *Risāla*.[16] By the late fifth/eleventh century many of the teachings of *malāmatiyya* and *futuwwa* had been integrated into the mainstream of mystical doctrine.[17] We shall see evidence of this in the mystical doctrines of the *Kashf al-asrār*.

During the second half of the fifth/eleventh and the first half of the sixth/twelfth centuries, probably the most significant development to take place in the Sufism of Khorasan was the evolution and coming to the fore of the mystical doctrines of love. This was accompanied by the emergence of Persian as a language for mystical discourse.[18]

Love always had a place in Islamic mysticism and could be sanctioned by words from the Qur'an itself, such as 'He loves them and they love Him' (Q. 5:54) and 'Say, if you love God, follow me; God will love you and forgive you your sins' (Q. 3:31). The doctrines of love among Muslim mystics may be traced back as far as the second/eighth and third/ninth centuries. Abū Nuʿaym, for example, attributes an early treatise on love to Ḥārith al-Muḥāsibī (d. 243/857).[19] The famous prayer associated with Rābiʿa al-ʿAdawiyya (d. 185/801) and quoted in the biographical work of ʿAṭṭār, exemplified the ideal of a pure, disinterested love of God:

> O my Lord, if I worship Thee from fear of Hell, burn me in Hell, and if I worship Thee from hope of Paradise, exclude me from thence, but if I worship Thee for thine own sake, then withhold not from me Thine Eternal beauty.[20]

After Rābiʿa and Muḥāsibī, other Sufis emphasized he importance of love. Abu'l-Ḥusayn al-Nūrī (d. 295/907) called himself *ʿāshiq* (lover), and numerous sayings about the love of God are attributed to him.[21] Hujwīrī refers to a tract on love, the *Kitāb al-maḥabba* of ʿAmr b. ʿUthmān al-Makkī (d. 297/910) and a treatise by Sumnūn al-Muḥibb (d. 300/913), in which all the stations of the mystical path are described in terms of love.[22] Ḥallāj (d. 309/922) was apparently the first Muslim mystic to have openly expressed in his writings the idea of a relationship of love with God which involved union.[23] Yet, even before Ḥallāj, some of the ecstatic utterances attributed to Bāyazīd Bisṭāmī certainly speak of the states of union and intoxication which he experienced in his love of God.[24] The philosopher/mystic Abu'l-Ḥasan ʿAlī al-Daylamī (fl. 400/1000), a disciple of Ibn Khafīf al-Shīrāzī (d. 371/982), wrote a substantial treatise on love, the *ʿAṭf al-alif al-ma'lūf ʿala'l-lām al-maʿṭūf*, which is a compendium of the views of mystics and philosophers on love.[25] For the most part, though, Sufi writers remained conservative about the place of love, and Sufi manuals contain no more than a chapter on the subject.[26]

Nevertheless, it appears that the ecstatic tradition of love and intoxication that had been associated with Bāyazīd was continuing in Khorasan. Hujwīrī contrasts the way of rapture (*ghalabāt*) and intoxication (*sukr*) of the followers of Bāyazīd (the Ṭayfūrīs), with the, in his view, superior way of sobriety (*ṣaḥw*) practised by the followers of al-Junayd al-Baghdādī (d. 298/910) (the Junaydīs).[27] Moreover, there is evidence to show that by the mid-fifth/eleventh century love was playing a more prominent role in the ritual practices of Sufism. The biography of Abū Saʿīd b. Abi'l-Khayr relates how, as a child, he had attended a gathering for spiritual recital (*samāʿ*) at which the words of a certain poem were repeatedly chanted until all present fell into a state of ecstasy. The poem reads as follows:

Love's affliction is the gift for the dervishes,
For them, friendship is their killing of the self.
The dignity of men is not in dirhams and dinars,
The way of noblemen is to sacrifice their lives.[28]

This poem is clearly describing the suffering and sacrifice of mystical love (here, *ʿishq*). But among some Sufis it had become customary to recite secular poetry about love and wine-drinking at such gatherings.[29] In his chapter on *samāʿ*, Hujwīrī takes issue with those Sufis who spend all their time 'listening to love-songs (*ghazal*) and descriptions of the face and hair and mole of the beloved'.[30] Abū Saʿīd is said to have included such poems in his sermons, and to have interpreted them in the light of his mystical experience.[31] By the turn of the sixth/twelfth century, the reciting of secular love poetry at *samāʿ* gatherings had become widespread enough for Abū Ḥāmid al-Ghazzālī to issue a *fatwā* authorising its permissibility under certain conditions, both in the *Iḥyāʾ*, and in the *Kīmiyā-yi saʿādat*.[32] He also wrote substantial chapters on love in both of these works, stressing its importance.[33]

By the early sixth/twelfth century, it can be said that the doctrine of love had become more fully established in the Sufism of Khorasan. Aḥmad Ghazzālī (d. 520/1126) had written a treatise in Persian, the *Sawāniḥ*, in which the entire mystical journey is described as a journey of love; the poet Sanāʾī was composing *ghazal*s about mystical love; and Maybudī was able to write a commentary on the Qur'an which included references to Laylī and Majnūn, and to Sultan Maḥmūd's love for Ayāz, and which defined the Qur'an itself as 'an epistle whose title is eternal love (*mihr-i qadīm*), and whose content is the story of love and lovers'.[34]

The emergence of the doctrines of love in Khorasani Sufism should perhaps be understood as a movement rather than a 'school',[35] for it embraced different interpretations of the concept of love and distinct approaches to the mystical path. Aḥmad Ghazzālī's *Sawāniḥ*, for example, is a metaphysical treatise in which love is understood as the Absolute in which ultimately both the lover and the Beloved are subsumed.[36] In the poetry of Sanā'ī, the theme of mystical love which is presented in his *ghazals* is offset by the sermonising on *zuhd*,[37] which features in many of his *qaṣīdas*.[28] While, as has been noted, love had a place in the doctrines of Abū Sa'īd, the predominant teaching which echoes through the numerous sayings collected in his biography is the need for humility, sincerity, and freedom from the self.[39]

In Maybudī's *Kashf al-asrār*, the doctrine of love is situated between two important theological principles: the doctrine of *taqdīr* (or *qaḍā'*) which teaches that everything is pre-ordained by God, and that all man's actions are created by Him,[40] and the doctrine which insists on the limits of rational knowledge, that whatever is received from the Book and the Sunna is to be accepted without question (*bi-lā kayf*) and must not be interpreted metaphorically. The following section will briefly discuss the way in which the mystical aspect of these two theological doctrines are associated with doctrine of love in the teachings of Maybudī, and the relationship which these have with the heritage of Anṣārī. This overview will provide a necessary background for the more detailed exposition of the mystical teachings of Maybudī which is to follow.

Maybudī's love mysticism and the heritage of Anṣārī

Chapters one and two presented two fundamental teachings of the *Kashf al-asrār*. The first insisted on adherence to the traditionalist dogma of the *ahl-i sunnat wa jamā'at*, and the second asserted the necessary interdependence of the outward law (*sharī'at*) and mystical realisation (*ḥaqīqat*).[41] A closer investigation of the mystical sections of the *Kashf al-asrār* reveals that theological doctrine also has its inner dimension and mystical aspect. Moreover, just as the observance and practice of the *sharī'a* is seen as the *sine qua non* for inner realisation, so too, acceptance of the creed (*'aqīda*) is understood as an essential pre-requisite for the attainment of mystical truth. Maybudī says, therefore, that the servant should be

> Sunnī in his belief (*ʿaqīdat*), pure in his conduct (*sīrat*), and virtuous in his way (*ṭarīqat*). From here opens the spring of wisdom, the truth of spiritual insight (lit. physiognomy, *firāsat*) and the light of gnosis (*maʿrifat*).[42]

While elsewhere he states:

> the noble ones of the way and wayfarers on the path of truth, are those whose hearts God kept pure of desires and innovation [...], who accepted what they heard, and went the way of acquiescence (*taslīm*), so that they escaped both from negating the divine attributes (*taʿṭīl*) and from anthropomorphism (*tashbīh*). They purified their hearts from the world and its contamination, until the light of gnosis shone in their hearts, and the springs of wisdom opened within them.[43]

In the *Kashf al-asrār*, the esoteric dimensions of two theological doctrines in particular are integrally linked both to each other and to the doctrine of love. The first of these is the doctrine of God's preordination and determination of things, denoted in Arabic by the terms *qaḍāʾ*, *qadar* and, more often in Maybudī's commentary, by the word *taqdīr*, which indicates God's 'implementation' or 'activation' of His eternally decreed destiny or portion for each person in time. Understood mystically, the doctrine of *taqdīr* teaches that however much the aspirant strives, he will only reach his goal by the intervention of divine grace. The second of the two doctrines is the doctrine of the limits of rational knowledge. This doctrine allows that God can only be known through gnosis (*maʿrifat*), which is not attained by mental effort but 'found' by the grace of unveiling (*mukāshafat*). Hence God is *nā daryāfta yāfta*, 'found yet uncomprehended'.[44] Such unveiling only takes place when the servant is rid of his own 'I', but this, again, only occurs by divine intervention.

If, in Maybudī's view, the servant may not approach God by way of knowledge, there can and should be no limit to his love and longing for God. If God chooses not to favour His servant with His grace, then his sense of longing and need will be increased. The pain which the lover suffers in separation from the Beloved is seen as a purifying fire which rids him of attachment to everything other than God. Naturally, the lover longs for union with the Beloved, but, again, this may only be attained by divine intervention, when the servant is delivered from his own "I" – that is, when he is brought to annihilation from himself (*fanāʾ*) and subsisting in God (*baqāʾ*).

These doctrines were not, of course, new to Sufism.[45] However, their constant reiteration and emphasis in the *Kashf al-asrār* shows their centrality to Maybudī's thinking. To what extent can this be said to represent a continuation or development of the teachings of Anṣārī? Given the uncertainty which exists concerning the authenticity of much of the corpus of works ascribed to Khwāja ʿAbd Allāh, and especially his Persian works, it is difficult to construct a reliable picture of his mystical doctrines.[46] Moreover, even if we accept the *Ṣad maydān* (Hundred Grounds) to be among those works which have 'a clearly defined connection' with Anṣārī,[47] several inconsistencies exist between this work and his two Arabic works on the same subject, the *Manāzil al-sāʾirīn* (Stages of the Wayfarers) and *ʿIlal al-maqāmāt* (Deficiencies of the Stations).[48] This divergence is particularly significant with regard to the place accorded to love in the teachings of Anṣārī. In the *Manāzil*, love is defined as the sixty-first station, the first in the category of mystical states (*aḥwāl*) and is defined as the point of transition between the level of the *ʿāmm*, and that of the *khāṣṣ*.[49] In the *ʿIlal*, love is not included among the stations of the *khawaṣṣ*.[50] In the *Ṣad maydān*, however, love is placed beyond the other stations, and is said to encompass them all.[51]

De Beaurecueil has proposed two possible reasons for this difference. The first is that the *Ṣad maydān* is a much earlier work and represents a preliminary sketch, as it were, for the much later *Manāzil al-sāʾirīn*.[52] The second is that in his later works Anṣārī wished to place more emphasis on the annihilation of self (*fanāʾ*); the 'deficiency' in the station of love was that it implied the continuing existence of the lover.[53] However, Bell has rightly observed that the third and highest degree of love defined by Anṣārī in both the *Ṣad maydān* and the *Manāzil* is equivalent to 'an ineffable state of *fanāʾ*'.[54] Another possible reason for discrepancies between the two works may be deduced from de Beaurecueil's observation that Anṣārī's Arabic works were more formal compositions intended for wider circulation, whereas his compositions in Persian were intended only for the more intimate circle of his immediate disciples.[55] We have, in effect, a twofold heritage of *Anṣāriyyāt*: on the one hand, his more formal and precise compositions in Arabic which were written down and in some cases authenticated with an *ijāza*; [56] on the other, his less formal teachings and prayers in Persian, which were preserved either in the notes or memories of his disciples.

The *Kashf al-asrār* certainly affirms the existence of this latter 'oral' (or semi-oral) tradition of Anṣārī's teachings. Although Maybudī may well have had access to Anṣārī's written works, citations of the master in the *tafsīr* are consistently preceded by the words *Pīr-i ṭarīqat guft*.[57] Since Maybudī was compiling his *tafsīr* within forty years of Khwāja ʿAbd Allāh's death, the diverse collection of Anṣārī's sayings assembled in the *Kashf al-asrār* could certainly add some authentic data to our knowledge of Anṣārī's mystical doctrines.[58] Maybudī undoubtedly regarded him as his authority on spiritual as well as theological matters, and quotations of Anṣārī are usually strategically placed as pithy or eloquent encapsulations of the subject under discussion. Hence, many of the mystical doctrines presented in the *Kashf al-asrār* are to be found echoed in some form in sayings of Anṣārī. For example, relating to the mystical understanding of *taqdīr* (or *qaḍāʾ*), we find two themes which recur in a number of his sayings. The first is the intense feeling of fear and helplessness at what God has pre-ordained:

> Ah, the fate that has gone before me! Alas, for what the self-willed (*khwadraʾī*) has already decreed. What use is it if I live in joy or distraction (*āshufta*)? I am in fear of what the Omnipotent has said in pre-eternity.[59]

Another is the belief in the role of divine intervention in the mystical path:

> O Lord! You know why I am happy? Because I did not find You by myself. Lord, You willed it not me. I found the beloved at my bedside when I awoke.[60]

The doctrine which insists on the limits of knowledge, and that only God can truly know Himself, is also represented in sayings of Anṣārī. For example, concerning a disagreement between Naṣrābādī[61] and Shāh[62] on whether or not it is possible to know God, Anṣārī is quoted as saying:

> Both are right. He who says it is not possible to know Him, is referring to the knowledge (*maʿrifat*) of the reality of God (*ḥaqīqat-i Ḥaqq*) to which no one has access, except that He in reality knows Himself. He who says it is possible to know God is referring to the knowledge of the commonalty (*ʿāmm*), that there is no God but He, Who has no partner [...].[63]

Likewise, on the subject of love and its centrality to the spiritual path numerous quotations of Anṣārī can be cited. For example he explains that

> Acquiescence (*riḍā'*) is the sign of finding the response to love (*dūstī*). Faithfulness brings freshness to love. Love's treasure is all light, the fruit of the love's tree is all joy [...].[64]

In another context Anṣārī relates a contest between sight or vision (*dīdār*)[65] and love (*mihr*) in which each tries to prove its superiority. Anṣārī's conclusion is clear:

> Sight is the share of the one who knows Him by created things (*ṣanā'i'*) and reaches Him through them [...] Love is the share of the one who knows Him by Him. The latter comes from Him to created things, not from created things to Him.[66]

Concerning the purifying fire of love, which will be discussed in detail later, the following is quoted from Anṣārī:

> Every fire burns the flesh, but the fire of love burns the soul. That soul-burning fire is unbearable.[67]

From this it would appear that doctrines which are central to the *Kashf al-asrār* formed part, at least, of the oral tradition of Anṣārī's teachings. Corroboration of the first two of these doctrines can be found in the *Manāzil*,[68] while parallels for all three can be seen in the *Ṣad maydān*.[69] The doctrines may be further corroborated by what is known historically about Anṣārī's preoccupation with the traditionalist beliefs of the Ḥanbalī school.[70] However, all these doctrines appear only in seminal form in quotations which Maybudī cites from Anṣārī. In the overall text of the *Kashf al-asrār*, they are substantially expanded and developed. That which is expressed in characteristically terse and elliptical style by Anṣārī, is unhurredly explained and illustrated by Maybudī, while scattered and fragmentary themes of Anṣārī's meditations and prayers are integrated into a doctrine which is for the most part consistently sustained throughout Maybudī's mystical commentary. Moreover, Anṣārī is by no means the only authority cited by Maybudī; in order to elucidate and endorse these doctrines he draws upon the entire heritage of Sufism, quoting masters of every 'school', including, for example, al-Ḥasan al-Baṣrī, Junayd, Ḥallāj and Bāyazīd.[71] In so doing, Maybudī gives his teachings a stamp of universality which takes them beyond the realm of a specifically 'Anṣārī' tradition.

Perhaps the most significant development in the *Kashf al-asrār*, when compared to the teachings of Anṣārī, is in the doctrine of love and the way it is expressed. A concrete example of the latter is the use of the word *ʿishq*. Anṣārī, when speaking of love, employs either the Arabic word *maḥabba* or the Persian words *dūstī* and *mihr*.[72] The word *ʿishq* (or its cognate derivatives *ʿāshiq* and *maʿshūq*) is never used in either the *Manāzil* or *Ṣad maydān*, and it appears in only three of the *munājāt* attributed to Anṣārī that are quoted in the *Kashf al-asrār*. Anṣārī's caution concerning the use of the word *ʿishq* may have been because the Ḥanbalī school disapproved of the use of that word to describe man's love for God,[73] or it may be that more generally, during the fifth/eleventh century, the use of the word *ʿishq* was still controversial.[74] Whereas the word *maḥabba*, implying either God's love for man or man's love for God, had its precedent in the Qur'an (for example in Q. 5:54 and Q. 3:31), the word *ʿishq* originally had either the sense of the love experienced between creatures (human beings), or an excessive love.[75] The word *ʿishq* was widely used in Persian secular love poetry, and must have been used at *samāʿ* gatherings where such poetry was chanted,[76] but was used only in a limited sense in Sufi treatises. The word really only gained currency in Sufi writings in the early sixth/twelfth century, when the doctrine of love was being more openly promulgated. Perhaps the two Ghazzālī brothers contributed to the establishment of the word *ʿishq* in Sufism. In the *Iḥyāʾ*, Abū Ḥāmid al-Ghazzālī employs the word for the love of God,[77] while in the *Sawāniḥ*, Aḥmad Ghazzālī uses the two words *maḥabbat* and *ʿishq* interchangeably and, more significantly, uses the word *ʿishq* both for man's love for God, and for God's love for man.[78]

Maybudī has no hesitation in using the word *ʿishq*, applying it to the mystic's love for God, to the Prophet's love for God,[79] and even to God's love for man.[80] Like Aḥmad Ghazzālī, Maybudī illustrates the theme of love with numerous poems and allegories, and he interprets numerous passages of the Qur'an in the light of the doctrine of love. In fact, while uncertainty remains over the place of love in the teachings of Khwāja ʿAbd Allāh, there can be no doubt about its importance for Maybudī. In the following chapters, we shall see that love is not only central to his interpretation of God's creation of the universe and of man, the fall of Adam, the covenant of *alast*, and the *miʿrāj* of the Prophet Muhammad, but also to his doctrine of the way of man's return to God.

NOTES

1 The 'myth' that mystics of the East were proponents of the way of intoxication (*sukr*) while those of Baghdad preferred the way of sobriety (*ṣaḥw*) is, in fact, an oversimplification based on a statement of Hujwīrī regarding the followers of Abū Yazīd and Junayd, see n. 27. See Terry Graham, 'Abū Saʿīd ibn Abi'l-Khayr and the School of Khurāsān', in L. Lewisohn, ed., *Classical Persian Sufism*, pp. 107ff; Javid Mojaddedi, *The Biographical Tradition in Sufism* (London, 2001), pp. 133–4.

2 On Ibrāhīm Adham see Richard Gramlich, *Alte Vorbilder des Sufitums* (Wiesbaden, 1995–6), I, pp. 135–282.

3 On the life and works of Tirmidhī see Bernd Radtke, *Al-Ḥakīm at-Tirmiḏī: ein islamischer Theosoph des 3./9. [i.e. 8./9.] Jahrhunderts* (Freiburg, 1980); Bernd Radtke and John O'Kane, *The Concept of Sainthood in Early Islamic Mysticism: Two Works by al-Ḥakīm al-Tirmiḏhī*, annotated trans. with intro. (Richmond, 1996); Sara Sviri, 'Words of power and the power of words: mystical linguistics in the works of al-Ḥakīm al-Tirmidhī', *Jerusalem Studies in Arabic and Islam* 27 (2002), pp. 204–44.

4 The sayings of Abū Yazīd Bisṭāmī have been published in ʿAbd al-Raḥmān Badawī, *Shaṭaḥāt al-ṣūfiyya* (Cairo, 1949). A selection of these has been translated into French by Abdelwahab Meddeb as *Les dits de Bistami: Shatahât* (Paris 1989). On Bisṭāmī see also Muhammad Abdur Rabb, *The Life, Thought and Historical Importance of Abū Yazīd al-Bisṭāmī* (Dacca, 1971); Roger Deladrière, 'Abū Yazīd al-Bisṭāmī et son enseignment spirituelle', *Arabica* 14 (1967), pp. 76–89; Annabel Keeler, 'Bāyazīd Bisṭāmī', in M.R. Isfandyār, ed., *Āshnāyān-i rah-i ʿishq* (Tehran, 2006), pp. 45–74.

5 The earliest primary source for the sayings of Kharaqānī is the anonymous *Nūr al-ʿulūm*, ed. Mujtabā Mīnuwī (Tehran, 1980). Sayings of Kharaqānī from the *Nūr al-ʿulūm* and ʿAṭṭār's *Tadhkirat al-awliyā'* have been translated into French by Christianne Tortel in her *Paroles d'un soufi* (Paris, 1998).

6 The biography and teachings of Abū Saʿīd were preserved in the late sixth/twelfth century by his descendant Ibn al-Munawwar in the *Asrār al-tawḥīd*.

7 On Aḥmad Ghazzālī see Nasrollah Pourjavady, *Sulṭān-i ṭarīqat* (Tehran, 1358sh/1980); idem, *ʿAyn al-Quḍāt wa ustādān-i ū* (Tehran, 1374sh/1995); idem, 'Aḥmad Ġazālī', *EI*[r], X, pp. 377–80.

8 On the Karrāmiyya see Clifford E. Bosworth, 'Karrāmiyya', *EI*[2], IV, pp. 667–9; idem, 'The rise of the Karrāmiyyah in Khurasan', *MW* 50 (1960), pp. 5–14; Chabbi, 'Remarques', pp. 33, 41–55, 61; Madelung, 'Sufism and the Karrāmiyya', pp. 39–53; Christopher Melchert, 'Sufis and competing movements in Nishapur', *Iran* 39 (2001), pp. 237–47; Josef Van Ess, *Ungenützte Texte zur Karrāmīya* (Heidelberg, 1980); Aron Zysow, 'Two unrecognised Karrāmī Texts', *JAOS* 108 (1988), pp. 583–87; Claude Vadet, 'Le Karramisme de la Haute-Asie au carrefour de trois sectes rivales', *REI* 48 (1980), pp. 25–50. On the early mystical love poetry of the Karrāmiyya see Muḥammad Riḍā Shafīʿī Kadkanī, 'Safīna'ī az shiʿrhā-yi ʿirfānī-yi qarn-i chahārum wa panjum', in M. Turābī, ed. *Jashn-nāma-yi Ustād Dhabīḥullāh Ṣafā* (Tehran, 1377sh/1998), pp. 340–60.

9 The principle source work on the Malāmatiyya is Abū ʿAbd al-Raḥmān al-Sulamī's *Risālat al-Malāmatiyya wa'l-ṣūfiyya wa ahl al-futuwwa*, ed. A. ʿAfīfī (Cairo, 1945). On the Malāmatiyya movement see also Sara Sviri, 'Ḥakīm Tirmidhī and the Malāmatī movement', in Lewisohn, ed., *Classical Persian Sufism*, pp. 583–613; R. Hartmann '*Futuwwa* und *Malāma*', *ZDMG* 72 (1918), pp. 193–8; Frederick de Jong, Hamid Algar and Colin H. Imber, 'Malāmatīya', *EI*², VI, pp. 223–8; Morris S. Seale, 'The ethics of the Malāmatiyya and the Sermon on the Mount', *MW* 58 (1968), pp. 12–23; Sulamī, *Risālat al-Malāmatiyya,* editor's introduction. Qushayrī's *Risāla* and Hujwīrī's *Kashf al-maḥjūb* also have chapters on *malāma.* Nasrollah Pourjavady, in his article, 'Manbaʿī kuhan dar bāb-i Malāmatiyyān-i Nīshāpūr', *Maʿārif* 15/1–2 (joint issue) (Farwardīn-Ābān 1377sh/November 1998), pp. 3–50, has edited and published another important source, a chapter on *malāmatiyya* in the *Tahdhīb al-asrār* of Abū Saʿd al-Khargūshī (d. 406 or 7/1015 or 16), ed. B.M. Bārūd (Abu Dhabi, 1999).

10 On the development of *futuwwa* in Sufism see Muhammad Jaʿfar Mahjub, 'Chivalry and early Persian Sufism', in Lewisohn, ed., *Classical Persian Sufism,* pp. 549–81; Chodkiewicz's introduction to al-Jerrahi's translation of Sulamī's *Kitāb al-futuwwa*, published as *The Book of Sufi Chivalry* (New York, 1983); Hartmann, '*Futuwwa* und *Malāma*'; Bulliet, *Islam, the View from the Edge,* pp. 162–5. Arabic sources on *futuwwa* include Sulamī's *Kitāb al-futuwwa al-ṣūfiyya* in *Risālat al-Malāmatiyya,* ed., A. ʿAfīfī; and a chapter on *futuwwa* in Qushayrī's *Risāla.* An earlier discussion of *futuwwa* or *jawānmardī* extracted from a Sufi 'manual' composed by an as yet unidentified fourth/tenth century mystic has recently been edited by Nasrollah Pourjavady in 'Du dastīna-yi kuhan dar taṣawwuf', *Maʿārif* 20/3 (March 2004), pp. 3–38.

11 Pourjavady, 'Manbaʿī kuhan', p. 12.

12 See statistical tables showing the occurrence of the terms *ʿābid, zāhid, ʿārif* and *ṣūfī* in the histories of Nishapur in Bulliet, *Patricians,* pp. 41, 42; also Chabbi, 'Remarques', pp. 20, 29ff. Pourjavady, ('Manbaʿī kuhan', pp. 12–13) notes that mystics of Transoxiana (for example, Tirmidhī and Abū Bakr al-Warrāq) were sometimes called *ḥakīm.* It is to be noted that Maybudī, writing in the early sixth/twelfth century, rarely uses the word *ṣūfī*, preferring to use terms such as *ʿārif, ahl-i ṭarīqat, jawānmardān-i ṭarīqat* or *ahl-i ḥaqīqat*, as mentioned in the preface.

13 Madelung, 'Sufism and the Karrāmiyya', p. 46; Bulliet, *Patricians,* p. 43; Malamud, 'Sufi organizations', pp. 429ff. Chabbi points out that Sulamī omits mystics connected to the Karrāmiyya movement from his *Ṭabaqāt al-ṣūfiyya.* See 'Remarques', pp. 20, 68–9.

14 With the exception of Kalābādhī, about whom little is known, all these Khorasani writers were connected through their teachers to the school of Iraq. For example, Sarrāj through Jaʿfar al-Khuldī (d. in Baghdad 348/960) and Aḥmad b. al-Sālim of Baṣra (d. 356/967); Sulamī to Abū Bakr al-Shiblī (d. 334/945) through Abu'l-Qāsim al-Naṣrābādī (d. 367/977–8); Qushayrī through Sulamī; and Hujwīrī through his two masters Abu'l-Faḍl Muḥammad al-Khuttalī (fl. 400/1000?) and Abu'l-Qāsim al-Kurrakānī (d. 469/1076).

15 Chabbi, 'Remarques', p. 69; Pourjavady, *Sulṭān-i ṭarīqat*, pp. 40–1.

16 As did Anṣārī in his *Manāzil al-sāʾirīn.* On the other hand, Hujwīrī, in his *Kashf*

al-maḥjūb, included a chapter on *malāma* but not on *futuwwa*.

17 Pourjavady, 'Manbaʿī kuhan', p. 3. For example, in Aḥmad Ghazzālī's *Sawāniḥ*, blame has been incorporated as a stage in the way of love. The integration of some of the teachings of *malāma* and *futuwwa* (or *jawānmardī*) into the doctrines of the *Kashf al-asrār* will be discussed in chapter six.

18 For an account of the development of love in Islamic mysticism see Marie-Louise Siauve, *L'amour de Dieu chez Ġazālī: une philosophie de l'amour à Baghdad au début du XIIe siècle* (Paris, 1986), pp. 79–101; Pourjavady, *Sulṭān-i ṭarīqat*, pp. 42ff; Carl W. Ernst, 'The stages of love in early Persian Sufism from Rābiʿa to Rūzbihān', in Lewisohn, ed., *Classical Persian Sufism*, pp. 435–55.

19 Preserved in Abū Nuʿaym al-Iṣfahānī, *Ḥilyat al-awliyā'* (Cairo, 1932–8), X, pp. 76–80. There is nonetheless doubt concerning the authorship of this work, for which see Gavin N. Picken, 'The concept of *Tazkiyat al-Nafs* in Islam in the light of the works of al-Ḥārith al-Muḥāsibī' (Ph.D dissertation, University of Leeds, 2005), p. 244, nn. 929–31. Many of the Qur'anic interpretations attributed to the earlier mystic and Shiʿi imam Jaʿfar al-Ṣādiq, place particular emphasis on mystical love, for which see Nwyia, *Exégèse coranique*, pp. 186–8. However, uncertainty still remains over the authenticity of these comments of Jaʿfar al-Ṣādiq. Böwering has gone so far as to call the author of the comments cited in the name of Jaʿfar al-Ṣādiq by Sulamī 'pseudo Jaʿfar al-Ṣādiq', and suggests that the latter may have lived in the first half of the fourth/tenth century rather than the second/eighth century. See Gerhard Böwering, 'The light verse: Qur'ānic text and Sufi interpretation', *Oriens* 36 (2001) p. 135.

20 ʿAṭṭār, *Tadhkirat al-awliyā'*, p. 87; trans. in Margaret Smith, *Rābiʿa the Mystic and Her Fellow Saints in Islām* (repr., Cambridge, 1984), p. 30.

21 See, for example, Rūzbihān Baqlī, *Sharḥ-i shaṭḥiyyāt*, p. 165. On Nūrī see Gramlich, *Alte Vorbilder*, I, pp. 381–446.

22 Hujwīrī, *Kashf al-maḥjūb*, pp. 398–9; tr. Nicholson, p. 309.

23 See, for example, the poems cited in Louis Massignon, *La passion d'Abū Manṣūr al-Ḥallāj, martyr mystique de l'Islam* (Paris, 1922), pp. 95 and 126, and those cited in Herbert Mason's translation, *The Passion of al-Ḥallāj; Mystic and Martyr of Islam* (Princeton, 1982), pp. 41–3.

24 For example: 'The torrent of His love (*ʿishq*) came and drowned all other than Him, and the One remained as He is eternally', Abu'l-Faḍl Muḥammad al-Sahlagī, *Kitāb al-nūr min kalimāt Abī Ṭayfūr*, ed. ʿA. Badawī in ʿA. Badawī, *Shaṭaḥāt al-ṣūfiyya* (Cairo, 1949), p. 109; or 'When they drink from the cup of His love, they fall into the sea of intimacy with Him, and delight in the ease of intimate communing with Him', ibid, p. 102; or words expressed during the so-called *miʿrāj* of Bāyazīd, ibid. pp. 138ff; trans. in A.J. Arberry, *Revelation and Reason in Islam* (London, 1957), pp. 98, 101.

25 Abu'l-Ḥasan ʿAlī b. Muḥammad al-Daylamī, *ʿAṭf al-alif al-ma'lūf ʿala'l-lām al-maʿṭūf*, ed. J.-C. Vadet (Cairo, 1962); French trans. by J.-C. Vadet as *Le traité d'amour mystique d'al-Daylami* (Geneva and Paris, 1980); trans. by J.N. Bell as *A Treatise on Mystical Love* (Edinburgh, 2005). After Daylamī, the philosopher Ibn Sīnā also wrote a treatise on love, the *Risāla fi'l-ʿishq* or *Risāla fī māhiyyat al-ʿishq*, in *Rasā'il al-Shaykh al-Ra'īs Abū ʿAlī al-Ḥusayn b. ʿAbd Allāh Ibn Sīnā fī asrār al-ḥikma al-mashriqiyya*, ed. A.F. Mehren (Leiden, 1899); study and French trans. by T. Sabri in '*Risāla fi'l-ʿishq*. Le traité sur l'amour d'Avicenne', *REI* 58

(1990), pp. 109–34. See also the Ikhwān al-Ṣafāʾ, *Risāla fī māhiyyat al-ʿishq*; trans. into Spanish by Ricardo Felipe Albert Reyna as, 'La "*Risāla fī māhiyyat al-ʿišq*" de las Rasāʾil Ijwān al-Ṣafāʾ,' *Anaquel de Estudios Árabes* 6 (1995), pp. 185–207.

26 This holds true for Kalābādhī's *Kitāb al-taʿarruf*, Sarrāj's *Lumaʿ*, Qushayrī's *Risāla*, Mustamlī's *Sharḥ al-taʿarruf* and Hujwīrī's *Kashf al-maḥjūb*. Nwyia (*Exégèse coranique*, p. 187), having discussed Jaʿfar al-Ṣādiq's understanding of mystical love, states: 'l'amour, chez les soufies, ne sera qu'une "station" parmi d'autres stations, ou alors il sera cet amour esthétique qui n'a rien à faire avec celui dont parle Ǧaʿfar dans le commentaire.' This is probably an indication that Nwyia was not familiar with later love mysticism, particularly developments which took place in Persian Sufism.

27 Hujwīrī, *Kashf al-maḥjūb*, pp. 228–30; tr. Nicholson pp. 184–9. On Hujwīrī's attribution of intoxication to Bāyazīd, see Mojaddedi, *Biographical Tradition*, pp. 133–4.

28 Ibn al-Munawwar, *Asrār al-tawḥīd*, p. 16.

29 On the use of such poetry in Persian mysticism and the development of the metaphorical language of wine and the beloved in Sufism, see Nasrollah Pourjavady, "Bāda-yi ʿishq", *Nashr-i Dānish*, Year 11/6 (1370sh/1991), pp. 4–13; Year 12/1 (1370–1sh/1992), pp. 4–18; 2, pp. 6–15; 3, pp. 26–32; 4, pp. 22–30; idem, *Būy-i jān* (Tehran, 1374sh/1995), ch. 4.

30 Hujwīrī, *Kashf al-maḥjūb*, p. 518; tr. Nicholson pp. 397–8. Mustamlī also shows his disapproval of such practices. See Mustamlī, *Sharḥ al-taʿarruf*, IV, p. 1812.

31 Ibn al-Munawwar, *Asrār al-tawḥīd*, editor's introduction, p. 109.

32 *Iḥyāʾ*, Part 2, Book 8, *Kitāb ādāb al-samāʿ waʾl-wajd*, ch. 1, p. 392; *Kīmiyā*, I, pp. 483–5.

33 For which see Siauve, *L'amour de Dieu*, and Richard Gramlich, *Muḥammad al-Ġazzālīs Lehre von den Stufen zur Gottesliebe: die Bücher 31–36 seines Hauptwerkes* (Wiesbaden, 1984).

34 *Kashf*, I, p. 278.

35 Although it has been termed *madhhab-i ʿishq*, for example in Pourjavady, *Sulṭān-i ṭarīqat*, p. 37. In the *Sawāniḥ* (ed. Pourjavady, p. 3), Aḥmad Ghazzālī himself speaks of 'our school' (*madhhab-i mā*), implying a 'school' of love, while Maybudī uses the expression *madhhab-i dūstī*, for example in *Kashf*, III, p. 730.

36 As opposed to Maybudī's understanding of God as the Beloved in Whom both love and the lover are ultimately subsumed, for which see chapter seven.

37 *Zuhd* is often translated with the English word 'asceticism', but in this context the term could more appropriately be rendered 'a disdain for, and withdrawal from the world'.

38 See Muḥammad Riḍā Shafīʿī Kadkanī, *Tāziyānahā-yi sulūk: naqd wa taḥlīl-i chand qaṣīda az Ḥakīm Sanāʾī* (Tehran, 1372sh/1993), pp. 25–34.

39 See, for example, Ibn al-Munawwar, *Asrār al-tawḥīd*, editor's introduction, p. 89; tr. O'Kane, introduction, p. 53.

40 They become man's only by acquisition (*kasb*). See *Kashf*, II, p. 445. On the doctrine of *kasb*, see ch. 1, p. 17 and n. 110.

41 See discussion pp. 17, 45–8 and 55–8.

42 *Kashf*, I, p. 127.

43 *Kashf*, III, p. 625.

44 See Anṣārī's *munājāt*, quoted p. 61.
45 That theological doctrine was important to earlier Sufis such as Sarrāj and Kalābādhī is indicated by the fact that they included sections on dogma in their Sufi manuals. On the doctrine of *taqdīr*, for example, see Kalābādhī, *Kitāb al-ta'arruf*, pp. 23ff; tr. Arberry, pp. 28ff; and on the limits of knowledge, see ibid, pp. 37–8; tr. Arberry, pp. 46–50. Schimmel says of Qushayrī's *Risāla* that it was written 'from the viewpoint of a full-fledged Ash'arite theologian'. See Annemarie Schimmel, *Mystical Dimensions of Islam* (Chapel Hill, 1975), p. 88. The importance of the doctrine of *taqdīr* is clearly exemplified in commentaries on *Sūrat Yūsuf* in both Sulamī's *Ḥaqā'iq* and Qushayrī's *Laṭā'if*. Louis Massignon has included a chapter on 'Mystical theology' in his *La passion d'Abū Manṣūr al-Ḥallāj*. On theology in early Sufism see Helmut Ritter, *Das Meer der Seele* (Leiden, 1978); trans. by J. O'Kane as *The Ocean of the Soul* (Leiden and Boston, 2003), ch. 4.
46 On which see Utas, 'The *Munājāt*', pp. 83–7.
47 The question of the authenticity of Anṣārī's Persian works has also been discussed by ibid., p. 83, and by Nasrollah Pourjavady, 'Iṣālat-i *Ṣad Maydān*-i Khwāja 'Abd Allāh Anṣārī', in 'A.A. Ṣādiqī, ed., *Yādnāma-yi Duktur Aḥmad Tafaḍḍulī* (Tehran, 1379sh/2001), pp. 1–15.
48 De Beaurecueil's edition of the *Ṣad maydān* may be found following his article 'Une ébauche persane' and his translation of the same work in his *Chemins de Dieu*. The text of *'Ilal al-maqāmāt* is included in de Beaurecueil, 'Un petit traité de 'Abdullāh Anṣārī sur les déficiences inhérentes à certaines demeures spirituelles', in Massignon, ed., *Mélanges Louis Massignon*, I, pp. 53–71, and the translation of this work in de Beaurecueil, *Chemins de Dieu*.
49 *Manāzil al-sā'irīn*, ed. with intro. and French trans. S. de Beaurecueil (Cairo, 1962), pp. 71–2, 104–6. See translator's note, p. 105, n. 1.
50 *'Ilal al-maqāmāt*, in de Beaurecueil, 'Un petit traité', pp. 164, 169.
51 Anṣārī, *Ṣad maydān*, text and French trans. in de Beaurecueil, 'Une ébauche persane', p. 30.
52 The *Manāzil al-sā'irīn* having been composed some twenty-five years after the *Ṣad maydān*. See de Beaurecueil, 'Une ébauche persane', pp. 5–6, 27; idem, *Khwādja 'Abdullāh Anṣārī*, p. 124.
53 As stated in Anṣārī's *'Ilal al-maqāmāt*, ed. de Beaurecueil, 'Un petit traité', p. 158; French tr. de Beaurecueil, *Chemins de Dieu*, p. 237. On the centrality of the doctrine of *fanā'* in Anṣārī's work and its relationship with the doctrine of love see Joseph N. Bell, *Love Theory in Later Hanbalite Islam* (Albany, 1979), pp. 171ff.
54 Bell, *Love Theory*, p. 75. In the *Ṣad maydān*, the highest degree of love is defined as 'not-being' (*nīstī*), and in the *Manāzil al-sā'irīn* as 'a ravishing love which cuts short expression, renders allusion too subtle [to attain it], and is beyond the realm of epithets'. The place of annihilation in the way of love according to the teachings of Maybudī's *Kashf al-asrār* will be discussed in chapter seven.
55 De Beaurecueil, *Chemins de Dieu*, pp. 37–8; Utas, 'The *Munājāt*', p. 83. Utas further suggests (ibid., p. 84) that Anṣārī may have used Arabic 'in strictly scholarly circles, a more or less literary Persian in public lectures, and a more vernacular style of Persian in the closer circle of pupils and friends'.
56 For example, the manuscript of *Manāzil al-sā'irīn* seen by Kāshānī. See de

Beaurecueil, 'Une ébauche persane', pp. 5–6.

57 See passim.

58 Although the absence of a critical edition of the *Kashf al-asrār* adds another difficulty here, for even supposing that the collection of Anṣārī's sayings was reasonably uncorrupted at the time that Maybudī had access to them, there remains the uncertainty over the text of the *tafsīr* itself. Nevertheless, it is reassuring to find that in one of the earliest known MSS of the work, namely that of the Āstān-i Quds, which is said to date from the sixth/twelfth century and covers from Q. 21:6 to the end of Q. 25, all the sayings of Anṣārī included in the published edition are present.

59 *Kashf*, I, p. 93; VII, p. 398, and X, p. 659. This *munajāt* appears in three variants in the printed text of *Kashf al-asrār*: the second two citations conform to MSS A and B, where citation 2 has *qismatī* and citation 3 *ḥukmī*. The first citation in the printed text has the erroneous *qismī* instead of *qismatī* and the variant *gar shād buwam* instead of *gar shād zīyam*, as in the second and third citations.

60 *Kashf*, IX, p. 507.

61 Abu'l-Qāsim Ibrāhīm b. Muḥammad Naṣrābādī al-Naysābūrī (d. 367/977–8).

62 It is not clear who this mystic is.

63 *Kashf*, V, p. 584. See also *Kashf*, V, p. 583.

64 *Kashf*, III, p. 155.

65 *Dīdār* can mean the faculty of sight, act of seeing, that which is seen, or a meeting.

66 *Kashf*, III, p. 639.

67 *Kashf*, I, p. 674.

68 On the doctrine of *taqdīr*, Stations 27, 28 and 29; and on the limits of knowledge Stations 30 and 41.

69 For example, on the importance of accepting the way of the Sunna, *Maydān*, 20; on *qaḍā'* and divine intervention, *Maydān*, 26 and 44; on the limits of knowledge, *Maydān*, 24, 51 and 67; and on love, *Maydān*, 18, 29, 40, 45, 51, 52, 75, 95 and conclusion.

70 For which see de Beaurecueil, *Khwādja 'Abdullāh*, and Afghānī, *'Abd Allāh al-Anṣārī al-Harawī*.

71 Another indication that by the fifth/eleventh and sixth/twelfth centuries it is no longer possible to speak of the two distinct schools of Khorasan and Baghdad.

72 That the word *dūstī*, which might be understood as friendship, could be used synonymously with *maḥabbat* is confirmed in the last chapter of *Ṣad maydān*, where Anṣārī speaks of love first as *maḥabbat* and then as *dūstī*. On several occasions Maybudī uses the word *dūstī* to translate the word *maḥabba* in an Arabic quotation, for example, *Kashf*, VII, p. 78 and VIII, p. 279. The same ambiguity exists in the French word *aimer* and in the modern Persian *dūst dāshtan*, both of which can mean either to like or to love.

73 See Louis Massignon, *Opera minora: textes recueillis, classés et présentés avec une bibliographie* (Beirut, 1963), II, pp. 248ff.

74 For example, in his *Risāla*, Qushayrī writes: 'There is no way that passionate love (*'ishq*) can be related to God, either from Him towards the servant, or from the servant towards God'; *Risāla*, p. 615; tr. Schlegel, p. 331. See also Hujwīrī, *Kashf al-maḥjūb*, pp. 400–1; tr. Nicholson, p. 310.

75 Abu'l-Faḍl Jamāl al-Dīn Mukarram b. Mukarram b. Manẓūr al-Miṣrī, *Lisān al-*

ʿArab (20 vols., Cairo, 1300–1307/1882–91), XII, p. 123; Qushayrī, *Risāla*, p. 61. For a discussion of the use of the term *ʿishq* in mysticism see Massignon, *Opera minora*, II, pp. 246–50; and in secular literature, Lois Anita Giffin, *Theory of Profane Love among the Arabs* (New York and London, 1971). See also Pourjavady, 'Bāda-yi ʿishq', Year 11/6 (1370sh/1991), p. 9; idem, *Sulṭān-i ṭarīqat*, p. 87. In Sulamī's commentary on *Sūrat Yūsuf*, the word *ḍalāl* (aberration) said of Jacob by Joseph's brothers (Q. 12:8 and 95), and of Zulaykhā by the women of Egypt (Q. 12:30), is glossed as *ʿishq* in comments attributed to Jaʿfar al-Ṣādiq.

76 For example in the poem quoted on p. 110, which was recited at the gathering which Abū Saʿīd attended during his childhood.

77 For example, *Iḥyāʾ*, Part 4, Book 6, *Kitāb al-maḥabba*, p. 207.

78 Aḥmad Ghazzālī, *Sawāniḥ*, *passim*.

79 *Kashf*, I, p. 53.

80 *Kashf*, I, p. 142; III, p. 732.

5

God and the creation

God in His Essence, His Attributes and His Acts

There are no ontological and philosophical discussions of the Deity in the *Kashf al-asrār*. Maybudī unequivocally states that any deliberation or inquiry concerning the divine essence or attributes conducted on the basis of [cerebral] knowledge (*ʿilm*) or the exercise of the rational faculty (*ʿaql*) is unlawful (*ḥarām*).[1] Discussions of the Divinity in the mystical sections of the *Kashf al-asrār* are therefore entirely centred on the tenets of belief (*ʿaqīda*). Often, they include poetic recitals of the divine attributes of God, and are written in rhyming and metred prose. The following passage is one among many emphasizing the unity of God in His Essence, His Attributes and His Acts. The context is Maybudī's commentary on the words 'Your Lord is one God' (Q. 2:163), and it is interesting to note that he has used both Arabic and Persian words to denote the divine attributes, including that of oneness:

> This is the quality of the one God (*Khudāwand-i yigāna*), the one Lord and King, in His greatness (*buzurgwārī*) and act (*kār-rānī*), one; in forbearance (*burdbārī*) and beneficence (*nīkūkārī*), one; in generosity (*karīmī*) and peerlessness (*bīhamtāʾī*), one; in kindness (*mihrabānī*) and in caring for His servant (*banda-nawāzī*), one. All grandeur (*kibriyāʾ*) is the mantle of His majesty (*jalāl*); all mightiness (*ʿaẓamat*) and omnipotence (*jabarūt*), the cloak of His divinity (*rubūbiyya*).[2] In this, He is one: in essence, one; in attributes, one; in His acts and His signs, one; in faithfulness and covenant, one; in grace (*luṭf*) and favour (*nawākht*), one; in love (*mihr*) and friendship (*dūstī*), one [...].[3]

In a number of contexts Maybudī shows how all of creation is proof of the oneness of God. Here, he is commenting on the verse 'Their messengers said: Can there be doubt concerning God, the Creator of the heavens and the earth?' (Q. 14:10):

> The prophets were amazed that there could be anyone in creation who doubted the oneness and unicity (*waḥdāniyyat wa fardāniyyat*) of God Almighty, for all of existence in its totality and in its smallest detail, indeed every being, is testimony and proof of His oneness and uniqueness.
>
> All that is needed is someone with a sense of smell
> Otherwise, the world is full of the scent of that zephyr.[4]

While all of existence is in itself evidence of God's oneness, existence is only maintained through the attestation of that oneness. In presenting this idea, Maybudī is expanding upon a tradition of the prophet. Here, he is commenting on Q. 9:36, 'The number of months with God is twelve':

> It is said that the wisdom in God's dividing the year into twelve months is so that it should tally with the number of letters in the words *lā ilāha illa'llāh*.[5] This confirms a saying of the Prophet that 'The heavens and earth subsist by the attestation of God's oneness (*tawḥīd*).'[6] The rotation of the spheres in the heavens, the cycles of time, and the years and months on earth depend on *tawḥīd*, and as long as those twelve letters are being uttered by those who attest to His oneness (*muwaḥḥidān*), the twelve months will continue their ordered succession. He made each letter the watchman over a month, and tied the continuance of the latter to the former. But that day, when the divine decree and pre-eternal destiny arrives, when God is about to untie the earth from the heavens, to scatter the earth and bring appointed time to an end, He will firstly remove *tawḥīd* from people altogether so that there is no longer any person bearing witness to His oneness.[7]

Thus, believers should realise the importance of the attestation of God's oneness. At the same time they must, paradoxically, be aware that only God in His transcendence can truly bear witness to that oneness, a principle that is expressed in the following Arabic poem, twice quoted from Anṣārī:

> There is no one who can attest to the oneness of the One
> For anyone who attests to that One denies It
> The attestation of oneness by One who describes It
> Is but an empty thing, annulled by the One.
> His oneness is that which is His oneness,
> And the one who describes Him is an apostate (*lāḥid*).[8]

The ineffability of God is here expressed differently by Maybudī:

> Seekers who hoped for apprehension [of Him] headed for a wilderness of searching, and lovers desirous of union with Him made heart and soul a target for the arrows of affliction; for the reality of His eternity (*ṣamadiyya*)[9] and the perfection of His oneness is inaccessible (*ʿazīz*). [That reality] transcends the limited capacity of the mind. He, mighty and glorious, made the whole universe content with just a whiff and a rumour of it. He gave not a drop from that cup to anyone. A man looks in the mirror and sees his image there before his eyes. From the way it appears, he might suppose that he could reach out his hand and take hold of that image. How wrong he would be! For it is a nearness that is distance itself. Even if he spent his whole life trying to attain that image, he would not reach it, nor would he grasp one atom of its existence:
>
> Out of love for You, a hundred thousand lives
> Were spent and not one found even a trace of union with You[10]

While maintaining the transcendence of God (*tanzīh*), Maybudī repeatedly insists on the belief that God has essence, attributes and acts, and, as discussed earlier, advocates a middle way that is free from *tashbīh* (anthropomorphism) on the one hand, and *taʿṭīl* (negation of the divine attributes) on the other.[11] He insists that *tashbīh* does not arise from affirming what is (i.e. God's having attributes), but from making comparisons.[12] In one context, he illustrates this principle with the word *wujūd*, which is applied both to creatures and to God; but while God is existent in His self-subsistence, in His being and His remaining, the creature is existent only by God's bringing it into existence (*ba-ījād-i Allāh*).[13]

Maybudī further distinguishes the attributes of God from those of created beings when he comments on Q. 51:49, 'And We have created all things in pairs, that you might reflect'. He begins by observing that God has created all accidents and engendered beings either in opposites or in pairs, such as male and female, night and day, sun and moon, strength and weakness and so on. He then continues:

> He created things thus, in pairs or opposites, so that they should be distinguished from the attributes of the Creator, and His oneness and unicity made manifest. For His glory is without ignominy, His power without incapacity, His strength without weakness, His knowledge without ignorance, His life without death, His joy without sadness, and His remaining without extinction.[14]

Thus, Maybudī maintains that the uniqueness of the divine attributes is in their perfection, by which he means in this context, their being purely as they are, without any trace of their opposite. Yet the divine attributes may *manifest* opposite effects in creation. Hence, among the names of God are *al-Qābiḍ* (He Who contracts), and *al-Bāsiṭ* (He Who expands), *al-Khāfiḍ* (the Abaser), and *al-Rāfiʿ* (the Exalter); *al-Muʿizz* (the Honourer) and *al-Mudhill* (He Who humbles).[15] Moreover, while the contrasting attributes of *jalāl* (majesty) and *jamāl* (beauty), *qahr* (coercion or wrath) and *luṭf* (gentleness or grace) imply no opposition or compromise in God, their opposite effects are essential to creation.

The divine *luṭf* and *qahr*, *faḍl* (favour) and *ʿadl* (justice) are manifested in the divine preordination of things, and particularly in the pre-eternal destiny of individual human beings and their ultimate end:

> He, be He glorified, had wrath and gentleness in perfection, and infinite majesty and beauty. He wishes to distribute these treasures. Thus it is that He places the crown of favour upon the head of one, in the garden of [His] grace, whilst He places the brand of wrath on the liver of another, in the dungeon of His justice. One He melts in the fire of His majesty, another He cherishes in the light of His beauty.[16]

In other contexts, Maybudī explains the opposite effects which the divine aspects of *jalāl* and *jamāl*, or the different names of God, can have on the state of the seeker. For example, commenting on the *basmala* at the commencement of *Sūrat al-Mulk* (Q. 67), Maybudī contrasts the effects of the name *Allāh* (here associated with the divine attributes of majesty and greatness), which engenders awe (*haybat*), and brings about annihilation from self (*fanāʾ*) and absence [from other than God] (*ghaybat*), with the effects of the names *al-Raḥmān* and *al-Raḥīm*, (associated with the divine aspect of gentleness, *luṭf*), which brings the servant from annihilation to subsisting [in God] (*baqāʾ*) or from awe (*haybat*) and bedazzlement (*dahshat*), to intimacy (*uns*).[17] Sometimes, however, when Maybudī discusses the effects of God's majesty and beauty, grace and justice, gentleness and coercion, it is in connection with the implementation of the divine preordination (*qaḍāʾ*) which brings felicity (*dawlat*) to some and misfortune (*shaqāwat*) to others.[18]

On one occasion, God's attribute of wisdom is linked to His mercy in mediating for the creation with respect to the implacability of His power.

Commenting on Q. 22:63, 'Do you not see [Prophet] how God sends down water from the sky?', Maybudī writes:

> God is omnipotent (*qadīr*) for He does whatever He wishes; He is wise, for He does not do all that He could. In this world He created not even an ant's foot or a gnat's wing but according to the requirements of His power (*qudrat*) and wisdom (*ḥikmat*) and in conformity with His will (*mashiyyat*). The divine wisdom and power work together in the ordering of creation. If there were not wisdom along with power, then the universe would be in chaos. God has attributes that are antagonistic towards the existence and acts of creatures; they are His qualities of glory (*ʿizzat*), might (*ʿaẓamat*), omnipotence (*jabarūt*), aloofness (*kibriyāʾ*) and complete independence (*istighnāʾ*). Then He has qualities which mediate for the existence and acts of creatures, such as wisdom and mercy (*raḥmat*), gentleness (*luṭf*) and kindness (*raʾfat*), goodness (*jawd*) and generosity (*karam*). These qualities of mercy and wisdom took hold of the reins of those qualities of glory and independence so that a handful of helpless creatures could live in the shade of His grace and mercy, according to His wisdom.[19]

Elsewhere, Maybudī seems to show the divine mercy to be a compensation for the divine preordination, *qaḍāʾ*. If God is the all-imposing (*jabbār*), 'the writing of Whose decree cannot be washed away with any water', He is also the generous (*karīm*), 'Whose grace and goodness are beyond all bounds'.[20] Further associated with God's mercy is His knowledge of man's weakness. For this reason He praises Himself, for He knows that man is incapable of praising Him adequately.[21] According to Anṣārī, it is a mercy from God that He keeps the realities of the unseen hidden, for neither could they be contained in this world, nor could the human intellect bear them.[22] This idea is differently expressed in an anecdote which Maybudī relates about Moses. One day he asks God, 'O Lord, are you far that I should call out loudly, or near that I should whisper?' The answer came, 'O Moses, even if We were to place a limit on Our farness you would never reach it, and even if We were to place a limit on Our nearness, you would not be able to bear it; you would be crushed beneath Our mightiness and majesty (*ʿaẓamat wa jalāl*).'[23] Maybudī then adds: 'God is both nearer to man than his jugular vein (Q. 50:16), and further away than anything in the universe. He is more evident than all that is in the universe, yet more hidden than that which is most concealed, and uniquely so.'[24]

Maybudī devotes numerous passages to God's love which, in particular, is directed towards humanity.[25] God's love for human beings preceded the existence of 'man and the world, the Throne (*'arsh*), the Tablet (*lawḥ*) and the Pen (*qalam*). It was before the existence of Heaven and Hell. In the absence of all these God said "He loves them, they love Him" [Q. 5:54]'.[26] Although, of course, God in His absolute independence (*istighnā'*) has no need of anything, yet Maybudī explains that His love for mankind is such that His longing for them can be greater than their longing for Him. Maybudī states that 'according to that dear one of the path', [27]

> The hearts of those who long [for God] are radiant with his light, and when the fire of their longing flares up, it illumines all that is in heaven and earth. God presents them to the angels saying 'These are the ones who long for Me. I attest that My longing for them is greater than their longing for Me.'[28]

The creation

Maybudī understands the divine purpose in creation as being for the sake of knowledge and love. In respect of knowledge, it is on the one hand, that God should be known, as in the well-known *ḥadīth qudsī*, 'I was a hidden treasure and I wished to be known. Therefore I created the creation so that I should be known',[29] and on the other, that His pre-eternal knowledge of the creation should be fulfilled. In his commentary on Q. 23:115, 'Did you think that We created you in vain?',[30] Maybudī glosses and expands upon a saying of Abū Bakr al-Wāsiṭī:[31]

> God Almighty, in His majesty and glory, and in His absolute omnipotence brought existents (*kā'ināt*) and originated beings (*muḥdathāt*) into being so that [His creatures] should know of His existence, and recognise His lordship and find proof of the perfection of His knowledge and power. And, according to His pre-eternal knowledge [of those creatures], He manifested the sign of friendship to His friends and the seal of enmity to [His] enemies.[32] He brought them into being from the concealment of non-existence according to His knowledge, for from pre-eternity He knew that he would create the universe and He wanted that creation to conform to his knowledge.[33]

Typically, however, Maybudī goes on to give love precedence over knowledge in the divine purpose of creation. Firstly, he provides a context for the *ḥadīth qudsī* alluded to previously. He relates that the prophet David once asked God why, in His absolute self-sufficiency and complete independence of everything, He had created the world, and what was the wisdom in bringing all these creatures into being? The answer came: 'I was a hidden treasure and I wished (lit. 'loved') to be known (*aḥbabtu an uʿrafa*). Therefore I created the creation that I should be known'.[34] Then Maybudī explains

> [The words] '*aḥbabtu an uʿrafa*' are an indication that mystical knowledge (*maʿrifat*) is based upon love (*maḥabbat*), and that wherever there is love there is knowledge, but wherever there is no love there can be no knowledge.[35]

In his discussion of the creation, Maybudī does not present any comprehensive system of cosmology. For him, cosmology seems to be principally centred on the creation of Muhammad and of Adam (that is, humankind), as will be seen in the sections which follow.

The Muhammadan light

First in all of creation, Maybudī explains, was Muhammad:

> The first essence to receive the robe of honour of the command *kun* ('Be!'), and the first upon whom the sun of God's grace shone was the pure spirit of that master.[36]

This 'pure spirit' of Muhammad had come to be known in Islamic mysticism as the Muhammadan light (*nūr Muḥammadī*).[37] Maybudī recalls this tradition when he interprets the words 'the likeness of his light' from the verse of light (Q. 24:35):

> Some commentators have said that 'his' here refers to Muṣṭafā on whom be blessings and peace, for his creation was light, his robe was light, his lineage was light and his birth was light. His contemplation (*mushāhadat*) was light and his dealing[s] (*muʿāmalat*) were light; his miracle (*muʿjizat*) was light, and he himself in his essence was 'light upon light' (Q. 24:35). [38]

Not only was Muhammad the first in creation, but he was the purpose for which the universe was created. In his interpretation of Q. 28:44, 'You [Muhammad] were not on the western side [of the mount]', Maybudī relates that Moses was told by God: 'Were it not for him [Muhammad] I would not have created the spheres'.[39] In another context Maybudī states that God created everything for Muhammad, and Muhammad for Himself. Glossing the words spoken by God to the Prophet, 'And put thy trust in the Mighty, the Merciful' (Q. 26:217), he writes:

> O rare incomparable pearl! We brought you forth from the depths of the ocean of Our omnipotence, and manifested you before the creatures of the world, so that the whole world could derive its nature from you. We created everything for you, and you for Ourself.'[40]

According to a tradition, Muhammad remained for an age alone in the Divine Presence. Maybudī relates this tradition in his commentary on Q. 32:1. Again, he is using the metaphor of light:

> It is said that when the Lord of Might, may He be exalted, created the light of Muhammad's nature (*fiṭrat*), He kept it in His glorious presence as He wished. And he (Muhammad) remained before God for 100,000 years (or it is said 2,000 years), and every day God looked upon him 70,000 times, and with every glance He adorned him with a new light and a new blessing.[41]

In his commentary on the account of the *miʿrāj* (night journey or ascension) of the Prophet (Q. 53:1–18), Maybudī again refers to the time when Muhammad was alone in creation, before all duality, heaven and earth, night and day, and he explains that everything that came into being after him was dependant on his existence.[42] Not only do all beings 'derive' their existence from Muhammad, but all the prophets derive their prophethood from him. The belief that Muhammad was both the first as well as the last prophet had its basis in the hadith, 'I was a prophet when Adam was between water and clay.'[43] Maybudī expands on this doctrine, again using the metaphor of light:

> O noble one! Who can know the worth of that master? What mind could have even a faint understanding of him? One hundred and twenty-four thousand prophets (lit. points of prophethood) have come and gone, and in comparison with him they were like stars. Although he was not yet visible, they all took the light of prophesy from him, just as, when the sun is absent [from view], the planets derive their light from it. But when the sun rises, the light of the planets is no longer visible because of the brightness of the

> sun. In the same way, all the prophets derived their light from Muhammad. But when he came into the world of form, they all disappeared.[44]

Muhammad's journey from the Divine Presence to the world of multiplicity began, Maybudī explains, when God shaped the light of his being in the form of Adam (*dar qālib-i Ādam*). Then he caused him to pass through 'the stages and degrees of vicissitude and stability (*talwīn wa tamkīn*) until he was seated on the throne of messengership in order to call people to religion. There follows a metaphorical account of this process:

> You might say that master was a falcon, trained upon the hand of grace, nurtured on the wing of proximity and intimacy. Then he was brought from the composure of beholding (*mushāhadat*) to the dispersion of calling (*daʿwat*), that he might go out and hunt a world and keep it before the wrath (*qahr*) and gentleness (*luṭf*) of God. Today he makes them his quarry by the law (*sharīʿat*). Tomorrow he will deposit them with God by his intercession (*shafāʿat*).[45]

The creation of Adam

If God created the universe in order that He should be known (and, according to Maybudī, loved, since *maʿrifat* is inseparable from *maḥabbat*), the sole creature destined for that knowledge and love was the human being. Commenting on Q. 39:6, 'We created you from a single soul', Maybudī writes:

> He created Adam and humanity to be the storehouse of His eternal secrets and the target for His generous favours. 'I was a hidden treasure and I wished to be known'. I had essence and attributes, transcendent, a knower was needed. I had majesty and beauty unending; a lover was needed. The sea of mercy and forgiveness had risen up; a beneficiary was needed. Other creatures had nothing to do with love, for they did not have that lofty aspiration.[46]

The idea of God 'needing' man in the capacity of knower and lover recalls a doctrine which appears in Aḥmad Ghazzālī's *Sawāniḥ* and in the *Tamhīdāt* of ʿAyn al-Quḍāt Hamadānī,[47] and which was later developed by Rūzbihān Baqlī.[48] However, in another context, Maybudī attempts to provide a theological corrective for this when he explains that, in respect of God's omnipotence, it would not have been impossible for Him to have created other creatures to fulfill this special role, but '[divine] jealousy (*ghayrat*) took hold of the reins of that omnipotence with the words "and [He] made binding on them the promise of obedience to God for that was more appropriate and fitting for them" (Q. 48:26)'.[49] 'It was possible [i.e. theologically allowable, *rawā*] for Him to create a hundred thousand like us in an instant, but from the point of view of love and jealousy it was not right (*na rawā*), for the secret of that unfathomable love was exclusively meant for us.'[50] This is why, even before God created the Throne, the Tablet and the Pen, before He created heaven and earth, in their absence He said, 'He loves them and they love Him' (Q. 5:54).[51] God singled out the human creature for His love even above the angels and hosts of heaven who had sung His praises for 700,000 years.[52] He even derived (*mushtaqq*) some of His names from His love for humanity such as *al-Ghafūr* (the Forgiving), *al-Wadūd* (the Loving), *al-Ra'ūf* (the Kind) and *al-Raḥīm* (the Compassionate).[53] There could be 'no other oyster for the pearl of love than Adam's breast. Other creatures came by way of creation, Adam by way of love.'[54]

In another context, Adam is described as the oyster for the pearl of mystical knowledge (*maʿrifat*):

> That day, when the beauty of Adam's pure spirit appeared from the world of the unseen, he was tall straight and upstanding, like an *alif*. Outward and inward had been brought together in him, and all the elements had been bonded in him by the Hand of Omnipotence. The angels could not see beyond the outer offence of his body. They did not know what oyster lay in the depths of the ocean of his breast, let alone what pearl was contained in that oyster. Because of their limitation they looked at his exterior and said, 'Will You place there one who will do harm there?' [Q. 2:30], until the call came from the unseen, 'You only see the form and the exterior, We see the end of the matter. Your eye is on the outward disobedience (*maʿṣiyyat*), but Our judgement is on the basis of that inward knowledge (*maʿrifat*).[55]

This passage speaks of the dual nature of the human being, combining both outward and inward. This principle is expressed in various ways by Maybudī: human beings are made up of vessels (*qawālib*) and deposits (*waḍāʾiʿ*), the containers are bodies and the deposits are spirits;[56] they are made of two things, earth (or clay, *ṭīnat*) and spirituality (*rūḥāniyyat*), the earth being of creation (*khalqī*), and the spirit from God's command (*amrī*);[57] or they are made of both earth and light.

> Know that the human being is two things: body and spirit. The spirit is of light and light is sublime, and the body is earth and earth is base. The spirit's wish is to ascend, while the body's wish is to descend. The Almighty King, hallowed and exalted be He, by His absolute power, bound them both together, the spirit tied to the body and the body to the spirit. These two are inseparable until the day of death, when the appointed term is finished and the servant's life comes to an end. Then the tie will be broken, the spirit will leave the body as a bird flies from a cage, and rise upwards towards its nest, and the body will return to earth.[58]

Humanity, then, needs to be reminded that without its association with light that earth would remain base, dark and helpless.[59] Yet, while we should be aware of our lowly origin, we should not despise it. Maybudī observes that God Himself preferred the sullied of the world below to the pure of the world above.[60] It is God's way, he reminds us, to hide the noblest and most precious things in the most worthless. Thus, He deposited silk in the silkworm, honey in the humble bee, the pearl in the oyster, and musk in the navel of the gazelle, while hard rock became the repository of gold, silver and turquoise.[61]

There are other reasons why earth should not be despised. Commenting on Q. 37:72, 'When your Lord said to the angels: I am about to create a mortal out of mire', Maybudī relates an anecdote according to which a dervish came to Bāyazīd and excitedly exclaimed, 'Oh, if only it weren't for this impudent earth!' Bāyazīd was outraged by this remark and shouted at him, 'If it wasn't for earth there would not be any of this burning in the breast. Were it not for earth, then there would have been neither the joy nor the grief of religion, and the fire of love would not have been lit. If there had not been earth, who would have perceived the perfume of pre-eternal love, and who would have become friends with the Eternal Being?'[62]

Elsewhere, Maybudī demonstrates the different virtues which earth (of which the human being was created) has over and above fire (of which Iblīs, or Satan, was created). For example, earth conceals faults whereas fire reveals them; fire causes things to separate, earth joins them; fire is proud and tries to go upwards, while earth is humble and seeks abasement.[63] But the greatest virtue of earth or clay is its malleability, so that a seal can be stamped upon it. Maybudī attributes the following explanation to God:

'The wisdom in Our creating Adam out of earth and clay was so that We could place the seal of trust (*amānat*) upon the clay of his heart as when We said "Lo, We offered the trust unto the heavens and earth and the hills but they shrank from bearing it and were afraid of it [...]"(Q. 33:72) [...] It was only Adam who in his manliness put out his hand to receive it.'[64]

Maybudī presents another explanation for why humanity alone in creation should have been able to bear not only 'the trust', but the meaning of the Qur'an:[65] it was because the human being has a heart.[66] It was on account of Adam's heart that God delayed his creation,[67] and it was for the sake of Adam's heart that the angels were commanded to prostrate themselves before him: 'it was on account of the heart (*dil*) not the clay (*gil*)'.[68]

In another context, Maybudī observes that the uniqueness of human beings is in the fact that all the elements are combined in them, whereas other created beings are made of a single element; for example, the angels of light, the jinn of fire, the sea of water and so on. Hence the human being represents a totality. Moreover, one can see the whole macrocosm, both the heavenly and sublunary realms, reflected in the microcosm of the human being. Maybudī expounds some of these correspondences at length in his commentary on Q. 22:5, 'O mankind! If you are in doubt concerning the resurrection, then remember that We created you from dust, then from a drop of seed, then from a clot'. Here, Maybudī observes that just as God created the seven spheres of heaven in order, so he made and ordered the seven limbs of the body,[69] firstly of water and clay, then of flesh, skin, vein, sinew and bone. Just as He divided the spheres into twelve constellations, He made in the body twelve orifices. Just as the seven planets, as some people think, govern a person's happiness or misfortune, so within the body, there are seven powers which govern the well-being of the body: those of sight, hearing, taste, smell, touch, speech and the intelligence.[70] After presenting other correspondences between the body and the realm of heaven, Maybudī continues, in more descriptive vein, by showing correspondences (he uses the word *iʿtibār*, meaning drawing a lesson from something) between the sublunary world and the body, such as the bones which are like mountains, the marrow like mines, the front like the east, the back like the west, the right like the south and the left like the north, breath like the wind and speech like thunder and so on. Adding a more spiritual note he compares the body to a throne on which sits a king, the heart. The king has no affinity with the unclean world, and, like a prisoner, he finds no peace or rest in that terrible prison. All he thinks of night and day is when he will be freed from that prison and return to the world of grace.[71]

In a number of passages quoted earlier, we saw that the Muhammadan substance or light was the first in all creation, that all other creatures were dependant on the existence of Muhammad, and that all prophets derived their light from him. In another passage, Maybudī ponders God's creation of the human being, whose various parts (e.g. bones, sinews, veins, eye, ear, brain and heart) first took shape as [individual] substances, and these substances were then drawn by God from the ocean of potentiality (*baḥr-i qudrat*) into the channel of composition (*silk-i tarkīb*). Maybudī then describes the different parts of the human make-up, using the metaphor of an adorned palace.[72] He continues by observing that when we look upon this human constitution [with our outward eye], it appears to be limited. However if we viewed it from the standpoint of the meanings and sublime realities that are deposited within it, we would see it to be a macrocosm (*ʿālam-i akbar*). Indeed, he adds, the heavenly bodies, the stars, the constellations, the sun and the moon, all derive their light from the heart of the believer, while the heart of the believer derives its light from the divine gaze (*naẓar-i Ḥaqq*).[73]

Thus, in Maybudī's cosmology, the believer, as true successor to Adam, continues to provide the link between God and the cosmos which was first brought into being through the pre-existential light or spirit of Muhammad.

Adam's slip (*zallat*) and banishment from Paradise

In his mystical commentary, Maybudī presents three principal reasons for Adam's slip and subsequent banishment from Paradise, all of which show these events in an entirely positive light, relating them to different aspects of the doctrine of love. They may be summarised as being: first, that Adam might truly realise the love of God for which he was destined; second, that he should suffer, for without pain there can be no real love; and third, that God's love and mercy should be fully manifested.

In his commentary on Q. 2:36, 'Satan caused them to slip (from there)', Maybudī relates that Khwāja ʿAbd Allāh Anṣārī was once asked whether

Adam was more perfect in the world or in Paradise, to which he answered 'in the world, for in Paradise he could be accused on account of himself (*dar tuhmat-i khwad būd*), but in the world he could be accused of love (*dar tuhmat-i 'ishq*)'. The disciples were then warned not to imagine that it was out of any baseness that Adam was expelled from Paradise; on the contrary, it was because of his lofty aspiration:

> The exactor of love (*mutaqāḍī-yi 'ishq*) knocked at the door of Adam's breast saying 'O Adam! The beauty of Reality has been unveiled; will you just stay here with all the comfort of Paradise?' Adam looked and saw infinite beauty, beside which the beauty of all the seven heavens was nothing. His noble aspiration took hold of his skirt saying, 'If ever you want to win love you must stake all this royal court [i.e. Paradise] for it'.[74]

Maybudī continues by explaining that love cannot be won without suffering:

> The command came, 'O Adam! Now that you have set foot on the path of love, leave Paradise, for this is the palace of ease, and what do the lovers of pain have to do with the Abode of Peace?[75] May the neck of lovers ever be caught in the snare of affliction![76]

The ability to suffer the pain of love is one of the virtues associated with 'manly' chivalry (*jawānmardī*).[77] So, in his commentary on Q. 6:2, 'He it is Who created you from clay', Maybudī relates how Adam imagined that he would eternally enjoy the security of Paradise, until the words came from God:

> O Adam! We want to make a man out of you
> How long will you sit there like women living for vain appearances?
> Set your sights on the way and go forth like a man.[78]
>
> O Adam, take your hand from the neck of Eve,
> And place it on the neck of the dragon of love.[79]

Another reason which Maybudī proposes for the exile from Paradise is that humanity should know its own weakness and dependence on God.[80] By realising their helplessness, servants are brought to the state of supplication and self-abasement that God requires of them.[81] Indeed, it is for this reason that God decreed that the prophets would slip.[82]

Thus far, Adam's slip has been understood in terms of the perfecting of his (i.e. humanity's) love, humility and 'manliness', but Maybudī also interprets the fall as being required by God for the complete manifestation of His attributes of mercy and love.[83] Adam is compared to a child whose mother sends him out wearing new clothes, warning him not to get them dirty. The child plays with his friends and returns with his clothes covered in mud, and is so ashamed that he hides in a corner. His mother knows well that the child is afraid of being punished and comfortingly calls out, 'O love of your mother's heart, come! I only sent you out so that I could set to work with soap and water.' So, like the mother, Maybudī explains, God sent man, dressed in the garment of innocence and the robe of trust, out into the world of dirt only when He had ready at hand the water of forgiveness and the soap of mercy.[84]

Since God knew that humanity would slip, even before He brought them into existence, He spread out the carpet of love and announced the favour of 'He loves them, they love Him', so that whatever they did would be forgiven and defended by the virtue (*ḥukm*) of love.[85] God's special favour to human beings could not really become manifest without their disobedience; for the real proof of favour is not that there should be kindness in times of agreement, but that there should be kindness at the time of opposition.[86] Moreover, man's abasement through sin makes him dearer to God, for, according to a tradition quoted more than once by Maybudī, God says 'The groaning of the sinner is dearer to Me than the chanting of those who praise Me'.[87]

Two other reasons are given for Adam's fall. Commenting on Q. 17:1, 'Glorified be He Who carried His servant by night', Maybudī explains that the secret of God's commanding Adam 'Go down' (Q. 7:13) was so that He could say to Muhammad, 'Rise'.[88] However, later in his commentary on Q. 20:115, 'And verily We made a covenant of old with Adam, but he forgot', Maybudī states:

> It is said that Adam had two existences: his first existence was for the world, not Paradise, and his second existence was for Paradise. The command came 'O Adam! Leave [Paradise] and go to the world. Stake all that dignity and glory[89] in the way of love, and get along with pain and suffering. Then we shall bring you back to this dear homeland and eternal abode with 100,000 honours and favours.'[90]

In other words, it was only by enduring the suffering of this world that humanity could win the rewards of Paradise.

The Covenant of *Alast*

The story of the covenant (*mīthāq*) which God made in pre-eternity with all the descendants of Adam has its basis in the following Qur'anic verse: 'And (remember, Muhammad) when your Lord brought forth from the children of Adam, from their reins, their seed, and made them testify of themselves (saying): Am I not your Lord (*a lastu bi-rabbikum*)? They said: Yes (*balā*), we do (so) testify' (Q. 7:172).

Prophetic hadiths commenting on this verse describe how God rubbed the back of Adam and brought forth his progeny, scattering them before Him like tiny ants (or particles),[91] after which He made each of them testify to His Lordship.[92] Several of these traditions link this covenant with divine preordination (*qaḍā'*) Some, for example, conclude with the words 'and the pen was dry with what was going to be from that day on till the day of resurrection', or 'and He wrote (ordained) their term (*ajal*) and their provision (*rizq*)'. More significant from the point of view of theological doctrine (and, as we shall see, for mystical doctrine in the *Kashf al-asrār*) is the tradition that God drew out Adam's progeny in two groups, one blessed and the other damned. According to different hadiths the former were drawn out by God's right hand and the latter by his left (or cast to the left);[93] or the former were drawn from Adam's right side and were white in colour, while the latter were drawn from his left side and were black.[94] To the first group God said 'Enter the Garden' and to the second, 'Enter the Fire. I do not care'.[95]

From early on, Sufis attached particular significance to the Covenant of *Alast*, or *rūz-i alast* or *rūz-i balā* as it is also called in Persian.[96] It was understood as the moment when man only existed through God, when he was in a state of annihilation from self (*fanā'*) and remaining in God (*baqā'*).[97] It was the moment when humanity was able to *see* God as well as hearing Him and, since vision is the mainspring of love, it was the moment when the seed of human love for God was sown.[98] On the Day of *Alast*, the primordial Revelation was placed in the human heart.[99] In this world, the spiritual vocation of the human being can be understood as the fulfilment of the pact agreed in pre-eternity with God; it is to return to that state of being with Him, cut off from all other.[100]

All these ideas are to be found in Maybudī's mystical commentary in various contexts where he raises the subject of the covenant. For example, the belief that on the Day of *Alast*, human beings were in the perfect state of annihilation from self and remaining in God, is expressed in a saying attributed by Maybudī to Anṣārī, according to which on the Day of *Alast* God was both the questioner and the answerer:[101]

> The King addressed the servant, and made him hear Him through Himself. In the servant's absence [from existence] He answered [on the servant's behalf] and then made the answer over to the servant. This was just as when God said '[...] You did not throw when you threw, but God threw' [Q.8:17].[102]

In his commentary on Q. 7:204, 'And when the Qur'an is recited give ear to it', Maybudī says that true audition (*samāʿ*) is a memory of the pre-eternal summons which was made [to man] on the Day of the Covenant.[103]

Like many other Sufis, Maybudī equates fulfilment of the covenant with the attainment of the goal of the mystical path.[104] Thus he states that the aspirants (*murīd*) of the 'first day' will never forget the spiritual intention (*irādat*) that they made then.[105] However, more central to Maybudī's discussions of the covenant are, typically, the doctrines of *qaḍāʾ* and of love. In his mystical commentary on Q. 2:63, 'And (remember) when We took the covenant with you'[106], Maybudī observes:

> God took the covenant from all men and all answered, but some responded willingly and others unwillingly.[107] The one who answered willingly had access to the witnessing of God and was protected by eternal love, whereas the one who responded unwillingly was left in darkness and alienation.[108]

He adds that at the time of the covenant God revealed Himself to the hearts of everyone, but to some it was a manifestation of punishment (*siyāsat*) and might (*ʿizzat*), and to others a manifestation of grace (*luṭf*) and generosity (*karāmat*).[109] So strongly is the Day of the Covenant associated with the predestination of mankind that Maybudī even calls it *rūz-i qabḍa* (the day of the 'handful').[110] Commencing on Q. 6:88, 'This is the guidance of God, He guided those of His servants whom He wished', Maybudī observes:

> Not everyone who set out reached his destination, and not everyone who arrived saw the Beloved. The one arrived who was effaced in himself, and the one who saw, had seen on the day of the handful.[111]

The theme of divine predestination appears again in Maybudī's mystical commentary on the Covenant verse itself. Here, however, pride of place is given to the theme of love with which the mystical commentary begins.

> From the point of view of understanding and in the language of truth, this verse has another mystery and reality:[112] it is an allusion to the beginning of the states of lovers, and the binding of the pact and covenant of love with them, that first day when God was present and reality attained.
>
> Cupbearer! [Let's drink] to Laylā and those nights
> When we were together with Laylā.
>
> How sweet was that day when the foundation of love was laid! How precious the time when the covenant of love was made! Those who aspire (*murīdān*) never forget that first day of spiritual intent (*irādat*). Those of anguished longing (*mushtāqān*) know that moment of union to be the crown of life and the focal point (*qibla*) of all time.[113]

Maybudī goes on to quote the verse 'Remind them of the days of God' (Q. 14:5), which he glosses in the following manner:

> The command came, 'O master [Muhammad]! Remind those servants of Mine who have forgotten Our pact and become busy with otherness. Remind them of that day when their pure spirits tied the covenant of love with Me, when We placed the collyrium of "Am I not your Lord?" on the eye of their longing.' O needful servant of God! Remember that day when the spirits (*arwāḥ*) and bodies (*ashkhaṣ*) of lovers drank the wine of affection (*maḥabbat*) from the cup of love (*ʿishq*) at the assembly of intimacy. The angels of highest heaven said, 'See now, how high these people are aiming. We have never even sipped this wine, nor even caught a whiff of it, but the clamour of those beggars calling "Is there any more?" has reached the Capella.'[114]
>
> Of that wine which is not forbidden in our religion
> You will not find our lips dry until the end of time.[115]

In other contexts Maybudī describes the bond of love (*paymān-i dūstī*) as being the first honour to have been given to humanity,[116] and defines the 'clear proof of the Lord (*bayyina*)' (Q. 11:17) as 'the seed of the pain of love which God sowed in the hearts of his lovers on the first day at the pre-eternal covenant'.[117]

In his commentary on Q. 33:72, 'Lo, We offered the trust unto the heavens and the earth and the hills but they shrank from bearing it and were afraid of it', Maybudī links humanity's taking on the trust (*amānat*) with his acceptance of the pact on the Day of *Alast*.[118] Here Maybudī is playing with the two words – *mihr* (love) and *muhr* (seal).

> It is customary for people, when they deposit something precious with someone, that they place a seal on it, and when they come to fetch it they check the seal. If it is in place they express their appreciation. On the Day of the Covenant the trust of 'Am I not your Lord?' was deposited with you and the seal of 'Yes' was placed upon it. When your life is ended and you are placed in the earth, that angel will enter and ask 'Who is your Lord?'[119] That is the way he checks to see if the seal of that first day is in place or not. O needful servant of God! From head to toe you have been filled with love and the seal [upon it] was of love. The seal (*muhr*) was placed there that the love (*mihr*) should remain there. [...] O [you with] burning heart that bears the seal of love, you are for Me and I am for you![120]

In these two passages we may note again the way that Maybudī attributes words to God. Though this is a common feature of Sufi exegesis, Maybudī uses it in a particular way in order to emphasize God's intimacy with human beings. This is one of numerous rhetorical devices which Maybudī has integrated into his exegetical narrative, which interweaves Qur'anic word, Prophetic hadiths, story telling, personification, rhyming prose and poetry.[121] In the following chapter we shall see that these features are sometimes, though not always, incorporated into discussions of the more practical and technical aspects of Sufi doctrine.

NOTES

1 *Kashf*, III, p. 294. It is to be noted that Maybudī understands *ʿaql* simply to be the rational faculty, unlike other Sufis, such as Ibn ʿArabī, who understood *ʿaql* to be also the Intellect, the locus of gnosis. On the use of the word *ʿaql* see Fazlur Rahman and William Chittick, 'ʿAql', *EIr*, II, pp. 194–8.

2 This recalls a *ḥadīth qudsī* related by Abū Dāwūd: 'Pride (or grandeur, *kibriyāʾ*) is My cloak and greatness (*ʿaẓama*) My robe, and he who competes with Me in respect of them I shall cast into Hell-fire.' See *Forty Hadith Qudsi*, selected and translated by E. Ibrahim and D. Johnson-Davies (Beirut, 1990), no. 19, p. 92.

3 *Kashf*, I, p. 439.

4 *Kashf*, V, p. 244; VI, p. 493; also IV, p. 302, where the same idea is quoted from Bāyazīd.

5 The first of the two Muslim attestations of faith (*shahādatayn*): 'There is no god but God.' In the Arabic script the number of letters does come to twelve.
6 The origin of this Prophetic saying is not clear. However, similar traditions exist, the closest being one related from Wahb b. Munabbih, according to which God said to the prophet Irmiyā when he was being sent to the Children of Israel: 'I am God, there is no one like Me, the heavens and earth and all that is in them subsist by My word (*bi-kalimatī*)'; related in Ṭabarī, *Jāmiʿ al-bayān,* Būlāq edition, XV, p. 27.
7 *Kashf*, IV, pp. 133–4.
8 *Kashf*, I, p. 582; II, p. 508. The last line could also be rendered: 'And the description of he who describes It (or Him) is an apostasy' (*wa naʿtu man yanʿatuhu lāḥid*). The poem appears at the very end of Anṣārī's *Manāzil al-sāʾirīn*, under the station of *Tawḥīd*, ed. de Beaurecueil. p. 113.
9 Both Arberry and Abdel Haleem translate the divine name 'al-Ṣamad' as 'eternal'. But Abdel Haleem has added the note that some interpretations of the divine name 'al-Ṣamad' include [God's being] 'self-sufficient' and 'sought by all'. Pickthall has therefore appropriately translated God's divine name 'al-Ṣamad' as 'the Eternally Besought of all'.
10 *Kashf*, X, p. 41.
11 See discussion on pp. 16–17.
12 *Kashf*, V, p. 374.
13 *Kashf*, I, pp. 254–5.
14 *Kashf*, IX, p. 325.
15 See Ghazzālī, *Al-Maqṣad al-asnā fī sharḥ maʿānī asmāʾ Allāh al-ḥusnā*, ed. F.A. Shehadi (Beirut, 1971); trans. by D.B. Burrell and N. Daher as *The Ninety-Nine Beautiful Names of God* (Cambridge, 1992). On the Divine names in Islamic theology see Daniel Gimaret, *Les noms divins en islam* (Paris, 1988). On 'opposition' or 'duality' within the Divine attributes see Sachiko Murata, *The Tao of Islam* (Albany) 1992, Part II. On Ibn ʿArabī and the Divine names and attributes from the point of view of manifestation see Toshihiko Izutsu, *Sufism and Taoism* (Berkeley, 1983), ch. 7.
16 *Kashf*, IX, p. 16. See also *Kashf*, V, pp. 230–1, where Maybudī explains that God's attribute of glory or might (*ʿizza*) comprises both light (*nūr*) and fire (*nār*). With the fire of His might He burns some, and with the light of His might He cherishes another.
17 *Kashf*, X, p. 178. See also *Kashf*, X, p. 431; VI, pp. 17, 342. This doctrine is also expressed by Hujwīrī, *Kashf al-maḥjūb*, p. 253; tr. Nicholson, p. 288.
18 For example, *Kashf*, X, p. 179; VII, p. 398.
19 *Kashf*, VI, pp. 408–9.
20 *Kashf*, X, p. 621.
21 *Kashf*, III, p. 138.
22 *Kashf*, IX, pp. 76–7.
23 *Kashf*, I, p. 498. Moses' question, with which this tradition begins, is found in a saying attributed by Ghazzālī to Kaʿb al-Aḥbār, but the divine response in the latter tradition is different: 'I sit with him who remembers Me'. See *Iḥyāʾ*, Part 2, Book 5, *Kitāb ādāb al-ulfa wa'l-ukhuwwa wa'l-ṣuḥba,* ch. 3, p. 303.
24 *Kashf*, I, pp. 439–40. See also the discussion of the word *qurb* (*Kashf*, X, p. 293) where Maybudī observes that whereas it is possible to describe the servant's

nearness to God, there is no way to conceive of, or describe, the nature of God's nearness to us, which is as He described it when He said, 'Nearer than his jugular vein'.

25 Indeed, it will be seen later that the main reason for God's creation of Adam was for love.

26 *Kashf*, IX, p. 117.

27 Possibly Anṣārī.

28 *Kashf*, VI, p. 322. A similar tradition is quoted in *Kashf*, V, p. 453: 'The longing of the righteous for the meeting with Me is never-ending, but indeed I long even more for the meeting with them.' Both these traditions appear in Aḥmad Samʿānī, *Rawḥ al-arwāḥ*, p. 22, while the latter tradition appears in Abū Nuʿaym al-Iṣfahānī, *Ḥilyat al-awliyā'* (Cairo, 1932–8), X, p. 91.

29 *Kuntu kanzan makhfiyan fa-aḥbabtu an uʿrafa, fa-khalaqtu'l-khalq likay uʿrafa.* This tradition is cited in Anṣārī's *Ṭabaqāt al-ṣūfiyya*, ed. S. Mawlā'ī, pp. 639, 645, and in a commentary on *Sūrat Yūsuf* (Q. 12) attributed to Aḥmad Ghazzālī, the *Baḥr al-maḥabba* (Bombay, 1898), p. 1. The hadith is listed, with slight variations in wording, by al-Sakhāwī, al-Qārī and al-ʿAjlūnī. See Shams al-Dīn Abi'l-Khayr Muḥammad b. ʿAbd al-Raḥmān al-Sakhāwī, *Al-Maqāṣid al-ḥasana fī bayān kathīr min al-aḥādīth al-mushtahira ʿala'l-alsina*, ed. ʿA.M. al-Ṣādiq (Beirut, 1979), § 838; Nūr al-Dīn ʿAlī b. Muḥammad b. Sulṭān (Mullā ʿAlī al-Qārī), *Al-Asrār al-marfūʿa fi'l-akhbār al-mawḍūʿa*, ed. M. Sabbagh (Beirut, 1971), § 353; Ismāʿīl b. Muḥammad al-Ajlūnī, *Kashf al-khafā' wa muzīl al-ilbās ʿammā ishtahara min al-aḥādīth ʿalā alsinat al-nās*, ed. A. al-Qālash (2 vols., Beirut, 1979), II, § 2016. A notable feature of these versions is the absence of the word hidden (*makhfiyan*). An early version of this tradition is to be found in the *Rasā'il* of the Ikhwān al-Ṣafā', where it begins: 'I was a hidden treasure of good and excellent things (*khayra wa faḍā'il*); I was not known and I wished to be known (note *aradtu* rather than *aḥbabtu*).' See *Rasā'il Ikhwān al-Ṣafā' wa khullān al-wafā'*, ed. B. al-Bustānī (4 vols., Beirut, 1957), III, 'Epistle on Causes and Effects', p. 356. The latter tradition is cited in Omar Ali de Unzaga, 'The conversation between Moses and God (*munāǧāt Mūsā*) in the *Epistles* of the Pure Brethren (*Rasā'il Iḫwān al-Ṣafā'*)', in D. de Smet, G. de Callataÿ and J.M.F. Van Reeth, eds., *Al-Kitâb: la sacralité du texte dans le monde de l'Islam* (Brussels, Leuven and Louvain-La-Neuve, 2004), p. 378.

30 Trans. Abdel Haleem.

31 On al-Wāsiṭī see Gramlich, *Alte Vorbilder*, II, pp. 267–400. Maybudī cites numerous comments from al-Wāsiṭī, most of which, including this, appear to have been somehow derived from Sulamī's *Ḥaqā'iq*.

32 Both the published edition of Sulamī's *Ḥaqā'iq* (ed. ʿImrān, II, p. 40) and MS Or. 9433 (fol. 200a) include only the following sentence of al-Wāsiṭī in this context: 'He caused the realms of engendered existence (*akwān*) to appear [in order] that the traces of friendship might be manifested to His friends and the traces of wretchedness to His enemies.'

33 *Kashf*, VI, p. 477; see also *Kashf*, VIII, p. 387. The discrepancy between the two versions here might suggest that Maybudī was using a variant manuscript or that he had derived it from an oral transmission. See ch. 1, p. 22 and nn. 133, 134.

34 In the *Rasā'il* of the Ikhwān al-Ṣafā', the *kuntu kanzan* hadith likewise

occurs as an answer from God to the same question posed by one of the prophets. See Ali de Unzaga, 'Conversation', p. 378.

35 *Kashf*, VI, p. 477. Ghazzālī also shows the interdependence of love and knowledge, for which see chapter seven.

36 *Kashf*, IX, p. 375.

37 For a history of the doctrine of *nūr-i Muḥammadī* see Annemarie Schimmel, *And Muḥammad is His Messenger* (Chapel Hill and London, 1985), ch. 7; Uri Rubin, 'Nūr Muḥammadī', *EI²*, VIII, p. 125; idem, 'Pre-existence and light: aspects of the concept of *Nūr Muḥammad*', *Israel Oriental Studies* 5 (1975), pp. 62–119; Tor Andrae, *Die Person Muhammeds in Lehre und Glauben seiner Gemeinde* (Stockholm, 1918). See also Tustarī's interpretation of the Muhammadan light in Böwering, *Mystical Vision*, pp. 149–53.

38 *Kashf*, VI, p. 546.

39 *Kashf*, VII, p. 334, Here Maybudī has substituted the Arabic pronoun *-hu* for *-ka* in the hadith: *law lāka la-mā khalaqtu'l-aflāk* (Were it not for thee I would not have created the spheres). This hadith resulted in the popular title given to Muhammad 'Lord of *law lāka*'. See Schimmel, *And Muḥammad*, p. 131. The hadith is listed in Qārī, *Asrār al-marfūʿa*, § 385; Ajlūnī, *Kashf al-khafāʾ*, § 2123.

40 *Kashf*, VII, p. 174. On the other hand, see *Kashf*, X, p. 328: 'Whatever We created, We created for Adam, and We created Adam for Ourself', by which Maybudī is referring to humanity.

41 *Kashf*, VII, p. 525. In his Persian gloss for this Arabic tradition, Maybudī adds: 'in every glance a new secret, a new mystery, a new favour and grace, and a new knowledge and understanding.' In the *Tamhīdāt* (ed. ʿA. ʿUsayrān [Tehran, 1962], p. 267), ʿAyn al-Quḍāt Hamadānī attributes this tradition to Sahl al-Tustarī, though in Tustarī's *tafsīr* it begins differently with the words: 'God created the light of Muhammad from His light. He formed it and brought it forth at His own hand. This light remained before God'; trans. in Böwering, *Mystical Vision*, p. 150.

42 Literally, everything was 'an uninvited guest' (*ṭufayl*) [hanging on] to his existence. *Kashf*, IX, p. 375.

43 This hadith is cited by Sakhāwī under his discussion of another hadith (listed as § 837), which reads: *kuntu awwal al-nabiyyīn fi'l-khalqi wa ākhirahum fi'l-baʿth*. He states that it resembles the hadith: *yā rasūl Allāh matā kunta* (or *kutibta*) *nabiyyan? qāla wa Ādam bayna'l-rūḥ wa'l-jasad*. With the latter ending the hadith is listed in Ibn Abī Shayba, *Al-Muṣannaf fi'l-aḥādīth wa'l-āthār*, ed. ʿA. Afghānī and A. al-Aʿzamī (15 vols., Bombay, 1979–83), XIV, *Kitab al-maghāzī*, ch. 2405 (Mā jāʾa fī mabʿath al-nabī), § 18402. It is listed in the same form by Ibn Ḥanbal, *Musnad*, V, p. 379. The popular form among the Sufis is, according to Sakhāwī, as in Maybudī's passage: *kuntu nabiyyan wa Ādam bayna'l-māʾi wa'l-ṭīn*.

44 *Kashf*, X, p. 202.

45 *Kashf*, IX, p. 375.

46 *Kashf*, VIII, p. 387.

47 See *Sawāniḥ*, ch. 11; also Nasrollah Pourjavady, 'Kirishma-yi ḥusn wa kirishma-yi maʿshūqī', in N. Pourjavady, *Būy-i jān* (Tehran, 1372sh/1993–4), pp. 179–97. Of course, there is no question of 'need' in the usual sense of that word; it is rather that the perfect *manifestation* of the Absolute requires the existence of lover and beloved. These two are already latently present as two aspects of the

One: *ḥusn* (the essence of beauty) and *ʿishq* (love). See *Sawāniḥ*, tr. Pourjavady, translator's commentary, pp. 94–6. ʿAyn al-Quḍāt Hamadānī expresses this idea differently with the following metaphor: 'The beauty of the face of Lordship is not perfect without the mole of slavehood, but the mole of slavehood would not even exist without the face of Lordship.' See *Tamhīdāt*, p. 275.

48 For example, when he speaks of the mystic (or indeed every atom of creation) as being the eye (*ʿayn*) with which God contemplates Himself. See Corbin, *En Islam iranien*, III, pp. 32ff., 66, 80.

49 Trans. modified with reference to Abdel Haleem's translation.

50 *Kashf*, IX, pp. 116–17. There is a subtle play of meaning between the two applications of the word *rawā* here.

51 *Kashf*, IX, p. 117.

52 *Kashf*, III, p. 571.

53 Ibid.

54 Ibid. See also *Kashf*, VIII, p. 545, where Maybudī states that human beings alone among creatures are privileged with the look of love (*naẓar-i maḥabbat*) from God.

55 *Kashf*, VII, p. 78. See also *Kashf*, IX, p. 154, where Maybudī states that the body of Adam was made the oyster for the pearl of the heart, the heart the oyster for the pearl of the secret (*sirr*), the secret the oyster for the pearl of the divine gaze.

56 *Kashf*, VI, p. 151.

57 According to the words of the Qur'an: 'They will ask you [Muhammad] about the spirit. Say, The spirit is by the command of my Lord' (Q. 17:85). *Kashf*, III, p. 297.

58 *Kashf*, VI, pp. 149–50.

59 Ibid. and *Kashf*, VII, pp. 455.

60 *Kashf*, III, p. 21.

61 *Kashf*, V, p. 422.

62 *Kashf*, VIII, p. 374.

63 *Kashf*, III, p. 50.

64 *Kashf*, VIII, pp. 100–1. This is an allusion to Q. 33:72, 'We offered the trust to the heavens and the earth and the mountains, but they refused to carry it; and man carried it.' The trust (*amāna*) is traditionally interpreted to mean obedience (*ṭāʿa*) and carrying out the obligatory duties (*farāʾiḍ*) prescribed by religion. According to Qushayrī (*Laṭāʾif*, III, p. 173), *amāna* is upholding what is obligatory according to the principles (*uṣūl*) and applications (*furūʿ*) [of *fiqh*], or it is *tawḥīd* in faith (*ʿaqdan*) and keeping the limits (*ḥifẓ al-ḥudūd*) in endeavours (*jahdan*). Maybudī interprets *amāna* here simply as love, as can be seen in the discussion of the Covenant of *Alast* on pp. 139–42 and esp. p. 142.

65 As in Q. 59:21, 'If We had caused the Qur'an to descend upon a mountain, you [Prophet] would have seen it humbled and split apart in awe of God.'

66 *Kashf*, VIII, p. 101; IX, p. 154.

67 *Kashf*, X, p. 328.

68 *Kashf*, VI, pp. 189–90.

69 Which were traditionally thought to be the head, the breast and back, the two arms and the two legs. See ʿAlī Akbar Dihkhudā, *Lughat-nāma* (Tehran, 1325–52sh/1946–73), XXXV, pp. 230 and 237.

70 *Kashf*, VI, pp. 343–4. This passage is reminiscent of a passage in the *Rasā'il* of the Ikhwān al-Ṣafā', II, p. 463. For example, according to the Ikhwān, the nine heavens (as opposed to Maybudī's seven) correspond to the nine substances of the body: bone, brain, flesh, veins, blood, nerve, skin, hair and nails, while the twelve constellations of the Zodiac correspond to the twelve orifices: two eyes, nostrils, ears, nipples of the breast, mouth, navel and channels of excretion (these latter are identical to the twelve orifices listed by Maybudī). Then the seven planets, whose influence governs the sublunary regions, are said to correspond to the seven powers of the body: attraction, sensation, digestion, repulsion, nutrition, sleep and imagination, and the seven spiritual powers: the five senses, the power of speech and the intellectual faculty. (Note: Here Maybudī has left out the bodily powers, but the spiritual powers correspond exactly to those mentioned by the Ikhwān.) See Seyyed Hossein Nasr, *Introduction to Islamic Cosmological Doctrines* (London, 1978), pp. 99–100.

71 Ibid.

72 This passage, again, bears some resemblance to a cosmological passage in the *Rasā'il*, where the Ikhwān al-Ṣafā' use the metaphor of a city though Maybudī has used the metaphor of a palace. He also has: 240 (as opposed to 248) pillars; 360 (as opposed to 390) rivulets; six servants (as opposed to seven artisans); the bodily powers such as attraction, sensation etc., listed in n. 70; and five watchmen assigned to its protection, namely the five senses. As in the previous passage, Maybudī ends with the king, whom he identifies with the heart, being seated on the throne of the palace (for the Ikhwān, the king is the intellect). *Rasā'il*, III, pp. 380–2. Nasr, *Islamic Cosmological Doctrines*, p. 100. Compare also Ghazzālī, *Kīmiyā*, I, p. 42.

73 *Kashf*, VI, pp. 424–5.

74 *Kashf*, I, p. 162. See also *Kashf*, X, p. 329, where Maybudī explains that it is only in separation that lovers become aware of their love. In Adam, the beauty of reality, i.e. the secret of love, was hidden beneath the comforts and blessings of Paradise.

75 One of the names for Paradise, according to Q. 10:25.

76 *Kashf*, I, p. 162. Or again, see *Kashf*, VI, p. 190, where, according to one of the spiritual masters, it was through Adam's disobedience that God wished to cook the provision of love (*'ishq*) in the oven of punishment (*siyāsat*).

77 The doctrines of *futuwwa* or *jawānmardī*, discussed on pp. 171–2.

78 This couplet is taken from a *qaṣīda* of Sanā'ī. It may be found in the *Dīwān-i Sanā'ī*, ed. M. Raḍawī (repr., Tehran, 1984), pp. 204–6.

79 *Kashf*, III, p. 298.

80 *Kashf*, III, p. 589.

81 *Kashf*, III, p. 640.

82 See, for example, *Kashf*, VIII, pp. 116–17, where David's slip is explained as being in order that he would come as a slave, full of burning anguish and indigence, instead of as a king.

83 This idea is also explored by Maybudī's near contemporary, Aḥmad Sam'ānī. See William Chittick, 'The myth of Adam's Fall in Aḥmad al-Sam'ānī's *Rawḥ al-arwāḥ*', in Lewisohn, ed., *Classical Persian Sufism*, pp. 337–59.

84 *Kashf*, III, p. 22.

85 *Kashf*, VII, p. 78.

86 *Kashf*, X, p. 329.
87 *Kashf*, III, pp. 21 and 640. What is implied is a groaning of pain, indigence and regret that is experienced by the sinner (mankind) as opposed to the 'complacency' of the angels. See the passage quoted in chapter three, pp. 93–4.
88 *Kashf*, V, p. 503.
89 Lit. crown, cap and sash (*tāj wa kulāh wa kamar*).
90 *Kashf*, VI, pp. 190–1.
91 In his *tafsīr*, Ṭabarī discusses the possible meaning of *dharr*, and opts for 'tiny ants', for which see Franz Rosenthal, trans. with introduction, *The History of Ṭabarī*, I, *From the Creation to the Flood* (Albany, 1989), p. 304, n. 836.
92 For the numerous hadiths commenting on this verse see Ṭabarī, *Jāmiʿ al-bayān*, ed. Shākir and Shākir, XIII, pp. 222–50; also idem, *History*, I, tr. Rosenthal, pp. 304–7. For an account of the development of the doctrines surrounding Q. 7:172, according to Sunni and Shiʿi thought as well as in Sufism, see Nasrollah Pourjavady, 'ʿAhd-i Alast: ʿAqīda-yi Abū Ḥāmid al-Ghazzālī wa jāygāh-i tārīkh-i ān', *Maʿārif* 7/2 (1990), pp. 3–47, now expanded and republished as the second chapter in idem, *Du mujaddid*.
93 Ṭabarī, *Jāmiʿ al-bayān*, ed. Shākir and Shākir, XIII, pp. 228, 234; idem., *History*, I, tr. Rosenthal, pp. 305–6.
94 Ṭabarī, *Jāmiʿ al-bayān*, ed. Shākir and Shākir, XIII, pp. 237–8, 242; idem., *History*, I, tr. Rosenthal, p. 307.
95 Ṭabarī, *Jāmiʿ al-bayān*, ed. Shākir and Shākir, IX, p. 76; idem., *History*, I, tr. Rosenthal, p. 305.
96 The Day of *Alast* ('Am I not?'), or Day of [saying] 'Yes'. For mystics, particularly those who adhered to the way of love, it was significant that the word *balā* could also be understood to mean affliction (when derived from the Arabic root *b-l-w*) and this allowed for a meaningful play on words in some later literature. Note the following line from a *ghazal* of Ḥāfiẓ: 'The Covenant of *Alast* was sealed with a "yes" (*balā*) that was for the purpose of affliction (*balā*).' See *Dīwān-i Ḥāfiẓ*, ed. P.N. Khānlarī (Tehran, 1359sh/1980–1), Ghazal 20. In the *Kashf al-asrār*, the Day of the Covenant is often alluded to simply by the words 'that day' (*ān rūz*).
97 This understanding of the Covenant of *Alast* was thought to have originated with Junayd. See Ali Hasan Abdel Kader, *The Life, Personality and Works of al-Junayd* (London, 1976), pp. 32, 41; Pourjavady, *Du mujaddid*, p. 34ff. However, Arberry has suggested that it may be traced to Bāyazīd's account of his so-called *miʿrāj* where he relates that God said to him: 'I was there when thou wast not, so be thou Mine when thou art not.' See Arberry, *Revelation and Reason in Islam*, pp. 103–4.
98 See Daylamī, *ʿAṭf al-alif*, p. 89; French tr. Vadet, p. 142. Pourjavady, 'ʿAhd', p. 17; idem, *Du mujaddid*, pp. 41–2.
99 Georges C. Anawati and Louis Gardet, *La mystique musulmane* (Paris, 1961), p. 131.
100 See Jaʿfar al-Ṣādiq's commentary on Q. 3:76, 'Le tafsîr mystique attribué à Ǧaʿfar Ṣâdiq, ed. Paul Nwyia, *Mélanges de l'Université St Joseph* 43 (Beirut, 1967), p. 192.
101 An idea earlier expressed by Ḥallāj. See Pourjavady, *Du mujaddid*, pp. 37–8, 66. See also Ḥallāj's commentary on the *mīthāq* (according to his numbering

Q. 7:171) in Massignon, *Essai*, p. 370.

102 *Kashf*, III, p. 796.

103 *Kashf*, III, p. 833. This recalls a statement of Kalābādhī on the subject of remembrance [of God] (*dhikr*), in his section on *samāʿ*. See Kalābādhī, *Kitāb al-taʿarruf*, pp. 126–7; tr. Arberry, pp. 166–7.

104 Schimmel, *Mystical Dimensions*, pp. 24, 172.

105 *Kashf*, III, p. 794.

106 This verse actually refers to the covenant made with the Children of Israel but the use of the word *mīthāq* here gives Maybudī the opportunity to introduce the theme of the Covenant of *Alast*. See also pp. 90–1.

107 This is probably a reference to the hadith narrated from Suddī (Ṭabarī, *Jāmiʿ al-bayān*, ed. Shākir and Shākir, XIII, p. 243; idem., *History*, I, tr. Rosenthal, p. 307), according to which some responded sincerely while others dissimulated (*ʿalā wajh taqiyya*). Daylamī (*ʿAṭf al-alif*, p. 89; French tr. Vadet, p. 143) describes some as responding with compliance (*ṭawʿan*) and some grudgingly (*karhan*).

108 *Kashf*, I, p. 219.

109 Ibid.

110 This is presumably a reference to the 'handful' of progeny which God took and cast to the right and the handful which He cast to the left, as in the hadith cited previously. Alternatively one might understand *qabḍa* as 'grip', that is, our being in the grip of divine destiny.

111 *Kashf*, III, p. 424.

112 Lit. taste (*dhawq*).

113 *Kashf*, III, p. 793.

114 The usage of the words *hal min mazīd* (Is there any more? Q. 50:30) is inspired by famous saying attributed to Bāyazīd, cited by Abū Nuʿaym al-Iṣfahānī, *Ḥilyat*, X, p. 40.

115 *Kashf*, III, pp. 793–4. This *bayt* is taken from Aḥmad Ghazzālī's *Sawāniḥ*, ed. Pourjavady, ch. 1, p. 3; tr. Pourjavady, p. 17. See also *Kashf*, IV, p. 254, where Maybudī again uses the image of drinking the wine of love with reference to the *mīthāq*.

116 *Kashf*, V, pp. 597–8.

117 *Kashf*, IV, p. 371.

118 On the *amāna* see n. 64.

119 A reference to one of the two angels, Munkar and Nakīr who, according to Islamic tradition, examine and, if necessary, punish the dead in their graves. See Arent J. Wensinck, 'Munkar and Nakīr', *EI*[2], VII, pp. 576–7.

120 *Kashf*, VIII, p. 101.

121 As discussed on pp. 92–6.

6

Aspects of spiritual guidance

This chapter will examine some of the teachings that Maybudī presents related to the theory and practice of spiritual wayfaring. It will begin by discussing the principal aim of the mystical path, namely the attainment of that which is described as 'union with God', also defined as the state of annihilation from self and subsisting in or through God, a state which requires the combating and conquering of the lower self or ego (*nafs*), known as the 'greater holy war'. The chapter will then discuss some of the more technical aspects of the theory of the mystical path, such as the stages of the way, and states and stations as they are explained in different contexts in the *Kashf al-asrār*. Finally it will look at some of the key hierarchies that are outlined by Maybudī, which both embrace and evaluate a range of approaches to the spiritual life, and it will show how among these, teachings of the Malāmatiyya and of the Futuwwa have become integrated into the doctrines of the *Kashf al-asrār*.

The goal of the mystical way

> O God! When shall I find again that day when You were for me and I was not.[1] Until I attain that time again I shall be caught between fire and smoke. If it cost me the two worlds to find that day again, I would have made a profit, and if I found Your being for myself by my own not-being then I would be content.[2]

This *munājāt* of Khwāja ʿAbd Allāh expresses in the form of a prayer the goal of the spiritual aspirant as it is consistently presented in the *Kashf al-asrār*: it is to be naughted in oneself so that only God remains; in other words, to attain the state of *fanāʾ* (annihilation from self) and *baqāʾ*

(subsisting in God). The following definition of *fanāʾ* and *baqāʾ* occurs in an intriguing passage attributed to Anṣārī, which consists of a dialogue between the heart (*dil*) and the spirit (*jān*). The heart is here in the position of the person who asks questions (*sāʾil*), and the spirit is the one authorised to give answers (*muftī*):

> The heart asked: 'What is *wafāʾ*, what is *fanāʾ* and what is *baqāʾ*?' The spirit answered: '*Wafāʾ* is fulfilling the covenant of love (*ʿahd-i dūstī-rā miyān bastan*). *Fanāʾ* is being freed from our own selfhood (*az khwadī-yi khwad barastan*). *Baqāʾ* is being united with the reality of God (*ba-ḥaqīqat-i Ḥaqq paywastan*).[3]

Although, as shall be seen in a number of passages cited in this chapter, the state of *baqāʾ* is not always mentioned, it is usually understood to 'follow on from' or be concomitant with the state of *fanāʾ*, and in Sufi manuals the two states are closely linked.[4] Maybudī explains the connection thus: '*fanāʾ* is in reality *baqāʾ*, for until you have become annihilated (*fānī*), you will not be subsistent (*bāqī*) in Him'.[5]

The spiritual goal is also described as the attainment of union with God, which was equated with *baqāʾ* in the previous passage, but is more often denoted by various derivations of the verbal root *W.Ṣ.L.*, such as: *waṣl, wiṣāl, wuṣla* or *muwāṣala* (opposite to *hijr* or *firāq*, meaning separation),[6] or by the term *jamʿ* (opposite to *tafriqa*).[7] An example of the former is Maybudī's explanation of the term *muwāṣala* in his commentary on Q. 6:163, 'Say: My worship and my sacrifice, my living and my dying are for God, Lord of the Worlds'.

> This verse concerning Muṣṭafā [i.e. Muhammad] is an allusion to the station of union (*muwāṣalat*). *Muwāṣalat* is being united with God (*ba-Ḥaqq paywastan ast*), and being freed from oneself. The sign of this condition is a heart alive with contemplation (*fikr*), and a tongue making remembrance (*dhikr*). [It means] being stripped of creatures, a stranger to oneself, in a state of serene detachment (*az taʿalluq āsūda*), and quiescent with God.[8]

Maybudī's usage of the term *jamʿ* may be exemplified by his explanation of the Qur'anic verse 'You did not throw when you threw, but God threw' (Q. 8:17).

> [These words] are an allusion to the very essence (lit. point, *nuqṭa*) of non-differentiation (*jamʿ*) and the realisation of isolation [from everything other

than God] (*tafrīd*). The eternal breeze blows, the lightning of oneness flashes, and the servant is snatched away from water and clay, duality annihilated. Reality has become unalloyed, and the borrowed 'I', killed.

> All the world's affliction is down to talk of 'You and me'
> Abandon 'me', may all the world be Your garden![9]

Maybudī explains that it is not enough for the servant to be rid of his own qualities so that he takes on the virtues or attributes of God, even though this in itself is considered to be an advanced stage of the way, and is recommended in two hadiths of the Prophet: 'Take on the virtues of God'[10] and 'Verily God is thus in "character" (*kadhālika khalqan*), whoever takes on just one of those characteristics will enter Paradise.'[11] The matter is clarified when Maybudī discusses these two hadiths in his commentary on the word '*rabbāniyyīn*' (servants of the Lord) in Q. 3:79:

> People of knowledge have said that what is meant by these virtues (*akhlāq*) is the qualities (*maʿānī*) of the ninety-nine names of God, through which the servant must pass in his wayfaring until he attains to union with God (*ba-wiṣāl-i Allāh risad*). The Khorasani master Abu'l-Qāsim Kurrakānī[12] said: 'As long as the servant is acquiring these qualities and all these attributes, he is still on the way, and has not reached the destination [...] As long as he is in gnosis he is deprived of the Known; as long as he is seeking love, he is ignorant of the Beloved.
> [...]
> One of the great masters was asked: 'When does the slave reach the Lord?' He answered: 'When he is annihilated in himself'. They asked, 'When [or how] does annihilation from self take place?' He answered: 'Seeking becomes effaced in the Sought, gnosis in the Known.' [13]

The 'greater holy war'

Maybudī presents in a number of ways the doctrine widely held among Sufis that the greatest obstacle and danger on the mystical path is man's lower self (*nafs*), or more specifically the self which incites to evil (*al-nafs al-ammāra bi'l-sūʾ*, often called simply the *nafs ammāra*).[14] He explains that while Satan is more harmful to man than a hundred hungry lions in a flock of sheep, a hundred Satans cannot do as much harm as the inciting self (*nafs-i ammāra*),[15] for Satan wants to bring about disobedience and sin, whereas the *nafs* wants to bring the servant to unbelief (*kufr*).[16] This is why the Prophet said: 'Your greatest enemy is your *nafs*, which is between your two sides.'[17]

In his commentary on Q. 3:160, 'If God is your helper none can overcome you, and if He withdraws His help from you, who is there who can help you?', Maybudī explains why, in another hadith, the Prophet described the war against the unbelievers as the 'lesser holy war' and the war against the *nafs* as the 'greater holy war'. First, the war against the unbelievers occurred only on occasions, whereas the war against the *nafs* is perpetual; second, the weapons of the unbelievers could be clearly seen, whereas the weapons of the *nafs*, its insinuation and concupiscence, are hidden. And finally, if in the battle against the unbelievers, the enemy receives divine assistance and the believer is killed, he is rewarded as a martyr; but if the enemy gains the upper hand in the battle with the *nafs*, the believer will face being cut off from God and the torments of Hell.[18] Conquering or 'killing' the *nafs* is therefore a vital necessity for the spiritual wayfarer. He must 'kill the *nafs* that his heart may come alive';[19] 'True kings are those who have conquered their *nafs-i ammāra*.'[20]

In another context Maybudī explains how in the 'greater holy war', as in the 'lesser holy war', strategies have to be used. So all kinds of spiritual exercises (*anwāʿ-i riyāḍāt*) and arts of combat (*funūn-i mujāhadāt*) are employed in order to subdue the *nafs*. Among these, none is more effective than restraining the *nafs* from its passions or lusts (*shahawāt*) and from those things which are familiar to it (*ma'lūfāt*). Dispensations and free interpretations of what is prescribed in the Qur'an and hadith are to be avoided, and whatever is harder and more difficult sought. Maybudī goes on to describe some of the lengths to which saints and prophets have gone in order to conquer the *nafs*. Abū Saʿīd Kharrāz (d. 286/899), for example, spent time standing on his head, while Jesus (according to al-Ḥasan al-Baṣrī) wore coarse wool, and ate wild plants and the leaves and bark of trees in the wilderness.[21] Eating little and wearing wool is a tradition advocated in one context by Maybudī,[22] but, as we shall see, he does not recommend extremes of physical rigour, for ascetic practices and even acts of worship can themselves become idols.[23] Thus, when Maybudī comments on the words 'Have you seen him who takes as a god his own desire?' (Q. 45:23), he says:

> One had money and trade before [his eyes]; another, his wife and child; yet another was thinking of reputation and honour. One remained enslaved to venerating his piety and self-restraint, and advanced no further than that; another made his obedience and worship into the focus of his attention (lit. *qibla*), and looking at and relying on that became a veil upon his way [...].[24]

In Maybudī's view, inner detachment and sincerity are more important than rigorous supererogatory practices. Indeed, he observes more than once that those who are advanced on the mystical path are able to maintain a balance between their inner and outer life, and he cites in support of this a saying of ʿAlī b. Abī Ṭālib: 'The best among this people are they whose [concern for] this world does not take their attention away from their [concern for] the other world, and whose [concern for] the other world does not take them away from their [concern for]this world.'[25]

Spiritual 'psychology'

Apart from the overall injunction to control and conquer the *nafs*, Maybudī presents a great deal more detailed information to assist the seeker in attaining the spiritual goal, and understanding mystical experiences to be encountered along the way. This information is diverse not only in content and but also in style of expression, ranging from the technical to the metaphorical and allusive. One would not expect these doctrines to be set out in any systematic order as in a Sufi manual, since they arise as spontaneous responses to the Qur'anic verses. However, even when all the data is assembled and collated, it is possible to find only a vaguely coherent system within the range of technical terms employed by Maybudī. On the whole, he avoids lengthy discussions of the technical side of mysticism, giving priority to a poetic and inspirational style that would appeal to the wide audience he was addressing, and that was, moreover, concordant with the mystical doctrines of love. Short passages of a more analytical and technical nature do occur from time to time, probably derived from earlier authors, but we shall see that even these tend to be transformed and appropriated into Maybudī's rhetorical style. In the examples which follow, readers will be frustrated if they try to find any system that is consistent in its detail. The formulations should be regarded as variations on a theme (or scheme) rather than any closely analysed system.

I have included under the general rubric of 'Sufi psychology' discussions of the inner make-up of the human being, schematic descriptions of progress on the mystical path, and explanations of spiritual states and stations.

The inner constitution of the human being

We have seen that that Adam (representing humankind) is made up of the two opposite elements of earth and spirit.[26] But Maybudī also repeatedly speaks of another opposition or polarity within the human being: that which exists between the lower self (*nafs*) and heart (*dil* or *qalb*). He informs us that the *nafs* derives from the lower, sublunary realm of matter (water and clay), and the heart derives from the subtle and lordly higher realm whose essence is pure light. The station of the *nafs*, therefore, became one of absence from the Divine Presence, while the station of the heart became that of witnessing.[27] This difference between *nafs* and heart is explained in a slightly different way in Maybudī's metaphorical interpretation of the words '[Who] set a barrier between the two seas' (Q. 27:61), where the 'two seas' are glossed as

> the *nafs* and the heart (*qalb*), [the barrier being] so that neither of these two should overcome the other. In the make-up of the human being there is the Ka'ba of the heart and the public bar (*maṣṭaba*) of the *nafs*. They are two opposite substances which in the natural created form (*khalqat*) of man have been brought together, but in the spiritual way (*ṭarīqat*) have been severed. Both are open to each other, but through the divine omnipotence a barrier has been placed between them. Whenever that inciting *nafs* makes a night assault on the abode of the heart, the heart in its affliction will go to seek redress at the court of the Almighty (*'Azīz*) and from the gardens of eternity will receive the honorary robe of God's [protective] glance. This is the secret of the hadith which states: 'Each day and night God looks at the hearts of His servants 360 times.'[28]

Another twofold explanation of the inner constitution of the human being contrasts the heart (*dil*) with the breast (*ṣadr*). In Maybudī's mystical commentary on the words 'Let there be no anguish in your breast' (Q. 7:2), he observes that the word *ṣadr* (breast) is used rather than *qalb* (heart), and likewise in Q. 15:97, 'We are well aware that your breast is oppressed by what they say'. This is because anguish and constriction may be attributed to the breast but not the heart, which is in the locus of witnessing (*shuhūd*), [and enjoys] the pleasure of beholding (*naẓar*), and perpetual intimacy (*dawām-i uns*).[29]

In these twofold formulations, the heart is clearly being identified with the contemplative function, and in this elevated role it is sometimes identified with a king or sultan.[30] However, in many instances, we find the heart depicted as one of several parts of the inner constitution of the human being. In these more complex formulations there is often the suggestion of an inner hierarchy, each organ or faculty being associated with a particular spiritual function, or stage of realisation.[31] For example, in his commentary on Q. 56:58–9, Maybudī outlines the functions of different parts and organs of the body, among which jealousy (*ḥasad*) is to be found in the liver (*jigar*), hatred or malice (*ḥiqd*) in the spleen, and the passions or desires (*shahawāt*) in the veins (*ʿurūq*); faith (*īmān*) is located in the heart (*dil*), love (*ʿishq*) in the secret (*sirr*), and gnosis in the spirit (*jān*).[32] Commenting on Q. 2:218, 'Indeed, those who believe and those who emigrate', Maybudī explains that inward migration means the servant going

> from the *nafs* to the heart (*qalb*), from the heart to the secret (*sirr*), from the secret to the spirit (*jān*) and from the spirit to God. For the *nafs* is the station of Islam, the heart the station of faith (*īmān*), the secret the station of gnosis (*maʿrifat*), and the spirit the station of divine unity (*tawḥīd*).[33]

Earlier we saw the breast (*ṣadr*) contrasted with the heart, in a twofold formulation in which the heart represented the contemplative function in man, and the *ṣadr* was equivalent to the *nafs*.[34] But in Maybudī's commentary on the word *shaghafa* (to penetrate the pericardium) in Q. 12:30, *ṣadr* becomes one of five layers or membranes (*parda*) of the heart, namely *ṣadr*, *qalb*, *fuʾād*, *sirr* and *shaghāf*, with the *ṣadr* evidently forming the outermost layer.[35] This fivefold definition may be an expansion of the fourfold formulation presented in the treatise known as *al-Farq bayna'l-ṣadr wa'l-qalb wa'l-fuʾād wa'l-lubb*.[36] Indeed, when this same definition reappears later in the *Kashf al-asrār*, we find that the five membranes have been reduced to four. The passage is worth quoting in full, since it shows how the somewhat technical opening, probably derived from the earlier treatise, gives way to Maybudī's own rhetorical style. It appears in the *Nawbat* III commentary on Q. 39:22, 'Is he whose breast God has expanded for surrender (to Him), so that he follows a light from His Lord (as one who disbelieves)?'

> Know that the human heart has four layers: the first is called *ṣadr*, it is the seat of the covenant of Islam (*mustaqarr-i ʿahd-i islām*), as in His words 'Is he whose breast God expanded for surrender (*islām*)?' [Q. 39:22]; the second is the *qalb*, and this is the locus of the light of faith (*maḥall-i nūr-i īmān*) as in His words 'in whose hearts He inscribed faith' [Q. 58:22]; [37] the third is the *fu'ād*, which is the domain of the witnessing of God (*sarāparda-yi mushāhadat-i Ḥaqq*), as in His words 'The heart did not lie (in seeing) what it saw' [Q. 53:11]; and the fourth is the *shaghāf*, the place where the caravans of love unload (*maḥaṭṭ-i raḥl-i ʿishq*), as in His words 'He has smitten her to the heart with love' [Q. 12:30].[38]
>
> Each of these four layers has [its own] characteristic and each a particular beneficial glance from God. When the Lord of the Worlds wishes to draw one untamed soul (*ramīda'ī*) to the path of His religion with the lasso of His favour, He looks first of all upon his *ṣadr* so that He might purify him of desires and innovation (*bidʿat*), and make him walk with rectitude on the highway of the Sunna; then He looks upon his *qalb*, so that he should become purified of worldly blemishes and vices, such as conceit (*ʿujb*) jealousy (*ḥasad*), arrogance (*kibr*), hypocrisy (*riyā'*), greed (*ḥirṣ*), enmity (*ʿidāwat*) and laxity (*ruʿūnat*), and begin to move on the way of scrupulous piety (*waraʿ*). Then He looks upon his *fu'ād* and cuts him off from all attachments to creatures, opening in his heart a spring of knowledge and wisdom, bestowing on him the light of guidance, as when He says: 'The earth will shine with the light of its Lord' [Q. 39:69]. Then He looks upon his *shaghāf*, and what a look is that! A look that brings beauty to the spirit, a look that makes the tree of happiness bear fruit, and awakens the eye of joy [...]; a look that is wine for the cup of the mystic's heart. When this look reaches his *shaghāf*, it snatches him away from water and clay, so that he steps into the alley of annihilation (*fanā'*). Thereupon, three things become naughted in three things: seeking becomes naughted in finding; knowing becomes naughted in the Known; and loving becomes naughted in the Beloved.[39]

Stages of progression on the spiritual way

We have seen that several of Maybudī's formulations of the inner constitution of the human being indicated some kind of progress through different stages of the spiritual way. But the stages of spiritual progression are described in a number of other ways in the *Kashf al-asrār*. Of these formulations, the simplest comprise two or, more often, three stages, while the more elaborate seem to comprise five or seven stages. The simpler threefold systems are often subdivided in some way, as in the following example, which occurs in Maybudī's mystical commentary on Q. 13:39, 'God effaces what He wills and establishes what He wills'. Here, the stages of the spiritual path are identified with three different aspects or levels of the 'highway of the religion of God' (*shāhrāh-i dīn-i Ḥaqq*), namely *islām, sunnat* and *ikhlāṣ*.[40] Each of these levels is associated with a particular state – *islām* with fear, *sunnat* with hope, and *ikhlāṣ* with love – and at each level there is both 'effacement' and 'establishment' (as in the Qur'anic verse). So, from the fearful heart God 'erases hypocrisy and establishes in its place certainty; removes meanness and establishes generosity; abolishes jealousy and establishes kindness', and so on. From the hopeful heart 'He removes choice and places in its stead submision [to the divine will]; effaces differentiation (*tafriqat*) and establishes non-differentiation (*jamʿ*)'. Finally, from the loving heart 'He erases the traces of humanity and puts in their place the evidences of reality (*ḥaqīqat*)'.[41]

One of the simplest threefold formulations of spiritual progress occurs in Maybudī's commentary on the words, 'Say: Praise be to God. He will show you His signs so that you will recognise them' (Q. 27:93).[42] Here, he is explaining the light of divine solicitude (*ʿināyat*) and safe-keeping (*riʿāyat*), which has been lit upon the way of God's servants:

> This way can be traversed in three stations (*manzil*): the first is being shown (*namāyish*), the second is making one's way (*rawish*), and the third is being drawn (*kashish*). *Namāyish* is alluded to in His words, 'He will show you His portents so that you shall know them'; *rawish* by His words, 'When He created you stage by stage' [Q 71:14][43] and 'That you will journey on from plane to plane' [Q. 84:19]; and *kashish* is alluded to in His words, 'Then he drew near and came down' [Q. 53:8].[44]

Yet another formulation of the stages of the way occurs in Maybudī's *Nawbat* III commentary on Q. 3:103, 'Hold fast (*wa-ʿtaṣimū*) all of you together to the rope of God'. In this fivefold scheme, he explains that the servant must first attain to *taqwā* (awareness of God) then he will proceed to *iʿtiṣām* (abstaining from what is unlawful), and from there he will attain *tawakkul* (complete trust in God). From *tawakkul* he will progress to *istislām* (total submission) and when he has reached *istislām* he will have become independant of all intermediaries, subsisting in God (*ba-Ḥaqq qāʾim*).[45]

Although, as we have seen, Maybudī often speaks of the need to 'kill' or subdue the *nafs*, Sufi doctrine also teaches that the inciting *nafs*, the *nafs ammāra*, can gradually be transformed through spiritual discipline into the *nafs* at peace (*nafs muṭma'inna*).[46] The different manifestations of the *nafs* during this process of transformation can be seen as another indication of stages of spiritual progress. Maybudī twice presents this doctrine in the *Kashf al-asrār*. The first occasion is when he comments on Q. 12:52, 'Indeed, the (human) soul incites to evil' (*inna'l-nafsa la-ammāratun bi'l-sū'*). Here, he explains that the *nafs* has four degrees (*rutbat*): the *nafs* that incites [to evil] (*nafs-i ammāra*), the deceiving *nafs* (*nafs-i makkāra*), the bewitching *nafs* (*nafs-i saḥḥāra*), and the *nafs* at peace (*nafs-i muṭma'inna*). He describes at length how the wayfarer has to ward off the ambushes of the first three of these before reaching the level of the *nafs* at peace – a level possessed by prophets and saints.[47] Interestingly, Maybudī has excluded from this explanation a stage that is commonly referred to by mystics, the blaming or self-reproaching *nafs* (*nafs lawwāma*), but he has occasion to explain this stage later when he comments on the verse which includes that term: 'By the self-reproaching soul! (*bi'l-nafs al-lawwāma*, Q. 75:2).[48] In this context, however, he mentions only the two stages of the blaming *nafs* and *nafs* at peace (*muṭma'inna*), the main point of his discussion being to show that while the servant is at the stage of blaming himself, he is trying to reach by way of himself a goal that can only be attained by the help of God-given success.[49] This latter doctrine will be examined in more detail in the section on *taqdīr* and divine intervention in chapter seven.

Sometimes the stages of the way are connected to ascending levels of contemplation or gnosis, as in this passage:

> First is the knowledge of reality (*'ilm-i ḥaqīqat*), and that is gnosis (*ma'rifat*); then is the essence of reality (*'ayn-i ḥaqīqat*), and that is finding (*wujūd*); then is the truth of reality (*ḥaqq-i ḥaqīqat*), and that is annihilation (*fanā'*).[50]

The next passage takes as an example stages in the Prophet's contemplation of God according to one of his intimate prayers:[51]

> These words [of the Prophet] allude to stages in the path of wayfaring towards God. It is a moving by way of spiritual aspirations (*himam*), not steps (*qadam*). The Prophet of God first contemplated the [divine] act (*fi'l*)

> and said, 'I seek refuge in Your forgiveness from Your retribution'; then he went beyond that station and contemplated the divine attribute and said, 'I seek refuge in Your good pleasure from Your anger.' Then he went beyond the divine attribute and contemplated the divine essence and said, 'I seek refuge in You from You.' Then he was stripped of his own attributes and said, 'I cannot encompass Your praise'. Then he made remembrance of the unicity (*fardāniyyat*) of God and said, 'You are as You praise Yourself.' The first is the station (*maqām*) of demonstrative reasoning (*istidlāl*); the second, the station of utter dependence (*iftiqār*); the third is the station of contemplation (*mushāhadat*); the fourth the station of perplexity (*ḥayrat*);[52] and the fifth the station of extinction (*fanāʾ*).[53]

Stages of the way are again connected to levels of gnosis in the following, from Maybudī's commentary on the words 'which the True Spirit (*al-rūḥ al-amīn*) brought down upon your heart' (Q. 26:193–4):

> Know that the heart has states and stations: the first is unveiling (*mukāshafat*); then there is witnessing (*mushāhadat*) and then direct witnessing (*muʿāyanat*); after that, the heart is overcome by proximity (*istīlā-yi qurb*), and thereafter is annihilation in proximity (*istihlāk dar qurb*).[54]

We can see that although Maybudī does include some formulations of a purely technical nature, such as the last passage cited here or the passage cited earlier on levels of reality (*ʿilm-i ḥaqīqat*, *ʿayn-i ḥaqīqat* and *ḥaqq-i ḥaqīqat*), he is more likely to represent the stages of progression by incorporating technical terms into passages of metaphor and allegory. He speaks, for example, of seven seas which must be crossed before the servant can reach the end of the alley of *tawḥīd*,[55] of five seas in which man is drowning and five ships which can save him,[56] or of twelve springs.[57] Metaphors of wine and drinking are also used; for example, he speaks of three different drinks which may be given to one who enters the door of affirmation (*taṣdīq*): sherbet, which will bring his heart to life with gnosis; poison, which will kill his inciting *nafs*; and wine, which will make him drunk and confounded with finding (*wujūd*).[58]

On occasion, a number of different metaphors are combined in one passage, as in Maybudī's commentary on the letters *Kāf Hā Yā ʿAyn Ṣād* at the beginning of *Sūrat Maryam* (Q. 19). He begins by quoting from Qushayrī, who has compared the separate letters to a wine of intimacy which God has poured out for His friends, and then continues:

When, in the orchard of grace, the friends of God drink this wine of intimacy from the holy cup, they experience joy (*ṭarab*). Their joy brings them to seeking (*ṭalab*) so that they break out of the cage of the world and fly upon the wings of love to the horizons of the unseen until they reach the Kaʿba of union (*waṣl*). When they arrive they are effaced in themselves, intellects drowned in [the divine] grace, and hearts annihilated in unveiling (*kashf*), the breeze of eternity (*nasīm-i azaliyyat*) wafting [to them] from the quarter of proximity, having lost themselves and found Him.[59]

States (*aḥwāl*) and stations (*maqāmāt*)

Most of the passages outlining the stages of spiritual progress include the mention of technical terms for stations, such as repentance (*tawba*), fear (*khawf*), hope (*rajāʾ*), patience (*ṣabr*), gratitiude (*shukr*), and for states, such as perplexity (*ḥayrat*), stupefaction (*dahshat*), awe (*haybat*), intimacy (*uns*), annihilation [from self] (*fanāʾ*), subsisting [in God] *baqāʾ*, and so on.[60] These terms are among those commonly discussed in manuals and other authoritative works on Sufism, where they are usually set out in a particular order and explained in some detail.[61] Lengthier discussions of individual states and stations do arise in the *Kashf al-asrār*, where they tend to occur as direct explanations of words which occur in the Qur'an, as part of digressions less directly related to the verses, as metaphorical interpretations of natural phenomena, or as allegorical interpretations of stories of the prophets.[62]

In these discussions, Maybudī frequently defines the states or stations according to different levels – sometimes two, occasionally four, but usually three.[63] This categorisation may be according to different levels of the microcosm; for example, the terms *zuhd* (renunciation [of the world])[64] and *ṣabr* (patience, forbearance) are defined at the levels of *nafs*, *dil* and *jān*. Or it might be according to different classes of believers, such as the worshippers (*ʿābidān*), mystics (*ʿārifān*) and lovers (*muḥibbān*),[65] or the commonalty (*ʿāmm*), elite (*khāṣṣ*) and elite of the elite (*khāṣṣ al-khāṣṣ* or *khāṣṣ al-khawāṣṣ*).[66] Such threefold definitions are reminiscent of Anṣārī's *Manāzil al-sāʾirīn* and *Ṣad maydān*,[67] but sometimes Maybudī ascribes them to other Sufi masters. For example, the definition of three levels of *tawakkul* (complete trust in God) is quoted from Abū ʿAlī Daqqāq (d. 405/1015),[68] the definition of three levels of *zuhd* is from Ḥallāj,[69] and of three levels of *tawḥīd* (realising the divine unity) from Abū Ḥafṣ Ḥaddād

(d. 260/873).[70] In any case, the threefold distinction between *ʿāmm*, *khāṣṣ* and *khāṣṣ al-khāṣṣ* (*khāṣṣ al-khawāṣṣ*) is ubiquitous in Sufi works.[71] These three terms were not to be understood as a static hierarchy among the spiritual travellers, but as levels of attainment, or stages of the way. Hence, Maybudī insists that no-one can reach the station of the elite (*khawāṣṣ*) unless he has passed through (or left behind) all the stations of the commonalty (*ʿawāmm*),[72] while in Abū ʿAlī Daqqāq's definition of *tawakkul*, the level *ʿāmm* is equated with *bidāyat* (the initial), the *khāṣṣ* with *wasāṭat* (the intermediate), and *khāṣṣ al-khāṣṣ* with *nihāyat* (the final).

Many of Maybudī's explanations of states and stations occur as part of his interpretations of stories of the prophets and will therefore be discussed in part three of this book. A few examples will nevertheless be examined here to illustrate his approach to such discussions. We find that the term *tawba* (repentance) is in one instance explained according to three levels and in another according to two. In both cases, the discussion occurs as a response to the mention of the word *tawba* (or other derivations from the same verbal root, such as *yatūbūna* or *tāʾib*) in the verse. The first instance occurs in Maybudī's mystical commentary on Q. 4:17, 'Forgiveness is only incumbent on God towards those who do evil in ignorance, [and] then turn quickly [in repentance] to God'. The following is the opening of a lengthy discussion and, as can be seen, indicates three stages of repentance:

> *Tawba* is the sign of the way, the 'master of ceremonies', a key to the treasure, an intercessor for union, the secret of all joy and the ferment (*māya*) of freedom. It begins with regret (*pashīmānī*) in the heart, then there is seeking forgiveness with the tongue, and finally, cutting oneself off both from bad itself and from bad people.[73]

On the other hand, *tawba* is defined in terms of two stages or levels in Maybudī's mystical interpretation of Q. 11:3, 'Ask forgiveness of your Lord and turn to Him repentant'. Here, he understands the two levels of *tawba* to be exemplified by the two commands in the verse itself, namely, to seek forgiveness and to repent:

> Seeking forgiveness (*istighfār*) is repentance (*tawba*), and repentance is seeking forgiveness, and the combining of these two words [in this verse] is a signal that you should come clean out of your sins as a snake comes out of its skin,[74] and then believe that your salvation comes not by your repentance but by His generosity and grace (may He be glorified). First seek forgiveness so

that you may be purified of your sins, then repent of reliance [on that repentance], so that you may be directed. First arise, and accomplish obedience and worship, as is commanded by the law, then rise above that rising as is indicated by reality. The former is the path of worshippers (*ʿābidān*), and the latter the way of mystics (*ʿārifān*) [...].[75]

The term *ṣabr* (patience) is likewise defined in different contexts according to two[76] and three levels. The threefold definition occurs in Maybudī's mystical commentary on the words 'O you who believe! Be patient (*iṣbirū*), have forbearance (*ṣābirū*) and hold fast in endurance (*rābiṭū*)' (Q. 3:200).[77] He first defines *ṣabr* according to three levels of the inner constitution of the human being on the basis of the three words for patience used in the verse, and second, on the basis of three categories of believers.

[With the word] *iṣbirū* he is addressing the *nafs*; with the word *ṣābirū*, the heart (*dil*) and with the word *rābiṭū*, the spirit (*jān*). To the *nafs* He says: 'Be patient in obedience and worship (*khidmat*)'; to the heart He says: 'Be patient with suffering and hardship; and to the spirit He says: 'Endure the burning anguish of longing and the pain of love'. And God is exceedingly patient (*Ṣubūr*).
[...]
And it is said: 'Be patient (*aṣbirū*) for the sake of God (*fi'llāh*); endure (*ṣābirū*) through God (*bi'llāh*), and be steadfast (*rābiṭū*) with God (*maʿa'llāh*). Being patient for the sake of God is the patience of worshippers (*ʿābidān*) in the station of worship, hoping for reward; having endurance through God is the patience of mystics (*ʿārifān*), in the station of reverence (*ḥurmat*) desiring union; and being steadfast with God is the patience of lovers in the station of witnessing (*mushāhadat*) at the moment of epiphany (*tajallī*), the eye gazing upon the object of contemplation (*dīda dar niẓāra nigarān*), the heart in bewilderment at [what] the eye [beholds], the spirit beside itself with love (*ba-mihr ba-faghān*).[78]

As with other aspects of mystical doctrine, explanations of states and stations in the *Kashf al-asrār* are often poetic and rich in metaphor. A typical example is Maybudī's discussion of *tabattul* (cutting oneself off from the world, or complete devotion to God) in his commentary on Q. 73:8, 'So remember the name of your Lord and devote yourself wholeheartedly to Him' (*tabattul ilayhi tabtīlan*):

Tabattul is one of the stations of [spiritual] wayfarers; those who in their states (*munāzilāt*) and unveilings have reached the point where Paradise with all its trees and rivers does not enter the beauty of their imagination, while hellfire with all its shackles and chains trembles in fear at the burning in their breasts. The venomous serpent of avidity for the world can never pierce with its fang their blissful state (*rūzigār-i ʿaysh*); nor can their skirt be caught by any thorn from the bush of envy and pride. No speck of dust from the inciting *nafs* can settle on the hem of the mantle of their Islam; nor any smoke from the darkness of passion affect their vision. They look upon creatures with a discerning eye,[79] speak with the tongue of compassion, and befriend people with hearts full of mercy. They are kings in nature, but beggars in appearance. They are the sultans of the way, yet they are clothed like orphans. They are wayfarers with no distance to travel (*rawandagān and wa masāfat dar miyān na*),[80] flyers with no need of feather or wing. They are intoxicated with the wine of love, alive with the life of proximity [to God].

They are people purified of everything other than Us,
They set fire to the heavens with the burning [lit. grieving] of their hearts
Once they were distanced from all but Us
They went beyond the Throne, and pitched their tent there.[81]

The spiritual community

Maybudī insists that the mystical path cannot be followed without the guidance of a spiritual master or, at least, the companionship of other seekers. Commenting on Q. 6:90, 'These were the people God guided, so follow the guidance [they received]', he writes:

Whoever is not serving a spiritual guide (*pīr*), attached to a teacher (*ustād*), accompanied by a fellow traveller (*rafīq*), or in the company of a master (*mihtar*) is on the brink of destruction. Without teacher or friend, he is [like] an uncultivated weed (*khwad-rust*), and nothing is produced from a weed. The person who is worthy to be followed and to be a master, is one who has himself been in the company of masters, trained by them and who has received the blessing of their supervision (*naẓar*).[82]

Maybudī further stipulates that no one is fit to become a guide (*pīr*) or accept spiritual aspirants (*murīds*) as disciples on the spiritual path unless he himself has passed safely through all its dangers:

He must have lost his way a thousand times and returned to it again before he can bring someone from being astray back to the path. For there must first be knowledge of the way *to* the path, and then the knowledge *of* the

> path. A person who has always been on the way knows the way but he does not know the way *to* the way. This is the secret of the slip[s] (*zallat*) of the prophets and the occurrence of lassitude in them. But God knows best.[83]

Maybudī suggests that everyone, regardless of their station, will benefit from the company of saints (more literally, 'friends of God', *awliyā*'). Commenting on Q. 18:18, concerning the Companions of the Cave and their dog, he states:

> As they (the companions) were going along the way, that little dog ran after them [calling]: 'You are honoured guests, and the honoured guest can bring along an uninvited guest (*ṭufayl*).' For those few small steps that the little dog went along with them, the believers will be reciting his story and celebrating him until the resurrection with the words 'and their dog stretching out his paws on the threshold' [Q. 18:18]. So, what say you about someone who spends his life in the company of the *awliyā*' and follows in their footsteps? Do you think that at the resurrection God would separate him from them? Absolutely not![84]

Maybudī also speaks of the spiritual power of the *awliyā*'. For example, he informs us that no more than a hint from Abū ʿAlī Siyāh (d. 424/1032) was enough to bring a group of Christian prisoners to Islam, where the [temporal] power of Sultan Maḥmūd had failed.[85] Such is the light of the friends of God that 'were a glimmer of its brightness to fall upon the world, stubborn unbelievers would all become believers in the oneness of God, and *zunnār* girdles would be changed for the belts of the religion of love'.[86] But God keeps them secretly in His protection, cherishes them lovingly in the fortress of His jealousy, and warns them not to reveal the pain of their love to any unseeing outsider.[87] The miracles of the *awliyā*' are also to be hidden, but for a different reason. Maybudī explains that the miracles (*karāmāt*) of saints are related to the miracles (*muʿjizāt*) of prophets. However, while the miracles of prophets were meant to be seen, since they constituted a proof for their claim to prophethood in their mission to call people [to the truth], the miracles of saints should be hidden from people, for they should not try to endorse any claim to sainthood, (i.e. they should not be making any claims) nor to call people [to their way]. Moreover, it should be understood that such miracles can be a manifestation of the divine ruse (*makr*).[88]

In Maybudī's view, the *awliyā*' are the successors to the prophets. He relates a saying of Muḥammad b. Aḥmad[89] according to which, when the Prophet died, the earth lamented that from that day no prophet would walk upon it until the Day of Resurrection; whereupon God replied, 'I will bring forth from this community people whose hearts will be like the hearts of prophets.'[90] Commenting on Q. 5:12, 'God made a covenant of old with the Children of Israel, and we raised among them twelve chieftains', Maybudī explains how 'just as there were leaders among the Children of Israel in a position of authority to whom they could refer, so, in the Muslim community there are *budalā'* (or *abdāl*, lit. substitutes), the *awtād* (tent pegs) of the world whose hearts are like the hearts of prophets.'[91] He then cites a saying of the Prophet, according to which there are in the community forty who embody the qualities of Abraham; seventy who embody those of Moses; three who embody the qualities of Jesus, and one who embodies the qualities of Muhammad. This hadith is followed by a saying of Abū ʿUthmān Maghribī (d. 373/983), who states that there are forty substitutes (*budalā'*), seven custodians (*umanā'*), three deputies (*khulafā'*) to the foremost (*a'imma*), and one 'pole' (*quṭb*). The *quṭb* is cognisant of them all and in charge of them, but no one knows his identity.[92]

Despite the power and authority that are ascribed to the *awliyā'*, there is no question that in Maybudī's teaching they rank lower in the spiritual hierarchy than the prophets (*anbiyā'*). He states, for example, that the end of the way (lit. matter) for the *awliyā'* is the beginning of the way for prophets.[93] The hierarchy of rank in faith and gnosis is set out as follows:

ulu'l-ʿazm (messengers of firm resolve)
payāmbarān-i mursal (messengers who bring a revelation)
anbiyā' (prophets)
ṣiddīqān (wholly sincere)
shahīdān (martyrs)
awliyā' (friends of God)
ʿāmma-yi mu'minān (commonalty of believers)

Higher than all of these is the Prophet Muhammad, whose station and degree of knowledge, Maybudī explains, God alone knows.[94] Thus, the *anbiyā'*, *awliyā'*, *shuhadā'* and *ṣiddīqān* galloped from the beginning to the end of their lives, spurring on their steeds, but finally only reached the first step of Muhammad.[95]

Among the spiritual wayfarers themselves there are also hierarchies. Maybudī explains that just as God created on the earth different kinds of topography, making some areas more fertile than others, so also, in the nature of the wayfarers (*ṭīnat-i sālikān*), He made differences, granting some more than others. People, he continues, may be compared to mines, some producing gold and some silver, some bitumen, and some tar.[96] Moreover, those of a lower station should not concern themselves with the stations of great mystics, lest they become despondent about their own rank. They should keep in mind that the princely army is not entirely made up of private soldiers and boon companions; there are also dog-keepers and grooms, and all have their role to play in the kingdom.[97]

Maybudī sets out the hierarchy among the spiritual wayfarers in a number of different ways in the *Kashf al-asrār*. Some of these hierarchical schemes, such as the *ʿāmm*, *khāṣṣ* and *khāṣṣ al-khawāṣṣ*, suggest different stages of realisation on the way, while others indicate different approaches to the spiritual path. An example of the latter is when Maybudī interprets God's 'treasuries on earth' (Q. 15:21) as the hearts of mystics and secrets of aspirants, which God adorned with shining pearls and precious deposits: 'the hearts of scholars (*ʿālimān*) are adorned with the subtleties of knowledge (*laṭāʾif-i ʿilm*), the hearts of worshippers (*ʿābidān*) are appointed with truths of the intellect (*ḥaqāʾiq-i ʿaql*), the hearts of mystics (*ʿārifān*) are adorned with wonders of the secret (*badāʾiʿ-i sirr*).[98] Another formulation clearly places the wholly sincere (*ṣiddīqān*) and mystics (*ʿārifān*) above ascetics or renunciants (*zāhidān*) and worshippers (*ʿābidān*).[99] In a discussion of the six ranks of travellers, the ascending order is presented as: *tāʾibān* (repentants), *ʿābidān*, *zāhidān*, *ʿālimān*, *ʿārifān*, *ṣiddīqān*.[100] In yet another formulation lovers (or friends) of God are placed above mystics: *zāhidān*, *ʿārifān*, *dūstān*.[101] Comparing three different approaches to the way, Maybudī explains that worshippers (*ʿābidān*), seek proximity through virtues (*faḍāʾil*), scholars (*ʿālimān*) through proofs (*dalāʾil*), and mystics (*ʿārifān*) by the abandoning of means (*ba-tark-i wasāʾil*).[102]

It can be seen that whether lovers (*dūstān*), mystics (*ʿārifān*) or the wholly sincere (*ṣiddīqān*) have been placed in the highest position, these three are consistently ranked higher than worshippers (*ʿābidān*), people of [outward] knowledge (*ʿālimān*) and renunciants (*zāhidān*).[103] Maybudī equates both the *ʿābid* and the *ʿālim* with the 'mercenary' (*muzdūr*) who worships and acts out of hope for reward (in the Hereafter), whereas the

ʿārif is compared to the guest (*mihmān*), who is neither concerned with reward or punishment, but hopes only for the vision of God.[104] When it comes to the *zāhidān*, we find that although ascetic practices are shown to have a place among spiritual disciplines, renunciation (*zuhd*) as a way in itself is seen as narrow and is not encouraged by Maybudī. He quotes a saying of Yaḥyā b. Muʿādh (d. 258/872) according to which the world is like a wedding. The worldly person spends his time adorning the bride. The *zāhid* tries to spoil her, pulling out her hair and tearing her dress. The *ʿārif*, on the other hand, is so occupied with the love of God that he does not have occasion either to love or hate the bride. On the Day of Resurrection, the worldly man will be called to account; if God is lenient with him it is because of His grace, but if He takes issue with him then it is what he deserves. The *zāhid* will be presented with all the pleasures of Paradise and told that he *must* enjoy them, while the *ʿārif* will be taken beyond the station of the dwellers of Paradise to the highest station, 'Firmly established in the favour of a Mighty King' (Q. 54:55).[105] This same idea is expressed more succinctly when Maybudī says, 'The *zāhid* tries to capture God from the world. The *ʿārif* tries to capture God from Paradise'.[106]

Malāmat and *jawānmardī*

Maybudī's gentle disparagement of asceticism in the previous passages may have been due, in part, to its association with the Karrāmiyya, though earlier mystics, such as Yaḥyā b. Muʿādh (quoted earlier) and Bāyazīd Bisṭāmī were also critical of *zuhd* when it appeared to become an end in itself.[107] Two other schools which had flourished in the spiritual climate of Khorasan, those of the Malāmatiyya and the Futuwwa, were regarded more favourably by Maybudī, and the influence of their doctrines is quite evident in the *Kashf al-asrār*. The principal doctrine of the Malāmatiyya, the 'School of Blame', was that in order to avoid falling into the snare of hypocrisy, pride and self-delusion, the aspirant must constantly subject his *nafs* to criticism and blame, both by himself and other people.[108] His piety and devotions should be kept hidden from others, and there should be nothing to distinguish him from the ordinary believers. The Malāmatiyya, therefore, maintained a common trade to earn their keep. Unlike the Sufis they did not wear wool, and they tended to avoid the practice of *samāʿ* and other rites which would attract attention to themselves.[109] From early on, the Malāmatiyya movement was subjected to criticism by those Sufis who considered the constant preoccupation with blaming the *nafs* to be a kind of dualism.[110] It was related that some Malāmatīs would even go to extreme lengths to attract the blame of others,[111] and this was criticised by mystics who saw this as an exploitation of the way of *malāma* for the sake of libertinism and antinomianism.[112]

The Malāmatī doctrine of seeking blame from others appears to be evinced in a number of aphorisms and anecdotes related in the *Kashf al-asrār*. One of these tells how Abū Saʿīd Kharrāz, disturbed by the excessive reverence which his followers held for him, moved to a place where he was certain to be held as a heretic (or fire-worshipper, *zindīq*), whereupon he was constantly pelted with stones and lived content.[113] Another anecdote relates how Ibrāhīm b. Adham (d. 160 or 174 /776 or 790) claimed that the happiest times in his life were when he was subjected to the greatest disdain and humiliation by people.[114] However, neither of these two mystics was attached to the Malāmatī movement; Kharrāz was a native of Baghdad at a time when the Malāmatiyya were centred in Nishapur, while Ibrāhīm b. Adham was a native of Balkh, and died before the movement had been established.[115] It is interesting to note that when Maybudī does quote from figures who were known to be masters of the Malāmatiyya, such as ʿAbd Allāh Munāzil (d. 331/943), to whom he refers as 'that unique one of his age and Shaykh of the People of Blame',[116] Abū Ḥafṣ Ḥaddād,[117] or Abū ʿUthmān Ḥīrī (d. 298/910),[118] it is not on the subject of *malāmat*.[119]

Nonetheless, several other doctrines expounded in the treatises on *malāmatiyya* or otherwise associated with the concept of blame are to be found in the *Kashf al-asrār*. These include the understanding that complete trust in God (*tawakkul*) does not require the abandonment of earning a living (*kasb*);[120] the teaching that a mystic's state should be concealed not only from others but from himself;[121] and the idea that blame purifies love,[122] and ultimately frees the lover from everything other than God.[123] Maybudī also includes couplets of the Qalandariyya type, albeit at times idiosyncratically, in an unusual way that reflects his own teachings.[124] For example, the following couplet appears in his commentary on Q. 56:3, 'Abasing [some] exalting others':

> Many a pious shaykh ended up without a mount.
> Many a reckless lad of the tavern (*rind-i kharābātī*) saddled a male lion.[125]

This Qalandarī poem is being used in a context in which Maybudī, typically, wishes to denounce innovation (*bidʿa*): a reckless young lad from the tavern who has [sound] belief (*jawān-i kharābāt-i muʿtaqid*) will be saved, while the shaykh of much prayer who is an innovator (*pīr-i munājāt-i mubtadiʿ*) will be condemned to the fire.

Another, one might say more conventional, citation of *qalandariyyāt* poetry occurs where Maybudī is explaining how love (*ʿishq*) is a privilege given not to the angels but to mankind, because 'unlike angels whose affair was single-hued (*yikrang*), man was subjected to the chameleon of destiny':

> You it was, O Beloved, who brought the way
> Of *qalandars* and gambling into this city.[126]

The word *qalandar* in this context probably implies a reckless abandonment of the world, while the mention of gambling (*qimār*), suggests a willingness to stake everything, two traits of character that are indispensable to the true lover of God. There is also the implication here of unruly behaviour which God should forgive, since He instituted love in man. The association between *qalandariyyāt* and love again occurs in a short and elegant passage of *sajʿ* (rhyming prose): 'For lovers, it is a good omen to be wounded in the alley of the Beloved; it is their wont to stake their lives in the gambling house of love (*dūstān-rā zakhm khwardan dar kūy-i dūst ba-fāl-i nīkū'st. Dar qimārkhāna-yi ʿishq īshān-rā jān bākhtan ʿādat-u khū'st*).[127]

Another instance of *qalandariyyāt* occurs when Maybudī comments on the word *maysir* (gambling) in Q. 5:90, 'O you who believe, strong drink and games of chance [...] are an infamy of Satan's handiwork'. He observes that the most highly esteemed and intrepid gambler is the one who stakes everything in one game (*kamzan*) and loses all (*pākbāz*).[128] He then explains that this is an allusion to 'the way of the *jawānmardān*' (lit. those who are 'young manly' or chivalrous), who throw themselves down on the highway of destiny, allowing themselves to be crushed under the feet of the basest people so that they may be freed from all desire for pomp and glory and consider themselves as nothing.

So long as you are tied to colour, nature, sky and star
Why should you say to others 'Live like a *qalandar*.'[129]

In this context it can be seen that the Qalandarī theme of the out-and-out gambler, the one who is ready to stake everything in one game, together with a fundamental principle of the Malāmatiyya, that is, to subject oneself to humiliation in order to escape from vainglory, have been defined as the way of the *jawānmardān*. In fact it can be said that in the *Kashf al-asrār*, Malāmatī doctrines have been subsumed within the ideals of *jawānmardī*, because for Maybudī *jawānmardī* (in Arabic, *futuwwa*) really implies an uncompromising and sincere dedication to the mystical path.[130] It is for this reason that the common vocative '*ay jawānmard!*' can simply be translated as 'O noble one [of the Path]!'

It has been suggested that the way of spiritual chivalry (*futuwwa* or *jawānmardī*) was primarily concerned with a person's relationship with their fellow human beings, whereas the way of *malāmat* concerned their relationship with God.[131] For Maybudī, however, *futuwwa* or *jawānmardī* included both a person's relationship with God and with their fellow human beings.[132] Concerning the latter, Maybudī states that the 'manly man' (*mard-i mardāna*)[133] is one who does not seek to reward ill with ill, for he knows that forgiveness is better.[134] Hence, Joseph was the prince of all the *jawānmardān* because, having received so much suffering at the hands of his brothers, he forgave them with the words 'Have no fear this day' (Q. 12:92).[135] Furthermore, the way of the *jawānmardān* (and Sufis) is that they should take upon themselves the sin of others and seek forgiveness for them.[136] They should be at peace with others and at war with themselves,[137] a mercy to others and an affliction to themselves.[138]

Concerning the servant's relationship with God, we learn that the *jawānmardān* are those who truly gird themselves up for the spiritual battle,[139] the first stage of which is to cut themselves off from all worldly vanity:

How long will you sit there like a woman concerned with vain appearances?
Set your sights on the way and go forth like a man.[140]

It is 'manliness' that enables people to see the signs of God in the world,[141] while anyone who makes the object of his attention other than what is evident from the miracles of creation does not have a foothold on the path of the *jawānmardān*.[142] It is only the valiant man (*mard-i nabard*) who is fit to be privy to the divine secrets in the Qur'an.[143] Commenting on the words, 'It is He (*huwa'l-ladhī*) Who has divided the two seas' (Q. 25:53), Maybudī discusses the divine name *Huwa* (He), and explains that it is only when the believer attains *jawānmardī*, that he will truly understand the reality of God's 'He-ness' (*huwiyyat*).[144] Such a person when he is asked 'Where have you come from?' answers '*Hū*', and when asked 'Where are you going?', he replies '*Hū*', and when asked 'What is your aim?', again, '*Hū*'. To every question he answers '*Hū*'.[145]

We have seen how in some contexts *qalandarī* was associated with love. *Jawānmardī*, also, has a part in the way of love. In his commentary on the *basmala* in *Sūrat al-Fātiḥa* (Q. 1.1), Maybudī explains that longing for the vision of the Beloved [in Paradise, as opposed to the pleasures of Paradise] is a quality of 'men'.[146] Perhaps the aspect of love most associated with *jawānmardī* in the *Kashf al-asrār* is the ability not only to bear, but also to enjoy the suffering that love brings. In the commentary on Q. 33:11, 'There the believers were sorely tested and deeply shaken',[147] Anṣārī is quoted as having said 'whoever complains at the wounds [inflicted by] the Beloved is not a *man* in loving Him',[148] and elsewhere, 'whoever is not happy in pain is not a *jawānmard*'.[149] Again, when Maybudī is commenting on Q. 70:5, 'But be patient [O Muhammad] with a patience fair to see', he explains that to have true patience requires the courage of a lion (*shīrmardī*) and lofty aspiration, so that in the way of religion the bitterer the drink the sweeter it will taste.[150]

Having discussed in detail various aspects of Maybudī's teachings concerning the spiritual path, we shall now return to the three fundamental and interrelated doctrines mentioned earlier, namely the mystical doctrines of *taqdīr*, knowledge and love.

NOTES

1 'That day' being a reference to *rūz-i alast*, the day of the Covenant of *Alast*, discussed pp. 139–42.

2 *Kashf*, V, p. 232; VII, p. 334. In the published edition, the latter passage has the incorrect *pur sūd* (full of profit) instead of *bar sūd* (in profit), and *būd-i khwad-rā* (for my own being) instead of *būd-i tu khwad-rā* (Your being for myself). These errors in the latter passage may be confirmed by a perusal of the manuscripts. In the case of the first discrepancy, both 'b' and 'p' are marked with

only one diacritic, and there is no obvious argument for reading *pur* instead of *bar*. In the case of the second, MS A has *būd-i khwad-rā* in the first citation and *būd-i tu khwad-rā* in the second, while MS B has *būd-i tu khwad-rā* in both citations. Since three out four citations have *būd-i tu khwad-rā*, and this makes more sense, I have taken this to be the correct variant.

3 *Kashf*, I, p. 60.

4 See, for example, in Kalābādhī's *Kitāb al-taʿarruf*, where *fanāʾ* and *baqāʾ* are discussed together in ch. 59, pp. 92–100; tr. Arberry, pp. 120–32; likewise in Qushayrī's *Risāla*, where they are discussed in one chapter, pp. 211–16; while in Anṣārī's *Manāzil al-sāʾirīn* they are discussed in consecutive chs. 92 and 93, pp. 104, 105; French tr. de Beaurecueil in ibid., pp. 129–32, and *Chemin de Dieu*, pp. 222–3; and likewise Anṣārī's *Ṣad maydān*, ed. de Beaurecueil, 'Une ébauche persane', chs. 99 and 100, pp. 60–1; French tr. de Beaurecueil, *Chemin de Dieu*, pp. 148–9.

5 *Kashf*, VII, p. 285.

6 For example, *Kashf*, II, p. 186; III, p. 544; V, p. 218, although in some cases (for example, *Kashf*, VI, p. 16) the term *wiṣāl* is used specifically to refer to being united with God in the next life.

7 For example, *Kashf*, IV, p. 230; and *Kashf*, V, p. 347. The term *jamʿ* has been translated by both Arberry (*Doctrine of the Sufis*, p. 114) and de Beaurecueil (*Manāzil al-sāʾirīn*, p. 135; *Chemins de Dieu*, p. 226) as 'concentration', and this is appropriate in so far as it indicates a unification of the aspiration, but misleading in that it conveys the idea of mental effort, whereas *jamʿ* is really an absorption in the One to the point that there is no longer any awareness of differentiation or separation – hence its opposition to the state of *tafriqa* (separation or differentiation). In the state of *jamʿ* it can be said that the servant no longer acts by his own volition. In the *Manāzil al-sāʾirīn* (p. 109), Anṣārī has placed *jamʿ* as the penultimate station, and in relation to it cited the Qur'anic verse: 'You did not throw when you threw, but God threw' (Q. 8:17). In his commentary on the *Manāzil al-sāʾirīn*, al-Iskandarī (638 or 639/1240 or 1241), as far as we know the earliest commentator on the *Manāzil al-sāʾirīn*, explains that in the state of *jamʿ*, the servant is freed from witnessing duality for he sees only the Lord, and is thereby negated from witnessing his witnessing. See ʿAbd al-Muʿṭī al-Lakhmī al-Iskandarī, *Sharḥ manāzil al-sāʾirīn*, ed. S. de Beaurecueil (Cairo, 1954), p. 225.

8 *Kashf*, III, p. 544.

9 *Kashf*, IV, pp. 230–1. The Persian construction also allows the last phrase to be 'the garden of You', which is more meaningful in this context, though less idiomatic in English.

10 The saying *takhalliqū bi-akhlāq Allāh* is cited by Ghazzālī in the *Iḥyāʾ*, Part 4, Book 6, *Kitāb al-maḥabba*, Section 2, p. 195, though he does not quote it as a hadith, but as an anonymous saying (introduced with the words *wa qīla*).

11 *Inna'llāha kadhā khalqan*. A similar hadith is cited by al-Ḥakīm al-Tirmidhī in his *Kitāb nawādir al-uṣūl fī maʿrifat aḥādīth al-rasūl*, ed. M.ʿA. ʿAṭāʾ (2 vols., Beirut, 1992), II, Principle 261, p. 295: 'Verily God has 117 virtues or attributes (*akhlāq*). Whoever attains one of them will enter Paradise.'

12 Kurrakānī (d. 469/1076) was one of Hujwīrī's spiritual masters.

13 *Kashf*, II, p. 186.

14 The term *nafs ammāra* originates from the words of the prophet Joseph, who observes (Q. 12:53): 'Indeed, the (human) soul enjoins to evil' (*inna'l-nafsa la-ammāratun bi'l-sū'*). The place of this term in Sufi doctrine is discussed on p.159.
15 *Kashf*, VII, p. 358.
16 *Kashf*, III, p. 153.
17 *Kashf*, VII, p. 358. This hadith is listed in Abū Bakr Aḥmad b. Ḥusayn al-Bayhaqī's *Kitāb al-zuhd al-kabīr*, ed. A.A. Ḥaydar (Beirut, 1987), § 343. Ghazzālī cites the hadith in the *Iḥyā'*, Part 3, Book 4, *Kitāb 'ajā'ib al-qalb*, Section 1, p. 114.
18 *Kashf*, II, p. 342. The hadith about the lesser versus the greater holy war takes various forms. Bayhaqī includes it in his *Kitāb al-zuhd al-kabīr*, § 373, though in his view the *isnād* has some weakness. According to this version, Jābir (probably Jābir b. 'Abd Allāh b. 'Amr, d. 78AH) reports that the Prophet said: 'You have come for the best; you have come from the lesser holy war to the greater holy war.' When asked what the greater holy war was, he said: 'The servant's struggle against his lust' (*mujāhadat al-'abd hawāh*). Qārī lists it in a variant form in his *Asrār al-marfū'a*, § 211: 'We have returned from the lesser holy war to the greater holy war', the greater holy war being defined as 'the war of the heart (*jihād al-qalb*)'. However, Sufis usually referred to it as a war or struggle against the *nafs*, as in Maybudī's passage cited on p. 153. Ghazzālī cites it in the *Iḥyā'*, Part 3, Book 1, *Kitāb 'ajā'ib al-qalb*, Section 3, p. 118, in the context of his discussion of combating the *nafs ammāra* and the passions (*shahawāt*).
19 *Kashf*, III, p. 717.
20 *Kashf*, I, p. 81.
21 *Kashf*, IV, p. 96.
22 *Kashf*, IX, p. 435.
23 *Kashf*, V, p. 281. It is partly for this reason, perhaps, that Maybudī places the *zāhid* and *'ābid* lower in the spiritual hierarchy than the *'ārif* and *'āshiq*, for which see pp. 167–8.
24 Ibid.
25 *Kashf*, V, pp. 209–10; 473. On this teaching see also *Kashf*, III, p. 560; V, p. 472; VI, p. 293.
26 See pp. 133–4.
27 *Kashf*, I, p. 605.
28 *Kashf*, VII, pp. 248–9. The metaphor of the *maṣṭaba* is used for the *nafs* elsewhere in the *Kashf al-asrār*, for example, *Kashf*, III, p. 717 and VIII, p. 362. A similar hadith to that cited at the end of this passage is listed by al-Ḥakīm al-Tirmidhī in his *Nawādir*, II, Principle 186, p. 29, which reads as follows: 'Verily each day God has 300 glances (*laḥẓa*) with which He looks at the people of the earth. Whoever is looked upon by that glance, God will avert from them the evil of this world and the next and grant them the good of this world and the next.'
29 *Kashf*, III, p. 557. See also *Kashf*, V, p. 333.
30 *Kashf*, VIII, p. 545; VI, p. 344. See chapter five, pp. 135–6 and n. 72.
31 This is also the case in earlier works of Sufism such as Abu'l-Ḥusayn al-Nūrī's *Maqāmāt al-qulūb*, ed. with intro. P. Nwyia, *Mélanges de l'Université Saint Joseph* 44 (1968), pp. 117–54; or the *Bayān al-farq bayn al-ṣadr wa'l-qalb wa'l-fu'ād*

wa'l-lubb, ed. N. Heer (Cairo, 1958); trans. by N. Heer in N. Heer and K.L. Honerkamp, *Three Early Sufi Texts* (Louisville, 2003), attributed to al-Ḥakīm al-Tirmidhī, and referred to previously as possibly being one of Maybudī's sources. See ch 1, n.139.

32 *Kashf*, IX, p. 469.

33 *Kashf*, I, pp. 581–2. Compare Nūrī (*Maqāmāt al-qulūb*, p. 130) where the *ṣadr* (instead of *nafs*) is the 'mine' (*ma'din*) of Islam, the heart the mine of faith (*īmān*), the *fu'ād* (instead of *sirr*) the mine of *ma'rifa*, and the *lubb* (instead of *jān*) the mine of *tawḥīd*. On occasion, Maybudī also uses the word *jān* (instead of *nafs*) to mean 'soul' or lower self, for example, *Kashf*, VI, p. 267, but usually he applies *jān* to mean spirit, as was indicated by its place above the heart in the spiritual hierarchy, and this is clearly confirmed when he discusses the 'command of God' (Q. 16:1), employing the word *rūḥ* in place of *jān* in a hierarchy which matches exactly some of the cited passages: 'The heart was commanded to be ever in watchfulness (*murāqaba*); the secret (*sirr*) ever in gnosis, was commanded to seek serenity (*ṣafāwa*), and the spirit (*rūḥ*), in the essence (*'ayn*) of contemplation (*mushāhadat*) was commanded to seek the immediacy of presence [with God] (*luzūm-i ḥaḍrat*). See *Kashf*, V, p. 360. Regarding the relative stations of the heart (*dil*) and the spirit (*jān*), see *Kashf*, IV, p. 57. See also Anṣārī's dialogue between the heart and spirit (*Kashf*, I, pp. 59–60) referred to on p. 151, where *dil* plays the part of the one who puts questions (*sā'il*) and *jān* the mufti. Moreover *dil*, we are told, is in the intermediate stage of depending upon mediation (*wāsiṭa*), while *jān* is said to be at the stage of direct experience (*'iyān*). In his *Risālat al-Malāmatiyya* (ed. A. 'Afīfī, p. 104), Sulamī presents a similar hierarchy going from *nafs* to *qalb* to *sirr* to *rūḥ*, whereas Qushayrī places the *sirr* above the *rūḥ*. See *Laṭā'if*, III, p. 62; *Risāla*, p. 257. For a discussion of the ordering of these terms in Sufism see Shigeru Kamada, 'A study of the term *sirr* (secret) in Sufi *laṭā'if* theories', *Orient* 19 (1983), pp. 7–28.

34 In Nūrī's formulation *ṣadr* was in an equivalent position to *nafs*.

35 *Kashf*, V, pp. 59–60.

36 Or indeed, that of Nūrī's *Maqāmāt al-qulūb*, in which case, Maybudī has substituted *shaghāf* for *lubb*. However, since in the introduction to the *Bayān al-farq*, the *shaghāf* is mentioned as being (inwardly) beyond *lubb*, perhaps Maybudī is substituting *sirr* for *lubb*.

37 Trans. Abdel Haleem.

38 One might compare this scheme – *ṣadr* (locus of *islām*), *qalb* (*īmān*), *fu'ād* (*mushāhada*), *shaghāf* (*'ishq*) – with the scheme quoted earlier – *nafs* (*islām*), *qalb* (*īmān*), *sirr* (*ma'rifa*), *jān* (*tawḥīd*).

39 *Kashf*, VIII, pp. 411–12.

40 By *sunna* Maybudī is here referring to what is exemplified in the speech and acts of the Prophet. The term *ikhlāṣ* is usually translated as sincerity. Anṣārī places *ikhlāṣ* as the twenty-fourth *manzil*, as part of his section on the initial steps (*bidāyāt*). See *Manāzil al-sā'irīn*, p. 31; French tr. de Beaurecueil in ibid., p. 72.

41 *Kashf*, V, p. 218. See also *Kashf*, VII, p. 265, where 'life' is made up of three things: fear, hope and love.

42 Trans. Abdel Haleem.

43 Trans. Abdel Haleem.

44 *Kashf*, VII, p. 265.

45 *Kashf*, II, pp. 238–9. See also *Kashf*, V, p. 231, where Maybudī presents another fivefold formulation based on the divine providence (*ʿināya*), each stage of which is endorsed with a quotation from the Qur'an or hadith, the first being God's acceptance; the second, His taking the servant's hand; the third, His binding his heart to Him; the fourth, that He causes the lightning flash of love to shine in his heart; and the fifth, that He blows to him the scent of union.

46 See, for example, al-Ḥakīm al-Tirmidhī, *Bayān al-farq*, pp. 80–3; tr. Heer, pp. 41–2. In the *Bayān al-farq*, however, the author's main concern is to relate these 'stages' of the *nafs* to different levels of the spiritual constitution of the human being: for example, the *nafs ammāra* is associated with the breast (*ṣadr*).

47 *Kashf*, V, pp. 92–4.

48 Trans. Abdel Haleem.

49 *Kashf*, X, pp. 309–10. This is precisely the argument made by al-Ḥakīm al-Tirmidhī against the Malāmatiyya, viz. that by focusing on blaming themselves, they were making themselves into a veil. See Sara Sviri, 'Ḥakīm Tirmidhī and the Malāmatī movement', in Lewisohn, ed., *Classical Persian Sufism*, pp. 609–12.

50 *Kashf*, VII, p. 196.

51 This prayer forms part of a prophetic tradition that is listed in a number of hadith collections. Muslim narrates it on the authority of ʿĀʾisha, in *Ṣaḥīḥ, Kitāb al-ṣalāt*, ch. 187 (Mā yuqālū fi'l-rukūʿ wa'l-sajda), no. 8, § 986; Tirmidhī, on the authority of ʿAlī b. Abī Ṭālib, in his *Jāmiʿ al-saḥīḥ wa huwa Sunan al-Tirmidhī*, ed. A.M. Shākir (Cairo, 1937), *Kitāb al-daʿwāt*, ch. 113 (Fī duʿāʾ al-witr), no. 1, § 3566; and Ibn Māja on the authority of ʿĀʾisha in his *Sunan*, ed. M.M. al-Aʿẓamī (Riyadh, 1983), *Abwāb al-duʿāʾ*, ch. 3 (Bāb taʿawwudh minhu rasūl Allāh), no. 4, § 3886. Ibn Ḥanbal lists this hadith a number of times on the authority of ʿAlī (*Musnad*, I, pp. 96, 118, 150), and twice on the authority of ʿĀʾisha (*Musnad*, VI, pp. 58, 201). All the hadiths narrated by ʿĀʾisha place the prayer during the Prophet's prostration (*sajda*), whilst those narrated by ʿAlī give the *witr* prayer as the context, with the exception of one citation of Ibn Ḥanbal which states that this prayer was 'towards the end of his time' (*Musnad*, I, p. 118). Al-Ḥakīm al-Tirmidhī cites the hadith in his *Nawādir*, II, Principle 276, p. 384. Maybudī, however appears to have reversed the order of the first two parts of the prayer, since all the versions in the hadith collections begin with seeking refuge in God's good pleasure from His anger.

52 The published edition has *ḥayat* (written *ḥaywat*), which is how the word appears in MS B. However, the earlier MS A has *ḥayra*, which seems more correct both given the words that are expressed from the state 'I cannot encompass Thy praise', and Maybudī's teachings on *ḥayra*, which will be discussed in chapter seven.

53 *Kashf*, IX, pp. 102–3.

54 *Kashf*, VII, p. 172.

55 *Kashf*, III, p. 297. These seas being the intoxication of ecstasy (*sukr-i wajd*); the lightning flash of unveiling (*barq-i kashf*); the perplexity of witnessing (*ḥayrat-i shuhūd*) the light of proximity (*nūr-i qurb*); the dominion of finding (*wilāyat-i wujūd*); the splendour of non-differentiation (*bahāʾ-i jamʿ*); and the reality of singleness (*ḥaqīqat-i ifrād*). Maybudī cites Abū Ṭālib al-Makkī's *Qūt al-qulūb*, ed. ʿA. al-Ḥifnī (2 vols., Cairo, 1991); German trans. with intro. and

commentary by R. Gramlich as *Die Nahrung der Herzen* (4 vols., Stuttgart, 1992–5), as the source for this metaphor. The same metaphor appears later (*Kashf*, VIII, p. 315) without the attribution to Makkī. In the printed edition the second citation has the erroneous *shukr-i wajd* instead of *sukr-i wajd*. MSS A and B have *sukr-i wajd* in both citations.

56 *Kashf*, V, p. 373. The five seas in which man is drowning are: occupation or preoccupation (*shughl*); grief (*gham*); greed (*ḥirṣ*); heedlessness (*ghafla*); and differentiation (*tafriqa*). The five ships of salvation are: complete trust in God (*tawakkul*), which will bring the servant from the sea of preoccupation to the shore of being unoccupied and free (*farāgha*); the ship of acquiescence (*riḍā'*) will bring him from the sea of grief to the shore of safety (*amn*); the ship of contentment (*qanā'a*) will bring him from the sea of greed to the shore of abstinence (*zuhd*); the ship of remembrance (*dhikr*) will bring him from the sea of heedlessness to the shore of wakefulness (*yaqẓa*); the ship of affirming God's oneness (*tawḥīd*) will bring him from the sea of differentiation to the shore of non-differentiation (*jam'*).

57 *Kashf*, III, p. 779. Maybudī may here have drawn Ja'far al-Ṣādiq's metaphorical interpretation of the twelve springs (Q. 7:160) from Sulamī's *Ḥaqā'iq*, though as stated earlier, Maybudī's version differs from that in Nwyia's edition of Ja'far al-Ṣādiq's commentary, as well as from the MS Or. 9433 and the edition published by 'Imrān.

58 *Kashf*, III, p. 203. See also *Kashf*, I, p. 592.

59 *Kashf*, VI, pp. 16–17.

60 Regarding the difference between stations (*maqāmāt*) and states (*aḥwāl*), Qushayrī writes that *aḥwāl* are gifts (*mawāhib*) and *maqāmāt* are attainments (*makāsib*), i.e. what is acquired by effort, that is 'states are bestowed from the essence of [divine] goodness (*min 'ayn al-jūd*), and stations are attained by taking pains (*bi-badhl al-majhūd*)'. See *Risāla*, pp. 191ff. Sarrāj (*Luma'*, pp. 41–2) distinguishes the two terms in a similar way, adding the observation that unlike stations, states are transient (*fa-lā tadūm*), and gives as examples of *maqāmāt*: *tawba*, *wara'*, *zuhd*, *faqr*, *ṣabr*, *riḍā'* and *tawakkul*; and of *aḥwāl*: *murāqaba*, *qurb*, *khawf*, *rajā'*, *shawq*, *uns* and so on.

61 For example, the *Kitāb al-ta'arruf* of Kalābādhī; *Sharḥ al-ta'arruf* of Mustamlī; *Risāla* of Qushayrī; the *Manāzil al-sā'irīn* and *Ṣad maydān* of Anṣārī.

62 See chapter three on the method of mystical commentary.

63 One exception is the station of fear which Maybudī categorises according to six levels. See *Kashf*, I, p. 177.

64 *Kashf*, X, p. 107.

65 *Kashf*, II, p. 400.

66 *Kashf*, II, p. 330.

67 Indeed, Maybudī's account of three levels of *dūstī* (*Kashf*, II, pp. 94ff.) appears to have been derived from the concluding section of Anṣārī's *Ṣad maydān*, ed. de Beaurecueil, 'Une ébauche persane', p. 61.

68 *Kashf*, II, p. 330.

69 *Kashf*, X, p. 107.

70 *Kashf*, V, pp. 405–6.

71 It is found in numerous contexts in Sarrāj's *Luma'*, Kalābādhī's *Kitāb al-ta'arruf*, Qushayrī's *Laṭā'if* and Hujwīrī's *Kashf al-maḥjūb*. Maybudī also uses this ternary

in other contexts, for example, when defining three kinds of believers who will inherit the earth (*Kashf*, II, pp. 573–4). The three terms are explained at length in a passage partly attributed to Junayd, *Kashf*, VI, p. 574.

72 *Kashf*, II, p. 273.

73 *Kashf*, II, pp. 452–3.

74 This expression resembles another famous metaphor coined by Bāyazīd: 'I shed my self as a snake sheds its skin, then I looked at myself and lo! I was He.' See Sahlagī, *Kitāb al-nūr*, p. 151.

75 *Kashf*, IV, p. 359. Alluded to here is the doctrine of repenting of repentance (*al-tawba min al-tawba*), which will be discussed in the chapter on Abraham.

76 *Kashf*, III, p. 729. That is, patience *from* God (*ṣabr az Ḥaqq*) and patience *in* or *through* God (*ṣabr ba-Ḥaqq*), as exemplified by the Qur'anic injunction to Muhammad: 'Endure patiently. Your endurance is only by (the help of) God' (Q. 16:127). The command is an indication of the need for fulfilling one's duty and servitude (*taklīf*, *'ubūdiyyat*), while the statement that follows it an indication of being praised and the attainment of the station of lordship (*ta'rīf*, *rubūbiyyat*). The former is the equivalent to *rawish* or *sulūk* and the latter, of *kashish* or *jadhb*, two terms which was discussed at length in chapter five. In another context (*Kashf*, X, p. 275), Maybudī contrasts patience in affliction with patience with divine bounty (*ni'mat*), the latter being the more difficult of the two.

77 Partly my translation.

78 *Kashf*, II, p. 400.

79 Lit. with an eye that draws the lesson from things (*chishm-i 'ibrat*).

80 Lit. without any intervening distance.

81 *Kashf*, X, p. 274. The image of pitching a tent beyond the Throne may be an allusion to one of the ecstatic and utterances (*shaṭḥiyyāt)* of Bāyazīd. It is included in Rūzbihān Baqlī's *Sharḥ-i shaṭḥiyyāt*, p. 86.

82 *Kashf*, III, p. 424.

83 *Kashf*, II, pp. 495–6.

84 *Kashf*, V, p. 671.

85 *Kashf*, IV, pp. 243–4. According to 'Abd al-Raḥmān Jāmī (*Nafaḥāt al-uns*, ed. M. 'Ābidī [Tehran, 1370sh/1991], p. 296), Abū 'Alī Siyāh was one of the great shaykhs of Merv. He associated with Abū 'Alī Daqqāq (d. 412/1021), the spiritual master of Qushayrī.

86 On the *zunnār* see ch. 2, n. 98.

87 *Kashf*, III, p. 777. Again this is a theme taught by the Malāmatiyya. See, for example, *Tahdhīb al-asrār*, in Pourjavady, 'Manba'ī kuhan', p. 33; Sulamī's *Risālat al-Malāmatiyya*, ed. 'Afīfī, p. 119. On divine jealousy, see pp. 96–7.

88 *Kashf*, VII, pp. 231–2. The divine ruse will be discussed in chapter eight.

89 Known by the *laqab* 'al-'Ābid' (the worshipper).

90 *Kashf*, VIII, p. 301.

91 For traditions about the substitutes (*abdāl* or *budalā'*) see Sakhāwī, *Al-Maqāṣid al-ḥasana*, § 8; Qārī, *Asrār al-marfū'a*, § 6; al-Ḥakīm al-Tirmidhī, *Nawādir*, I, Principle 51, p. 165; II, Principle 222, p. 103.

92 *Kashf*, III, p. 65. According to 'Abd al-Raḥmān Jāmī, Sa'īd b. Sallām (Abū 'Uthmān Maghribī) was originally from Qayrawan, and later moved to Mecca where he spent years as a mystic and was 'unique among the shaykhs'. He ended his days in Nishapur. See Jāmī, *Nafaḥāt al-uns*, pp. 87–8.

93 *Kashf*, I, pp. 709–10. Yet he follows this statement with an argument that typifies his mystical doctrine of love, namely that sometimes God is kinder to those who are weaker, because they consider themselves to be impure, and whoever is more helpless is nearer to the Beloved.
94 *Kashf*, IV, p. 177.
95 *Kashf*, III, p. 386.
96 *Kashf*, V, p. 166. See also V, p. 192.
97 *Kashf*, III, p. 257.
98 *Kashf*, V, p. 310. Compare *Kashf*, VI, p. 17: the *ʿārifān* have the unveiling of the divine majesty (*mukāshafa-yi jalāl*), the *ʿāshiqān* have the witnessing of the divine beauty (*mushāhada-yi jamāl*).
99 *Kashf*, IV, p. 279.
100 *Kashf*, I, p. 177.
101 *Kashf*, I, p. 130.
102 *Kashf*, III, pp. 121–2.
103 Again, see *Kashf*, X, p. 492, where in his commentary on the words single (*witr*) and pair (*shafʿ*), Maybudī states that the *ʿābid* and *zāhid* go in pairs whereas the *murīd* goes alone; or *Kashf*, IV, p. 279, where Maybudī states that *ʿābidān* and *zāhidān* travel by land while *ʿārifān* and *ṣiddīqān* travel by sea. The former is an allusion to *sulūk* or *rawish* and the latter to *jadhb* or *kashish*, which is discussed on pp. 185 and 219–22.
104 *Kashf*, VII, p. 152. In another context (*Kashf*, III, p. 294), he states that the language of outer knowledge (*ʿilm*), alluded to in the law, is the stock in trade (*māya*) of wage-earners (*muzdūrān*) and capital (*sarmāya*) for Paradise-seekers, while mystics and knowers of God have another language; theirs is the language of unveiling (*kashf*) and mystery of love (*ramz-i maḥabbat*). The language of knowledge is by narration (*riwāyat*) and the language of unveiling by divine grace (*ʿināyat*). The person of narration is the wage-earner and the seeker of houris, the person of divine grace is in the ocean of direct witnessing, immersed in light. See also *Kashf*, V, p. 260.
105 *Kashf*, V, p. 167. There is an allusion here to the idea that mystics should neither fear Hell nor hope for Paradise, but only love God, as is expressed in the prayer of Rābiʿa al-ʿAdawiyya (d. 185/801) cited p. 109.
106 *Kashf*, VI, p. 390.
107 See ch. 4, n. 13, regarding Sulamī's omitting to mention the Karrāmiyya in his work. Concerning *zuhd*, Bāyazīd is reported to have remarked: 'What value does this world have that [a person] needs to talk about abstaining from it?' See Sahlagī, *Kitāb al-nūr*, p. 120. See also ibid., pp. 54, 79, 128; Abū Nuʿaym al-Iṣfahānī, *Ḥilyat al-awliyāʾ* (Cairo, 1932–8), X, p. 37.
108 For references on the Malāmatiyya see ch. 4, n. 9.
109 See, for example, Khargūshī's comments in Pourjavady, 'Manbaʿī kuhan', p. 34, and Sulamī, *Risālat al-Malāmatiyya*, ed. ʿAfīfī, p. 101.
110 For the mystic should go beyond his self and think only of God. See, for example, Kalābādhī, *Kitāb al-taʿarruf*, p. 70; tr. Arberry, p. 91; Mustamlī, *Sharḥ al-taʿarruf*, III, p. 1286; Hujwīrī, *Kashf al-maḥjūb*, pp. 75–6; tr. Nicholson, pp. 67–8; Sviri, 'Ḥakīm Tirmidhī and the Malāmatī movement', pp. 610f.
111 Although this does not appear to be one of the principles set out in either Khargūshī's or Sulamī's treatise. Examples of these excesses are given by

Mustamlī, *Sharḥ al-taʿarruf*, III, p. 1286.

112 See, for example, Anṣārī, *Ṭabaqāt al-ṣūfiyya*, ed. Ḥabībī, p. 104; ed. Mawlāʾī, p. 122. Anṣārī's remarks indicate that he was not against the earlier Malāmatīs or the genuine practice of their doctrines, for he says: 'The doctrine [of *malāmat*] does not mean that you don't follow the Shariʿa; it means that you don't follow your *nafs*, or look upon yourself with approbation. *Malāmat* is not that a person should act indecently, to draw the blame of other people; it is that in serving God (*dar kār-i Allāh*), he should have no fear of them; he should open his inmost secret to God, keeping it pure for Him, and should have no fear of the ill that others [may do to or think of him].'

113 *Kashf*, VII, p. 417.

114 The high point being when a shameless fellow entered the mosque where he was sitting and passed water on his face; *Kashf*, VII, pp. 417–8. Hujwīrī relates this anecdote, with one or two differences, in his chapter on *malāmat*. See *Kashf al-maḥjūb*, p. 76; tr. Nicholson, p. 68.

115 In his *Risālat al-Malāmatiyya*, Sulamī cites several mystics who were not in fact attached to the movement, such as Bāyazīd, Yaḥyā b. Muʿādh and Abū Bakr al-Wāsiṭī. This may have been, as Pourjavady suggests ('Manbaʿī kuhan', p. 11), in order to lend authority to his inclusion of the Malāmatiyya as part of 'mainstream' Sufism. On the other hand, certain aspects of Malāmatī doctrine would be part of any spiritual outlook. For example, in a passage on *ikhlāṣ* in the *Kashf al-asrār*, Dhu'l-Nūn al-Miṣrī relates how on the night of the *miʿrāj* the Prophet was completely unaffected by the praise of the angels and told them that he could not wait to be sent back to Abū Jahl's 'threshold of oppression' so that he could be addressed as: 'You magician! You liar!'; *Kashf*, I, p. 328.

116 *Kashf*, I, p. 481; V, p. 407.

117 *Kashf*, III, p. 18; V, pp. 405–6.

118 *Kashf*, II, p. 40; VI, p. 559; IX, p. 258.

119 For example, the sayings of ʿAbd Allāh Munāzil comprise an expression of his longing for death, which is contrasted with the states of Abū Saʿīd b. Abi'l-Khayr and Bishr al-Ḥāfī who wept in awe and apprehension at the impending encounter with God (*Kashf*, I, p. 481), and words of admonition to a wealthy man (*Kashf*, V, p. 407). To Abū Ḥafṣ Ḥaddād (*Kashf*, III, p. 18, *Nawbat* II) is attributed the saying: 'Perfection in religion consists of two things: gnosis of God and following the *sunna* of Muṣṭafā, and a discussion of three levels of *tawḥīd*' (*Kashf*, V, pp. 405–6). To Abū ʿUthmān Hīrī, who was also known as a hadith scholar, are ascribed sayings concerning acquiescence (*riḍāʾ*) and divine preordination (*qaḍāʾ*, *Kashf*, II, p. 40, *Nawbat* II) and *sunna* versus *bidʿa* (innovation) (*Kashf*, VI, p. 559, *Nawbat* II), and the following aphorism: 'Brotherhood in religion is a stronger [bond] than brotherhood through kinship' (*Kashf*, IX, p. 258, *Nawbat* II), and maybe also a mystical interpretation of the good tree (*Kashf*, III, pp. 642–3), and an aphorism concerning respect for parents (*Kashf*, V, p. 551). Both these sayings are cited in the name of Abū ʿUthmān. Maybudī clearly regarded these figures as authoritative scholars and mystics rather than exclusively as masters of the Malāmatī movement.

120 *Kashf*, VII, pp. 56–7; V, p. 245. This principle is discussed in Khargūshī's *Tahdhīb al-asrār* (see Pourjavady, 'Manbaʿī kuhan', p. 34, n. 13) and Sulamī, *Risālat al-Malāmatiyya*, ed. ʿAfīfī, p. 101. Thus Melchert's bracketing together

of the Karrāmiyya and Malāmatiyya as 'Renunciant schools' appears to be an oversimplification that ignores some of the doctrines of the latter, as stated in the works of Sulamī and Khargūshī. See Melchert, 'Sufis and Competing Movements in Nishapur', p. 237.

121 *Kashf*, II, p. 548; V, pp. 563–4; III, p. 779; VIII, p. 180, as discussed in Khargūshī's *Tahdhīb al-asrār* (see Pourjavady, 'Manbaʿī kuhan', p. 33) and Sulamī's *Risālat al-Malāmatiyya,* p. 119.

122 *Kashf al-maḥjūb*, p. 68; tr. Nicholson. p. 62.

123 A doctrine expounded by Aḥmad Ghazzālī in the *Sawāniḥ*, chs. 4, 5 and 6.

124 The Qalandariyya emerged as a movement in the early seventh/thirteenth century manifesting an extreme antinomian form of the Malāmatiyya. See Sviri, 'Ḥakīm Tirmidhī and the Malāmatī Movement', p. 584. However, as de Bruijn has pointed out, Qalandarī motifs appeared in Persian literature at least a century earlier. See Johannes T.P. de Bruijn, *Of Piety and Poetry: the Interaction of Religion and Literature in the Life and Works Of Ḥakīm Sanā'ī of Ghazna* (Leiden, 1983), p. 4; idem, 'The *Qalandariyyāt* in Persian Mystical poetry, from Sanā'ī onwards', in L. Lewisohn, ed., *The Legacy of Mediaeval Persian Sufism* (London, 1992), pp. 77–86. Apart from the wild and reckless figure of the *qalandar* himself, such poetry usually includes the image of the tavern (*kharābāt*), drinking, and gambling (*qimār*). See ibid., pp. 84–5.

125 *Kashf*, IX, p. 454.

126 *Kashf*, III, p. 571.

127 *Kashf*, II, p. 356.

128 *Kashf*, III, pp. 235–6. See also *Kashf*, VIII, p. 179, where Maybudī has quoted part of a *qaṣīda* of Sanā'ī, including the recommendation that one should take up the occupation of the gambler who stakes all (*pīsha-yi pākbāzī gīr*).

129 *Kashf*, III, p. 236.

130 See, for example, *Kashf*, I, pp. 229–30, where he speaks of the *jawānmardān* who 'in a state of perfected humanity, stepped onto the battlefield of the way, and proceeded with rectitude, so that their unification (*aḥadiyyat*) became dyed with the colourless colour of love'. The metaphor of colour derives from the description of the calf to be sacrificed in Q. 2:69, upon which these words are commenting. See also *Kashf*, I, p. 605, and III, p. 483. For sources on *futuwwa*, see ch. 4, n. 10.

131 Kadkanī, introduction to his edition of Ibn Munawwar's *Asrār al-tawḥīd*, I, pp. 86–7.

132 This is also evidenced in Sulamī's *Kitāb al-futuwwa*. For example he writes: 'There is a *futuwwa* fit for your behaviour towards God, another towards the Prophet, another towards your companions'. See Sulamī, *Kitāb al-futuwwa*, ed. S. Ateş (Ankara, 1397/1977); repr. in N. Pourjavady, *Majmūʿa-yi āthār-i Abū ʿAbd al-Raḥmān Sulamī* (2 vols., Tehran, 1369sh/1990), pp. 228–9; trans. by T.B. al-Jerrahi al-Helvati as *The Book of Sufi Chivalry* (New York, 1983), p. 36.

133 I believe Maybudī's usage of the words *mardī* and *mardānagī* is equivalent to *jawānmardī*, and not to the Arabic *muruwwa* (lit. [mature] manliness), which is often translated as the possession of good moral character, although Qushayrī (*Risāla*, p. 473) includes *muruwwa* as a branch of *futuwwa*. For the distinction between these two terms see the relevant articles in *EI*[2].

134 *Kashf*, II, p. 759.

135 *Kashf*, V, p. 669.
136 *Kashf*, III, p. 751. Exemplified by Moses' response to the Children of Israel's worshipping of the calf (Q. 5:150–1).
137 *Kashf*, II, p. 341.
138 *Kashf*, VII, p. 475.
139 *Kashf*, II, p. 341.
140 *Kashf*, I, p. 606. This *bayt* from a *qaṣīda* of Sanā'ī occurs at least five times in *Kashf al-asrār*. The *bayt* may be found in the *Dīwān* of Sanā'ī (repr. Tehran, 1984), p. 205. Interestingly, Maybudī has preceded this *bayt* with one that comes later in the same *qaṣīda*.
141 *Kashf*, IV, p. 302.
142 *Kashf*, X, p. 375.
143 *Kashf*, II, p. 613.
144 *Huwiyya*, lit. He-ness, is really a reference to the divine ipseity.
145 *Kashf*, VII, p. 56.
146 *Kashf*, I, p. 31.
147 Trans. Abdel Haleem.
148 *Kashf*, VIII, p. 31.
149 *Kashf*, IV, p. 429; VII, p. 439. The need for suffering in the way of love is further discussed in chapters seven and ten.
150 *Kashf*, X, p. 232.

7

Mystical theology and the way of love

Taqdīr and divine intervention

The doctrine that man's happiness or misfortune in this world and the next is determined by God's pre-eternal decree (*qaḍā'*, *taqdīr*) is reiterated throughout the mystical sections of the *Kashf al-asrār*.[1] It is the mystics, Maybudī explains, who are truly aware of the implication of *qaḍā'*: 'the *'ābid* has his eye on *abad* (his eternal end), whereas the *'ārif* has his eye on *azal* (what was decreed in pre-eternity)'.[2] The intense feeling of apprehension and helplessness in face of this pre-eternal decree is powerfully expressed in a *munājāt* of Anṣārī, cited in chapter four (see p. 114). It is quoted in a number of contexts by Maybudī:

> Ah, the fate that has gone before me! Alas for what the Self-willed has already dictated! What use is there in my being happy or upset? I am in fear of what the Omnipotent has decreed in pre-eternity.[3]

In the *Kashf al-asrār*, the divine decree is shown to be Satan's excuse for refusing to prostrate himself before Adam, and his subsequent alienation from God.[4] Maybudī relates how Sahl al-Tustarī questions Iblīs (Satan) about his disobedience. In reply, the latter deplores his alienation from the Divine Presence, and explains in a poem that it was inevitable because 'his kilim was woven black' (i.e. misfortune was woven into his very nature). When Iblīs is again questioned by Bāyazīd, he states in his defence that the matter of opposing (*mukhālafat*), or complying with (*muwāfaqat*) God's command was out of his hands; since all opposition or compliance comes from Him, we have no power over it.[5] In another context, where Satan is again questioned over his refusal to obey the command to prostrate himself before Adam, he answers: 'Command is one thing and nature (*nihād*, lit. make-up, constitution) is another. The command was *to* me but the nature was *in* me. I had no remedy for changing my nature'.[6]

The awareness that everything has been pre-ordained does not mean that people should abandon their efforts; whoever supposes that he can reach his destination without making an effort is under an illusion, but whoever imagines he can arrive [simply] by making an effort is no less deluded.[7] There must be exertion through worship (*ṭāʿat*), but attaining degrees [of spirituality] is through God-given help (*tawfīq*).[8] The servant should be aware that acceptance by God is 'by His grace (*faḍl*) not by his own act (*ʿamal*)',[9] and should not expect to find Him either by means of his act or of his intellect (*ʿaql*).[10]

The only way out of this apparent impasse is to have complete trust in God (*tawakkul*), and commit one's affairs to Him (*tafwīḍ*). True *tawakkul*, Maybudī explains, is that a person should 'rise above the way of his own choice (*ikhtiyār*), and abandon (lit. become blind to) his own power of disposal (*taṣarruf*). He should pitch the tent of acquiescence and surrender (*riḍā wa taslīm*) in the alley of destiny and decree (*qaḍāʾ wa qadar*)'.[11] For this reason Sahl al-Tustarī recommends that the soundest of prayers is remembrance (*dhikr*), because we should leave aside choice (*ikhtiyār*).[12] Abandoning choice with an awareness of one's utter neediness (*iftiqār*) is the point of the compass of the way.[13] As long as the servant is 'managing his own affairs (*dar tadbīr-i khwīsh*) he is in the darkness of ignorance, and as long as he entrusts his affairs to God (*tafwīḍ*), he is in the radiance of gnosis and the light of guidance.'[14]

In fact, it is the seeker's effort and the seeker himself that impedes him, for otherwise God is already present. This is expressed in the *munājāt* of Anṣārī: 'You are present, so what need have I to seek?'[15] Indeed, as Anṣārī repeatedly points out, it is only because the servant has already found God that he seeks Him:

> Whatever can be found by seeking is worthless. The finding of God [comes to] the servant before his seeking, [nonetheless] seeking is its prerequisite. The gnostic found seeking from finding, not finding from seeking, just as the devotee found worship from sincerity, not sincerity from worship, and the means from the end, not the end from the means. O God! Finding You precedes both seeking and the seeker, but the servant seeks You because he is overcome by restlessness.[16] The seeker is seeking and the One sought has been found before he even seeks. See, what a strange affair is this![17]

This paradox may be explained by the teaching that the divine act precedes all acts, and everything comes from God.[18] So again, Anṣārī is cited as having said: 'The light of faith comes from finding, not finding from the light of faith' and similarly, Ḥallāj: 'He who seeks God by the light of faith is like someone who looks for the sun by the light of a star.'[19]

Thus, while the servant must exert himself and seek God, he only finds Him (again) when he is released both from his effort and from himself by divine intervention. Anṣārī therefore prays:

> O God! You cleansed [me] with 1000 waters until you had acquainted me with love, yet still one cleansing remains to be done: that You should cleanse me of myself so that I can rise out of myself and only You will remain. O God! Shall we never have one day together without the trouble of myself? That I might open my eye and not be confronted with my 'I'?[20]

The moment when the servant is released from himself is called *jadhb* or *jadhba*, (lit. attraction or pulling). In Sufi literature the Arabic term *jadhb* is paired with its opposite, *sulūk* (journeying), while in Persian the equivalent terms *kashish*[21] and *rawish*, or sometimes, *kashish* and *kūshish* (effort), or *rawanda* (going) and *rubūda* (snatched) are used. Maybudī describes the experience of *jadhba* in his commentary on Q. 10:22, 'It is He Who enables you to travel on land and sea'[22]:

> In the language of allusion, travelling on land means making one's way on the highways of the law, by means of demonstrative reasoning and the [revealed] Message. Travelling by sea alludes to the divine overpowering which in an ecstatic moment seizes the reins of the servant's steed without any intermediary, taking him through the stations of reality to the holy places of witnessing. Just as a journey that would take one month on land can be made in one day by sea, so in the field [of spiritual wayfaring] this noble one travelled the distance of a whole lifetime with one rapture (*jadhba*) from God. This is why it has been said: 'A rapture from God is equal to the work of the *thaqalayn*.'[23]

Another aspect of the mystical application of the doctrine of *qaḍāʾ* appears in Maybudī's emphasis on the alternation of opposite states, such as fear (*khawf*) and hope (*rajāʾ*), contraction (*qabḍ*) and expansion (*basṭ*), awe (*haybat*) and intimacy (*uns*).[24] Most of the Sufi manuals understand the alternation of states as belonging to those who are in the station of *talwīn* (changeability or vacillation), while those in the higher station of *tamkīn* (stability) are no longer affected by the alternation of states. Hujwīrī, for example, writes: 'The signification of *talwīn* is change and turning from one state to another [...] he who is steadfast (*mutamakkin*) is not vacillating (*mutaraddid*) for he has carried all that belongs to him into the presence of God',[25] while Qushayrī states that '*talwīn* is an attribute of the people of states (*aḥwāl*), and *tamkīn* an attribute of the people of realities (*ḥaqā'iq*)'.[26] Occasionally, Maybudī complies with this idea, as when, for example, he compares the sun to the possessor of *tamkīn* who is eternally in the radiance of gnosis, and the moon to the possessor of *talwīn* whose states are changing, so that he goes from expansion (*basṭ*), which elevates him to union, and then returns to lassitude falling into the state of contraction (*qabḍ*).[27] However, more consistently Maybudī maintains that the alternation of states affects all the ranks of spiritual travellers and even prophets.[28] The difference lies in the states between which the mystics move, according to their level of attainment. Thus, for initiates, the 'two seas' (Q. 35:12) represent fear and hope, while for adepts they represent contraction and expansion, because 'just as the worship of the aspirant at the beginning of his seeking (*irādat*) must be subject to fear and hope, so at the final stage, in the perfection of his gnosis, his state is not devoid of contraction and expansion.'[29]

There were precedents for this view among earlier mystics. For example, discussing the terms *talwīn* and *tamkīn*, Abū Naṣr al-Sarrāj states that there are two opinions regarding *talwīn*: according to the first, *talwīn* is a sign of the attainment of realised truth (*ḥaqīqa*), because it is the manifestation of the power of the Omnipotent which brings about change; according to the second, the sign of realised truth is the removal of *talwīn*. The former concerns the changing of hearts and inner realities which are purified for God (*talwīn al-qulūb wa'l-asrār al-khāliṣa li'llāh*), and the latter, the changing of states (*talwīn al-aḥwāl*).[30] Hujwīrī relates an exchange between Ḥallāj and Junayd on the subject of sobriety (*ṣaḥw*) and intoxication (*sukr*), and Massignon, commenting on this passage, contrasts the theory of Junayd, 'for whom God is the lone author of contrasting psychic states that He alternates in His own way in the souls of mystics, to whom he remains inaccessible', with Ḥallāj's idea of the gradual removal of the consideration of all intermediaries, including spiritual states, in the attainment of immediate and essential union of God.[31] The predominant view presented in the *Kashf al-asrār*, clearly concurs with the first view in Sarrāj's definition, and the view of Junayd in Massignon's observation.

Maybudī explains the need for the alternation of states in various ways. We have already seen the sense of caution expressed in the quotation from Anṣārī (see p. 60), where he advocated an oscillation between an awareness of God's transcendence and His immanence.[32] Some of the reasons given for the alternation of unveiling and concealment are that man does not have the capacity for direct or perpetual vision of the realities,[33] or that it is part of the way of love.[34] But above all, the insistence on the alternation of states appears to be connected to Maybudī's mystical doctrine of divine decree and intervention. Thus, he explains that the contraction (*qabḍ*) and expansion (*basṭ*) of the mystics (*ʿārifān*) are a divine ruling (*ḥukm-i ilāhī*) and kingly decree (*taqdīr-i pādshāhī*),[35] and again, 'God's way (*sunna*) with prophets (*anbiyāʾ*) and saints (*awliyāʾ*) is that He sometimes keeps them in non-differentiation (*jamʿ*) and sometimes in differentiation (*tafriqa*).'[36] The doctrine is further illustrated in Maybudī's commentary on the words 'and We caused them to turn over to the right and the left' (Q. 18:18), said of the Companions of the Cave while they were sleeping. Maybudī explains that this is an allusion to those who have risen out of themselves and reached their Lord. At that moment all mediation is removed and God acts and disposes for them, just as when it was said of those noble ones 'We caused them to turn to the right and the left', it means 'we turned them from the state of annihilation to subsistence, from unveiling to veiling from manifestation to concealment'.[37]

Knowledge

Maybudī's mystical understanding of the doctrine of *taqdīr* and divine intervention also appears in the realm of knowledge. According to a saying of Anṣārī, the reality of *tawḥīd* cannot be attained by rational demonstration (*istidlāl*) or endeavour (*ijtihād*), but is found, unsought (*nā khwāsta dar āmada*) in a state of 'inadvertence' (*ghaflat*).[38] While the language of knowledge is through transmission (*ba-riwāyat*) the language of unveiling is by [divine] favour (*ʿināyat*).[39] This doctrine is, in effect, a mystical application of the 'traditionalist' attitude towards reason. To accept without comprehending (*nā daryāfta padhīrufta*) and to be suspiscious of the rational faculty (*tuhmat bar ʿaql nihāda*) constitutes, according to Maybudī, not only the Sunni credo, but the recommended way from which opens the 'spring of wisdom, truth of spiritual insight, and the light of gnosis'.[40]

This is not to say that knowledge does not have its place. Various passages in the *Kashf al-asrār* indicate the importance both of the rational faculty (*ʿaql*) and of knowledge (*ʿilm*). For example, Maybudī understands the words 'We shall show them Our signs on the horizons and in themselves until it will be clear to them that it is the Truth' (Q. 41:53) to be, in part, a reminder to humanity that they should look at themselves and ponder the wonder of their existence. In particular they should realise that their value (*qīmat*) lies in the rational faculty, and their magnificence (*hishmat*) in their knowledge.[41] Commenting on the words 'Is not He [best] Who made the heavens and earth?' (Q. 27:60), Maybudī interprets the earth to be an allusion to the lower soul (*nafs*), and the heavens to be an allusion to noble and lofty reason (*ʿaql*), and adds: 'there is no nobler and more elevated quality than this.'[42] Elsewhere he compares faith to a pair of scales, the two pans of which are fear and hope, and the pointer, love (*dūstī*). These two pans are suspended from knowledge, for knowledge is indispensable: fear without knowledge is the fear of the Khārijīs; hope without knowledge is the hope of the Murjiʾīs, while love without knowledge is the love of the libertines (*ibāḥatiyyān*).[43] In another context, when commenting on the 'people who have understanding (*qawm yaʿqilūn*)' (Q. 2:164), Maybudī writes:

> Reason is the tether of the heart (*ʿaql ʿiqāl-i dil ast*), that is, it keeps the heart from other than the Beloved and restrains it from unworthy sentiments. According to the school of the *ahl-i sunnat*, reason is light, and its locus is in the heart, not the brain. It is the prerequisite for God to address man (*sharṭ-i khiṭāb*), not the cause (*mūjib*) of His command, and in gnosis it is purely the tool, not the origin.[44]

In this passage, Maybudī is already placing limits on *ʿaql*. Commenting on the words 'Say, [O Muhammad, to mankind]: If you love God, follow me; God will love you and forgive your sins' (Q. 3:31), Maybudī warns that *ʿaql* is only a watchman (*pāsbān*). It is not a guide (*rāhbar*), that you should put the reins in its hand, nor is it a way that you should set out upon.[45] Moreover, *'aql* is a gift from God (*mawhibat*), which is of no use without God-given success (*tawfīq*). To endorse this point Maybudī quotes a hadith of the Prophet which relates how when God created *'aql*, He commanded it 'Rise!' and it rose, then 'Be seated!', and it sat down, then 'Come!' and it came, then 'Go!', and it went, then 'See!', and it saw. Then He said, 'By My Glory and Majesty, I have not created anything more noble and excellent than you. By you I am worshipped and by you I am obeyed. Thus far the hadith is well-known, though with some variations.[46] However, Maybudī adds a somewhat unusual conclusion:

> At this praise an element of conceit appeared in *'aql*. God did not allow this, and commanded: 'O *'aql*! Look again and see what you can see.' *'Aql* looked and saw a form more excellent and beautiful than itself. It asked: 'What are you?' It replied: 'I am that without which you are useless, I am *tawfīq*.'[47]

The second part of this tradition is consistent with Maybudī's belief that the knowledge of God is not 'acquired' but 'found' by divine intervention. More than once he states that until God makes Himself known to the heart of His servants, they will never have cognisance (*shinākht*) of Him.[48] According to this principle, Maybudī defines three categories of knowledge, to each of which is assigned a teacher: the knowledge of *sharī'at* may be learned, and its teacher is the *ustād*; the knowledge of *ṭarīqat* is to be practised, and its teacher is the *pīr*; and the knowledge of *ḥaqīqat* can only be found, and God entrusted the teaching of this to Himself.[49]

This moment of 'finding' the knowledge of God is, as Maybudī indicates, none other than the moment of annihilation from self.[50] He explains this doctrine in another passage where he defines three levels of knowledge. Here he is using the metaphor of light.

> Three lights are cast into the heart of the servant at three stages [lit. times]: in the beginning the light of reason (*'aql*); at the intermediate stage, the light of knowledge (*'ilm*); and at the end, the light of gnosis (*'irfān*). [...] By the light of the beginning he knows his own fault; by the light of the intermediate stage he recognises what is harmful to him, and by the light of the end he discovers his own non-existence. By the light of the beginning he is freed from idolatry (*shirk*), by the light of the intermediate stage he is freed from opposition (*khilāf*), and by the light of the end he is freed from himself.[51]

In yet another formulation, this time comprising four levels of knowledge, Maybudī defines the highest level as being that of the one who is 'snatched from himself' (*az khwad rubūda*).[52] For this reason, people of spiritual realisation, the *ahl-i ḥaqīqat*, are unable to express, or even give an indication of their experience. It must be kept hidden not just from the unworthy but from awareness at an outer level in themselves.[53] The following saying is quoted from Junayd:

> Whenever I supposed that I had arrived somewhere, the call came from my secret: 'When you thought you had found Me you lost Me, when you thought you had lost me you found Me'.[54]

Nor should gnosis be sought, for 'whoever seeks gnosis is seeking a portion (*naṣīb*), and whoever seeks a portion is fostering and worshipping their self.'[55]

The way in which God reveals Himself at moments of unveiling is sometimes described in theological terms, according to the divine acts, attributes and essence. For example, commenting on the words 'Verily in the creation of the heavens and earth [...] are signs for people who have understanding' (Q. 2:164), Maybudī explains that God reveals Himself to the *ʿāmm* through His creation, to the *khāṣṣ* through His Attributes, and to the *khāṣṣ al-khāṣṣ* in His Essence.[56] In other contexts, however, he allows that only Muhammad has the capacity to contemplate the Divine Essence.[57]

Moments of unveiling and encounter with God are often described using words which suggest vision, for example, the Arabic words *shuhūd*, *mushāhadat*, *kashf*, *mukāshafat*, *ʿiyān*, *muʿāyanat*, and the Persian word *dīdār*. However, on several occasions Maybudī stipulates that, in this life, the vision of the divine reality is a vision of the heart, not of the eyes.[58] The experience of unveiling at its highest level is shown to be a fleeting experience, and is often depicted through the metaphor of light.[59] For example, Anṣārī describes the theophany (*tajallī*) as a sudden lightning flash (*barq*).[60] Maybudī explains the reason for the transient nature of this experience in his commentary on the words 'Such as remember God, standing, sitting and reclining, and reflect upon (*yatafakkarūna*) the creation of the heavens and earth' (Q. 3:191).[61] He firstly relates the admonition, 'Do not contemplate God, because you cannot encompass His measure', and then explains:

He says 'Do not ponder the essence of God because you will not attain His measure (*ba qadr-i ū narasīd*), nor will you be able to know Him as is fitting for Him.' [Indeed] you cannot even reach the outskirts of His glorious Majesty. Not that His majesty is hidden from creatures. No, on the contrary it is because it is so evident and clear, but human sight is very weak and cannot bear to perceive it. Rather, it is dazzled, bewildered and confounded by it, just like the bat who does not come out during the day because its eye is too weak to bear the light of the sun. This is the level of the commonalty of believers (*ʿawāmm*). However, great ones and those who are truly realised (*buzurgān wa ṣiddīqān*) do have the strength for this vision (*naẓar*) but only intermittently (*gāh gāh*), not for any duration. Similarly, people take no more than a glimpse at the orb of the sun, for if they looked at it for any time they would go blind. So, if one wishes to contemplate, then one should contemplate the wonders of His creation, for all that is in existence is a light from the light of the power and greatness of God be He glorified.[62]

Love

The pre-eminence of love

Maybudī uses various arguments to justify the centrality of love. First, he claims that the way of love was a part of the divine revelation. Commenting on the words 'Follow, [O Muhammad], that which has been revealed to you by your Lord' (Q. 6:106), he distinguishes between two kinds of revelation sent to Muhammad: one which was sent outwardly through the mediation of Gabriel, defined as *risālat* (message); and the other which came to him 'from secret to secret (*sirran bi-sirr*)', in the seclusion of 'or nearer (*aw adnā*)' (Q. 53:9). Concerning the contents of *risālat* (presumably the words of the Qur'an) which was sent down to his outer self, the Prophet was commanded 'communicate it to people', but regarding the contents of *waḥy*, the revelation that he received in seclusion (*ba-khalwat*), Maybudī states: 'that was the secret of love (*dūstī*)' which the Prophet was commanded to 'listen to and follow'.[63] If in this passage love was shown to be an inward revelation separate from the Qur'an, in another context, as we have seen, the Qur'an itself is defined as 'God's keepsake with His lovers, an epistle whose title is Eternal Love and whose contents are the story of love and lovers'.[64]

On a number of occasions Maybudī shows love to be the highest station of the mystical path. For example, when defining three stages of the way

Maybudī begins with 'knowledge of the outward law' (*sharīʿat*); after this he places 'inner striving and spiritual discipline' (*ṭarīqat*); and finally (equivalent to *ḥaqīqat*), he places 'the story of the heart, heartsease and lovers (*ḥadīth-i dil wa dil-ārām wa dāstān-i dūstān*)'.[65] In another threefold definition of religion, the third stage, *ikhlāṣ* (sincerity) is said to consist in being a lover (*muḥibb*).[66] When he comments on the words 'Say, [O Muhammad to mankind], If you love God, follow me; God will love you and forgive your sins' (Q. 3:31), Maybudī compares the saying of Abraham that whoever followed him would be of his people, to the saying of Muhammad that whoever followed him would be the friend of God, and adds, 'There is no higher state than that of love'.[67] A tradition about Jesus relates how he considers the most radiant among the spiritual wayfarers he encounters to be the lovers of God.[68]

We have seen how in Maybudī's interpretation of the hadith 'I was a hidden treasure and I wished to be known (*aḥbabtu an uʿrafa*)', he gives love precedence over gnosis, seeing this tradition as proof that 'mystical knowledge (*maʿrifat*) is based upon love (*maḥabbat*)' and that 'wherever there is love there is knowledge, but wherever there is no love there can be no knowledge'.[69] The dependence of spiritual knowledge and realisation on love is shown elsewhere: for example, when Maybudī states that the mystics (*ʿārifān*) and the truly sincere (*ṣiddīqān*) have reached a perfect state only when love (*ʿishq*) has complete sovereignty over them,[70] or that 'the people who have hearkened to the call of God, accepted with heart and soul the summons of the Prophet and fufilled the Covenant of *Alast* are those who place heart and soul in the censer of *maʿrifat* on the fire of *maḥabbat*.'[71]

The purifying fire of love

In his mystical commentary on the words 'and purify My house' (Q. 22:26), which are understood exoterically to be a command to cleanse and purify the Kaʿba in preparation for the Pilgrimage, Maybudī relates a tradition according to which the prophet David is commanded by God: 'Purify a house for me that I may come and dwell there'. David asks 'Which house?' to which the reply is given, 'The heart of My believing servant'. David then asks, 'And how can it be purified?' to which God answers, 'Set alight the fire of love therein to burn all that is not related to Me'. David further asks, 'Where can I find a heart worthy of Your Majesty and Might?' and God replies, 'Wherever you see a harvest burnt by the fire of love in the quest for Me'. Maybudī then observes that all things that are burnt become valueless except the heart, which increases in value.[72]

In another context Maybudī shows, through an anecdote about Abū Bakr al-Shiblī (d. 334/945), that the servant whose heart is burnt will not be touched by the fires of Hell in the Afterlife, and quotes the following poem.

> Roast your heart in the fire of love,
> And then turn from your heart to your soul,
> Then, if you should meet the Beloved on the way,
> Sacrifice both of these at His feet.[73]

The fire of love may be more precisely defined as the feeling of intense need (*niyāz*) and longing (*shawq*), which the lover experiences in separation from the Beloved. Maybudī quotes the following tradition concerning the longing (*ishtiyāq*) for God:

> The hearts of those who yearn (*mushtāqān*) are lit by the light of God, and when their longing is aroused [its] light illumines all that is between heaven and earth.[74]

According to Anṣārī, there can be no better means for the lover than need (*niyāz*),[75] while Maybudī explains that a suffering soul that is full of need, anguish (*gudāz*, lit. melting) and burning of the heart (*sūz-i dil*) should be considered as booty.[76]

The object of longing in this world may be for unveiling (*kashf*), inner witnessing (*mushāhadat*) of, or union (*waṣl*) with God, but as we have seen, such experiences are only fleeting. Anṣārī complains of the transient nature of these moments of unveiling:

> O most Precious of the two worlds! Sometimes You are hidden, sometimes manifest. My heart is perplexed and my soul going mad. How long will this concealing and revealing go on? Tell me, when will the unending revealing be?[77]

The transient experience of unveiling produces two effects in the seeker: one is a sense of perplexity or consternation (*ḥayrat* or *taḥayyur*), sometimes defined as stupefaction or bedazzlement (*dahshat*),[78] and the other is an intensification of the sense of longing. [79] Both of these are often described in the *Kashf al-asrār* with the metaphors of being drowned or intoxicated, or of being afflicted by an unquenchable thirst. Such effects are more fully portrayed in the following passages, most of which include *munājāt* of Anṣārī:

> The one who seeks is in the whirlpool of woe (*ḥasrat*), the one who finds is perplexed (*ḥayrān*) in the inundation of light. In that perplexity, [the one who finds] keeps saying in that state of bedazzlement:
>
> I am in bewilderment at You, O take my hand
> You, who are the Guide for the one who is perplexed at You.
>
> The Master of the Way (Anṣārī) said: 'Everyone laments their perplexity, but I am joyful at it [...]. I cling to the fire of perplexity as a moth does to the [burning] lamp; neither is my soul troubled by its overwhelming heat, nor my heart by its painful brand. O God! I have water in my head and fire in my heart. Inwardly I am cosseted (*nāz dāram*)[80] and outwardly destitute. I have embarked upon a sea that has no shore. I have a pain in my soul for which there is no cure. My eye came upon something which no tongue can describe.[81]
>
> 'How did I know that the mercenary (*muzdūr*) is the one who sets store by Paradise,[82] but the mystic (*ʿārif*) is the one who desires [just] one moment of union (*wiṣāl*)? How did I know that perplexity (*ḥayrat*) is the way to union with You, and he seeks You the more who is drowned in You?'[83]
>
> O You Who are found and only to be found! What sign do they give of being drunk save having lost themselves. Everyone finds affliction in being far away, this poor one in being near. Everyone is thirsting from lack of water, but I from being full [...].[84]

Maybudī uses similar imagery when he describes the state of *dahshat* (stupefaction or bedazzlement).[85] He explains that first, by unveiling His majesty (*jalāl*), 'God drowns [the servant] in a wave of *dahshat* so that in the overpowering of intimacy (*uns*) he is released from himself. [It is a state] in which the body has no longer any endurance, the heart cannot get along with reason (*ʿaql*), [86] nor can the eye (*naẓar*) be steady enough for discrimination (*tamyīz-rā napāyad*)'.[87] He then remarks at how many intoxicated ones (*mastān*) have entered the valley of *dahshat* thirsting (*ʿaṭshān*), bewildered (*ḥayrān*), sometimes laughing, sometimes crying, and constantly pleading with God about the painful and burning anguish which they have no power to bear.[88] It is perhaps for this reason that Maybudī states that lovers need to have a special kind of patience – *al-ṣabr maʿa'llāh* (patience with God) in the state of witnessing (*mushāhadat*) at the time of manifestation (*tajallī*).[89]

Ultimately the longing of seekers is for the vision of God in the Afterlife for, as Maybudī explains, in this life 'lovers will have only a glimpse of the lights of those secrets and a scent of the perfume of those traces. Only Muhammad had the capacity for direct witnessing (*ʿiyān*)';[90] or 'today there can only be a witnessing of the heart (*mushāhada-yi dil*), tomorrow there will be direct witnessing with the eyes (*muʿāyana-yi chashm*)'.[91] For this reason, Anṣārī explains, true lovers of God long for death: 'Everyone hopes for something, and the hope of the mystic is for the vision [of God] (*dīdār*). Everyone loves life, and death is difficult for them, but the mystic has need of death for the sake of vision'.[92]

Yet even vision of God in the Afterlife will not reduce the sense of longing. So, Maybudī insists:

> O noble one! Take care that you don't imagine that tomorrow, when those who have travelled the straight path in religion, those who long for the court of God, and are immersed in the ocean of certainty, attain the vision of the Majestic Lord, their longing (*shawq*) will be reduced by one iota – in the liver of a fish there is a thirst which will never be assuaged by one jot, even if you were to assemble for it all the oceans of the world. Today they are in the fount of longing; tomorrow in the fount of direct experience, too, they will be in the ardour of longing.[93]

Suffering and the perfection of love

In the way of love the seeker must be prepared to suffer every kind of affliction. The inevitable connection between love and suffering is explained in the following passage of Anṣārī, where there is a play on the two words *maḥabbat* (love) and *miḥnat* (affliction) which look identical in the Arabic script apart from the placing of a diacritical point:

> *Maḥabbat* and *miḥnat* look alike [as words], and *miḥnat* and *maḥabbat* are old friends. The elixir of love does not cost nothing, but whatever the affliction, it is not costly for the soul. You should readily give a thousand souls for the Beloved. With the desire of Him, His trials are sweet, even if they be all blood and fire.[94]

In the *Kashf al-asrār* we are told that 'God prescribes affliction (*balāʾ*) for His lovers',[95] that 'He sends a sherbet of suffering along with the robe of love',[96] and that 'in the society of love they wear only affliction'.[97] Apart from the suffering which lovers must inevitably experience in times of separation – for as Maybudī states 'a person cannot have the sweetness of union without having tasted the bitterness of the colocynth of separation'[98] – there is also the suffering which God inflicts on His lovers to test and perfect their love. Maybudī relates a tradition according to which the seed of Adam was divided into a thousand groups and honoured with love. To begin with all were desirous of love. Then He placed the world before them with all its beauty. All became entranced by it, except one group. Then this group was again divided into a thousand parts, and all stood firm in their love until God presented them with the comforts of Paradise. They, too, became bewitched with the shade, the rivers and houris and remained with that, except for one group. This group in turn was divided into a thousand groups which this time were brought to the alley of affliction. All the groups turned away except for one whose members 'headed for that alley like lovers, having no regard either for suffering or for hardship, and said, "We regard it great good fortune to be bearing Your grief and suffering Your affliction." '[99]

Lovers of God should feel honoured to suffer for 'whoever has a higher station in love, the greater is their suffering'. Maybudī includes this statement in his commentary on the story of Job, and endorses it with the hadith of the Prophet: 'Verily the ones who suffer most are the prophets, and then the saints, and then people like them.'[100] Thus lovers should not simply accept their suffering, they should enjoy it.[101] Indeed, Maybudī even goes further to observe that there can be no ease of the heart or peace for the soul without the pain of love (*gham-i ʿishq*).[102]

Jealousy and the way of love

Jealousy is inseparable from the way of love. In Anṣārī's words 'love (*mihr*) and jealousy (*ghayrat*) are partners (*anbāz*)'. [103] There is jealousy on the part of God, and jealousy on the part of the lover. The divine jealousy has the dual function of perfecting and protecting the love of His friends. If, when the servant has been 'granted access to God's favour, clothed with the cloak of His love and graced by His generosity', he becomes bold, then

God will 'keep him moving between jealousy and love. Sometimes jealousy will close the door, so that the servant will be brought to asking; sometimes love will open the door so that he enjoys direct witnessing [of God]'.[104] In his commentary on the words 'Those who spread slander' (Q. 24:11), Maybudī states that God is 'jealous (*ghayūr*) for the hearts of the elite among His servants'. He keeps watch over their hearts and, should they turn their attention to other than Him, they will experience the 'whip of His chastisement'.[105] In another context, Maybudī speaks of the 'sword of eternal jealousy' which God keeps above the heads of His lovers to prevent them from looking at, or desiring, other than Him.[106] At the same time, the divine jealousy conceals the states of His closest servants from others.[107]

On the part of the servant, jealousy has two levels. Maybudī relates that once, in a state of ecstasy, Shiblī was heard to say, 'O Lord, in the next world (lit. tomorrow) make everyone blind so that no one but I can see You'. On another occasion he was heard to say 'O Lord make Shiblī blind. It would be a shame if along with me [my eye] should see You.' Maybudī explains that the first saying was out of the jealousy of others, and the second was out of the jealousy of his own eye, and adds that in the way of noble ones (*jawānmardān*) the latter is more precious and perfect than the former.[108] The same idea is expressed in part of Maybudī's commentary on the words, 'Say, He, God is One' (Q. 112:1):

> O Muhammad! To those who are madly in love say 'He'. Do not mention His name or attribute, for they are the jealous ones; they cannot bear to see or hear another mention the name or attribute of the Beloved, not even their own heart or eye or tongue! So it is that they say:
>
> My passion for You has reached the point
> That I do not even allow my own eye to see Your face.[109]

The culmination of the way of love

We have seen that in various descriptions of the spiritual journey, Maybudī shows the highest degree to be annihilation from self (*fanā'*).[110] The state of *fanā'* is likewise shown to be the highest stage in the way of love. In his commentary on the words 'and know that God comes between a man and his own heart' (Q. 8:24), Maybudī explains:

> The heart is the way and the Beloved is the homeland. Once [the seeker] has reached that homeland what need does he have for travelling? To begin with the heart is essential (*nāchār*) but at the end it is a veil. [...] At the beginning the heart is needed because it is impossible to travel the way of the law without it [...] but at the end to remain with the heart is duality (*dū-gānagī*), and duality is far from God.[111]

In this respect, Maybudī's understanding of the way of love may be compared to that of Aḥmad Ghazzālī, that is to say the aim is to go beyond all duality. However, since in Aḥmad Ghazzālī's metaphysical system love itself is viewed as the Absolute, for him duality remains in the concept of the lover and the beloved.[112] Maybudī, on the other hand, identifies the Absolute with the Beloved. Thus, when commenting on the virtues of 'those who pray for forgiveness' (Q 3:17), he states that they are the ones who:

> go beyond gnosis to 'see' the Known (*maʿrūf*), and go beyond love (*dūstī*) to 'see' the Beloved (*dūst*).[113]

In another context he explains that as long as the servant continues to seek love he is unaware (*bī khabar*) of the Beloved:

> Rush on towards love, and then don't get caught there
> Go on beyond love (*ʿishq*) and being in love (*ʿāshiqī*).

He then adds, 'A great master was once asked "When will the servant reach his Lord?", to which he replied "When he is annihilated from himself".'[114]

In an explanation of the three stages or stations of *ʿishq*, the third station is defined as *nīstī* (non-existence).[115] The progress towards *nīstī* is described as follows:

> *Nīstī* is that you should be effaced in love [so that] you exist neither for this world nor the next. The two worlds were consumed by love (*dar dūstī shud*) and love by the Beloved. Now I can neither tell whether it is I or He.[116]

In the poetic language of love this concept is expressed in various ways: for example, with the popular metaphor of the moth and candle[117] or of the candle which only gives out light by sacrificing itself;[118] or in the language of gambling, with the metaphor of 'staking one's life in the gambling-house of love'.[119] Perhaps one of the clearest expositions of the progress through love to annihilation from self and subsistence in God is presented in Maybudī's explanation of the reason for God's institution of the month of fasting. Here he is using the metaphor of the experience of fasting for the experience which the lover undergoes:

> The masters of gnosis understand another mystery about Ramadan. They say that during this month the Lord of Might cleanses the mystics from other than Him. Then He burns them with His love [or love for Him], sometimes keeping them in fire, sometimes in water, sometimes thirsting, sometimes drowning. Neither when they drown is there any quenching, nor when they thirst any sleep.[120] And these lines express their state:
>
> If He burns, say 'Burn!' and if He soothes say 'Soothe!'
> It is best for the lover that he should be between fire and water.
> So that in one he should be burnt and in the other drowned.
> Once he becomes free of himself the Beloved will be in his arms.
>
> This is why the master of the way (Anṣārī), when he was asked about composure (*jamʿiyya*), answered that 'it is that you should fall into the grip (*qabḍa*) of God, and whoever falls into the grip of God, is burned away in Him and God remains in his place'.[121]

By adding this saying to his interpretation, Maybudī is clearly bringing together the two doctrines of love and divine determination in the mystical path. In following the way of love the seeker must allow himself to 'fall into the grip of God', to submit to the divine dictates which alternately burn and drown him, in order to perfect his love and ultimately free him from himself.[122]

Having examined the hermeneutics of the *Kashf al-asrār* in part one, and the mystical doctrines of the work in part two, in the final part of this book, part three, I shall set about illustrating the ways in which these two elements of mystical hermeneutics and doctrine interact in Maybudī's interpretations of the Qur'anic stories of Abraham, Moses and Joseph. We shall see how through these interpretations Maybudī is able not only to expound 'technical' knowledge about the states and stations of the spiritual path in a non-technical manner, he is also able to convey many aspects of the way of mystical love.

NOTES

1 See, for example, *Kashf*, I, p. 219; V, pp. 230–1; VI, pp. 60, 91–2; VII, p. 398; X, p. 179.
2 *Kashf*, V, p. 260.
3 Occurs in *Kashf*, I, p. 93; VII, p. 398; X, p. 659.
4 On the divine decree and Iblīs see Peter Awn, *Satan's Tragedy and Redemption: Iblīs in Sufi Psychology* (Leiden, 1983), pp. 96–109.
5 *Kashf*, I, p. 161.
6 *Kashf*, I, p. 563.
7 *Kashf*, II, p. 496.
8 *Kashf*, IV, p. 441.
9 *Kashf*, VII, pp. 40–1.
10 *Kashf*, IX, pp. 201–2.
11 *Kashf*, VIII, p. 13.
12 *Kashf*, V, p. 526. Sahl al-Tustarī's admonition is to be found, word for word, in the same context (Q. 17:11) in his commentary, *Tafsīr al-Qur'ān al-ʿaẓīm*, p. 57.
13 *Kashf*, VI, p. 255.
14 *Kashf*, III, p. 297. See also Maybudī's interpretation of the sleepers in the cave (*Sūrat al-Kahf*, Q. 18), *Kashf*, V, p. 260; VII, p. 153.
15 *Kashf*, III, p. 358.
16 Restlessness (*bī qarārī*) does not have a negative sense here but implies an impatience on the part of the seeker to be with God. Note that in the *Ṣad maydān* (ed. de Beaurecueil, 'Une ébauche persane', pp. 33–4) *bī qarārī* is shown by Anṣārī to be one of the signs of *uns* (intimacy) in the lover.
17 *Kashf*, II, pp. 496–7. See also *Kashf*, I, p. 35. This teaching is also to be found in the *Ṣad maydān*, *Maydān*, 44, on *ṭalab* (seeking).
18 Compare the words of Bāyazīd: 'At the beginning [of my wayfaring] I was mistaken in four things: I supposed that I remembered Him and knew Him and loved Him and sought Him. When I had become advanced [on the way] (*nahaytu*), I saw that His remembrance preceded my remembrance, His gnosis preceded my gnosis, His love came before my love, and that He sought me first so that I would seek Him.' Cited by Abū Nuʿaym al-Iṣfahānī, *Ḥilyat al-awliyā'* (Cairo, 1932–8), X, p. 34. See also Samʿānī, *Rawḥ al-arwāḥ*, pp. 306–7.
19 *Kashf*, VII, p. 196.
20 *Kashf*, VII, p. 398.
21 The substantive from the present participle of the verb *kashīdan* (or *kishīdan*), to draw, pull.
22 Trans. Abdel Haleem.
23 *Kashf*, IV, pp. 278–9. The source of this latter quote is unclear. For a discussion of its attribution see Badīʿ al-Zamān Furūzānfar, *Aḥādīth wa qiṣaṣ-i Mathnawī*, re-edited by Ḥ. Dāwūdī (Tehran, 1376sh/1997). In Q. 55:31, the word *thaqalān* is usually interpreted to mean jinn and human beings. Lane, however, in his *Arabic-English Lexicon*, ed. S. Lane-Poole (repr., Cambridge, 1984), I, p. 344, quotes the following hadith: 'Verily I am leaving you two objects of high esti-

mation and care (*thaqalayn*), the Book of God, and my kindred, or my near kindred (*ʿitratī*).' It is listed with this latter meaning in various forms by Ibn Ḥanbal, *Musnad*, III, pp. 14, 17, 26, 59; IV, 367, 371; while Dārimī lists a hadith in which the *thaqalayn* are the Book and the *Ahl al-Bayt*. See ʿAbd Allāh b. ʿAbd al-Raḥmān al-Dārimī, *Sunan*, *Kitāb faḍāʾil al-Qurʾān*, ed. ʿA.Ḥ.Y. al-Madanī (Cairo, 1966), ch. 1 (Faḍl man qaraʾa al-Qurʾān), no. 11, § 3319. Here, however, Maybudī clearly intends the expression to mean jinn and human beings.

24 For example in *Kashf*, I, pp. 520, 615; III, pp. 501, 833; V, pp. 91, 165, 311; VI, pp. 87, 236, 342; VII, pp. 14, 397; VIII, pp. 179, 387; IX, pp. 33, 127–8, 317; X, pp. 593, 655.

25 *Kashf al-maḥjūb*, p. 486; tr. Nicholson, p. 372.

26 *Risāla*, p. 232.

27 *Kashf*, VIII, p. 234. Though it should be pointed out that the passage in question, occurring in Maybudī's commentary on Q. 18:39, has been taken from Qushayrī's *Laṭāʾif* (III, p. 217) and may have been added for good measure, not because it was representative of Maybudī's doctrines. Two other instances where Maybudī presents this view are: *Kashf* II, p. 93, and *Kashf*, V, p. 282, though in the latter case, while the interpretation is not identical in its wording, the idea is very similar to that presented in Qushayrī's commentary on the same verse (Q. 14:25). See *Laṭāʾif*, II, p. 255.

28 *Kashf*, II, p. 329.

29 *Kashf*, VIII, p. 179. See also *Kashf*, IX, p. 421, where the two seas (Q. 55:19) represent fear and hope for the *ʿāmm*, contraction and expansion for the *khāṣṣ*, and awe and intimacy for the *ṣiddīqān*. In fact, Qushayrī also speaks of an alternation between *fanāʾ* and *baqāʾ* in ascending degrees in his *Tartīb al-sulūk* (ed. Meier in *Essays on Islamic Piety and Mysticism*, pp. 93–133). In his discussion of Qushayrī's *Tartīb al-sulūk*, Kamada has observed that: 'he [the aspirant] is raised up to the final state by repeatedly experiencing *fanāʾ* and *baqāʾ*. Like a spiral, passing through the paired experiences of *fanāʾ* and *baqāʾ* several times, he gradually proceeds to a deeper experience.'

30 Sarrāj, *Lumaʿ*, p. 366.

31 *Kashf al-maḥjūb*, pp. 235–6; tr. Nicholson, p. 189. See Massignon, *The Passion of al-Ḥallāj, Mystic and Martyr of Islam*, tr. H. Mason, abridged (Princeton, 1994), p. 64.

32 *Kashf*, VI, p. 111. A similar note of caution may be seen in another passage of Anṣārī (*Kashf*, IX, p. 317), where he advocates that the servant should look first upon proximity [with God] (*qurb*) so that intimacy (*uns*) is born, and then upon the Glory [of God] (*ʿizzat*) so that reverence (*ḥurmat*) is born.

33 This will be discussed in the section on knowledge, which follows.

34 This also will be discussed in the section on love, pp. 193 and 197.

35 *Kashf*, VI, p. 236.

36 *Kashf*, II, p. 329.

37 *Kashf*, V, p. 671.

38 *Kashf*, II, pp. 508–9.

39 *Kashf*, III, p. 294.

40 *Kashf*, I, p. 127. Quoted in full on p. 112.

41 *Kashf*, VIII, p. 545.

42 *Kashf*, VII, p. 247.

43 *Kashf*, III, p. 255; also III, p. 369. This idea is to be found in Anṣārī's *Ṣad maydān* (*Maydān*, 73; de Beaurecueil, 'Une ébauche persane', p. 44), while the metaphor of the pair of scales appears in *Maydān*, 43 (de Beaurecueil, 'Une ébauche persane', pp. 60–1). By 'fear without knowledge' Maybudī is probably referring to the Khārijī doctrine that anyone who has committed a major sin, whether a believer or not, will be damned in the Afterlife, whilst by 'hope without knowledge' he is referring to the Murji'ī doctrine that faith (*īmān*) is a matter of verbal attestation rather than acts. On the Khārijīs see G. Levi Della Vida, 'Khāridjites', *EI²*, IV, pp. 1074–7. On the Murji'īs see Wilferd Madelung, 'Murdji'a', *EI²*, VII, pp. 605–7.

44 *Kashf*, I, p. 442. On the use of the metaphor of light for knowledge see Franz Rosenthal, *Knowledge Triumphant: the Concept of Knowledge in Medieval Islam* (Leiden, 1970), ch. 6. On the limitations of *ʿaql* in the view of Persian mystics see Chittick and Rahman, 'ʿAql', *EIr*, II, pp. 195–6.

45 *Kashf*, II, p. 91.

46 See Bayhaqī, *Al-Jāmiʿ li-shuʿab al-īmān*, ed. ʿA.ʿA. Ḥāmid (14 vols., Riyadh, 2003), VI, (Fī faḍl al-ʿaql), p. 349, § 4312; Sulaymān b. Aḥmad Abu'l-Qāsim b. Aḥmad al-Ṭabarānī, *Muʿjam al-awsaṭ*, ed. A. Ibn Muḥammad and ʿA. al-Ḥusaynī (10 vols., Cairo, 1415/1994–5), II, p. 235, § 1845; al-Ḥakīm al-Tirmidhī, *Nawādir*, II, Principle 206, p. 60. Ghazzālī cites it in *Iḥyā'*, Part 1, *Kitāb al-ʿilm*, ch. 7, p. 109.

47 *Kashf*, I, p. 442. Compare the dialogue between God and *ʿaql* in Kalābādhī, *Kitāb al-taʿarruf*, p. 136. This hadith is quoted in Samʿānī's *Rawḥ al-arwāḥ*, p. 63, but without Maybudī's conclusion.

48 *Kashf*, III, p. 467.

49 *Kashf*, V, p. 394 and again II, p. 774. Compare also *Kashf*, VI, pp. 292–3, on knowledge of *tafsīr*, *ta'wīl* and *fahm*, quoted p. 80.

50 For this reason it is sometimes said that only God can know Himself. See, for example, Kalābādhī, *Kitāb al-taʿarruf*, p. 39; tr. Arberry, pp. 54–5.

51 *Kashf*, III, p. 485. See *Ṣad maydān*, *Maydān*, 80, where Anṣārī shows these three to be stages of *istislām*: the first is *az shirk rastan* (to be freed from polytheism), the second, *az khilāf rastan* (to be freed from opposition), and the third, *az khwad rastan* (to be freed from one's self). The passage may also be compared with others cited pp. 159–60, where Maybudī defines stages of progress on the spiritual path in terms of levels of contemplation.

52 *Kashf*, III, p. 374. Another reference to *jadhb* or *kashish*.

53 *Kashf*, VI, pp. 477–8. Again this may be compared to the Malāmatiyya doctrine discussed in ch. 6, n. 109.

54 *Kashf*, V, p. 359. See also V, pp. 583–4, where the same theme is quoted from Abū Bakr al-Ṣiddīq and Abū ʿAlī Daqqāq.

55 *Kashf*, III, p. 438.

56 *Kashf*, I, p. 441.

57 *Kashf*, IV, p. 381.

58 For example, *Kashf*, I, pp. 549–50, [*ḥusna-yi*] *īn jahānī shuhūd-i asrār*, [*ḥusna-yi*] *ān jahānī ru'yat-i abṣār*. See also *Kashf*, I, p. 341; V, p. 384; X, p. 664. On the question of the vision of God, in both Islamic theology and mysticism see

the comprehensive study by Nasrollah Pourjavady, *Rū'yat-i māh dar āsmān* (Tehran, 1375sh/1996); Eric Chaumont, ed., *Autour du regard* (Louvain, 2003).

59 For example, *Kashf*, VI, p. 493; III, p. 439; VI, p. 553; VIII, p. 443.

60 *Kashf*, VI, p. 222, and V, p. 165.

61 Trans. amended with reference to Abdel Haleem's translation.

62 *Kashf*, II, p. 397. The bat metaphor appears in the *Kitāb al-maḥabba* of Ghazzālī's *Iḥyā'*, Part 4, Book 6, Section 8, p. 213; idem., *Kīmiyā*, II, p. 595.

63 *Kashf*, III, p. 457.

64 *Kashf*, I, pp. 278–9.

65 *Kashf*, IX, p. 419.

66 *Kashf*, V, p. 218.

67 *Kashf*, II, p. 94.

68 *Kashf*, VII, p. 78; IX, p. 91. This story also appears in Ghazzālī's *Iḥyā'*, Part 4, Book 6, *Kitāb al-maḥabba*, p. 182; idem., *Kīmiyā*, II, p. 571.

69 *Kashf*, VI, p. 477. See pp. 129–30.

70 *Kashf*, I, pp. 239–40.

71 *Kashf*, V, p. 476. See also *Kashf*, I, p. 592, where Maybudī speaks of those who have drunk the wine of *ma'rifat* and are intoxicated from the cup of *maḥabbat*.

72 *Kashf*, VI, p. 371; IV, p. 37. See also *Kashf*, I, p. 604.

73 *Kashf*, I, pp. 674–5. Some mystics spoke of the burning of the *nafs* (for example, Abū Sa'īd, according to Ibn al-Munawwar, *Asrār al-tawḥīd*, I, pp. 295–6), or the heart (for example, Abu'l-Ḥasan Kharaqānī, quoted in 'Aṭṭār, *Tadhkirat al-awliyā'*, p. 706), but essentially the principle is the same: a purification from other than God.

74 *Kashf*, I, p. 430, quoted from *ān 'azīz-i rūzigār* (that venerable one of the age).

75 *Kashf*, III, p. 763.

76 *Kashf*, VIII, p. 116. On the spiritual function of separation according to Aḥmad Ghazzālī and 'Ayn al-Quḍāt Hamadānī see Awn, *Satan's Tragedy*, pp. 144–5.

77 *Kashf*, V, p. 165. Partly attributed to Bāyazīd in VIII, p. 388.

78 Among Abū Ṭālib al-Makkī's seven seas which must be traversed in the way of *tawḥīd*, the third is *ḥayrat-i shuhūd*, as related by Maybudī, *Kashf*, III, p. 297. See ch. 6, n. 55.

79 This is confirmed by a saying of Sulamī (*Darajāt al-mu'āmalāt*, ed. A.Ṭ. 'Irāqī, in *Majmū'a*, ed. Pourjavady, I, p. 492): 'Longing in [the state of] witnessing (*mushāhada*) is more intense than longing in absence (*ghayba*) [...]. True longing does not go away either in proximity or separation.'

80 The word *nāz* here has the sense of God-given aplomb which accompanies the bestowal of divine favour.

81 *Kashf*, III, pp. 20–1.

82 Lit. 'is the one who has deposited his capital (*ra's al-māl*) in Paradise'. *Muzdūr* is a person who worships God out of hope for the rewards of Paradise in the Afterlife and is contrasted with the *'ārif* who worships purely out of love for God and whose hope in the Afterlife is only for the vision of God.

83 *Kashf*, IX, p. 90. The printed edition has left out the *chi* the second time (i.e. *man dānistam* instead of *man chi dānistam*, as at the beginning of the *munājāt*). The former conforms to MS E, though the earlier MSS A and B both have *man chi dānistam* both times, which is more likely to be correct.

84 *Kashf*, VII, p. 310.

85 Much of this passage has, in fact, been derived from Anṣārī's definition of *dahshat*, in the 96th *Maydān* of Anṣārī's *Ṣad maydān*.

86 Anṣārī adds here: 'because the spirit (*rūḥ*) summons it.'

87 *Ṣad maydān* has *nayābad* (does not find) instead of *napāyad* (does not look steadily at) while the published edition of *Kashf al-asrār*, and both MSS A and B, all have the latter.

88 *Kashf*, V, p. 219. The connection which Maybudī has made in this passage between *uns* and *dahsha* appears to have been taken from Anṣārī's *Ṣad maydān* (de Beaurecueil, 'Une ébauche persane', pp. 58–9). However, more commonly among Sufi writers (including Maybudī later in the same passage and elsewhere), the state of *dahsha* and/or *ḥayra* is associated with the state of awe (*hayba*) which is aroused in the seeker when God reveals Himself in His aspect of rigour and majesty according to His name *al-Jalāl*, as opposed to the state of *uns* (intimacy), aroused when God reveals His attribute of gentleness and beauty according to His name *al-Jamāl*, for example, *Kashf*, IV, p. 279; V, pp. 219, 230, 550; X, p. 178. See p. 127 re effects of the Divine Attributes of *qahr* (wrath) and *luṭf* (gentleness).

89 *Kashf*, II, p. 400. This passage is quoted in full on p. 163.

90 *Kashf*, V, p. 165; VI, p. 87.

91 *Kashf*, V, p. 384.

92 *Kashf*, III, pp. 732–3. On this subject see Pourjavady, *Rū'yat-i māh*, pp. 232ff.

93 *Kashf*, VII, p. 53 and VIII, p. 530.

94 *Kashf*, VI, p. 461. This version is taken from Anṣarī's *Rasā'il-i fārsī-yi Khwāja ʿAbd Allāh Anṣārī*, ed. S. Mawlā'ī (Tehran, 1372sh/1993), I, p. 356.

95 *Kashf*, VIII, p. 30.

96 *Kashf*, VI, p. 294.

97 *Kashf*, VIII, p. 388.

98 *Kashf*, IX, p. 376.

99 *Kashf*, VIII, pp. 30–1.

100 *Kashf*, VI, p. 294. The hadith is most commonly found without the mention of saints, that is: 'Those who suffer the most are the prophets and those most like them and those most like them' (*al-anbiyā' wa'l-amthāl wa'l-amthāl*). See Tirmidhī, *Jāmiʿ*, *Kitāb al-zuhd*, ch. 56 (Mā jā'a fī'l-ṣabr maʿa'l-balā'), no. 3, § 2398; Ibn Māja, *Sunan*, *Abwāb al-fitan*, ch. 23 (Bāb al-ṣabr ʿala'l-balā'), no. 1, § 4072; al-Dārimī, *Sunan*, *Kitāb al-raqā'iq*, ch. 67 (Bāb fī ashadd al-nās balā'an), no. 1, § 2786; Ibn Ḥanbal, *Musnad*, I, pp. 172 (this version of the hadith includes the righteous (*ṣāliḥūn*) after the prophets), 174, 180; IV, p. 369.

101 *Kashf*, VI, p. 62; VIII, p. 31.

102 *Kashf*, II, p. 80.

103 *Kashf*, I, p. 60.

104 *Kashf*, III, p. 763. This is another allusion to the alternation of states, see pp. 185–7.

105 *Kashf*, VI, pp. 511–12.

106 *Kashf*, II, p. 418. For Aḥmad Ghazzālī's teaching on the different swords of jealousy and their role in the perfecting of love see *Sawāniḥ*, ch. 4.

107 *Kashf*, II, pp. 417–18; VI, p. 478; X, p. 107.

108 *Kashf*, IX, p. 33.

109 *Kashf*, X, p. 666.

110 With the concomitant state of subsistence in God (*baqā'*) being understood, though less often mentioned.
111 *Kashf*, IV, pp. 36–7.
112 *Sawāniḥ*, chs. 4 and 65. See also ibid., tr. Pourjavady, translator's commentary, pp. 88, 111.
113 *Kashf*, II, p. 57.
114 *Kashf*, II, p. 187. In one context (*Kashf*, VII, p. 475), however, when explaining the reality of *tafrīd*, Maybudī quotes the following poem:

Here there is neither love nor beloved nor lover
You are all 'youness', take enmity out of the way!

115 *Nīstī* is also the third stage of love (*maḥabbat*) in Anṣārī's final section of *Ṣad maydān* (in Beaurecueil, ed., 'Une ébauche persane', p. 30), following after the grounds of *fanā'* and *baqā'*. However, Anṣārī merely lists the stages of love: *rāstī*, *mastī* and *nīstī*, without explaining them.
116 *Kashf*, II, pp. 94–5.
117 *Kashf*, I, pp. 423, 571.
118 *Kashf*, I, pp. 496, 571–2.
119 *Kashf*, II, p. 356.
120 Sic. (*khwāb*) in both published edition and MSS A and B.
121 *Kashf*, I, p. 496.
122 It is interesting to note that Aḥmad Ghazzālī, too, introduces a chapter on the need to abandon free will, almost at the conclusion of the *Sawāniḥ* (ch. 75).

PART THREE

MAYBUDĪ'S MYSTICAL INTERPRETATION OF THE STORIES OF THE PROPHETS

PROLEGOMENON

Prophets in the Qur'an and in Sufi exegesis

The Biblical prophets have an important place in the Qur'an. In part, they are there to show continuity; not the continuity of a chosen people and its religion, as in the Old Testament, but the continuity of a message. All the prophets, whether they brought a scripture (*rusul*) or not (*anbiyā'*), were witnesses to their people of the oneness of God, and warners of the coming meeting with Him.[1] The Prophet Muhammad was simply 'confirming that which had gone before'.[2] The stories of the prophets also offered reassurance for Muhammad. Like him they had suffered persecution, and the rejection of their message by many of their people, but were eventually made triumphant over their adversaries who inevitably faced the consequences of their denial of the Revelation.

Events in the lives of the prophets are widely dispersed in the Qur'an. Unlike the Bible, the Qur'an does not present a chronicle of the prophets' lives. With the exception of Joseph, whose life is set forth in a continuous narration to make up the whole of Sura 12, the stories of the prophets usually appear in the Qur'an as isolated incidents, summarily narrated, with little indication as to the order in which they occurred. The same event may be told more than once, and in forms which vary from one sura to another. One tendency in Orientalist scholarship has been to study particular stylistic features of the Qur'an, or its content, in order to support the theory that it was in some way derived from Biblical and Midrashic sources.[3] Another approach has been not to challenge the Qur'an as revealed scripture, but to understand these stylistic features as having a logic proper to the Qur'an's own purpose.[4] From this point of view, the terse, elliptical way in which the stories of the prophets are told in the Qur'an need not be explained merely as an indication that the stories were already familiar to the Arabs through their contact with the Jewish communities of the Arab Peninsula; it can be seen as an essential part of the Qur'anic rhetoric. Thus the stories, stripped of their details, are lifted from the level of Biblical history to the level of the universal message which contains them.[5] Events in the lives of the prophets become parables or 'comparisons (*amthāl*) which God coins for men' (Q. 13:17; 24:35 and 29:43).[6] On the one hand, they remain an integral part of the revelation as a whole; on the other, they are in themselves signs to be pondered upon (Q. 12:111; 17:9).

Understood as parables, the stories of the prophets gave Sufi commentators on the Qur'an great scope for expounding states and stations of the mystical way.[7] In chapter three, we saw how in Maybudī's mystical interpretation of a story of Abraham, the concern was no longer with Abraham as prophet, and with all that might be expected of him as such, but with Abraham as a universal prototype of the spiritual wayfarer. We also saw how in one interpretation Abraham was represented as one of the worshippers (*ʿābidān*) who found comfort in the contemplation of God's creation, whilst in another interpretation he was represented as a mystic (*ʿārif*) who had realised the divine oneness (*tawḥīd*) in the profoundest sense of cutting himself off from all but the one. In the chapters that follow we shall see how Abraham and other prophets are sometimes shown at the stage of initiates in the mystical path in the position of '*murīd*', and sometimes at the stage of adepts as '*murād*'.

This apparent belittling of the station of a prophet was not uncommon in Islamic literature. Often shortcomings and weaknesses in earlier prophets were used as a foil to show the faultlessness and excellence of the Prophet Muhammad.[8] Maybudī does sometimes use this method to emphasize the pre-eminence of the Prophet Muhammad, but more often, if he speaks of a prophet being in a 'lower' station, it is to show how he subsequently advanced to a higher one. There can be little doubt that Maybudī's purpose in this was to give encouragement to his audience. Since the possibility of spiritual realisation was, according to his interpretation, evidenced in the Qur'an by the stories of the prophets, the spiritual wayfarer could aspire not to prophethood, of course, but to follow their precedent in the path of spiritual realisation. Furthermore, as stated earlier, the seeker would gain insights into the different stages and stations of the path. Maybudī provides justification for this principle in the words of Junayd. When asked by Abū Bakr al-Kattānī about the metaphors in the stories, he replied, 'They are among God's armies with which He strengthens the states (*aḥwāl*) of His seekers.' When Abū Bakr further inquired if there was any basis for this in the Book, Junayd replied 'Yes, in God's words, "So [Muhammad] We have told you the stories of the prophets to make your heart firm, and in these accounts truth has come to you, as well as lessons and reminders for the believers"' (Q. 11:120).[9]

In the chapters which are to follow, it will be seen that there are effectively three different prophetologies at work in Maybudī's *Kashf al-asrār*. At one level, the prophets are presented in their conventional role as prophets, and here Maybudī fleshes out the Qur'anic version of their stories with material added from *Isrāʾīliyyāt* traditions and the *qiṣaṣ al-anbiyāʾ* corpus. At another level, the prophets are viewed as prototypes of the spiritual wayfarer. Here the stories are open to a number of different interpretations, as was demonstrated in the case of the Abraham story. Finally, there is the level of 'meta-history', where the role of each prophet is placed within the greater divine plan of creation and salvation. Here, the Prophet Muhammad is understood to be the first and last in creation, as being both the *raison d'être* of the universe[10] and its culmination. At this level, as we have seen, Maybudī compares Muhammad to the sun from which, even before it has risen, the planets (i.e. the other prophets) derive their light. Once the sun has risen, the light of the planets vanishes in its greater light.[11] Or again, in his commentary on the heavenly ascension (*miʿrāj*) of the Prophet, where Maybudī explains that Adam was commanded 'Fall down!' (Q. 2:36), so that later Muhammad might be commanded 'Arise!'.[12]

These three levels of prophetology co-exist as analogical parallels. The fire of Nimrod might be a real fire, its coolness to Abraham being a divine miracle to demonstrate his prophethood; equally, it might be the fire of base desires which is unable to harm the purified soul. The love of Zulaykhā for Joseph might be the passionate infatuation of a mistress for her slave, but it could at the same time be interpreted as the unperfected love of a human being for God.[13] The ease with which Maybudī moves between these levels, without the intervention of a comparison or simile, is an indication that what Meisami has termed 'the analogical mode of thought' was at this time being manifested in the realm of Sufi exegesis as much as in other genres of literature.[14] Some of this fluidity was perhaps lost in later mystical commentaries, which reflect a more systematized form of Sufi thought, such as the *Tafsīr* of ʿAbd al-Razzāq al-Kāshānī, where figures in the stories of the prophets are often interpreted as symbols to represent different aspects of the human microcosm.[15] Maybudī's interpretations, in any case, typify an earlier period of Sufism, when the main concern was with the path, and with explaining states and stations to the wayfarer, in contrast to later theosophical schools which focused on the exposition of metaphysical perceptions attained at the culmination of the way.

The discussion which follows is intended to convey the way in which not only doctrines that were of particular importance to Maybudī, but also detailed knowledge about the states and stations of the Sufi path, are expounded *through* the exegesis of the Qur'an. Therefore, although I have to some extent rearranged the material according to the progressive stages of the spiritual way, I have at the same time tried to maintain the close connection between these doctrinal expositions and episodes in the life of each prophet as they are related in passages and verses of the Qur'an. Reference to other Sufi sources has been made only as required to provide clarification for doctrines not fully explained by Maybudī. As explained in the preface, a brief general survey of the place which the prophets hold in the Qur'an, in hadith literature, and in the Islamic tradition will precede the discussion of the esoteric interpretation of their stories. In some instances reference will be made to material within the exoteric commentary where this appears to have some bearing on the mystical interpretation of the verse, or where the esoteric reading represents a significant departure from the exoteric.

NOTES

1 On the application of the terms *rasūl* and *nabī* see Toufic Fahd, 'Nubuwwa', *EI*², VIII, pp. 93–7; Arent J. Wensinck, 'Rasūl', *EI*², VIII, pp. 454–5.

2 Q. 2:41, 89, 91; 35:31.

3 For example, Abraham Geiger, *Was hat Mohammad aus dem Judenthume aufgenommen?* (Leipzig, 1902); Haim Schwarzbaum, *Biblical and Extra-Biblical Legends in Islamic Folk Literature* (Walldorf-Hessen, 1982); Norman Calder, 'From Midrash to scripture: the sacrifice of Abraham in early Islamic tradition', *Le Muséon* 101 (1988), pp. 375–402. For a critique of this approach see Brannon M. Wheeler's discussion in his *Moses in the Qur'an and Islamic Exegesis* (London, 2002), Introduction, especially pp. 1–6.

4 Mary R. Waldman, in her 'New approaches to "Biblical" materials in the Qur'ān', *MW* 75/1 (1985), pp. 1–16, has pointed out the inadequacy of an

exclusively literary-historical approach to the study of the Qur'an. She states (p. 1): 'When scholars investigate the apparent transmission of material from one monotheistic scripture to another, they tend to assume that earlier materials are normative and later ones derivative. This tendency, if unmitigated, makes it difficult to appreciate either earlier or later materials in and of themselves, and it affects scholars' attitudes to the whole of the Judeo-Christian-Islamic tradition and each of its various parts.' On this 'new approach' to narratology see also Barbara Herrstein Smith, 'Narrative versions, narrative theories', *Critical Inquiry* 7 (1980), pp. 213–36.

5 Again see Waldman, 'New approaches', where this idea is interestingly illustrated through a comparison of the Biblical and Qur'anic stories of Joseph.

6 See Cyril Glasse, 'Koran', *CEI*, p. 230, and this volume, pp. 76 and 86–7.

7 The particular scope for allegorical and mystical interpretation that was to be found in the Qur'anic accounts of the stories of the prophets has been pointed out by Nwyia in his *Exégèse coranique*, pp. 68, 178.

8 It is already present in the hadith of intercession, for which see Bukhārī, *Saḥīḥ*, *Kitāb aḥādīth al-anbiyā'*, ch. 3 (Laqad arsalnā nūhan ilā qawmihi), no. 4, § 3340; *Kitāb al-riqāq*, ch. 51 (Bāb ṣiffat al-janna wa'l-nār), no. 20, § 6565. It also appears in later Islamic literature, for example, in Ibn 'Arabī's chapter on Joseph in his *Fuṣūṣ al-ḥikam*, ed. A. 'Afifī (Cairo, 1946; repr., Beirut, 1980); trans. by R.W.J. Austin as *Bezels of Wisdom* (London, 1980).

9 *Kashf*, IV, p. 463.

10 See the discussion ch. 5, pp. 130–1 and n. 39 concerning the hadith, *Law lāka la-mā khalaqtu'l-aflāk* (Were it not for you I would not have created the spheres).

11 *Kashf*, X, p. 202. See pp. 131–2.

12 *Kashf*, V, p. 503. Again, see p. 138.

13 Although Zulaykhā is not herself a prophet, I am including her in my discussion of prophetology because she plays an important role of the story of Joseph.

14 Julie Scott Meisami, *Medieval Persian Court Poetry* (Princeton, 1987), p. 33.

15 For example, Adam represents the Heart of the World (*qalb al-ʿālam*) or the Universal Rational Soul (*al-nafs al-nāṭiqa al-kulliyya*), and Eve the Animal Soul (*al-nafs al-ḥayawāniyya*). See Kāshānī's commentary on Q. 4:1, *Tafsīr al-Qur'ān al-karīm*, ed. 'Alī, I, p. 137; Zachariah represents the Spirit (ibid., II, p. 6, commenting on Q. 19:1-3); Jacob represents the Active Intellect, Joseph the Heart, and his brothers the Psychic Forces (ibid., *passim*, commenting on Sura 12). Lory, in his *Les Commentaires*, p. 82, states: 'Le schéma d'interprétation appliqué par Qāshānī est pratiquement le même dans chaque cas et ne comporte d'un récit à l'autre que quelques variantes d'importance secondaire.' See also Ronald L. Nettler's discussion of the prophets in Ibn 'Arabī's *Fuṣūṣ al-ḥikam* in his *Sufi Metaphysics and Qur'ānic Prophets: Ibn 'Arabī's Thought in the Fuṣūṣ al-ḥikam* (Cambridge, 2003); the discussion of Simnānī's interpretations of the prophets in Henri Corbin, *En Islam Iranien*, III, Book II, ch. 4; and the discussion of allegory, this volume, pp. 84–6.

8

The story of Abraham

In Islam, Abraham has the special position of being the 'Father of Prophets' both in a physical sense, as the progenitor of the Biblical prophets through Isaac and of Muhammad through Ishmael, and in a spiritual sense, in having, through his prayer and covenant, guaranteed the perpetuation of the Revelation through the prophets that followed.[1] There is particular significance in the fact that, in the Qur'an, this covenant is associated with the building of the Kaʿba, since it is through the Revelation brought by Muhammad that believers turn their faces to the Kaʿba in prayer, an act symbolic of the return to the recognition of the oneness of God.

It is said more than once in the Qur'an, 'Follow the religion of Abraham' (Q. 3:95; 4:125; 16:123), and Abraham is traditionally viewed as an example of the submission and obedience that is to be understood by the word 'Islam'.[2] In being 'true or upright' (*ḥanīf*) (Q. 2:130; 3:95; 4:125; 6:162; and 16.120, 123), he is identified with the 'true religion' (*al-ḥanīfiyya*).[3] He is also praised in the Qur'an for being veracious (*ṣiddīq*) (Q. 19:41), faithful (*al-ladhī waffā*) (Q. 53:37), clement (*ḥalīm*) (Q. 11:75), and for bringing to God a 'whole or sound heart' (*qalb salīm*) (Q. 37:84). In Islamic tradition he is seen as having initiated the rites of pilgrimage and as the originator of important customs, such as circumcision, clipping the nails and moustache, and hospitality. The events in the life of Abraham which are related in the Qur'an are listed in table 8.1.

Abraham, *Khalīl Allāh*

Central to all of Maybudī's interpretations of the stories of Abraham is the Sufi understanding of the Qur'anic designation of Abraham as 'Friend of

Table 8.1 The life of Abraham

1) The building of the Kaʿba, covenant and prayer.	Q. 2:125–9; 3:96–7; 14:35–41
2) Abraham sees the star, moon and sun and calls them his lord.	Q. 6:75–9
3) Argument with Nimrod about God.	Q. 2:258
4) Prayer for God to show him how he brings the dead to life.	Q. 2:260
5) Confrontation between Abraham and his father and people over idol worship.	Q. 6:80–3; 19:42–8; 21:52–7; 37:83–90
6) Destruction of idols and being thrown into the fire.	Q. 21:58–70; 37:91–8
7) Angels coming as guests and bringing Abraham news of a son;	Q. 11:69–73; 15:51–6; 51:24–30
8) and news of the destruction of Lot's people.	Q. 11:74–6; 15:58–60; 51:32–4
9) The sacrifice of Isaac/Ishmael.	Q. 37:102–7

God' (*Khalīl Allāh*). In fact, all the events which happened to Abraham are seen as directly linked to his fulfilment of the requirements of friendship (*khulla*). Abraham is given the epithet *Khalīl* only once in the Qur'an (Q. 4:125), whereas he is praised seven times for being true or upright (*ḥanīf*), a name by which he is also known. But, since *Khalīl* was a title reserved exclusively for him, it became the honorific (*laqab*) by which he is popularly known, just as Moses is known as *Kalīm Allāh* (Interlocutor of God) and Muhammad as *Ḥabīb Allāh* (Beloved of God).

It has been suggested that Abraham was already known as 'Friend of God' before the coming of the Islamic Revelation.[4] Commentators on the Qur'an do not throw any light on this matter. Their concern has been to investigate how the word *khalīl*, meaning friend, comes to be derived from the various significations of its root *KH.L.L.*, and why the title should have been given to Abraham.

Ṭabarī sees *khulla* on Abraham's part as comprising both enmity and friendship: enmity on behalf of God [towards those who oppose Him] (*al-ʿadāwa fī'llāh wa'l-bughḍ fīhī*) and friendship for God and love for Him (*wa'l-wilāya fī'llāh wa'l-ḥubb fīhī*). *Khulla* on God's part is the help which He granted Abraham in protecting him from his enemy Nimrod, and in other honours which He bestowed upon him.[5]

Bayḍāwī looks more closely at the origin of the word. According to him it might be from *khilāl* (boring, drilling), 'for it is love which penetrates (*takhallala*) and fuses with the soul (*khālaṭahā*)'; or it may be from *khalal* (flaw, fissure), 'for each of the two friends fills the gap in the other'; or from the word *khall* (a path in the sand), 'for two friends accompany each other on the way'; or from *khalla* (quality), 'for each of the two are compatible in their qualities'.[6] It is interesting that Bayḍāwī does not make any connection between these ideas about the derivation of the word *khalīl* and the significance of the epithet for Abraham.[7] In glossing the words 'and God took Abraham for a friend', he says, 'He chose him and distinguished him with a token of His esteem similar to that with which a friend honours his friend', and adds that this declaration was made to encourage people to follow the 'religion of Abraham', because Abraham had reached the 'ultimate virtue and human perfection'.[8]

Many exoteric commentaries include the account of a miracle through which the name *Khalīl* became associated with Abraham. The following is taken from Ṭabarī's version:

> Once, when the people in his area were stricken with a famine, Abraham went to a friend of his of the people of Mosul, or according to others of Egypt, to request provision for his family, but the friend was unable to help. As Abraham was nearing home again, he passed by a sandy desert. He thought that if he were to fill his sacks with sand, then his family would not be upset upon his arrival thinking he had returned empty-handed, but would imagine he had brought them something. He did accordingly, but the sand inside the sacks changed into flour. When he got home he went to sleep. His family opened the sacks and found the flour, with which they speedily made dough and baked bread. When Abraham woke he asked them where they had got the flour to bake the bread and they answered, 'It was some of the flour that you brought from your friend.' Then he realised what had happened and said 'Yes, from my friend, God.' So it is that God called him friend.[9]

In none of these exoteric commentaries is any particular significance attached to the name *Khalīl*. It was simply a title with which God had honoured Abraham, for his faithfulness and virtue or as an indication of the special protection accorded to him. For the Sufis, however, *khulla* implied the perfect and uncompromising love of God. If for the *ahl-i sharīʿat* it was the religion (*millat*) of Abraham that was to be followed, for the *ahl-i ṭarīqat* it was in his example as the true friend of God, *Khalīl*, that he was to be emulated.

In Maybudī's mystical interpretations, the perfect love exemplified in the friendship of Abraham also meant the profound inner realisation of all the virtues for which he is praised in the Qur'an. Or, put another way, true friendship with and love of God is inseparable from the perfection of these virtues – Maybudī frequently shows how a virtue practised at its minimal, outer level by the *ʿāmm* or *ahl-i sharīʿat* must be realised at a more profound level by the *khāṣṣ* or *ahl-i ṭarīqat*. Thus Abraham's faithfulness (Q. 53:37) was not merely his fulfillment of all God's commands, but the fact that, at the moment of greatest trial, his only refuge was in God;[10] his submission (Q. 2:131; 37:103) involved not just accepting the trials placed upon him, but rejoicing in them,[11] and his not being one of the idolaters (*mushrikīn*) (Q. 3:67) meant freeing himself from all worldly attachments, especially concern for his own soul. Ultimately, *khulla* signified the realisation of *tawḥīd*, for, as Maybudī shows, this is the true meaning of Abraham's words, 'I am free of all that you associate (with Him)' and 'I have turned my face towards Him Who created the heavens and the earth' (Q 6:78, 79).

If true friendship with God required perfection of the virtues, it therefore implied attainment of the end of the spiritual journey. In his various interpretations, Maybudī sometimes shows Abraham to be in the state of perfect friendship, having reached the end of the path, and sometimes to be still travelling, one of the *rawandigān*, a spiritual aspirant (*murīd*) rather than one who is 'sought' (*murād*). At other times he shows that Abraham is in essence to be identified with friendship. Friendship was 'written' for Abraham before Adam came into existence. God creates His friends from the 'clay of Abraham'. Finally, he shows how true friendship with and love of God must inevitably be subject to tests and trials.

The following analysis of Maybudī's mystical commentaries on the different episodes in the story of Abraham will attempt to show how he saw in them a depiction of the spiritual journey. Because of the diversity of these interpretations, the material will not be arranged according to the temporal order of events, or the order in which they appear in the Qur'an, but rather according to the mystical themes which prevail in the commentary.

Abraham's spiritual journey

*Murīd / murād, rawish / kashish, tafriqa / jam*ʿ

> People are of three kinds in this matter. There is the person who acts either from fear or hope, gazing towards love, accompanied by diffidence (*ḥayā*ʾ). He is called *murīd*. There is the person who is snatched away from the valley of differentiation to the valley of non-differentiation (*jam*ʿ) He is called *murād*. Whoever is in neither of these two positions is an imposter, crazed and deluded.[12]

> Just as by sea, the journey that would take one month on land can be made in one day, so in the field [of spiritual wayfaring] that noble one travelled the distance of a whole lifetime with one *jadhba* from God.[13]

Both of these statements express the teaching that the spiritual wayfarer can only go so far through his own efforts and good actions. In order for him to attain to the state of union, to 'cross the sea', he depends upon the intervention of the divine attraction (*jadhb*).[14] Maybudī sees an illustration of this doctrine in the story of Abraham. Here he associates the pair of terms *murīd/murād* (seeking/sought) with the terms *rawish/kashish*, the Persian equivalents of the Arabic words *sulūk* (journeying in the sense of an effort on the part of man) and *jadhb* or *jadhba* (the divine attraction, a rapture or drawing forth by God, without human effort). The context is the last part of the prayer made by Abraham as he and Ishmael were laying the foundations of the Kaʿba, and the words of God which follow (Q. 2:129, 130):

> 129. 'Our Lord! Raise up in their midst a messenger from among them who will recite to them Your revelations, instruct them in the scripture and in wisdom, and make them grow. You, only You, are the Mighty, the Wise.'
> 130. Who but a fool would forsake the religion of Abraham? We chose him in the world and he will rank among the righteous in the Hereafter.[15]

Maybudī takes the words 'a messenger from among them' to refer to Muhammad (*Ḥabīb*), and the second verse clearly refers to Abraham (*Khalīl*). He begins his mystical commentary on these two verses by comparing the stations of these two prophets:

> These two were both prophets, cherished, worthy and adorned with divine favour, yet there is a difference between Ḥabīb and Khalīl. Khalīl is *murīd* and Ḥabīb is *murād*. The *murīd* seeks, the *murād* is sought. The *murīd* is going (*rawanda*), the *murād* is snatched (*rubūda*). The *murīd* is making his way (*dar rawish-i khwad*) in the station of servitude, the *murād* is with the divine rapture (*dar kashish-i Ḥaqq*) upon the carpet of communion.

Maybudī then brings this doctrine to bear on the story of Abraham's calling the star, moon and sun his Lord. In this passage he introduces the term *makr*, which is often translated as a 'divine ruse', and could be defined as an illusion created by God to test the spiritual wayfarer.

> The path of one who is making his way is not free of the divine ruse (*makr*). This is why Khalīl, despite the greatness of his state, was subject to delusion. When the star of *makr* rose upon his path he said, 'This is my Lord.' And so it was when the Dominion sent forth an ambush of *makr* through the moon and sun in turn, until the divine protection (*'iṣmat*) from error took hold of the reins of his friendship and brought him from the world of *makr* to Himself. Then Khalīl said, 'Verily I have turned my face to the One Who fashioned the heavens and earth as one upright.' As for Muṣṭafā, who was under the attraction of God, the ambush of *makr* had not the power to come in his way. Indeed all of creation that night took refuge in him from *makr* and sought the protection of his law from deception and decline.[16] And he, blessings be upon him, was so upheld in the attraction of God that not even out of the corner of his eye did he look at anything: 'His eye did not swerve nor did he transgress' [Q. 53:17].[17]

Kalābādhī defines the *murīd* as 'the man whose spiritual striving (*ijtihād*) preceded his unveilings (*kushūf*)', whilst the *murād* is 'he whose unveilings preceded his spiritual striving.'[18] Qushayrī states that, according to the Sufis, the *murīd* is a novice (*mubtadī'*), whereas the *murād* is an adept (*muntahī*), and goes on to observe that God's way with His seekers differs: 'most have to go through struggles and trials before they are brought to illumination, whereas some are given unveiling at the beginning, attaining to that which others do not reach even through their toiling. These latter nevertheless return from these graces to complete the disciplinary practices that they had passed by.'[19]

In Maybudī's interpretation Abraham, as *murīd*, has to go through trials and be subject to the ambushes of *makr* before he is brought to the truth, whereas Muhammad, as *murād*, is brought directly. Whether this transformation takes place at the beginning (*bidāya*) or at the end (*nihāya*), it is through the intervention of God. This important doctrine is explained further by Maybudī with a reference to Moses in which the terms *rawish* and *kashish* are again discussed. Maybudī here is commenting on the verse 'Mention Moses in the Scripture. Indeed, he was chosen' (Q. 19:51) and discussing whether the last word, the predicate for Moses, should be read with *kasra*, to form the active participle *mukhliṣ*, or with *fatḥa* to form the passive, *mukhlaṣ*:

> If you read it with *kasra* [*mukhliṣ*], it refers to Moses' station in the beginning, when he was making his way (*dar rawish-i khwad*), but if you read it with *fatḥa* [*mukhlaṣ*], it alludes to his state at the end when he came under the divine attraction (*kashish-i Ḥaqq*). That is, Moses was *mukhliṣ* (purifying himself) in his travelling the way of prophethood. Then We freed him (*khallaṣnāhu*) from his travelling, drew him forth and delivered him (*akhlaṣnāhu*) [indicated by the words] 'And We brought him nigh in communion' [Q. 19:52]. Moses had both *rawish* and *kashish*. 'Moses came to Our appointed tryst' [Q. 7:143] alludes to his state of differentiation (*tafriqa*) in the state of journeying, whist in His words 'We drew him nigh in communion', God is drawing him to the point of non-differentiation (*dar nuqṭa-yi jamʿ*).'

Maybudī now speaks again of the danger that remains as long as the traveller is not free from himself.

> As long as a man is making his way, his foot is on dangerous ground, as is meant by the saying, 'Those that are purifying themselves (*mukhliṣūn*) are in great danger.' This is until he reaches the point of non-differentiation and the attraction of God intervenes. Then the world of danger cannot affect his foot, indeed his foot only remained as long as he was making his way (*dar rawish*). When the divine attraction came, his foot was abandoned, neither step nor path remained (*na qadam mānd wa na qadamgāh*). [20]

In the previous passage Abraham found divine protection from the ambushes of *makr*. Here, first Moses, then more generally man, finds deliverance (*ikhlāṣ*) by being freed from himself, as expressed in the words 'neither step nor path remained'. The state of journeying or making one's way (*rawish*) is here allied to the state of differentiation (*tafriqat*), whilst the state of divine attraction is related to the state of non-differentiation (*jamʿ*).[21] Thus God's 'taking the reins' out of the servant's hands is none other than, to use the words of Ḥallāj, His taking the 'I am from in between'.[22]

We find this clearly explained by Hujwīrī in the *Kashf al-maḥjūb*:

> Absence from one's self is presence with God and vice versa. God is Lord of the human heart. When a divine rapture (*jadhbat*) overpowers the heart of the seeker, the absence of his heart becomes equivalent to its presence with God, partnership (*shirkat*) and division (*qismat*) disappear, and the relationship to self comes to an end.[23]

Defining the terms *jamʿ* and *tafriqa* according to their usage by the Sufis he says:

> Whenever they use the term *tafriqat* [...] they attach to it the meaning of 'human actions' (*makāsib*), eg. self-mortification, and by *jamʿ* they signify 'divine gifts' (*mawāhib*), eg. contemplation.' [24]

Hujwīrī goes on to quote the well-known hadith, 'My servant continually seeks access to Me by means of acts of supererogation until I love him and when I love him, I am his ear and his eye and his hand and his heart and his tongue. Through Me he hears and sees and speaks and grasps'.[25] In light of this hadith, he justifies the well-known saying of Bāyazīd, 'Glory to me', concluding that 'the fact is, when the Divine Omnipotence manifests Its dominion over humanity, It transports a man out of his own being, so that his speech becomes the speech of God.'[26]

Returning to the story of Abraham, we find a similar doctrine expressed by Maybudī. Here it is not that in the state of union man's speech becomes God's speech, but that God speaks for man. The implication is nonetheless the same: God is 'present' and man is 'absent'. Again, a comparison is being made between the state of the prophet Abraham and that of the Prophet Muhammad. Commenting on Abraham's words, 'I have surrendered' (Q. 2:131). Maybudī writes:

If someone should ask what is the wisdom in the fact that Abraham was told 'Surrender' and answered, 'I have surrendered', whereas Muṣṭafā was told 'So know' [Q. 47:19] but did not answer, 'I know', the answer is that if Muṣṭafā did not [himself] answer, God stood in for him (*niyābat dāsht*) and answered on his behalf: 'The messenger believes' [Q. 2:285]. [...] This was more perfect than the state of Abraham, who answered from the essence of differentiation (*az ʿayn-i tafriqat*), which is why he spoke himself. But Muṣṭafā was at the very point of non-differentiation (*nuqṭa-yi jamʿ*), having reached God and having lost himself in God. Needless to say God took his place and said on his behalf what needed to be said about him. This is the meaning of the prophetic pronouncement, 'Whoever is for God, God is for him'.[27]

Tajrīd and tafrīd

Several of Maybudī's mystical commentaries on the story of Abraham seeing the star, moon and sun and saying, 'This is my Lord' (Q. 6:75–9), occur as elaborations of his comments on other verses, but two interpretations are given in the context of the passage itself. The first of these will be discussed later. The second concerns the process of purification and 'isolation' of the soul for God, defined in the Sufi manuals by the closely allied terms *tajrīd* (literally 'stripping away') and *tafrīd* ('making single'). Maybudī here quotes from an unnamed source, to whom he refers as 'that noble one of the path':

When from the Court of Oneness (*aḥadiyyat*), by the divine quality of kindness and mercy, Khalīl received the accolade of 'and God took Abraham for a friend'. The command then came, 'O Khalīl! There can be no standing still in the path of friendship. Go beyond the station of "I have surrendered to the Lord of the Worlds" [Q. 2:131]. Make the journey which they call the journey of *tafrīd*, "Those who are alone [for God] will arrive first".'[28] Khalīl was a swift-footed seeker, who sought the Keepsake of Eternity (*yādgār-i azal*). He placed the sandal of determination upon the foot of aspiration and set upon the journey of 'I am going unto my Lord' [Q. 37:99]. From the ambush of the unseen the treasuries of glory opened, and from them pearls and wondrous treasures in abundance were poured down upon the path of 'I am going'. Khalīl was still a traveller (*rawanda*), tied to 'I am going'. He had not yet reached the point of non-differentiation. He looked back, saw the booty and became occupied with it. The beauty of *tawḥīd* veiled its face from him, saying 'Why did you look back?' So he sought forgiveness and said, 'I do not like things that set' [Q. 6:77]. But then again he saw the pearls

of the unseen and he stopped again, saying, 'This is my Lord, this is my Lord', for those pearls were so beguiling and absorbing. Khalīl was told, 'You should not have stopped! You set upon the path of "I am going" and then looked back at the booty and treasures. Why did you not restrain the eye of your aspiration and observe the practice of that master of the world and attribute of that lord of the sons of Adam? For on that night of propinquity and intimacy the greatest signs revealed themselves on his path but his way was that of "His eye did not swerve" [Q. 53:17]. O Khalīl! What is one who is seeking the Keepsake of Eternity, the Mystery of the Lord of Beneficence, doing with treasures and booty?'
[...]
Khalīl took the hand of *tajrīd* from the sleeve of *tafrīd* and struck the face of secondary causes (*asbāb*), saying, 'I have turned my face to the One Who created the heavens and the earth, as one by nature upright, and I am not of the idolators' [Q. 6:79], which means 'I have singled out my purpose for God. I have purified my covenant from other than God, kept my commitment concerning God for God, and made my ecstasy in sincerity for God. I am for God, nay effaced in God, *wa'llāh, Allāh*.' [29]

In the Sufi manuals the stations of *tafrīd* and *tajrīd* are always placed together as a complementary pair, but *tajrīd* invariably precedes *tafrīd*. However in this passage *tafrīd* is alluded to first. What Maybudī seems to be saying is that *tafrīd* cannot be accomplished without *tajrīd*; that is, the seeker's purpose could not effectively 'be singled out for God' until his 'covenant had been purified from other than God'. According to 'Abd al-Muʿṭī al-Iskandarī (d. 638 or 9/1240–41), in his commentary on Anṣārī's *Manāzil al-sā'irīn*, *tafrīd* can only be after *tajrīd* because *tajrīd* is cutting off from other than God and *tafrīd* is singling out God by predilection (*īthār*).[30]

The booty, treasures and pearls of the unseen are probably the states (*aḥwāl*) which are granted to the seekers as they progress on the way, from which, however delightful, they must also preserve detachment. This is clear from Mustamlī's commentary on Kalābādhī's *Taʿarruf*, in which he defines three levels of *tajrīd*:

Outwardly it is the servant's shedding of accidents (*aʿrāḍ*), inwardly it is his being stripped of the idea of recompense (for the things of the world that he has left), and thirdly it is that his inmost being is stripped of seeing the stations to which he attains or the states he experiences. That is, if, once he has freed himself outwardly from worldly accidents and inwardly from recompense in this world and the next, a state or station should appear to him and he takes satisfaction in it or is at ease with it, then he becomes a worshipper of that moment (*waqt*) or that station, not a worshipper of God.[31]

Al-tawba min al-tawba

Maybudī speaks about another idol which can be a deflection from the truth in his commentary upon one of Abraham's prayers: 'My Lord! Make this territory safe and preserve me and my sons from idolatry'. This verse is the beginning of the long prayer made by Abraham on the occasion of his leaving Ishmael and Hagar in an 'uncultivated valley near the Holy house' (Q. 14:35–41). Maybudī's exoteric commentary on this verse in *Nawbat* II is brief and is concerned firstly with what is meant by 'safe' – that no bird should be hunted nor any tree cut down, and secondly with the idea that *ujnubnī* (avert me, Q. 14:21) in fact means *thabbitnī 'ala'l-ijtināb* (make me firm in averting [idol worship]).

In the esoteric commentary, *Nawbat* III, Maybudī looks at the symbolic significance of the two halves of the verse for the soul. When Abraham asked God to keep this territory safe he was requesting two things: one, the safety of Mecca from the invasion of enemies; the other 'the safety of the heart from the conquest of the sultan of desire'. This symbolic meaning, Maybudī explains, is alluded to in the second part of the verse, 'preserve me and my sons from idolatry'. These idols, he says, are 'whatever keeps you from God, whatever your heart tends towards other than God, as has been stated in God's words "Have you not seen him who takes for a god his own desire?"' (Q. 18:27). After explaining what these idols might be for most men – for example, money, children or reputation – Maybudī warns of those things which can become idols for pious men. For instance, some people become locked into venerating their piety and abstinence, while others focus all their attention on their obedience and devotion, which then becomes a veil for them.[32]

Maybudī then quotes the verse 'Turn to God altogether, O believers, that you may succeed' (Q. 24:31), which is also cited in Anṣārī's chapter on *al-tawba* (repentance) in the *Manāzil al-sā'irīn,* where the highest level of repentance is *al-tawba min al-tawba* (repenting of repentance). Defining the third subtlety of repentance, Anṣārī explains that 'it is that the servant's contemplation of the divine decree does not allow him to consider a good action as virtuous or a bad action as ugly because he has risen above all such ideas to the idea of the divine decree.'[33] In his commentary on Anṣārī's discussion of *al-tawba*, Iskandarī writes:

> The summit of all stations is the attainment of the station of realising the divine unity (*tawḥīd*), and that is being freed from all other causes, worldly, religious, repentance or otherwise. Firstly the servant returns from what is other than God. Then he returns from looking upon that return, fearing that his soul might be content with the perfection of his repentance, for that would constitute an imperfect repentance. Then he repents of looking upon that imperfection, fearing that his soul will relax in the knowledge of the imperfection. So he purifies himself of what is other than his Lord and his heart will not be at peace with other than Him.[34]

Maybudī brings this teaching, an essential doctrine of the Malāmatiyya,[35] to bear on the second part of Abraham's prayer, 'Keep me and my sons from idol worship' (Q. 14:35), which he turns into an exhortation to 'avert your gaze from your obedience, in order that you might realise His favour. Free yourself from your being that you might taste His friendship.' He then cites an interpretation that is attributed to Jaʿfar al-Ṣādiq, firstly in Arabic and then, in an expanded form, in Persian: 'O Lord! You gave me friendship, avert my gaze from looking upon it, that I should not see it as coming from myself. And You gave my children prophethood. Keep them from being tied to [regard for] their actions and themselves.' Ibn ʿAṭā's interpretation of this same supplication provides a further illustration of this teaching:

> Abraham completed the building of the Kaʿba as he had been commanded and then prayed, 'Lord, accept this from us.' The reprimand came from God, 'We commanded you to build the house. We favoured you [with this command] and granted you success in it that you should not be bashful about being blessed. But you say "Accept this from us", forgetting My favour to you and thinking of it as your deed and your doing a favour.'[37] Abraham therefore prayed, 'Keep me and my sons from worshipping idols', that is, 'O God! Seeing our own actions and attributing them to ourselves is an idol which ambushes my path of friendship and my children's path of prophesy. By Thy grace remove this idol from before us, remove our being from before us and maintain Thy favour upon us.' [38]

Faith, certainty and tranquillity

> And when Abraham said [unto his Lord], 'My Lord! Show me how You give life to the dead.' He said, 'Do you not believe, then?' Abraham said, 'Yes, but [I ask] in order that my heart should be at ease.' His Lord said, 'Take four birds and train them to come back to you. Then place a part of them on each hill and then call them. They will quickly come back to you. And know that God is mighty, wise.'(Q. 2:260)[39]

Most commentaries on this verse are to some extent apologetic: Abraham's request was not because of any lack of faith on his part; he only wished to see with his eyes what he already knew, to add certainty to faith, or to find greater certainty.[40] Some commentators add the pretext that Abraham wished to be able to argue more convincingly with Nimrod, who, when Abraham had stated that his Lord brings the dead to life, had retorted, 'I also give life and cause death' (Q. 2:258). In his *Nawbat* II commentary Maybudī explains further the reasons for Abraham's request:

> When God said, 'Do you not believe, then?' [...] Abraham replied, 'Yes, I believe and I am certain, but I wish that my eyes could see the miracles of Your making and the wonders of Your power, so that the knowledge of certainty (*ʿilm al-yaqīn*) might become the eye of certainty (*ʿayn al-yaqīn*), and the faith [that I attained] through rational demonstration (*ba-istidlāl*) should change to faith [which I attain] through perception (*īmān ḥissī*), for the evil whisperings can have access to the way of reasoning and indirect knowledge,[41] but not to perception and direct experience (*ḥiss wa ʿiyān*). Then the heart will find peace and be safe from evil suggestions.[42]

Anṣārī's explanation of the progression from *ʿilm al-yaqīn* to *ʿayn al-yaqīn* is similar: '*ʿAyn al-yaqīn* is being able, through comprehension, to go beyond rational demonstration, and by means of direct experience to go beyond indirect or 'reported' knowledge. It is tearing away the veil of knowledge, through direct witnessing.'[43] The connection between certainty, born of direct vision and peace at heart, which is already indicated in the wording of the same Qur'anic verse (Q. 2:260) (*li-yaṭma'inna qalbī*), is also present in Anṣārī's definition of *ṭuma'nīna* in the *Manāzil al-sā'irīn*: 'Tranquillity is a repose (*sukūn*) which is strengthened by a true security similar to direct experience (*amn ṣaḥīḥ shābih bi'l-ʿiyān*).[44]

Maybudī explains *ṭuma'nīna* in a different way in the *Nawbat* III section, where he gives a symbolic interpretation of the second part of the verse, which refers (by implication) to the killing of the four birds:

When Abraham asked God to show him how he gives life to the dead, he was seeking life of the heart (*dil*) and tranquillity in his secret (*sirr*), for he knew that until his heart was alive, tranquillity would not descend to it; and until he had found tranquillity, he would not reach the ultimate goal of the mystics. That goal is the spirit of intimacy, the heart's witnessing and the persistence of love, the tongue in remembrance, the heart enjoying the mysteries, the spirit enjoying the Beloved's coquetry; the tongue in invocation, the heart in contemplation, the spirit in love; the tongue expressing [what is] elucidated through the heart and experienced directly by the spirit. Abraham was told, 'Since life is in dying, and remaining (*baqāʾ*) in annihilation (*fanāʾ*), go, kill four birds. Outwardly carry out this command out of respect for My authority to show your servanthood. Inwardly carry out the command upon your person. Sever the head of the peacock of vain beauty (*zīnat*); take no repose in the pleasure and vanity of the world. [...] Kill the raven of greed; do not covet that which is transient and soon comes to an end [...][45] Break the cockscomb of desire; allow no concupiscence to enter your heart lest you be deprived of Me [...] Kill the vulture of expectation; do not extend your hopes nor set your heart on this world of play and trifles. Only thus may you reach that life which is [truly] good. O Abraham! The good life *is* that life in the heart and peace of the secret that you are seeking.'[46]

From knowledge to gnosis

The beginning of gnosis is demonstrative but its end intuitive, just as technical knowledge is first acquired and finally becomes instinctive.[47]

We return now to the first of Maybudī's mystical interpretations of the story of Abraham's looking at the star, moon and sun and calling them his Lord, when he is specifically commenting on the verses in question, namely Q. 6:75–9. The interpretation is quite clear and will be quoted in full:

'Thus did We show Abraham the kingdom of the heaven and earth.' Firstly he was shown the kingdom of heaven and earth so that by means of rational demonstration (*ba-istidlāl*) he could find proof of the existence of the Creator. He looked at the star and said, 'This is my Lord'; that is to say, this is the proof of my Lord, for my Lord is Eternal and this sets and 'I do not like that which sets'. Then eventually the beauty of reality showed its face to him. He went beyond the way of rational demonstration and proof (*istidlāl wa burhān*) to witnessing and direct experience (*mushāhadat wa ʿiyān*). He turned aside from everything and said, 'Indeed, they are all an enemy to me save the Lord of the Worlds' [...] First he went as an *ʿālim* and then he came as an *ʿārif*.

Al-Wāsiṭī says, 'People of the world are going towards Him. The mystics are coming from Him. If someone says, "I know God through proof", ask him "How did you know that proof?"' Yes, in the beginning proof is necessary, just as it was for Khalīl. To begin with, when each proof came upon his way, the star, the moon and the sun, whatever proof he came upon he clung to it, saying 'This is my Lord'. Then when he went beyond the stage of proofs, he saw the beauty of *tawḥīd* with the eye of direct experience (*'iyān*). He said, 'O my people! See, I am free of all that you associate [with Him]'; that is, I am free of the need to prove the Creator through created things, for there is no proof of Him other than Him. This is why that master of religion said, 'I know God through God and I know other than God through His Light'.[48]

Perfect friendship with God

The interpretations discussed in the previous section have shown Abraham making the journey towards annihilation in God, knowledge through God, and purification from all that is not God that was required of him as *Khalīl*. However there are many instances in the mystical sections of the *Kashf al-asrār* where Maybudī shows Abraham as having realised the state of perfect friendship and as an example to be followed in virtue.

Playing upon the triliteral root *KH.L.L.*, Maybudī states that Khalīl was 'the friend (*dūst*) in whose friendship (*dūstī*) there was no flaw (*khalal*)'.[49] He was an example of the way of *tawḥīd* and the reality of *tafrīd*.[50] He showed signs of the sincerity in *tawḥīd* when first of all he saw this world in the form of a star, then the other world in the form of the moon, and then the soul which incites [to evil] (*nafs ammāra*) and his love for Ishmael in the form of the sun. He saw that they did not have the traces of eternity and permanence and turned away from them with the words 'I have turned my face to the One who created the heavens and the earth.' (Q. 6:79)[51]

Speaking of the whole or sound heart (*qalb salīm*) which Abraham is said to possess (Q. 37:84), Maybudī says that it was free of idolatry (*shirk*), doubt (*shakk*), pure of any blemish, safe from any attachment.[52] Such was Abraham's complete trust in God (*tawakkul*) that he was prepared to leave Ishmael and Hagar in an 'uncultivated valley'.[53] Abraham is given as an example of charity in Maybudī's commentary on Q. 9:79. He explains that the charity of the people who concern themselves with the fulfilment of the religious law is different from that of the people of spiritual realisation.

The former, slaves of the way of the law, give five dirhams out of every two hundred, seeking thereby God's good pleasure and the eternal bliss of Paradise. But the latter, the people of spiritual retreat and witnessing (*ahl-i khalwat wa mushāhadat*), the masters of finding and communing [with God] (*khudāwandān-i yāft wa ṣuḥbat*) are different; they are like *Khalīl*,

> who took the hand of complete trust [in God] (*tawakkul*) from the sleeve of acquiescence (*riḍā'*), and struck the face of secondary causes and attachments. In the path of God they gave up all worldly considerations, placed heart and soul in the slave's robe of trial and grief and strove against the enemy, by manifesting the religion of Islam and upholding the Divine Word. Even then they saw themselves to be inadequate in the way of God.[54]

Abraham's devotion to God, Maybudī observes, was such that he did not sleep at night but stayed awake to contemplate the signs of his Lord: 'When night came upon him he saw a star' (Q. 6:77).[55] Moreover, he had reached the highest degree of piety, that of those who will be granted the most blessed Paradise, the Paradise of God's good pleasure (*al-riḍwān al-akbar*). This was because

> he considered anything having the stamp of being an accident to be his enemy, [saying]: 'Indeed, they are all an enemy to me save the Lord of the Worlds' [Q. 26:77]. He turned his face from everything so that he might, with a heart that is free, concern himself with the pain of loving the truth, and knowing for certain that strangers cannot be contained alongside the pain of this love, he cut heart and soul off from all else.' [56]

In this passage, Maybudī is equating Abraham's piety with his perfect love of God. This love is understood to be the essence of his consummate friendship, a friendship which Maybudī says was written for him in eternity.

> Adam was still in the concealment of non-existence when the Lord of Might placed the seal of friendship upon Abraham, kindling within him the fire of desire for Him, and the beauty of love for the eternal revealed itself to him. This is what is meant by His words, 'Long ago We bestowed on Abraham his right conduct' [Q. 21:51]. Thus, when he came into existence, that day when he stood upon the plain of bewilderment (*taḥayyur*) his heart ablaze with love for the eternal and his soul drunk with the wine of annihilation, in that moment when lovers take their morning drink, in the drunken

unruliness of those who have lost their hearts in the wine-sickness of non-existence, whatever he looked upon, in that ecstatic state he said, 'This is my Lord'. He found himself annihilated in witnessing the majesty and beauty of God, no longer aware of creatures or himself. Of course God increased the honour upon him by saying: 'Indeed, Abraham was a nation (*umma*) obedient to God, by nature upright' [Q. 16:120]. Abraham said: 'O God! You were all, and all is You.' Because Abraham was single-mindedly for God, God called him '*umma*'.[57]

The test and proof of friendship

The word *balā*ʾ is used to mean trial or affliction and its derivative *ibtilā*ʾ to mean test, trial or, by extension, misfortune. According to Sufi doctrine, trials may come from God simply because, as Maybudī says, 'It is His way (*sunnat*) to found joy wholly upon suffering',[58] or they may be a result of God's jealousy, and hence a means of purification;[59] they may be a test to verify the truth of a claim, or they may just be an inevitable consequence of loving Him, as where Maybudī speaks of the 'pain of loving the truth' (see p. 230).[60]

The Qur'an itself uses the word *ibtilā*ʾ in connection with Abraham: 'And [remember] when his Lord tried Abraham with His commands' (Q. 2:124). Maybudī interprets these trials first as a purification from other than God: 'O Abraham! Whoever wants Us must be wholly for Us. As long as one jot of human desire and intransigence of soul remains, you will not come from the pain of effort (*kūshish*) to the ease of attraction (*kashish*)'.[61] Second, they are a result of Abraham's claim, 'I have surrendered' (Q. 2:131), for God tells Abraham 'every claim must have a meaning, just as every truth (*ḥaqq*) must have a reality (*ḥaqīqa*), therefore stand by for the test (*imtiḥān*).' Abraham was then tested in three ways: by 'other than him' (*ba-ghayr-i khwīsh*), by 'part of him' (*ba-juz*ʾ*-i khwīsh*), and by 'all of him' (*ba-kull-i khwīsh*). The test by other than him was in his wealth, to see how much he was prepared to give away in order to hear Gabriel, disguised in human form, call out God's name '*yā Quddūs*!' – and, of course, he was willing to give away all his flocks of sheep and himself as well. The test by part of him was the command to sacrifice his son; and the test by all of him was his being placed in the fire of Nimrod.[62]

The phrases 'by part of him' and 'by all of him' are expressive of the way the respective importance of these two trials was evaluated by the Sufis.

From an exoteric point of view Abraham's near sacrifice of his son was seen, both in the Judeo-Christian and Islamic traditions, as an example of total submission and obedience, the fulfillment of the ultimate test of devotion that could be placed on any human being.[63] But for Islamic mysticism the story of Abraham in the fire of Nimrod, and the profound symbolism of the fire which was 'coolness and peace', represented a more perfect sacrifice.[64] In fact, Muslim tradition presents the story of Abraham's near sacrifice of his son as more of a two-sided affair, focusing as much upon the virtue of Ishmael's willingness to offer up his life as upon Abraham's readiness to sacrifice him.[65] In the *Kashf al-asrār* we find Abraham and Ishmael each arguing the case that his suffering was greater: Ishmael, that he was giving up life which was precious to him; and Abraham, that Ishmael's suffering would soon be over whereas he would have to live on with his.[66]

Maybudī's exoteric and esoteric commentaries on the sacrifice story are significantly different. The exoteric commentary largely consists of a dramatic narrative full of emotion and suspense, but based on traditions that are included in the commentaries of Ṭabarī, Ṭabarṣī, Bayḍāwī and others.[67] The torment of Abraham, who first agonises over whether the command in his dream was from God or from the devil, and then weeps and complains to God of the harshness of a trial 'which neither heaven nor earth could bear', is contrasted with the calm detachment and practical acceptance of Ishmael, whose virtue is shown even more by his concern both for his parents and for the correct execution of the rite: he must be tied firmly lest his limbs twitch at the moment of death and Abraham's clothes become spattered with blood, which would invalidate the righteous deed, and he must be placed face down so that he might die in a state of prostration and lest Abraham be moved with pity not to carry out the deed, or he himself feel regret at being parted from his father and become disobedient to God's command. Firm in their resolution, the two are making their way towards the mountain when they are assailed by Satan, who, having had no success in arousing Hagar's maternal instincts to prevent the sacrifice, now approaches Ishmael and Abraham in turn. Abraham's awareness of the difficulty of maintaining his resolve for this momentous task is indicated by the fact that the means to which he resorts in order to elude Satan are both physical; first he runs away, then he throws stones at him.[68] The Qur'an states that God called Abraham (to stop the sacrifice) 'when he had flung him on his face' (Q. 37:103),[69] but Maybudī's commentary goes further to say that Abraham drew the knife across his throat but it did not cut because Gabriel intervened by turning the blade of the knife the other way.[70]

Passing on to the mystical commentary we find that Maybudī gives only one explanation for the sacrifice story: that it was the result of divine jealousy. Abraham had become too attached to Ishmael, therefore the command came,

> 'O Abraham! You claimed to be Our friend and came like a *murīd* on the path of discipleship saying, "I have turned my face to the One Who created the heavens and the earth". You disdained creatures and attachments with the words "They are all an enemy to me save the Lord of the Worlds". Now you have gone and spent the heart that was reserved for the love of the Mighty and Beautiful upon him [Ishmael], and placed the seal of love upon him. Make a sacrifice to Me and cut yourself off for Me. Rise and carry out the order, and if you want Me then cure your own sickness.'[71]

Maybudī uses this argument to answer the question posed in many commentaries as to how, when Abraham did not actually kill his son, he could be said to have fulfilled the divine command. He states, 'God said, "O Abraham! The aim was that you should cut your heart free of him. Now that you have cut it free, We have intervened for you [in preventing the sacrifice]."'[72]

If in Judaic tradition the story of Abraham's sacrifice of Isaac is said to represent 'the culminating drama of Abraham's life, the true end to his spiritual and emotional growth',[73] Maybudī's interpretation of the story suggests that Abraham had not yet reached the 'true end', but was still in the process of being freed from other than God. Even in Maybudī's exoteric interpretation Ishmael seems to have greater detachment, and we find him almost in the role of Abraham's teacher.[74]

In the commentaries upon the story of Abraham in the fire of Nimrod (Q. 21:68, 69) there is no torment, no temptation. Abraham has already reached that state of complete attachment to and dependence upon God, which is why, according to a tradition, Abraham said that he was never happier than when he was in the fire of Nimrod.[75] This total dependence upon God, which Maybudī understands as one of the meanings of the word *khalīl*,[76] is emphasized in the *Nawbat* II section of the commentary, at the moment when Abraham was cast into the fire:

> Angels, heaven and all upon earth aside from men and jinn cried out: 'Our Lord! Abraham, the only one on earth who worships You, is being burned for Your sake. Allow us to help him.' God gave them permission: 'He is My friend, My only friend; I am his God, his only God. If he asks for rain to come down, rain down upon him. If he asks for help, then help him. But if he asks for help from none other than Me, then leave us to ourselves.' The keeper of the waters offered the service of the waters and the keeper of the wind offered the service of the wind, but Abraham would have none of it. He looked up and said, 'You are alone in heaven and I alone on earth. God is my sufficiency, a most excellent protector!'[77]

Still in the *Nawbat* II section, the dialogue which follows between Abraham and Gabriel shows Abraham to be in a state of intimacy with God which is accorded to human beings but not to angels:

> When they threw Abraham into the fire, Gabriel came before him and asked, 'Do you need anything?' and he answered, 'From you, no.' Then Gabriel told him, 'Ask your Lord.' And he replied, 'His knowledge of my state obviates the need for my request.'[78]

The fire of divine love

Maybudī begins his mystical commentary on the story of Abraham in the fire of Nimrod by showing that this fire was the fire of divine love, a love whose intensity only one such as Abraham could bear. He skillfully links the commentary on Q. 2:51, 'Long ago We gave Abraham his right conduct', with his commentary on Abraham in the fire (Q. 21:68–9), in a passage which is among the most beautiful in the *Kashf al-asrār*:

> Khalīl was still in the concealment of non-existence when the Tailor of Grace had sewn his waistcoat of *tawḥīd*. He had not yet set foot in the orbit of existence when the Bountiful Druggist had mixed his palatable drink. Obviously, when he came into being, even at the beginning of his childhood, the sun of friendship began to shine in him and the fountains of knowledge and wisdom opened in the courtyard of his breast. At the time of his youth, the light of guidance was made his special gift, and a girdle of honour was tied around his waist. He was brought to such a position that the hosts of heaven bit the finger of amazement and were saying, 'O God! We are baffled at the graces of honour and distinction that are being bestowed upon Khalīl from Your Mighty presence [...]', until the call came from the glorious court of the Majestic Lord: 'O hosts of heaven! If We were to bring into the open

that fire which We have placed in the grate of Abraham's soul, with its sparks We should burn heavens and the earth, angels and men.'[79]

Maybudī further develops this idea in what appears at first to be a surprising interpretation of the words, 'Be coolness and peace for Abraham' (Q. 21:69):

This call was made to the fire which was laid in the grate of Abraham's soul. When Nimrod placed him in the catapult (*manjanīq*), Abraham placed his secret in the catapult of contemplation. Just as he came near to the fire of Nimrod, when he was about to sigh from the ardour of witnessing [God], and would have extinguished Nimrod's fire, the call came, 'O fire!', that is, 'O fire of witnessing! Be cool to Nimrod's fire and do not impose your power over it, for We have decreed that in the middle of the fire We shall bring forth a garden of flowers and lights as a favour to Our friend, to make known his miracle [...]'.[80]

What is meant here is that, because of the nature of Abraham's inner fire, there would have been no need for God to have said to the fire, 'Be cool', for it would not have touched him anyway. The outward appearance of coolness and the garden of flowers was decreed as a miraculous manifestation to the world of Abraham's state of prophethood.[81]

There follows a mystical interpretation of a kind which is unusual for Maybudī, and more typical of later commentators such as Kāshānī, where the characters and elements in the story are interpreted as symbols.[82] Maybudī introduces it as a 'subtlety' (*laṭīfa*):

Your *nafs* is represented by Nimrod, its passion is the fire and the purified [lit. burnt] heart (*dil-i sūkhta*) is represented by Khalīl. The *nafs* ignited the fire of desire, and, with the chains of deception and the shackles of concupiscence, placed the heart into the catapult of disobedience and cast it into the fire of desire.[83]

These symbols would later be used by Rūmī,[84] but Maybudī now introduces another element, *'aql* (the rational faculty), symbolised in the story by Gabriel:

When the heart had not yet entered the fire, 'Aql, in a state of astonishment, approached to offer its service to the heart saying, 'Do you need anything?' The heart answered, 'From you, no. O 'Aql! Do you remember when it was said to you, "Come", and you came, then, "Go", and you went. Then, when you were asked, "Who are you? ", you were at a loss to answer. That day you had no access to yourself; today, how can you truly know what I need?'[85]

Typically, in this passage *ʿaql*, which Maybudī understands to be the faculty of discursive reasoning rather than the locus of mystical vision (see ch. 5, n. 1), has been transcended. Explaining the coolness of the fire, Maybudī says, 'When the heart had entered the fire of desire, the command came, "Be cool"; in other words, "Be cool to the heart, for it is already burned with Our love."'

Since Abraham has already been put through the purifying fire of divine love there was nothing left in him (of his lower soul) to be burned in the fire of passion. The 'trial' in the fire of Nimrod was thus the proof of his complete spiritual transformation, his realisation of perfect friendship with God.

NOTES

1 See Q. 2:125–9; 3:96–7; 14:35–41.

2 For example, *Kashf*, III, p. 128.

3 Ṭabarī argues in favour of traditions which interpret *ḥanīf* to mean upright (*mustaqīm*), as opposed to others which interpreted *ḥanīf* to be one who makes the pilgrimage or is circumcised. See *Jāmiʿ al-bayān*, ed. Shākir and Shākir, III, pp. 104–7. According to a tradition cited by Maybudī (*Kashf*, IV, pp. 210–11), the Prophet was asked by Abū ʿĀmir, the monk: 'What [religion] do you profess?' to which he replied, 'I profess the "Ḥanīfī" religion' (*jiʾtu bi'l-ḥanīfiyya*), which Maybudī glosses as 'the true and pure religion of Abraham'. The relevant hadith is listed, but with the word *baʿathtu* instead of *jiʾtu*, by Ibn Ḥanbal, *Musnad*, V, p. 266; VI, pp. 116, 233; and by Ṭabarānī, *Muʿjam al-awsaṭ*, II, pp. 235–6, § 1845.

4 Firestone goes so far as to say that the honorific is probably 'derived from Jewish sources' since Abraham is referred to as 'Your friend' (*ohavakha*) in Chronicles 20: 7 and as 'My friend' (*ohavi*) in Isaiah 41: 18. He further states: 'It would be natural for the special names of Abraham and Isaac to have evolved within a Jewish community living in an Arabic-speaking environment that commonly used the honorific title.' See Reuven Firestone, 'Abraham's son as intended sacrifice', *Journal of Semitic Studies* 34 (1989), pp. 118–9, n. 78; idem, *Journeys in Holy Lands* (Albany, 1990), p. 201, n. 25. It is worth noting, however, that *ohav* is related to the Arabic root *Ḥ.B.B.*, not *KH.L.L.*

5 *Jāmiʿ al-bayān*, ed. Shākir and Shākir, IX, p. 251.

6 Bayḍāwī, *Anwār al-tanzīl*, p. 233.

7 In the interpretation of Kāshānī, on the other hand, it is by taking the word

khalīl back to its root form, *KH.L.L.* meaning to penetrate or permeate, that the key is found to understanding Abraham's title: 'He [God] treated him as a friend, that is, He entered him by penetrating his essence and qualities, to the extent that nothing remained of them.' See Kāshānī, *Tafsīr al-Qur'ān al-karīm*, ed. ʿAlī, I, p. 289. See also Ibn ʿArabī, *Fuṣūṣ al-ḥikam* (Cairo, 1946), pp. 80–4, and Austin's introduction to his translation of ch. 5 in *Bezels*, p. 90. On the significance of *khalīl* and *takhallul* in Ibn ʿArabī's understanding of the prophet Abraham see Nettler, *Sufi Metaphysics*, ch. 5.

8 Bayḍāwī, *Anwār al-tanzīl*, p. 287.

9 *Jāmiʿ al-bayān*, ed. Shākir and Shākir, IX, pp. 251–2. Maybudī's version of the story begins with a description of Abraham's hospitality, *Kashf*, II, pp. 710–11.

10 *Kashf*, IV, p. 367. See the account of Abraham in the fire, p. 234.

11 *Kashf*, VI, p. 62.

12 Anṣārī, *Manāzil al-sā'irīn*, p. 4.

13 *Kashf*, IV, p. 279.

14 See the section on *qaḍā'* and divine intervention in chapter seven, p. 185.

15 Trans. modified with reference to Abdel Haleem's translation.

16 'That night' is a reference to the 'ascension by night' (*miʿrāj*) of the Prophet Muhammad (Q. 17:1 and 53:1–18).

17 *Kashf*, I, p. 367.

18 Kalābādhī, *Kitāb al-taʿarruf*, p. 107; tr. Arberry, pp. 155–6, with slight modification.

19 Qushayrī, *Risāla*, p. 438.

20 *Kashf*, VI, pp. 62–3.

21 For definitions of these terms see ch. 6, n. 7.

22 Ḥallāj:

Between You and me there is an 'I am' that baffles me,
So take away, by Your Grace, this 'I am' from in between.

See Ḥusayn b. Manṣūr al-Ḥallāj, *Dīwān*, ed. L. Massignon (Paris, 1955), p. 90; trans. in Carl W. Ernst, *Words of Ecstasy in Sufism* (Albany, 1985), p. 27. See also the *munājāt* of Anṣarī cited p. 185.

23 Hujwīrī, *Kashf al-maḥjūb*, pp. 319–20; tr. Nicholson, p. 248.

24 Hujwīrī, *Kashf al-maḥjūb*, p. 326; tr. Nicholson, pp. 252–6.

25 References for this hadith are given in ch. 3, n. 137.

26 Hujwīrī, *Kashf al-maḥjūb*, p. 326; tr. Nicholson, pp. 253–4.

27 *Kashf*, I, pp. 370–1. This interpretation, though mystical in content, appears in the *Nawbat* II section of the commentary. A similar hadith is listed without comment in ʿAjlūnī, *Kashf al-khafā'*, § 2578, with the wording: *man kāna maʿa'l-lāh kāna'llāhu maʿahu.*

28 A hadith of the Prophet quoted by Anṣārī in the introduction to his *Manāzil al-sā'irīn,* p. 5. The hadith is listed by Bayhaqī, *Al-Jāmiʿ li-shuʿab al-īmān*, II, ch. 10 (Bāb fī maḥabbat Allāh), § 503 and § 504; al-Ḥakīm al-Tirmidhī, *Nawādir,* Principle 1832, II, p. 104.

29 *Kashf*, III, p. 410. The last sentence in this passage is taken from Qushayrī's *Laṭā'if* (I, p. 485) and Maybudī's version of it endorses the corrections made by the editor of the published edition.

30 Iskandarī, *Sharḥ manāzil al-sā'irīn*, pp. 223–4.

31 Mustamlī, *Sharḥ al-taʿarruf*, IV, p. 1426. This extract is translated from

Mustamlī, *Khulāṣa-yi sharḥ al-taʿarruf*, ed. A.ʿA. Rajāʾī (Tehran, 1349sh/1970) p. 362.

32 *Kashf*, V, p. 281. Perhaps there is also a suggestion here that the *ʿārif* goes beyond the states of the *zāhid* and the *ʿābid*. See pp. 167–8.

33 Anṣārī, *Manāzil al-sāʾirīn*, p. 11.

34 See Iskandarī, *Sharḥ manāzil al-sāʾirīn*, p. 25.

35 As discussed in ch. 6, p. 169 and n. 121. See Sulamī, *Risālat al-Malāmatiyya*, ed. ʿAfīfī, repr. in Pourjavady, ed., *Majmūʿa*, II, p. 435; French tr. Deladrière, pp. 58–9; Khargūshī, *Tahdhīb al-asrār*, in Pourjavady, 'Manbaʿī kuhan', p. 33.

36 *Kashf*, V, p. 282. Also in *Ḥaqāʾiq*, ed., Nwyia, *Mélanges*, p. 204.

37 Note again here, the attribution of words to God.

38 *Kashf*, V, p. 282. This comment of Ibn ʿAṭāʾ appears in Sulamī's *Haqāʾiq*, ed. ʿImrān, I, p. 347; ed. Nwyia, *Trois œuvres inédites*, pp. 70–1.

39 Trans. modified with reference to the translation of Abdel Haleem.

40 Bayḍāwī, *Anwār al-tanzīl*, p. 134; Tustarī, *Tafsīr al-Qurʾān al-ʿaẓīm*, p. 11; *Laṭāʾif*, I, p. 201; *Kashf*, I, p. 712.

41 Lit. reported knowledge, of which one is informed (*khabar*).

42 *Kashf*, I, pp. 712–13. Maybudī gives the same explanation for Jesus' disciples' asking for the table to be sent down, related in Q. 5:114. See *Kashf*, III, p. 265. This is another example of the *Nawbat* II commentary entering the realm of mystical interpretation.

43 Anṣārī, *Manāzil al-sāʾirīn*, pp. 53–4.

44 Ibid., p. 68.

45 The metaphors here are probably derived from similes used in an anonymous comment in Sulamī's *Ḥaqāʾiq*, ed. ʿImrān, I, p. 78; MS Or. 9433, fol. 19b.

46 *Kashf*, I, p. 718. This passage is preceded by a quite different interpretation which explains Abraham's request as being simply because of the desire to hear God speak. Similar interpretations are found in Sulamī's *Ḥaqāʾiq*, ed. ʿImrān, I, p. 78; MS Or. 9433, fol. 19b.

47 Abū ʿAlī Daqqāq and Shaykh Abū Sahl Ṣuʿlūkī, quoted by Hujwīrī, *Kashf al-maḥjūb*, p. 349; tr. Nicholson p. 272.

48 *Kashf*, III, pp. 409–10. Maybudī does not name this 'master of religion' but Sahlagī has attributed the saying to Bāyazīd. See Sahlagī, *Kitāb al-nūr*, pp. 129, 133.

49 *Kashf*, II, p. 712.

50 *Kashf*, II, p. 163.

51 *Kashf*, IV, pp. 120–1.

52 *Kashf*, VIII, p. 285.

53 *Kashf*, V, p. 283.

54 *Kashf*, IV, p. 186.

55 *Kashf*, I, pp. 253–4. This interpretation was discussed on p. 77–8.

56 *Kashf*, II, pp. 42–3, commenting on Q. 3:15.

57 *Kashf*, V, p. 474. A similar passage occurs in *Kashf*, I, p. 351, where it is said that Jacob had love, Moses intoxication, but Abraham had both love and intoxication.

58 *Kashf*, V, p. 117. This statement occurs in the *Nawbat* II section.

59 See chapter seven, pp. 196–7.

60 *Kashf*, II, p. 43. See also *Kashf*, I, p. 423 where, commenting on Q. 2:155, Maybudī has God say: 'Whoever seeks union or proximity with Us will inevitably bear the burden of affliction and taste the sherbet of pain'.

61 *Kashf*, I, p. 375.
62 *Kashf*, I, pp. 375–6.
63 The Qur'an does not give the name of the son who was to be sacrificed, and traditionists and exegetes were divided as to whether it was Isaac or Ishmael. Firestone shows how numerous traditions supporting each of the two as the intended sacrifice exist, but that most earlier traditionists and the earlier exegetes considered Isaac to be the intended sacrifice, whereas virtually all exegetes after Ṭabarī supported Ishmael. See Firestone, 'Abraham's son', and idem, *Journeys*, ch. 16 and Appendix 2. Maybudī gives arguments for both sides but opts for Ishmael, except for one occasion, when he names the intended sacrifice as Isaac.
64 That is, sacrifice in the original sense of the word, 'making sacred', a transformation of the material by the spiritual.
65 See, for example, Ṭabarī's *History*, II, trans. by W.M. Brinner as *Prophets and Patriarchs* (Albany, 1987), pp. 93–4, 97. This is in line with the Qur'anic account of the story according to which Ishmael knows that Abraham has been commanded to sacrifice him, whereas in the Biblical account (Genesis 22:6–13) Abraham hides this, so that when Isaac asks: 'Where is the lamb for the burnt offering?' he says: 'The Lord will take care of the lamb.' It is interesting to note, however, that in the Midrash Isaac is fully aware that Abraham is to sacrifice him and accepts God's command willingly. See Norman Calder, 'Tafsīr from Ṭabarī to Ibn Kathīr: problems in the description of a genre, illustrated with reference to the story of Abraham', in G.R. Hawting and A.K. Shareef, eds., *Approaches to the Qur'ān* (London and New York, 1993), p. 379.
66 *Kashf*, VIII, p. 300.
67 For a comprehensive survey of traditions relating to the sacrifice see Firestone, *Journeys*, ch. 14.
68 *Kashf*, VIII, pp. 290–1.
69 Note God speaking here, not Gabriel as in the Biblical version.
70 This provides the occasion for a digression (*Kashf*, VIII, p. 292) to assert the principle that a knife does not cut nor fire burn by its nature, but in accordance with the custom (*ʿāda*) established by God, a doctrine which was held by the Ashʿarīs (and, evidently, by traditionalist Shāfiʿīs, like Maybudī). On the doctrine of *ʿāda* see Gardet and Anawati *Introduction à la théologie musulmane*, p. 353.
71 *Kashf*, VIII, p. 300.
72 *Kashf*, VIII, p. 292.
73 David Shulman, *The Hungry God: Hindu Tales of Filicide and Devotion* (Chicago, 1993), p. 135.
74 It is interesting to note that in the Targums on the *Akedah*, Isaac, who offers himself willingly for the sacrifice, is favoured with a heavenly vision; according to the Tosefta fragment of Targum Yerushalmī, commenting on Genesis XXII, 10: 'the eyes of Abraham were turned to the eyes of Isaac, but the eyes of Isaac were turned to the angels of heaven. Isaac saw them but Abraham did not see them', or, in the Targum on verse 14: 'the glory of the *Shekīnah* of the Lord was revealed to him.' See Vermes, *Scripture and Tradition in Judaism*, pp. 194–5.
75 *Kashf*, VI, p. 268.
76 *Kashf*, II, p. 710. *Khalīl* can mean *faqīr*, when *khulla* implies want, need. See Lane, *Arabic-English Lexicon*, I, p. 780.
77 According to a hadith of the Prophet, these words (Q. 3:173) were first said by

Abraham in the fire of Nimrod. The hadith is indexed in Bayhaqī's *Al-Jāmiʿ li-shuʿab al-īmān* as § 295789.

78 *Kashf*, VI, p. 267.

79 *Kashf*, VI, p. 271.

80 *Kashf*, VI, p. 273.

81 According to Islamic tradition, each prophet had a miracle as a proof to the world of his prophethood, for example the ring of Solomon, the rod of Moses and so on.

82 See ch. 3, p. 84 and n. 80, and Prolegomenon, pp. 211–12 and n. 15.

83 *Kashf*, VI, p. 274.

84 On Rūmī's allegorical interpretations of the Prophets and other stories see Taqī Purnāmdāriyān, *Dāstān-i payāmbarān dar Kulliyāt-i Shams* (Tehran, 1369sh/1990). On prophets in Rūmī's poetry see John Renard, *All the King's Royal Falcons* (Albany, 1994).

85 *Kashf*, VI, p. 274. See Kalābādhī, *Kitāb al-taʿarruf*, p. 39, for a slightly different version of this allegory in which ʿAql is asked by God not 'Who are you?' but 'Who am I?' ʿAql's inability to answer until God had opened its eyes by the 'light of unicity' (*waḥdāniyya*) is taken to show that ʿAql cannot know God save through Him. See also ch. 7, p. 189 and n. 50.

9

The story of Moses

In a well-known traditional account of the ascension (*mi'rāj*) of the Prophet Muhammad, it is said that when he had ascended through the seven heavens and been taken into the Divine Presence, the duty of fifty prayers a day was placed upon him. The Prophet relates:

> On my return I passed by Moses, and what a fine friend of yours he was! He asked me how many prayers had been laid upon me and when I told him fifty he said, "Prayer is a weighty matter and your people are weak, so go back to your Lord and ask him to reduce the number for you and your community." I did so and He took off ten. Again, I passed by Moses and he said the same again, and so it went on until only five prayers for the whole day and night were left. Moses again gave me the same advice. I replied that I had been back to my Lord and asked Him to reduce the number until I was ashamed, and I would not do it again. He of you who performs those [five prayers] in faith and trust will have the reward of fifty.[1]

The conversation between the two prophets related here illustrates Moses' importance in Islam as Muhammad's predecessor: he is advising Muhammad from his own experience as a prophet charged with bringing the divine law to his people. Moses, as William Brinner has rightly said, is the prophet 'whose career as a messenger of God, lawgiver and leader of his community most closely parallels that of Muhammad'.[2]

It is perhaps for this reason that Moses is mentioned more in the Qur'an than any other pre-Islamic prophet.[3] All the main events in his life that are narrated in the Bible are to be found dispersed through the chapters of the Qur'an with, in addition, a story which is not given in the Bible, that of Moses' encounter with one of God's servants, unnamed in the Qur'an but later identified as al-Khiḍr. A list of the events in the life of

Moses as they appear in the Qur'an can be found in table 9.1. The Qur'anic accounts of these stories sometimes vary in detail from their Biblical counterparts. For example, Moses is adopted by Pharaoh's wife and not by his daughter, and it is Moses himself and not Aaron who demonstrates the miracle of the rod turning into a serpent and a hand turning white.

More significantly, there is a different emphasis in the stories, which have been woven into the Qur'anic narrative to echo and endorse its essential themes. We find, for example, only a few cursory references to the Exodus, and these seem to be as much concerned with the punishment of Pharaoh as with the salvation of the Children of Israel. This is consistent with the Qur'an's constant warning of doom to oppressors and deniers of the Revelation. On the other hand, much is made of Moses' continuing struggle with the intransigence and disobedience of the Children of Israel, and this may have been partly to act as an admonition directly addressed to Jews who were exposed to the Islamic Revelation,[4] and partly to provide a parallel for Muhammad in his struggle with members of his own tribe. The miracle of the rod and hand, as it is demonstrated first to Moses and then to Pharaoh, is told in detail four times, and brings to mind the recurrent theme in the Qur'an of the signs (*āyāt*) of God – signs which point the believers in the direction of the truth, but to which the unbelievers will always be blind.[5] Even the story of Moses' being entrusted to the waters of the Nile, adopted by Pharaoh's family and eventually nursed by his own mother, is told in the context of God's giving reassurance to Moses that He will always protect him from his adversaries, a reassurance that was clearly intended for Muhammad and his followers.

Moses, *Kalīm Allāh*

In the Qur'an, Moses is shown not only as a prophet with a divine mission to his people and to Pharaoh; he is also the prophet who was 'brought close in communion [with God]' (Q. 19:52), who experienced the theophany in the burning bush at the Valley of Ṭuwā and on Mount Sinai, and to whom God spoke unmediated, for which privilege he was given the honorary title, *Kalīm Allāh*, the Interlocutor of God.[6]

The Qur'anic account of the theophany at Mount Sinai is particularly

Table 9.1 The life of Moses

1) His infancy.	Q. 20:38–40; 28:7–13
2) His youth and the killing of an Egyptian.	Q. 20:40; 28:14–20
3) His escape to Midian, marriage to the daughter of Shuʿayb and the undertaking of ten years' hired labour.	Q. 20:40; 28:21–9
4) Hearing God speak from the burning bush.	Q. 20:10–16; 27:7–9; 28:29–30
5) He is shown the miracles of the rod turning into a snake and the hand turning white, and his being commanded to take God's message to Pharaoh.	Q. 20:17–36; 27:10–12; 28:31–5
6) He goes to Pharaoh with the message and the miracles, and Pharaoh rejects them.	Q. 7:103–27; 20:49–73; 43:46–54
7) The plagues.	Q. 7:130–5; 17:101–2; 43:48–50
8) The exodus and the drowning of Pharaoh.	Q. 2:50; 17:103; 20:77–9; 43:55–6
9) His mission to the Children of Israel. The covenant, their worship of the golden calf.	Q. 2:51–64, 67–74, 92–3; 5:20–4; 7:138–41
10) His retreat on Mount Sinai, the theophany, the writing on the tablets.	Q. 7:142–8
11) The encounter with Khiḍr.	Q. 18:60–82

significant for the Islamic perception of Moses and, as we shall see, for Sufism. Although Moses' period of forty days retreat at Mount Sinai is alluded to elsewhere in the Qur'an (Q. 2:51), the theophany itself is related only once, in verses 143–5 of *Sūrat al-Aʿrāf* (Q. 7). The account reads as follows:

143. And when Moses came to Our appointed tryst and His Lord had spoken to him, he said: My Lord! Show me [Yourself] that I may see You. He said You will not see Me, but look at the mountain! If it stands in its place, then you will see Me. And when his Lord revealed [His] glory to the mountain He sent it crashing down. And Moses fell down senseless. And when he woke he said: Glory be to You! I turn to You in repentance, and I am the first of the [true] believers.
144. He said: O Moses! I have chosen you over other people for My messages and by My speaking [to you]. So hold to that which I have given you, and be among those who are thankful.
145. And We inscribed for him, upon the tablets, the lesson to be drawn from all things and the explanation of all things, then [bade him]: Hold on to them firmly; and command your people that they should grasp their excellent [teachings]. I shall show you the abode of sinners.[7]

Once again, we find that the Qur'anic account of this story has quite a different emphasis from its Biblical counterpart. Verse 145 speaks of the tablets, but that which was inscribed on them is only summarily described. Rather, our attention is focused upon the nature of Moses' experience. Comparing the Biblical and Qur'anic versions of this story, Brinner has observed that 'in the Islamic account Moses' meeting with God and his speaking to him are central; whereas in the Jewish tradition, although this experience is without doubt important and valued, what becomes central is a tangible product of the meeting rather than the meeting itself.'[8]

In fact, in the Qur'anic account the drama is centred upon Moses' request for the vision of God, and God's refusal. While in the Bible this is explained by 'a man shall not see Me and live' (Exodus 33:20), the Qur'an does not give any reason for the refusal. Instead, we are shown the tremendousness of the manifestation of the divine glory in its effect upon the mountain and Moses. The story was to be cited by both sides in doctrinal debates about the possibility or otherwise of seeing God, either in this life or in the Hereafter,[9] but more relevant to the present discussion is the fact that it provided a scriptural basis for the distinction in rank which Islamic tradition was to make between the prophets Moses and

Muhammad. At the end of a long passage in which Maybudī lists all the aspects of Moses' life that are mentioned in the Qur'an, he says, 'God mentioned all this that the people of the world should know his special position, intimacy and proximity [with God], yet, with all this distinction and rank, he did not go beyond the foot of obedience to the Prophet Muhammad', and to this statement he adds a hadith of the Prophet, 'If Moses were alive he could have done no more than follow me.'[10]

Hearing versus seeing

The Qur'an does not state that Muhammad saw God, but it does not state that he was refused the vision of God either, and it is widely held in Sunni tradition that on the night of the *miʿrāj*, when Muhammad had gone beyond the 'lote tree of the uttermost end' (Q. 53:12), he did see God, although there is a difference of opinion as to whether it was a vision of the eyes or the heart.[11] Moses' experience on Mount Sinai inevitably came to be compared with the *miʿrāj* of Muhammad, and in Qur'anic commentaries we find such comparisons being made as 'God spoke to Muhammad without a veil, whereas He spoke to Moses from behind a veil'; and 'God divided hearing His speech and seeing Him between Moses and Muhammad: Moses heard God speak twice and Muhammad saw Him twice';[12] or the more mystical:

> Moses had not found the delight of witnessing (*mushāhadat*), had gone no further than listening and mentioning, but Muṣṭafā went beyond the bounds of listening to the point of non-differentiation (*nuqṭa-yi jamʿ*) [...] Remembrance was effaced in the Remembered, the sun in light itself, the soul in direct witnessing (*ʿiyān*). Immersion in such witnessing is beyond the reach of expression (*bayān*).

and elsewhere, having described how God spoke to Moses in words that could be counted, Maybudī states:

> About the speech which passed between God and Muhammad on the *miʿrāj* nothing can be said, 'He revealed to His servant that which He revealed' [Q. 53:10].[14]

Reference has already been made to the way in which the 'lesser perfection' of other prophets is often used in Islamic literature as a foil to show the pre-eminence of the Prophet Muhammad,[15] but Moses appears to be cited more than any other prophet in such comparisons. This is perhaps because of his particular similarity to Muhammad or because, as Maybudī says, 'in the court of glory, other than Muṣṭafā, no prophet enjoyed the openness and proximity [with God] that Moses had.'[16] In the *Kashf al-asrār*, the frequency of comparisons between Moses and Muhammad is certainly conspicuous.[17] The area for comparison is not always their respective experiences at Mount Sinai and during the *miʿrāj*, although this is the most frequently cited example; it might be the personal attributes of the two prophets, or the revelations which they brought, or their peoples, that is, the Children of Israel and the Muslims. Generally, the comparisons do not appear to be intended polemically. As often as not, they occur in the *Nawbat* III sections of the work, and seem to perform one of three functions in Maybudī's rhetoric: to explain aspects of the mystical path and inspire the aspirant to strive to reach a higher spiritual state; to foster love and reverence for Muhammad; or to encourage the virtue of gratitude for the special mercies which are inherent in the final Revelation. Some examples of these are briefly outlined here.

In his commentary on the words 'We have appointed mansions for the moon' (Q. 36:38), Maybudī compares the sun to the possessors of the state of *tamkīn* who are 'ever in the radiance of knowledge of Him, for whom the sun of His knowledge has permanently risen from the zodiac (*burūj*) of their fortune, never to be eclipsed, nor obscured by clouds'. The moon, on the other hand, may be compared to the servant 'whose states are changing (*fī tanaqqul*), who is possessed of *talwīn* (vacillation). From the state of expansion (*basṭ*) he has that which brings him to the bounds of union (*ḥadd-i wiṣāl*), then he returns to lassitude (*fatra*) and falls into the state of contraction (*qabḍ*).'[18] The prophet Moses, then, was in a state of *talwīn* since, as Maybudī explains, when God spoke to him he went from one state to another, and change and alteration came over him, so that no one could look at his face (because of its dazzling brightness). Muhammad, on the other hand, was of the people of *tamkīn*. At the moment of vision and speaking with God he remained in a state of stability and firmness (*istiqāmat wa tamakkun*), and 'not a hair on his body showed any alteration'.[19]

Maybudī relates how, when Moses returns from Mount Sinai and finds the Children of Israel worshipping the calf, he prays to God: 'Distinguish between us [Aaron and himself] and the people who are doing wrong'

(Q. 5:25). He remarks on how different this is from Muhammad who, on the night of the *mi'rāj*, was brought to the Highest Presence and greeted with 'Peace be upon you, O Prophet, and the mercy of God and His blessings!', and yet did not forget his people, but said, 'Peace be upon us and upon the righteous servants of God!'[20]

In discussing the second form of the verbal root *N.Z.L.* as it is used to speak of the revelation of the Qur'an (Q. 3:2) Maybudī explains that it implies a gradual process of revelation over years, verse by verse, as was necessary, whereas the Torah was revealed all at once, 'seventy camel-loads, of which one part would take a year to read'.[21]

Commenting on Moses' prayer, 'O my Lord! Relieve my heart' (Q. 20:25),[22] a prayer which is answered by God, Maybudī adds that whatever favour or blessing God bestowed upon Moses, He bestowed upon Muhammad's people:

> It was said to Moses, 'Your prayer is granted' [Q. 20:36] and concerning them it was said, 'And He gives you all you ask of Him' [Q. 14:34]. God said 'O Muhammad! I have honoured you; every favour which I granted to Moses and every kindness which I showed him I have granted to your people, according to their rank: I said to Moses "I have showered you with love from Me" [Q. 20:39], while about your people I said "He loves them and they love Him" [Q. 5:54]; [...] of Moses I said "We drew him close [to Us] in communion" [Q. 19:52], and to your people I said "Prostrate yourself and draw near" [Q. 96:19], and "We are nearer [Q. 50:16]".'[23]

'A man like yourselves'

In this last example we find Moses presented not as the forerunner of Muhammad, but as the forerunner of Muhammad's people, the *umma*. Maybudī relates more than once the tradition according to which Moses, having been told by God about the virtues of Muhammad's people, begs that if he cannot become their prophet he may be made one of them.[24] This brings to mind another role which Moses performs in Islamic literature in general, and in the *Kashf al-asrār* in particular, where moral teachings are presented either in the form of an exhortation addressed to Moses or as an anecdote about him. This is often a spontaneous exhortation beginning with words such as 'It was revealed to Moses...', but it might be preceded by the report of some oversight or shortcoming on Moses' part.[25] For example, Ghazzālī writes that God sent the following revelation to

Moses: 'Whoever obeys his mother and father I shall record him as obedient, and whoever obeys Me but disobeys them, I shall record him as disobedient.'[26]

In explaining the intense and painful longing that the aspirant must have if he is to reach his Lord, Maybudī relates the following anecdote:

> A dervish groaned at Moses' assembly. Moses shouted at him impatiently. Immediately Gabriel appeared and said, 'O Moses! God says that in your gathering the one possessed of suffering and a heart was that man, who came for His sake to your gathering. You shouted at him. Even though you are a dear one and Kalīm, yet you do not see the secret which He has placed beneath this man's misfortune (lit. black kilim).' [27]

A saying attributed to Jaʿfar al-Ṣādiq states that at the time of Moses' communing with God he was warned, 'Do not extend your possessions in this world lest your heart become hardened, and one whose heart is hardened is far from Me'.[28]

Examples such as these abound in Islamic literature of all kinds. On the one hand, it appears that Moses can act as the recipient for exhortations "from God" for homiletic purposes, without there being any need for, or possibility of, verification (i.e. by *isnād*) in a way that was impossible with respect to the Prophet Muhammad. On the other, Moses can represent a kind of 'Everyman' with which the Muslim believer is able to identify.[29] Just as in their explanations of aspects of the mystical path, Muslim exegetes chose to show prophets other than Muhammad progressing from a 'lower spiritual station' to a 'higher' one, from being seeker (*murīd*) to being sought (*murād*), or from a novice (*ahl-i bidāyat*) to an adept (*ahl-i nihāyat*), so it was more acceptable to show the 'human' side of a prophet other than Muhammad when preaching the importance of a particular virtue to the generality of believers. Of course Muhammad is to be seen as 'a man like yourselves' (Q. 18:110), but at the same time he is, Maybudī reminds us, 'not the father of one of you' (Q. 33:40). 'He is like them in form (*ba-ṣūrat*), but unlike them in attribute (*ba-khāṣṣiyyat*), which is why the Prophet said, "I am not like any one of you".'[30]

The foregoing has shown some aspects of Moses' importance in the Qur'an and in Islamic tradition, and themes which predominate in Maybudī's exoteric commentary on the stories of Moses. In summarising these, it might be said that Moses' importance is both in his being special, and in his being not as special as the Prophet Muhammad. Some of these themes are discussed in the *Nawbat* III sections of the *Kashf al-asrār* although they are not strictly speaking mystical; that is, they are not concerned with the journey towards, or experience of God. It is to Moses' significance for Sufism and mystical exegesis that we shall now turn.

Moses in Sufi exegesis

Just as Sufis who commented on the stories of Abraham had explored the implications of his being called *Khalīl Allāh*, so when it came to the stories of Moses they took inspiration from his title, *Kalīm Allāh*. It is significant that the Sufis refer to Moses' experience of hearing God speak as *munājāt*, the term which they apply to their own intimate prayer and communing with God. In fact, the word *munājāt* derives from the root *N.J.W.* (here, in its third form, meaning confiding, conversing in whispers), and the Qur'an says of Moses, 'We brought him close in communion (*najīyan*) (Q. 19:52).

In his study of early Sufi exegesis and the development of the language of mysticism, Paul Nwyia states 'from early on, the Qur'anic accounts of Moses spurred Muslim exegesis to meditate upon his experience as being the entry into a direct relationship with God, so that later the Sufis would come to regard him as the perfect mystic, called to enter into the mystery of God.' He goes on to observe that the Qur'an contains a more fully developed idea of this religious experience than the Bible, since it makes a clear distinction between the auditive and visual experience.[31]

However, whilst Sufi exegetes did consider the hearing/seeing distinction, they had far more to say about two key events in the story of Moses; every detail of the Qur'anic narrative relating to Ṭuwā and Sinai is interpreted to provide a more precise understanding of his spiritual state and experience. For example, the removal of his sandals at Ṭuwā, the extension of his period of retreat at Sinai from thirty to forty days and his being commanded to look at the mountain, all have a particular spiritual significance. According to Ghazzālī, the removal of the two sandals refers to cutting off his attachment to the two worlds;[32] according to Kāshānī, the extra ten days' fasting were added because, at the end of thirty days he used a *miswāk* (toothstick), representing that part of himself from which he had not been freed,[33] and according to Ibn ʿAṭāʾ, God made Moses busy himself with the mountain, because if, at the moment of manifestation, his attention had not been diverted he would have died.[34]

The interpretation of these details might differ, of course, from one commentator to another, or within one commentary, and especially with regard to the events at Mount Sinai. For example, when God says 'You shall not see Me' it might be an admonition to Moses that he, a mere mortal (*fānin*), cannot have access (*sabīl*) to the immortal (*bāqī*),[35] or it might indicate that Moses had attained the mystical state of *baqāʾ*, since here it is God who is speaking, whereas when he asks 'show me [Yourself] that I may look at You' he is still in possession of his own 'I'.[36]

It can be seen from these examples, and will be evident from Maybudī's mystical commentary as a whole, that Moses is not necessarily shown as the 'perfect mystic' but often as the mystic in the process of being perfected. Moses is the only prophet who was, to use Maybudī's words, 'sent to the school (*dabīristān*) of Khiḍr', and for whom Khiḍr became a 'furnace (*kūra*) of spiritual discipline' (*riyāḍat*), in which he could be purified like silver ore.[37] The encounter between Moses and Khiḍr (Q. 18:60–82) is often seen as a prototype of the relationship between disciple and spiritual master, in which, traditionally, the disciple must accept without question his master's guidance.[38] More than this, perhaps, the particular affinity which Sufis feel towards Moses is because by boldly requesting the vision of God, he represents the heroic determination of the spiritual traveller, the true *jawānmard*, who longs for union with the One.

Moses' spiritual journey

Maybudī's mystical commentary on the story of Moses is mainly focused upon four events, which he describes as four journeys:[39]

The Journey of Fleeing (*harab*): Moses flight to Midian
The Journey of Seeking (*ṭalab*): Moses' encounter with the burning bush in the Valley of Ṭuwā
The Journey of Joy (*ṭarab*): the theophany at Mount Sinai
The Journey of Toil (*taʿab*): the meeting with Khiḍr

Within the scheme of these four journeys, I shall examine Maybudī's interpretations of the story of Moses; as in the story of Abraham, the material will be arranged according to the mystical themes that Maybudī expounds through his interpretations.

The journey of fleeing: the flight to Midian

The battlefield of ḥayrat and miḥnat

> And as he turned his face towards Midian he said: It may be that my Lord will guide me on the right road (Q. 28:22).

Maybudī begins his commentary on this verse by explaining that the way to gnosis necessarily involves trials:

> In pre-eternity (*sabq-i sabq*), when the orchard of gnosis (*maʿrifat*) was adorned with the trees of love (*maḥabbat*), a battlefield of bewilderment (*ḥayrat*) and affliction (*miḥnat*)[40] was placed before it and made the way to it. [As the Prophet said] 'Paradise is surrounded by hardships'.[41] Whomsoever God wished to bring to the orchard of gnosis, He brought first to the field of perplexity and made his head a ball for the polo-stick of affliction, so that he might savour the taste of perplexity and torment before he attained the perfume of love. This was the situation of Moses; when God wished to place upon him the gown of prophethood (*nubuwwat*) and bring him to the court of messengership (*risālat*) and of conversing [with Him] (*mukālamat*), first of all He placed him in the crook of the polo-stick of affliction (*baliyyat*) so that he should be cooked through trials and ordeals – as the Lord of Might said, 'and We tried you with a heavy trial' [Q. 20: 40]; that is, We cooked you thoroughly so that you should become pure and free from all other.[42]

Maybudī here employs metaphors which were to become widely used in Persian poetry to express the suffering which the lover must be put through by the beloved. He is also possibly following Anṣārī (see the passage cited p. 195) in his play upon the words *maḥabbat* (love) and *miḥnat* (affliction or trial) which look identical in the Arabic script apart from the placing of a dot.

In his commentary on the story of Abraham, Maybudī explained that Abraham's claim to have submitted to God was tested in three ways: by his wealth, his son and himself.[43] These were all trials of sacrifice. Here

Moses is subjected to a different trial, that of *ḥayrat.*

Ḥayrat, or sometimes *taḥayyur*, is usually translated as perplexity, consternation or amazement, and has various applications in Islamic mysticism. It can have the negative sense of being dazed by the world and unable to understand God, or baffled by too much questioning and doubt concerning God. In chapter seven, the state of *ḥayrat* or *dahshat* was said to arise from the experience of unveiling, especially when God reveals Himself in His aspect of majesty (*jalāl*). This application of the term *ḥayrat* occurs later in Maybudī's commentary on the story of Moses, but here it is coupled with the idea of *miḥnat*. It is the bewilderment of one who must submit totally to the divine will, and 'become a ball for the polo-stick', so that God can guide him to the truth. Relevant here is a saying of Ibn ʿAṭāʾ concerning the prophet Joseph:

> We caused Joseph to pass through all sorts of trials and kept him a long time in the station of bewilderment in the terrain of affliction, until We brought him to the station of favour and exaltedness and caused him to taste the wine of proximity and intimacy.[44]

Returning to the story, Maybudī tells us that Moses is fleeing from Egypt, he is perplexed (*ḥayrān*), looking to the right and left, in fear of his life (Q. 28:21). In desperation he pleads for God's help, 'Deliver me from the wrongdoing folk'. God assures him that he will have His protection as before, and peace (*sakīna*) comes into his heart. It is now that the next stage of perplexity occurs: 'Moses set off for the wilderness (*biyābān*), not intent on Midian but because of (or for the sake of) spiritual openings (*bar futūḥ*).'[45] The wilderness or desert conveys the idea of being cut off from the world with God as the only guide. To further illustrate the theme of hardship and perplexity Maybudī introduces a story of Abraham (Q. 6:75–9) as he comments on the next verse, 'It may be that my Lord will guide me on the right path' (Q. 28:22):

> From the point of view of allusion in the language of unveiling, 'the right path' (*sawāʾ al-sabīl*), is regularly directing the soul (*muwāẓabat-i nafs*) through service (*khidmat*), and peace of the heart through rectitude (*istiqāmat*).[46] The man travelling the path cannot enter the quarter of divine unity (*sar-i kūy-i tawḥīd*) until he has passed through the stations of that path. To begin with, when Khalīl (Abraham) was being brought to the royal court, first he was taken to the quarter of the star, so he said, 'This is my

Lord'. Then he went to the quarter of the moon and thence to the quarter of the sun. In every quarter he found a fault [...] He realised that this was not the royal road of rectitude nor the end of the street of *tawḥīd*. All roads were blocked to him. With the foot of reflection (*tafakkur*) he stood at the end of the street of bewilderment (*taḥayyur*), dazed, thirsty, seeking the Beloved, so that everyone who saw him would say, 'This man is a captive of the dust of the end of the street of [the Beloved]'.

The dust at the end of the Beloved's street became like jasmine petals
Whoever passes through that dust will become as I am.

[...] The manly man (*mard-i mardāna*)[47] is not the one who travels mounted, upon the highway, a wide, open road; the true man is he who, at darkest night, upon a narrow road, goes to the end of the street of the Friend without a guide.[48]

The principle that it is necessary to enter a stage of perplexity and hardship, abandoning completely what is known and trusting in the guidance of God, has here been expressed using two metaphors: that of a narrow, uncharted road in the depths of the night, in the case of Abraham; and that of the desert or playing field, in the case of Moses.

Ghaybat and ḥuḍūr, fanāʾ fi'llāh

Maybudī now uses different imagery to convey another stage in Moses' 'spiritual journey', that of attaining to the divine oneness (*tawḥīd*). As he comments upon the next verse, 'When he reached the waters of Midian' (Q. 28:23), he writes:

Outwardly he came to the waters of Midian but in his heart he came to the springs of intimacy. The springs of intimacy (*uns*) are the courts of divine unity (*sāḥāt-i tawḥīd*) [...]. When the servant reaches the courts of divine unity he becomes drowned in the light of witnessing (*mushāhadat*), absent from himself (*ghāʾib*), present (*ḥāḍir*) in God. Seeking is extinguished in What is found, knowing in the Known, seeing in the Seen. Attachments are cut off, [secondary] causes vanish, regulations have no validity, limits disappear, and allusion and expression are annulled. Rain loses itself when it reaches the sea, stars become invisible in the light of day. Be annihilated in yourself (*burasīd*) that you might reach the Lord (*birasīd*).[49]

Parts of this passage are evidently drawn from Qushayrī's commentary on the same verse in the *Laṭāʾif al-ishārāt*, which reads:

> Outwardly he reached the springs of Midian, but in his heart he reached the springs of intimacy and ease (*uns wa rawḥ*). There are different springs: the springs of the heart (*qalb*) are the gardens of expansion (*riyāḍ al-basṭ*) [where they experience] the revelations of being present [with God] (*kushūfāt al-muḥāḍara*) and delight in all kinds of [divine] graces (*mulāṭafa*); the springs of spirits (*arwāḥ*) are the places of witnessing where they experience the revelation of the lights of contemplation and become absent (*yughībūna*) from all perception of themselves (*'an kull iḥsās bi'l-nafs*); the springs of secrets (*asrār*) are the courts of divine unity (*tawḥīd*), and there the control is God's – for *there* is no self and no perception, no heart and no intimacy, it is annihilation in the eternal (*istihlāk fi'l-ṣamadiyya*) and effacement in the all (*fanā' bi'l-kul-liyya*).[50]

Both of these passages appear to link the states of absence from self (*ghayba*) and presence in God (*ḥuḍūr*) with annihilation from self (*fanā'*), though Maybudī's passage, which is slightly less technical than that of Qushayrī, gives the impression that one who is absent from self and present in God is *virtually* in a state of annihilation from self. Qushayrī, on the other hand, who actually introduces the term *fanā'*, indicates this to be the experience of 'secrets', by which he is probably alluding to a higher or deeper experience within the human inner make-up than that of the heart and spirit, which experience presence and absence respectively.[51]

Referring to the Sufi manuals, we find that according to Sarrāj, a *ghayba* of the heart signifies its being absent from witnessing creatures (*mushāhadat al-khalq*) because of its presence in, and contemplation of, God.[52] Kalābādhī states that *ghayba* signifies a person's 'absence to the enjoyments (*ḥuẓūẓ*) of his self, although they still persist in him – only he is absent from them because he is present with what belongs to God.'[53] In his *Risāla*, Qushayrī describes *ghayba* as absence from awareness or perception (*ḥiss*) of oneself, and states that people vary in their *ghayba* according to their state.[54] In defining *ḥuḍūr*, both Sarrāj and Qushayrī explain that the servant is present (with God) to the extent that he is absent from creatures.[55] Neither explicitly mentions the state of annihilation (*fanā'*) in this connection.

The journey of seeking: in the valley of Ṭuwā

In Maybudī's discussion of Moses' four journeys, he explains that the journey of seeking took place on 'the night of fire'; that is, when Moses went in search of fire. In Maybudī's interpretation of the story of Abraham we saw that the fire of Nimrod symbolised the fire of divine love, a fire that burns away separateness (*tafarruq*), a fire of purification from other than God. It was 'coolness and safety' for Abraham because he was already freed from the two worlds and himself, and had realised divine unity (*tawḥīd*) – 'one who has been burnt cannot be burned again'. In Maybudī's interpretation of the story of Moses, the fire of the burning bush (expressed in Persian as 'tree') is described as the fire of gnosis and guidance,[56] the fire of love,[57] and we shall see that it is also interpreted as the fire of divine unity.[58] All of these Maybudī shows to be ultimately one and the same.

The fire of gnosis and guidance

Before Moses experiences the epiphany of the burning bush (or tree), he has to undergo further hardship and perplexity in order to prepare him for the guidance he is to receive from God. To emphasize the idea that these hardships have been imposed by God, Maybudī states that the road was *commanded* to be hidden, the clouds were *commanded* to rain, his family were *commanded* to wail, and so on.[59] In another passage where he comments on Moses' words, 'For sure, I can see a fire' (Q. 27:7),[60] Maybudī sets the scene in greater detail, demonstrating his skill in dramatic narrative:

> That night when Moses fell into bewilderment (*taḥayyur*) in the desert, having left Midian and set off for Egypt, whence he intended to bring his mother and two sisters [...], fear of Pharaoh filled his heart. Suddenly he lost his way in the desert. The night was dark and the way narrow. It was a moonless night and he was severely troubled. He was stranded and confused in that desert amidst the rain, the wind and the boundless cold. Lightning flashed, thunder clapped and his wife kept crying in the pain of childbirth. He took up flints and tinder and struck many times but there was no spark. In desperation he threw them to the ground. The Lord of the Worlds caused them to speak to him. They said, 'O Moses! Do not be angry with us for we are at the command of a King. Within, we are full of fire but we have been ordered not to let out one spark of it.' That night the command came to all the fires in the world that they should not leave their mines. For God said, 'This night is the night that We shall guide a friend to Us by fire and shall favour him.'[61]

Here, the fire of the burning bush is shown as the fire by which God was to 'guide a friend to Himself'. As he continues his commentary on this verse Maybudī describes six kinds of fire mentioned in the Qur'an, among which the fire of the burning bush is the fire of 'gnosis and guidance' (*maʿrifat wa hidāyat*).[62] However, more predominant in Maybudī's interpretations of this story is the idea of the fire of divine love:

> The journey of seeking was on the 'night of the fire' when Moses went in search of fire. What kind of fire was it that set the whole world aflame? Whenever there is talk of the fire of Moses just the allusion to it fills the whole world with the scent of love. Moses sought fire and found light. This noble one went in search of light and found fire. If Moses reached without intermediary the sweetness of hearing the speech of God, no wonder if some of its fragrance reached his friends.[63]

The soul-consuming fire of divine love

For Moses the fire of love might, for the sake of rhetoric, be shown as an outward manifestation:

> If the fire of Moses was manifest, the fire of these noble ones is hidden. And if the fire of Moses was in the tree, the fire of these noble ones is in the soul. He who has it will know: all fires burn the body but the fire of love burns the soul. The soul-burning fire is unbearable.[64]

or it might be understood as an inner fire:

> Moses was searching for fire to light the house, he found a fire that burns heart and soul.[65]

This statement occurs in Maybudī's commentary on the story as it is narrated in Q. 20:9 ff. He follows it with a definition of three different kinds of fire from the point of view of mysticism.

> There are different kinds of fire: the fire of shame (*sharm*), the fire of yearning (*shawq*) and the fire of love (*mihr*). The fire of shame burns separateness (*tafarruq*); the fire of yearning burns patience (*ṣabr*); and the fire of love burns the two worlds so that nothing but God remains. The proof of finding love is the burning of the two worlds; the sign of the realised soul is not having to do with other than God; and the indication of being noughted is being annihilated from oneself – rain is no more when it reaches the sea. That person is effaced when he reaches the Lord.[66]

Tajrīd and tafrīd

The fire of the burning bush, in burning the two worlds, becomes the fire of *tawḥīd*; but Moses, like Abraham[67] is told to go beyond the first realisation of *tawḥīd*. In the words of Anṣārī, '*Tawḥīd* is not just that you should know Him as one (*ū-rā yigāna dānī*), the true *tawḥīd* is that you should *be* one [i.e. isolated] for Him (*ū-rā yigāna bāshī*).'[68] As Maybudī continues his commentary on the story, where Moses hears the voice of God from the burning bush (Q. 20:12–4), he writes:

> Moses, having reached the head of the spring of *tawḥīd*, when he heard the words 'I, even I, am your Lord' [Q. 20:12], was commanded, 'Enter the world of *tafrīd*', so he stamped upon the two worlds and made his aspiration single-mindedly for God.[69]

In the chapter on Abraham, it was seen that *tafrīd* (isolation of the self [for God]) is not possible without *tajrīd* (stripping away [of other than God]).[70] The necessity for *tajrīd* is symbolised in the story of Moses by the command for him to remove his sandals, 'So take off your shoes, for you are in the holy valley of Ṭuwā' (Q. 20:12). Qushayrī explains that these words are an allusion to freeing the heart from the two worlds, to becoming free, stripped of all other for God, by [attaining] the quality of being solely for Him (*tajarrud li'l-Ḥaqq bi-naʿt al-infirād*)'.[71] This is expressed by Maybudī in the following manner:

> O Moses! Be [undividedly] one (*yigāna*) for the [Undividedly] One (*Yigāna*), first by subjecting your intention to stripping away (*tajrīd*), then in the breeze of intimacy. Be done with the two worlds so that the breeze of familiarity might blow from the plain of 'He is evermore' (*lam yazal*), the veil of division having been taken from before you and the summons of [divine] grace having reached your soul. [72]

Only thus prepared could Moses be brought to the station of proximity represented by the burning bush:

> Moses saw the fire of [outward] form upon the tree, but in the depths of his heart he saw the fire of love (*ʿishq*) – such a fierce fire, such an overpowering Lord, such a relentless burning!
>
> You placed fire in my heart and oil in my soul
> Then You say 'Keep My secret hidden'!

> Moses, burnt with love and ravaged by want (*faqr*), stood a moment under that tree. The tree that is in the garden of union (*wuṣlat*) has its roots in the earth of love, its branches in the sky of purity, and its leaves are nearness and proximity. Its fragrant blossom is ease and pure joy, and its fruit 'I, even I, am the Lord' [Q. 20:12]. Moses stood beneath that tree, effaced in his attributes (*mutalāshī-yi ṣifāt*), annihilated in his essence (*fānī-yi dhāt*). All of him had become ear, and his differentiation (*tafriqat*) had become non-differentiation (*jamʿ*). Suddenly the call came from God: 'O Moses! "I, even I, am your Lord".' At that moment, the branch of providence (*ʿināyat*) brought forth the fruit of guidance (*hidāyat*). The ocean of friendship (*wilāyat*) sent forth the pearl of sufficiency (*kifāyat*).
> [...]
> Moses donned the robe of propinquity and sipped the wine of intimacy. He saw the honoured place (*ṣadr*) of union (*wuṣlat*) and smelt the fragrant herb of mercy.[73]

Here Maybudī is clearly interpreting Moses' experience of the theophany in the burning bush as his being taken from the state of differentiation (*tafriqat*) to the state of non-differentiation (*jamʿ*) and union (*wuṣlat*).[74] However, he finds the opportunity to discuss other states as the Qur'anic story proceeds.

Haybat and dahshat

In his interpretation of the event which follows the epiphany of the burning bush, namely the miracle of Moses' rod (Q. 20:17–21), Maybudī explains that when the call 'I, even I, am your Lord' reached Moses, he was overcome with awe (*haybat*), bewilderment (*ḥayrat*) and amazement (*dahshat*). This use of the term *ḥayrat* differs from the perplexity that Maybudī depicted in his interpretation of Moses' turning towards Midian; the *ḥayrat* and *dahshat* he is describing here is the bewilderment that accompanies the experience of unveiling, as discussed in chapter seven (pp. 193–5):

> [...] Under this attack of awe there could be no calm, the body could not forbear, nor the heart listen to reason;[75] until the Lord of the Worlds restored his heart with a call of gentleness (*luṭf*), by bringing up the subject of his rod, 'What is in your hand, O Moses?' (Q. 20:17).[76]

To clarify further the state to which Maybudī is alluding here, it will be helpful to refer to another passage where he describes the experience in more detail. The context is his commentary on the *Basmala* at the commencement of *Sūrat al-Mulk* (Q. 67:1):

> *Bismi'llāhi'l-raḥmāni'l-raḥīm.* Hearing the name 'Allāh' necessarily induces awe (*haybat*), and brings about annihilation and absence [from self] (*fanā' wa ghaybat*) [...] The one who hears this word, through that experience of awe, becomes effaced in such a way that not even his imagination will remain to him, and he will elude any sign that might be given [to identify] him.
> [...]
> Then through hearing the name 'al-Raḥmān al-Raḥīm' he is brought from the the narrow pass of stupefaction (*dahshat)* to the open plain of familiarity (*uns*), and his state of annihilation (*fanā'*) changes to subsistence (*baqā'*). This is the way of God, may His greatness be glorified and His names be hallowed: He reveals His divinity (*ilāhiyyat*) which brings about stupefaction and bewilderment (*dahshat wa ḥayrat*). Then He provides a salve (*marham*) by [revealing] His attributes of gentleness and mercy (*luṭf wa raḥmat*). [The name] 'Allāh' is an allusion to His majesty, might and divinity; the names al-Raḥmān and al-Raḥīm are an allusion to His gentleness and mercy.[77]

In light of this passage, it appears that Maybudī is interpreting Moses' experience as a manifestation of that state of *dahshat* which is particularly aroused by the revelation of God's majesty, but which is relieved by the 'opposite' state of *uns*, the latter being brought about by the revelation of His mercy and gentleness, in this case represented by God's raising the subject of the rod.[78] Of course this passage also refers to the states of *fanā'* and *baqā'* – and it should be noted that here again, Maybudī is linking absence from self (*ghaybat*) to annihilation (*fanā'*). But the concomitant states of *fanā'* and *baqā'* are more fully alluded to in the context of Maybudī's interpretation of the theophany on Mount Sinai.

The journey of joy: the theophany on Mount Sinai

The pain of longing and the wine of love

Before Moses was ready for the meeting with his Lord he had to complete a period of retreat and fasting: 'And [remember] when We did appoint (*wa'adnā*) for Moses thirty nights [of solitude] and added to them ten' (Q. 7:142). Maybudī begins his mystical commentary on this verse in the language of love. He speaks firstly of how precious the promise or pledge (*waʿda*) is in love, and how noble it is to sit at the meeting place (waiting for the beloved). The addition of ten days to the period of retreat, which in his *Nawbat* II commentary Maybudī had explained as a penalty for his use of the *miswāk* to sweeten the smell of his breath, he interprets here very differently:

> How sweet is the breaking of an appointment in the religion of love. The master of the way [Anṣārī] said 'The trysts of lovers are pleasing when they are broken,' Then he said:
>
> Delay me and put me off
> Promise me but do not keep your word.
>
> To put off an appointment or delay a meeting by days is not acceptable except in the religion of love (*madhhab-i dūstī*), for in love inconstancy is the essence of constancy, it is the playful aloofness of love (*nāz-i dūstī*). Do you not see that God acted in just this way with Moses?[79]

There is no one word equivalent for the Persian word *nāz* in English. It can mean soothing, caressing or fondling, or it can indicate an independence and self-sufficiency, sometimes even a haughty disdain on the part of the beloved, in contrast to the need and dependence (*niyāz*) of the lover. It can also signify coquetry, cajoling, or flirting, that is, both putting off and giving encouragement at the same time. *Nāz* is desirable because it has the effect of increasing the love and longing for the beloved. Hence Maybudī says that Moses was happy for this delay, for he saw the thirty days as 'capital' (*māya*) and the extra ten days as profit (*sūd*). Also involved here is the idea that the true lover is happy with whatever the beloved dictates, and that as long as the meeting is delayed, it is still to be hoped for and to come. This is a sign of God's love for Moses as well as Moses' love for God.

Commenting on the same verse, Maybudī points out that Moses' state during this period of retreat was such that he had no thought of food or drink, and was not aware of hunger. This was, Maybudī says, because he was 'borne by God (*maḥmūl*) on a journey of grace (*karāmat*), waiting for communion with God (*munājāt*)', whereas on his first journey, when they sent him in search of knowledge to Khiḍr, 'he could not bear even half a day of hunger before he was saying "Bring us our breakfast" (Q. 18:63), for that was a journey of correction (*ta'dīb*) and toil (*mashaqqat*), and he was in the elementary stage of making his way (*rawish*), bearing rather than borne (*mutaḥammil lā maḥmūl*).[80] He was aware of the discomfort because he was with himself (*bā-khwad būd*), and he saw the signs of hunger because he was on the path of created things.'[81]

Maybudī continues by interpreting the events which took place on Mount Sinai as he comments on verse Q. 7:143.

> Moses' journey of seeking was on the night of fire. [...] His journey of joy was 'When Moses came to Our appointed tryst'. Moses came free of himself, lost to himself (*az khwad bī khwad gashta*), having sipped the wine of love from the holy cup. The pain of desire for what he wanted to say was pressing inside him, and from the seas of love the wave of 'Show me [Yourself]' had risen up. He walked about the camp of the Children of Israel and put together the words of their messages and requests, so that when he came into the Divine Presence his conversation would be long.
>
> I hold it forbidden to speak with others
> But with you I speak at length.
>
> But then, when he reached the august state of communing [with God] (*ḥaḍrat-i munājāt*), he became drunk with the wine of longing, burnt by hearing the speech of God, and forgot all that. In that state there was only one thing [that he could] say: 'Show me [Yourself] that I may see You.'[82]
>
> The angels cast the stone of blame at his desire, saying, 'O son of menstruating woman! Do you desire to see the Glorious Lord? [...] What has happened to earth and water that it is speaking of eternity? How can it be fitting for "he-who-was-not-and-then-was" to seek to attain to "He-was-always-and-ever-shall-be?"' Moses, out of his intoxication and rapture answered in the voice of *tafrīd*, 'You must forgive me for I did not come to this by myself. It was His willing, not mine.'
>
> I saw the beloved at my bedside when I awoke.
> You it was who first spoke of love
> Treat us now as You should!

Then, Maybudī relates, God commanded the angels to forgive Moses:

> 'Leave Moses, for one who has drunk the wine of "I have chosen you for Myself" [Q. 20:41] from the cup of "And I have showered you with love from Me" [Q. 20:39)] is bound to be as wine-sick as this.' In those realities of unveiling (*ḥaqā'iq-i mukāshafāt*) Moses tasted the wine of love from the cask of the house of grace. His heart soared with desire for unicity (*fardāniyya*). From the quarter of proximity, a breeze from the intimacy of union blew upon his soul. The fire of love began to show its flames. Patience fled from his heart, and he lost control of himself. He said, 'Show me [Yourself] that I may see You – at least one look.'[83]

Fanāʾ and baqāʾ

Commenting on the words 'And when his Lord revealed His glory to the mountain he sent it crashing down' (Q. 7:143), Maybudī speaks first of the annihilation of the mountain: 'When a fragment of the signs of might and the traces of the glory of oneness reached that mountain, it returned to the state of non-existence and not a sign of it remained'. Then he indicates that the mountain represented the part of Moses' humanity which still remained to be extinguished:[84]

> 'And Moses fell down senseless' [Q. 7:143]. When, in that swoon Moses' existence left him and his humanity was given to the mountain, the essential Reality [of God] (*nuqṭa-yi ḥaqīqī*) was revealed with the words 'Behold it is We. Since you have gone from in between, *We* are seeing (*mā dīdawarīm*).'[85]

Again, to clarify Maybudī's interpretation of Moses' experience we shall have recourse to a passage from elsewhere in the *Kashf al-asrār*. The passage is quoted from Abū Saʿīd Kharrāz, and occurs in the context of Maybudī's commentary on Q. 5:55:

> When God wishes to befriend (*yuwālī*) one of His servants He [firstly] opens to him a door of His remembrance, and when he delights in that remembrance God opens for him the door of propinquity (*qurb*). Then He raises him to the private chamber of intimacy (*uns*), and after that He places him upon the throne of unity (*tawḥīd*). He then lifts the veils from him and brings him into the abode of unicity (*fardāniyya*) and reveals His majesty and grandeur (*jalāl wa ʿaẓama*) and when he beholds (lit. when his sight falls upon) the might and grandeur, he subsists [in God] by his own not being (*bi-lā huwa*). The servant becomes effaced (*fānī*), falling into God's protection (be He glorified), and is freed from any awareness of [lit. claim to] his own selfhood.[86]

Fardāniyya in this passage is equivalent to the phrase *nuqṭa-yi ḥaqīqī* in Maybudī's interpretation. At the manifestation of the essential reality of God (*nuqṭa-yi ḥaqīqī*), Moses' own qualities, symbolised by the mountain, are annihilated, so that in his selflessness only God remains. Thus he attains the state of subsistence in God (*baqāʾ fīʾllāh*), which is alluded to in Maybudī's interpretation by the words '*We* are seeing'.[87]

Tafriqa and jamʿ

In his interpretation of the moment of the theophany (*tajallī*) at Mount Sinai, Maybudī's allusion to the states of *fanāʾ* and *baqāʾ* is framed by two interpretations in which he discusses the need for complete submission to the divine will. It will be recalled that earlier he had indicated that Moses' being effaced in his attributes brought him from the state of differentiation (*tafriqat*) to non-differentiation (*jamʿ*).[88] Here, he is equating *tafriqat* with the persistence of the human will, as opposed to *jamʿ*, which he associates with the annihilation of the human will in the divine will.[89]

Thus, when he comments on God's refusal to grant Moses the vision of Him (Q. 7:143), Maybudī writes:

> It is said that Moses' station at the moment when he heard God say 'You shall not see Me' was higher than at the moment when he said 'Show me [Yourself]', for in the former he was under God's will and in the latter he was with his own will. [...] The latter is *tafriqa* and the former is *jamʿ*. The essence of *jamʿ* is undoubtedly more perfect.[90]

The same theme of submission to the divine will returns in Maybudī's commentary on the words which follow the theophany, 'When he regained consciousness he said "Glory be to You, I turn unto You repentant"'. He begins with what appears to be a theological point:

> When Moses regained consciousness he said 'O Lord! Your absolute perfection is beyond the point that any human being should desire to attain Your Eternity (*ṣamadiyya*), or that a person should seek You by himself, or that a heart or soul should speak of seeing You today [i.e. in this life]. O God! I have repented.'
>
> They [the angels?] said: 'O Moses! Do people give up the battle so soon?[91] Do they turn back so quickly and easily?'

In Maybudī's interpretation of Moses' reply, 'I repent to You', there is a return to the theme of submission to the divine will:

> I wanted union with Him but He wanted my separation
> I abandoned what I wished for what He wished.[92]
>
> What should I have done when my aim was not achieved? Once again I returned to the state of servitude, and the station of the impotence of slavery [...].[93]

Although Maybudī does not here, as in the earlier passage, explicitly equate this submission to the divine will with the state of *jamʿ*, it is implied in the following saying of Aḥmad Ghazzālī: 'Separation that is willed by the Beloved is more union than union that is willed by the lover' (*firāq ba-ikhtiyār-i maʿshūq wiṣāltar buwad az wiṣāl ba-ikhtiyār-i ʿāshiq.*[94]

The journey of toil: Moses and Khiḍr

This most arcane of stories, narrated once in the Qur'an in *Sūrat al-Kahf* (Q. 18:60–82), has raised several questions among Muslim historians and exegetes.[95] First of all, why should Moses have undertaken this arduous journey to find 'one of God's servants' who will teach him of his knowledge? Who exactly was this servant of God, unnamed in the Qur'an, but identified in Islamic tradition as al-Khiḍr or al-Khaḍir (lit. the Green One)? What was his status, and what was the nature of his knowledge that Moses, a prophet, should be sent to learn from him? It is interesting to find that in exoteric commentaries the first three of these questions are discussed in detail, but very little is said about the last, whereas in esoteric commentaries it is by understanding the last – that is, the nature of Khiḍr's knowledge (*ʿilm ladunī*, knowledge from [God's] presence) that answers are provided for the first three.

In his *Nawbat* II commentary on the story, Maybudī narrates two traditions attributed to Ibn ʿAbbās which explain the reason for Moses' being sent in search of Khiḍr. The first tradition relates how once Moses was preaching to the Children of Israel and was asked whether there was anyone more knowledgeable than him. When he answered that there was not, God reprimanded him and Gabriel brought him the message that he was to go to the meeting of the two seas, for there was one wiser than him from whom he was to learn.[96] According to the second tradition, it was Moses who asked God which of His servants was more knowledgeable, to which God replied: 'The one who continues to learn and adds the knowledge of others to his own so that he might find a word which will bring him to My guidance or drive him away from My rejection.' Then Moses prayed to God that if there was one more knowledgeable than himself, he should be guided to him so that he can learn from him. God answered that there was, in the person of Khiḍr, and gave him directions to find him.[97]

Maybudī discusses various opinions about the identity of Khiḍr, or

Khaḍir, and the reasons for his being given this *laqab*, such as the tradition that when he prayed green herbage sprang up around him.[98] On the question of Khiḍr's status, Maybudī explains that some consider him to be a *nabī* (prophet) and others a *walī* (one guided or befriended by God). The preferred opinion appears to be that he was a prophet, perhaps because it was doctrinally less acceptable that a prophet should need to be taught by less than a prophet.[99] In his commentary on Q. 18:66, which begins 'They found one of Our servants to whom We had given mercy (*raḥma*) from Us', Maybudī glosses the word *raḥma* as 'prophesy (*nubuwwa*) and knowledge (*ʿilm*), obedience (*ṭāʿat*) and longevity (*ṭūl al-ḥayāt*)'.[100]

In his *Nawbat* II commentary, Maybudī presents only brief definitions of *ʿilm ladunī* (Q. 18:66), which he first glosses as 'knowledge of the Unseen which others do not know'. Then, in his commentary on Khiḍr's words to Moses, 'You will not be able to bear with me patiently' (v. 68), he has Khiḍr explain: 'because I have been taught the Unseen of my Lord's knowledge'. In his commentary on the next verse (v. 69), 'How could you be patient in matters beyond your comprehension?',[101] he adds the gloss: 'those matters which you do not know, which are outwardly reprehensible (*munkar*), the inner meaning of which differs from their outer meaning.'[102]

Mystical commentaries provide more detailed insights into the nature of *ʿilm ladunī*. In the *Ḥaqāʾiq al-tafsīr*, for example, Sulamī cites Ibn ʿAṭāʾ's definition of *ʿilm ladunī* as 'knowledge without the intermediary of unveiling (*kushūf*) or formal instruction (*talqīn al-ḥurūf*), [which is] received by the witnessing of spirits (*mushāhadat al-arwāḥ*)';[103] while Qāsim states that 'knowledge by elicitation (*istinbāṭ*) is by effort and intermediaries, whereas *ʿilm ladunī* is without either effort or intermediaries'.[104] Qushayrī presents several different but complementary definitions. For example, he defines *ʿilm ladun Allāh* as that which is gained by inspiration (*ilhām*) without the effort (*takalluf*) of seeking (*taṭallub*); that which God teaches the elite among His servants; and that which God teaches His friends concerning that wherein lies the well-being of His servants (*ṣalāḥ ʿibādihi*). This [knowledge] is one, Qushayrī continues, which will benefit God's servants rather than its possessor, and he concludes: 'It is knowledge the possessor of which has no way of denying, nor has he any absolute proof of its correctness, and if you ask him to prove it he will not be able to find any evidence for it. And the most powerful knowledge is the furthest from proof.'[105]

In some Sufi interpretations, understanding the nature of *ʿilm ladunī* may provide a solution for the problem of the respective statuses of Moses and Khiḍr, for in the Qur'anic account, Khiḍr does appear to be 'by far the superior of the two figures'.[106] In Sulamī's *tafsīr*, Fāris solves the problem by seeing Moses as being superior to Khiḍr in one kind of knowledge, and Khiḍr as superior to Moses in another. The apparent limitation of Moses was due to his providential function as a messenger (*rasūl*), but both kinds of knowledge come from one source.

> Moses was more knowledgeable than Khiḍr (may God's peace be upon them both) in that which he learned from God, and Khiḍr was more knowledgeable than Moses concerning that which Moses was impelled into.[107] Furthermore, Moses was given to abide in his qualities that others might learn from his conduct.[108] [...] Khiḍr was in a state of extinction (*fānī*), annihilated (*mustahlak*), and for one who is annihilated there can be no ruling (*ḥukm*). Moses was remaining (*bāqī*) in God and Khiḍr was effaced in God and there was no difference between them because they both spoke from one source (*maʿdan*).[109]

This bears some similarity to the later interpretation of Ibn ʿArabī, who identifies Khiḍr 'with the inward aspect of spiritual understanding as compared with the outward aspect of divine truth expressed in the form of the law represented by Moses'.[110] However, Maybudī's mystical commentary on this story presents an interpretation of *ʿilm ladunī* and the relationship between Moses and Khiḍr which is perhaps more in keeping with a school (or period) of Sufism that was concerned with the states and stations of the spiritual journey rather than the metaphysical understanding of prophetic knowledge versus gnosis. In fact, Maybudī sees Khiḍr's knowledge not as alternative to the knowledge of the law, but as the fruit of the true realisation of it.

> [*ʿIlm ladunī*] is that with which the Lord of the Worlds blessed Khiḍr when He said concerning him 'And We taught him knowledge from Us'. Whoever can dedicate his qualities entirely to the sacred law, We shall engrave the secrets of the knowledge of Reality upon his heart as 'We taught him knowledge from Us'. The one who enunciates this knowledge is the realised person (*muḥaqqaq*) who speaks from his finding [ie. by direct vision]. Light radiates from his speech, acquaintance [with God] is visible in his face and devotion evident from his conduct. A flash of illumination (*barq*) from the Greatest Light shines in his heart, the lamp of gnosis is lit [within him] and the

secrets of the Unseen revealed to him, as was the case with Khiḍr concerning the ship, the boy and the wall.

Maybudī then presents an unusual interpretation to explain the status of Khiḍr in relation to Moses and the reasons for Moses being sent to learn from him:

> See that you do not imagine, even though Moses, God's interlocutor, was sent to Khiḍr's school (*dabīristān*), that Khiḍr was in any way greater than Moses. Absolutely not! For in the Court of Glory, after Muṣṭafā no prophet had that joyful conversation and proximity [with God] that Moses had. But Khiḍr became Moses' furnace of spiritual discipline (*kūra-yi riyāḍat*). It is just as when a person wants to purify silver and puts it into a furnace, the silver is more excellent than the fiery furnace and not the other way round. When Khiḍr said 'You will not be able to bear with me patiently' (v. 68), what [we should] understand by his allusion is: 'O Moses! Your inmost nature has such communion with the evidences of God that you should have said: "Lord show me [Yourself]", and I, Khiḍr, do not have the power or the strength to allow such words to enter my heart, nor even to entertain such a thought. Your greatness will not bear with the affliction of my deprivation, "You will not be able to bear with me patiently."'[111]

In the story as it is told in the Qur'an, Khiḍr gives explanations to justify the apparently outrageous deeds that he has committed: he damaged the ship because it belonged to some poor men, and there was behind it a tyrannous king who was taking every ship by force; he killed the youth because his parents were devout believers and he feared that the boy would oppress them with rebellion and unbelief, and he hoped that God would grant them a better son; and lastly, he repaired the wall without taking payment because it belonged to two orphans in the city, and beneath it was a treasure left to them by their righteous father – God wished that they should come of age and discover the treasure. These explanations could stand on their own from a moral point of view, yet they seem to beg for some sort of mystical interpretation. It is surprising, therefore, to find that almost no commentary is made on these three deeds and Khiḍr's explanations of them in either Sulamī's *Ḥaqāʾiq al-tafsīr* or Qushayrī's *Laṭāʾif al-ishārāt*. Maybudī, however, does comment on them, pointing out the importance of the truths behind them:

As for the wrecking of the ship, the killing of the youth and the repairing of the wall, each one when understood according to the perception of people of ecstatic experience (*ahl-i mawājīd*), alludes to a great principle.

The sea [represents] the sea of gnosis into which more than 120,000 prophets have dived with their people in the hope that in the net (lit. skirt) of their seeking they might catch pearls of *tawḥīd* – for [the Prophet] has said: 'He who knows himself knows his Lord'.[112] The ship represents the ship of humanity, which Khiḍr in his kindness decided to wreck. The owners of the ship were poor men, whose quality was that of profound peace (*sakīna*); concerning such people [the poor] the word from the Court of Eternity has stated, 'He it is that has sent down tranquility into the hearts of the believers' (Q. 48:4), while Muṣṭafā, seeing the felicity which the splendour of truth manifested in their hearts, said, 'O God! Make me live as a poor man, and die as a poor man, and resurrect me in the company of the poor'.[113] When Khiḍr, with the hand of compassion, wrecked the ship of humanity, Moses saw its outer appearance fairly adorned and flourishing from the grooming (*pīrāya*) of the law and the way. He said, 'Did you wreck it to drown its people?' Khiḍr answered that there was behind the flourishing a king, a devil, who had planned an ambush that he might by his force and cunning (*makr*) seize the ship and have access to it day and night, as it is said, 'Satan has become second nature to man.' We removed that adornment and flourishing out of kindness, so that when Satan comes in the guise of a king, he will see the exterior wrecked and will leave it alone.[114]

There is perhaps here a reference to the teachings of the Malāmatiyya. The idea is that virtues and spiritual qualities should be disguised for the sake of the *ghayrat* (jealousy) which protects God's secrets from the unworthy and from drawing the attention of the Satan of complacency.[115] Maybudī continues,

The killing of the youth to which Moses took objection, is an allusion to desire (*munā*) and self-delusion (*pindāsht*) which rear their heads from man's [lower] nature in the battlefield of spiritual discipline and the furnace of spiritual striving. He (Khiḍr) said, 'We have been commanded that we should slay with the sword of jealousy (*ghayrat*) whatever is not in conformity with faith. The result of this self-deception, if it [is allowed] to develop,[116] is that the youth will become an infidel of the Path. We cut him off from the path of *kufr* in the very beginning so that he should proceed once more with [awareness] of his own limits.'

As for the wall which he repaired, it is an allusion to the soul at peace (*nafs-i muṭma'inna*). When he (Khiḍr) saw that Moses had become completely purified (*pāk wa pālūda*) in the furnace of spiritual striving

> (*mujāhadat*), and would have become annihilated, he said, 'O Moses! Do not allow it (the soul) to become annihilated, for in that court it has just claims (*ḥuqūq*) for its service. Building up its exterior as well as taking care of its interior are an obligation for each individual (*farḍ ʿayn*), for it is said "verily your soul has its due". And beneath it treasuries of the secrets of the eternal have been placed. If that wall of the soul is laid low, the treasury of Lordly secrets will be out in the open and any unworthy or base person will covet them. The secret of these words is that the treasure of the truth has been placed in the attributes of humanity, and the condition and constitution[117] of dervishes made its veil.'[118]

It is possible to see in these three interpretations references to the *nafs al-lawwāma*, the *nafs al-makkāra* and the *nafs al-muṭma'ina* respectively.[119] The interpretation of Khiḍr's repairing of the wall seems to embody several teachings. When Maybudī speaks of *ḥuqūq* (privileges or just claims) and, likewise, of the 'qualities of humanity' (*ṣifāt-i bashariyya*) and the 'condition and constitution of dervishes', he may mean an existence and nature granted them by God, after complete purification in the furnace of spiritual discipline.[120] There may also be here the idea of the condition of the veracious (*ṣiddīqān*), whose station is such that attending to their outer needs does not distract them from the contemplation of God, as is explained in the saying of ʿAlī b. Abī Ṭālib referred to above: 'The best among this people are they whose [concern for] this world does not take their attention away from their [concern for] the other world, and whose [concern for] the other world does not take them away from their [concern for] this world.'[121] The idea that if the [purified] soul is destroyed the Lordly secrets will be 'out in the open' and exposed to the unworthy, is perhaps an allusion to the situation of Ḥallāj, who, by his lack of attention to the world, exposed the secrets to those who could not possibly understand them. Also relevant here might be Jāmī's definition of two groups among the people of attainment (*ahl-i wuṣūl*):

> [There are] those to whom the primordial grace and loving-kindness has granted salvation after their being submerged in complete union in the wave of *tawḥīd*, [taking them out] of the belly of the fish of 'annihilation' to the shore of non-differentiation (*tafriqat*) and the arena of permanent subsistence (*baqā'*), so that they might lead the people towards salvation.[122] The others are those who are completely submerged in the ocean of unity, and have been so completely noughted in the belly of the fish of 'annihilation' that never any news or trace comes to the shore of separation and the direction

> of subsistence [...] and the sanctity of perfecting others is not entrusted to them.[123]

The mention of the 'furnace of spiritual discipline' in the interpretation of the killing of the youth, and the 'furnace of spiritual striving' in the interpretation of the repairing of the wall, brings us again to Maybudī's idea that Moses was sent to Khiḍr to be purified through the process of *riyāḍat*. This raises certain questions. Why should Moses need to be subjected to such disciplines when he had already reached the exalted state of communing with God? Is the journey to Khiḍr to be understood as preceding his experiences at Ṭuwā and Mount Sinai, despite the fact that, according to the histories, the journey to Khiḍr took place after the Exodus? One possible answer is that mystical interpretations fall outside the realm of historical chronology; each event narrated in the Qur'an is interpreted for the spiritual significance it conveys in its own right. This can explain the reason why historically Abraham's sacrifice of Ishmael follows his being placed in the fire of Nimrod, but spiritually the fire "follows" the sacrifice, in that Abraham is shown to be in a more perfect station.[124] However, in the case of Moses and Khiḍr another answer is plausible according to Sufi doctrine: a servant may be brought without effort to a very high station and then afterwards be required to pass through the preliminary stages of spiritual discipline. This was explained in Qushayrī's definition of the *murīd* referred to earlier:

> God's way with His seekers differs: most have to go through struggles and trials before they are brought to illumination, whereas some are given unveiling at the beginning, attaining to that which others do not reach even through their toiling. These latter, nevertheless, return from those graces to complete the disciplinary practices they had passed by.[125]

NOTES

1 A Prophetic hadith transmitted by ʿAbd Allāh b. Masʿūd in Muḥammad b. Isḥāq, *Kitāb al-mubtadaʾ waʾl-mabʿath waʾl-maghāzī*, known as *Sīrat Ibn Isḥāq*, ed. M. Ḥāmid Allāh (Rabat, 1976); trans. by A. Guillaume as *The Life of Muhammad: A Translation of Isḥāq's Sīrat Rasūl Allāh* (London, 1955), p. 186. The hadith is also related in Bukhārī, *Saḥīḥ*, *Kitāb badʾ al-khalq*, ch. 6 (al-Malāʾika), no. 1, § 3207, and *Kitāb Aḥādīth al-anbiyāʾ*, ch. 5 (Dhikr Idrīs), no. 1, § 3342.

2 William M. Brinner, 'An Islamic Decalogue', in W.M. Brinner and S.D. Ricks, eds., *Studies in Islamic and Judaic Traditions II* (Atlanta, 1989), p. 68.
3 According to Johns, there are 502 verses in the Qur'an relating to Moses as compared with 235 relating to Abraham, 131 to Noah, and 93 to Jesus. See Anthony H. Johns, 'Moses in the Qur'an', in R.B. Crotty, ed., *The Charles Strong Lectures 1972–1984* (Leiden, 1987), p. 123.
4 Johns (ibid., p. 124) points out that this part of Moses' story is more fully developed in the Medinan period of the revelation of the Qur'an.
5 See for example Q. 2:252, 266; 3:112; 5:75; 10:5–6; 11:96; 16:79, 104; 17:59; 18:9, 17, 57; 20:22–3; 27:81–2; 36:46; 43:46; 45:4, 13. In the Qur'an the rod, the hand and the plagues are all referred to as *āyāt*.
6 The words *kallama'llāhu Mūsā taklīman* (Q. 4:164), from which this *laqab* was probably taken, have been translated by Pickthall, Yusuf Ali, Arberry and Abdel Haleem to mean that God spoke to Moses *directly*. Maybudī explains that the cognate accusative is used here to emphasise that the speech was without intermediary (*Kashf*, II, p. 768). Qushayrī (*Laṭā'if*, I, p. 390) writes that the statement informs us of God's 'singling out (*takhṣīṣihi*) Moses for hearing His speech without intermediary', which is endorsed by the words of Q. 7:144: 'He said, O Moses! I have preferred thee above mankind by My messages and by My speaking unto thee.'
7 Trans. modified with reference to Abdel Haleem's translation.
8 Brinner, 'Islamic Decalogue', p. 72.
9 Maybudī discusses this issue in his *Nawbat* II commentary on this passage, *Kashf*, III, p. 727. He begins by countering the Mu'tazilī claim that God's words 'You shall not see me' (*lan tarānī*) are proof of the impossibility of seeing God, firstly with the argument that wherever the word *lan* is used as a negative it implies a limited time, not an eternity; hence what God means here is either: 'You shall not see Me in this world, with the mortal eye', or: 'You shall not see Me through asking and prayer, but by favour and bestowal', or: 'You shall not see Me before Muhammad and his people'; and secondly with the argument that it is inconceivable that a prophet could make the mistake of requesting that which is impossible. See *Kashf*, III, p. 725. For an account of theological and mystical doctrines concerning the possibility or otherwise of seeing God, see Pourjavady, *Rū'yat-i māh*. On the theme of the vision of God, see also Chaumont, ed., *Autour du regard*.
10 *Kashf*, VII, p. 286. A variant form of this hadith is included in Ibn Abī Shayba, *Kitāb al-muṣannaf*, *Kitāb al-adab*, Section 1071 (Min karh al-naẓar fī kutub ahl al-kitāb), § 6472.
11 See numerous traditions on this subject quoted in Ṭabarī, *Jāmi' al-bayān*, Būlāq edition, XXVII, pp. 26–9; Bayḍāwī, *Anwār al-tanzīl*, pp. 392–3; *Kashf*, IX, pp. 359–60.
12 A hadith narrated by Ka'b al-Aḥbār in Ṭabarī, *Jāmi' al-bayān*, Būlāq edition, XXVII, p. 27.
13 *Kashf*, I, p. 53.
14 *Kashf*, I, pp. 676–7.
15 See p. 210.
16 *Kashf*, V, p. 728.
17 See, for example, *Kashf*, I, pp. 52, 57–8, 104, 194, 195, 198, 262, 677, 780; II,

pp. 6, 93, 568–9; III, pp. 88, 89, 534, 762; IV, pp. 336–7, 397; V, p. 535; VI, pp. 134–5, 188–9; VII, pp. 30, 53, 110, 185–7, 287, 312, 458; VIII, p. 372; IX, pp. 44, 378; X, p. 202.

18 *Kashf*, VIII, p. 234. I have read *talwīn* for *takwīn* here. The passage is almost identical to Qushayrī's commentary on the same verse, *Laṭā'if*, II, p. 217, where the fifth form of the same verbal root (*talawwun*) is used.

19 *Kashf*, II, p. 93. The Moses/Muhammad comparison is also used by Qushayrī in his section on *talwīn* and *tamkīn* in the *Risāla*, pp. 232–5. See also Sulamī's *Risālat al-Malāmatiyya*, ed. ʿAfīfī, repr. in Pourjavady, ed., *Majmūʿa*, p. 403; French tr. Deladrière, p. 30.

20 *Kashf*, III, pp. 89–90.

21 *Kashf*, II, p. 6.

22 Yusuf Ali has the more literal 'Expand me my breast', while Pickthall has 'Relieve my mind', and Abdel Haleem 'Lift up my heart.' However, Abdel Haleem has 'Did We not relieve your heart?' for the same Arabic construction in Q. 94:1.

23 *Kashf*, VI, pp. 134–5.

24 *Kashf*, I, pp. 57–8, 677. See also Moses' prayer to become part of Muhammad's *umma* in al-Ḥakīm al-Tirmidhī, *Khatm al-awliyā'*, ed. ʿU.I. Yaḥyā (Beirut, 1965), p. 317; ʿAyn al-Quḍāt Hamadānī, *Tamhīdāt*, p. 133. This tradition is discussed by Uri Rubin in his *Between Bible and Qur'ān: The Children of Israel and the Islamic Self-Image* (Princeton, 1999), ch. 5, pp. 110ff. See also Ali de Unzaga, 'Conversation', pp. 273–4.

25 Such anecdotes and exhortations do appear in the name of other prophets (quite often David), but they most commonly involve Moses.

26 Ghazzālī, *Kīmiyā*, I, p. 430.

27 *Kashf*, IV, pp. 267–8. See also Ghazzālī, *Kīmiyā*, I, p. 421, where Moses prays: 'O Lord! Where shall I seek Thee?' and God replies: 'With the broken-hearted'; and Rūmī's *Mathnawī*, II, lines 1720ff., for the story of Moses and the shepherd.

28 *Kashf*, VIII, p. 403; III, p. 352.

29 Netton has also compared Moses to Everyman in his article on the story of Moses and Khiḍr, where he sees Moses as having ordinary knowledge, the 'literalist' imagination of Everyman, who is confronted with one endowed with 'supernatural' knowledge in the person of Khiḍr. See Ian R. Netton, 'Theophany as a paradox: Ibn al-ʿArabī's account of al-Khiḍr in his *Fuṣūṣ al-Ḥikam*', *Journal of the Muhyiddin Ibn 'Arabi Society* 11 (1992), pp. 11–22.

30 *Kashf*, III, p. 422. The hadith is listed with the same wording (*lastu ka-aḥadikum*) in Tirmidhī, *Jāmiʿ*, *Abwāb al-ṣawm*, ch. 62 (Bāb mā jā'a fī karāhiyyat al-wiṣāl li'l-ṣā'im), no. 1, § 778; *Abwāb al-aṭʿima*, ch. 14 (Bāb mā jā'a fī rukhṣa fī akal al-thūm maṭbūkhan), no. 3, § 1810; and in Ibn Ḥanbal, *Musnad*, II, p. 23. It is listed with different wording (*lastu mithlakum*) in Muslim, *Saḥīḥ*, *Kitāb al-ṣiyām*, ch. 415 (Bāb al-nahī ʿan al-wiṣāl fi'l-ṣawm), no. 2, § 2427; and in Ibn Ḥanbal, *Musnad*, II, pp. 252 and 377.

31 Nwyia, *Exégèse coranique*, p. 83.

32 Ghazzālī, *Mishkāt al-anwār*, ed. and trans. by D. Buchman as *The Niche of Lights* (Utah, 1998), p. 30.

33 Kāshānī, *Tafsīr al-Qur'ān al-karīm* (Beirut, 1968), I, p. 448.

34 *Ḥaqā'iq*, ed. Nwyia, *Trois œvres inédites*, p. 52.

35 Quoted from Jaʿfar al-Ṣādiq, *Ḥaqā'iq*, ed. Nwyia, 'Le tafsîr mystique', p. 196.

36 *Laṭāʾif*, I, p. 567.
37 *Kashf*, V, p. 728.
38 Khiḍr allows Moses to accompany him on condition that he will not question what he does.
39 *Kashf*, V, pp. 726–7. Kristen Sands has indicated that Maybudī may have derived this scheme of four journeys (through Qushayrī) from al-Thaʿlabī's *Qiṣaṣ al-anbiyāʾ*. However, since al-Thaʿlabī attributes the scheme of five journeys he outlines to 'the sages' (*al-ḥukamāʾ*), it is also possible they were all drawing on a common, possibly oral, source. See K. Sands, *Ṣūfī Commentaries on the Qurʾān in Classical Islam*, London and New York, 2006, p. 89; Abū Isḥāq al-Thaʿlabī, *Qiṣaṣ al-anbiyāʾ al-musammā biʾl-ʿArāʾis al-majālis*, Beirut, 1985, p. 237.
40 The published edition has the incorrect *maḥabba* here, instead of *miḥna*, which is in both MSS A and B.
41 This hadith is listed in Bukhārī, *Ṣaḥīḥ, Kitāb al-riqāq*, ch. 29 (Ḥujibat al-nār biʾl-shahawāt), no. 1, § 6487; and in a number of forms in Ibn Ḥanbal, *Musnad*, II, pp. 333, 354, 380. It is also listed in Nawawī's *Forty Ḥadīth Qudsī*, Arabic text and trans. E. Ibrahim and D. Johnson-Davies (6th repr., Lebanon, 1990), no. 19. The translators note: 'The Arabic word used here is *makārih*, the literal meaning of which is "things which are disliked". In this context it refers to forms of religious discipline, positive and negative, that man usually finds onerous.' See ibid., p. 140, n. 2. However, Maybudī is here putting the hadith to the service of a mystical meaning.
42 *Kashf*, VII, pp. 307–8.
43 See p. 231.
44 *Kashf*, V, p. 117.
45 *Kashf*, VII, p. 308. Maybudī gives no explanation for his use of the word *futūḥ* here, but reference to Qushayrī's *Laṭāʾif* (III, p. 60) is helpful: 'He turned himself in the direction of Midian, without intending Midian or anywhere else, for he went out upon (or for the sake of) spiritual openings (*futūḥ*), and he turned his heart towards his Lord, expecting that He would lead him to the place that was best for him.' In another context (*Kashf*, VIII, p. 169), Maybudī explains *futūḥ* as being something which comes unasked for or unsought from the Unseen. This may either be some form of provision (*rizq* or *ʿaysh*), or it may be knowledge from the Divine Presence (*ʿilm ladunī*) which is not [formally] learned or heard (i.e. received through the oral tradition), but is in conformity with the Sharīʿa, and familiar to the heart.
46 *Istiqāma* implies also integrity, constancy and stability.
47 An expression used in the tradition of *jawānmardī*, for which see pp. 171–2.
48 *Kashf*, VII, p. 309.
49 *Kashf*, VII, pp. 309–10.
50 *Laṭāʾif*, III, p. 62.
51 See ch. 6, n. 32. Qushayrī is also linking the ascent through different states to different levels within the inner make-up of the human being. See ch. 6, especially pp. 156–7 and n. 33.
52 Sarrāj, *Lumaʿ*, p. 340.
53 *Kitāb al-taʿarruf*, p. 87; tr. Arberry, p. 112.
54 *Risāla*, pp. 214ff. Note that in the *Laṭāif* he uses the words *iḥsās biʾl-nafs*.

55 Sarrāj, *Luma'*, p. 340; Qushayrī, *Risāla*, p. 216.
56 *Kashf*, VII, p. 186.
57 *Kashf*, VI, p. 113; V, p. 727.
58 Ibid.
59 *Kashf*, VII, p. 310.
60 Trans. Abdel Haleem.
61 *Kashf*, VII, pp. 185–6.
62 The other fires are: the beneficial fire (*ātash-i manfa'at*), in the context of Q. 56:71; the fire of assistance (*ātash-i ma'ūnat*), Q. 18:96; the fire of humiliation (*ātash-i madhallat*), Q. 7:12; the fire of punishment (*ātash-i 'uqūbat*), Q. 22:72; and the miraculous fire (*ātash-i karāmat*), Q. 21:69.
63 *Kashf*, V, p. 727.
64 *Kashf*, V, p. 727; VI, pp. 112–13. See also *Kashf*, I, p. 674.
65 *Kashf*, VI, p. 112.
66 *Kashf*, VI, p. 113.
67 See pp. 223–4.
68 *Kashf*, IV, p. 287.
69 *Kashf*, VI, p. 113.
70 Again, see pp. 223–4.
71 *Laṭā'if*, II, p. 447.
72 *Kashf*, VI, p. 113.
73 *Kashf*, VII, p. 311.
74 For a discussion of these terms see ch. 6, pp. 151–2, and ch. 8, pp. 219–23.
75 This is almost word for word Maybudī's/Anṣarī's definition of *dahsha*. Again, see p. 194. An interpretation attributed to Ja'far al-Ṣādiq (*Ḥaqā'iq*, ed. Nwyia, 'Le tafsîr mystique', p. 209) speaks of Moses' state of stupefaction (*dahsh*) and annihilation (*fanā'*) at hearing the words of God in the epiphany of the burning bush.
76 *Kashf*, VI, p. 113.
77 *Kashf*, X, p. 178.
78 See ch. 7, n. 88.
79 *Kashf*, III, p. 730. Although Maybudī has attributed the saying and poem in the first paragraph of this passage to *pīr-i ṭarīqat*, by which he usually means Anṣārī, the saying and poem are cited word for word by Sulamī, who attributes them to one of the recent [commentators]. See *Ḥaqā'iq*, ed. 'Imrān, I, p. 237. The poem is also cited by Qushayrī, *Laṭā'if*, I, p. 563. It is quite possible that the saying and poem were current in the oral tradition, and would have been cited by Anṣārī too.
80 In the *Qiṣaṣ al-anbiyā'* tradition, the theophany at Mount Sinai precedes Moses' encounter with Khiḍr, and elsewhere (*Kashf*, V, pp. 726–7) Maybudī places it last on his list of Moses' journeys. But, as indicated on p. 76 ff., Sufi interpretation is not concerned with the historical chronology of events but with their spiritual significance as parables. Clearly, in this context it fits in with the mystical interpretation to understand the journey with Khiḍr as a prior, less advanced journey. On the contrast between 'bearing' and 'being born' see the discussions of *rawish* and *kashish* in relation to Abraham in ch. 8, pp. 219–20.

81 *Kashf*, III, pp. 730–1. This interpretation is also given by Qushayrī in his commentary on Q. 18:63. See *Laṭā'if*, II, p. 406.
82 Thus far, much of this passage appears to have been derived from Qushayrī's interpretation of the same verse. See *Laṭā'if*, I, p. 565.
83 *Kashf*, III, p. 732. Again note that the temporal sequence of events has been eclipsed by the inspired dynamic of the interpretation.
84 This had been represented by the *miswāk* in Kāshānī's commentary. See pp. 249–50.
85 *Kashf*, III, p. 733.
86 *Kashf*, III, p. 156.
87 The same idea is alluded to in Qushayrī's interpretation where he states 'God after the annihilation of Moses was better for Moses than Moses' remaining to Moses', and continues 'the witnessing of the realities through God is more perfect than the creature's remaining through the creature' (*shuhūd al-ḥaqā'iq bi'l-Ḥaqq atamm min baqā' al-khalq bi'l-khalq*). See *Laṭā'if*, I, p. 566. (The Köprülü 117 MS has *shuhūd al-Ḥaqq bi'l-Ḥaqq*, which might be translated as 'witnessing God by or through God', and is perhaps more appropriate here.) In Maybudī's words '*We* are seeing'; the object of vision or witnessing is not specified, as in Qushayrī's interpretation.
88 See p. 258.
89 These two states are discussed in the context of the story of Abraham. See ch. 8, pp. 222–3.
90 *Kashf*, III, p. 733; also in Qushayrī's *Laṭā'if*, I, p. 565.
91 Lit. 'Is the shield to be put down so soon?'
92 This poem appears in Qushayrī's *Laṭā'if*, I, p. 567, and Rūzbihān Baqlī's *'Arā'is al-bayān fī ḥaqā'iq al-Qur'ān*, litho. (Lucknow, 1315/1898), p. 411.
93 *Kashf*, III, p. 734.
94 *Sawāniḥ*, p. 35.
95 For an account of aspects of the development of Muslim exegesis of Q. 18:60–85, and for an assessment of various orientalist opinions concerning the 'provenance' of this Qur'anic story, see Wheeler, *Moses in the Qur'an*.
96 *Kashf*, V, pp. 713–14. A similar tradition is narrated on the authority of Ubayy b. Ka'b in Ṭabarī's *History*, III, trans. W.M. Brinner as *The Children of Israel* (Albany, 1991), p. 5.
97 *Kashf*, V, p. 714. This tradition also appears in Ṭabarī's *History*, III, tr. Brinner, p. 13.
98 *Kashf*, V, p. 718. Among the traditions he cites is one from an unnamed source according to which Khiḍr was actually called Baliya' b. Mulkiyān b. Yaqtān, another that he was a king's son, or a son of Pharaoh. Like Elias (Ilyās) (with whom he would meet every year) he would remain alive as long as the Qur'an was on earth; once the Qur'an left the earth, the two of them would die. For a full discussion of the person of Khiḍr, his identification or otherwise with the prophets Elijah or Elias, see George K. Anderson, *The Legend of the Wandering Jew* (Providence, 1965); Israel Friedlander, 'Khiḍr', *Encyclopaedia of Religion and Ethics*, ed. James Hastings (New York, 1915), VII, pp. 693–5; Nancy K. Sanders, *The Epic of Gilgamesh* (Harmondsworth, 1972); Leo Shaya, 'The Eliatic Function', *Studies in Comparative Religion* (Winter-Spring 1979), pp. 31–40; Irfan

Omar, 'Khiḍr in the Islamic Tradition', *MW* 83/3–4 (1993), pp. 279–91; Wheeler, *Moses in the Qur'an*, pp. 19ff.

99 It may have been for this reason that some agreed with the tradition of Ibn Isḥāq that the Moses who went in search of Khiḍr was another Moses, one Mūsā b. Ifraʾīm b. Yūsuf. But Maybudī (*Kashf*, V, p. 718) discounts this view as being unlikely (*baʿīd*), citing a tradition of Bukhārī on the authority of Saʿīd b. Jubayr. Ṭabarī likewise discounts the view that Khiḍr was not the companion of Moses the prophet. See Ṭabarī, *History*, III, tr. Brinner, pp. 5–6.

100 *Kashf*, V, p. 718.

101 Trans. Abdel Haleem.

102 *Kashf*, V, p. 719. Bayḍāwī says only a little more here: *ʿilm ladunī* is 'knowledge which is concerned with Us and is only learned by Our providence (*tawfīqinā*) and that is the knowledge of the Unseen'. See *Anwār al-tanzīl*, p. 568.

103 *Ḥaqāʾiq*, ed. Nwyia, *Trois œuvres inédites*, p. 83.

104 *Ḥaqāʾiq*, MS Or. 9433, fol. 165b; ed. ʿImrān, I, p. 414. ʿImrān's edition has Haytham instead of Qāsim.

105 *Laṭāʾif*, II, pp. 407–8. Corrected with reference to the MS Köprülü fol. 170a.

106 C.f. Netton, 'Theophany as a paradox'.

107 That is, the tests set by Khiḍr.

108 This is his function as a messenger (*rasūl*).

109 *Ḥaqāʾiq*, MS Or. 9433, fol. 165b; ed. ʿImrān, I, p. 414.

110 Cf. Johns, 'Moses in the Qur'an', p. 137. Austin (*Bezels*, p. 250) explains the difference between the two prophets as illustrating 'the perennial tension between the Sacred Law, represented by Moses and expressing the divine truth, and the mystic, or esoteric knowledge of the gnosis that perceives not only the necessity for and validity of that law, but also the inescapable validity and necessity of those aspects of cosmic becoming that elude the law, as also the synthesis of both in the oneness of being'. Netton ('Theophany as a paradox', p. 20) also states: 'There can logically and finally be no *real* tension between the relative ranks of al-Khaḍir and Moses, between the servant of God and the Messenger of God, if all are manifestations of the Divine Theophany as Paradox.' Again this is reminiscent of Fāris' interpretation quoted above.

111 *Kashf*, V, p. 728.

112 This tradition is listed in Sakhāwī, *Al-Maqāṣid al-ḥasana*, § 1149, and Qārī, *Asrār al-marfūʿa*, § 506. Sakhāwī claims that the saying originates with the third/ninth century mystic Yaḥyā b. Muʿādh. Ghazzālī cites this saying several times in the *Iḥyāʾ*, but not as a hadith of the Prophet, for example Part 3, Book 1, *Kitāb ʿajāʾib al-qalb*, introductory section, p. 112.

113 This hadith is listed in Ibn Māja, *Sunan*, *Abwāb al-zuhd*, ch. 7 (Mujālasat al-fuqarāʾ), no. 2, § 4178, and the *Mishkāt al-masābiḥ*, trans. by J. Robson (Lahore, 1975), II, Book 25 (Words that Soften the Heart), ch. 2 (Excellence of the Poor), Section 2.

114 *Kashf*, V, pp. 728–9.

115 See the discussion of this doctrine in the teachings of the Malāmatiyya on pp. 168ff.

116 Lit. 'if he reaches maturity in it'.

117 Lit. 'mould of the clay' (*aṭwār-i ṭīnat*).

118 *Kashf*, V, p. 729.

119 See discussion p. 159.

120 A comparable teaching is presented in Kāshānī's commentary on *Sūrat Yūsuf*, when Joseph, representing the heart, has been purified from all otherness in the prison of spiritual retreat, and attained to the state of *fanāʾ* or *jamʿ*. On his release, he enters the state of *baqāʾ*, which Kāshānī understands as a return to multiplicity after Unity and to *tafriqa* from *jamʿ*. According to the tradition, Joseph also marries Zulaykhā, who represents the soul at peace (*nafs muṭmaʾinna*), and his marriage to Zulaykhā is interpreted by Kāshānī to mean the heart's compensating the *nafs* with the pleasures it requires after it has become purified – equivalent to the rebuilding of the wall. See Kāshānī, *Tafsīr al-Qurʾān al-karīm,* ed. ʿAlī, I, p. 324.

121 *Kashf*, V, p. 473.

122 This conforms exactly with Maybudī's description of the situation of the Prophet Muhammad (see p. 132). See also Fāris' interpretation of the respective knowledge of Khiḍr and Moses (p. 266), which refers precisely to the contrast between the states of *fanāʾ* and *baqāʾ*.

123 *Nafaḥāt al-uns*, pp. 5–6; trans. in Schimmel, *Mystical Dimensions*, pp. 6–7.

124 This point was alluded to above in this chapter, n. 80.

125 *Risāla*, p. 437.

10

The story of Joseph

The stories of prophets, as noted in the Prolegomenon, tend to be dispersed through the suras of the Qur'an and presented as isolated events, or sequences of events, often with no indication as to the chronological order in which they occurred. One exception is the Qur'anic story of Joseph, which begins with his childhood and ends with his mature years as ruler of Egypt, and is related in its entirety to form the greater part of the twelfth sura of the Qur'an, *Sūrat Yūsuf*.

Introduced as the 'best' or 'fairest' of stories (v. 3), the sequence of events in Joseph's life forms a continuous narrative that is only briefly interrupted by divine comments and exhortations such as 'and God was aware of what they did' (v. 19), or 'God always prevails in His purpose, though most people do not realise it' (v. 21),[1] or 'God rewards the charitable' (v. 88). Often these comments are integrated into the dialogue, as when Jacob says: 'God it is Whose help is to be sought in the (predicament) you are describing' (v. 18) or Joseph: 'This is God's bounty to us and to mankind; but most men do not give thanks' (v. 38). Outside *Sūrat Yūsuf*, the name of the prophet Joseph is mentioned only twice in the Qur'an, in Q. 6:85 and Q. 40:34. The sequence of events in Joseph's life as narrated in *Sūrat Yūsuf* are briefly outlined in table 10.1.

Table 10.1 The life of Joseph

Q. 12:4–20	Joseph relates to his father a dream in which he has seen eleven stars, the sun and moon bowing down before him. Jacob advises him not to tell his brothers. The brothers, out of jealousy, take Joseph from Jacob and cast him into a pit. They bring his shirt to Jacob stained with 'false blood' claiming a wolf has eaten him. Jacob is suspicious of their story. Merchants find Joseph, and he is sold (to them) for a 'trifling sum'.

Q. 12:21–29	In Egypt, Joseph is purchased by ʿAzīz, who advises his wife that they should treat Joseph well, for he might be like a son to them.[2] God 'establishes' him there and teaches him the interpretation of dreams. The lady of the house (Zulaykhā) attempts to seduce him. He (having seen 'the proof of his Lord') flees. The two meet her husband at the door, she tries to implicate Joseph. The fact that his shirt is torn at the back is seen as proof of his innocence.
Q. 12:30–35	Gossip about Zulaykhā's act and her attachment to Joseph spreads among the women of Egypt. Zulaykhā invites them to a feast, and brings Joseph before them. Overwhelmed by the sight of his beauty, they cut their hands by mistake.[3] Zulaykhā threatens Joseph with prison if he does not bend to her will. He chooses prison rather than yield to their desires.
Q. 12:36–54	Joseph interprets the dreams of two fellow prisoners, one of whom, as he predicts, goes to serve the King. After some years, through the ex-prisoner, Joseph is summoned to interpret the King's dream. Before doing so he insists that Zulaykhā exonerate him.
Q. 12:55–82	The King puts Joseph in charge of the storehouses. A famine in Canaan brings Joseph's brothers to Egypt to request provisions. Joseph demands that they bring 'a certain brother' (Benjamin). The brothers return to ask Jacob to allow Benjamin to come. When they return to Egypt, Joseph reveals his identity to Benjamin. As the brothers leave with their provisions, Joseph's cup is found in Benjamin's possession, and he is detained.
Q. 12:83–93	Jacob is informed that Benjamin has been detained. He advocates patience, though he has already gone blind with grieving for Joseph. The brothers return to Egypt to plead for Benjamin's release. Joseph reveals his identity to his brothers. They seek, and are granted his forgiveness. As they leave, Joseph commands that they throw his shirt over his father's face to cure his blindness.
Q. 12:94–101	As the caravan sets out for Canaan, Jacob already senses the fragrance of Joseph's shirt. The shirt cures his blindness, and the brothers ask his (their father's) forgiveness. Joseph receives them all in Egypt. He places his parents on a dais and they all bow down to him, Joseph realises that this is the fulfillment of the dream he had had long ago. Joseph prays to God, showing appreciation for His blessings and protection, and asking that he should die in submission (to God) and be one of the righteous.

As can be seen from the summary in table 10.1, the key events in Joseph's life are related in chronological sequence. Yet, as several comparative and textual studies have demonstrated, the Qur'anic account of Joseph is far from being a chronicle of the prophet's life.[4] Moreover, while in the Biblical account, Joseph's life 'continues the story of the patriarchs of the family of Abraham'[5] and 'constitutes a key moment in the history of the Hebrew people',[6] the Qur'anic story of Joseph is 'self-contained – enclosed by the prediction of the (Joseph's) initial dream and its fulfillment'.[7] In addition to its not being 'part of a larger historical narrative', the Qur'anic story is 'decontextualised' in another way: apart from Joseph and Jacob, no other character is directly named.[8] Furthermore, an economy of style in the Qur'anic account, which is predominantly dialogue-led, allows the action to move forward as a sequence of 'dramatic scenes'.[9] All these features serve to focus the mind on the significance of the events themselves, and on the lessons of the story.

The didactic function of the story of Joseph, and of other prophets, is clearly stated both early on and in the concluding verse of the sura: 'In [the story of] Joseph and his brothers there are signs for those who have inquiring [minds]' (v. 7); 'and in their [the messengers'] story there is a lesson (*ʿibra*) for men of understanding' (v. 111). The two over-riding 'lessons' or themes in the Qur'anic story of Joseph seem to be firstly, the invincibility of the divine will – the inevitable prevailing of *taqdīr* (God's pre-ordaining and determining of things) over *tadbīr* (human contrivance and design), and secondly, God's guidance and protection of the righteous. At a more personal level, the *ʿibra* is said to be a message of reassurance to Muhammad, especially since the sura was revealed during a period of extreme hardship for the Prophet.[10]

Joseph, *al-Ṣiddīq*

Joseph's *laqab*, like that of other prophets, has its origin in the Qur'an. *Al-Ṣiddīq*, an intensive adjectival form of the verbal root *Ṣ.D.Q.*, may be translated as 'the extremely veracious, completely truthful'.[11] Joseph is addressed with this title by the 'cup-bearer' (his ex-fellow prisoner) when he comes to request an interpretation for the king's dream (v. 46). In this context, therefore, Joseph's title may allude to his complete veracity both in the interpretation of dreams and foretelling of events. However, another form of the same root, *Ṣ.D.Q.*, occurs in two other contexts in the sura: 'If his shirt is torn from behind then she has lied and he is truthful (lit. one of the truthful, *ṣādiqūn*) (v. 27), and 'Now the truth is out. I asked of him an evil act, and he is indeed truthful' (v. 51). Thus, the *laqab* might also serve to assert the fact that Joseph spoke the truth (as opposed to Zulaykhā, who lied), a fact which is inseparably associated with the chastity of the prophet and his resistance (albeit with God's intervention) to Zulaykhā's attempts to seduce him.

The Qur'an clearly shows Joseph to be in the line of Abrahamic prophets. In one of two references to Joseph which occur outside *Sūrat Yūsuf* it is said: 'Joseph brought you clear proofs before, yet you did not cease to doubt what he brought you until, when he died, you said: God will not send any messengers after him' (Q. 40:34); while in *Sūrat Yūsuf* itself we see Joseph in his prophetic role when he preaches to his fellow prisoners (vs. 37–40), and when he addresses his brothers (vs. 92, 98) and his father (v. 100), and when he prays (v. 101).

Like his father, who is referred to as 'a lord of knowledge' (v. 68), Joseph is endowed with God-given wisdom and understanding. The emphasis throughout the sura is that knowledge is divinely taught: 'Thus your Lord will teach you the interpretation of events (*aḥādīth*)' (v. 6); Jacob is a lord of (or possessed of) knowledge 'because We taught him' (v. 68); 'We raise by grades of mercy whomsoever We will, and above every lord of knowledge there is one more knowing' (v. 76), and 'When he reached his prime, We gave him knowledge (*ḥukm*) and wisdom (*'ilm*)' (v. 22).[12] Joseph himself acknowledges that his knowledge has been taught him by God (v. 37).

Joseph's knowledge evidently extends beyond the realm of dream interpretation to the practical domain of administration.[13] He is, by his own admission a 'skilled custodian' (*ḥafīẓ 'alīm*) and the choice of words here not only confirms his trustworthiness, as acknowledged by the king (v. 54), but his ability to administer wisely the supplies of the kingdom. Moreover, he is shown to have diplomacy and psychological insight, firstly when he ensures that his name is cleared before entering the presence of the king, and secondly in the manner in which he treats his brothers when they come to Egypt. Other virtues which Joseph displays in the Qur'anic story are humility (v. 53), a sense of honour and awareness of his obligation to his master, 'Azīz, (vs. 23 and 52), and justice (v. 79).

However, more than any of these qualities, more even than the virtue of truthfulness for which he is named al-Ṣiddīq, the attribute which is most associated with the prophet Joseph is his great beauty.[14] While this is not explicitly mentioned in the Qur'an, it is implied in the astonishment of the women of Egypt, who on seeing him utter, 'This is not a human being, this is no other than a gracious angel' (v. 31). Joseph's beauty is, besides, firmly attested in a number of Prophetic traditions. In his history, Ṭabarī cites a hadith transmitted through Anas which states that half the beauty in the world was given to Joseph and his mother Rachel, while the other half was shared out among the rest of creation.[15] Maybudī relates a similar tradition, without *isnād*, according to which half of all beauty was given to Joseph alone,[16] and another which tells how Adam, having been commanded to give Joseph a paternal gift, declares: 'I have bestowed on him two thirds of the beauty of all my offspring.'[17] In another hadith cited by Maybudī, the Prophet relates that on the occasion of his heavenly ascent (*miʿrāj*), he saw the prophet Joseph 'like a full moon'.[18] As a metaphor, the full moon suggests not only great beauty but also radiance. The luminosity of Joseph's presence is described in a saying of Isḥāq b. ʿAbd Allāh b. Abī Farwa (d. 144/761), who relates: 'When Joseph passed through the streets of Egypt his face lit up the walls [of the city] as the sun's rays light up the world.'[19]

According to Sufi exegesis, this radiance emanated not from Joseph's external beauty, but from his inner qualities. Maybudī cites the observation of Ibn ʿAṭā' that there are two kinds of beauty: outward and inward.[20] He (Maybudī) then explains that outward beauty is adornment of character (*ārāyish-i khalq*) and fair appearance (*ṣūrat-i zībā*), whereas inward beauty is impeccability of character (*kamāl-i khalq*) and virtuous conduct (*sīrat-i nīkū*). Joseph's brothers saw no more than his outer beauty, so it is not surprising that they sold him for a paltry sum, but ʿAzīz, having been shown just one atom of that inner beauty, said 'Receive him honourably' (v. 21).[21]

The significance of Joseph's beauty, both in Islamic literature in general and in Sufi exegesis in particular, is that it made him the object of love. It will be seen, in fact, that Joseph differs from the prophets Abraham and Moses in that the mystical interpretation of his story does not centre on his Qur'anic *laqab*.[22] It is rather as the embodiment of perfect beauty that he becomes not only the object of love at the human level but also a symbol of the divine Beloved.

The mystical interpretation

Two themes are central to Maybudī's mystical interpretation of the story of Joseph. The first springs from the predominant 'lesson' of the sura itself, namely that God is the Controller and Provider of all things and that man must have complete trust (*tawakkul*) in Him. The second, only a subsidiary theme in the Qur'anic story but given much greater prominence by Maybudī, is the theme of love. The story of Joseph, therefore, provides Maybudī with the scope to expound and develop two doctrines that are, according to his understanding, fundamental to the mystical path.

It is only in the first of these two themes that Joseph acts as a subject who could be viewed as a model or prototype of the spiritual wayfarer. Here, he has an active role, along with his brothers, his father Jacob and, to a lesser extent, Zulaykhā. In the second theme, the theme of love, Joseph has no path to travel; that is to say, we see him, momentarily, as the perfect loving son, grieving in separation from his father, but not in the state of *ḍalāl* (lit. aberration), but according to some interpreters 'excessive love' for which both Jacob (vs. 8 and 95) and Zulaykhā (v. 30) are criticised.[23] In this theme, Joseph's role is principally as the object of Jacob's and Zulaykhā's love, which is where, from a mystical point of view, both the interest and the development lies.

God as controller and provider of all things

This theme which, as has been stated, is central to the Qur'anic story of Joseph, is highlighted at various points in Maybudī's mystical commentary on the sura. Joseph's brothers attempted by their scheming (*makr*) 'to cast one who was singled out for favour into the dust of degradation. They could not, for they had no power over a destiny which had been dealt out and the decree that had been issued'.[24] Likewise, 'Zulaykhā had a stratagem, by her mortal devising (*tadbīr-i basharī*) she locked the doors of her private chamber, but God, by His pre-eternal decree (*taqdīr-i azalī*) opened the doors of protection from sin (*ʿiṣmat*) to Joseph'.[25]

While affliction is often an inescapable part of the destiny of human beings – Maybudī even states that affliction (*balāʾ*) *is* divine preordination (*qaḍāʾ*), however much it may not be what we choose or like[26] – human beings may, paradoxically, bring affliction upon themselves by their actions. In Maybudī's mystical commentary on *Sūrat Yūsuf*, we discover that there can be two reasons for this humanly precipitated suffering, both of which are essentially a form of deviation from the realisation of divine unity (*tawḥīd*). It may be, as we shall see later, a consequence of loving other than God, or it may be due to a lapse in awareness of God as the sole source of all goodness and protection. Thus, according to a comment quoted from Ibn ʿAṭāʾ, Jacob made the mistake of relying on the number of Joseph's brothers, taking assurance from their claim 'We shall take good care of him' (v. 12),[27] to which Maybudī adds: 'Inevitably, that prop (*takya-gāh*) was made into an ambush of suffering, and the very spot where he had placed his trust became a source of treachery. But that day when he sent Benjamin to Egypt, he said "God is the best protector" (v. 64), so Benjamin was returned to him quickly.'

Joseph himself is twice shown to suffer the consequences of not having complete trust in God's protection. On the first occasion, when Zulaykhā threatens him with imprisonment if he does not bend to her will, he says, 'Prison is dearer to me than that which they are urging me [to do...]' (v. 33). Maybudī observes that by expressing a preference Joseph has made a choice. He relates the adage 'Choosing goes hand in hand with being tested' (*al-ikhtiyār maqrūn al-ikhtibār*),[28] and then explains:

> Joseph made a choice for himself; of course he became embroiled in trials and testing [...] for as the tradition relates 'If he had asked for safety (*ʿāfiyat*) and not asked for prison, it would have been granted to him'.[29] But he chose affliction (*balāʾ*), so veracity (*ṣidq*) in [that preference for] affliction was demanded of him, and his suffering increased.[30]

On the second occasion, Joseph asks the fellow prisoner who was destined to become cup-bearer to the king to 'remember me in the presence of your lord' (v. 42). Here Maybudī cites a well-known hadith of the Prophet transmitted through al-Ḥasan: 'May God have mercy on my brother Joseph. If he had not said "Remember me in the presence of your lord"' he would not have remained in prison for a further seven years after the five.'[31]

Conversely, a person may be rewarded for submitting to the divine 'control' of things. According to tradition, after many years of suffering in separation from Joseph, and after the death of ʿAzīz, Zulaykhā prays that she should be able to marry Joseph. Maybudī relates that Gabriel is sent to Joseph with this message from God: 'Until now Zulaykhā sought you by her own cunning and scheming, and of course she did not gain you. Now she seeks you from Me, and for your sake has made her peace with Me. Go and fulfill her need.'[32]

Love

While the subject of divine pre-ordination (*taqdīr*) does have importance in Maybudī's mystical interpretation of the story of Joseph, there can be no doubt that pride of place has been given to the theme of love. So central is love to his interpretation that in his mystical commentary on verse 3, 'Verily We narrate unto thee the best of stories', he identifies the story of Joseph simply as 'the story of lover and beloved.[33] He writes:

> How beautiful is the story of Joseph! It is a story of lover and beloved, a tale of separation and union. A grief-stricken soul is needed to read the story of those who suffer; a lover is needed to know the pain of love and the agony that lovers go through. Only one who has been burnt in the fire of love can be moved by the burning anguish of those who long for the Beloved. I'm the slave of that yearning soul which burns with passion at the end of the Beloved's street. I'm jealous of the eye that weeps in absence of the loved One's love. I'll sacrifice heart and soul for that crazed lover who tells the story of those in love.
>
> In the town my heart tends towards that one, sweetheart,
> Who talks about your love.[34]

In this passage it can be seen how, in developing the theme of love, Maybudī has made liberal use of imagery and motifs associated with love poetry, such as the one who suffers (*dardzadaʾī*) and who is burnt (*sūkhtaʾī*) by love, the one who sighs at the end of the Beloved's street (*bar sar-i kūy-i dūst*) and rains down tears (*ashk bārad*). We may also note in passing some aspects of Maybudī's rhetoric, for example his use of repetition – 'a grief-stricken soul is needed (*dardzadaʾī bāyad*)', 'a lover is needed (*ʿāshiqī bāyad*)' and so on – and the way he is indirectly calling for these qualities, the qualities of the lover, from his listener or reader. Then, in order to press this demand further, he shows how humble, jealous and devoted he feels towards one who has such qualities, at the same time indicating his own commitment to the way of love.

In his commentary on the story of Joseph, Maybudī explores not only the many states and stages experienced in the way of love, but also love at its various levels, from the love of one human being for another to the purest love of God. Since, as Maybudī demonstrates, love at the human level may lead to, or be a manifestation of, divine love – that is, mystical love or love for God (*ʿishq-i ilāhī*) – it is not surprising to find correspondences and, at times overlapping between these levels. For example, the trials undergone by, and the demands made upon the lover of another human being are equally to be borne by the lover of God. Both suffer intense pain in separation from their beloved, both are expected to face the blame of others for their love, and both may experience jealousy. These correspondences are clearly demonstrated in Maybudī's commentary, and show how naturally human love can become a symbol for mystical love.

Zulaykhā's love for Joseph

The Qur'anic verses relating to 'the wife of ʿAzīz' tell of the following: she is instructed by her husband to treat Joseph well; she becomes infatuated with Joseph; she attempts to seduce him and then to implicate him; she presents him to the women of Egypt; she threatens to imprison him; and, later, she admits her own guilt before the king. Muslim tradition adds much detail to this account and resolves Zulaykhā's story with a happy ending. According to this tradition, after admitting her guilt she suffers for years in separation from Joseph, losing her sight and beauty and becoming old, bent and destitute, languishing in an ever-increasing love for Joseph. Finally, after the death of ʿAzīz, she abandons idolatry, adopts the religion of Joseph, miraculously regains her youth and beauty, marries Joseph and bears him two sons.[35] Thus resolved, Zulaykhā's story could provide an important moral and religious teaching, demonstrating the rewards for repentance from sin and for adopting the true faith. It could also, as in Maybudī's commentary, be interpreted as the story of a journey from human to divine love.

From human to divine love

Maybudī presents this interpretation of Zulaykhā's love in the *Nawbat* II sections of the *Kashf al-asrār*. However, since the transformation from the love of a human being to the love of God was understood to be, in some cases, a first step on the way of mystical love,[36] and since the larger story of this transformation acts as a frame for the mystical interpretations, it will be discussed here.

Maybudī's somewhat sympathetic treatment of Zulaykhā from the beginning seems to prefigure the noble outcome of her story. It also prepares us for her role not simply as the temptress of Joseph but also, analogically, as a lover of God.[37] While much of the material in Maybudī's account is derived from traditional sources, the details and comments that he adds seem to slant it in Zulaykhā's favour.[38] For example, we learn that when bidding for Joseph begins, Zulaykhā, out of good manners (*adab*), remains silent and waits for her husband to make the first offer. That done, however, she insists that the money for his purchase should come entirely from her own purse.[39] Unlike Joseph's brothers who sold him for a paltry sum, Zulaykhā (and ʿAzīz) could see beyond Joseph's outward beauty to his inner qualities which is why they were prepared to pay so much for him.[40]

The powerful effect which Joseph's beauty had on people, and especially women, is indicated not only in the Qur'an, in the episode of the women of Egypt, but in a number of traditions. One such tradition relates that when Joseph was first presented before the public for auction 'several girls began to menstruate and countless people became infatuated with him (*dar fitna uftādand*)'.[41] Another tradition tells how, once established in ʿAzīz's house, Joseph would busy himself with his devotions and would recite the scriptures in such a beautiful voice that 'no-one could hear it without being entranced by it' (again, *dar fitna uftādī*).[42] It is no surprise, then, that Zulaykhā should become enamoured of him. She invites Joseph to come and read to her every day, even though she admits that she can understand none of it. As he reads to her she falls completely in love with him (*Zulaykhā-rā dar dil ʿishq-i Yūsuf bar kamāl būd*).[43] Yet, Maybudī adds, 'she constrained herself to endure it and be patient, taking consolation in the fact that he would sit and talk to her'.[44] In this scene, and likewise later in the seduction scene, Joseph seems to be in the role of teacher to Zulaykhā. For example, when out of shame she naively covers her idols lest they witness her sin, Joseph says, 'Do you feel shame before one who neither hears nor sees nor has the power to harm or benefit, yet you have no shame before the One Who created the world and all that is in it and Who knows the state of all people whether it be revealed or hidden?'[45]

Maybudī certainly relates, from traditional accounts, some of the wiles which Zulaykhā uses in her attempt to seduce Joseph: for example, her requesting her husband to have a special mansion built, furnished with idols, for the adornment of which she sent for gold and jewels to be brought from her mother and brothers, who were then rulers of Yemen;[46] or her lowering her veil in front of Joseph, to reveal her head and neck.[47] Yet, even in the midst of her attempt to seduce Joseph, Maybudī has her profess her ardent love for him, accusing him of hard-heartedness and reciting the following poem:

> God knows (*yaʿlamu'llāh*), my darling, if I can tell night from day,
> For night and day I am dazed (*madhūsh*) and confused (*sargardān*) in my love for you.[48]

The inclusion of this love poem, although it occurs in the *Nawbat* II section, suggests that Zulaykhā is being viewed here not simply as the would-be seductress of Joseph, but as the epitome of all lovers, including lovers of God. Indeed, from this point on, Zulaykhā appears more in the *Nawbat* III sections of the commentary. The *Nawbat* II sections mainly clarify what is recounted in the sura itself, up to the commentary on Zulaykhā's admission of her guilt before Joseph and the king (vs. 51). Here, we are presented with the traditional account, outlined earlier, of Zulaykhā's years of suffering and grief, followed by her conversion to the religion of Joseph and, finally, her marriage to him. Significantly, Maybudī adds narrative detail to this account, in order to emphasize the magnitude of her suffering, destitution and helplessness, all of which, according to his understanding, will certainly have aided her spiritual transformation.[49] To demonstrate that Zulaykhā has truly been led from human love to divine love, Maybudī relates how she becomes so avid in her devotions to God that she is not free for a moment. When Joseph desires to be alone with her she refuses. He expresses concern that she might have ceased to love him, at which she replies that of course she loves him but, 'that time when I sought you I was heedless of God, now that I have come to know Him, I will not attend to you until I have completed my worship of Him'.[50]

From *ghalabāt-i ʿishq* to *wilāyat-i ʿishq*

In his commentary on the words 'And they raced with one another to the door and she tore his shirt from behind' (v. 25), Maybudī observes that 'Joseph was fleeing and Zulaykhā was running after. The former had seen proof of his Lord and was overcome (*maghlūb*) with fear of God Most High; the latter was driven to insanity by the overwhelming(s) of love (*ghalabāt-i ʿishq*)'.[51]

As a Sufi term, the word *ghalaba* (pl. *ghalabāt*)has been defined by Kalābādhī as a 'state which arises in the servant during which he can neither perceive causes nor observe propriety of conduct'.[52] In his commentary on Kalābādhī's *Kitāb al-taʿarruf*, Mustamlī explains that the *ghalaba* may be the 'overwhelming of a sense of awe at the majesty and greatness of God, such that even the calamity of hell disappears from the servant's mind, or an awareness of the generosity and grace of God such that all other blessings fade from his mind'.[53] Kalābādhī has placed his chapter on *ghalaba* immediately before the chapter on *sukr* (intoxication), while, in the *Kashf al-maḥjūb*, Hujwīrī has likewise linked the state of *ghalaba* (translated by Nicholson as 'rapture') to intoxication (*sukr*),[54] and in another passage, where Hujwīrī places the state of sobriety (*ṣaḥw*) in opposition to intoxication, he places the state of *tamkīn* (stability) in opposition to *ghalabāt*.[55] The relevance of the opposing of these two terms will be seen later in Maybudī's interpretation of Zulaykhā's story.

The use of the Sufi term, *ghalabāt*, although it occurs in the *Nawbat* II section of Maybudī's commentary, is perhaps another indication of the ambiguity of, and the overlapping between, Zulaykhā's role as lover of Joseph and as prototype of the lover of God. Turning to the *Nawbat* III section and the mystical commentary on the same verse (v. 25), we find that Maybudī again uses the words fleeing (*gurīzān*) and running (*dawān*), recalling the earlier '*ghalabāt*' passage. However, here we learn of the deficiency of Zulaykhā's love. Commenting on the second part of the verse, 'and they met her lord and master at the door. She said: What shall be the reward for one who wishes to dishonour your wife [...]?', Maybudī explains that Zulaykhā put the blame on Joseph because 'there was no truth (*ṣidq*) in her love. Of course, as a result, there was no truth in her words. She did not choose Joseph above herself and did not subdue her own self-interest'.[56] It was only later, when 'the love of Joseph had gained complete dominion (*wilāyat*) over her breast, and reached the pericardium of her heart, that she set aside her own interest and spoke the truth: "Now the truth is out. I asked of him an evil act, and he is surely of the truthful"' (v. 51).[57] The mention in this passage of the pericardium of the heart (*shaghāf*) leads Maybudī to verse 30, in which the related word *shaghafa* is used: 'Indeed he has smitten her to the heart with love'. This presents him with the opportunity to develop further the doctrine of complete possession or domination (*wilāyat*) by love.

First, he explains that the *shaghāf* is the innermost of five layers or membranes (*parda*) of the heart. The first layer is the *ṣadr*, seat of the covenant of Islam (*mustaqarr-i ʿahd-i islām*); the second is the *qalb*, locus of the light of faith (*maḥall-i nūr-i īmān*); the third is the *fuʾād*, site of the glance of God (*mawḍiʿ-i naẓar-i Ḥaqq*); the fourth is the *sirr*, safe deposit of the treasure of sincerity (*mustawdaʿ-i ganj-i ikhlāṣ*), and the fifth is the *shaghāf*, the place where the caravans of love unload (*maḥaṭṭ-i raḥl-i ʿishq*).[58] Maybudī then quotes the following definition from Sumnūn al-Muḥibb:

> They speak of *shaghāf* when the membranes of the heart become full of love, so that nothing [else] remains there. [...] This is as it was when Majnūn was asked: 'Who is more excellent, Abū Bakr or ʿUmar?' and replied: 'Laylā is more beautiful'![59]

The explanation is completed with a comment cited in the name of Jaʿfar al-Ṣādiq: 'The *shaghāf* is like a cloud;[60] it obscures his (i.e. the lover's) heart from contemplating other than Him (i.e. the Beloved) and from preoccupation with other than Him.'[61]

The inevitable consequence of complete conquest by love is blame. It is here that Zulaykhā's two roles as lover of Joseph and lover of God unquestionably overlap. Maybudī writes:

> When that poor creature succumbed to Joseph, and love had taken complete possession of her, the tongues of censure began to wag and the women of Egypt shot arrows of blame at her saying: 'The ruler's wife is asking of her slave-boy an evil act [...]' [v. 30)] She took comfort in the thought that a fair beloved is worth being blamed for.

He continues:

> The very capital of lovers is blame. How can one who does not bear the burden of blame even be called a lover? [Zulaykhā] said to herself, 'Yes, I shall show them my beloved so they shall know that,
>
> Love for such a face, is a crown upon one's head
> Even though there come from it a hundred thousand headaches!'

The state of *wilāyat-i ʿishq* is now linked to the state of stability (*tamkīn*) as Maybudī comments on the scene in which Zulaykhā presents Joseph before the women of Egypt. He relates that when they saw the beauty of Joseph,

> some fainted, some died, some were dazed and others bewildered (*sarāsīma wa mutaḥayyir*). They all said: 'This is not a human being, this is no other than a gracious angel' [Q. 12:31].[62]

Maybudī observes that when Joseph revealed his beauty, the women of Egypt cut their hands but Zulaykhā did not. They all became bewildered and showed alteration in their state (*mutaḥayyir wa mutaghayyir gashtand*), whereas Zulaykhā did not. He explains:

> This is because her state had become strong (*qawī*) due to the prolongation of her encounter with him. The vision of him had become her food and custom (*ghadhāʾ wa ʿādat*), so it did not affect her. Alteration (*taghayyur*) is an attribute of novices in this affair [i.e. the mystical path]; when their experience of reality (*maʿnā*) becomes prolonged, then alteration ceases.[63]

To endorse this teaching further, Maybudī continues by quoting a saying of Abū Bakr al-Ṣiddīq, in which he relates that he once saw a man who had recently entered Islam weeping, upon which he remarked:

> This is how we were until our hearts became hardened (*qasat qulūbunā*), that is to say, became strong and firm. It is the same with an earthenware pot: the first time water is poured into it, it hisses, but once it has got accustomed to the water and absorbed it, then it no longer makes any sound.[64]

This tradition of Abū Bakr appears in another passage in the *Kashf al-asrār* where the connection between *wilāyat-i ʿishq* and *tamkīn* (or *tamakkun*) is confirmed and further clarified. Here, Maybudī is commenting on the words 'Then your hearts were hardened' (Q. 2:74). Having stated that in the ignorant, hardness of heart is unkindness and cruelty and remoteness from the way of God, he explains that in mystics and masters of truth and purity, it is strength of heart, stability (*tamakkun*), perfection of gnosis, and the state of purity (*ṣafwat*). At this point he alludes to the aforementioned saying of Abū Bakr and explains:

> The novice shouts and groans and wails because his love [or the love of God, *ʿishq-i way*] has not yet gained its complete dominion over him. Once the affair reaches its perfection, purity of gnosis (*ṣafwat-i maʿrifa*) has become strong, and the sultan of love has completely gained its dominion (*wilāyat*) over him, all that crying and wailing ceases and is replaced by happiness and joy. So the poet said:
>
> To begin with, when love for my beloved was new to me,
> My neighbour could not sleep at night for my wailing,
> But as my love increased my wailing decreased,
> When fire fully takes hold, it gives off less smoke.[65]

To summarise: in the beginning, Zulaykhā was enraptured and overwhelmed by love, but this love was not 'true', that is to say it had neither penetrated the depths of her being, nor gained complete dominion over her. Later, however, as love increased and took total possession of her, she attained a state of stability (*tamkīn*). Unlike the women of Egypt who, as novices in love, were overcome by the sight of Joseph and showed alteration and confusion in their state, Zulaykhā was now an adept. She was no longer outwardly affected by her experience of love, since there was no longer anything in her consciousness but the beloved.

Jacob's love for Joseph

With the exception of one passage, Jacob is consistently presented in Maybudī's mystical commentary as a prototype of the lover of God.[66] As Jacob's beloved, however, Joseph's role shifts in the course of Maybudī's exposition of different aspects of the way of mystical love. At different points he is a human focus for the love of God, a symbol of the divine Beloved, a rival distracting Jacob from the love of God, and an earthly mirror for the contemplation of God.

Love's suffering

Jacob's centrality as prototype of lover of God is indicated by the fact that he is introduced even before Joseph in Maybudī's mystical commentary. Having identified 'the best of stories' as being 'the story of lover and beloved, separation and union' (see the passage quoted on p. 285), he writes:

> When the seeds of the pain of love were being scattered in the hearts of [God's] friends, Jacob was [already] on the highway of this affair. Stripped of all otherness (*tajrīd*) and in pure isolation for God (*tafrīd*), he had been brought to [a state of] sincerity (*ikhlāṣ*) in the crucible of spiritual discipline (*riyāḍat*) and had become worthy of the seed of the pain of love.[67]

Jacob was, therefore, in pre-eternity destined to be an adept in the way of divine love. In a state of spiritual perfection, he was ready to receive the seed of the pain of love. Maybudī continues:

> When that seed reached the soil of his heart, it was tended with the water of 'He poured upon them of His light',[68] until the jasmine of the covenant [of love] (*'abhar-i 'ahd*) came up.[69]

Hitherto, the pain which was latent in that seed of love had not manifested itself, nor had Jacob's love been tested through the trials of suffering. For this to take place, the divine love must be turned towards a human object:

> Then by way of pretext (*bahāna*), the Joseph-beauty was made into his *qibla*, humanity was shown the way to its own kind,[70] and the cry went up 'Jacob's neck has been hooked in the snare of desire for Joseph'. From behind the veil of jealousy the very essence of truth (*nuqṭa-yi ḥaqīqat*) said 'Call me Arsalān so no-one should know who I am'.[71]

Divine love took on the form of love for Joseph not only in order that Jacob's love should be perfected through suffering, but also, as can be seen in the previous passage, so that Jacob's love of God, Who is referred to here as the very essence of truth, could be concealed (by the veil of jealousy) from others who could not understand it (Joseph's brothers). This explains the statement 'Call me Arsalān so that no-one should know who I am'.[72] Maybudī develops the idea of Joseph as a '*qibla*' for divine love later in his commentary, but for the time being he takes up the theme of suffering.

In order to experience more fully the bitterness of separation, Jacob was first to taste the sweetness of union. We are told that Joseph's brothers saw their father 'with that blossoming spring, that full moon seated before him, the mat of union spread out in the tent of his beauty'.[73] The brothers beg their father to allow Joseph to accompany them, and Jacob gives his consent; not, Maybudī points out, at their request, but at Joseph's. Here Jacob, unlike Zulaykhā, is the true lover, constantly wishing to fulfill the beloved's wish, and preferring his own discomfort and hardship (for the beloved's sake) over his own pleasure.[74]

The traditional account of Jacob's subsequent period of suffering in separation from Joseph, and of mourning in the 'House of Sorrows' (*bayt al-aḥzān*)[75] is elaborated in a poetic manner by Maybudī:

> When they [the brothers] reached the wilderness, they drew the poisoned dagger from the scabbard of destiny, cast that sun- and moon-like face into the pit, and burned the liver of Jacob in separation from that radiant full moon. The birds of the air slumbered, the fishes of the sea slept, and the beasts of the desert took their rest, but the old prophet could neither sleep nor rest in comfort [...] When he entered his hermitage he would weep and wail in such a way that all the people of Canaan, men and women alike, wept with him in his grief.[76]

Another opportunity to describe the extent of Jacob's grieving occurs when Maybudī relates a tradition according to which a merchant from Canaan passes by Egypt, and Joseph (here also, the grieving lover) inquires after his father. The merchant informs Joseph that his father has taken upon himself 'such grieving that not even a mountain could bear, let alone a human being'.[77]

Maybudī often refers to Jacob's House of Sorrows as a hermitage or spiritual retreat (*ṣawma'a*), and shows how in his state of mourning Jacob is fully occupied with his devotion to God. Thus, when the merchant from Canaan, mentioned in the tradition above, returns from Egypt and, in the middle of the night, goes to Jacob's hermitage hoping to give Jacob the good news of his encounter with Joseph, he hears a voice from inside call out: 'I will not come out until dawn. Now, I am busy with my devotions and with my worship of God. I cannot leave that to become occupied with other than God.'[78] In another context, Maybudī refers to Jacob's retreat as the House of the Sorrow(s) of Poverty (*bayt al-aḥzān-i faqr*). Commenting on the words 'Alms are only for the poor' (Q. 9:60), he admonishes those who have not known inner poverty or want (*faqr*) saying: 'O you whose heart has never for one day been in the company of the pain of want! You who have never in your life spent one hour like Jacob in the House of Sorrows of Poverty!' and tells them that they are wrong to imagine that without tasting the sherbet of poverty or donning the clothes of spiritual discipline they could ever join the ranks of the poor among the companions and the stations of the elite in the Hereafter.[79]

Even more than the virtue of Jacob's seclusion for the sake of the remembrance and worship of God, Maybudī emphasizes the spiritual benefit of suffering itself. For example in his commentary on v. 58, 'And when Joseph's brethren came and presented themselves before him', Maybudī relates that Joseph commanded the servants to bring his brothers' merchandise for him to examine himself. He describes how the servants are baffled to know why, when gold, silver and priceless jewels are brought, Joseph never orders that they be opened before him, yet when these worthless ass-loads of sheep's wool and old shoes are brought, he insists that they should be opened before his throne. Maybudī then explains:

> Of course, there is a secret in this. It is that every strand of that wool carried a loving thought, a painful sigh of Jacob. If [all] that pain and love of Jacob had not been there, what use would he have had with the fleeces, let alone with opening the sacks himself?

An analogy is then drawn:

> O noble one! The Lord of Might cast a hundred thousand years of Satan's worship to the wind, in the desert of 'It means nothing to Me', while He accepted into His presence a single sigh of pain from the dervish saying: 'The groaning of sinners is dearer to me than the murmuring of worshippers.'[80]

Maybudī's purpose here is to show how a state of need and helplessness brings the servant closer to God and is endearing to Him. Later, when commenting on Jacob's words 'I perceive Joseph's scent' (v. 94), Maybudī demonstrates the spiritual transformation which has taken place:

> It is strange that the person carrying the shirt did not perceive the scent of it at all, while Jacob perceived it at a distance of eighty parasangs. This is because it was the scent of love, and the scent of love wafts only to the lover.

> Moreover, it does not always reach him, for until a person is cooked (*pukhta*) by love, and trampled (*kūbīda*) under love's affliction that scent will not reach him. Don't you see that early on at the beginning of the story, when Joseph had been taken from Jacob and thrown into the pit only a short distance away, Jacob had no knowledge of his [presence there] and could not perceive his scent?[81]

In another interpretation of the same verse, Maybudī presents a different explanation of Jacob's receptivity to the scent of Joseph's shirt. According to a saying quoted in the name of Jaʿfar al-Ṣādiq by Sulamī, the zephyr (*rīḥ al-ṣabā*) asked permission from God to bring Jacob the good news (of his imminent reunion with Joseph), and this permission was granted.[82] No reason for this is given in Sulamī's commentary, but Maybudī provides a clear explanation: God commanded the zephyr to bring the scent of Joseph to Jacob so that (and Maybudī is attributing these words to God) 'before Joseph's messenger brings him the news he should receive it from My messenger (i.e. the zephyr) and will recognise the completeness of My kindness and grace towards him.' The mystical significance of this is then explained:

> According to the experience [lit. tasting, *dhawq*] of mystics, this is that divine breath (*nafḥa-yi ilāhī*) which, unobserved, moves around the world and about the breasts of believers and those who affirm the oneness of God, until it sees a breast that is pure, a secret (*sirr*) that is empty. Then it alights there.
>
> Her love came to me before I even knew what love was
> So it chanced upon a heart that was free and settled there.
>
> It is to this that the Prophet was alluding when he said 'Verily there are in your life's destiny [lit. in the days of your time, (*ayyām dahrikum*)] divine winds [of mercy] blowing'.[83]

This poem is cited in several other contexts in *Kashf al-asrār* where Maybudī (or Anṣārī) speaks of the state of freedom from all attachments and otherness, and annihilation from self, such that God is found not by the servant's own seeking, but simply by his being absent from himself. For example, the poem follows the statement: 'These are the noble ones who, when they are given access to direct experience [of the truth], are prepared; who, when the veil is lifted are [already] freed from all creatures, and who have kept the skirt of realities out of reach of the hand of attachments;'[84] or the saying of Anṣārī, 'O God, you know why I am happy? Because I did not come upon You by myself. It was Your willing, O Lord, not mine – the beloved was at my bedside when I awoke.'[85] It was only in this state of pure emptiness that Jacob could receive the scent of Joseph's shirt.

Love's jealousy

In the pain of separation from the beloved, it is natural for the lover to try to find solace (*tasallī*) in another. However, the beloved's jealousy will not tolerate any such substitution, which is seen as a betrayal on the lover's part.[86] In Maybudī's commentary on Joseph's command to his brothers, 'Bring me the brother of yours [who is with] your father' (v. 59), we see that Jacob has found solace (*tasallī*) in Benjamin, and Joseph now takes on the role of the jealous beloved:

> It is said that Joseph summoned Benjamin because he had heard that Jacob had found all his heart's ease in looking at him, that he loved Benjamin and had placed him in his stead. He became jealous at this and protested, 'He claims to love me and then takes another in my place and consoles himself with him! Snatch Benjamin away from Jacob and bring him to me. Let the dust of others not settle on the page of affection, for there can be no sharing in love, and no room for two beloveds in one heart [...].'[87]

Later, in his commentary on verse 81, where Joseph tells his brothers to inform their father that he is keeping Benjamin prisoner, Maybudī explains in more detail the psychology of taking consolation (*tasallī*). He relates that Jacob, in his desolation and helplessness in the pain of separation from Joseph, wanted to 'turn some memento of Joseph into a salve for his wound, and to find diversion in loving one of Joseph's relations.' Benjamin, who had 'drunk from the same cup and been brought up with him' became this memento and a comfort for his grief. Maybudī further explains:

> The lover's heart will always incline towards one who has some connection with the beloved or who resembles them in some way. So it was that Majnūn went out into the desert and captured a gazelle. He saw a likeness to Laylā in its eyes and neck. He kept stroking its neck and kissing its eyes saying, 'Your eye is her eye and your neck is her neck'.[88]

However, neither love's requirement for suffering nor its jealousy would allow this prop of comfort:

> When Jacob attached his heart to Benjamin, and found some solace in him, once again the poisoned dagger was drawn from the scabbard of destiny. Benjamin was kept from his father with the accusation of being a thief. Affliction was added to affliction, salt was poured into the wound and he who had already been burnt was burned again. Just as fire ignites readily with burnt tinder (*ḥurqa-yi sūkhta*), so the pain of separation settles best in a burnt heart [...]. As long as Jacob saw Benjamin, he found consolation in him for [as they say] 'Whoever is deprived of seeing [the beloved] takes comfort in some trace of him'. But when he was deprived of seeing Benjamin, his suffering reached its limit. From the pain in his heart he cried out, and in desolation said, 'Alas my grief for Joseph' (v. 84).[89]

This time, it is God's jealousy that is aroused. The reprimand comes from the Divine Presence:

> O Jacob! How long this sorrow and regret at being apart from Joseph? How long this grieving and sighing? Now, stop all this grieving altogether. Know that you are keeping apart from Us as long as you remain occupied with him. [...] Now Jacob! See that after this you do not mention the name of Joseph, or I'll have your name removed from the register of prophets.[90]

At this rebuke, Jacob no longer mentions the name of Joseph until,

> from the court of majesty, by way of mercy and grace, the command was given to Gabriel: 'Go to Jacob and return Joseph to his memory again.' Gabriel came and brought the name of Joseph. Jacob sighed and the revelation came from God: 'O Jacob! I know what was behind your sighs and, by My glory, if he [Joseph] had died I would have brought him back to life for you because of the excellence of your fidelity.'[91]

The 'bringing back' of Joseph's name suggests two things: first, that Jacob had completely submitted to the divine command by relinquishing his remembrance of Joseph; and second, the legitimacy in God's eyes of Joseph as the object of Jacob's love. This brings us again to the idea of a human focus or '*qibla*' for divine love,[92] a concept which is further developed in the section which follows.

Love and the contemplation of God

Maybudī's reflections on the significance of Joseph's command that his shirt be thrown over Jacob's face (v. 93), and the immediate curing of Jacob's blindness, provide insights into both the reason for Jacob's loss of sight, and the nature of Jacob's love for Joseph. Earlier in his mystical commentary on the words: 'And his eyes turned white with the sorrow that he was suppressing' (v. 84), Maybudī includes a comment of Abū ʿAlī Daqqāq that 'Jacob wept for a created being, therefore he lost his sight, whereas David wept more than Jacob and did not go blind because his weeping was for God.[93] This view is later mollified by the observation that 'God's words were "*abyaḍḍat ʿaynāhu*" (his eyes were whitened), not "*ʿamā Yaʿqūb*" (Jacob went blind), for *ʿamā* indicates a blindness of the heart, as when it is said: "For indeed it is not the eyes that go blind, but it is the hearts, which are within their breasts, that grow blind" (Q. 22:46). Jacob had perfect vision and lucidity of heart, but his eyes were veiled from seeing others, for to see others in place of the beloved in the school of love is polytheism itself.'[94]

Here, Maybudī has explained Jacob's blindness according to the law of human, and clearly analogously divine, love. However, later he provides another explanation according to the understanding of spiritual psychology. Commenting on verse 96, 'Then, when the bearer of good tidings came to him and laid it (the shirt) on his face, immediately he saw again', Maybudī draws from Qushayrī's *Laṭāʾif* the observation that if Joseph's shirt had been thrown over the face of any other blind person in the world, their sight would not have returned; Jacob's sight returned by means of Joseph's shirt because his sight had gone through separation from him.[95] The spiritual psychology behind this phenomenon is then explained by Maybudī:

> In Jacob, love for Joseph had become mingled with his spirit. The seat [lit. capital, *dār al-mulk*] of the spirit is the brain. It lends strength to the eye, and clarity of vision [derives] from it. When Joseph went, the beauty of seeing and clarity of vision went, for that strength and clarity of vision was held in the person and scent of Joseph [...]. Of course, when the shirt was brought to Jacob, Joseph's scent arrived with it, and clarity of vision also returned. Thus you should know that in reality the beloved takes the place of the eye and spirit; separation from the beloved brings about a deficiency (*nuqṣān*) in the eye and the spirit, while union strengthens them.

I said: O Idol! I thought you were my beloved,
Now that I look well, I see that you are my very soul.
I'll lose my faith if you turn away from me,
O [my] soul and [my] world, you are my faith and infidelity![96]

An explanation for this passage may be found in chapters one and two of Aḥmad Ghazzālī's *Sawāniḥ*,[97] and, particularly, in the translator's commentary from which the following quotation is taken:

> After the unification of love with the spirit, and the purification of the heart, which is the means of gnosis, the inner eye opens and intuition or vision begins. The perceiver here is not the spirit alone, but the spirit as unified with love. [...] As the spirit advances along the path, he [it] becomes weaker and weaker, while love becomes stronger and stronger. [...] The last stage of this experience is when the spirit is annihilated, and thereby what is reflected in the mirror is love in the form of the beloved[...].[98]

It is no coincidence that the quatrain with which Maybudī ends this passage also appears in chapter two of *Sawāniḥ*, and Aḥmad Ghazzālī's comment on the third hemistich is especially pertinent to Maybudī's interpretation:

> [...] He [the writer] should have said, 'I shall lose my soul[99] if you turn away from me.' But these were the words of a poet, and he was bound by metre and rhyme.[100]

We may note that in this interpretation, Jacob's love is shown to have begun where Zulaykhā's love ended – that is, at the point where love has complete control (*wilāyat*), and the lover sees nothing but the beloved everywhere, even in place of his own soul.[101]

Yet another interpretation of the nature of Jacob's love for Joseph occurs at the beginning of this *Nawbat* III section, where Maybudī comments on Joseph's words 'Take this shirt of mine'. Maybudī observes that beneath the miracle of the curing of Jacob's blindness lies a great secret which may be explained thus:

> For Jacob, to look at Joseph was, by intermediary (*ba-wāsaṭa'ī*), to witness (*mushāhada*) God. Whenever Jacob saw Joseph with his bodily eye, the eye of his secret (*sirr*) gazed in the witnessing of God. So, when the vision of Joseph was veiled from his sight, the witnessing of God was likewise veiled from his heart. All Jacob's grieving was for the loss of the witnessing of God,

> not for the loss of Joseph's company, and all that sorrow and lamentation for Joseph was because he had lost his mirror.[102] He did not weep at the loss of the mirror itself,[103] but for the intimate companion (*mūnis*) of his heart,[104] which he no longer saw, and for this loss he burned [in anguish] (*mīsūkht*). Of course, that day when he saw Joseph again he fell down in prostration, for his heart found [once more] the witnessing of God. That prostration was made in his witnessing of God, for only God is worthy of prostration.[105]

More than a human focus or '*qibla*' for divine love, Joseph has here been identified as a theophany of God. Although Maybudī does not mention love in this passage, it is implied in the use of the words *mūnis* (intimate companion) and *mīsūkht* (burned).[106] Jacob's perfect love is here shown to be none other than the gnosis of God, or, put another way, it was only through perfect love that God could be perceived in the mirror of Joseph's beauty.[107] When Jacob lost that mirror, in the form of the beloved, he was also deprived of the witnessing of God. Thus it can be seen that in the way of love, gnosis (*ma'rifa*) and love (*maḥabba*) are inseparable.[108]

As in his esoteric interpretations of the stories of Abraham and Moses, so also in his commentary on *Sūrat Yūsuf*, Maybudī has been able to explain in detail different stages and stations of the mystical path. However the story of Joseph has allowed him particular scope to expound in a comprehensive manner his doctrines of the way of mystical love. In his exposition, Joseph has mainly been viewed as a symbol of the divine Beloved, and Jacob and Zulaykhā as prototypes of lovers or potential lovers of God. While Zulaykhā's love gradually evolves from human love to divine love, and from love which is partial (in both senses of that word) and therefore selfish, to love which has complete possession and leaves no room for the consideration of self, Jacob's love is shown from the beginning to have been potentially the perfect love for God – the 'seed of the pain of love' that was sown in his heart from pre-eternity. It is partly out of divine jealousy, in order to conceal Jacob's love for God from those who could not understand it, but mainly to perfect that love for God, that Joseph was made into a focus or '*qibla*' for Jacob's love. Thus Jacob could be 'cooked' and 'beaten about' by his years of suffering in separation from Joseph.

It is in Maybudī's interpretation of the final part of *Sūrat Yūsuf*, namely the healing of Jacob's sight by Joseph's shirt, and his bowing down before Joseph, that we begin to see a more contemplative side to the love mysticism of Maybudī, one that recalls the teachings of Aḥmad Ghazzālī and looks forward to later developments in love mysticism by Rūzbihān Baqlī, where the human beloved is seen as a theophany of God. However, most of Maybudī's commentary is expressive of a way of mystical love that teaches the need for suffering and intense longing for the Beloved, a purifying fire that eventually purifies the seeker from all other than God. It is these doctrines that were to become the predominant themes of later Persian mystical literature, as exemplified par excellence in the poetry of ʿAṭṭār, Rūmī and Ḥāfiẓ.

NOTES

1 Trans. Abdel Haleem. 'His purpose' rather than 'his [Joseph's] career' (Pickthall) for *amrihi* makes more sense here.

2 Ṭabarī's *History*, II, tr. Brinner, p. 153, n. 362, names Joseph's purchaser (referred to as ʿAzīz in the Qur'an as either Qaṭafir or Iṭfir b. Rawhib, both being Arabic equivalents to the Biblical name Potiphar. Ṭabarī states that ʿAzīz was a ruler who was in charge of the Egyptian treasury. On the etymology of the name Potiphar see Alan Richard Schulman and Itaim Zʾew Hirschberg, 'Potiphar', *EJ*, XIII, p. 934. ʿAzīz's wife is unnamed in the Qur'an. According to Ṭabarī, *History*, II, tr. Brinner, p. 154, n. 365, and Thaʿlabī, *ʿArāʾis al-majālis* (Cairo, n.d.), p. 128, she was called Rāʿīl, but many sources also give her name as Zalīkah or Zulaykhā. Thaʿlabī (ibid.) gives another alternative: Bakā bint Fiyūsh.

3 The widely held tradition being that she gave them citrons or oranges to eat, and they cut their hands instead of the fruit.

4 See for example Waldman, 'New approaches'; Muhammad Abdel Haleem, 'The story of Joseph in the Qurʾān and the Old Testament', *ICMR* 1/2 (1990), pp. 171–91. Other studies on the Qur'anic story of Joseph include: John Macdonald, 'Joseph in the Qurʾān and Muslim commentary', *MW* 46 (1956) pp. 113–31, 207–24; Paul Nwyia, 'Un cas d'exégèse soufie'; Anthony H. Johns, 'Joseph in the Qurʾān: dramatic dialogue, human emotion and prophetic wisdom', *Islamochristiana* 7 (1981), pp. 29–55; Samuel M. Stern, 'Muḥammad and Joseph: a study in Koranic narrative', *JNES* 44 (1985), pp. 193–204; Mustansir Mir, 'The story of Joseph: plot, themes and characters', *MW* 76 (1986), pp. 1–15; Laroussi Gasmi, 'Les réseaux connotatifs dans le texte coranique (le récit de Joseph: Sourate XII, v. 4–102)', *Arabica* 33 (1986), Fasc. 1, pp. 1–48; Gary A. Rendsburg, 'Literary structures in the Qurʾānic and Biblical stories of Joseph', *MW* 75 (1985), pp. 118–20; Jaako Hämeen-Anttila, '"We will tell you the best of stories". A study on surah XII', *Studia Orientalia Helsinki* 67 (1991), pp. 7–32; Gayane K. Merguerian and Afsaneh Najmabadi, 'Zulaykha and Yusuf: whose "best story?"', *IJMES* 29 (1997), pp. 485–508; James W. Morris, 'Dramatizing the sura of Joseph: an introduction to the Islamic humanities', *Journal of Turkish Studies* 18 (1994), pp. 201–24.

5 Abdel Haleem, 'Story of Joseph', p. 172.
6 Waldman, 'New approaches', p. 5.
7 Ibid., p. 6.
8 Ibid., p. 6; Abdel Haleem, 'Story of Joseph', p. 174. Jacob is only directly named once (v. 68). Elsewhere, when his name is mentioned, it is among other patriarchs, for example, 'upon the family of Jacob' (v. 6) and 'the religion of my fathers, Abraham, Isaac and Jacob' (v. 38).
9 See Johns, 'Joseph in the Qurʾān', pp. 31ff.; Abdel Haleem, 'Story of Joseph', p. 174; Hämeen-Anttila, 'Best of stories', p. 19.
10 *Kashf*, V, p. 150; Abdel Haleem, 'Story of Joseph', p. 188. Both Johns ('Joseph in the Qurʾān'), and Stern ('Muḥammad and Joseph'), have pointed out parallels between the situation of Joseph (and Jacob in his bereavement) and the Prophet Muhammad at the time the sura was revealed.
11 William Wright, ed., *A Grammar of the Arabic Language*, trans. from German by Caspari, 3rd edn, revised by W. Robertson Smith and M.J. de Goeje (Cambridge, 1967), pp. 137–8. While Joseph is presented as the epitome of veracity in the Qur'an, it is interesting to note that according to Jewish legend he was, in his childhood, given to slandering his brothers, which is why he was sold into slavery. See Louis Ginzberg, *Legends of the Jews*, trans. from German by H. Szold (Philadelphia, 1909–38), II, pp. 5–6.
12 These two words *ḥukm* and *ʿilm* are variously interpreted to mean intellect (*ʿaql*) and knowledge (*ʿilm*) before he attained prophethood (Mujāhid, quoted in Ṭabarī, *Jāmiʿ al-bayān*, ed. Shākir and Shākir, XVI, p. 23); or prophethood (*nubuwwa*) and knowledge of religion (*fiqh al-dīn*) (*Kashf*, V, p. 37). According to Maybudī, Joseph received revelation (*waḥy*) when he was in the well or pit, but when he reached adulthood he was made to manifest his calling (of people to the faith) (*iẓhār al-daʿwa*).
13 Another parallel here with the Prophet Muhammad.
14 Later, Shihāb al-Dīn al-Suhrawardī was to identify Joseph with beauty, Zulaykhā with love and Jacob with sorrow. See Shihāb al-Dīn Yaḥyāʾ b. Ḥabash al-Suhrawardī, *Fī ḥaqīqat al-ʿishq* (known also as *Mūnis al-ʿushshāq*), Persian text in *Majmūʿa-yi āthār-i Shaykh-i Ishrāq, Shihāb al-Dīn Yaḥyā Suhrawardī*, III: *Majmūʿa-yi āthār-i farsī-yi Shaykh-i Ishrāq*, ed. S.H. Nasr (Tehran, 1970); trans. by W.M. Thackston as *The Mystical and Visionary Treatises of Shihabuddin Yahya Suhrawardi* (London, 1982). This treatise is discussed by Corbin, *En Islam iranien*, II, pp. 361ff. See also Nwyia, 'Un cas d'exégèse soufie', p. 410.
15 Ṭabarī, *History*, II, tr. Brinner, p. 148.
16 *Kashf*, V, p. 12. The same is related in a hadith listed by Muslim, *Saḥīḥ*, *Kitāb al-īmān*, ch. 75 (Bāb al-isrāʾ bi'l-rasūl), no. 1, § 309.
17 *Kashf*, V, p. 13.
18 *Kashf*, V, p. 12. Related in Ibn Isḥāq, *Kitāb al-mubtadaʾ wa'l-mabʿath wa'l-maghāzī*, tr. Guillaume, p. 186.
19 *Kashf*, V, p. 12. Also cited by Thaʿlabī, *ʿArāʾis al-majālis*, p. 118.
20 Maybudī's source here is probably Sulamī's *Ḥaqāʾiq*, ed. Nwyia, *Trois œuvres inédites*, p. 60, where Ibn ʿAṭāʾ's comment reads: '"They sold him for a paltry sum"; thus you should know that outward beauty has no value with God be He exalted. True beauty is inward beauty.'
21 *Kashf*, V, p. 42.

22 An exception being Ibn ʿArabī's *Fuṣūṣ al-ḥikam* where the chapter on Joseph is centred on the idea of truth.

23 Among the commentators who interpret *ḍalāl* as 'excessive love' are: Jaʿfar al-Ṣādiq, who when asked about *ʿishq* called it *ḍalāl* (*Ḥaqāʾiq*, ed. Nwyia, 'Le tafsīr mystique', p. 201); Ṭabarī, *Jāmiʿ al-bayān*, ed. Shākir and Shākir, XV, pp. 8, 95; Maybudī, who describes it as *maḥabbat-i mufriṭ* (excessive love) (*Kashf*, V, p. 15); and Bayḍāwī, who uses the expression *li-tarkihi al-taʿdīl fi'l-maḥabba* (on account of his abandoning moderation in love) (*Anwār al-tanzīl*, p. 453).

24 *Kashf*, V, p. 25.

25 *Kashf*, V, pp. 46–7.

26 *Kashf*, V, p. 45.

27 *Kashf*, V, 27. Also in Sulamī's *Ḥaqāʾiq*, ed. Nwyia, *Trois œuvres inédites*, p. 59.

28 *Kashf*, V, p. 70. This saying and part of the interpretation that follows appears in Qushayrī's *Laṭāʾif*, II, p. 173. The same idea is presented in quotes from Sahl (al-Tustarī) and others in Sulamī's *Ziyādāt ḥaqāʾiq al-tafsīr*, p. 64.

29 This saying is quoted from Ibn ʿAṭāʾ in Sulamī's *Ḥaqāʾiq*, ed. Nwyia, *Trois œuvres inédites*, pp. 62–3.

30 *Kashf*, V, pp. 70–1.

31 *Kashf*, V, p. 70. A similar hadith transmitted through al-Ḥasan (possibly Ḥasan al-Baṣrī), cited in Ṭabarī (*Jāmiʿ al-bayān*, ed. Shākir and Shākir, XVI, p. 112) concludes: 'He would not have stayed in prison as long as he did.' However, other traditions cited by Ṭabarī (ibid, XVI, pp. 113–14) specify the period of seven years.

32 *Kashf*, V, p. 89.

33 Whereas in Qushayrī's *Laṭāʾif* (II, pp. 166–7) the 'mention of lovers' is given as one among several reasons for the sura's designation as 'the most beautiful of stories'. This is just one example of the greater emphasis which Maybudī places on love in his commentary, as compared with the mystical commentaries of Sulamī and Qushayrī.

34 Or: 'love for you'. *Kashf*, V, p. 11.

35 *Kashf*, V, pp. 87–9. One tradition of Ibn ʿAbbās cited by Maybudī states merely that when ʿAzīz died the king gave Zulaykhā in marriage to Joseph. Kisāʾī relates how Zulaykhā suffers hardship and hunger during the period of famine. She sells her possessions and becomes Joseph's slave. Later, she converts to monotheism and Joseph, having freed her and restored her to her former wealth, marries her. See Muḥammad b. ʿAbd Allāh al-Kisāʾī, *Qiṣaṣ al-anbiyāʾ*, trans. by W.M. Thackston as *The Tales of the Prophets of al-Kisāʾī* (Boston, 1978), pp. 179–80. In the *Qiṣaṣ al-anbiyāʾ* of Abū Isḥāq Ibrāhīm b. Manṣūr b. Khalaf al-Naysābūrī, ed. Ḥ. Yaghmāʾī (Tehran, 1340sh/1961), pp. 145–9, a whole section is devoted to the end of Zulaykhā's story. In Naysābūrī's version ʿAzīz divorces Zulaykhā before he dies.

36 See Pourjavady, 'Bāda-yi ʿishq', 12/2, p. 7; Merguerian and Najmabadi, 'Zulaykha and Yusuf', p. 498. This view is clearly stated by the ninth/fifteenth century mystic poet, ʿAbd al-Raḥmān Jāmī, who in his *mathnawī Yūsuf wa Zulaykhā* writes:

Don't turn away from love, even though it be [mere] metaphor (*majāz*),
For it may bring you to that [love] which is real (*ḥaqīqī*).

See Jāmī, *Haft awrang*, ed. M.M. Gīlānī (Tehran, 1337sh/1958), p. 594.

The use of the terms 'metaphorical' or relative love (*ʿishq-i majāzī*) and real love (*ʿishq-i ḥaqīqī*) are equivalent in meaning to human (or natural) love (*ʿishq-i basharī* or *ṭabīʿī*) and divine love (*ʿishq-i ilāhī*.) See Pourjavady, 'Bāda-yi ʿishq', 12/2, pp. 8ff.

37 A role which she unequivocally plays in Jāmī's *mathnawī* of the story.

38 Sympathetic comments are to be found in other commentaries too. For example, in Aḥmad b. Muḥammad b. Zayd Ṭūsī's (fl. fifth/eleventh or sixth/twelfth century) early Persian commentary on *Sūrat Yūsuf*: when it is discovered that Joseph's shirt is torn at the back, and Zulaykhā's guilt is revealed, Joseph is commanded by Gabriel not to oppose or blame Zulaykhā, but to be aware that she has a right to union with him just as she has a right to gnosis of God. See Aḥmad b. Muḥammad b. Zayd Ṭūsī, *Tafsīr-i Sūra-yi Yūsuf: al-sittīn al-jāmiʿ li-laṭāʾif al-basāṭīn*, ed. M. Rawshan, Persian Texts Series 35 (Tehran, 1967), p. 341.

39 *Kashf*, V, p. 35.

40 *Kashf*, V, p. 42.

41 *Kashf*, V, p. 35.

42 *Kashf*, V, p. 37.

43 *Kashf*, V, p. 38.

44 Ibid.

45 *Kashf*, V, p. 58.

46 *Kashf*, V, p. 37.

47 *Kashf*, V, p. 40.

48 *Kashf*, V, p. 39.

49 *Kashf*, V, pp. 87–8. Maybudī's doctrine concerning the role of suffering in the perfecting of love was discussed in Chapter Seven and will be discussed with reference to Jacob below.

50 *Kashf*, V, pp. 89–90.

51 *Kashf*, V, p. 52.

52 *Kitāb al-taʿarruf*, p. 83. In his translation of this work, Arberry has rendered the word *ghalaba* as 'overmastery'. See *Doctrine of the Sufis*, p. 108.

53 *Kitāb al-taʿarruf*, IV, p. 1469.

54 *Kashf al-maḥjūb*, p. 229; tr. Nicholson p. 184.

55 Ibid., p. 275; tr. Nicholson p. 226. See pp. 185–7 for a discussion of the word *tamkīn*.

56 *Kashf*, V, p. 59. For the true lover submits his will to that of the beloved, as we shall see in the case of Jacob.

57 Ibid. Compare with Naysābūrī (*Qiṣaṣ al-anbiyāʾ*, p. 112), who states that when Zulaykhā's love (*ʿishq*) was base desire (*shahawa*) she blamed the beloved for her crime, but when her love was real (or a reality, *ḥaqīqa*) she admitted her guilt.

58 *Kashf*, V, pp. 59–60. Another version of this definition was discussed in part two, pp. 156–7.

59 *Kashf*, V, p. 60.

60 The printed edition and MS A has the erroneous *ʿayn* instead of *ghayn*. MS B, however, and Nwyia's edition of Jaʿfar al-Ṣādiq's commentary from the *Ḥaqāʾiq* ('Le tafsīr mystique', p. 201) have the more likely *ghayn*.

61 *Kashf*, V, p. 60. In chapter two of the *Sawāniḥ*, Aḥmad Ghazzālī also connects the idea of domination by love with seeing nothing but the beloved, not even

oneself: 'Love veils the spirit from seeing himself and so it overwhelms the eye of his inspection. As a result, love has taken the place of the spirit's image in the mirror and the spirit sees it instead of himself.' This is where he says:

I have your image in my eye so much
That whatever I perceive, I think it is you.

See Aḥmad Ghazzālī, *Sawāniḥ*, ed. Pourjavady, p. 4; tr. Pourjavady, p. 18. Aḥmad Ghazzālī uses the term *wilāyat* in the sense of complete domination by the 'sultan of love' in two other contexts: in chapter 24 and chapter 45, where it is applied to the state in which the lover goes beyond the point where his love is subject to increase or decrease. See *Sawāniḥ*, ed. Pourjavady, p. 38;tr. Pourjavady, p. 61. See also ibid., the translator's commentary p. 109.

62 *Kashf*, V, p. 60.

63 *Kashf*, V, p. 61. Also in Qushayrī's *Laṭā'if*, II, p. 182. Compare Naysābūrī, *Qiṣaṣ al-anbiyā'*, p. 103: 'when a person gets used to something (*khū karda*) they no longer fear it.'

64 *Kashf*, V, p. 61.

65 *Kashf*, I, pp. 239–40. This passage is almost certainly based on chapter 24 of Aḥmad Ghazzālī's *Sawāniḥ*, ed. Pourjavady, pp. 23–4; tr. Pourjavady, pp. 43–4, although there is some variation in the way it is worded. The first hemistich of the poem is also slightly different.

66 The passage in question (*Kashf*, V, p. 27) presents a 'meta-historical' explanation for the psychological phenomenon that parents find separation from their children harder than children separation from their parents.

67 *Kashf*, V, p. 11.

68 An allusion to the following hadith: 'Verily God created the creatures in darkness, and then He poured upon them some of His Light', which is again cited in *Kashf*, VI, p. 543. It is cited in the same form in Ghazzālī's *Mishkāt al-anwār*, ed. and tr. Buchman, p. 12. This appears to be a variation of a hadith which is listed in Ibn Ḥanbal's *Musnad*, II, pp. 176 and 197, and by Tirmidhī, *Jāmi'*, *Kitāb al-īmān*, ch. 18 (Mā jā'a fī iftirāq hādhihi'l-umma), no. 3. In all of these versions the hadith has 'cast' instead of 'poured', and it is extended with the statement: 'Whosoever was touched by that light found guidance and whomsoever it missed went astray.' In the latter form it is cited and explained by Maybudī in *Kashf*, I, p. 570. Al-Ḥakīm al-Tirmidhī also lists this hadith more than once; in II, Principle 287, p. 413 we find one version with 'poured' and another with 'cast'.

69 Maybudī is possibly alluding here to the *'ahd-i alast*, which he interprets as a covenant of love as was seen in chapter five, p. 141–2. Moreover, the words *'abhar-i 'ahd* are reminiscent of the expression *'abhar-i 'ishq* used by Aḥmad Ghazzālī in the *Sawāniḥ*, ed. Pourjavady, p. 44. Maybudī may even have borrowed the metaphor of sowing the seed of love from Aḥmad Ghazzālī, although he uses it in a different way.

70 Or humanity was shown the way to divine love *through* its own kind.

71 *Kashf*, V, p. 11. Note in this passage the expression *jamāl-i yūsufī* (Joseph-beauty) is used instead of *jamāl-i Yūsuf* (the beauty of Joseph). Perhaps Maybudī has used this adjectival form to emphasise the abstract and universal nature of the phenomenon.

72 The 'veil of [divine] jealousy' (*parda-yi ghayrat*) is mentioned in other contexts, for example in *Kashf*, VI, p. 512. See also *Kashf*, VIII, p. 180, where the Companions of the Prophet are said to conceal their inner wealth with outer poverty, and once more the words 'Call me Arsalān [...]' are used; and yet again (*Kashf*, VIII, p. 204) where the veil of jealousy hides the beauty of the Prophet from any unworthy person. For a discussion of the different kinds of Divine jealousy see pp. 196–7.

73 *Kashf*, V, p. 25. The word used for 'mat' here is *naṭʿ*, which literally means a leather mat which was spread out for the playing of chess or the beheading of a person.

74 *Kashf*, V, p. 26. Qushayrī presents a slightly different version of the same idea: 'the lover gives the comfort of the beloved preference over his own likes.' See *Laṭāʾif*, II, p. 172. The shift in Maybudī's version is interesting, given the emphasis in his doctrines of the need for suffering in the way of love.

75 The House of Sorrows or Grief(s) (*bayt al-aḥzān*) is neither mentioned in Ṭabarī's history nor in his *tafsīr*, but it is mentioned in Kisāʾī's *Qiṣaṣ al-anbiyāʾ*, tr. Thackston, p. 173.

76 *Kashf*, V, p. 26.

77 *Kashf*, V, pp. 44–5. This tradition appears in Kisāʾī's *Qiṣaṣ al-anbiyāʾ* (tr. Thackston, pp. 172–3) though, as we shall see below, the ending differs.

78 *Kashf*, V, p. 45. But according to Kisāʾī (*Qiṣaṣ al-anbiyāʾ*, tr. Thackston, p. 173) when the merchant returns to Canaan, Jacob runs to meet him, and when he hears the news of Joseph, falls into a swoon.

79 *Kashf*, IV, p. 167.

80 *Kashf*, V, p. 105.

81 *Kashf*, V, p. 140.

82 *Ḥaqāʾiq*, ed. Nwyia, 'Le tafsîr mystique', p. 202.

83 *Kashf*, V, p. 139. This hadith is listed in Ṭabarānī's *Al-Muʿjam al-kabīr* (Cairo, 1426/2005), Book 19, p. 233, no. 519 and his *Muʿjam al-awsaṭ*, Book 3, p. 180, § 2856 and Book 6, p. 221, § 6234. Ghazzālī cites it in the *Iḥyāʾ*, Part 1, Book 4, *Kitāb asrār al-ṣalāt*, ch. 5 (Fī faḍl al-jumʿa wa ādābihā), Section 4, p. 247; and in Part 3, Book 1, *Kitāb ʿajāʾib al-qalb*, Section 4, p. 120.

84 *Kashf*, VII, p. 265.

85 *Kashf*, V, p. 475. See also *Kashf*, II, p. 509; VII, p. 415; IX, p. 507. A similar interpretation of the scent of Joseph's shirt is to be found in Samʿānī's *Rawḥ al-arwāḥ*, pp. 306–7. Note that the words 'The beloved was at my bedside when I awoke' were used in connection with Moses, see p. 261.

86 Aḥmad Ghazzālī shows that 'consolation (*salwat*) in love is a sign of imperfection' which has to be removed (*Sawāniḥ*, ed. Pourjavady, p. 23; tr. Pourjavady, p. 43).

87 *Kashf*, V, pp. 105–6.

88 *Kashf*, V, pp. 127–8. Aḥmad Ghazzālī also relates this story of Majnūn. In his version, Majnūn sets the gazelle free instead of killing it, and when asked for an explanation says 'there is something in it which is like Laylā'. Ghazzālī explains that this is still the beginning of love; at a higher stage, the lover comes to know 'that [transcendent] perfection belongs [only] to the beloved, and he finds nothing other than the beloved like unto her.' Then, 'his intimacy with others will cease, except with what pertains to her, such as the dog in the

quarter of the beloved or the dust on her doorstep'. See *Sawāniḥ*, ed. Pourjavady, pp. 22–3; tr. Pourjavady, p. 43. Maybudī's statement that: 'The lover's heart will always be drawn to one who is connected to the beloved or resembles them in some way', appears to have brought together that which Ghazzālī has more precisely defined as two stages in the way of love.

89 *Kashf*, V, p. 128.

90 Ibid. A similar threat appears in Ṭūsī's *Al-Sittīn*, but there the words are spoken by Gabriel, not God. See *Al-Sittīn*, p. 585.

91 *Kashf*, V, p. 129.

92 See p. 293.

93 *Kashf*, V, p. 129. The saying is probably taken from Qushayrī's *Laṭā'if*, II, p. 200. A similar interpretation appears in Sulamī's *Ḥaqā'iq* quoted from Ibn ʿAṭā', but in this case the comparison is made between Adam and Jacob. See *Ḥaqā'iq*, ed. Nwyia, *Trois œuvres inédites*, p. 64.

94 *Kashf*, V, p. 130. Again, this comment may be based on a saying of Abū ʿAlī Daqqāq quoted by Qushayrī, *Laṭā'if*, II, p. 200, though interestingly Qushayrī does not use the term 'school of love'.

95 *Kashf*, V, p. 141; *Laṭā'if*, II, p. 207.

96 *Kashf*, V, p. 141. The published edition has *jān-i jahān*, which would be translated 'soul or spirit of the world', but Pourjavady ('Jān wa jahān kīst yā chīst', *Maʿārif* 13/2 [November 1996], pp. 161–78) has argued that the more correct version is *jān wa jahān* 'soul and world', and this indeed is how it appears in MS A.

97 *Sawāniḥ*, ed. Pourjavady, pp. 3–5; tr. Pourjavady, pp. 17–20.

98 Pourjavady, *Sawāniḥ*, *Inspirations*, p. 86. The translator continues thus: 'This, however is not the final stage of the journey. It started with love, and it must also end with love, not in the form of the beloved or her attribute [...]'. However, as stated previously (p. 198), Maybudī's doctrine of love differs from that of Aḥmad Ghazzālī in as much as Maybudī does not perceive love, but the Beloved as the Absolute.

99 That is, rather than faith.

100 *Sawāniḥ*, ed. Pourjavady, p. 5; tr. Pourjavady, p. 20.

101 See pp. 289–92 and especially the quotation from *Sawāniḥ* in note 57.

102 That is, the means by which he contemplated God. Compare *Kashf*, III, p. 778: 'The *ʿārif* is a mirror; he who looks upon it sees his Lord.'

103 i.e., the person of Joseph.

104 i.e., the contemplation of God.

105 *Kashf*, V, pp. 139–40.

106 The relevance of love to this passage is further clarified in the later mystical commentary by Rūzbihān Baqlī on the words: 'And his eyes turned white with the sorrow he was suppressing' (Q. 12:84):

> The wisdom in the fact that Jacob's sight was lost, but Adam and David's sight remained [despite their weeping] is that Jacob's weeping was the weeping of a grief that had been kneaded (*maʿjūn*) with the pain of separation. This was because of the loss of the theophany (*tajallī*) of God's beauty, which was held in the mirror of Joseph's countenance. Jacob enjoyed, from God, the special privileges of love (*khaṣā'iṣ al-ʿishq*) [or, Jacob was distinguished by God with the special qualities of love]. From the

station of love he had received the subtleties of *iltibās* [God's theophany in creation which veils us from His sublime reality], and when that intermediary (*wāsiṭa*) was lost, so also was the beholding (*muṭāla'a*) of the beauty of God [...].

See Rūzbihān Baqlī, *'Arā'is al-bayān fī ḥaqā'iq al-Qur'ān*, p. 637. On Rūzbihān Baqlī's use of the term *iltibās* see Carl Ernst, *Rūzbihān Baqlī: Mysticism and the Rhetoric of Sainthood in Persian Sufism* (Richmond, 1996), p. 104, n. 56. For a discussion of *iltibās* in the context of Rūzbihān's commentary on *Sūrat Yūsuf*, see my study, 'Towards a prophetology of love: the figure of Jacob in Sufi commentaries on *Sūrat Yūsuf*, in Annabel Keeler and Sajjad Rizvi, eds., *The Spirit of the Letter: Approaches to the Esoteric Interpretation of the Qur'an* (Oxford, 2016), pp. 136–42.

107 In another passage, Maybudī quotes Anṣārī as praying, 'O God, You have manifested Your light in the hearts of Your lovers [...] making their hearts into Your mirror and pristine abode; You are evident there, but in the two worlds You are invisible in Your evidentness'. See *Kashf*, VI, p. 572.

108 See chapter five, p. 130 and chapter seven, p. 192.

Conclusion

This study has set out to introduce an important but little-known figure in the history of Sufism, the sixth/twelfth-century scholar and mystic, Rashīd al-Dīn Maybudī and his Persian commentary, the *Kashf al-asrār wa ʿuddat al-abrār*. It has examined the mystical hermeneutics and doctrines of this work and explored the interaction of these two elements in his interpretation of the Qur'anic stories of the prophets Abraham, Moses and Joseph.

Although no new data has emerged concerning Maybudī's life, the close study of the text of his commentary has yielded considerable information about his doctrines, tastes and interests. A Shāfiʿī in *fiqh*, Maybudī was a fervent traditionalist who championed a number of Ḥanbalī doctrines, although he never claimed any formal allegiance to that school and preferred to place himself under the ubiquitous banner of the *ahl al-sunna wa'l-jamāʿa*. Like his spiritual forebear Khwāja ʿAbd Allāh Anṣārī, he condemned speculative theology (*kalām*), philosophy and, in fact, all attempts at comprehending God by means of discursive reasoning. The rational faculty (*ʿaql*) does have its role to play, but only in the realm of outward knowledge and at the service of *sharīʿa*. Thus he writes: 'Do not tie your heart to *ʿaql*; it is but a policeman (*pāsbān*), and can be neither a guide [...] nor the way' (*Kashf*, II, 91). In the inner quest for God, all cogitation must be abandoned; gnosis (*maʿrifa*) cannot be attained through mental effort, but comes to those who are freed from themselves, by the grace of divine unveiling (*mukāshafa*).

Like other mystics of his period, Maybudī believed that the observance of *sharīʿa*, though it might guarantee salvation, was not complete without the inner realisation of truth (*ḥaqīqa*). Likewise, *ḥaqīqa* can have no existence without *sharīʿa*. The two, he explains, are inseparably linked like body and soul. Spiritual realisation further presupposes the rigorous control, or more precisely crushing, of the ego (*nafs*) through the disciplines of the mystical way (*ṭarīqa*). These two clearly defined but interdependent elements of *sharīʿa* (embodying the dogma of the *ahl al-sunna*) and *ḥaqīqa* (the culmination of *ṭarīqa*) constitute for Maybudī the mainstays of religious life, and it is these two principles which determine the form and content of his commentary on the Qur'an.

Taking the term hermeneutics to designate the aims, criteria and method of interpretation, we have seen that Maybudī's overall purpose in writing the *Kashf al-asrār* was to provide spiritual guidance (*irshād*). At the level of exoteric exegesis, this involved the inclusion of a substantial amount of homiletic material in addition to what was strictly required for the explanation of the Qur'anic verses. A closer analysis of the mystical hermeneutics of the *Kashf al-asrār*, on the other hand, indicated that the aim of esoteric interpretation is *intrinsically* one of *irshād*; that is to say, while exoteric interpretation attempts to explain the verses, esoteric interpretation seeks to elucidate the states and stations of the mystical path in the light of, or through the inspiration of, the verses. Thus the overall function of *irshād* in the *Kashf al-asrār* appears to comprise three levels, corresponding to the tripartite arrangement of the *tafsīr*: the first is to provide a basic comprehension of the Scripture through the translation of the verses (*Nawbat* I); the second, to facilitate a more thorough understanding of the verses by means of exoteric exegesis (*Nawbat* II); and the third, to encourage advancement to greater sincerity in the practice of what is understood (*Nawbat* III). These three levels might be said to correspond to the traditional designation of *ʿāmm*, *khāṣṣ* and *khāṣṣ al-khawāṣṣ*.

Maybudī appears to have held significantly different criteria for the exoteric and for the esoteric interpretation of the Qur'an. The parameters for exoteric interpretation were strictly defined by his traditionalist beliefs. Thus, while he insists that *tafsīr bi'l-maʾthūr* should be combined with *tafsīr bi'l-raʾy*, and even condones attempts to interpret the *mutashābihāt*, he does not permit any metaphorical interpretation or *taʾwīl* of the anthropomorphic verses; these are to be left without being interpreted, *bi-lā kayf*. For esoteric interpretation, on the other hand, no criteria are set down save the condition that its practitioner must have completely purified his soul. At the level of mystical exegesis, the shackles of literalism fall away because here the agent is not discursive reasoning but divine illumination. Within the *Nawbat* II and *Nawbat* III sections, Maybudī had the scope to develop fully these two distinct approaches to Qur'anic interpretation. In addition, by juxtaposing the exoteric and esoteric sections of his commentary he was able to endorse, by implication, the interdependence of *sharīʿa* and *ḥaqīqa*, and to uphold the importance of the literal meanings of the verses. The structure of the *Kashf al-asrār* clearly indicates that he intended the three sections to be read together – the esoteric was to be seen not as an alternative, but as complementary to the exoteric.

By writing his commentary in Persian, Maybudī almost certainly intended to reach a broad audience with varied levels of scholarly and spiritual attainment. This is indicated by the range of content and the lively narrative style in parts of the *Nawbat* II sections, and by the more accessible style (as compared with the recondite commentary of Qushayrī, for example) of the *Nawbat* III sections. The choice of Persian also provided Maubudī with greater scope and freedom to develop the rhetorical style of his mystical commentary, for which he brought together rhyming and metred prose, poetry, story-telling and a rich language of metaphors. All these elements, together with the more intimate and direct tone provided by his own native tongue, assisted him in the expression of themes related to the mystical way of love, which so pervades his work.

The examination of the mystical teachings of the *Kashf al-asrār* revealed three key, inter-related doctrines. Two of these constitute an inner dimension of traditionalist beliefs: the doctrine of God's pre-ordination of all things, and intervention in the affairs of men; and the doctrine that imposes limits on rational knowledge. Only the third, the doctrine of love, can really be seen as a way or means of spiritual return. As de Beaurecueil has stated concerning the doctrine of love in Anṣārī's *Ṣad maydān*: 'L'amour [...] est le moteur de toute cheminement spirituelle.'[1] Maybudī seems to want us to understand three things about God, and three things about man. God is the All-powerful, He is the All-knowing, and He has infinite love and mercy towards man. Man is weak and incapable of knowing God; yet he can and should love Him with all his being. Overall it is the theme of love that is the unifying dynamic of Maybudī's mystical commentary, inspiring its content and transforming its literary style.

Through his mystical interpretations of the stories of the prophets, Maybudī expounds these three principal doctrines as well as many of the terms used by Sufis to define the conditions, states and stations of the mystical path: what it means to be *murīd* or *murād*, *mukhliṣ* or *mukhlaṣ*; or to experience *haybat* and *uns*, *tafriqa* and *jamʿ*, *fanāʾ* and *baqāʾ*; and so on. However, Maybudī does not simply explain these aspects of mystical doctrine in the mode of a Sufi manual; he presents them in a homiletic way, drawing into his rhetoric the drama of the story as well as the poetic imagery of his time. When Abraham, for example, becomes beguiled by 'pearls of the unseen', he is scolded by the 'beauty of *tawḥīd*' and told to observe the custom of 'his eye did not swerve'. On entering the valley of Ṭuwā, Moses is told to go beyond the first realisation of *tawḥīd* and subject his intention to the stripping away of *tajrīd* (symbolised by the removal of his sandals). Jacob, we are informed, is able to catch the scent of Joseph only once he has been cooked by love and trampled down by love's suffering. In such instances, the prophets' stories have truly become parables, allowing admonitions and exhortations to be obliquely directed to the reader or listener. It is here, in the interpretations of the stories of the prophets, that we find most fully exemplified the hermeneutics of *irshād*.

While in these esoteric interpretations Abraham, Moses and Jacob are viewed as prototypes of the spiritual wayfarer, their conventional 'exoteric' role as prophets is never far away. We may assume that when those whom Maybudī was addressing read or listened to his mystical commentary on these stories, they would still have fresh in their minds the more literal interpretation. For Maybudī this did not entail any contradiction: the fire of Nimrod could be a real burning fire, which miraculously did no harm to Abraham's body, and it could analogically be the fire of desire which has no affect on the purified soul; the throne (*ʿarsh*) of God could (and in Maybudī's view should) be affirmed as His Throne in heaven, but equally, *on earth* it could be the heart of His believing servant. The Throne did not have to be interpreted metaphorically as a symbol of divine power. The Throne, simply by being 'throne', could invoke corresponding significations of 'throneness' according to a person's level of spiritual understanding.

As he wrote the *Kashf al-asrār*, Maybudī was evidently aware that there would always be those whom he calls mercenaries or wage-earners (*muzdūrān*) or paradise-seekers (*bihisht-jūyān*), who had no aspiration to go beyond the level of outward observance of the religious law. For them he provided not only an explanation of the verses, but also a comprehensive guide to what was required by the *sharīʿa*, as well as what was praiseworthy or reprehensible according to the traditions of the Prophet. In addition, through his mystical interpretations, he gave them a taste of what could be experienced by striving to look beyond 'the blessing (*niʿma*)' to 'the One Who blesses (*munʿim*)', at the same time giving encouragement and solace to those who were already aspiring to transcend themselves. In this pragmatic and catholic approach one might detect the influence of Ghazzālī's *Iḥyā'* or *Kīmiyā-yi saʿādat*, or perhaps it is simply an indication of Sufism's growing outreach during this period.

Maybudī has never been feted as a great mystic or religious thinker; in the history of Sufism his name was almost completely eclipsed by that of Anṣārī, the celebrated Master of the Heart whom he so revered. Yet in his role as an enthusiast, who assembled a vast treasury of traditional knowledge, popular legend and Sufi lore, and as a masterly communicator who knew how to convey this knowledge in an appealing and often compelling style, he has made an invaluable contribution both to the heritage of Islamic mysticism and to Persian literature. This is acknowledged by the number of times Maybudī's *Kashf al-asrār* has been copied over the centuries and, more recently, by the fact that the ten-volume edition has been reprinted seven times since the 1950s.

Yet the importance of this commentary, particularly for those who wish to study Islamic mysticism, deserves to be far more widely appreciated. It is to be hoped that this book has gone some way towards demonstrating the significance of Maybudī's *Kashf al-asrār* for this field. It is further to be hoped that the recent publication of William C. Chittick's abridged translation of the mystical sections of *Kashf al-asrār* alongside other Sufi commentaries for the Great Commentaries on the Holy Qur'an Series,[2] and his inclusion of many translated passages from the work in his anthology, *Divine Love: Islamic Literature and the Path to God*,[3] may serve to make the text more widely known.

In Maybudī's commentary, we find fully and eloquently expressed doctrines that were central to later Sufi authors. Indeed, Maybudī's expositions of these subjects can assist our understanding of Sufi works in both poetry and prose, for in the former the doctrines are often only subtly alluded to, whereas in the latter their expression may be highly technical, or dry and restrained. More generally, therefore, this study may serve to reaffirm the significance that Sufi exegesis holds as a source for understanding the doctrines of Islamic mysticism. As Böwering has stated, and demonstrated with his own study of Tustarī's commentary, the spontaneous comments preserved in mystical interpretations of the Qur'an often represent freer and more direct expressions of Sufi ideas than are to be found in most Sufi sources of this period.[4] Perhaps this study will also have confirmed that texts written in Persian should not escape the purview of anyone wishing to gain a comprehensive knowledge of the religious sciences of Islam, and particularly of mysticism.

There is plenty of scope for further academic research on the *Kashf al-asrār*. A comprehensive study needs to be made of the sources of Maybudī's commentary, particularly the mystical sections. This might throw more light on the provenance of the *Kashf al-asrār*, and answer such questions as how much of Maybudī's commentary derives from Anṣārī, and whether Anṣārī's original was written in Persian or Arabic. Another valuable study would be to trace the influence of *Kashf al-asrār* not only on later *Persian tafsīrs* but also on other works of Sufi literature.

Maybudī's commentary remains a vast but relatively untapped source of information on hagiography and Sufi lore. The difficulty is that the material is scattered throughout the ten volumes of the work. Progress on a new critical edition is underway, one which is being made on the basis of many more manuscripts than were used for the Hekmat edition. However, it will probably be some time before this arduous task is completed. If it were to be available in a digitised and searchable form, it would be an even greater service to scholarship on Qur'anic exegesis and Sufism. Meanwhile, the text is now available at https://ganjour.net, and therefore in principle should be searchable, and in Japan a database of the *Nawbat* III sections of *Kashf al-asrār* is under development at http://kashf-al-asrar.tufs.ac.jp. Beyond this, if time allows, I intend to complete an analytical index of the Maybudī's mystical commentary. Once the data is made more accessible in these ways, then the *Kashf al-asrār* might, in time, come to be valued alongside Sarrāj's *Kitāb al-Lumaʿ*, Kalabādhī's *Kitāb al-taʿarruf*, Mustamlī's *Sharḥ al-taʿarruf*, Qushayrī's *Risāla*, and Hujwīrī's *Kashf al-maḥjūb* as a key source text on the history and doctrines of Sufism.

NOTES

1 De Beaureueil, *Chemins de Dieu*, p. 43.
2 *Kashf al-asrār: The Unveiling of Mysteries*, abridged translation by William C. Chittick, Great Commentaries on the Holy Qur'an Series (Kentucky, 2015). Available at http://www.altafsir.com.
3 William C. Chittick, *Divine Love: Islamic Literature and the Path to God* (New Haven, 2013).
4 Gerhard Böwering, 'The Qur'an commentary of al-Sulamī', in W. B. Hallaq and D.P. Little, eds., *Islamic Studies Presented to Charles J. Adams* (Leiden, 1990), p. 55.

Bibliography

Primary Sources

Abu'l-Futūḥ Rāzī, Ḥusayn b. ʿAlī. *Rawḍ al-jinān wa rawḥ al-janān*, also known as *Tafsīr-i Shaykh Abu'l-Futūḥ al-Rāzī*, ed. Muḥammad Jaʿfar Yāḥaqqī and Muḥammad Mahdī Nāṣiḥ, 20 vols. Mashhad, Āstān-i Quds-i Riḍawī, Bunyād-i pizhūhishhā-yi Islāmī, 1371–5sh/1992–6.

Abū ʿUbayda Maʿmar b. al-Muthannā al-Taymī. *Majāz al-Qur'ān*, ed. Fu'ad Sezgin, 2 vols. Cairo, Maktabat al-Khānjī, 1954–62.

Abū ʿUbayd al-Qāsim b. Sallām. *Kitāb al-nāsikh wa'l-mansūkh*, ed. John Burton. Cambridge, Gibb Memorial Trust, New Series, 1987.

al-ʿAjlūnī, Ismāʿīl b. Muḥammad. *Kashf al-khafāʾ wa muzīl al-ilbās ʿammā ishtahara min al-aḥādīth ʿalā alsinat al-nās*, ed. Aḥmad al-Qalāsh, 2 vols. Beirut, Muʾassasat al-risāla, 1979.

Anṣārī, ʿAbd Allāh. *ʿIlal al-maqāmāt*, text in Serge de Laugier de Beaurecueil, 'Un petit traité de ʿAbdullāh Anṣārī sur les déficiences inhérentes a certaines demeures spirituelles', in Louis Massignon, ed., *Mélanges Louis Massignon*. Damascus, Institut Français de Damas, 1956, I, pp. 153–71. French translation reprinted in Serge de Laugier de Beaurecueil, *Chemins de Dieu*. Paris, Sindbad, 1985.

_____. *Manāzil al-sāʾirīn*, ed. with introduction and French translation by Serge de Laugier de Beaurecueil. Cairo, Institut Français d'Archéologie Orientale, 1962.

_____. *Rasāʾil-i Fārsī-yi Khwāja ʿAbd Allāh Anṣārī*, ed. Sarwar Mawlāʾī. Tehran, Intishārāt-i Ṭūs, 1372sh/1993.

_____. *Ṣad maydān*, text and French translation in Serge de Laugier de Beaurecueil, 'Une ébauche persane des *Manāzil as-Sāʾirīn*: Le *Kitāb-e Ṣad maydān* de ʿAbdullāh Anṣārī', *Mélanges Islamologues d'Archéologie Orientale* 2 (1954), pp. 1–90. French translation reprinted in Serge de Laugier de Beaurecueil, *Chemins de Dieu*. Paris, Sindbad, 1985. English translation by Nahid Angha as *Stations of the Sufi Path: The Hundred Fields (Ṣad maydān) of Abdallah Anṣārī of Herat*. Cambridge, Archetype, 2010.

_____. *Ṭabaqāt al-ṣūfiyya*, ed. ʿAbd al-Ḥayy Ḥabībī. Kabul, Historical Society of Afghanistan, 1962; ed. Sarwar Mawlāʾī. Tehran, Intishārāt-i Ṭūs, 1362sh/1983–4.

al-Ashʿarī, Abu'l-Ḥasan ʿAlī b. Ismāʿīl. *Kitāb al-ibāna ʿan uṣūl al-diyāna*. Cairo, Idārat al-ṭibāʿa al-munīriyya, 1348/1929. Translated by Walter C. Klein as *Abu'l-Ḥasan ʿAlī ibn Ismāʿīl al-Aśʿarī's Kitāb al-Ibāna ʿan uṣūl al-diyāna* (*The Elucidation of Islam's Foundation*). New Haven, American Oriental Society, 1940.

ʿAṭṭār, Farīd al-Dīn. *Ilāhīnāma*, ed. Fu'ād Rawḥānī. Tehran, Kitābfurūshī-yi Zawwār, 1339sh/1960. Translated by John A. Boyle as *The Book of God*. Manchester, Manchester University Press, 1976.

_____. *Tadhkirat al-awliyāʾ*, ed. Muḥammad Istiʿlāmī. Sixth reprint, Tehran, Intishārāt-i Zawwār, 1346sh/1967–8. Partial translation by Arthur J. Arberry in *Muslim Saints and Mystics: Extracts from Attār's Tadhkirat al-auliyāʾ*. Persian Heritage Series. Chicago, University of Chicago Press, 1966.

al-Aʿwār, Hārūn b. Mūsā al-Qārī. *Kitāb al-wujūh wa'l-naẓāʾir fi'l-Qurʾān al-karīm*, ed. Ḥātim Ṣālim al-Damīm. Baghdad, Wizārat al-thaqāfa wa'l-iʿlām, dāʾirat al-āthār wa'l-turāth, 1988.

ʿAyn al-Quḍāt, ʿAbd Allāh b. Muḥammad Hamadānī. *Shakwat al-gharīb*, ed. ʿAfīf ʿUsayrān. Tehran, Tehran University Press, 1962.

_____. *Tamhīdāt*, ed. ʿAfīf ʿUsayrān. Tehran, University of Tehran, 1962.

_____. *Zubdat al-ḥaqāʾiq*, Arabic text, ed. ʿAfīf ʿUsayrān, with Persian translation by Mahdī Tadayyun. Tehran, Iran University Press, 1379sh/2000.

Baqlī, Rūzbihān b. Abī Naṣr. *ʿArāʾis al-bayān fī ḥaqāʾiq al-Qurʾān*, 2 vols. Lithograph edition, Lucknow, Newal Kishore, 1315/1898.

_____. *Sharḥ-i shaṭḥiyyāt*, ed. Henri Corbin. Tehran, Anjuman-i Īranshināsī-yi farānsa dar Īrān, 1966.

al-Bayḍāwī, ʿAbd Allāh b. ʿUmar. *Anwār al-tanzīl wa asrār al-taʾwīl*, published as *Baidhawi Commentarius in Coranum*, ed. Heinrich Leberecht Fleischer (Henricus Orthobius). Leipzig, Vogel, 1846–8.

al-Bayhaqī, Abū Bakr Aḥmad b. Ḥusayn. *Al-Jāmiʿ li-shuʿab al-īmān*, ed. ʿAbd al-ʿAlī ʿAbd al-Ḥamīd Ḥāmid, 14 vols. Riyadh, Maktabat al-rushd, 2003.

_____. *Kitāb al-zuhd al-kabīr*, ed. Amīr Aḥmad Ḥaydar. Beirut, Dār al-jinān, 1987.

al-Bukhārī, Muḥammad b. Ismāʿīl. *Al-Jāmiʿ al-ṣaḥīḥ*, ed. Ludolf Krehl and Theodoor W. Juynboll. Leiden, Brill, 1862–1909. Arabic text and translation in Muhammad Muhsin Khan, *The Translation of the Meanings of Sahih al-Bukhari*, 9 vols. Riyadh, Darussalam, 2004.

Burūsawī, Ismāʿīl Ḥaqqī. *Ruḥ al-bayān*, ed. Aḥmad ʿUbayd ʿInāya. Beirut, Dār iḥyāʾ al-turāth al-ʿArabī, 1421/2001.

al-Dārimī, ʿAbd Allāh b. ʿAbd al-Raḥmān. *Sunan al-Dārimī*, ed. ʿAbd Allāh Ḥāshim Yamānī al-Madanī. Cairo, Dār al-maḥāsin li'l-ṭibāʿa, 1966.

Dawlatshāh Samarqandī. *Tadhkirat al-shuʿarāʾ*, ed. Edward G. Browne. London, Luzac and Leiden, Brill, 1901.

al-Daylamī, Abu'l-Ḥasan ʿAlī b. Muḥammad. *ʿAṭf al-alif al-maʾlūf ʿalaʾl-lām al-maʿṭūf*, ed. Jean-Claude Vadet. Cairo, Al-Maʿhad al-ʿilmī al-Faransī li'l-āthār al-sharqiyya, 1962. Translated into French by J.-C. Vadet as *Le traité d'amour mystique d'al-Daylami*. Geneva, Droz and Paris, Champion, 1980. Translated into English by Joseph N. Bell as *A Treatise on Mystical Love*. Edinburgh, Edinburgh University Press, 2005.

al-Farrāʾ, Yaḥyā b. Ziyād. *Kitāb maʿānī al-Qurʾān*, ed. Aḥmad Yūsuf Najātī. Cairo, Dār al-kutub al-Miṣriyya, 1374/1955.

Farāhī, Muʿīn al-Dīn. *Tafsīr ḥadāʾiq al-ḥaqāʾiq*, ed. Jaʿfar Sajjādī. Tehran, Iran University Press, 1346sh/1967–8. Reprint, Tehran, Amīr Kabīr, 1985.

Ghaznawī, Khwāja Sadīd al-Dīn Muḥammad. *Maqāmāt Zhinda Pīl*, ed. Ḥishmat Allāh Muʾayyad Sanandjī. Tehran, Bungāh-i tarjuma wa nashr-i kitāb, 1340sh/1961.

al-Ghazzālī, Abū Ḥāmid Muḥammad. *Faḍāʾiḥ al-bāṭiniyya*, ed. ʿAbd al-Raḥmān Badawī. Cairo, al-Dār al-qawmiyya li'l-ṭibāʿa wa'l-nashr, 1964.

_____. *Fayṣal al-tafriqa bayn al-islām wa'l-zandaqa*, ed. Sulaymān Dunyā. Cairo, Dār iḥyāʾ al-kutub al-ʿArabiyya, Maṭbaʿat Muṣṭafā al-Bābī al-Ḥalabī, 1961. Translated by Richard J. McCarthy in *Freedom and Fulfillment*. Boston, Twayne, 1980. Translated by Sherman Jackson as *On the Boundaries of Theological Tolerance in Islam: Abū Ḥāmid al-Ghazālī's Fayṣal al-tafriqa bayna al-Islām wa al-zandaqa*. Oxford, Oxford University Press, 2002.

_____. *Iḥyāʾ ʿulūm al-dīn*, 6 vols. Damascus, Dār al-khayr, 1417/1997.

Kitāb al-ʿilm, translated by Nabih Amin Faris as *The Book of Knowledge*. Lahore, Sh. Muhammad Ashraf, 1962.

Kitāb jawāhir al-Qurʾān, translation with introduction and annotation by Muhammad Abul Quasem as *The Jewels of the Qurʾān: al-Ghazālī's Theory*. Bangi, Malaysia, University of Malaya Press, 1977.

Kitāb al-maḥabba wa'l-shawq wa'l-riḍāʾ wa'l-uns, translated into French by Marie-Louise Siauve as *Livre de l'amour, du désir ardent, de l'intimité et du parfait contentement*. Paris, J. Vrin, 1986. Translated into German by Richard Gramlich as *Muḥammad al-Ġazzālīs Lehre von den Stufen zur Gottesliebe: die Bücher 31–36 seines Hauptwerkes*. Wiesbaden, Franz Steiner, 1984.

Kitāb qawāʿid al-ʿaqāʾid, translated by Nabih Amin Faris as *Foundations of the Articles of Faith*. Lahore, Sh. Muhammad Ashraf, 1963.

Kitāb riyāḍat al-nafs and *Kitāb kasr al-shahwatayn*, translated with introduction by Timothy J. Winter as *On Disciplining the Soul and on Breaking the Two Desires*. Cambridge, Islamic Texts Society, 1995.

Kitāb tilāwat al-Qurʾān, translated by Muhammad Abul Quasem as *The Recitation and Interpretation of the Qurʾān: al-Ghazālī's Theory*. Bangi, Malaysia, Jabatan usuluddin dan falsafa, University of Kebangsaan, 1979.

_____. *Iljām al-ʿawāmm ʿan al-kalām*, ed. Muḥammad al-Muʿtaṣim bi'llāh al-Baghdādī. Beirut, Dār al-kitāb al-ʿArabī, 1985.

_____. *Al-Iqtiṣād fi'l-iʿtiqād*, ed. Ibrahim Agâh Çubukçu and Hüseyin Atay. Ankara, Nur Matbaası, 1962.

_____. *Kīmiyā-yi saʿādat*, ed. Ḥusayn Khadīwjam, 2 vols. Third reprint, Tehran, Intishārāt-i ʿilmī wa farhangī, 1364sh/1985.

_____. *Al-Maqṣad al-asnā fī sharḥ maʿānī asmāʾ Allāh al-ḥusnā*, ed. Fadlou A. Shehadi. Beirut, Dār al-Mashriq, 1971. Translated by David B. Burrell and Nazih Daher as *The Ninety-Nine Beautiful Names of God*. Cambridge, Islamic Texts Society, 1992.

_____. *Mishkāt al-anwār*, ed. Abu'l-ʿAlāʾ ʿAfīfī. Cairo, Dār al-qawmiyya li'l-ṭibāʿa wa'l-nashr, 1964. Translated by William H.T. Gairdner as *Al-Ghazzali's Mishkāt al-anwār*. Lahore, Sh. Muhammad Ashraf, 1952. Arabic text edited with translation in David Buchman, *The Niche of Lights*. Utah, Brigham Young University Press, 1998.

_____. *Al-Munqidh min al-ḍalāl*, ed. Farid Jabre. Beirut, al-Lajna al-Lubnāniyya li-tarjamat al-rawāʾiʿ, 1969; ed. Rashid Ahmad (Jullandri). Lahore, Awqāf Board Government of the Punjab, 1971. Translated into French with introduction and notes by Farid Jabre as *al-Munqiḏ min aḍalāl* [sic]*: Erreur et délivrance*. Beirut, Commission internationale pour la traduction des chefs d'oeuvre, 1959. Translated into English by Richard J. McCarthy in *Freedom and Fulfillment*. Boston, Twayne,1980.

_____. *Qānūn al-taʾwīl*, ed. Muḥammad Zāhid al-Kawtharī. Cairo, Maṭbaʿat al-anwār, 1359/1940.

_____. *Tahāfut al-falāsifa*, ed. Sulaymān Dunyā. Cairo, Dār iḥyāʾ al-kutub al-ʿArabiyya, 1947. Translated by Sabih Ahmad Kamali as *al-Ghazālī's Tahafut al-falasifah: Incoherence of the Philosophers*. Lahore, Pakistan Philosophical Congress, 1958.

Ghazzālī, Aḥmad. *Baḥr al-maḥabba*. Bombay, n.p., 1898.

_____. *Sawāniḥ*, ed. Nasrollah Pourjavady. Tehran, Bunyād-i farhang-i Īrān, 1359sh/1980; ed. Helmut Ritter. Istanbul, Maṭbaʿat al-maʿārif li-jamʿiyyat al-mustashriqīn al-Almāniyya, 1942. Translated with an introduction and glossary by Nasrollah Pourjavady as *Sawāniḥ, Inspirations from the World of Pure Spirits*. London, Kegan Paul International, 1986.

Ḥāfiẓ, Shams al-Dīn Muḥammad. *Dīwān-i Ḥāfiẓ*, ed. Parvīz Nātil Khānlarī. Tehran, Intishārāt-i Khwārazmī, 1359sh/1980–1.

al-Ḥakīm al-Tirmidhī, Muḥammad b. Alī. *Bayān al-farq bayn al-ṣadr wa'l-qalb wa'l-fuʾād wa'l-lubb*, ed. Nicholas Heer. Cairo, Dār iḥyāʾ al-kutub al-ʿArabiyya, 1958. Translated by Nicholas Heer in N. Heer and Kenneth L. Honerkamp, *Three Early Sufi Texts*. Louisville, Fons Vitae, 2003.

_____. *Khatm al-awliyāʾ*, ed. ʿUthmān Ismāʿīl Yaḥyā. Beirut, Imprimerie Catholique, 1965.

_____. *Kitāb Nawādir al-uṣūl fī maʿrifat aḥādīth al-rasūl*, ed. Muṣṭafā ʿAbd al-Qādir ʿAṭāʾ, 2 vols. Beirut, Dār al-kutub al-ʿilmiyya, 1992.

al-Ḥallāj, Ḥusayn b. Manṣūr. *Dīwān*, ed. Louis Massignon. Paris, Paul Geuthner, 1955. French translation by Louis Massignon. Paris, Éditions des Cahiers du Sud, 1955.

Hamadānī, ʿAbd Allāh b. Muḥammad. *See* ʿAyn al-Quḍāt.

Hujwīrī, ʿAlī b. ʿUthmān Jullābī. *Kashf al-maḥjūb*, ed. Valentin Zhukovski. Leningrad, Maṭbaʿa-yi dār al-ʿulūm, 1926. Translated by Reynold A. Nicholson as *Kashf al-maḥjūb: The Oldest Persian Treatise on Sufism*. London, Gibb Memorial Trust, 1911.

Ibn Abī Shayba. *Kitāb al-muṣannaf fi'l-aḥādīth wa'l-āthār*, ed. ʿAbd al-Khāliq Afghānī and Amīr al-ʿUmarī al-Aʿẓamī, 15 vols. Bombay, Dār al-Salafiyya, 1979–83.

Ibn ʿAjība, Abū'l-ʿAbbās Aḥmad b. Muḥammad b. al-Mahdī. *Al-Baḥr al-madīd*, ed. Aḥmad ʿAbd Allāh al-Qurashī, 6 vols. Cairo, Ḥasan ʿAbbās Zakī, 1999–2001; ed. ʿUmar Ahmad al-Rāwī, 8 vols. Beirut, Dār al-kutub al-ʿilmiyya, 2002; ed. Wahīd Quṭub, 8 vols. Cairo, al-Maktaba al-tawfiqiyya, n.d.; Turkish translation by Dilaver Selvi as İbn Acîbe el-Hasenî, *Bahru'l-Medîd*, 11 vols. Istanbul, Semerkand yayınları, 2015; Partial English translation by Mohamed Fouad Aresmouk and Michael Abdurrahman Fitzgerald as *The Immense Ocean: Al-Baḥr al-Madīd. A Thirteenth Century Quranic Commentary on the Chapters of the All-Merciful, the Event, and Iron*. Louisville, Fons Vitae, 2009.

_____. *Tafsīr al-fātiha al-kabīr*, ed. Bassām Muḥammad Bārūd, 2 vols. Abu Dhabi, al-Majmaʿ al-Thaqāfī, 1999.

Ibn ʿArabī, Muḥyī al-Dīn. *Fuṣūṣ al-ḥikam*, ed. Abu'l-ʿAlāʾ ʿAfīfī. Cairo, Dār iḥyāʾ al-kutub al-ʿArabiyya, 1946. Reprint, Beirut, Dār al-kitāb al-ʿArabī, 1980. Translated by Ralph W.J. Austin as *Bezels of Wisdom*. Classics of Western Spirituality. London, SPCK, 1980.

Ibn Barrajān, *Iḍāḥ al-ḥikma bi aḥkām al-ʿibra (Wisdom Deciphered, the Unseen Discovered)*, edited by Gerhard Böwering and Yousef Casewit under the title *A Qurʾān Commentary by Ibn Barrajān of Seville (d. 536/1141)*. Leiden and Boston, Brill, 2015.

_____. *Sharḥ asmāʾ Allāh al-ḥusnā*, ed. Purificación de la Torre. Madrid, Consejo Superior des Investigaciones Científicas, 2000.

Ibn Ḥanbal, Aḥmad. *Al-Musnad*, 6 vols. Cairo, Al-Maṭbaʿa al-Maymaniyya, 1895.

Ibn Isḥāq, Muḥammad. *Kitāb al-mubtadaʾ wa'l-mabʿath wa'l-maghāzī*, known as *Sīrat Ibn Isḥāq*, ed. Muḥammad Ḥāmid Allāh. Rabat, Maʿhad al-dirāsat wa'l-abḥāth li'l-taʿrīb, 1976. Translated by Alfred Guillaume as *The Life of Muḥammad: A Translation of Ibn Isḥāq's Sīrat Rasūl Allāh*. London, Oxford University Press, 1955.

Ibn al-Jawzī, ʿAbd al-Raḥmān b. ʿAlī. *Talbīs Iblīs*. Cairo, Idārat al-ṭibāʿa al-munīriyya, 1369/1950. Translated by David S. Margoliouth as *The Devil's Delusion*, *IC* 9, (1935), pp. 1–21, and 12 (1938), pp. 235–40.

Ibn Māja, Abū ʿAbd Allāh Muḥammad b. Yazīd. *Mishkāt al-masābiḥ*, tr. J. Robson, 2 vols. Lahore, Sh. Muhammad Ashraf, 1975.

_____. *Sunan*, ed. Muḥammad Muṣṭafā al-Aʿẓamī. Riyadh, Wizārat al-maʿārif, 1983.

Ibn Manẓūr, Abu'l-Faḍl Jamāl al-Dīn Muḥammad b. Mukarram al-Miṣrī. *Lisān al-ʿArab*, 20 vols. Cairo, Maṭbaʿat Būlāq, 1882–91.

Ibn al-Munawwar, Muḥammad. *See* Mayhanī.

Ibn Qutayba, ʿAbd Allāh b. Muslim. *Tafsīr gharīb al-Qur'ān*, ed. Aḥmad Ṣaqr. Beirut, Dār al-kutub al-ʿāmma, 1978.

_____. *Ta'wīl mushkil al-Qur'ān*, ed. Aḥmad Ṣaqr. Cairo, Dār iḥyāʾ al-kutub al-ʿArabiyya, 1954.

Ibn Rajab, ʿAbd al-Raḥmān b. Aḥmad al-Baghdādī. *Dhayl ʿalā ṭabaqāt al-Ḥanābila*, ed. Henri Laoust and Sāmī al-Dahhān, 2 vols. Damascus, Institut Français de Damas, 1370/1951.

Ibn Sīnā, Abū ʿAlī b. ʿAbd Allāh. *Risāla fi'l-ʿishq* or *Risāla fī māhiyyat al-ʿishq*, in *Rasā'il al-Shaykh al-Ra'īs Abū ʿAlī al-Ḥusayn b. ʿAbd Allāh Ibn Sīnā fī asrār al-ḥikma al-mashriqiyya*, ed. August Ferdinand Mehren. Leiden, Brill, 1889. Study and French translation by Tahini Sabri in '*Risāla fi'l-ʿishq*. Le traité sur l'amour d'Avicenne', *REI* 58 (1990), pp. 109–34.

Ibn Ṭāhir al-Baghdādī, ʿAbd al-Qāhir. *Uṣūl al-dīn*. Istanbul, Madrasat al-ilāhiyyāt bi-dār al-funūn al-Turkiyya, 1928.

Ikhwān al-Ṣafāʾ. *Rasā'il Ikhwān al-Ṣafāʾ wa khullān al-wafāʾ*, ed. Buṭrus al-Bustānī, 4 vols. Beirut, Dār al-Ṣādir, 1957.

ʿIlm al-taṣawwuf, ta'līf dar ḥudūd-i sāl-i 400 hijrī az mu'allif-i nā shinākhta, ed. Nasrollah Pourjavady. Tehran, Muʾassasa-yi pizhūhishī-yi ḥikmat wa falsafa-yi Īrān wa Dānishgāh-i Āzād-i Berlīn, 1390sh/2011.

al-Iṣfahānī, Abū Manṣūr Muʿammar. *Kitāb nahj al-khāṣṣ*, ed. with French introduction by Serge de Laugier de Beaurecueil in ʿAbd al-Raḥmān Badawī, ed., *Mélanges Taha Husain*. Cairo, Dār al-maʿārif, 1962; ed. with Persian introduction by Nasrollah Pourjavady, *Taḥqīqāt-i Islāmī* 3/1–2 (1988–9), pp. 94–149.

al-Iṣfahānī, Abū Nuʿaym. *Ḥilyat al-awliyāʾ*, 10 vols. Cairo, Maktabat al-Khānjī and Maṭbaʿat al-saʿāda, 1932–8; ed. Muṣṭafā ʿAbd al-Qādir ʿAṭāʾ, 11 vols with index. Beirut, Dār al-kutub al-ʿilmiyya, 1997.

Isfarāyinī, Abu'l-Muẓaffar Shāhfūr. *Tāj al-tarājim fī tafsīr al-Qur'ān li'l-aʿājim*, ed. Najīb Māyil Harawī and ʿAlī Akbar Ilāhī Khurāsānī, 3 vols., incomplete. Tehran, Mīrath-i maktūb, 1374sh-/1995–.

al-Iskandarī, ʿAbd al-Muʿṭī al-Lakhmī. *Sharḥ manāzil al-sā'irīn*, ed. Serge de Laugier de Beaurecueil. Cairo, Institut Français d'Archéologie Orientale, 1954.

Ja'farī, Ja'far b. Muḥammad. *Tārīkh-i Yazd*, ed. Iraj Afshar. Persian Text Series 2. Tehran, Bungāh-i tarjuma wa nashr-i kitāb, 1338sh/1960.

Jāmī, 'Abd al-Raḥmān. *Haft awrang*, ed. Murtaḍā Mudarris Gīlānī. Tehran, Kitābfurūshī-yi Sa'dī. 1337sh/1958.

_____. *Nafaḥāt al-uns*, ed. Maḥmūd 'Ābidī. Tehran, Intishārāt-i Iṭṭilā'āt, 1370sh/1991.

al-Jaṣṣāṣ al-Rāzī, Aḥmad b. 'Alī. *Aḥkām al-Qur'ān*, 4 vols. Istanbul, Maṭba'at al-awqāf al-Islāmiyya, 1335–38/1916–19 or 20. Reprinted in 3 vols, Beirut, Dār al-kitāb al-'Arabī, 1978.

al-Kalābādhī, Abū Bakr Muḥammad b. Isḥāq. *Kitāb al-ta'arruf li-madhhab ahl al-taṣawwuf*, ed. Arthur J. Arberry. Cairo, Maṭba'at al-sa'āda, 1934. Translated by Arthur J. Arberry as *Doctrine of the Sufis*. Cambridge, Cambridge University Press, 1935. Reprinted 1977.

al-Kāshānī, 'Abd al-Razzāq. *Tafsīr al-Qur'ān al-karīm*, also known as *Ta'wīlāt al-Qur'ān*, and popularly and erroneously known as the *Tafsīr Ibn 'Arabī*, 2 vols. Beirut, Dār al-yaqẓa al-'Arabiyya, 1968; ed. 'Abd al-Wārith Muḥammad 'Alī. Beirut, Dār al-kutub al-'ilmiyya, 2001. Partially translated by Feras Hamza as *Tafsīr al-Kāshānī. Part I, Sūrahs 1–18*. Louisville, Fons Vitae, forthcoming (available at http://www.altafsir.com).

Kāshifī, Ḥusayn al-Wā'iẓ. *Mawāhib-i 'Aliyya, yā Tafsīr-i Ḥusaynī*, ed. Muḥammad Riḍā Jalālī Nā'īnī, 4 vols. in 2. Tehran, Intishārāt-i Iqbāl, 1317–29sh/1938–50.

Khalīfa, Ḥājjī (Kâtip Çelebi). *Kashf al-ẓunūn*, 2 vols. Istanbul, Maṭābi' wikālat al-ma'ārif al-jalīla, 1941–7.

Kharaqānī, Abu'l-Ḥasan. *Aḥwāl wa aqwāl-i Shaykh Abu'l-Ḥasan Kharaqānī, muntakhab-i Nūr al-'ulūm, manqūl az nuskha-yi khaṭṭī-yi Landan*, ed. Mujtabā Mīnuwī. Tehran, Kitābkhāna-yi Ṭahūrī, 1980.

al-Khargūshī, Abū Sa'd 'Abd al-Malik b. Muḥammad. *Tahdhīb al-asrār*. MS Berlin Ahlwart 2819; ed. Bassām Muḥammad Bārūd. Abu Dhabi, Al-Majma' al-thaqāfī, 1999.

al-Kisā'ī, 'Alī b. Ḥamza. *Kitāb al-mutashābih fi'l-Qur'ān*, ed. Muḥammad Muḥammad Dāwūd. Cairo, Dār al-manār, 1998.

al-Kisā'ī, Muḥammad b. 'Abd Allāh. *Qiṣaṣ al-anbiyā'* (*Vita prophetarum auctore Muḥammed ben 'Abdallah al-Kisā'ī*), ed. Isaac Eisenberg, 2 vols. Leiden, Brill, 1922–3. Translated by William M. Thackston as *The Tales of the Prophets of al-Kisā'ī*. Boston, Twayne, 1978.

al-Maḥallī, Jalāl al-Dīn Muḥammad b. Aḥmad and Jalāl al-Dīn 'Abd al-Raḥmān b. Abī Bakr al-Suyūṭī. *Tafsīr al-Jalālayn*. Damascus, Maktabat al-mallāḥ, 1960; ed. 'Abd Allāh Rabī' Maḥmūd. Beirut, Maktabat Lubnān, 2000.

al-Makkī, Abū Ṭālib. *Qūt al-qulūb fī mu'āmalat al-maḥbūb*, ed. 'Abd al-Mun'im al-Ḥifnī, 2 vols. Cairo, Dār al-rashād, 1991. Translated into

German with introduction and commentary by Richard Gramlich as *Die Nahrung der Herzen*, 4 vols. Stuttgart, Franz Steiner, 1992–5.

Maybudī, Abu'l-Faḍl Rashīd al-Dīn. *Kashf al-asrār wa ʿuddat al-abrār*, ed. Ali Asghar Hekmat *et al.* Tehran, Amīr Kabīr, 1331–9sh/1952–60. Reprinted several times. Extracts translated in Feras Hamza and Sajjad Rizvi, with Farhana Mayar, eds., *An Anthology of Qur'anic Commentaries. Vol. 1: On the Nature of the Divine*. Oxford, Oxford University Press in association with the Institute of Ismaili Studies, 2008; abridged translation into English by William C. Chittick as *The Unveiling of Mysteries and Provision of the Righteous*. Louisville, Fons Vitae, 2015 (also available at http://altafsir.com/).

Mayhanī, Muḥammad b. al-Munawwar b. Abī Saʿd b. Abī Ṭāhir b. Abī Saʿīd. *Asrār al-tawḥīd fī maqāmāt Shaykh Abī Saʿīd*, ed. Muḥammad Riḍā Shafīʿī Kadkanī, 2 vols. Tehran, Intishārāt-i Āgāh, 1366sh/1987. Translated with an introduction and notes by John O'Kane as *The Secrets of God's Mystical Oneness*. California, Mazda and Bibliotheca Persica, 1992.

Mujāhid b. Jabr. *Tafsīr al-imām Mujāhid b. Jabr*, ed. ʿAbd al-Raḥmān al-Ṭāhir b. Muḥammad al-Sūratī, 2 vols. Islamabad, Islamic Research Institute, 1976; ed. Muḥammad ʿAbd al-Salām Abu'l-Nīl. Cairo, Dār al-fikr al-Islāmī al-ḥadītha, 1410/1989.

Muqātil b. Sulaymān. *Kitāb al-ashbāh wa'l-naẓā'ir fi'l-Qur'ān al-karīm*, ed. ʿAbd Allāh Maḥmūd Shiḥāta. Cairo, al-Hayʾa al-Miṣriyya al-ʿāmma li'l-kitāb, 1395/1975.

_____. *Tafsīr al-khams miʾat āya min al-Qurʾān*, ed. Isaiah Goldfeld. Shfaram, Dār al-Mashriq, 1980.

_____. *Tafsīr Muqātil ibn Sulaymān*, ed. ʿAbd Allāh Maḥmūd Shiḥāta, 4 vols. Cairo, al-Hayʾa al-Miṣriyya al-ʿāmma li'l-kitāb, 1979–89.

Muslim b. al-Ḥajjāj al-Qushayrī (al-Naysābūrī). *Ṣaḥīḥ bi-sharḥ al-Nawāwī*, 18 vols. in 9 parts. Cairo, al-Maṭbaʿat al-Miṣriyya bi'l-Azhar, 1929–30.

Mustamlī Bukhārī, Abū Ibrāhīm Ismāʿīl b. Muḥammad. *Khulāṣa-yi Sharḥ al-taʿarruf*, ed. Aḥmad ʿAlī Rajāʾī. Tehran, Bunyad-i farhang-i Īrān, 1349sh/1970.

_____. *Sharḥ al-taʿarruf li-madhhab ahl al-taṣawwuf*, ed. Muḥammad Rawshan. Tehran, Intishārāt-i asāṭīr, 1363sh/1984.

Mustawfī, Muḥammad Mufīd (Bāfiqī). *Jāmiʿ-i Mufīdī*, ed. Iraj Afshar, 3 vols. Tehran, Kitābfurūshī-yi Āzādī, 1961–4.

al-Naḥḥās, Abū Jaʿfar Aḥmad b. Muḥammad. *Kitāb al-nāsikh wa'l-mansūkh*, ed. Muḥammad ʿAbd al-Salām Muḥammad. Kuwait, Maktabat al-falaḥ, 1408/1988.

al-Nasafī, ʿAbd Allāh b. Aḥmad. *Madārik al-tanzīl wa ḥaqāʾiq al-taʾwīl*, ed. Marwān Muḥammad al-Shaʿʿār, 4 vols. Beirut, Dār al-nafāʾis, 1996.

al-Nawawī, Abū Zakariyya Yaḥyā b. Sharaf. *An-Nawawī's Forty Ḥadīth*, Arabic text and translation by Ezzadin Ibrahim and Denys Johnson-Davies. Fifth reprint, Lebanon, The Holy Qur'an Publishing House, 1980.

_____. *Forty Hadith Qudsi*, Arabic text and translation by Ezzadin Ibrahim and Denys Johnson-Davies. Sixth reprint, Beirut, The Holy Qur'an Publishing House, 1990.

al-Naysābūrī, Abū Isḥāq Ibrāhīm b. Manṣūr b. Khalaf. *Qiṣaṣ al-anbiyāʾ*, ed. Ḥabīb Yaghmāʾī. Tehran, Bungāh-i tarjuma wa nashr-i kitāb, 1340sh/1961.

Niẓāmī ʿArūḍī. *Chahār Maqāla*, ed. Muḥammad Qazwīnī. Gibb Memorial Series. Leiden, Brill, 1910. Revised translation by Edward G. Browne as *Four Discourses*. Gibb Memorial Series. London, Luzac, 1921.

Niẓām al-Mulk. *Siyar al-mulūk* or *Siyāsat-nāma*, ed. Hubert Darke. Persian Text Series 8. Tehran, Bungāh-i tarjuma wa nashr-i kitāb, 1340sh/1962. Reprint, 1347sh/1968. Translated by Hubert Darke as *The Book of Government*. London, Routledge Kegan Paul, 1960.

Nūr al-Dīn ʿAlī b. Muḥammad b. Sulṭān (Mullā ʿAlī al-Qārī). *Al-Asrār al-marfūʿa fi'l-akhbār al-mawḍūʿa*, ed. Muḥammad al-Sabbagh. Beirut, Dār al-amāna, 1971.

al-Nūrī, Abu'l-Ḥusayn. *Maqāmāt al-qulūb*, ed. with introduction by Paul Nwyia in *Mélanges de l'Université Saint-Joseph* 44 (1968), pp. 117–54.

Philo of Alexandria. *De opificio mundi*, Greek text with translation in Francis H. Colson and George H. Whitaker, *Philo*. 12 vols. London and Harvard, Loeb Library, 1929.

Qatāda b. Diʿāma. *Kitāb al-nāsikh wa'l-mansūkh fī Kitāb Allāh taʿalā*, ed. Ḥātim Ṣāliḥ al-Dāmin. Beirut, Muʾassasat al-risāla, 1404/1984.

al-Qazwīnī, ʿAbd al-Jalīl b. Abi'l-Ḥasan. *Kitāb al-naqḍ, maʿrūf bi-baʿḍ mathālib al-nawāsib fī naqḍ baʿḍ fadāʾiḥ al-rawāfiḍ*, ed. Jalāl al-Dīn Muḥaddith Urmawī, 3 vols. Tehran, n.p., 1358sh/1980.

al-Qushayrī, Abu'l-Qāsim ʿAbd al-Karīm b. Hawāzan. *Laṭāʾif al-ishārāt*, ed. Ibrāhīm Basyūnī, 3 vols. Cairo, Dār al-kitāb al-ʿArabī, 1968–71. MS Fazıl Ahmed Paşa 117, Köprülü Library, Istanbul. Partially translated by Kristin Zahra Sands as *Subtle Allusions. Part I: Sūrahs 1–4*. Louisville, Fons Vitae, 2017 (also available at http://www.altafsir.com).

_____. *Al-Risāla al-Qushayriyya fī ʿilm al-taṣawwuf*. Cairo, Dār al-kutub al-ḥadītha, 1966. Translated by Barbara Von Schlegel as *The Principles of Sufism*. Berkeley, Mizan Press, 1990. German translation with introduction and commentary by Richard Gramlich as *Das Sendschreiben al-Qušayrīs über das Sufitum*. Stuttgart, Franz Steiner Verlag, Wiesbaden, 1989. English translation by Alexander D. Knysh as *Al-Qushayri's Epistle on Sufism*. Reading, Garnet, 2007.

___. *Tartīb al-sulūk*, ed. Fritz Meier in F. Meier, *Essays on Islamic Piety and Mysticism*, tr. John O'Kane. Leiden, Brill, 1999, pp. 93–133.

al-Rāwandī, Muḥammad b. ʿAlī b. Sulaymān. *Rāḥat al-ṣudūr wa āyat al-surūr*, ed. Muḥammad Iqbāl. Tehran, Amīr Kabīr, 1364sh/1985.

Rāzī, *see* Abu'l-Futūḥ Rāzī.

al-Rāzī, Fakhr al-Dīn Muḥammad. *Al-Tafsīr al-kabīr*, known also as *Mafātīḥ al-ghayb*, 32 vols. in 16. Cairo, al-Maṭbaʿat al-bahiyya al-Miṣriyya, 1938.

Rāzī, Najm al-Dīn ʿAbd Allāh b. Muḥammad al-Rāzī (known as Dāya). *Baḥr al-ḥaqāʾiq wa'l-maʿānī fī tafsīr al-sabʿ al-mathānī*, vol. I, ed. with an introduction by Moḥammad Movahedī. Tehran, Muʾassasa-yi pizhūhishī-yi ḥikmat wa falsafa-yi Īrān, 1392sh/2013.

_____. *Mirṣād al-ʿibād min al-mabdaʾ ila'l-maʿād*, ed. Muḥammad Amīn Riyāḥī. Tehran, Bungāh-i tarjuma wa nashr-i kitāb, 1973. Translated by Hamid Algar as *The Path of God's Bondsmen from Origin to Return*. Delmar, New York, Caravan Books, 1982.

al-Rāzī, Sayyid Murtaḍā. *Tabṣirat al-ʿawāmm fī maʿrifat maqālāt al-anām*, ed. ʿAbbās Iqbāl. Reprint, Tehran, Intishārāt-i asāṭīr, 1984.

Rūmī, Jalāl al-Dīn al-Balkhī. *The Mathnawī*, ed. with translation and commentary by Reynold A. Nicholson, 8 vols. London, Gibb Memorial Trust, 1925–40.

al-Sahlajī (Sahlagī), Abu'l-Faḍl Muḥammad. *Kitāb al-nūr min kalimāt Abī Ṭayfūr*, ed. ʿAbd al-Raḥmān Badawī in ʿA. Badawī, *Shaṭaḥāt al-ṣūfiyya*. Cairo, Maktabat al-nahḍa al-Miṣriyya, 1949.

al-Sakhāwī, Shams al-Dīn Abi'l-Khayr Muḥammad b. ʿAbd al-Raḥmān. *Al-Maqāṣid al-ḥasana fī bayān kathīr min al-aḥādīth al-mushtahira ʿala'l-alsina*, ed. ʿAbd Allāh Muḥammad al-Ṣādiq. Beirut, Dār al-kutub al-ʿilmiyya, 1979.

al-Samʿānī, Abū Saʿd ʿAbd al-Karīm b. Muḥammad b. Manṣūr. *Kitāb al-ansāb*, ed. Muḥammad ʿAbd al-Qādir ʿAṭāʾ. Beirut, Dār al-kutub al-ʿilmiyya, 1998.

Samʿānī, Shihāb al-Dīn Aḥmad. *Rawḥ al-arwāḥ fī sharḥ asmāʾ al-Malik al-Fattāḥ*, ed. Najīb Māyil Harawī. Tehran, Intishārāt-i ʿilmī wa farhangī, 1368sh/1989.

Sanāʾī al-Ghaznawī, Abu'l-Majd Majdūd b. Ādam. *Diwān-i Sanāʾī*, ed. Mudarris Raḍawī. Tehran, Shirkat-i ṭabʿ-i kitāb, 1320sh/1941–2. Reprint, Kitābkhāna-yi Sanāʾī, 1984.

_____. *Ḥadīqat al-ḥaqīqa wa sharīʿat al-ṭarīqa*, partially edited with translation by Major John Stevenson. Calcutta, Baptist Mission Press, 1910; ed. Mudarris Raḍawī. Tehran, Tehran University Press, 1329sh/1950.

al-Sarrāj, Abū Naṣr ʿAbd Allāh b. ʿAlī (al-Ṭūsī). *Kitāb al-lumaʿ fi'l-taṣawwuf*, ed. with synopsis in English by Reynold A. Nicholson. Gibb Memorial Series 22. London, Luzac and Leiden, 1914.

Shabistarī, Maḥmūd, *Gulshan-i rāz*, Persian text with translation and notes, chiefly from the commentary of Muḥammad b. Yaḥyā Lāhījī, by Edward H. Whinfield. London, Trübner, 1880; ed. Ṣamad Muwaḥḥid in *Majmūʿa-yi āthār-i Shaykh Maḥmūd Shabistarī*. Second reprint, Tehran, Ṭahūrī, 1371sh/1992.

al-Shahrastānī, Abu'l-Fatḥ Muḥammad b. ʿAbd al-Karīm. *Kitāb al-milal wa'l-niḥal*, ed. William Cureton. Leipzig, Otto Harrassowitz, 1842. Partial translation by ʿAbd al-Karīm Kāzī and J.G. Flynn as *Muslim Sects and Divisions: The Section on Muslim Sects in the Kitāb al-milal wa'l-niḥal*. London and Boston, Kegan Paul International, 1984.

_____. *Mafātīḥ al-asrār wa maṣābīḥ al-abrār*, facsimile edition with introduction and index, 2 vols. Tehran, Markaz-i intishārāt-i nusakh-i khaṭṭī, 1368sh/1989.

al-Sijistānī, Muḥammad b. ʿUzayr. *Tafsīr gharīb al-Qur'ān*, ed. Muḥammad al-Ṣādiq al-Qamḥāwī. Cairo, Maktabat al-Jundī, 1970.

al-Sirjānī, Abu'l-Ḥasan ʿAlī b. al-Ḥasan. *Al-Bayāḍ wa'l-sawād*, ed. Muḥsin Pūrmukhtār. Tehran, Muʾassasa-yi pizhūhishī-yi ḥikmat wa falsafa-yi Īrān wa Dānishgāh-i Āzād-i Berlīn, 1390sh/2011; ed. Bilal Orfali and Nada Saab and published as *Sufism, Black and White: A Critical Edition of* Kitāb al-Bayāḍ wa-l-Sawād *by Abū l-Ḥasan al-Sīrjānī (d. ca. 470/1077)*. Leiden, Brill, 2012.

al-Subkī, Tāj al-Dīn ʿAbd al-Wahhāb b. ʿAlī. *Ṭabaqāt al-Shāfiʿiyya al-kubrā*, ed. Maḥmūd Muḥammad al-Ṭanāḥī and ʿAbd al-Fattāḥ Muḥammad al-Ḥulw. Cairo, Ḥajar li'l-ṭibāʿa wa'l-nashr, 1992.

Sufyān al-Thawrī, Abū ʿAbd Allāh Sufyān b. Saʿīd b. Masrūq. *Tafsīr al-Qur'ān al-karīm*, ed. Imtiyāz ʿAlī ʿArshī. Rampur, n.p., 1965. Reprinted as *Tafsīr Sufyān al-Thawrī*. Beirut, Dār al-kutub al-ʿilmiyya, 1403/1983.

al-Suhrawardī, Shihāb al-Dīn Yaḥyā b. Ḥabash. *Fī ḥaqīqat al-ʿishq* (known also as *Mūnis al-ʿushshāq*), Persian text in *Majmūʿa-yi muṣannafāt-i Shaykh-i Ishrāq, Shihāb al-Dīn Yaḥyā Suhrawardī*, III: *Majmūʿa-yi āthār-i Fārsī-yi Shaykh-i Ishrāq*, ed. Seyyed Hossein Nasr. Tehran, Anjuman-i shāhanshāhī-yi falsafa-i Īrān, 1970. Translated by William M. Thackston as *The Mystical and Visionary Treatises of Shihabuddin Yahya Suhrawardi*. London, Octagon, 1982.

al-Sulamī, Muḥammad b. al-Ḥusayn Abū ʿAbd al-Raḥmān. *Darajāt al-muʿāmalāt*, ed. Aḥmad Ṭāhirī ʿIrāqī in Nasrollah Pourjavady, ed., *Majmūʿa-yi āthār-i Abū ʿAbd al-Raḥmān Sulamī*, 2 vols. Tehran, Iran University Press, 1369sh/1990.

_____. *Ḥaqā'iq al-tafsīr*. MS British Library Or. 9433; ed. Sayyid ʿImrān. Beirut, Dār al-kutub al-ʿilmiyya, 2001. Comments attributed to Jaʿfar al-Ṣādiq ed. with introduction by Paul Nwyia in 'Le tafsîr mystique attribué a Ğaʿfar Ṣâdiq', *Mélanges de l'Université Saint-Joseph* 43 (1967), pp. 179–230. Translated into English by Farhana Mayer as *Spiritual Gems: The Mystical Qur'an Commentary Ascribed to Imam Jaʿfar al-Ṣādiq, as Contained in Sulamī's Ḥaqāʾiq al-tafsīr*. Louisville, Fons Vitae, 2011. Comments of Ibn ʿAṭāʾ al-Adamī ed. Paul Nwyia in *Trois oeuvres inédites de mystiques musulmanes: Šaqīq Balḫī, Ibn ʿAṭā, Niffārī*. Beirut, Dar el-Machreq, 1973. Comments attributed to Ḥallāj ed. Louis Massignon in idem. *Essai sur les origines du lexique technique de la mystique musulmane*. Paris, Paul Geuthner, 1922. These extracts have been reprinted in Nasrollah Pourjavady, ed., *Majmūʿa-yi āthār-i Abū ʿAbd al-Raḥmān Sulamī*, 2 vols. Tehran, Iran University Press, 1369sh/1990.

_____. *Kitāb al-futuwwa*, ed. Süleyman Ateş. Ankara, n.p., 1397/1977. Reprinted in Nasrollah Pourjavady, ed., *Majmūʿa-yi āthār-i Abū ʿAbd al-Raḥmān Sulamī*, 2 vols. Tehran, Iran University Press, 1369sh/1990. Translated by Sheikh Tosun Bayrak al-Jerrahi al-Helvati as *The Book of Sufi Chivalry*. New York, Inner Traditions, 1983.

_____. *Laṭāʾif al-miʿrāj*, tr. Frederick S. Colby as *The Subtleties of the Ascension: Early Mystical Sayings on Muḥammad's Heavenly Journey*. Louisville, Fons Vitae, 2006.

_____. *Masāʾil wa taʾwīlāt ṣūfiyya li-Abī ʿAbd al-Raḥmān al-Sulamī/Sufi Inquiries and Interpretations of Abū ʿAbd al-Raḥmān al-Sulamī and a Treatise of Traditions by Ismāʿīl al-Naysābūrī*, ed. Bilal Orfali and Gerhard Böwering. Beirut, Dar el-Machreq, 2010.

_____. *Rasāʾil ṣūfiyya li-Abī ʿAbd al-Raḥmān al-Sulamī (d. 412/1021)*, ed. Gerhard Böwering and Bilal Orfali. Beirut, Dar el-Machreq, 2009.

_____. *Risālat al-Malāmatiyya wa'l-ṣūfiyya wa ahl al-futuwwa*, ed. Abu'l-ʿAlāʾ ʿAfīfī. Cairo, Maṭbaʿat ʿĪsā al-Bābī al-Ḥalabī, 1945. Reprinted in Nasrollah Pourjavady, ed., *Majmūʿa-yi āthār-i Abū ʿAbd al-Raḥmān Sulamī*, 2 vols. Tehran, Iran University Press, 1369sh/1990. Translated into French by Roger Deladrière as *Sulami: La lucidité implacable (Épître des hommes du blâme)*. Paris, Arléa, 1991.

_____. *Ṭabaqāt al-ṣūfiyya*, ed. Johannes Pedersen. Leiden, Brill, 1960.

_____. *Ziyādāt ḥaqāʾiq al-tafsīr*, ed. with introduction by Gerhard Böwering. Beirut, Dār al-Mashriq, 1995.

_____. [Various] as *Abū ʿAbd ar-Rahmān as-Sulamī: Collected Works on Sufism. Vol. 3*, ed. Nasrollah Pourjavady and Mohammad Soori. Tehran, Iranian Institute of Philosophy and Institute of Islamic Studies with the Free University of Berlin, 2009.

al-Suyūṭī, Jalāl al-Dīn ʿAbd al-Raḥmān. *Al-Itqān fī ʿulūm al-Qurʾān*, ed. Muḥammad Abu'l-Faḍl Ibrāhīm, 4 parts in 2 vols. Cairo, Maktabat wa maṭbaʿat al-mashhad al-Ḥusaynī, 1967.

al-Ṭabarānī, Sulaymān b. Aḥmad Abu'l-Qāsim b. Aḥmad al-Lakhmī al-Shāmī. *Al-Muʿjam al-awsaṭ*, ed. Abu'l-Maʿādh b. Muḥammad and ʿAbd al-Muḥsin al-Ḥusaynī, 10 vols. Cairo, Dār al-Ḥaramayn, 1415/1994–5.

_____. *Al-Muʿjam al-kabīr*. Cairo, Dār akhbār al-yawm, 1426/2005.

al-Ṭabarī, Abū Jaʿfar. *Jāmiʿ al-bayān ʿan taʾwīl āy al-Qurʾān*, published under the title *Jāmiʿ al-bayān ʿan tafsīr al–Qurʾān*, 30 parts in 10 vols., with 1 vol. index. Cairo, Maṭbaʿat al-Maymanīya, 1321/1903; ed. Maḥmūd Muḥammad Shākir and Aḥmad Muḥammad Shākir, vols. 1–16, incomplete. Cairo, Dār al-maʿārif, 1955–69. Abridged translation with introduction of vol. I by John Cooper as *The Commentary on the Qurʾān*, Oxford, Oxford University Press, 1987.

______. *Taʾrīkh al-rusul waʾl-mulūk*, ed. Muḥammad Abu'l-Faḍl Ibrāhīm, 10 vols. Cairo, Dār al-maʿārif, 1960–9. Translated as *The History of al-Ṭabarī*, I: *From the Creation to the Flood*, translated with general introduction by Franz Rosenthal. Albany, SUNY, 1989; II: *Prophets and Patriarchs*, translated by William M. Brinner. Albany, SUNY, 1987; III: *The Children of Israel*, translated and annotated by William M. Brinner. Albany, SUNY, 1991.

al-Ṭabrisī (Ṭabarṣī), al-Faḍl b. al-Ḥasan. *Majmaʿ al-bayān fī tafsīr al-Qurʾān*. Qum, Maktabat Āyatullāh al-ʿUẓmā al-Marʿashī, 1403/1983–4.

al-Thaʿlabī, Abū Isḥāq Aḥmad b. Muḥammad. *Al-Kashf waʾl-bayān* also known as *Tafsīr al-Thaʿlabī*, ed. ʿAlī ʿĀshūr. Beirut, Dār iḥyāʾ al-turāth al-ʿArabī, 2002.

_____. *Qiṣaṣ al-anbiyāʾ al-musammā biʾl-ʿArāʾis al-majālis*. Cairo, Dār al-manār, n.d. Translated by William M. Brinner as *ʿArāʾis al-majālis fī qiṣaṣ al-anbiyāʾ or: Lives of the Prophets as recounted by Abū Isḥāq Aḥmad b. Muḥammad b. Ibrāhīm al-Thaʿlabī*. Leiden and Boston, Brill, 2002.

al-Tirmidhī, Muḥammad b. ʿĪsā. *Al-Jāmiʿ al-ṣaḥīḥ wa huwa Sunan al-Tirmidhī*, ed. Aḥmad Muḥammad Shākir. Cairo, Maṭbaʿat Muṣṭafā al-Bābī al-Ḥalabī, 1937.

al-Ṭūsī, Abū Jaʿfar Muḥammad b. al-Ḥasan. *Al-Tibyān fī tafsīr al-Qurʾān*, ed. Aḥmad Shawqī al-Amīn and Aḥmad Ḥabīb Qaṣīr al-ʿĀmilī, 10 vols. Najaf, al-Maṭbaʿat al-ʿilmiyya, 1959–63.

Ṭūsī, Aḥmad b. Muḥammad b. Zayd. *Tafsīr-i Sūra-yi Yūsuf: al-sittīn al-jāmiʿ li-laṭāʾif al-basāṭīn*, ed. Muḥammad Rawshan. Persian Texts Series 35. Tehran, Bungāh-i tarjuma wa nashr-i kitāb, 1967.

al-Tustarī, Sahl b. ʿAbd Allāh. *Tafsīr al-Qurʾān al-ʿaẓīm*. Cairo, Dār al-kutub al-ʿArabiyya al-kubrā, 1329/1911; ed. Muḥammad Bāsil ʿUyyūn al-Sūd and published as *Tafsīr al-Tustarī*. Beirut, Dār al-Kutub al-ʿIlmiyya, 2002. Translated by Annabel Keeler and Ali Keeler as *Tafsīr al-Tustarī*. Louisville, Fons Vitae, 2011 (also available at http://www.altafsir.com).

al-Zamakhsharī, Abu'l-Qāsim Maḥmūd b. ʿUmar. *Al-Kashshāf ʿan ḥaqāʾiq al-tanzīl*, 4 vols. Cairo, Maṭbaʿat Muṣṭafā al-Bābī al-Ḥalabī, 1972.

Secondary Sources

Abdel Haleem, Muhammad A.S. 'The story of Joseph in the Qurʾān and the Old Testament', *ICMR* 1/2 (1990), pp. 171–91.

_____. *Understanding the Qurʾān*. London, IB Tauris, 1999.

_____. *The Qur'an: A New Translation*. Oxford, Oxford University Press, 2004.

Abdel-Kader, Ali Hasan. *The Life, Personality and Works of al-Junayd*. London, Gibb Memorial Trust, 1976.

Abdur Rabb, Muhammad. *The Life, Thought and Historical Importance of Abū Yazīd al-Bisṭāmī*. Dacca, Academy for Pakistani Affairs, 1971.

Abrahamov, Binyamin. *Islamic Theology: Traditionalism and Rationalism*. Edinburgh, Edinburgh University Press, 1998.

_____. 'The *bi-lā kayfa* doctrine and its foundation in Islamic theology', *Arabica* 42 (1995), pp. 165–79.

Abul Quasem, Muhammad. 'Al-Ghazālī in defence of a Sufistic interpretation of the Qurʾān', *IC* 53 (1979), pp. 63–86.

al-Afghānī, Muḥammad Saʿīd. *ʿAbd Allāh al-Anṣārī al-Harawī, mābādiʾuhu wa ārāʾuhu'l-kalāmiyya wa'l-rūḥiyya*. Cairo, Dār al-kutub al-ḥadītha, 1968.

Afshar, Iraj. 'Iḥtimālī dar bāb-i muʾallif-i *Kashf al-asrār*', *Yaghmā* Year 14 (1340sh/1962), p. 312.

_____. 'Sang-i qabr-i barādar-i muʾallif-i *Kashf al-asrār*', *Yaghmā* Year 20 (1346sh/1968), pp. 190–2.

_____. 'Dukhtar-i Maybudī', *Yaghmā* Year 21 (1347sh/1969), p. 440.

_____. 'Two 12th century gravestones of Yazd in Mashhad and Washington', *Studia Iranica* 2/2 (1973), pp. 203–11.

______. 'Khāndān-i Jamāl al-Islām', *Yaghmā* Year 31 (1357sh/1979), pp. 624–8.

Ahmad, Rashid (Jullandri). 'Qurʾānic exegesis and classical *tafsīr*', *IQ* 12 (1968), pp. 71–119.

_____. 'Tafsīr in Sufi literature with particular reference to Abū al-Qāsim al-Qushayrī'. Ph.D Thesis, University of Cambridge, no. 6351, October 1968.

_____. 'Abū al-Qāsim al-Qushayrī as a theologian and commentator', *IQ* 13 (1969), pp. 6–69.

Aigle, Denise, ed. *Saints Orientaux*. Paris, De Boccard, 1995.

Ali de Unzaga, Omar. 'The conversation between Moses and God (*munāǧāt Mūsā*) in the *Epistles* of the Pure Brethren (*Rasāʾil Iḫwān al-Ṣafāʾ*)', in Daniel de Smet, Godefroid de Callatäy and Jan M.F. Van Reeth, eds.,

Al-Kitâb: la sacralité du texte dans le monde de l'Islam. Brussels, Leuven and Louvain-La-Neuve, Société belge d'études orientales, 2004, pp. 371–87.

Allard, Michel. 'En quoi consiste l'opposition faite a al-Ashʿarī par ses contemporains Ḥanbalites?', *REI* 28 (1960), pp. 93–108.

Alshaar, Nuha, ed. *The Qur'an and* Adab*: The Shaping of Literary Traditions in Classical Islam*. Oxford, Oxford University Press in association with the Institute of Ismaili Studies, 2017.

Amir-Moezzi, Mohammad Ali, ed. *Le voyage initiatique en terre d'Islam*. Louvain, Peeters, 1996.

Anawati, Georges C. and Louis Gardet. *La mystique musulmane*. Paris, Vrin, 1961.

_____. *Introduction a la théologie musulmane*. Third edition, Paris, Vrin, 1981.

Anderson, George K. *The Legend of the Wandering Jew*. Providence, Brown University Press, 1965.

Andrae, Tor. *Die Person Muhammeds in Lehre und Glauben Seiner Gemeinde*, Stockholm, Kungl. boktryckeriet. P.A. Norstedt & söner, 1918.

Anzābī-nizhād, Riḍā. *Guzīda-yi tafsīr-i Kashf al-asrār, ta'līf-i Rashīd al-Dīn Maybudī*. Tehran, Jāmī, 1374sh/1995.

Arberry, Arthur J. *The Koran Interpreted*. London, George Allen and Unwin, 1955. Numerous reprints from several publishers.

_____. *Revelation and Reason in Islam*. London and New York, George Allen and Unwin, 1957.

Ateş, Süleyman. *İşârî tefsir okulu*. Ankara, Ankara Üniversitesi Basımevi, 1974.

Awn, Peter. *Satan's Tragedy and Redemption: Iblīs in Sufi Psychology*. Leiden, Brill, 1983.

Ay, Mahmut. 'The Sufi hermeneutics of Ibn ʿAjība (d. 1224/1809): a study of some eschatological verses of the Qur'an', in Annabel Keeler and Sajjad Rizvi, eds., *The Spirit and the Letter: Approaches to the Esoteric Interpretation of the Qur'an*. Oxford, Oxford University Press in association with the Institute of Ismaili Studies, 2016, pp. 415–41.

Aydin, Mehmet S. 'Al-Ghazâli on metaphorical interpretation', in Ralph Bisschops and James Francis, eds., *Metaphor, Canon and Community*. Bern, Peter Lang, 1999, pp. 242–55.

Ayoub, Mahmoud M. 'The speaking Qurʾān and the silent Qurʾān: a study of the principles and development of Imāmī Shīʿī *tafsīr*', in Andrew Rippin, ed., *Approaches to the History of the Interpretation of the Qurʾān*. Oxford, Clarendon and New York, Oxford University Press, 1988, pp. 77–98.

Badawī, ʿAbd al-Raḥmān, ed. *Mélanges Taha Husain*. Cairo, Dār al-maʿārif, 1962.

_____. *Shataḥāt al-Ṣūfiyya*. Cairo, Maktabat al-naḥda al-Miṣriyya, 1949.

Bāhir, Muḥammad. *Abu'l-Futūḥ al-Rāzī wa tafsīr-i rawḍ al-jinān*. Tehran, Khāna-yi kitāb, 2009.
Bar-Asher, Meir M. *Scripture and Exegesis in Early Imāmī Shi'ism*. Leiden and Boston, Brill and Jerusalem, Magnus Press, 1999.
Bauer, Karen, ed. *Aims, Methods and Contexts of Qur'anic Exegesis (2nd/8th–9th/15th C.)*. Oxford, Oxford University Press in association with the Institute of Ismaili Studies, 2013.
Bausani, Alesssandro. 'Religion in the Saljuq period', *CHI* V, pp. 283–302.
De Beaurecueil, Serge de Laugier. 'Une ébauche persane des *Manāzil as-Sā'irīn*: Le *Kitāb-e Ṣad maydān* de ʿAbdullāh Anṣārī', *Mélanges Islamologiques d'Archéologie Orientale* 2 (1954), pp. 1–90.
_____. 'Un petit traité de ʿAbdullāh Anṣārī sur les déficiences inhérentes a certaines demeures spirituelles', in Louis Massignon, ed., *Mélanges Louis Massignon*, 3 vols. Damascus, Institut Français de Damas, 1956, I, pp. 153–71.
_____. *Khwādja ʿAbdullāh Anṣārī, mystique Ḥanbalite*. Beirut, Imprimerie Catholique, 1965.
_____. *Chemins de Dieu*. Paris, Sindbad, 1985.
Bell, Joseph N. *Love Theory in Later Hanbalite Islam*. Albany, SUNY, 1979.
Bellamy, James A. 'The mysterious letters of the Koran: old abbreviations of the Basmalah', *JAOS* 93/3 (1973), pp. 267–85.
Bello, Iysa A. *The Medieval Islamic Controversy between Philosophy and Orthodoxy*. Leiden, Brill, 1989.
Bernstein, Marc S. *Stories of Joseph: Narrative Migrations between Judaism and Islam*. Detroit, MI, Wayn State University Press, 2006.
Bisschops, Ralph and James Francis, eds. *Metaphor, Canon and Community*. Bern, Peter Lang, 1999.
Bosworth, Clifford E. 'The rise of the Karrāmiyyah in Khurasan', *MW* 50 (1960), pp. 5–14.
_____. 'Kākūyids', *EI*², IV, pp. 465–7.
_____. 'Karrāmiyya', *EI*², IV, pp. 667–9.
_____. 'The political and dynastic history of the Iranian world (AD 1000–1217)', *CHI* V, pp. 1–202.
Böwering, Gerhard. *The Mystical Vision of Existence in Classical Islam: The Qur'ānic Hermeneutics of the Ṣūfī Sahl at-Tustarī (d. 283/896)*. Berlin and New York, Walter de Gruyter, 1980.
_____. 'Sufi hermeneutics and medieval Islam'. Discussion paper given at the Tokyo Sophia University, Tokyo, 1987. Published in *Revue des études islamiques* 55–7 (1987–8), pp. 255–70.
_____. 'The Qur'ān commentary of al-Sulamī', in Wael B. Hallaq and Donald P. Little, eds., *Islamic Studies Presented to Charles J. Adams*. Leiden, Brill, 1990, pp. 41–56.

_____. 'The light verse: Qur'ānic text and Sufi interpretation', *Oriens* 36 (2001), pp. 113–44.

_____. 'The Scriptural senses in medieval Ṣūfī Qur'ān exegesis', in Jane Dammen McAuliffe *et al.*, ed., *With Reverence for the Word: Medieval Exegesis in Judaism, Christianity, and Islam.* Oxford and New York, Oxford University Press, 2003, pp. 346–75.

_____. 'The interpretation of the Arabic letters in early Sufism: Sulamī's *Sharḥ maʿānī al-ḥurūf*', in Annabel Keeler and Sajjad Rizvi, eds., *The Spirit and the Letter: Approaches to the Esoteric Interpretation of the Qur'an.* Oxford, Oxford University Press in association with the Institute of Ismaili Studies, 2016, pp. 86–124.

Brinner, William M. 'An Islamic decalogue', in William M. Brinner and Stephen D. Ricks eds., *Studies in Islamic and Judaic Traditions II.* Atlanta, Ga., Scholars Press, 1989, pp. 67–84.

_____ and Stephen D. Ricks, eds. *Studies in Islamic and Judaic Traditions*, 2 vols. Atlanta, Ga., Scholars Press, 1989.

De Bruijn, Johannes T.P. *Of Piety and Poetry: The Interaction of Religion and Literature in the Life and Works of Ḥakīm Sanā'ī of Ghazna.* Leiden, Brill, 1983.

_____. 'The *Qalandariyyāt* in Persian mystical poetry, from Sanā'ī onwards', in Leonard Lewisohn, ed., *The Legacy of Mediaeval Persian Sufism.* London, Khaniqahi Nimatullahi Publications, 1992, pp. 77–86.

Bulliet, Richard. *The Patricians of Nishapur: A Study in Medieval Islamic Social History.* Cambridge Mass., Harvard University Press, 1972.

_____. 'The political-religious history of Nishapur in the eleventh century', in Donald S. Richards, ed., *Islamic Civilisation: 950–1150.* Oxford and London, Cassirer, 1973, pp. 80–91.

_____. *Islam, the View from the Edge.* New York, Columbia University Press, 1994.

Burge, Stephen R., ed., *The Meaning of the Word: Lexicology and Qur'anic Exegesis.* Oxford, Oxford University Press in association with the Institute of Ismaili Studies, 2015.

Calder, Norman. 'From Midrash to scripture: the sacrifice of Abraham in early Islamic tradition', *Le Muséon* 101 (1988), pp. 375–402.

_____. 'Tafsīr from Ṭabarī to Ibn Kathīr: problems in the description of a genre, illustrated with reference to the story of Abraham', in Gerald R. Hawting and Abdul-Kader Shareef, eds., *Approaches to the Qur'ān.* London and New York, Routledge, 1993, pp. 101–40.

Casewit, Yousef, *The Mystics of al-Andalus: Ibn Barrajān and Islamic Thought in the Twelfth Century.* Cambridge, Cambridge University Press, 2017.

Chabbi, Jacqueline. 'La fonction du ribat a Baghdad du Ve siecle au début du VIIe siecle', *REI* 42 (1974), pp. 101–21.

_____. 'Remarques sur le développement historique des mouvements ascétiques et mystiques au Ḫurāsān', *SI* 46 (1977), pp. 6–72.

_____. 'Khānḳāh', *EI²*, IV, pp. 1025–6.

Chaumont, Eric, ed. *Autour du regard.* Louvain, Peeters, 2003.

_____. 'al-Shāfiʿī' *EI²*, IX, pp. 181–5.

Chittick, William. 'The myth of Adam's fall in Aḥmad Samʿānī's *Rawḥ al-arwāḥ*', in Leonard Lewisohn, ed., *Classical Persian Sufism from its Origins to Rumi.* London and New York, Khaniqahi Nimatullahi Publications, 1993, pp. 337–59.

_____. *Divine Love: Islamic Literature and the Path to God.* New Haven, Yale University Press, 2013.

_____, tr. with introduction. *The Unveiling of Mysteries and Provision of the Righteous. See* Primary Sources, Maybudī, *Kashf al-asrār.*

Colby, Frederick S. *Narrating Muḥammad's Night Journey: Tracing the Development of the Ibn ʿAbbās Ascension Discourse.* Albany, SUNY, 2008.

_____, tr., *The Subtleties of the Ascension. See* Primary Sources, al-Sulamī, *Laṭāʾif al-miʿrāj.*

Colson, Francis Henry and George Herbert Whittaker. *Philo of Alexandria.* London, Heinemann, 1929–62.

Corbin, Henri. 'L'intériorisation du sens en herméneutique soufie', *Eranos Jahrbuch* 26 (1957), pp. 57–187.

_____. 'Herméneutique spirituelle comparée, I. Swedenborg - II. Gnose Ismaélienne', *Eranos-Jahrbuch* 33 (Zurich 1965), pp. 71–176.

_____. *L'Homme de lumiere dans le soufisme iranien.* Paris, Éditions présence, 1971. Translated by Nancy Pearson as *Man of Light in Iranian Sufism.* London, Shambala, 1978. Reprint, New Lebanon, Omega, 1994.

_____. *En Islam iranien.* Paris, Gallimard, 1971–2.

_____. *Avicenne et le récit visionnaire: étude sur le cycle des récits avicenniens.* Paris, Berg International, 1979. Translated by Willard R. Trask as *Avicenna and the Visionary Recital.* London, Routledge and Kegan Paul, 1960–1.

Crotty, Robert B., ed. *The Charles Strong Lectures, 1972–1984.* Leiden, Brill, 1987.

Dabashi, Hamid. *Truth and Narrative: The Untimely Thoughts of ʿAyn al-Quḍāt al-Hamadhānī.* Richmond, Curzon Press, 1999.

Daftary, Farhad. *The Ismāʿīlīs: Their History and Doctrines.* Cambridge, Cambridge University Press, 1990.

Damghānī, Aḥmad Mahdawī. *Ṣawābnāma-yi aghlaṭ-i chāpī-yi mujalladāt-i dahgāna-yi tafsīr-i sharīf-i Kashf al-asrār wa ʿuddat al-abrār*, ed. Saʿīd Wāʿiẓ. Tehran, Ayene-ye Miras, 2007.

Dānishpazhūh, Muḥammad Taqī. '*Fuṣūl*-i Rashīd al-Dīn Maybudī', *Farhang-i Īrān-zamīn* Year 16 (1348sh/1969), pp. 44–89.

Dashtī, Mihdī. 'Ta'ammul dar bara-yi tafsīr-i *Kashf al-asrār*-i Maybudi', *Majalla-yi Safīna* (Winter 1382/2003). (Available at http://www.maarefquran.org/index.php/page,viewArticle/LinkID,10658)

Deladrière, Roger. 'Abū Yazīd al-Bisṭāmī et son enseignment spirituelle', *Arabica* 14 (1967), pp. 76–89.

_____. 'Les niveaux de conscience selon l'exégèse d'al-Qāšānī', *Bulletin d'études orientales* 29 (1977), pp. 115–20.

Dhahabī, Muḥammad Ḥusayn. *Al-Tafsīr wa'l-mufassirūn*, 3 vols. Reprint, Beirut, Dār al-Yūsuf, 2000.

Dihkhudā, ʿAlī Akbar. *Lughat-nāma*, 50 vols. Tehran, Tehran University Press, 1325–52sh/1946–73.

Ernst, Carl W. *Words of Ecstasy in Sufism*. Albany, SUNY, 1985.

_____. 'The stages of love in early Persian Sufism from Rābiʿa to Rūzbihān', in Leonard Lewisohn, ed., *Classical Persian Sufism from its Origins to Rumi*. London and New York, Khaniqahi Nimatullahi Publications, 1993, pp. 435–55.

_____. *Rūzbihān Baqlī: Mysticism and the Rhetoric of Sainthood in Persian Sufism*. Richmond, Curzon Press, 1996.

Fahd, Toufic. 'Nubuwwa', *EI*[2], VIII, pp. 93–7.

Farhadi, A.G. Ravan. *ʿAbdullāh Anṣārī of Herāt (1006–1089): An Early Sufi Master*. Richmond, Surrey, Curzon, 1996.

Fikrat, Muhammad Asif. *Munājāt wa guftār-i Pīr-i Harāt Khwāja ʿAbdu'llāh-i Anṣārī-yi Harawī*. Kabul, Bayhaqī, 1355sh/1976.

Firestone, Reuven. 'Abraham's son as intended sacrifice', *Journal of Semitic Studies* 34 (1989), pp. 95–131.

_____. *Journeys in Holy Lands*. Albany, SUNY, 1990.

Furūzānfar, Badīʿ al-Zamān. *Sharḥ-i aḥwāl wa naqd wa taḥlīl-i āthār-i Farīd al-Dīn Muḥammad ʿAṭṭār-i Nīshāpūrī*. Kitābfurūshī-yi Dihkhudā, Tehran, 1363sh/1984.

_____. *Aḥādīth wa qiṣaṣ-i Mathnawī*, re-edited by Ḥusayn Dāwūdī. Tehran, Amīr Kabīr 1376sh/1997.

Frank, Richard M. 'Elements in the development of the teaching of al-Ashʿarī', *Le Muséon* 104 (1991), pp. 141–90.

_____ 'al-Ghazālī on *taqlīd*: scholars, theologians and philosophers', *Zeitschrift für Geschichte der arabisch-islamischen Wissenschaften* 7 (1991–2), pp. 207–52.

_____. *Creation and the Cosmic System: al-Ghazālī and Avicenna*. Heidelberg, Carl Winter Universitätsverlag, 1992.

_____. *Al-Ghazālī and the Ashʿarite School*. Durham and London, Duke University Press, 1994.

Friedlander, Israel. 'Khiḍr', *Encyclopaedia of Religion and Ethics*, ed. James Hastings. New York, 1915, VII, pp. 693–5.

Frye, Richard N. *The Histories of Nishapur*. Harvard Oriental Series 45. Cambridge, Mass., Harvard University Press, 1965.

Gasmi, Laroussi. 'Les réseaux connotatifs dans le texte coranique (le récit de Joseph: Sourate XII, v. 4–102)', *Arabica* 33 (1986), Fascimile 1, pp. 1–48.

Geiger, Abraham. *Was hat Mohammad aus den Judenthume aufgenommen?* Leipzig, M.W. Kaufmann, 1902.

Gianotti, Timothy J. *Al-Ghazālī's Unspeakable Doctrine of the Soul*. Leiden, Brill, 2001.

Giffin, Lois Anita. *Theory of Profane Love among the Arabs*. New York, New York University Press, 1971.

Gilliot, Claude. 'Parcours exégétiques: de Ṭabarī a Rāzī (Sourate 55)', *Études arabes, analyses, théorie* 1 (1983), pp. 87–116.

_____. *Exégese, langue et théologie en Islam: l'exégese coranique de Ṭabarī (m. 311/923)*. Paris, Vrin, 1990.

_____. 'The beginnings of Qur'ānic exegesis', in Andrew Rippin, ed., *The Qur'ān: Formative Interpretation*. Ashgate, Variorum, 1999, pp. 1–27.

Gimaret, Daniel. 'Théories de l'acte humain dans l'école Ḥanbalite', *BEO* 29 (1977), pp. 157–78.

_____. *Théories de l'acte humaine en théologie musulmane*. Paris, Vrin and Leuven, Peeters, 1980.

_____. *Les noms divins en islam*. Paris, Éditions du Cerf, 1988.

Ginzberg, Louis. *Legends of the Jews*. Translated from the German manuscript by Henrietta Szold, 7 vols. Philadelphia, Jewish Publication Society of America, 1909–38.

Glassé, Cyril. *Concise Encyclopaedia of Islam*. Revised edition, London, Stacey International, 2001.

Godlas, Alan. 'Influences of Qushayrī's *Laṭā'if al-ishārāt* on Sufi Qur'anic commentaries, particularly Rūzbihān al-Baqlī's *'Arā'is al-bayān* and the Kubrawī *al-Ta'wīlāt al-najmiyya*', *Journal of Sufi Studies* 2/1 (2013), pp. 78–92.

Goldziher, Ignaz (or Ignác). *Muhammedanische Studien*. Halle, M. Niemeyer, 1888–90. Translated by C.R. Barber and Samuel M. Stern as *Muslim Studies*. London, George Allen and Unwin, 1967–71.

_____. *Streitschrift des Ġazalī gegen die Bātinijja-Sekte*. Leiden, Brill, 1916.

Görke, Andreas and Johanna Pink, eds. *Tafsīr and Islamic Intellectual History: Exploring the Boundaries of a Genre*. Oxford, Oxford University Press in association with the Institute of Ismaili Studies, 2014.

Graham, Terry. 'Abū Sa'īd ibn Abi'l-Khayr and the school of Khurāsān', in Leonard Lewisohn, ed., *Classical Persian Sufism from its Origins to Rumi*. London and New York, Khaniqahi Nimatullahi Publications, 1993, pp. 83–135.

Gramlich, Richard. *Muḥammad al-Ġazzālīs Lehre von den Stufen zur*

Gottesliebe: die Bucher 31–36 seines Hauptwerkes. Wiesbaden, Franz Steiner, 1984.

_____. *Abu'l-ʿAbbās b. ʿAṭāʾ: Sufi und Koranausleger.* Stuttgart, Franz Steiner Verlag, 1995.

_____. *Alte Vorbilder des Sufitums*, 2 vols. Wiesbaden, Harrassowitz, 1995–6.

Grant, Robert M. (with David Tracy). *Short History of the Interpretation of the Bible.* Second edition, revised and enlarged, London, S.C.M. Press, 1984.

Griffel, Frank. *Apostasie und Toleranz im Islam: die Entwicklung zu al-Ġazālī's Urteil gegen die Philosophie und die Reaktionen der Philosophen.* Leiden, Brill, 2000.

Haji, Hamid. *A Distinguished Dāʿī under the Shade of the Fāṭimids: Ḥamīd al-Dīn Kirmānī (d.c. 411/1020) and His Epistles.* London, H. Haji, 1998.

_____. *Founding the Fatimid State: The Rise of an Early Islamic Empire.* London and New York, IB Tauris in association with the Institute of Ismaili Studies, 2006.

Hallaq, Wael B. and Donald P. Little, eds. *Islamic Studies Presented to Charles J. Adams.* Leiden, Brill, 1990.

Hämeen-Anttila, Jaakko. '"We will tell you the best of stories". A study on surah XII', *Studia Orientalia Helsinki* 67 (1991), pp. 7–32.

Hamza, Feras and Rizvi, Sajjad, with Farhana Mayer. *An Anthology of Qur'anic Commentaries. Vol. 1: On the Nature of the Divine.* Oxford, Oxford University Press in association with the Institute of Ismaili Studies, 2008.

Harris, Joseph and Karl Reichl, eds. *Prosimetrum: Cross-Cultural Perspectives on Narrative in Prose and Verse.* Woodbridge, D.S. Brewer, 1997.

Hartmann, Richard. '*Futuwwa* und *Malāma*', *ZDMG* 72 (1918), pp. 193–8.

Hawting, Gerald R. and Abdul-Kader Shareef, eds. *Approaches to the Qurʾān.* London and New York, Routledge, 1993.

Heath, Peter. 'Creative hermeneutics: a comparative analysis of three Islamic approaches', *Arabica* 36 (1989), pp. 173–210.

_____. *Allegory and Philosophy in Avicenna (Ibn Sīnā): With a Translation of the Book of the Prophet Muḥammad's Ascent to Heaven.* Philadelphia, University of Pennsylvania Press, 1992.

_____. 'Allegory in Islamic Literatures', in Rita Copeland and Peter T. Struck, eds., *The Cambridge Companion to Allegory.* Cambridge, Cambridge University Press, 2010, pp. 83–100.

Heer, Nicholas. 'Abū Ḥāmid al-Ghazālī's esoteric interpretation of the Qurʾān', in Leonard Lewisohn, ed., *Classical Persian Sufism from its Origins to Rumi.* London and New York, Khaniqahi Nimatullahi Publications, 1993, pp. 235–57.

Heffening, Willi. 'al-Shāfiʿī', *EI*[1], VIII, pp. 252–4.

Heinen, Anton M. 'The notion of *taʾwīl* in Abū Yaʿqūb al-Sijistānī's *Book of Sources (Kitāb al-manābiʿ)*', *Hamdard Islamicus* 2/1 (1979), pp. 35–46.

Hekmat, Ali Asghar. 'Une exégese coranique du XII siecle en Persan', *Journal Asiatique* 238 (1950), pp. 91–6.

Herrstein-Smith, Barbara. 'Narrative versions, narrative theories', *Critical Inquiry* 7 (1980), pp. 213–36.

Hodgson, Marshall G.S. *Venture of Islam: Conscience and History in a World Civilization*, 3 vols. Chicago, University of Chicago Press, 1974.

Isfandyār, Maḥmūd Riḍā, ed. *Āshnāyān-i rah-i ʿishq*. Tehran, Iran University Press and Sāzmān-i farhang wa irtibāṭāt-i Islāmī, 2006.

Izutsu, Toshihiko. *God and Man in the Koran: Semantics of the Koranic Welttanschauung*. Tokyo, Keio Institute of Cultural and Linguistic Studies, 1964.

_____. *Ethico-religious Concepts in the Qurʾān*. Montreal, McGill University Press, 1966.

_____. *Sufism and Taoism*. Berkeley, University of California Press, 1983.

Jackson, Sherman. *On the Boundaries of Theological Tolerance in Islam: Abū Ḥāmid al-Ghazālī's Fayṣal al-tafriqa bayna al-Islām wa al-zandaqa*. Oxford, Oxford University Press, 2002.

Jeffery, Arthur. 'The mystic letters of the Koran', *MW* 14 (1924), pp. 247–60.

Johns, Antony H. 'Joseph in the Qurʾān: dramatic dialogue, human emotion and prophetic wisdom', *Islamochristiana* 7 (1981), pp. 29–55.

_____. 'al-Rāzī's treatment of the Qurʾānic episodes telling of Abraham and his guests: Qurʾānic exegesis with a human face', *Mélanges de l'Institut Dominicain d'Études Orientales du Caire* 17 (1986), pp. 81–114.

_____. 'Moses in the Qur'an', in Robert B. Crotty, ed., *The Charles Strong Lectures, 1972–1984*. Leiden, Brill, 1987, pp. 123–38.

Johnson, Kathryn V. 'A mystical response to the claims of philosophy: Abu'l-Majd Majdūd Sanāʾī's *Sayr al-ʿibād ilā'l-maʿād*', *IS* 34/3 (1995), pp. 253–95.

Jones, Alan. 'The mystical letters of the Qurʾan', *SI* 16 (1962), pp. 5–11.

De Jong, Frederick (with Hamid Algar and Colin Imber), 'Malāmatiyya', *EI*^{2}, VI, pp. 223–8.

Kadkanī, Muḥammad Riḍā Shafīʿī. *Tāziyānahā-yi sulūk: naqd wa taḥlīl-i chand qaṣīda az Ḥakīm Sanāʾī*. Tehran, Intishārāt-i Āgāh, 1372sh/1993.

_____. 'Safīnaʾī az shiʿrhā-yi ʿirfānī-yi qarn-i chahārum wa panjum', in Muḥammad Turābī, ed., *Jashn-nāma-yi Ustād Dhabīḥullāh Ṣafā*. Tehran, Nashr-i Shahāb, 1377sh/1998, pp. 340–60. (see ch. 4, n. 8)

_____. *Qalandariyya dar tārīkh: digardīsīhā-yi yik aydiʾuluzhī*. Tehran, Sukhan, 1386sh/2007.

_____. '"Pīr-i Hirī ghayr az Khwāja ʿAbd Allāh Anṣārī" ast!' *Nāma-yi Bahāristān*, Year 10 (1388sh/2009), vol. 15, pp. 185–92.

Kamada, Shigeru. 'A study of the the term *sirr* (secret) in Sufi *laṭāʾif* theories', *Orient* 19 (1983), pp. 7–28.

Karamustafa, Ahmet T. *Sufism: The Formative Period*. Edinburgh, Edinburgh University Press, 2007.

Keeler, Annabel. 'Bāyazīd Bisṭāmī', in Maḥmūd Riḍā Isfandyār, ed., *Āshnāyān-i rah-i ʿishq*. Tehran, Iran University Press and Sāzmān-i farhang wa Irtibāṭāt-i Islāmī, 2006, pp. 35–74.

_____. 'Persian, Language of the Heart in Maybudī's *Kashf al-asrār*', in Fereydun Vahman and Claus V. Pederson, eds., *Religious Texts in Iranian Languages*. Copenhagen, The Royal Danish Academy of Science, 2006.

_____. 'Exegesis iii, In Persian', *EIr*, IX, Fascimile 2, pp. 119–23.

_____. 'Joseph: in Qurʾānic Exegesis', *EIr*, XV, pp. 34–41.

_____. 'Ṣūfī *tafsīr* as a mirror: Qushayrī the *murshid* in his *Laṭāʾif al-ishārāt*', *Journal of Qur'anic Studies* 7 (2006), pp. 1–21.

_____. 'Towards a prophetology of love: the figure of Jacob in Sufi commentaries on *Sūrat Yūsuf*', in Annabel Keeler and Sajjad Rizvi, eds., *The Spirit and the Letter: Approaches to the Esoteric Interpretation of the Qur'an*. Oxford, Oxford University Press in association with the Institute of Ismaili Studies, 2016, pp. 125–53.

_____. 'The concept of *adab* in early Sufism with particular reference to the teachings of Sahl b. ʿAbd Allāh al-Tustarī (d. 283/896)', in Francesco Ciabotti, Eve Feuillebois-Pierunek, Catherine Mayeur-Jaouen and Luca Patrizi, eds., *Ethics and Spirituality in Islam: Sufi Adab*. Leiden, Brill, 2016, pp. 63–101.

_____ and Sajjad Rizvi, eds., *The Spirit and the Letter: Approaches to the Esoteric Interpretation of the Qur'an*. Oxford, Oxford University Press in association with the Institute of Ismaili Studies, 2016.

_____ and Ali Keeler, tr. *Tafsīr al-Tustarī*. *See* Primary Sources, al-Tustarī, *Tafsīr al-Qurʾān al-ʿaẓīm*.

Khurramshahi, Baha ud-Din. 'L'Explication du Coran par le Coran lui-meme', *Aux Sources de la Sagesse* 2/6 (1995), pp. 7–20.

Kinberg, Leah. 'Muḥkamāt and Mutashābihāt (Q. verse 3/7). Implication of a Qurʾānic pair of terms in medieval exegesis', *Arabica* 35 (1988), pp. 143–72.

Kiyānī, Muḥsin. *Tārīkh-i khānaqāh dar Īrān*. Tehran, Ṭahūrī, 1369sh/1990.

Lagarde, Michel. 'De l'ambiguité dans le Coran', *Quaderni di Studi Arabi* 3 (1985), pp. 45–62.

Landolt, Hermann. 'Ghazālī and "*Religionswissenschaft*"', *Asiatische Studien* 45/1 (1991), pp. 19–72.

_____. 'Two types of mystical thought in Muslim Iran', *MW* 68 (1978), pp. 187–204.

Lane, Edward W. *Arabic-English Lexicon*, ed. Stanley Lane-Poole. Reprint, Cambridge, Islamic Texts Society, 1984.

Laoust, Henri. 'Les premieres professions de foi ḥanbalites', in Louis Massignon, ed., *Mélanges Louis Massignon*. Damascus, Institut Français de Damas, 1956, III, pp. 7–35.

_____. *La profession de foi d'Ibn Batta*. Damascus, Institut Français de Damas, 1958.

Lazarus-Yafeh, Hava. 'Are there allegories in Sufi Qur'ān interpretation?', in Jane Dammen McAuliffe *et al.*, ed., *With Reverence for the Word: Medieval Exegesis in Judaism, Christianity, and Islam*. Oxford and New York, Oxford University Press, 2003, pp. 366–75.

Levi Della Vida, G. 'Khāridjites', *EI²*, IV, pp. 1074–7.

Lewisohn, Leonard, ed. *The Legacy of Mediaeval Persian Sufism*. London, Khaniqahi Nimatullahi Publications, 1992. Reprinted as vol. II in L. Lewisohn, ed. *The Heritage of Sufism*. Oxford, One World, 1999.

_____, ed. *Classical Persian Sufism from its Origins to Rumi*. London and New York, Khaniqahi Nimatullahi Publications, 1993. Reprinted as vol. I in L. Lewisohn, ed., *The Heritage of Sufism*. Oxford, One World, 1999.

Loewinger, David S. and József Somogyi, eds. *Ignace Goldziher Memorial Volume*, 2 vols. Budapest, n.p., 1948.

Lory, Pierre. *Les Commentaires ésotériques du Coran d'apres ʿAbd al-Razzâq al-Qâshânî*. Paris, Les Deuz Océans, 1980.

_____. *La science des lettres en Islam*. Paris, Dervy, 2004.

_____. 'Eschatology and Hermeneutics in Kāshānī's *Ta'wīlāt al-Qur'an*', in Annabel Keeler and Sajjad Rizvi, eds., *The Spirit and the Letter: Approaches to the Esoteric Interpretation of the Qur'an*. Oxford, Oxford University Press in association with the Institute of Ismaili Studies, 2016, pp. 325–43.

Lumbard, Joseph E.B. 'From *ḥubb* to *ʿishq*: the development of love in early Sufism', *JIS* 18/3 (2007), pp. 345–85.

Macdonald, John. 'Joseph in the Qur'ān and Muslim commentary', *MW* 46 (1956), pp. 113–31, 207–24.

Madelung, Wilferd. *Religious Schools and Sects in Medieval Islam*. London, Variorum, 1970.

_____. 'Sufism and the Karrāmiyya', in W. Madelung, *Religious Trends in Early Islamic Iran*. New York, Biblioteca Persica, 1988, pp. 39–53.

_____. *Religious Trends in Early Islamic Iran*. New York, Biblioteca Persica, 1988.

_____. 'Hishām b. al-Ḥakam', *EI²*, III, pp. 496–8.

_____. 'Murdjiʿa', *EI²*, VII, pp. 605–7.

Mahjub, Muhammad Jaʿfar. 'Chivalry and early Persian Sufism', in Leonard Lewisohn, ed., *Classical Persian Sufism from its Origins to Rumi*. London and New York, Khaniqahi Nimatullahi Publications, 1993, pp. 549–81.

Makdisi, George. 'Muslim institutions of learning in eleventh-century Baghdad', *BSOAS* 24 (1961), pp. 1–56.

_____. 'Ashʿarī and the Ashʿarites in Islamic religious history', *SI* 17 (1962), pp. 37–80 and *SI* 18 (1963), pp. 19–39.

_____. *Ibn ʿAqīl et la résurgence de l'Islam traditionaliste au XIe siecle.* Damascus, Institut Français de Damas, 1963. Translated by the author as *Ibn ʿAqil: Religion and Culture in Classical Islam*. Edinburgh, Edinburgh University Press, 1997.

_____. 'The Sunni revival', in Donald S. Richards, ed., *Islamic Civilisation: 950–1150*. Oxford and London, Cassirer, 1973, pp. 155–68.

_____. *The Rise of Colleges*. Edinburgh, Edinburgh University Press, 1981.

_____. *L'Islam hanbalisant*. Paris, Paul Geuthner, 1983.

_____. 'Al-Ghazâlî, disciple de Shâfiʿî en droit et théologie', in *Ghazâlî, la raison et le miracle: table ronde Unesco, 9–10 décembre 1985*. Islam d'hier et d'aujourd'hui 30. Paris, Maisonneuve et Larose, 1987, pp. 45–55.

Malamud, Margaret. 'Sufi organizations and structures of authority in medieval Nishapur', *IJMES* 26 (1994), pp. 427–42.

Masarrat, Ḥusayn. *Kitābshināsī-yi Rashīd al-Dīn Maybudī*. Tehran, Anjuman-i āthār wa mafākhir-i farhangī, 1374sh/1995.

Massey, Keith. 'Mysterious Letters,' *EQ*, III, pp. 471–6.

Massignon, Louis. *Essai sur les origines du lexique technique de la mystique musulmane*. Paris, Paul Geuthner, 1922. Translated by Benjamin Clark as *Essay on the Origins of the Technical Language of Islamic Mysticism*. Paris, University of Notre Dame Press, 1997.

_____. *La passion d'Abū Manṣūr al-Ḥallāj, martyr mystique de l'Islam*, 2 vols. Paris, Paul Geuthner, 1922. Translated by Herbert Mason as *The Passion of al-Ḥallāj: Mystic and Martyr of Islam*, 4 vols. Princeton, Bollingham, 1982. Abridged translation by Herbert Mason as *The Passion of al-Ḥallāj: Mystic and Martyr of Islam*. Princeton, Princeton University Press, 1994.

_____. *Mélanges Louis Massignon*, 3 vols. Damascus, Institut Français de Damas, 1956.

_____. *Opera minora: textes recueillis, classés et présentés avec une bibliographie*, 3 vols. Beirut, Dār al-maʿārif, 1963.

McAuliffe, Jane Dammen. 'Qurʾānic hermeneutics: the views of Ṭabarī and Ibn Kathīr', in Andrew Rippin ed., *Approaches to the History of the Interpretation of the Qurʾān*. Oxford, Clarendon and New York, Oxford University Press, 1988, pp. 46–62.

_____, Barry D. Walfish and Joseph W. Goering, eds. *With Reverence for the Word: Medieval Scriptural Exegesis in Judaism, Christianity, and Islam*. Oxford and New York, Oxford University Press, 2003.

McDermott, Martin J. 'Abu'l-Fotūḥ Rāzī', *EIr*, I, p. 292.

Meddeb, Abdelwahab. *Les dits de Bistami: Shatahât*. Paris, Fayard, 1989.

Meier, Fritz. 'Ḫurāsān und das Ende der klassischen Ṣūfik', in *Atti del Convegno Internazionale sul tema: La Persia nel Medioevo (Roma 31 marzo-5 aprile)*. Rome, Academia dei Lincei, 1971, pp. 131–56. Translated by John O'Kane in Fritz Meier, *Essays on Islamic Piety and Mysticism*. Leiden, Brill, 1999.

_____. *Essays on Islamic Piety and Mysticism*. Translated by John O'Kane. Leiden, Brill, 1999.

Meisami, Julie Scott. *Medieval Persian Court Poetry*. Princeton, Princeton University Press, 1987.

_____. 'Mixed prose and verse in medieval Persian literature', in Joseph Harris and Karl Reichl, eds., *Prosimetrum: Cross-Cultural Perspectives on Narrative in Prose and Verse*. Woodbridge, D.S. Brewer, 1997, pp. 295–319.

Melchert, Christopher. 'Sufis and competing movements in Nishapur', *Iran* 39 (2001), pp. 237–47.

_____. 'The piety of the ḥadīth folk', *IJMES* 34 (2002), pp. 425–39.

_____. 'The interpretation of three Qur'anic terms (*siyāḥa*, *ḥikma* and *ṣiddīq*) of special interest to the early renunciants', in Stephen R. Burge, ed., *The Meaning of the Word: Lexicology and Qur'anic Exegesis*. Oxford, Oxford University Press in association with the Institute of Ismaili Studies, 2015, pp. 89–116.

Merguerian, Gayane K. and Afsaneh Najmabadi. 'Zulaykha and Yusuf: whose "Best Story"?', *IJMES* 29 (1997), pp. 485–508.

Mez, Adam. *Die Renaissance des Islams*, ed. Hermann Reckendorf. Heidelberg, C. Winter, 1922. Translated by Salahuddin Bukhsh and David S. Margoliouth as *The Renaissance of Islam*. London, Luzac, 1937.

Mir, Mustansir. 'The story of Joseph: plot, themes and characters', *MW* 76 (1986), pp. 1–15.

Mojaddedi, Javid. *The Biographical Tradition in Sufism*. London, Curzon, 2001.

Morris, James W. 'Dramatizing the sura of Joseph: an introduction to the Islamic humanities', *Journal of Turkish Studies* 18 (1994), pp. 201–24.

Munzawī, Aḥmad. *Fihrist-i nuskhahā-yi khaṭṭī-yi fārsī*, 6 vols. Tehran, Regional Cultural Institute, 1374–6sh/1995–7.

Murata, Sachiko. *The Tao of Islam*. Albany, SUNY, 1992.

Nafīsī, Saʿīd. *Sukhanān-i manẓūm-i Abū Saʿīd-i Abi'l-Khayr*. Sixth reprint, Tehran, Īrānmihr, 1376sh/1997.

Naḥwī, Akbar. 'Barkhī az manābiʿ-i fārsī-yi *Kashf al-asrār*', in Mehdī Malik Thābit, ed., *Yādnāma-yi Abu'l-Faḍl Rashīd al-Dīn Maybudī*, vol. II. Yazd, Intishārāt-i nīkū rawish, 1379sh/2000, pp. 272–84.

Nasr, Seyyed Hossein, ed. *Mélanges offerts à Henri Corbin*. Tehran, Kitābfurūshī-yi Ṭahūrī, 1977.

_____. *Introduction to Islamic Cosmological Doctrines*. London, Thames and Hudson, 1978.

Nettler, Ronald L. *Sufi Metaphysics and Qur'ānic Prophets. Ibn 'Arabī's Thought in the Fuṣūṣ al-ḥikam*. Cambridge, Islamic Texts Society, 2003.
Netton, Ian R. 'Theophany as a paradox: Ibn al-ʿArabī's account of al-Khiḍr in his *Fuṣūṣ al-Ḥikam*', *Journal of the Muhyiddin Ibn 'Arabi Society* 11 (1992), pp. 11–22.
Nguyen, Martin. *Sufi Master and Qur'an Scholar: Abū'l-Qāsim al-Qushayrī and the Laṭā'if al-ishārāt*. Oxford, Oxford University Press in association with the Institute of Ismaili Studies, 2012.
_____. '*Al-Tafsīr al-kabīr*: an investigation of al-Qushayrī's major Qur'an commentary', *Journal of Sufi Studies* 2/1 (2013), pp. 17–45.
_____. 'Exegesis of the *ḥurūf al-muqaṭṭa'a*: polyvalency in Sunni traditions of Qur'anic interpretation', *Journal of Qur'anic Studies* 14/2 (2012), pp. 1–28.
_____. 'Letter by letter: tracing the textual genealogy of a Sufi *tafsīr*', in Karen Bauer, ed., *Aims, Methods and Contexts of Qur'anic Exegesis (2nd/8th–9th/15th C.)*. Oxford, Oxford University Press in association with the Institute of Ismaili Studies, 2013, pp. 217–40.
_____. 'Qushayrī's exegetical encounter with the *mi'rāj*', in Annabel Keeler and Sajjad Rizvi, eds., *The Spirit and the Letter: Approaches to the Esoteric Interpretation of the Qur'an*. Oxford, Oxford University Press in association with the Institute of Ismaili Studies, 2016, pp. 241–70.
Nicholson, Reynold A. *Studies in Islamic Mysticism*. 1921. Reprint, Cambridge, Cambridge University Press, 1978.
Nwyia, Paul. 'Le tafsîr mystique attribué a Ǧaʿfar Ṣâdiq', Arabic text and introduction, *Mélanges de l'Université Saint-Joseph* 43 (1967), pp. 179–230.
_____. *Exégese coranique et langue mystique*. Beirut, Dar el-Machreq, 1970.
_____, ed. *Trois oeuvres inédites de mystiques musulmanes: Šaqīq Balḫī, Ibn 'Aṭā, Niffārī*, Beirut, Dar el-Machreq, 1973.
_____. 'Un cas d'exégese soufie: l'histoire de Joseph', in Seyyed Hossein Nasr, ed., *Mélanges offerts à Henri Corbin*. Tehran, Ṭahūrī, 1977, pp. 407–23.
Omar, Irfan. 'Khiḍr in the Islamic tradition', *MW* 83/3–4 (1993), pp. 279–91.
Patton, Walter M. *Aḥmad ibn Ḥanbal and the Miḥna*. Leiden, Brill, 1897. Reprint, 1971.
Paul, Jürgen, 'Au début du genre hagiographique au Khorassan', in Denise Aigle, ed., *Saints Orientaux*. Paris, de Boccard, 1995, pp. 15–38.
Pedersen, Johannes. 'The Islamic preacher: *wā'iẓ, mudhakkir, qāṣṣ*', in David S. Loewinger and József Somogyi, eds., *Ignace Goldziher Memorial Volume*, 2 vols. Budapest, n.p., 1948, I, pp. 226–51.
_____, [G. Makdisi]. 'Madrasa', Part 1, *EI*², V, pp. 1123–34.
Picken, Gavin N. 'The concept of *Tazkiyat al-Nafs* in Islam in the light of the works of al-Ḥārith al-Muḥāsibī'. Ph.D Thesis, University of Leeds, 2005.

Pickthall, Marmaduke. *The Meaning of the Glorious Koran*. London, Al-Furqan Publications Ltd., 1930. Numerous reprints from different publishers.
Pindarī, Yad Allāh Jalālī, ed. *Yādnāma-yi Abu'l-Faḍl Rashīd al-Dīn Maybudī*, vol. I. Yazd, Intishārāt-i Yazd, 1378sh/1999.
Poonawala, Ismail. 'Ismāʿīlī *ta'wīl* of the Qurʾān', in Andrew Rippin, ed., *Approaches to the History of the Interpretation of the Qurʾān*. Oxford, Clarendon and New York, Oxford University Press, 1988, pp. 199–222.
_____. 'Taʾwīl', *EI²*, X, pp. 390–2.
Pourjavady, Nasrollah. *Sulṭān-i ṭarīqat*. Tehran, Intishārāt-i Āgāh, 1358sh/1980.
_____. 'Abū Manṣūr Iṣfahānī: Ṣūfī-yi Ḥanbalī', *Maʿārif* 4/1 (November 1989), pp. 3–80.
_____. "Ahd-i Alast: ʿAqīda-yi Abū Ḥāmid al-Ghazzālī wa jāygāh-i tārīkh-i ān', *Maʿārif* 7/2 (November 1990), pp. 3–47.
_____. 'Bāda-yi ʿishq', *Nashr-i Dānish*, Year 11/6 (1370sh/1991), pp. 4–13; Year 12/1 (1370–1sh/1992), pp. 4–18; 2, pp. 6–15; 3, pp. 26–32; 4, pp. 22–30.
_____. *Būy-i jān*. Tehran, Iran University Press, 1372sh/1993–4.
_____. *ʿAyn al-Quḍāt wa ustādān-i ū*, Tehran, Iran University Press, 1374sh/1995.
_____. 'Sag-i kūy-i dūst wa khāk-i rāhash', *Nashr-i dānish* Year 15/3 (1374sh/1995), pp. 9–16.
_____. 'Jān u jahān kīst yā chīst?', *Maʿārif* 13/2 (November 1996), pp. 161–78.
_____. *Rūʾyat-i māh dar āsmān*. Tehran, Iran University Press, 1375sh/1996.
_____. 'Manbaʿī kuhan dar bāb-i Malāmatiyyān-i Nīshāpūr', *Maʿārif* 15/1–2 (joint issue) (Farwardīn-Ābān 1377/November 1998), pp. 3–50.
_____. 'Iṣālat-i *Ṣad Maydān*-i Khwāja ʿAbd Allāh Anṣārī', in ʿAlī Ashraf Ṣādiqī, ed., *Yādnāma-yi Duktur Aḥmad Tafaḍḍulī* (*Tafazzoli Memorial Volume*). Tehran, Intishārāt-i Sukhan, 1379sh/2001, pp. 1–15.
_____. 'Laṭāʾif-i Qurʾānī dar Majālis-i Sayf al-Dīn Bākharzī'. *Maʿārif* 18/1 (March 2001), pp. 3–24.
_____. *Du mujaddid*. Tehran, Iran University Press, 1379sh/2002.
_____. 'Zabān-i ḥāl dar adabiyyāt-i Fārsī', Part 1, *Nashr-i dānish* Year 17/2 (1379sh/2001), pp. 25–42.
_____. 'Du dastīna-yi kuhan dar taṣawwuf', *Maʿārif* 20/3 (March 2004), pp. 3–38.
_____. 'Aḥmad Ġazālī', *EIʳ*, X, pp. 377–80.
_____. *Zabān-i ḥāl dar ʿirfān wa adabiyyāt-i Pārsī*. Tehran, Intishārāt-i Hirmis, 1385sh/2006.
Purnāmdāriyān, Taqī. *Dāstān-i payāmbarān dar Kulliyāt-i Shams*. Tehran, Muʾassasa-yi muṭālaʿāt wa taḥqīqāt-i farhangī, 1369sh/1990.

Radtke, Bernd. *Al-Ḥakīm at-Tirmiḏī: ein islamischer Theosoph des 3./9. [i.e. 8./9.] Jahrhunderts*, Freiburg, K. Schwarz, 1980.

_____ and John O'Kane. *The Concept of Sainthood in Early Islamic Mysticism: Two Works by al-Ḥakīm al-Tirmidhī*. Richmond, Curzon, 1996.

Rahman, Fazlur, and William Chittick. 'ʿAql', *EIr*, II, pp. 194–8.

Renard, John. *All the King's Royal Falcons*. Albany, SUNY, 1994.

Rendsburg, Gary A. 'Literary structures in the Qurʾānic and Biblical stories of Joseph', *MW* 75 (1985), pp. 118–20.

Richards, Donald S., ed. *Islamic Civilisation: 950–1150*. Oxford and London, Cassirer, 1973.

Ridgeon, Lloyd. *Jawanmardi: A Sufi Code of Honour*. Edinburgh: Edinburgh University Press, 2011.

Rippin, Andrew, ed. *Approaches to the History of the Interpretation of the Qurʾān*. Oxford, Clarendon and New York, Oxford University Press, 1988.

_____, ed. *The Qurʾān: Formative Interpretation*, Ashgate, Variorum, 1999.

Ritter, Helmut. 'Philologica II', *Der Islam* 17 (1928), pp. 249–57.

_____. 'Philologica VIII', *Der Islam* 22 (1934), pp. 89–105.

_____. *Das Meer der Seele*. Leiden, Brill, 1978. Translated by John O'Kane as *The Ocean of the Soul*. Leiden and Boston, Brill, 2003.

Rizvi, Sajjad. 'The existential breath of al-Raḥmān and the munificent grace of al-Raḥīm: the *Tafsīr Sūrat al-Fātiḥa* of Jāmī and the school of Ibn ʿArabī', *Journal of Qur'anic Studies* 8 (2006), pp. 58–87.

Rosenthal, Franz. *Knowledge Triumphant: The Concept of Knowledge in Medieval Islam*. Leiden, Brill, 1970.

Rubin, Uri. 'Pre-existence and light: aspects of the concept of *Nūr Muḥammad*', *Israel Oriental Studies* 5 (1975), pp. 62–119.

_____. *The Eye of the Beholder: The Life of Muḥammad as Viewed by the Early Muslims*. Princeton, Darwin, 1995.

_____. *Between Bible and Qur'an: The Children of Israel and the Islamic Self-Image*. Princeton, Darwin, 1999.

_____. 'Nūr Muḥammadī', *EI²*, VIII, p. 125.

Ruknī-Yazdī, Mahdī. *Laṭāʾifī az Qurʾān-i karīm*. Mashhad, Intishārāt-i Āstān-i Quds-i Riḍawī, 1372sh/1993.

_____. *Jilwahā-yi tashayyuʿ dar Kashf al-asrār-i Maybudī*. Tehran, Intishārāt-i Yazd, 1374sh/1995.

Sādiqī, ʿAlī Ashraf, ed. *Yādnāma-yi Duktur Aḥmad Tafaḍḍulī* (*Tafazzoli Memorial Volume*). Tehran, Intishārāt-i Sukhan, 1379sh/2001.

Sajjādī, Jaʿfar. *Farhang-i iṣṭilāḥāt wa taʿbīrāt-i ʿirfānī*. Reprint, Tehran, Ṭahūrī, 1370sh/1991.

Saleh, Walid A. *The Formation of the Classical Tafsīr Tradition. The Qur'an Commentary of al-Thaʿlabī (d. 427/1035)*. Leiden and Boston, Brill, 2004.

_____. 'The last of the Nishapuri school of *tafsīr*: al-Wāḥidī (d. 468/1076) and his significance in the history of Qur'anic exegesis', *JAOS*, 126/2 (2006), pp. 223–43.

Sanders, Nancy K. *The Epic of Gilgamesh*. Harmondsworth, Penguin, 1972.

Sands, Kristin Z. *Ṣūfī Commentaries on the Qur'ān in Classical Islam*. London and New York, Routledge, 2006.

_____. 'On the popularity of Husayn Vaʿiz-i Kashifi's *Mawahib-i ʿaliyya*: a Persian commentary on the Qur'an', *Iranian Studies* 36 (2003), pp. 469–83.

_____. 'On the subtleties of method and style in the *Laṭā'if al-ishārāt* of al-Qushayrī, *Journal of Sufi Studies* 2/1 (2013), pp. 7–16.

_____. 'Making it plain: Sufi commentaries in English in the twentieth century', in Annabel Keeler and Sajjad Rizvi, eds., *The Spirit and the Letter: Approaches to the Esoteric Interpretation of the Qur'an*. Oxford, Oxford University Press in association with the Institute of Ismaili Studies, 2016, pp. 155–76.

_____, tr. *Abū'l-Qāsim al-Qushayrī's* Laṭā'if al-ishārāt. *Subtleties of the Allusions. See* Primary Sources, al-Qushayrī, *Laṭā'if al-ishārāt*.

Ṣayfī, ʿAlī Asghar. 'Ta'thīr-i *Rawḥ al-arwāḥ* dar tafsīr-i *Kashf al-asrār*', in Yad Allāh Jalālī Pindarī, ed., *Yādnāma-yi Abu'l-Faḍl Rashīd al-Dīn Maybudī*, vol. I. Yazd, Intishārāt-i Yazd, 1378sh/1999, pp. 356–94.

Schimmel, Annemarie. *Mystical Dimensions of Islam*. Chapel Hill, University of North Carolina Press, 1975.

_____. *And Muḥammad was His Messenger*. Chapel Hill and London, University of North Carolina Press, 1985.

Schwarzbaum, Haim. *Biblical and Extra-Biblical Legends in Islamic Folk Literature*. Walldorf-Hessen, Verlag für Orientkunde Dr H. Vorndran, 1982.

Seale, Morris S. 'The ethics of Malāmatīya Sufism and the sermon on the Mount', *MW* 58, (1968), pp. 12–23.

Sharīʿat, Muḥammad Jawād. *Fihrist-i Kashf al-asrār wa ʿuddat al-abrār*. Tehran, Amīr Kabīr, 1363sh/1984.

Shaya, Leo. 'The Eliatic Function', *Studies in Comparative Religion* (Winter-Spring 1979), pp. 31–40.

Shulman, David. *The Hungry God: Hindu Tales of Filicide and Devotion*. Chicago, University of Chicago Press, 1993.

Siauve, Marie-Louise. *L'amour de Dieu chez Ġazālī: une philosophie de l'amour a Baghdad au début du XIIe siecle*. Paris, Vrin, 1986.

Sidersky, David. *Les Origines des légendes musulmanes dans le Coran*. Paris, Paul Geuthner, 1933.

Silvers[-Alario], Laury. 'The teaching relationship in early Sufism: a reassessment of Fritz Meier's definition of the *shaykh al-tarbiya* and *shaykh al-taʿlīm*', *MW* 93 (2003), pp. 69–97.

_____. *A Soaring Minaret: Abu Bakr al-Wasiti and the Rise of Baghdadi Sufism*. Albany, SUNY, 2010.

de Smet, Daniel, Godefroid de Callataÿ and Jan M.F. Van Reeth, eds. *Al-Kitâb: la sacralité du texte dans le monde de l'Islam*. Brussels, Leuven and Louvain-La-Neuve, Société belge d'études orientales, 2004.

Smith, Jane Idleman. 'The Understanding of *nafs* and *rūḥ* in contemporary Muslim considerations of the nature of sleep and death', *MW* 49/3 (1979), pp. 151–62.

Smith, Margaret. *Rābiʿa the Mystic and Her Fellow Saints in Islām*. Reprint, Cambridge, Cambridge University Press, 1984.

Stern, Samuel M. 'Muhammad and Joseph: a study in Koranic narrative', *JNES* 44 (1985), pp. 193–204.

Storey, Charles A. *Persian Literature*, 2 vols. London, Luzac, 1927; Second edition, London, Luzac, 1953.

Sviri, Sara. 'Ḥakīm Tirmidhī and the Malāmatī movement', in Leonard Lewisohn, ed., *Classical Persian Sufism from its Origins to Rumi*. London and New York, Khaniqahi Nimatullahi Publications, 1993, pp. 583–613.

_____. 'Words of power and the power of words: mystical linguistics in the works of al-Ḥakīm al-Tirmidhī', *Jerusalem Studies in Arabic and Islam* 27 (2002), pp. 204–44.

_____. 'The early mystical schools of Baghdad and Nīshāpūr, or: in search of Ibn Munāzil', *Jerusalem Studies in Arabic and Islam* 30 (2005), pp. 450–82.

_____. 'The countless faces of understanding: on *istinbaṭ*, listening and mystical exegesis', in Annabel Keeler and Sajjad Rizvi, eds., *The Spirit and the Letter: Approaches to the Esoteric Interpretation of the Qur'an*. Oxford, Oxford University Press in association with the Institute of Ismaili Studies, 2016, pp. 51–85.

Swartz, Merlin L. *A Medieval Critique of Anthropomorphism: Ibn al-Jawzī's Kitāb Akhbār aṣ-ṣifāt*. Leiden, Brill, 2002.

Syamsuddin, Sahiron. '*Muḥkam* and *Mutashābih*: an analytical study of al-Ṭabarī's and al-Zamakhsharī's interpretations of Q.3:7', *Journal of Qur'anic Studies* 1/1 (1999), pp. 63–79.

Ṭabāṭabāʾī, Muḥammad Muḥīṭ. 'Dāstān-i tafsīr-i Khwāja Anṣārī', *Dānish* 1 (1328sh/1949), pp. 193–200.

Thābit, Mehdī Malik, ed. *Yādnāma-yi Abu'l-Faḍl Rashīd al-Dīn Maybudī*, vol. II. Yazd, Intishārāt-i nīkū rawish, 1379sh/2000.

The Oxford English Dictionary. Second edition, Oxford, Oxford University Press, 1989.

The Shorter Oxford Dictionary. Fifth edition, Oxford, Oxford University Press, 2002.

Tibawi, Abdul Latif. 'Origin and character of *al-Madrasah*', *BSOAS* 25 (1962), pp. 225–38.

Todd, Richard. *The Sufi Doctrine of Man: Ṣadr al-Dīn Qūnawī's Metaphysical Anthropology*. Leiden, Brill, 2014.

Torjesen, Karen J. *Hermeneutical Procedure and Theological Method in Origen's Exegesis*. Berlin and New York, De Gruyter, 1986.

Tortel, Christiane. *Paroles d'un soufi: Abû'l-Ḥasan Kharaqânî (960–1033)*. Paris, Éditions du Seuil, 1998.

Turābī, Muḥammad, ed. *Jashn-nāma-yi Dhabīḥullāh Ṣafā*. Tehran, Nashr-i shahāb, 1377sh/1998

Tyan, Émile. "Iṣma', *EI*², IV, pp. 182–4.

Utas, Bo. 'The *Munājāt* or *Ilāhī-nāmah* of ʿAbdu'llāh Anṣārī', *Manuscripts of the Middle East* 3 (1988), pp. 83–7.

Vadet, Claude. 'Le Karramisme de la Haute-Asie au carrefour de trois sectes rivales', *REI* 48 (1980), pp. 25–50.

Vahman, Fereydun and Claus V. Pederson, eds. *Religious Texts in Iranian Languages*. Copenhagen, The Royal Danish Academy of Science, 2006.

Van Ess, Josef. *Die Gedankenwelt des Ḥāriṯ al-Muḥāsibī*. Bonn, Selbstverlag des Orientalischen seminars der Universität Bonn, 1961.

_____. *Ungenützte Texte zur Karrāmīya*. Heidelberg, C. Winter, Universitätsverlag, 1980.

_____. 'Le miʿrāj et la vision de Dieu dans les premieres spéculations théologiques en Islam', in Mohammad Amir-Moezzi, ed., *Le voyage initiatique en terre d'Islam*. Paris and Louvain, Peeters, 1996, pp. 27–56.

_____. 'Tas̲h̲bīh wa tanzīh', *EI*², X, pp. 341–4.

Vermes, Geza. *Scripture and Tradition in Judaism*. Leiden, Brill, 1961.

Von Grünebaum, Gustav E. 'Iʿd̲j̲āz', *EI*², III, pp. 1018–20.

Waldman, Mary R. 'New approaches to "Biblical" materials in the Qurʾān', *MW* 75/1 (1985), pp. 1–16.

Wansbrough, John E. 'Majāz al-Qurʾān: periphrastic exegesis', *BSOAS* 33 (1970), pp. 247–66.

_____. *Quranic Studies*. London Oriental Series 31. Oxford, Oxford University Press, 1977.

Watt, W. Montgomery, 'The origin of the Islamic doctrine of acquisition', *JRAS* (1943), pp. 234–7.

_____. *Free Will and Predestination in Early Islam*. London, Luzac, 1948.

_____. *Muslim Intellectual: A Study of Al-Ghazali*. Edinburgh, Edinburgh University Press, 1963.

_____. *The Formative Period of Islamic Thought*. Edinburgh, Edinburgh University Press, 1973.

Wensinck, Arent J. *Concordance et indices de la tradition musulmane*, 8 vols. in 4. Second edition, Leiden, Brill, 1992.

_____. 'Munkar and Nakīr', *EI*², VII, pp. 576–7.

_____. 'Rasūl', *EI*², VIII, pp. 454–5.

Wheeler, Brannon M. *Moses in the Qur'an and Islamic Exegesis*. London, Routledge Curzon, 2002.
Whittingham, M. *Al-Ghazālī and the Qur'ān: One Book, Many Meanings*. New York, Routledge, 2007.
Widengren, Geo. *Muḥammad, the Apostle of God and his Ascension*. Uppsala, Lundequistska Bokhandeln, 1955.
Wild, Stefan. 'The self-referentiality of the Qur'ān: sura 3:7 as an exegetical challenge', in Jane Dammen McAuliffe *et al.*, ed., *With Reverence for the Word: Medieval Scriptural Exegesis in Judaism, Christianity, and Islam*. Oxford and New York, Oxford University Press, 2003, pp. 422–36.
Williams, Wesley. 'Aspects of the creed of Aḥmad ibn Ḥanbal: a study of anthropomorphism in early Islamic discourse', *IJMES* 34 (2002), pp. 441–63.
Wright, William, ed. *A Grammar of the Arabic Language*. Translated from the German of Caspari. Third edition, revised by W. Robertson Smith and M.J. de Goeje. Cambridge, Cambridge University Press, 1967.
Yusuf Ali, Abdullah. *The Holy Qur'an: Text, Translation and Commentary*. Cairo, al-Manār, 1938.
Zadeh, Travis. *The Vernacular Qur'an: Translation and the Rise of Persian Exegesis*. Oxford, Oxford University Press in association with the Institute of Ismaili Studies, 2012.
Zargar, Cyrus. *Sufi Aesthetics: Beauty, Love and the Human Form in the Writings of Ibn ʿArabī and ʿIrāqī*. Columbia, SC, University of South Carolina Press, 2011.
Zarrīnkūb, ʿAbd al-Ḥusayn. *Justujū dar taṣawwuf-i Īrān*. Tehran, Amīr Kabīr, 1363sh/1984.
Zhukovsky, Valentin. 'Persian Sufism, being a translation of Professor Zhukovsky's introduction to his edition of the *Kashf al-maḥjūb*', *BSOAS* 5 (1928–30), pp. 475–88.
Zysow, Aron. 'Two unrecognised Karrāmī texts', *JAOS* 108 (1988), pp. 583–87.

Index of Qur'anic citations

Sura	verse	page
1	1	172
	4	52
	6	52
	7	54
2	1	53, 54
	2	87
	3	88
	4	59
	5	59
	7	82
	10	87
	17	86
	18	86
	22	90, 91–2
	25	83
	26	86, 89
	30	86, 89, 93, 133
	36	136, 211
	40	88
	41	212n. 2
	50	243
	51	234, 244
	51–64	243
	54	85
	57	95
	58	85
	62	83–4, 100n. 72
	63	90, 140
	67–74	243
	69	181n. 130
	74	91, 291–2
	77	77, 78
	78	91
	85	85
	86	87
	89	212
	91	212
	92–3	243
	96	88
	104	87
	106	85
	116	89
	124	86, 231
	125	88
	125–9	216, 236n. 1
	129	219
	130	215, 219
	131	218, 222–3, 223, 231
	141	81
	144	89
	163	124
	164	188, 190
	165	21
	218	156
	252	271n. 5
	258	216, 227
	260	216, 227
	266	271n. 5
	269	40
	285	223
3	2	247
	7	41, 42, 43, 44, 62n. 8
	17	198
	31	109, 116, 188, 192
	67	218
	79	152
	85	56
	95	215
	96–7	216, 236n. 1
	103	158
	112	271n. 5
	160	153
	173	239–40n. 77

Sura	verse	page
	191	190
	200	163
4	17	162
	82	49
	103	58
	125	215, 216
	147	59
	164	271n. 6
5	12	166
	20–4	243
	25	247
	54	60, 109, 116, 129, 133, 247
	55	262
	60	52
	63	65n. 28
	64	16, 30n. 99
	75	271n. 5
	90	170
	114	238n. 42
	116	65n. 32
	150–1	182n. 136
6	2	137
	3	60
	19	34n. 133
	75–9	74–9, 216, 223, 228–9, 252
	77	223, 230
	78	218
	79	218, 224, 229
	80–3	216
	85	278
	88	140–1
	90	164
	91	60
	103	60
	106	191
	162	215
	163	151
7	2	155
	13	138
	12	274n. 62
	54	30n. 98
	103–27	243
	129	42
	130–5	243

Sura	verse	page
	138–41	243
	142	259
	142–8	243
	143	221, 261, 262, 263
	143–5	244
	144	271n. 6
	157	91
	172	139, 148n. 92
	204	140
8	4	57
	17	140, 151, 173n. 7
	24	197–8
9	23	78
	36	125
	60	295
	79	229–30
10	4	30n. 98
	5–6	271n. 5
	22	185
	25	147n. 75
11	3	162
	17	141
	69–73	216
	74–6	216
	75	215
	96	271n. 5
	120	211
12		278–80
	3	278, 285
	4–20	278
	6	281, 303n. 8
	7	280
	8	283
	12	284
	18	278
	19	278
	21	51–2, 278, 282
	21–9	279
	22	281
	23	281
	25	289
	27	280
	30	156, 157, 283, 290
	30–5	279

Sura	verse	page
	31	282, 291
	33	284
	36–54	279
	37	281
	37–40	281
	38	278, 303n. 8
	42	284
	46	280
	51	281, 288, 290
	52	159, 281
	53	174n. 14, 281
	54	281
	55–82	279
	58	295
	59	297
	64	284
	68	281, 303n. 8
	76	281
	79	281
	81	297
	83–93	279
	84	298, 299, 308n. 106
	88	278
	92	171, 281
	93	299
	94	295–6
	94–101	279
	95	283
	96	299
	98	281
	100	281
	101	281
	111	210, 280
13	2	30n. 98
	13	46
	17	47, 97n. 12, 99n. 36, 210
	39	158
	41	18
14	5	141
	10	125
	21	225
	25	201n. 27
	34	247
	35	226
	35–41	216, 225, 236n. 1
15	21	167
	51–6	216
	58–60	216
	97	156
16	1	175n. 33
	79	271n. 5
	104	271n. 5
	120	215, 231
	123	215
	127	178n. 76
17	1	138, 237n. 16
	9	210
	11	200n. 12
	44	65n. 35
	59	271n. 5
	70	42
	85	146n. 57
	101–2	243
	103	243
18	9	271n. 5
	16	85
	17	271n. 5
	18	86, 165, 187
	27	225
	39	201n. 27
	57	271n. 5
	60–82	243, 250, 264
	63	260–1
	66	265
	68	265, 267
	69	265
	77	46, 47
	96	274n. 62
	110	248
19	1	160
	41	215
	42–8	216
	51	221
	52	221, 242, 247, 249
20	5	30n. 98, 59, 60
	9	256
	10–16	243
	12–14	257–8

Sura	verse	page
	17	258
	17–21	258
	17–36	243
	22–3	271n. 5
	25	247, 272n. 22
	36	247
	38–40	243
	39	247, 261
	40	243, 251
	41	261
	46	53
	49–73	243
	77–9	243
	114	60
	115	138
21	51	230
	52–7	216
	58–70	216
	68	233
	68–9	234
	69	233, 235, 274n. 62
	101	21
22	5	135
	19	46
	26	192
	46	299
	63	128
	72	274n. 62
23	115	129
24	11	197
	31	225
	35	99n. 36, 130, 210
25	53	172
	59	30n. 98
26	77	79, 230
	193–4	160
	217	131
27	7	255
	7–9	243
	10–12	243
	60	188
	61	155
	81–2	271n. 5
	93	158
28	7–13	243
	14–20	243
	21	252
	21–9	243
	22	251, 252–3
	23	253–4
	29–30	243
	31–5	243
	44	130
	88	65n. 32
29	43	99n. 36, 210
30	39	65n. 32
32	1	131
	4	30n. 98
	17	21
33	11	172
	40	248
	72	135, 142, 146n. 64
35	12	186
	31	212n. 2
36	38	246
	46	271n. 5
	70	30n. 99
37	72	134
	83–90	216
	84	215, 229
	91–8	216
	99	223
	102–7	216
	103	218, 233
38	29	41
	67–8	21
	75	65n. 28
	76	30n. 99
39	6	132
	22	157
	56	65n. 32
	69	157
40	16	52
	19	77, 78
	34	278, 281
	56	15
41	11	46, 65n. 35
	53	188
42	11	65n. 32
43	46	271n. 5
	46–54	243

Sura	verse	page
	48–50	243
	55–6	243
45	4	271n. 5
	13	271n. 5
	23	153
47	19	223
48	4	268
	10	30n. 99
	26	133
50	16	128, 247
51	24–30	216
	32–4	216
	49	126
53	1–18	131, 237n. 16
	8	158
	9	191
	10	245
	11	157
	12	245
	17	220, 224
	37	215, 218
54	1	46
	55	168
55	19	201n. 29
	27	65n. 32
	31	200n. 23
56	3	169–70
	58–9	156
	71	274n. 62
	85	60
57	1	46, 47
	3	60
	4	30n. 98, 60
58	22	157
59	21	146n. 65
67		127
	1	259
	8	46
	17	65n. 30
70	5	172
71	14	158
73	8	163–4
75	2	159
	22	60
84	19	158
94	1	272n. 22
96	19	247
112	1	197

Index

Aaron 242, 246
abad (eternal end, post-eternity) and *azal* (pre-eternity) 183
ʿābid pl. *ʿābidūn/ʿābidān* (worshipper) 88, 103, 118n. 12, 161, 163, 167, 174n. 23, 179n. 103, 183, 210, 238n. 32
Abraham 74-9, 215-36, 314
  endowed with love in pre-eternity 230
  faithfulness 218
  and hospitality 215, 237n. 9
  as *Khalīl Allāh* (Friend of God) 215-19, 220, 229-34, 236-7n. 7, 252
  and *khulla* (friendship) & root *KH.L.L.* 216-18, 236n. 4, 236-7n. 7, 239n. 76
    perfect friendship with God 229-31
    test and proof of friendship 231-6
  mystical interpretations xxv-xxiv, 74-9, 91, 210, 219-236
  prayers 216, 219, 225, 226
  religion (*milla/millat*) of Abraham 217, 218
  spiritual journey in Maybudī's mystical interpretations 219-229, 253
  story
    covenant 215, 216
    in fire of Nimrod 231, 234-6, 255, 270
    laying foundations of Kaʿba 219
    leaving Ishmael and Hagar 225
    sacrifice of son 231-3, 270
  seeing star, moon and sun 74-9, 98n. 29, 220, 223-4, 228-9, 252-3
  submission 218
  see also Ishmael; Nimrod
Abū ʿAbd Allāh b. Karrām 108
Abū ʿAlī Siyāh 165
Abū Bakr al-Kattānī 210-11
Abū Bakr al-Ṣiddīq 202n. 54, 290-1
Abū Bakr al-Warrāq 118n. 12
Abū Bakr al-Wāsiṭī 22, 108, 129, 144nn. 31 and 32, 180n. 115, 229
Abū Dardā 73
Abū Jahl 180n. 115
Abū Manṣūr Waraqānī 26n. 32
Abū Sahl Ṣuʿlūkī 238n. 47
Abū Saʿīd b. Abiʾl-Khayr 1, 4, 107, 117n. 6
  at *samāʿ* gatherings 110, 123n. 76
  awe at the prospect of death 180n. 119
  on burning of the *nafs* 203n. 73
  regulation of *khānaqāh*s 5, 26n. 28
  rubāʿī attributed to 68n. 91
  supervision of disciples 5, 25nn. 24, 25
  teachings on love 110-111
Abū ʿUthmān Hīrī 169, 180n. 119
Abū ʿUthmān al-Maghribī (Saʿīd b. Sallām) 166
Abū Yazīd Bisṭāmī (Bāyazīd) 107, 110, 115, 117nn. 1 and 4, 178n. 81, 180n. 115
  on the Covenant of *Alast* 148n. 97
  criticism of *zuhd* 168, 179n. 107
  on finding and seeking 200n. 15
  followers (Ṭayfūrīs) 117n. 1
  and *hal min mazīd* 149n. 114
  on knowing God through God 238n. 48
  on love, intoxication and union 109, 119n. 24
  and *malāma* 180n. 115
  metaphor of snake shedding its skin 178n. 74
  metaphor of pitching tent beyond the Throne 178n. 81
  on the need for earth 134
  on preordination 200n. 18
  questioning Satan 183
  on self-evidentness of God 142n. 4
  shaṭḥiyyāt 222
  way of intoxication (*sukr*) 110

Abu'l-Futūḥ Rāzī, *Rawḍ al-jinān wa rawḥ al-janān* 3, 19, 27n. 50, 33n. 120, 62n. 2
Abu'l-Qāsim al-Kurrakānī 118n. 14, 152, 173n. 12.
Abu'l-Qāsim al-Naṣrābādhī 118n. 14
Abu'l-Qāsim Yūsuf b. al-Ḥusayn b. Yūsuf al-Harawī 18
acquisition *see kasb*
ʿāda/ʿādat (habit) 86
  doctrine of 239n. 70
adab (courtesy, good manners, propriety) 287
  towards God 89
Adam 131, 155, 218, 230, 308n. 93
  bestows beauty on Joseph 282
  creation of 42, 93-4, 132-6, 144n. 25
  descendants 139
  elements combined in him 135
  heart as reason for angels' prostration 135
  lofty aspiration 132, 137
  oyster for pearl of gnosis (*maʿrifa*) 133
  seed of, those who are lovers of God 196
  slip (*zallat*) 211
    and banishment from Paradise 136-9, 147n. 76
  as symbol in Kāshānī's commentary 213n. 15
  two existences 138
  weeping for God 308nn. 93 and 106
Afshar, Iraj 13
aḥdiyya (unification, oneness) 181n. 130, 223
ʿahd-i alast see Covenant of *Alast*
aḥkām (rulings, pl. of *ḥukm*), *aḥkām al-Qur'ān* 9
  bayān al-aḥkām 19
ahl al-sunna wa'l-jamāʿa/ahl-i sunnat wa jamāʿat 17, 53, 54, 111, 188, 311-12
ahl-i ḥaqīqat (people of spiritual realisation) xxvi, 59, 88, 190, 118n. 12, 229
ahl-i sharīʿat (people concerned with religious law) 88, 218, 229
ahl-i ṭarīqat (person or people of the spiritual path) xxvi, 118n. 12, 218
Aḥmad b. Ḥanbal
  opposition to metaphorical interpretation 45
  persecution of 30n. 96
  citation by Maybudī 17
  Qur'an's uncreatedness 53
Aḥmad b. al-Sālim of Baṣra 118n. 14
aḥruf 96n. 6
aḥwāl 88, 113, 177n. 60, 186, 211, 224
  and *maqāmāt* 161-4
  see also *ḥāl*; spiritual states; stations
ʿĀ'isha 176n. 51
Akedah see Isaac, sacrifice
akhbār al-awwalīn (tales of the ancients) 85
akhbār wa āthār (hadiths and traditions) 19
alast see Covenant of *Alast*
ʿAlī b. Abī Ṭālib 176n. 51
  exegetical methods 73
  on levels of meaning in the Qur'an 70
  Maybudī's respect for 15
  on spiritual balance 154, 269
ʿālim pl. *ūlamā'/ʿālimān* (scholar, learned person) 167, 228
  see also ulema
Allāh see God
Allard, Michel 17
allegory 71, 72, 160
  use in mystical exegesis 84-6, 90, 101n. 79, 161
Alp Arslān 2, 23n. 4
amāna/amānat (the 'trust') 146n. 64
  identified with Covenant of *Alast* 135, 142, 146n. 64, 149n. 118
ʿāmm also *ʿawāmm*, *ʿāmma* (commonalty) 6, 57, 66n. 47, 80, 161-2, 167, 191, 201n. 29, 218, 312
  God's revelation to 190
  practise of virtues 218
  understanding of the Qur'an 63n. 13
ʿāmm, khāṣṣ, and *khāṣṣ al-khāṣṣ/khāṣṣ al-khawāṣṣ* 26-7n. 40, 66n. 39, 80, 88, 113, 161-2, 167, 177-8n. 71, 190, 312
amthāl (parables/comparisons) 210, 314
  coining of 86
  see also mathal

analogy (*qiyās*), in the stories of the prophets 211
use in mystical exegesis 82-4
anbiyā' (sing. *nabī*) *see* prophets
andīsha (meditation, thought), three kinds on the Qur'an 49
angels 149n. 119, 216
complacency 148n. 87
intervention with God in the testing of Abraham through the fire of Nimrod 234
not privileged with love (*'ishq*) 170
reactions to Moses during his journey to Sinai 261, 263
wonderment at creation of Adam 133
wonderment at Abraham's distinction 234
annihilation
of attributes 152
from self 152, 186, 189, 197, 198, 230, 253, 256, 258, 269
of human will in divine will 263
see also fanā', *nīstī*
Anṣārī, 'Abd Allāh (*Pīr-i ṭarīqat*) xix, 1, 12, 14, 15, 17, 18, 311, 313, 315
on Adam's expulsion from Paradise 136-7
on alternation of states 60, 187
on al-Ash'arī, quoted by Ibn Rajab al-Baghdādī 31n. 104
on the burning of the heart 193
on certainty and tranquillity in faith 227
on Covenant of *Alast* 140
on *dahshat* 204nn. 85 and 88, 274n. 75
dogmas in 114-15, 122n. 68
on *dūstī* 177n. 67
on knowledge with fear, hope and love 202n. 43
dialogue between *dil* and *jān* 151
on *fanā'* and *baqā'* 151, 173n. 4
on finding God by His willing 297
on finding preceding seeking 184, 200n. 17
on goal of the mystical way 150
on God's light manifested in the hearts of His lovers 309n. 107
on God's mercy 128
on God's oneness 125
on God's Throne 59-60
and Ḥanbalī school 17, 31n. 104, 115
on *ikhlāṣ* 175n. 40
'Ilal al-maqāmāt 113
inclusion of *malāmat* and *futuwwa* 118n. 16
on *'ishq* and *jawānmardī* 172
on *jam'* 173n. 7
on *jam'iyya* 199
Kitāb al-arba'īn 18, 32n. 116
on longing for God 194-5
on love 260, 274n. 79
on love and divine determination (*taqdīr*) 199
on love (*mihr*) and jealousy (*ghayrat*) 196
love mysticism, contrasted with Maybudī's views 111-16
on the Malāmatiyya 180n. 112
Manāzil al-sā'irīn xxi, 113, 115-16, 118n. 16, 121nn. 52 and 54, 161
as source for Maybudī 22
and Maybudī 14-15, 33n. 126, 40, 115
Munājāt, the corpus xvi, 33n. 126, 61, 94-5
munājāt (intimate communings with God) 21, 33n. 126, 114, 116
on perplexity 194
play upon the words *maḥabbat* and *miḥnat* 195, 251
prayer to be annihilated from self 150, 185
on promises in love 260
on God's pre-eternal decree 183
Qur'an commentary and its use by Maybudī 20-1, 40
on restlessness 200n. 16
Ṣad maydān 113, 115, 121n. 54, 161
as source for Maybudī 22
on seeking God 184-5
on spiritual states of different classes of believers 161
on stages of love 205n. 115
on suffering and perfection in love for God 195
Ṭabaqāt al-ṣūfiyya xxi-xxii, 25n. 21, 144n. 29
on *tafrīd* and *tajrīd* 224

Anṣārī, ʿAbd Allāh (*Pīr-i ṭarīqat*) (*cont.*):
tafsīr 56
on *al-tawba* 225
on *tawḥīd* 187, 257
on transient nature of moments of unveiling 193
threefold definitions of states and stations 102n. 103, 161
on transendence and imminence of God 60-1
use of Arabic and Persian 113, 121n. 55
Anṣāriyyāt 14, 125n. 33
twofold heritage of 113
anthropomorphism 16-17, 112, 126
in the Qur'an 16, 30nn. 98 and 99
Shāfiʿī school and 32n. 11
see also tashbīh
Anūshīrvān the Just 12
ʿaqīda (tenets of belief), as basis for belief in God's oneness 111, 124
ʿaql (rational faculty, reason) 17, 142n. 1, 167, 188-9, 194, 235-6, 303n. 12, 311
God's creation of (hadith) 189, 202n. 46, 235-6
God's dialogue with 202n. 47
light of 87, 202n. 47
limits of 47-8, 184, 202n. 44
not the basis for knowledge of God 124, 184
and Qur'anic interpretation 47, 101n. 79
role of 188
symbolised in the story of the fire of Nimrod 235-6, 240n. 85
and *tawfīq* 189, 202n. 47
use for traditionalists 32n. 113
Arabic language
Abu'l-Futūḥ Rāzī's use of 33n. 120
Anṣārī's use of 113, 121n. 55
grammar 52
as language of the Qur'an xxi
Maybudī's use of in *Kashf al-asrār* 19-20, 92
poetry 52
ʿārif pl. *ʿārifān* (mystics/possessors of mystical knowledge or gnosis) xxvi, 60, 77, 78, 88, 118n. 12, 161, 163, 167, 174n. 23, 179nn. 98, and 103-4, 187, 192, 194, 203n. 82, 210, 228, 238n. 32
see also spiritual hierarchy
asbāb al-nuzūl (circumstances of revelation) 9, 50, 99n. 52
sabab-i nuzūl 19
asceticism *see zuhd*
al-Ashʿarī, Abū Mūsā 65n. 32
al-Ashʿarī, Abu'l-Ḥasan ʿAlī b. Ismāʿīl 17
al-Anṣārī's views of 31n. 104
Kitāb al-ibāna ʿan uṣūl al-diyāna 31n. 102
Ashʿarīs 15, 16, 17
persecution by al-Kundurī 2, 23n. 4
views on metaphorical interpretation 45
on Qur'an being uncreated in meaning 14-15, 67n. 65
Ashʿarism, Ashʿarī school 23n. 5
Maybudī's criticisms of 15-16
within Niẓāmiyya *madrasas* 2-3
theology 2, 23-4n. 6
ʿāshiq pl. *ʿāshiqān* (mystical lover) xxvi, 174n. 23, 179n. 98, 264, 285
Nūrī as 109
see ʿishq
ātash see fire
ʿAṭṭār, Farīd al-Dīn xviii, xxii, 1, 8, 109, 203n. 73
attributes (divine) *see* God
audience addressed by Maybudī 57-8, 95, 313-15
awe (*hayba*) 127, 161, 314
and intimacy (*uns*) 185
see also hayba
awliyāʾ, sing. *walī* ('saints', friends of God) 55, 66n. 47, 80, 165, 187
light of, power of 165
as successors to prophets 165-6
awtād (lit. tent pegs) 166
āyat pl. *āyāt* 242, 271n. 5
ʿAyn al-Quḍāt, ʿAbd Allāh b. Muḥammad Hamadānī 1, 24n. 18, 145n. 41
Shakwat al-gharīb 27n. 41
Tamhīdāt
on God's 'need' of man 132, 146n. 47
on spiritual function of separation 203n. 76

ʿAzīz (Zulaykhā's husband) 279, 281, 282, 284, 286, 287, 302n. 2, 304n. 35

Bābā Ṭāhir 25n. 25
Baghdad 14
  Madrasas 2, 24n. 6
Baghdadi/Iraqi and Khorasani schools of mysticism 108, 117n. 1, 118n. 14, 122n. 71
balā (Yes) 139
  play on two meanings of *balā* 148n. 96
balāʾ (affliction) 231, 283-4
  see also ibtilāʾ; love
baqāʾ (subsistence in God) 127, 161, 259, 262-3, 266, 269, 314
  and *fanāʾ* (annihilation from self) 150-1, 173n. 4, 197, 201n. 29, 204-5n. 110, 228, 262-3, 277n. 120
bāqī (one who subsists) 250, 259, 266
Baqlī, Rūzbihān b. Abī Naṣr 1, 302
  ʿArāʾis al-bayān xxi, 275n. 92
    on Jacob's blindness 308n. 106
  Sharḥ-i shaṭḥiyyat 27n. 41, 178n. 81
    on ecstatic utterances 99n. 46
  on God's 'need' of man 132, 146n. 48
al-Barbahārī 17, 31n. 102
baṣīra/baṣīrat (insight) 82
Basmala 50-1, 52
basṭ (expansion) 254
  and *qabḍ* (contraction) 185, 186-7, 246
bāṭin, baṭn (inner) xxiv, 69-73, 81, 96n. 6
  see also esoteric
baṭn 71, 73, 96n. 6
al-Bayḍāwī, ʿAbd Allāh b. ʿUmar 19, 64n. 23, 217, 276n. 102, 304n. 23
bayt al-aḥzān (House of Sorrows) 294-5
bayt al-aḥzān-i faqr (House of the Sorrow(s) of Poverty) 295
de Beaurecueil, Serge de Laugier 20, 21, 33n. 124, 113, 173n. 7, 313
beauty
  ḥusn 146n. 47
  jamāl 127
  Joseph's beauty 282, 287, 303n. 18, 306n. 71
Bell, Joseph N. 113
Benjamin (Joseph's brother) 279, 284, 297-8
Bewilderment 163
  see also ḥayra
Biblical stories of the prophets *see* prophets
bidʿa/bidʿat (innovation in religion) 157, 170, 180n. 19
bidāya/bidāyat (beginning, elementary stage) 162, 221, 248
bihisht-jūyān see paradise seekers
bi-lā kayf (doctrine of the limits of rational knowledge) 31n. 102, 111, 312
Bishr al-Ḥāfī 180n. 119
blame *see malāma*
Bosworth, Clifford E. 13
Böwering, Gerhard xxiii, xxiv, 21-2, 70-2, 103n. 118, 119n. 19, 316
breast *see ṣadr*
Brinner, William M. 241, 244
al-Bukhārī, Muḥammad b. Ismāʿīl 9, 270n. 1, 276n. 99
burning bush 242, 255-8
  see also Moses
Burūsawī, Ismāʿīl Ḥaqqī, *Rūḥ al-bayān* xxii, 316

certainty *see yaqīn*
Children of Israel 182n. 136, 242, 246, 261, 264
  covenant with, 90, 149n. 106
Chittick, William C. xxvii, 315
choice *see ikhtiyār*
Christians, salvation, 83-4
  see also exegesis, Christian
Companions of the Cave ('Sleepers in the Cave') 85-6, 103n. 134, 165, 187
Consolation *see tasallī*; *salwāt*
Contemplation levels 159
Cosmology 130, 136, 147n. 72
Covenant (*mīthāq* or *ʿahd*) of *Alast* 90-1, 116, 139-42, 149n. 106, 172n. 1, 192
  ʿahd-i alast 306n. 69
  referred to in Anṣārī's *munājāt* 150, 172n. 1, 192
  rūz-i alast, rūz-i balā 139
  rūz-i qabḍa (day of the 'handful') 140-1
creation 129-30
  of Adam 132-3
  divine purpose in 129
  Muḥammad first in 130-2

creatures, existence, distinguished from that of God 126

dahshat (amazement/stupefaction) 127, 161, 194, 252, 258-9
and *uns*, 194, 204n. 88
ḍalāl (lit. aberration, understood as excessive love) 283, 304n. 23
Daqqāq, Abū ʿAlī 161, 162, 178n. 85, 202n. 54, 238n. 47, 299, 308n. 94
ḍarb al-amthāl (coining of similitudes) *see amthāl*
al-Dārimī, ʿAbd Allāh b. ʿAbd al-Raḥmān 201n. 23
David 78
anecdotes about 272n. 25
questions God about the cleansing of the heart 192-3
questions God about creation 129
slip 147n. 82
weeping for God 299, 308n. 106
al-Daylamī, Abu'l-Ḥasan ʿAlī
ʿAṭf al-alif al-maʾlūf ʿala'l-lām al-maʿṭūf 109
on the Covenant of *Alast* 149n. 107
dhawq (lit. tasting, mystical experience) 296
dhikr (remembrance) 151, 177n. 56, 184
Dhu'l-Nūn al-Miṣrī, on *ikhlāṣ* 180n. 115
dīdār (sight/vision), and *mihr* 115, 190, 195
dil see heart
dūst pl. *dūstān* (friend, lover) 167, 229
dūstī (friendship, love) 116, 122n. 72, 197, 229
of God 124
three levels of 177n. 67
see also love
duwayras 5
see also khānaqāh; ribāṭ

earth 134-5
as an metaphor for lower soul (*nafs*) 188
Bāyazīd's views on 134
Egypt, women of, in the story of Joseph 282, 287, 290-2
esoteric, concept xxvi
see also bāṭin; exegesis
esoteric exegesis
aim of 77
digression in Maybudī's 79
diversity of meanings in 76-80
edification within 89-90
as *irshād* 79-82
Maybudī's aim in 79
methods of 81-90, 101n. 79
preconditions for 48-9
theories 69-74
see also allegory; hermeneutics
Eve, as a symbol 213n. 15
Exegesis xxiii, 86-8
Christian, late Patristic 71, 72, 97n. 17, 97-8n. 23, 100n. 59
fourfold theory of meanings 71, 72
Jewish, fourfold theory 71
Jewish and theological problems concerning Exodus 99n. 29
Maybudī's approach to 39-50
Sufi 28n. 53
see also esoteric exegesis; hermeneutics; mystical commentary
exoteric and esoteric exegesis xxvi, 74-80, 312-13, 314
on Q. 6:76-80 compared 74-81
see also ẓāhir; *bāṭin*
Exodus 99n. 29, 242, 244

fahm (understanding) 43, 70, 71, 73, 80
faith *see īmān*
fanāʾ (annihilation from self), 113, 121n. 54, 127, 157, 159, 161, 189, 197, 254, 259, 262, 263, 274n. 75, 277n. 120, 314
and *baqāʾ* 112, 150-1, 173n. 4, 201n. 29, 204-5n. 110, 205n. 115, 228, 250, 262, 263, 277nn. 120 and 122
connection with Covenant of *Alast*, 139, 148n. 97
and love 113, 121nn. 53 and 54
fānī (one who is annihilated from self) 250, 262, 266
faqīh pl. *fuqahāʾ* (jurisprudent) 2, 10
faqr (poverty in the spiritual path) 258, 295
as a station 177n. 60
Farāhī, Muʿīn al-Dīn *Ḥadāʾiq al-ḥaqāʾiq* xxii

farḍ ʿayn (what is obligatory for all) 269
farḍāniyya 125, 160, 261, 262
Fāriʿa 52
Fāris 266
Fasting 199
Fāṭima bint Rashīd al-Dīn (daughter of Maybudī) 13, 30n. 80
Fatimids 2
fatra/fatrat (lassitude) 83, 165
fear
with hope and love as life 175n. 41
six levels of 177n. 63
without knowledge 188, 202n. 43
see also khawf
fikr (thought, contemplation, reflection) 42, 48, 151
finding (God), 80, 87, 184, 187, 189, 230, 296
see also wujūd; *yāft*
fiqh see jurisprudence
firāq (separation) 196, 203n. 76, 263
see also love
fire (*ātash*)
of desire 314
of divine love 234-6, 256, 257
of gnosis and guidance 255-6
as opposed to earth 134
mentioned in the Qur'an 255-6, 274n. 62
within mysticism 256
Footstool 93, 94
friendship (*khulla*) 216-18
as perfection of virtues 218
see also Abraham
fu'ād 156, 157, 175n. 33, 290
Fuḍayl b. ʿIyāḍ 108
futūḥ 252, 273n. 45
Futuwwa (spiritual chivalry) 168
futuwwa/jawānmardī 99n. 44, 108, 118n. 10, 170-2, 181nn. 132 and 133

Gabriel 231
and Abraham's friendship with God 234
bringing revelation to Muhammad 191
commanded to remind Jacob of Joseph 298
commands Moses to meet al-Khiḍr 264
prevents the sacrifice of Ishmael 233
relays God's command to Joseph to marry Zulaykhā 285
as the symbol of *ʿaql* within the story of the fire of Nimrod 235-6
gambling (*maysir*) 170-1
Gāzurgāh 14, 29n. 67
ghafla/ghaflat (inadvertence, heedlessness) 177n. 56, 187
ghalaba pl. *ghalabāt* (overwhelming, rapture) 289, 305n. 52
as a way 109
ghayba/ghaybat (absence from self) 127, 253, 254, 259
and *ḥuḍūr* (presence in God) 254, 259
ghayrat (jealousy) 133, 196
see also jealousy
ghazal (love songs) 7, 110, 111
Ghaznavids 2, 25n. 25
al-Ghazzālī, Abū Ḥāmid Muḥammad 1, 2, 3, 23n. 5, 24n. 8, 143n. 23
and Ashʿarī school 23n. 5, 45
contribution to Sufism 6
fatwa on administration of endowments of *khānaqāh*s 6
fatwa on love poetry 110
hermeneutics 48, 64nn. 25, 26 and 27
and anthropomorphic verses in the Qur'an 45, 65n. 35
on metaphorical interpretation (and *ta'wīl*) 45, 55, 64n. 26, 65n. 35, 66n. 47, 97n. 20
on plurality of meanings in the Qur'an 55, 73
Ihyā' ʿulūm al-dīn 1, 6, 10, 45, 173n. 10, 276n. 112, 315
as source for Maybudī 22, 34n. 141
Kimiyā-yi saʿādat 6, 110, 315
as source for Maybudī 22, 34n. 141
on lesser and greater holy wars 174n. 18
on *lisān al-ḥāl* 65n. 35
Mishkāt al-anwār 272n. 32, 306n. 68
on Moses 247-8, 249
Al-Munqidh min al-ḍalāl 6
on philosophy 3, 24n. 16
Tahāfut al-falāsifa 3, 64n. 27
on use of word *ʿishq* for love 116
Ghazzālī, Aḥmad 7, 107, 144n. 29, 181n. 123, 302

Ghazzālī, Aḥmad (*cont.*):
on God's 'need' of man 132
on Majnūn and the gazelle 307n. 88
metaphysics of love 7, 110, 111, 198
on need to abandon free will 205n. 122
on *salwat* 307n. 86
Sawāniḥ 7, 149n. 115, 306n. 69
as source for Maybudī 14, 22, 24
on 'school of love' 120n. 35
significance for love mysticism 7, 110, 111
on submission to God's will as equivalent to the state of *jam'* 264
on unification with the spirit 300
use of word *'ishq* for love 116
on way of love 198
on *wilāyat-i 'ishq* 306n. 61
Gilliot, Claude 10, 53, 71, 99n. 47
gnosis (*ma'rifa/ma'rifat*) 112
attainment 311
as against knowledge of God 228-9
levels 159
masters of (*arbāb-i ma'rifat*) 18
not to be sought 190
see also ma'rifa (gnosis)
God
'adl (justice) 127
aḥadiyya (oneness) 91
Allāh divine name
effect contrasted with that of *al-Raḥmān* and *al-Raḥīm* 127, 279
attributes (*ṣifāt*) 16, 17, 45-6, 66n. 39, 124-9, 143n. 16, 313
involving no opposition in God 126, 143n. 15
attributes and acts 51
attribution of comments to in exegesis 88, 95
'aẓama/'aẓamat (majesty, mightiness of God) 124, 128, 262
being 'above' 59
as the Beloved 120n. 36
contemplation of 190-1
creation, reason for 129-30
revealing Himself through creation, attributes and essence 190
desiring friendship with human beings 95
essence (*dhāt*) 60, 66n. 39
and attributes 125
Essence, Attributes and Acts 124
contemplation of according to rank 66n. 39
Prophet's contemplation of 159-60, 176n. 51
'face' (*wajh*), 65n. 32
found through detachment from all things 296-7
see also finding; *yāft*; *wujūd*
'hand of' 16, 45-6, 65nn. 28 and 32
'hearing' and 'sight' 53-4
as 'hidden treasure' 129-30, 132, 144n. 29, 192
Hū/Huwa (He), referring to God 172, 197
huwiyya (He-ness), divine ipseity 182n. 144
ineffability 126, 190-1
intervention
see taqdīr and preordination
istighnā' (complete independence of God) 128, 129
'izza/'izzat (glory or might) 128, 140
comprising both light and fire 143n. 16
jalāl (majesty of God) 124, 147, 179n. 98, 194, 262
jamāl (beauty) 127, 179n. 98
kibriyā' (grandeur, of God) 124, 128, 142n. 2
kindness to the spiritually weak 179n. 93
light 293, 306n. 68
longing for the righteous 144n.28
love
for human beings 90, 128-9
for Muhammad 89
and mercy manifested through Adam's slip (*zallat*) 138
majesty and might 193, 259
manifest, yet unseen 61
mercy 127-8, 138
Names 50-1, 52, 54-5, 127, 133, 172, 204n. 88, 259
nearness (*qurb*) 60, 143-4n. 24
and farness 128
'need' of man 132, 145-6n. 47

not needing a son 89
power and wisdom 91
qahr and *luṭf* (coercion or wrath) and *luṭf* (gentleness) opposite attributes of God 127, 132, 204n. 88
al-Raḥīm 50, 55, 127, 259
al-Raḥmān 50, 54, 127, 259
transcendence (*tanzīh*) 60, 126
and imminence 60, 187
unity 124-5 *see also tawḥīd*
unveiling 179n. 104, 193-5, 252-3, 258, 311
see also mukāshafa; *kashf*
will, in the story of Joseph 280
submission of human will to 263-4
wisdom 127-8
combined with omnipotence 128
guidance *see hidāya*; *hudā*; *irshād*

Ḥabīb Allāh (Beloved of God) Muhammad as 216, 220
see also Muhammad
ḥadd (level of meaning in the Qur'an) 70, 71, 73
Ḥaddād, Abū Ḥafs 161, 169, 180n. 119
hadith 9, 15, 142n. 2
on the *akhlāq* of God 152, 173n. 11
on *balā'* 204n. 100
on creation of *'aql* 189, 202n. 46, 235-6
on God's creating the creatures in darkness 293, 306n. 68
on 'greater and lesser holy war' 153, 174n. 18
on God's being a 'hidden treasure' 129-30, 144n. 29, 192
of *law lāka* 145n. 39
on *mi'rāj* of the Prophet 241, 270n. 1
on *nafaḥāt* 296, 307n. 83
on Paradise being surrounded by *makārih* 251, 273n. 41
on supererogatory works (*al-nawāfil*) 103-4n. 137
Ḥāfiẓ, Shams al-Dīn Muḥammad 30n. 90, 148n. 96, 302
Hagar 225, 229, 232
ḥakīm among the terms for mystics 118n. 12
al-Ḥakīm al-Tirmidhī 34n.139, 107, 117n. 3, 118n. 12
Bayān al-farq bayn al-ṣadr wa'l-qalb wa'l-fu'ād wa'l-lubb 22, 156, 174-5n. 31, 176n. 46
on stages of the *nafs* 176n. 46
criticism of the Malāmatiyya 176n. 49
Kitāb nawādir al-uṣūl fī ma'rifat aḥādīth al-rasūl 173n. 11, 174n. 28
on Moses' prayer to become part of Muhammad's *umma* 272n. 24
on the Prophet's contemplation of God 176n. 51
ḥāl pl. *aḥwāl* 85
see also aḥwāl
hal min mazīd (Is there any more?) 141, 149n. 114
see also Abū Yazīd Bisṭāmī
ḥalāl and *ḥarām* 51, 70, 71
al-Ḥallāj, Ḥusayn b. Manṣūr 10, 109, 269
on Covenant of *Alast* 148-9n. 101
love involving union with God 109
on purification as pre-requisite for esoteric exegesis 49
on light of faith 185
on need to be freed from the self 222, 237n. 22
on sobriety (*ṣaḥw*) and intoxication (*sukr*) 186
on *zuhd* 161
Hamadan 32n. 111
Ḥamdūn al-Qaṣṣār 108
Ḥanbalī school, Ḥanbalīs 17
Anṣārī and 31n. 104, 115
on anthropomorphisms in the Qur'an 16, 30-31n. 100, 65n. 32
on *bi-lā kayf* 31n. 102
influence on Maybudī 16-17, 311
on *kasb* 31-2n. 110
with Shāfi'ī tendencies 32n. 111
ḥanīf (true/upright), Abraham as 215-16, 236n. 3
al-ḥanīfiyya (true religion), Abraham identified with 215, 263n. 3
ḥaqā'iq sing. *ḥaqīqa* (inner truths, realities) 55, 70, 87, 96n. 2, 167, 186, 296
ḥaqīqa/*ḥaqīqat* (realised truth, spiritual or inner realisation) 21, 33n. 124, 43, 44, 49, 57, 61, 62, 111, 158, 186, 189, 231, 293, 311-13

ḥaqīqa/ḥaqīqat (*cont.*):
and love 192, 305n. 57
ʿilm-i ḥaqīqat, *ʿayn-i ḥaqīqat* and *ḥaqq-i ḥaqīqat* 159, 160
and *sharīʿa* 56-7, 59, 311-13
see also sharīʿa; *ṭarīqa*
ḥasad (envy) 156, 157
al-Ḥasan al-Baṣrī 10, 80, 115, 153, 284, 304n. 31
ḥayāʾ (diffidence) 102n. 103, 219
hayba/haybat (awe) 49, 127, 161, 258-9, 314
and intimacy (*uns*) 185, 204n. 88
ḥayra/ ḥayrat (perplexity, bewilderment) 160, 161, 163, 176n. 55, 193-4, 203n. 78, 204n. 88, 251-3, 258, 259
heart (*qalb*, *dil*)
Adam's heart 135-6, 146n. 55
burning of 203n. 73
burnt 235
coming live through killing of *nafs* 153
contrast with the breast (*ṣadr*) 155-6
God's treatment, in the spiritual journey 146n. 75, 158
as a house 192
as king or sultan 136, 147n. 72, 156
layers of 157, 290
locus of faith (*īmān*) 156, 157, 175n. 38, 290
opposition to the lower self (*nafs*) 155, 174n. 28
prayer to keep safe from sultan of desire 225
role in path to God 197-8
states and stations of 160
hardening of from God 248
vision of/in 299
dil 156, 161, 163, 175n. 33, 188
dialogue with *jān* 151
dil-i sūkhta (burnt heart cannot be burned again) 235
qalb 156-7, 175n.33, 175n. 38, 254, 290
qalb salīm (whole or sound heart) of Abraham 215, 229
see also fuʾād; *shaghāf*
Hekmat, Ali Asghar 12
Herat 2, 32n. 111, 107
Heresiography 3, 24n. 11
hermeneutics 312-13, 314
definition of xxiii-xxiv
theories of compared 69-74
Qur'anic hermeneutics,
criteria 40-50, 76-7
development 8-12
exoteric and esoteric compared 74-81
of Ghazzālī 45, 48, 73
in the *Kashf al-asrār* 39-50, 74-81
Maybudī's theory 49-50, 79-80
of esoteric commentary on the Qur'an 69-96
criteria 47-9, 55, 73-4, 76-7
and language of mystical expression 95-6
methods of, (Maybudī and Qushayrī) 81-92
and religious practice 55-62
see also exegesis; *istinbāṭ*; *tafsīr*; *taʾwīl*
hermenoia 100n. 57
hidāya/hidāyat (guidance) 256, 258
see also hudā
hierarchy in faith and gnosis 166
see also spiritual hierarchies
ḥikma/ḥikmat (wisdom) 40, 42, 128,
Ḥikmat al-ishrāq (Philosophy of illumination) 1
ḥirṣ (greed) 157, 177n. 56
Ḥishāmiyya 45
Hodgson, Marshall G.S. 6, 23nn. 3 and 5, 26-7n. 40
Holy war
'lesser holy war' 152-3, 174n. 18
'greater holy war' 150, 152-4, 174n. 18
homily, and *tafsīr* 50-5
hope
without knowledge 188, 202n. 43
see also rajāʾ
House of Sorrows *see bayt al-aḥzān*
hudā 87, 103n. 125
Ḥudhayfa b. Yamān 80
ḥuḍūr (presence in God) 253-4
Hujwīrī, ʿAlī b. ʿUthmān Jullābī 118n. 14
contrasts way of the Ṭayfurīs and Junaydīs 109-10
critical of love poetry 110
on way of sobriety (*ṣaḥw*) and intoxication (*sukr* or *ghalabāt*) 109-110, 117n. 1, 186-7, 289

on *ghalaba* 289
on Ibrāhīm b. Adham and *malāma* 180n. 114
on *jadhba* 222
Kashf al-maḥjūb 25n. 20, 108, 118n. 14, 118-19n. 16, 120n. 25, 177n. 71, 238n. 47
on love mysticism 109, 120n. 26
on *malāma* and *futuwwa* 118-9n. 16
on mystics of the East and Baghdad 117n. 1
on *shaṭḥiyyāt* 222
on *tamkīn* 186, 289
ḥukm 281, 303n. 12
human beings
correspondences with macrocosm 135-6, 147nn. 70, 72
creation 132-6
inner constitution 155-7
loved by God 128-9
made up of vessels and deposits, body and spirit, darkness and light 133-4
nature 313
see also Adam
Ḥusayn b. al-Qāḍī ʿAlī 18
Ḥusayn Miftāḥ 29n. 67
ḥusn see beauty
Huwa (He) *see* God

ibāḥatiyyān (libertines) 188
ʿibāra/ʿibārat (what is explicit) 55, 96n. 2
Iblīs *see* Satan
Ibn ʿAbbās, ʿAbd Allāh 8, 65n. 32, 69, 70, 75, 96n. 7, 97n. 8, 264, 304n. 35
Ibn Abī Shayba 145n. 43
Ibn ʿArabī, Muḥyī al-Dīn 237n. 7, 266, 304n. 24
Ibn ʿAṭāʾ al-Adamī 10, 22, 66n. 39, 237n. 7, 226
on beauty 282, 303n. 20
on *ʿilm ladunī* 265
on Jacob's afflictions 284
on Jacob's blindness 308n. 93
on Joseph's afflictions 252
on Moses' experience at Sinai 250
on purification of soul for esoteric interpretation 48-9
Ibn Baṭṭa 17
Ibn Bishr 9
Ibn Ḥanbal *see* Aḥmad b. Ḥanbal
Ibn Isḥāq, Muḥammad 270n. 1, 276n. 99, 303n. 18
Ibn al-Jawzī
on interpretation of anthropomorphic verses 65n. 32
Talbīs Iblīs 27n. 41
Ibn Kathīr 99n. 32
Ibn Khafīf al-Shīrāzī 109
Ibn Māja 276n. 113
Ibn Masʿūd, ʿAbd Allāh 70, 73, 270n. 1
Ibn al-Munawwar 26n. 28, 203n. 73
Ibn Qutayba 8, 21
Ibn Rajab al-Baghādī 20, 31n. 104, 33n. 124
Ibn Sīnā 24-5n. 18, 64n. 24
Risāla fi'l-ʿishq (*Risāla fī māhiyyat al-ʿishq*) 119n. 25
Ibn Yaʿlā 32n. 111
ʿibra (lesson to be drawn) 280
Ibrāhīm b. Adham 12, 107, 117n. 2, 169, 180n. 114
ibtilāʾ (test/trial/misfortune) 231
idolaters (*mushrikīn*) 218
idolatry (*shirk*) 90
Abraham's opposition to 216
in the spiritual path 153, 225-6
see also polytheism
iftiqār (utter neediness) 160, 184
iʿjāz 42, 63n. 10
ijtihād (spiritual striving) 80, 187, 220
ikhlāṣ (sincerity) 158, 175n. 40, 180n. 115, 192, 221-2, 290, 293
ikhtiyār (choice) 184, 284
Ikhwān al-Ṣafāʾ (Brethren of Purity) *Rasāʾil* 120n. 25, 144n. 29, 144-5n. 34, 147nn. 70 and 72
ilhām (inspiration) 80, 265
ʿilm see knowledge
ʿilm ladunī 264, 265-7
ʿilm al-mukāshafa 48
ʿilm al-yaqīn see yaqīn
Ilyās 275n. 98
'Imām al-Ḥaramayn' 13, 29n. 72
see also al-Juwaynī
īmān (faith) 202n. 43
located in the heart 156, 175n. 38

īmān (faith) (*cont.*):
with certainty and tranquillity 227-8
intellect *see 'aql*
intimacy *see uns*
intoxication (*sukr*, *mastī*) 99n. 46, 164, 176n. 55, 186, 194, 203n. 71, 205n. 115
as opposed to sobriety (*ṣaḥw*) 109-110, 117n. 1, 186-7, 289
irāda/irādat (spiritual intention, 'aspirancy') 86, 102n. 92, 141
Iran xvi, 2
'irfān (mysticism, gnosis) xxvi, 189
irshād (spiritual guidance) 79-80, 81-2
in the hermeneutics of esoteric interpretation 82-9, 100n. 58, 312, 314
Isaac 215, 216, 231-3, 239nn. 63, 65 and 74
see also Abraham
Isfahan 32n. 111
al-Iṣfahānī, Abū Nu'aym 22, 25n. 21, 109, 144n. 28, 200n. 18
Isfarāyinī, Abu'l-Muẓaffar Shāhfūr, *Tāj al-tarājim* 11, 33n. 120
Isḥāq b. 'Abd Allāh b. Abī Farwa 282
ishāra/ishārat (allusion, what is allusive) 49, 55, 57, 85, 96n. 2
ishārāt-i ṣūfiyān (allusions of Sufis) 19
Ishmael 79, 215, 216, 219, 225, 229
sacrifice 216, 231-3, 239 nn. 63 and 65, 270
see also Abraham
'ishq (passionate love or love) 110, 116, 122n. 74, 123n. 75, 141, 146n. 47, 156, 170, 192, 198, 257, 287, 290, 291, 304n. 23, 308n. 106
see also love; *dūstī*; *maḥabba*
'ishq-i basharī (human [or natural] love) 305n. 36
'ishq-i ḥaqīqī (real love) 304-5n. 36
'ishq-i ilāhī (divine love) 305n. 36
'ishq-i majāzī ('metaphorical' or relative love) 304-5n. 36
al-Iskandarī, 'Abd al-Mu'ṭī al-Lakhmī 173n. 7, 224, 226
islām (submission) 56-7, 158, 215
ism 52
'iṣma (immunity/protection from error) 76, 86, 99n. 29
Ismailis 3, 24n. 8, 27n. 50, 101n. 81
metaphorical and allegorical interpretation 44, 84
isnād (chain of transmission) 9, 53, 67n. 63, 248
Israel *see* Children of Israel
Isrā'īliyyāt traditions 99n. 32, 211
istidlāl (demonstrative reasoning, rational deduction) 76, 160, 187, 227, 228-9
and *burhān* (proof) 228
as opposed to *'iyān* 227, 228
istighfār (seeking forgiveness) 162
istinbāṭ 10, 44, 49-50, 63n. 18, 66n. 41, 73-4, 265
see also mustanbaṭāt
istislām (self-surrender) 56-7, 96n. 2, 158, 202n. 51
istithnā' 16, 30n. 97
'iyān (direct experience) 190, 195, 227, 228

Jacob 278, 279, 281, 283, 303n. 8, 305n. 56
afflictions 284
arousing jealousy 297-8
blindness 299-302, 308n. 106
identified with love 238n. 57
identified with sorrow 303n. 14
love for Joseph 292-302, 307n. 74, 314
prototype of lover of God 292
suffering 293-7
as symbol 213n. 15
and *tawakkul* 284
jadhb/jadhba (divine attraction, rapture) 178n. 76, 185, 219
as opposed to *sulūk* 219
see also kashish
Ja'far al-Ṣādiq 10, 33n. 119, 34n. 133, 72, 79, 119n. 19, 120n. 26, 248, 296
ascription of interpretations to 119n. 19
on levels of meaning for different classes of believers 55, 70, 98n. 25
on Covenant of *Alast* 148n. 100
on Moses state of *dahsha* and *fanā'* 274n. 75
on *ḍalāl* as *'ishq* 304n. 23

interpretation of twelve springs 177n. 57
on levels of meaning in the Qur'an 70, 98n. 25
on *shaghāf* 290
on the veiling of the heart 248
Jahmīs 15
Jām, Aḥmad (*Zhinda Pīl*) 5, 25n. 24, 26n. 25
jam' 151, 158, 173n. 7, 176n. 55, 177n. 56, 187, 219, 222, 245, 258, 263-4, 277n. 120, 314
Jamāl al-Islām Abū Sa'd b. Aḥmad b. Mihrīzād 12-13
Jāmī, 'Abd al-Raḥmān xxii, 178nn. 85 and 92
on *ahl-i wuṣūl* 269-70
on graduating from human to divine love 304n. 36
jān (spirit) 60, 156, 161, 163
as *muftī* with *dil* 150
locus of gnosis 156
as soul or self 175n. 33
jawānmard pl. *jawānmardān* (spiritually chivalrous person) 103n. 134, 170-2, 181n. 130, 197, 250
jawānmardī (spiritual chivalry) 108, 137, 170-2, 181nn. 130 and 133
and love 172
see also futuwwa; *mard*; *mardānagī*
jealousy (*ghayra/ghayrat*) 196-7, 285, 297-8
God's jealousy 133, 196-7, 231, 233, 268, 293, 298, 301, 307n. 72
mystic lover's jealousy 197
'veil of jealousy' 293, 307n. 72
Jerusalem in Christian exegetical theory 71
Jesus 72
disciples' request concerning faith 238n. 42
spiritual wayfarers as lovers of God 192
war against the *nafs* 153
Jews
salvation 83-4
see also Israel
Job, 196
Joseph 51-2, 199, 278-302
beauty 282, 287, 294, 301, 303nn. 14 and 18, 306n .71
brothers 279, 283, 294, 295
brought near to God through afflictions 252
endowed with knowledge 281, 303n. 12
healing of Jacob's blindness 299-302
Jacob's love for 292-302, 314
as jealous beloved 297-8
in Jewish legend 303n. 11
love in story of 285-302
as mirror of God 301, 308n. 106
mystical interpretation 283-302
as the prince of all the *jawānmardān* 171
as a prophet 281
in the Qur'an 209, 278-9 Table 10.1, 280
reassurance in his story for Muhammad 280, 303n. 10
shirt 294, 295-7, 299-300, 305n. 38
scent of 294, 295-7, 299, 307n. 85
as *al-Ṣiddīq* 280-1
on the soul's propensity to evil *nafs ammāra* 174n. 14
as symbol of divine Beloved 282, 292, 301
allegorical interpretation 101n. 80, 213n. 15
virtues 281-2
Zulaykhā's love for 211, 286-92
Judaism, exegetical methods 71-2
see exegesis
al-Junayd al-Baghdādī 110, 115, 186, 190
on Covenant of *Alast* 148n. 97
on finding 190
on levels of meaning in the Qur'an 97n. 12
on metaphors in stories of the prophets 210-11
Junaydīs (followers of al-Junayd) 117n. 1, 178n. 71
mysticism contrasted with that of the Ṭayfūrīs 109-10
jurisprudence (*fiqh*) 15, 51
Shāfi'ī school 32n. 111
al-Juwaynī, 'Abd al-Malik ('Imām al-Ḥaramayn') 2, 29n. 72

Ka'b al-Aḥbār, on Moses questioning God 143n. 23
Ka'ba 192, 215, 216, 219, 226
Kākūyids 13-14
al-Kalābādhī, Abū Bakr Muḥammad b. Isḥāq 118n. 14, 177n. 71
on *fanā'* and *baqā'* 173n. 4
on *ghalaba* 289
on *ghayba* 254
Kitāb al-ta'arruf li-madhhab ahl al-taṣawwuf 25n. 20, 108
on love 120n. 26
on *murīd* and *murād* 220
on *sukr* 289
discussion of theological dogma 121n. 45
kalām (speculative theology) 15, 311
use in Ash'arī school 30n. 92
Kalīm Allāh (Interlocutor of God) *see* Moses
Karrāmiyya 3, 24n. 9, 45, 108, 117n. 8, 118n. 13, 168, 179n. 107
kasb (doctrine of 'acquisition') 17, 31-2n. 110, 120n. 40
kasb (earning a living) 169
al-Kāshānī, 'Abd al-Razzāq
on Abraham as *Khalīl Allāh* 236-7n. 7
allegorical interpretations 84, 101n. 80, 276-7n. 120, 211-12
exegetical methods 98nn. 25 and 28
on Moses' experience at Sinai 249
Tafsīr al-Qur'ān al-karīm (*Ta'wīlāt al-Qur'ān*/*Tafsīr Ibn 'Arabī*)
use of *taṭbīq* 100n. 67
kashf pl. *kushūf* (unveiling) 161, 176n. 55, 179n. 104, 190, 193, 220, 254, 265
see also mukāshafa
Kashf al-asrār wa 'uddat al-abrār xv-xxi, 10, 19-22, 29n. 65, 311, 315-16
audience 20, 51, 56-7, 92, 154
authorship 12
Nawbat I 54-5
Nawbat II 54, 56, 58-9, 62
Nawbat III 56, 57-9, 62
rhetorical style and scope 11-12, 21, 92-6, 154, 285, 313
sources 20-2
structure 19-20, 21, 54-5, 57-9, 80, 92, 99n. 37
use of Arabic in 19-20, 92
use of Persian in 3, 19-20, 92, 313
see also Maybudī, Abu'l-Faḍl Rashīd al-Dīn
Kāshifī, Kamāl al-Dīn Ḥusayn Wā'iẓ, *Mawāhib-i 'Aliyya* xxii, 29n. 65
kashish (attraction, rapture from God) 80, 158, 178n. 76, 185, 202n. 52, 219-21
see also jadhb/jadhba rawish
KH.L.L. 216, 229, 236nn. 4 and 7
al-Khaḍir (lit. the Green One) *see* al-Khiḍr
Khalīfa, Ḥājjī 12, 28-9n. 65
Khalīl Allāh (Friend of God) *see* Abraham
khānaqāh (Sufi lodge) 5-6, 13, 14, 26n. 28, 33n. 126
Kharaqānī, Abu'l-Ḥasan 25n. 25, 107, 117n. 5, 203n. 73.
Khargūshī, Abū Sa'd 'Abd al-Malik 28n. 57, 63n. 18, 179nn. 109 and 111, 180n. 120, 181n. 121
Khārijīs 188
al-Kharrāz, Abū Sa'īd 153, 169, 262
khāṣṣ pl. *khawāṣṣ* (elite) 6, 11, 44, 55, 57, 63nn. 13 and 17, 66n. 39, 80, 83, 161-2, 167, 190, 201n. 29, 218, 312
khāṣṣ al-khāṣṣ/*khāṣṣ al-khawāṣṣ* (elite of the elite) 6, 63n. 13, 80, 83, 161-2, 167, 190, 312
khawf (fear) 161
and *rajā'* (hope) 177n. 60, 185
al-Khiḍr 241, 243, 250, 260, 264-70, 272n. 29, 273n. 38, 275n. 98
khilāf (opposition) 189
see also mukhālafa
Khorasan xix, 3, 4, 5, 11, 14, 23n. 6, 96, 168
love mysticism in 109-11
Maybudī's links with 14-15
mysticism in 107-9
Khorasani school of mysticism, and Baghdadi school 100n. 65, 122n. 71
khulla (friendship) *see* Abraham
knowledge 187-91
divinely taught 47-8, 281
finding as opposed to 112
Ghazzālī's threefold hierarchy of 6
of God 47, 66n. 46, 114, 189-91, 228-9, 301

going beyond knowledge to the Known 152, 157, 198
knowing oneself to know one's Lord 268
from knowledge to gnosis 228-9
rational knowledge, limits 46-7, 112-13, 114, 124, 311, 313
subordinate to love in the divine purpose of creation 129
see also *'aql*; gnosis; *'ilm*; *ma'rifa*
al-Kundurī, Abū Naṣr 2, 23n. 4
al-Kurrakānī *see* Abu'l-Qāsim
kūshish (effort) 185, 231
on Anṣārī's Qur'an commentary 20, 21
al-Kutubī, Abū 'Abd Allāh Ḥusayn 33n. 124

lā ilāha illa'llāh (first Muslim attestation of faith) 125, 143n. 5
language, literary xvii, 7, 12, 15, 109, 313
see also poetry, story telling
laṭīfa pl. *laṭā'if* (subtlety, grace) 167, 235
laṭā'if in Sufi interpretation 55, 70, 32-3n. 119
laṭa' if-i mudhakkirān ('associations' of preachers) 19
Laylā (and Majnūn) 141, 290, 297, 307n. 88
Lazarus-Yafeh, Hava 84, 101n. 79
light, analogy for knowledge 189
of God 293, 306n. 68
Muhammadan 130-2
lisān al-ḥāl 65n. 35
literalism 46, 312-13, 314
longing for God *see shawq*
love
doctrines of in *Kashf al-asrār* 111-16, 191-9
and contemplation 299-302
contrasted with those of Anṣārī 111-16
and the Covenant of *Alast* 139, 141-2
culmination of the way of love 152, 197-9
God's love for humans 128-9, 136-9
Going beyond love to Beloved 152, 157, 198
human love and love for God 7, 285, 286, 287-8, 301
and *jawānmardī* 172
jealousy and the way of love 196-7, 297-8
knowledge based on/inseparable from 130
as mystical way 301, 308n. 88, 313
precedence over knowledge in the divine purpose of creation 129
pre-eminence 191-2
purifying fire of 115, 192-5, 199, 261, 302
seeds of love, metaphor 141, 293, 294, 301, 306n. 69
separation in 147n. 74, 196, 294, 297, 299, 301, 308n. 106
stations of 198, 205n. 115
and suffering or affliction 137, 110, 172, 195-6, 251, 293-7, 305n. 49
language of 94, 259-61
metaphysics of 7, 111, 198
poetry 7
'school of' 111, 120n. 35, 260
in the story of Joseph 283-302
without knowledge 188
words used for 116
see also love mysticism; *dūstī*; *'ishq*; *maḥabba*; *mihr*
love mysticism 7, 15, 96, 107-16
lover/lovers of God
rank in spiritual hierarchy 167
spiritual states 161
submission of will to that of Beloved 294, 305n. 56
willingness to stake lives 170
see also *'āshiq*; *muḥibb*
lubb (core), spiritual 156, 175nn. 33 and 36
luṭf (gentleness or grace) 124, 127-8, 132, 140, 258, 259

McAuliffe, Jane Dammen, definition of hermeneutics xxiii-xxiv
Madrasas 26n. 38
Merv 2
Niẓāmiyya 2-3
maḥabbat/ maḥabbat 116, 122n. 72, 130, 192, 195, 205n. 115, 251
cup of 141, 203n. 71
ma'rifat based on, inseparable from 130, 192, 301

maḥabbat/ maḥabbat (*cont.*):
and *miḥnat* (affliction or trial) 195, 251
see also love; *dūstī*; *ʿishq*; *mihr*
al-Maḥallī, Jalāl al-Dīn, *Tafsīr al-Jalālayn* 19
Maḥmūd (sultan) 165
and Ayāz 110
encounter with Abu'l-Ḥasan Kharaqānī 25n. 25
Maḥmūd Barkyārūq (son of Malik-Shāh) 14
Maḥmūd Shabistarī, *Gulshan-i rāz* 27n. 43
majāz al-Qur'ān 9
majlis pl. *majālis* P. *majlis-hā* (session) in structure of *Kashf al-asrār* 19, 20, 57, 68n. 76
Majnūn (and Laylā) 290, 297, 307n. 88
Makdisi, George 2, 23nn. 4 and 5, 23-4n. 6, 32n. 111
al-Makkī, Abū Ṭālib 203n. 78
Qūt al-qulūb, as source for Maybudī 22, 176n. 55
al-Makkī, ʿAmr b. ʿUthmān, *Kitāb al-maḥabba* 109
makr (divine ruse) 76, 99n. 38, 165, 220, 221, 268, 283
malāma/malāmat (blame) 168, 180n. 112, 290-1
Malāmatiyya (School of Blame) 108, 118n. 9, 168-9, 171, 178n. 87, 180n. 115, 181n. 124, 226, 268, 276n. 115
Mālik b. Anas 31n. 102
Malik Shāh (Saljuq sultan) 2, 14
al-Ma'mūn (Caliph) 30n. 96
manzil (station or stage) on the spiritual path 158
maqām pl. *maqāmāt* (station) on the spiritual path 80, 102n. 103, 161-4,
and *aḥwāl* 161-4, 177n. 60
see also spiritual states and stations
mard-i mardāna ('manly' man), allusion to ideals of Sufi chivalry 76, 253
mardānagī 171, 181n. 133
maʿrifa /maʿrifat (gnosis) 17, 49, 66n. 47, 112, 114, 130, 133, 156, 159, 175nn. 33 and 38, 251, 256, 292, 301, 311
based on and inseparable from *maḥabbat* 130, 192, 301
wine of 203n. 71
trials on the way to 251
see also gnosis (*maʿrifa*); *ahl-i maʿrifat*
Massignon, Louis xv, xxiii, 71, 186-7
mastī see intoxication
mathal 76
see also amthāl
mathnawī 8
maṭlaʿ var. *muṭṭalaʿ* 70, 71, 73, 96n. 4, 97nn. 10 and 12
Maybudī, Abu'l-Faḍl Rashīd al-Dīn 12-17
ancestry 12-13
authorship of *Kashf al-asrār* 12
full title 12, 29n. 67
hermeneutics 16-17, 39-50, 74-81, 90-6, 312-13
jurisprudence 15
Kitāb al-fuṣūl 15, 18-19, 29n. 67
Kitāb-i arbaʿīn 15, 18
links with Khorasan 14-15
mystical doctrines 111-16, 124-42, 150-72
religious beliefs 15-17, 311
rhetoric *see Kashf al-asrār*
on *ta'wīl* 44-5, 46-7
traditionalism 15-18, 111-12, 124
use of Arabic 19-20
use of Persian 3, 10-12, 19-20, 92, 313
works 18-20
see also Kashf al-asrār wa ʿuddat al-abrār
maysir (gambling) 170-1
see also gambling; *qimār*
Meisami, Julie Scott 103n. 130, 211
Melchert, Christopher, on the Karrāmiyya and Malāmatiyya 180-1n. 119
mercenaries *see muzdūr*
metaphorical interpretation, by philosophers, Muʿtazilī 44-6
Ghazzālī's views on (and *ta'wīl*) 45, 55, 64n. 25, 65n. 35, 66n. 47, 97n. 20
Maybudī's condemnation of, concerning anthropomorphic verses 16, 44-6, 59-60, 312
see also allegory; symbol
metaphors 313
bat 191, 203n. 62
of human love for divine love 7, 94
moth and candle 198

for states and stations 160, 163, 176-7n. 55, 177n. 56,
in stories of the prophets 210-11
of wine drinking 160
wine of annihilation 231-2
wine of intimacy 160
wine of love 141, 164, 259, 261
wine of *ma'rifat* 203n. 71
miḥnat (affliction) 92, 251-2
and *maḥabbat* (love) 195, 251
mihr (love) 115, 116, 142, 196, 256
debate with *dīdār* (vision) 115
of God 124
miracles 165
of Abraham and flour 217
Abraham and the garden in the midst of Nimrod's fire 235
see also mu'jizat (prophetic miracle)
mi'rāj (ascension of the Prophet Muhammad) 131, 180n. 115, 211, 220, 237n. 16, 241, 245, 247, 270n. 1, 282, 303n. 18
mirror
heart/secret as 300-1, 306n. 61, 309n. 107
'ārif as 308n. 102
Joseph as 308n. 106
months, number as a reflection of God's oneness 125
moon
called lord by Abraham 74-79, 216, 220, 223, 228-9, 253
compared to possessors of the state of *talwīn* (vacillation) 246
as metaphor 282
as symbol 84, 101n. 78
Moses 221-2, 241-3, 243 Table 9.1
comparison with Muhammad 244-9
as 'Everyman' 248, 272n. 29
as a forerunner of Muhammad's people (*umma*) 247
identified with intoxication 238n. 57
as *Kalīm Allāh* (interlocutor of God) 216, 242-5
as Muhammad's predecessor 131, 221, 241
mystical interpretations 250-70
prayers 247, 272n. 74
in the Qur'an 241-2, 243 Table 9.1, 244-5, 182n. 136
rod representing Shari'a 84
spiritual journey 250-70
flight to Midian 251-4, 255
meeting with al-Khiḍr 260-1, 264-70, 274n. 80
theophany on Mount Sinai 242, 244, 245-6, 249, 250, 259-64, 270, 274n. 80
in the valley of Ṭuwā 249, 254-9, 270, 314
in Sufi exegesis 249-50
mu'āyana/mu'āyanat (direct witnessing) 190, 195
see also 'iyān
muḥaddith (traditionist, scholar of hadith) 15, 32n. 112
Muhammad (Muṣṭafā)
adab (courtesy) towards God 89
beauty of hidden by veil of divine jealousy 307n. 72
capacity for direct witnessing (*'iyān*) of God 190, 195
capacity to contemplate the divine essence 190
compared to Abraham 220-1, 222-3
compared to Moses 241, 244-7
contemplation of God 159-60, 176n. 51
created when Adam between water and clay 131
encouragement of love and respect for 81, 89
eye not swerving (*mi'rāj*) 220, 224
first and last in creation 130-2, 211
God's creation of the spheres for the sake of 131
as *Ḥabīb Allāh* (Beloved of God) 216, 220
on *ḥanīfiyya* 236n. 3
heart of as source of knowledge of God 47
intimacy with God 94
on Joseph 82, 284
journey to the world from divine presence 132
like other men but unlike them 248
loved by God 89, 130-1

Muhammad (Muṣṭafā) (*cont.*):
and *malāma* 180n. 115
Muhammadan light (*nūr Muḥammadī*) 130-2, 136
as *murād* 221
prayers 159-60, 176n. 51, 268, 276n. 113
pre-eminence 210
prophets derive their light from him 211, 131-2
as the Prophet 209-11
receiving two kinds of revelation 191
shaped in the form of Adam 132
in state of *jam*ʿ 222-3
spiritual rank 166
in state of *tamkīn* 246
as a sun 131, 211
vision of God 245
*see also mi*ʿ*rāj*
Muḥammad (son of Malik Shāh) 14
Muḥammad b. Aḥmad al-ʿĀbid 166
Muhammadan light (*nūr Muḥammadī*) 130-2, 136
al-Muḥāsibī, Ḥārith 71, 97n. 12, 109, 119n. 19
muḥkam (unequivocal) and *mutashābih* pl. *mutashābihāt* (ambiguous) verses 9, 39, 41-4, 62-3n. 8, 63nn. 12, 13 and 15, 312
muhr (seal) 83, 142
Mujāhid b. Jabr 9, 21, 40, 65n. 32, 303n. 12
mujāhada/mujāhadat (spiritual struggle, combat) 153, 268-9, 270
Mujassima corporealists 45
muʿjizat pl. *muʿjizāt* (prophetic miracle) 130, 165, 179n. 98, 240n. 81
mukāshafa/mukāshafat (unveiling) 48, 49, 103n. 125, 112, 160, 179n. 98, 261, 311
mukhālafa/mukhālafat (opposition), opposite to *muwāfaqat* (conformity) 183
mukhlaṣ/mukhliṣ 221, 314
mulḥid heretic 53
munājāt 249
see also Anṣārī, *Munājāt*
Munāzil, ʿAbd Allāh 169, 180n. 119
munāzilāt (states) 163
see also ḥāl; aḥwāl; spiritual states
Munkar and Nākir *see* angels
Muqātil b. Sulaymān 8, 21
murād 210, 218, 219-21, 248, 314
murāqaba/murāqabat 175n. 33, 177n. 60
murīd 140, 164, 179n. 103, 210, 218, 219-21, 233, 248, 270, 313
murīd and *murād* 218-21
Murjiʾīs 188, 202n. 43
muruwwa 181n. 133
Mūsā b. Ifrāʾīm b. Yūsuf 275n. 99
mushāhada/mushāhadat (witnessing, inner beholding of God) 96n. 2, 193, 130, 132, 157, 160, 163, 175nn. 33 and 38, 179n. 98, 190, 195, 203n. 79, 229, 235, 245, 253, 265, 300-1
mushrikīn (idolaters, polytheists) 218
mushtāqān (those who long for God) 129, 141, 144n. 28, 193
Muslim 9, 176n. 51
Mustamlī, Abū Ibrāhīm Ismāʿīl b. Muḥammad 25n. 20, 120nn. 26 and 30, 179-80n. 111, 224-5, 289
mustanbaṭāt 28n. 57, 63n. 18
see also istinbāṭ
mutakallimūn (scholastic theologians) 15
see also kalām
mutashābih (ambiguous) verses *see muḥkam* and *mutashābih*
Muʿtazilīs 3, 9, 31n. 100, 46, 97n. 20, 44, 54, 65n. 32, 271n. 9
muwāṣala/muwāṣalat (union) 151
muzdur pl. *muzdurān* (mercenaries) 167, 179n. 104, 194, 203n. 82, 314-15
mystical exegesis *see* esoteric exegesis
mystical way
goal 150-2
combating the *nafs* 152-4
spiritual communities 164-8
stages of progression 157-61
states (*aḥwāl*) and stations (*maqāmāt*) 161-4
see also spiritual 'psychology'
mysticism
importance of Maybudī's *Kashf al-asrār* for study of 315-16
in Khorasan 107-9

see also love mysticism
mystics *see 'ārif/'ārifān*

nabī see prophets
nafs (lower self, ego or soul) 60, 82, 87, 65n. 32, 161, 163, 175n. 33, 179n. 110, 180n. 112, 188, 235
combating and conquering 150, 152-4
crushing through *ṭarīqa* 312
earth as an analogy for 188
locus of Islam 175n. 38
ḥuqūq (rights, or just claims) 269, 277n. 120
killing (with sword of spiritual striving) 85, 153
as obstacle on the mystical path 152-3
opposition to the heart (*dil/qalb*) 155
association with *ṣadr* (breast) 156, 176n. 46
symbolised in the story of the fire of Nimrod 235
stages of transformation, degrees of the *nafs* 159
nafs ammāra (inciting nafs) 79, 87-8, 152, 155, 159, 160, 164, 229
Joseph's words 174n. 14
nafs lawwāma (self-reproaching *nafs*) 159, 269
nafs al-makkāra 159, 269
nafs-i muṭma'inna (*nafs* at peace) 159, 268, 277n. 120
nafs saḥḥāra (bewitching *nafs*) 159
Nākir and Munkar *see* angels
al-Nasafī, 'Abd Allāh b. Aḥmad, *Madārik al-tanzīl wa ḥaqā'iq al-ta'wīl* 64n. 23
al-nāsikh wa'l-mansūkh (abrogating and abrogated verses) 9
Naṣrābādhī, Abu'l-Qāsim 114
*nawbat*s (turns) xvi, 19-22, 54-5, 57-9, 80, 92, 99n. 37, 312-13
see also Kashf al-asrār; structure
al-Naysābūrī, Abū Isḥāq Ibrāhīm 304n. 35, 305n. 57, 306n. 63
nāz 194, 203n. 80, 260
naẓar (beholding, contemplating, or a look, glance) 156
naẓar-i Ḥaqq (divine gaze, glance) 136, 155
naẓar-i maḥabbat (look of love) from God 146
Nicholson, Reynold A. 289
nihāya/nihāyat (end, final stage) 162, 221, 248
ni'ma/ni'mat (blessing, bounty) 43, 178n. 76, 315
walī-yi ni'mat (Bestower of blessing) 43
Nimrod 75, 211, 216, 255, 270, 314
see also Abraham
Nishapur 2, 14, 23n. 4, 26n. 38, 30n. 85, 169
nīstī (not being) 198, 205n. 115
see also annihilation
niyāz (need) 193, 295
Niẓām al-Mulk 2-3, 4-6, 32n. 111
N.J.W. 249
nūr Muḥammadī (Muhammadan light) 130-2, 136
al-Nūrī, Abu'l-Ḥusayn 34n. 139, 109, 175nn. 33 and 34
Maqāmāt al-qulūb 34n. 139, 174n. 31, 175n. 36
Nwyia, Paul xxiii-iv, 79, 81, 98n. 27, 120n. 26, 249
N.Z.L. 247

Origen, exegetical theory and proceedure 72, 97n. 20, 97-8n. 23, 100n. 59

pākbāz (one who is willing to lose all in gambling) 170, 181n. 128
parables *see amthāl*; *mathal*
Paradise 82-3, 251
Adam's banishment from, and the doctrine of love 136-9
mystics' view of 163-4, 168, 179n. 105
paradise seekers (*bihisht-jūyān*) 179n. 104, 314-15
al-riḍwān al-akbar (Paradise of God's good pleasure) 230
state of believers in 83
surrounded by *makārih* (undesirable things) 251, 273n. 41
patience 161, 163, 172
see also ṣabr
Paul, Jürgen 11, 25n. 24, 28n. 63
People of the Book, salvation 83-4

perplexity (*ḥayrat*) 161, 193-4
see also ḥayrat
Persian language
farsī-yi ẓāhir (literal Persian) 19
Anṣārī's use 113, 121n. 55
Isfarāyinī's use 33n. 120
as language for mystical expression 15, 109, 313
Maybudī's use 3, 92, 313
prose development in 7
secular love poetry 116
use for wider audience 8
use in *Kashf al-asrār* xvi, 19
use in writings on love mysticism 7
Pharaoh 242, 243
Philo of Alexandria 97n. 20
philosophers, philosophy 3, 24n. 18, 44, 45, 47, 109, 311
pīr (shaykh, spiritual master) 5-6, 11, 26n. 29, 164-5
see also spiritual master
poetry 93, 94, 142, 313, 314, 315
love poetry 7, 110
disapproval of its use in mysticism 120n. 30
qalandariyyāt 169-170, 181n. 124
use by preachers 12, 28n. 64, 104n. 139
use in prose 93, 103n .130
use in Persian mysticism 120n. 29
polemics in exegesis 53-4
polytheism 202, 299
see also idolatry
Potiphar 302n. 2
Pourjavady, Nasrollah 118n. 12, 180n. 115, 308nn. 96 and 98
prayer, canonical 58, 184
prayers
of Abraham 216, 219, 225, 226
of Moses 247, 272n. 24 and 27
of Muhammad 159-60, 176n. 51, 268, 276n. 113
number of daily prayers 241
preordination (*qaḍā'*, *qadar, taqdīr*) 17, 61, 90, 111, 112, 114, 127, 128, 140, 180n. 119, 183-7, 248, 283-5, 313
and Covenant of *Alast* 139-42
qaḍā', *qadar* and *taqdīr*, definition 112
taqdīr 112, 183-91
prevailing over *tadbīr* (human contrivance and design) 280, 283, 285
prophetologies in *Kashf al-asrār* 211
prophets 125, 209-12, 278, 280
Abraham as father of 215
in Bible, as compared with the Qur'an 209-10, 241-2, 244, 249
historical chronology, mystical interpretations fall outside 270, 274n. 80
al-Khiḍr identified as 265
miracles 165, 240n. 81
mystical interpretations of their stories xix, xxv-vi, 211-12, 270, 274n. 80, 313-14
nabī pl. *anbiyā'* 166, 209
place in spiritual hierarchy 166
qiṣaṣ al-anbiyā' corpus of stories of the prophets 9, 51-2, 211
rasūl pl. *rusul* (prophet bringing scripture) 209
payāmbarān-i mursal 166
slipping, slips (*zalla* pl. *zallāt*) 165
spiritual progression 210, 248
stories of 9, 51-2, 209-11, 278, 313-14
in allegorical interpretation 85
subject to alternation of states 186
ūlu'l-'aẓm (messengers of firm resolve) 166
see also Abraham; Joseph; Moses
prose, poetical prose 93-6, 142
rhyming (*musajja'*) 94
see also saj'

qabḍ (contraction), and *basṭ* (expansion) 60, 84, 92, 185, 186, 187, 246
see also basṭ
qaḍā' see preordination
qadar 112
see also preordination
Qādirī Creed (*al-I'tiqād al-Qādirī*) 16
Qādirīs, metaphorical interpretations 46
qāḍīs 2, 18, 23n. 3
qahr and *luṭf see* God
qalandar 170, 181n. 124
Qalandarī motifs 169-71
Qalandariyya 181n. 124

qalandariyyāt see poetry
qalb see heart
qanāʿat (contentment) 177n. 56
al-Qazwīnī, ʿAbd al-Jalīl b. Abi'l-Ḥasan, *Kitāb al-naqḍ* 24n. 11
qibla as focus for divine love 89, 293, 298, 301
qimār (gambling) 170, 181n. 124
see also gambling; *maysir*; metaphors
qimārkhāna (gambling house) 170
of love 198-9
qirāʾa/qiraʾat (variant readings) 9, 19, 50, 52
qiṣaṣ al-anbiyāʾ see prophets
qiyās (analogy) 17, 82-4
qudrat (power, omnipotence) of God 46, 128, 133
Qur'an
allegorical interpretation 84-5
anthropomorphic expressions 16, 39, 45-6, 67n. 62
commenting upon the Qur'an 52-3
epistle whose title is eternal love 110, 191
literary-historical approaches to 212-13n. 4
mysterious letters commencing suras 53, 58
revelation, compared with that of Torah 247
as revelation of God's love 191
style and rhetoric in 46, 209-10
theories of levels of meaning 33n. 119, 55-6, 70-1, 72-4
uncreatedness 16, 53
see also exegesis; hermeneutics
qurb 143n. 24, 160
al-Qushayrī, Abu'l-Qāsim ʿAbd al-Karīm b. Hawāzan 1, 4, 11, 14, 22, 28n. 52, 56, 107, 118n.14
on Abū ʿAlī Daqqāq on polytheism 308n. 94
as an Ashʿarī 121n. 45
audience addressed in his commentary 68n. 82, 92
comparison of Moses with Muhammad 272n. 19
exegetical methods 82-90, 101n. 78
on *fanāʾ* 254
and *baqāʾ* 173n. 4, 201n. 29
on *futuwwa* 108
on *ghayba* and *ḥuḍūr* 254
on God speaking to Moses directly (Q. 4:164) 271n. 6
on *ʿilm ladunī* 265
on the inner constitution of the human being 175n. 33
on *ʿishq* 122n. 74
on Jacob's blindness 308n. 93
on Joseph's healing of Jacob's blindness 299
Laṭāʾif al-ishārāt xvi, 33n. 119
comparison with *Kashf al-asrār* 11, 90-2
mystical exegesis xxv, 81, 82-90
rhetorical style and scope 11, 90-1
as a source for Maybudī 14, 22, 34n. 135, 90
on love 120n. 26, 274n. 79
on Moses' journey to Sinai 275n. 87
on Moses' meeting with al-Khiḍr 267
on *murīd* 270
and *murād* 220-1
on *muruwwa* and *futuwwa* 181n. 133
Al-Risāla al-Qushayriyya fī ʿilm al-taṣawwuf 25n. 20, 120n. 25
as a source for Maybudī 22
on *sharīʿa* and *ḥaqīqa* 56
on states (*aḥwāl*) and stations (*maqāmāt*) in the mystical way 177n. 60
on suffering in love 307n. 74
Al-Tafsīr al-kabīr 28n. 52
on *talwīn* and *tamkīn* 186
on terms *ʿāmm, khāṣṣ* and *khāṣṣ al-khawāṣṣ* 63n.17, 177n. 71
quṭb (spiritual pole or axis) 166

Rābiʿa al-ʿAdawiyya 109, 179n. 105
Rachel (Joseph's mother) 282
al-Raḥīm and *al-Raḥmān* divine names of mercy 50, 133, 259
effects on mystic contrasted with name *Allāh* 127
raḥma/raḥmat (mercy) 265
see also God
rajāʾ (hope) 161, 185

rakʿa/rakʿat bowing, in canonical prayer 58
Ramadan 199
Rashīd al-Dīn *see* Maybudī
rasūl see prophets
rawanda pl. *rawandagān* (one who is making his way) 185, 218, 220, 223
see also rawish
rawish (going, making one's way) opposite of *kashish* 158, 178n. 76, 185, 219–22, 260, 274n. 80
ra'y (reasoned opinion) 42
see also tafsīr bi'l-ra'y
Rāzī, Abu'l-Futūḥ *see* Abu'l-Futūḥ Rāzī
al-Rāzī, Fakhr al-Dīn Muḥammad 24n. 17
Al-Tafsīr al-kabīr 19
al-Rāzī, Sayyid Murtaḍā
Tabṣīrat al-ʿawāmm 24n. 11, 32n. 111
reason *see ʿaql*
religious belief *see uṣūl al-dīn; ʿaqīda*
remembrance (*dikhr*) 184, 245
renunciation [of the world] *see zuhd*
repentance *see tawba*
resurrection 89, 103n. 125
restlessness (*bī qarārī*) 184, 200n. 16
revelation (*waḥy*) 48, 191, 303n. 13
riʿāya/riʿāyat (observance) 62
ribāṭ 5, 26n. 28
see also duwayra; *khānaqāh*
riḍā' (acquiescence) 115, 177nn. 56 and 60, 180n. 119, 184, 230
as a station 177n. 60
rind (reckless lad) 170
risāla (message) 191
riwāya/riwāyat (narration, [oral] transmission) 179n. 104, 187
riyāḍa/riyāḍat (spiritual disciplinary practice) 153, 250, 270, 267, 293
rubūbiyya/rubūbiyyat (divine Lordship) 124, 178n. 76
rubūda (snatched) 185
rūḥ pl. *arwāḥ* (spirit) 141, 160, 175n. 33, 204n. 86
Rūmī, Jalāl al-Dīn 1, 8, 97n. 12, 235, 240n. 84, 302
rumūz-i ʿārifān (allegories of mystics) 19
ruʿūna/ruʿūnat (stupidity, laxity, weakness, self-adornment) 157
rūz-i alast, rūz-i balā, rūz-i qabḍa see Covenant of *Alast*

ṣabā (zephyr) 296
sabab-i-nuzūl see asbāb al-nuzūl
ṣabr (patience) 161, 163, 177n. 60, 178n. 76, 256
as a station 177n. 60
ṣadr (breast) 156-7, 175nn. 33 and 38
contrast with the heart (*dil*, *qalb*) 155-6
as locus of Islam 157, 290
Ṣafā' and Marwā, symbolic interpretation 84
ṣaḥw (sobriety) 110, 186, 289
contrasted with *sukr* (intoxication) 109-110, 117n. 1, 186-7, 289
Saʿīd b. Jubayr 276n. 99
Saʿīd Ghiyāth al-Dīn ʿAlī Munshī 13
Saʿīd Muwaffaq al-Dīn Abī Jaʿfar b. Abī Saʿīd b. Aḥmad b. Mihrīzad 13
Saints, lit. friends of God (*awliyā'*) 165
sajʿ 94
sakīna (profound peace) 252, 268
Saljuqs 2, 4, 5, 13, 25n. 25
Salmān al-Fārisī 100n. 72
salwat (consolation, solace) 307n.86
samāʿ (spiritual recital) 5, 110, 116, 123n. 76
ṣamadiyya (God's eternity, for His being eternally besought of all) 126, 143n. 9, 254, 263
Samʿānī, Aḥmad 34-5n. 142, 147n. 83
Rawḥ al-arwāḥ 144n. 28
as a source for Maybudī 22
Sanā'ī, Abu'l-Majd Majdūd 1, 8, 147n.78
*ghazal*s on mystical love 110, 111
on levels of meaning in Qur'an 98n. 25
and philosophy 24-5n. 18
poetry in the *Kashf al-asrār* 14, 30n. 87
qalandariyya motifs and theme of gambling 181n. 124, 182n. 140
*qaṣīda*s 111, 147n. 78
quoted by Maybudī 14
al-Sarrāj, Abū Naṣr ʿAbd Allāh b. ʿAlī
on *ghayba* and *ḥuḍūr* 254
on *istinbāṭ* 73-4, 79
Kitāb al-lumaʿ fi'l-taṣawwuf 22, 25n. 20, 108, 120n. 26, 177n. 71

as a source for Maybudī 22
on states (*aḥwāl*) and stations (*maqāmāt*) in the mystical way 177n. 60
on *talwīn* and *tamkīn* 186
Sarwar Mawlā'ī 18
Satan (Iblīs) 134, 152, 268, 295
as the cause of Adam's slip (*zallat*) 136
and divine decree 183-4, 200n. 4
excuse 183-4
made of fire 134
and the sacrifice of Ishmael 232
as 'second nature' to man 268
Ṣ.D.Q. 280, 281
seas, as spiritual metaphor 160, 176-7nn. 55 and 56
seeking God 184-5
see also finding (God)
separation *see* love, *firāq*
al-Shāfi'ī 17, 53
and 'Alī b. Abī Ṭālib 30n. 89
Shāfi'ī school 2, 15, 32n. 111, 53
and Sufism 108
shaghāf (pericardium of the heart) 157, 175n. 36, 290
locus of *'ishq* 175n. 38
shaghafa (to penetrate the pericardium) 156-7
shahīd pl. *shuhadā'*, *shahīdān* (martyr) 166
shahwa pl. *shahawāt* (passion, lust, desire) 153, 156, 305n. 57
al-Sharastānī, Abu'l-Fatḥ Muḥammad b. 'Abd al-Karīm, *Kitāb al-milal wa'l-niḥal* 28n. 11
Mafātīḥ al-asrār wa masābīḥ al-abrār 24n. 15
sharī'a/sharī'at 13, 51, 56-7, 59, 84, 111, 132, 189
and *ḥaqīqa* 55-7, 58, 59, 192, 311–13
shaṭḥ pl. *shaṭḥiyyāt* (ecstatic utterances) 99n. 46, 222
shawāhid (textual evidence) 52
shawq (longing, yearning, ardour), for God 193-5, 203n. 79, 256
shaykhs (*pīrs*) 5-6, 11, 26n. 29, 28n. 63
al-Shiblī, Abū Bakr 118n. 14, 193, 197
Shihāb al-Dīn 'Alī, *Sharḥ al-hawī* 13
Shihāb al-Dīn Muḥammad 13
al-Shīrāzī, Abu Isḥāq 23n. 3
shukr (gratitude) 59, 161
ṣiddīq/ṣiddīqān (veracious) 166-7, 179n. 103, 191-2, 201n. 29, 215, 269
Sinai *see* Moses
sinners, groaning of (dear to God) 138, 148n. 87
sirr pl. *asrār* (secret) 66n. 49, 146n. 55, 156, 167, 175nn. 33 and 36, 228, 296, 299, 300
locus of *ma'rifa* 175n. 38
sirran bi-sirr (from secret to secret) revelation of love to Muhammad 191
Sleepers in the Cave *see* Companions of the Cave
Spirit *see rūḥ, sirr*
spiritual hierarchies 164-8, 174n. 23
spiritual master (shaykh, *pīr*) need for, qualifications for 164-5
spiritual path, stages of 157-61
spiritual 'psychology' 154-64, 299
inner constitution of the human being 155-7
spiritual states and stations 92, 161-4, 177n. 60, 211, 301, 313-14
alternation of 60, 185-7, 196-7, 204n. 104
need for detachment from 224-5
see also ḥāl; maqām
Storey, Charles A. 12, 29n. 65, 54
story-telling 8, 93-4, 104n. 139, 313-14
al-Suhrawardī, Shihāb al-Dīn 1, 303n. 14
ṣūfī as a term xxvi, 108, 118n. 12
Sufism
apologetics in 27n. 41
concept of xxvi
historical development 1-8
and love mysticism 108-11
manuals xxv, 4, 25n. 20, 154, 161, 316
and theology 121n. 45
see also mysticism
Sufyān al-Thawrī 9, 21
sukr (intoxication) 109-10, 186
and *ghalaba* 289
see also ṣaḥw
al-Sulamī, 'Abd al-Raḥmān xvi, 1, 73, 108, 203n. 79, 267
citing 'Alī b. Abī Ṭālib, on levels of meaning in the Qur'an 70

al-Sulamī, ʿAbd al-Raḥmān (*cont.*):
citing Ibn ʿAṭāʾ al-Adamī 265, 303n. 20, 308n. 93
citing Jaʿfar al-Ṣādiq 98n. 25, 177n. 57, 296
citing Junayd, on levels of meaning in the Qur'an 97n. 12
exclusion of Karrāmiyya 118n. 13
on *futuwwa* 181n. 132
Ḥaqāʾiq al-tafsīr 10, 28n. 56, 70, 81
use by Maybudī 22, 34n. 133
Kitāb al-futuwwa 181n. 132
on longing for God 203n. 79
on love 274n. 79
on Moses' meeting with al-Khiḍr 266, 267
Risālat al-Malāmatiyya 175n. 33, 180n. 115
Ṭabaqāt al-ṣufiyya 25n. 21, 108, 118n. 13
Ziyādat ḥaqāʾiq al-tafsīr 10, 97n. 12, 98n. 25
sulūk (journeying) 185, 219
see also rawish
Sumnūn al-Muḥibb 109, 290
sun
called lord by Abraham 216, 220, 223, 228-9, 253
compared to the possessors of the state of *tamkīn* 246
as symbol 84, 101n. 78
sunna/sunnat 157, 158, 175n. 40, 180n.119
as source of knowledge 47
al-Suyūṭī, Jalāl al-Dīn, *Tafsīr al-Jalālayn* 19, 62-3n. 8
symbolism
in the stories of the prophets 101nn. 76, 78 and 80, 212
use in mystical exegesis 84-6
within the story of Nimrod's fire 235

Ṭabāʾiʿiyān 15, 30n. 93
ṭabaqāt works 4
al-Ṭabarī, Abū Jaʿfar 10-11, 40, 42, 50, 52, 63n. 12, 100n. 72, 232, 236n. 3, 239n. 63, 276n. 99, 302n. 2, 304n. 24, 304n. 31
on Abraham as *Khalīl Allāh* 217
criteria for assessing interpretations 99n. 47
Jāmiʿ al- bayān ʿan taʾwīl āy al-Qurʾān 8, 9-10, 19, 40, 53, 62n. 13
as source for Maybudī 21, 33n. 127
on *al-Raḥīm* 50
on *al-Raḥmān* 50
on levels of meaning in the Qur'an 70-1
on Q. 3:7 42, 62-3n. 8
use of polemic 53
use of the word *taʾwīl* 62n. 2
tabattul (cutting oneself off from the world/complete devotion to God) 163-4
al-Ṭabrisī (Tabarṣī), al-Faḍl b. al-Ḥasan, *Majmaʿ al-bayān fī tafsīr al-Qurʾān* 3, 27n. 50, 232
tadbīr (human contrivance and design), no power against *taqdīr* 184, 280, 283
tafakkur (reflection) 47, 253
see also fikr
tafarruq 255, 256, 258
see also tafriqa
tafrīd (isolation of the self for God) 152, 205n. 114, 229, 261
and *tajrīd* 223-5, 257, 293
tafriqa/tafriqat 151, 158, 177n. 56, 187, 221-2, 258, 263, 314
opposed to *jamʿ* 173n. 7, 187, 221-2, 263-4, 269, 277n. 120
see also tafarruq
tafsīr 44, 67n. 50, 73, 80
categories 40-1, 69, 70
and *taʾwīl* 44, 60, 66n. 23, 80
and homily 50-5
see also exegesis; hermeneutics
tafsīr bi'l-maʾthūr 9, 39, 41, 44, 49, 75, 100n. 60, 312-13
tafsīr bi'l-raʾy 9, 39, 41, 44, 49, 99n. 33, 100n. 60, 312-13
al-Taftazānī 12
tafwīḍ (committing one's affairs to God) 184
taḥayyur 193-4, 252
see also ḥayra
tajallī (theophany, epiphany, manifestation, of God) 163, 190, 195, 301, 302, 308nn. 106 and 107

tajrīd
three levels of 224-5
and *tafrīd* 152, 205n. 114, 223-5, 229, 257, 261, 293, 314
ṭalab (seeking) 161, 250
talwīn (vacillation) 84, 132, 185-6, 246 (as *taghayyur*, 291)
tamkīn (stability) 84, 132, 185-6, 289, 246, 291-2
and *wilāyat-i ʿishq* 291-2
tanzīh (transcendence of God) 31n. 100, 126
Targum 239n.74
taqdīr see preordination
taqwā (piety, awareness of God) 87, 102n. 103, 158
ṭarīqa/ṭarīqat (spiritual path) 62, 112, 155, 189, 192, 312
and *sharīʿa* 56-7, 189, 192
tasallī (consolation, solace) 297-8
see also salwat
tashbīh 16-17, 112, 126
see also anthropomorphism
taslīm (submission, surrender, acquiescence) 60, 112
taṭbīq 100n. 67
see also analogy and exegesis, esoteric, methods of
taʿṭīl (negation of the divine attributes) 16, 126
tawakkul (complete trust in God) 61, 158, 161-2, 169
as response to pre-ordination 184
in the story of Joseph 283-5
tawba (repentance) 161
stages 162-3
al-tawba min al-tawba 178n. 75, 225-6
tawfīq (God-given success) 184, 189, 202n. 47
tawḥīd (unity, of God) 76, 78, 96n. 6, 160, 161, 175nn. 33 and 38, 177n. 56, 180n. 119, 187, 203n. 78, 210, 218, 223, 226, 229, 234, 252-3, 255, 257, 262, 268-9, 284, 314
taʾwīl pl. *taʾwīlāt* 40, 44-5, 47, 49, 55, 64nn. 20, 23 and 24, 66n. 47, 80, 97n. 9, 100n. 60, 312
taʾwīl ʿaqlī (exertion of reason) 44
taʾwīl kashfī (mystical unveiling) 44
Ṭayfūrīs, mysticism contrasted with that of the Junaydīs 109-10
al-Thaʿlabī, Abū Isḥāq Aḥmad b. Muḥammad 273n. 39, 302n. 2
Throne of God (*ʿarsh*) 16, 45, 59-60, 61, 65n. 32, 89, 93, 129, 164, 314
Throne, Tablet (*lawḥ*) and Pen (*qalam*) 129, 133
tilāwa (recitation) 70-1
al-Tirmidhī, al-Ḥakīm *see* al-Ḥakīm
al-Tirmidhī, Muḥammad b. ʿĪsā 9, 272n. 24, 306n. 68
Torah 247
Torjesen, Karen J. 97-8n. 23
traditionalism, traditionalist 17, 32n. 112, 61, 311
Tughril Beg 23n. 4, 25n. 25
ṭumaʾnīna 227-8
al-Ṭūsī, Abū Jaʿfar Muḥammad b. al-Ḥasan, *Al-Tibyān fī tafsīr al-Qurʾān* 19, 27n. 50, 62n. 2, 63n. 9
Ṭūsī, Aḥmad b. Muḥammad b. Zayd. *Tafsīr-i Sūra-yi Yūsuf* 305n. 38, 308n. 90
al-Tustarī, Sahl b. ʿAbd Allāh 23n. 54
on levels of meaning in the Qur'an 70-3, 96n. 7
on the *nūr Muḥammadī* 145n. 41
on prayer and remembrance (*dhikr*) 184, 200n. 12
questioning Satan 183
Tafsīr al-Qurʾān al-ʿaẓīm 10, 70
as a source for Maybudī 22
Twelver Shiʿa, exegesis 27n. 50, 46

ulema (scholars, of exoteric knowledge) 4, 6, 11, 44, 56, 83
umma/ummat 11, 231, 247
ummī 91
union (with God) union with 61, 150-2, 193 299, 263, 269
see also jamʿ; *muwāṣala*; *W.Ṣ.L.*; *wiṣāl*; *wuṣla*
uns (intimacy) 127, 156, 160-1, 177n. 60, 194, 200n. 16, 201n. 32, 253-4, 259, 262, 314
and awe (*haybat*) 185
and *dahsha* 194, 204n. 88

unveiling 187, 190-1, 193
  see also kashf; *mukāshafa*
uṣūl al-dīn (fundamentals of religious belief) 15

variant readings *see qirā'a*
virtues (*akhlāq*) 218
  taking on virtues of God 152, 173n. 11
vision (of God) 190-1, 202n. 58, 244-5, 271n. 9

Wahb b. Munabbih 143n. 6
waḥy see revelation
walī (one guided or befriended by God) 265
  see also awliyā'
wara' (scrupulous piety) 157, 177n. 60
waṣl (union with God) 151, 161, 193
waṣl (union) 151
  see also muwāṣala
wilāya/wilāyat (friendship) 258
wilāyat-i 'ishq (dominion, complete control by love) 289-92, 300-1
  Aḥmad Ghazzālī on 305-6n. 61
wine and drinking, spiritual metaphors 160
  see also metaphors
wiṣāl (union or attainment) 151-2, 173n. 6, 194, 246, 264
wool, wearing of 153
worshipper *see 'ābid*
W.S.L. 151
wujūd as existence 126
  as finding 159-60, 176n. 55
  see also finding; *yāft*
wujūh wa naẓā'ir (analogues) 9, 19
wujūh-i ma'ānī (facets of meaning) 19
wuṣlat (union) 151, 258

yāft (finding) 80, 184
  masters of 230
Yaḥyā b. Mu'ādh 168, 180n. 115, 276n. 112
yaqīn (certainty)
  'ilm al-yaqīn, *'ayn al-yaqīn*, *ḥaqq al-yaqīn* 227
Yazd 13-14, 32n. 111

Zachariah, as symbol 213n. 15
zāhid pl. *zāhidān* (renunciant) 88, 118n. 12, 167-8, 174n. 23, 238n. 32
  see also zuhd
ẓāhir or *ẓahr* (outer, exoteric) xx, 70-3, 96n. 6
  and *bāṭin* (inner, esoteric) xxiv, 55-62, 69
  see also bāṭin; *baṭn*
zalla/zallat pl. *zallāt* (slipping, slips) 136, 165
al-Zamakhsharī, Abu'l-Qāsim 3
  Al-Kashshāf 'an haqā'iq al-tanzīl 9, 62n. 2, 63n. 8
zuhd (renunciation, disdain for, withdrawal from the world) 111, 120n. 37, 161, 168, 177n. 60
Zulaykhā 51-2, 213n. 13, 279, 281, 283-4
  attempt to seduce Joseph 288
  and blame 290-1
  conversion 286, 288
  and *ḍalāl* (excessive love) 283
  identified with love 303n. 14
  love for Joseph 211, 286-92, 300, 305nn. 38 and 57
  marriage to Joseph 277n. 120, 288, 304n. 35
  as prototype of lover 301
zunnār (belt or girdle worn by People of the Book) 61, 165